Current Personality Theories

Current Personality Theories

Edited by Raymond J. Corsini

F. E. PEACOCK PUBLISHERS, INC.   ITASCA, ILLINOIS 60143

To Edgar F. Borgatta

A great thorough-going man does not confine himself to one school, but combines many schools, as well as reads and listens to the arguments of many predecessors.

KUO HSI

Table of Contents

Chapter	Page Number	
1.	1	INTRODUCTION *Raymond J. Corsini*
2.	15	PSYCHOANALYSIS *Peter L. Giovacchini*
3.	45	INDIVIDUAL PSYCHOLOGY *Heinz L. Ansbacher*
4.	83	ANALYTICAL PSYCHOLOGY *Renaldo J. Maduro and Joseph B. Wheelwright*
5.	125	PERSON-CENTERED THEORY *T. L. Holdstock and Carl R. Rogers*
6.	153	PERSONALISM *William S. Sahakian*
7.	177	BEHAVIORISM: OPERANT REINFORCEMENT *Robert W. Lundin*
8.	203	PERSONAL CONSTRUCTS THEORY *Lee Sechrest*
9.	243	EXISTENTIAL PERSONALITY THEORY *Suzanne C. Kobasa and Salvatore R. Maddi*
10.	277	SOCIOLOGICAL THEORIES OF PERSONALITY *Anselm Strauss*
11.	303	CONSTITUTIONAL THEORIES OF PERSONALITY *Franklin C. Shontz*
12.	335	SOVIET PERSONALITY THEORY *Isidore Ziferstein*
13.	367	ASIAN PERSONALITY THEORY *Paul B. Pedersen*
14.	399	A MEDLEY OF CURRENT PERSONALITY THEORIES *Raymond J. Corsini*
		Karen Horney's *Psychosocial Theory* J. L. Moreno's *Sociometric Theory* Abraham Maslow's *Self-Actualization Theory* Henry A. Murray's *Needs-Press Theory* Eric Berne's *Transactional Analysis* Erik Erikson's *Developmental Theory* Frederick Perls's *Gestalt Therapy* Albert Ellis's *Rational-Emotive Theory* William Glasser's *Reality Theory* Albert Bandura's *Social Learning Theory* Hans J. Eysenck's *Typology Theory* Harold Greenwald's *Direct Decision Theory*
	433	Glossary

Preface

This volume provides a text for courses in personality theory. It is intended as a teaching tool definitive in character.

A truly definitive book must be written by authorities. This calls for an edited book. To this end 15 authorities were invited to write 12 chapters for the various theories selected.

Edited books are frequently uncoordinated and undisciplined. They are usually difficult to read. The solution to these problems was met in this book by asking each authority to write to a common outline (for each chapter) and to devote equivalent space to each topic within each chapter.

Thus, each author gives his authoritative views on a particular theory, and yet the book is disciplined and readable. This is particularly important when a book can be read "horizontally," from section to section, a procedure recommended for those interested in comparisons between theories.

The issue of selecting theories represents a heavy burden for an editor. How it was solved in *Current Personality Theories* is discussed at length in the Introduction. My first intention was to have ten theories, each representative of a different perception about the nature of human nature. However, after selections were made, a chapter on Asian theories and one on Soviet personality theory were added. And this was still not enough. In the final chapter I added twelve more theories, briefly summarized, to give a fuller picture of the scene currently in personality theory and application. These accounts were subsequently reviewed by experts. The twelve theories in Chapter 14 are as follows: Karen Horney's Psychosocial Theory, J. L. Moreno's Sociometric Theory, Abraham Maslow's Self-Actualization, H. A. Murray's Needs-Press Theory, Eric Berne's Transactional Analysis, Erik Erikson's Developmental Theory, Fritz Perls's Gestalt Theory, Albert Ellis's Rational-Emotive Theory, William Glasser's Reality Theory, Albert Bandura's Social Learning Theory, Hans J. Eysenck's Typological Theory and Harold Greenwald's Direct Decision Therapy Theory.

Current Personality Theories is truly a group effort. Some 50 people were involved in its production in one way or another. My major adviser and consultant was Dr. Edgar F. Borgatta, the coeditor of a massive handbook on personality theories[1] and

[1] E. F. Borgatta and W. W. Lambert (Eds.), *Handbook of Personality Theory and Research.* Chicago: Rand McNally, 1968.

also the author of the section on personality theories in the *Encyclopaedia Britannica,* 15th Edition. He was an unfailing source of ideas and assistance throughout the five years of planning and production.

In Hawaii I had an informal consortium of people on whom I called for all sorts of assistance: advice, suggestions, judgments. They include (listed alphabetically): Drs. Jack Annon, Gary Beck, Milton Bloombaum, Minnie Boggs, Irving Copi, Milton Diamond, Laurence Jacobs, Hillavi Kroon, Anthony Marsella, Floyd Matson, Jerrold Shapiro, and Arnold Schwartz. Others elsewhere were of help in various aspects, including Drs. Heinz Ansbacher, Ledford Bischof, Vincent Calia, Richard Coan, Albert Ellis, Harold Greenwald, Nira Kefir, Arthur Lerner, H. A. Murray, and Howard Parad.

My wife, Dr. Kleona Rigney, helped in several important ways: giving her common-sense opinions about the suitability of contents and clarity of writing, and also by doing some of my chores while I was surrounded by piles of manuscripts. Parts of the typing and clerical work of this book were done by Maureen Dinker, Brenda Nishimura, and Roberta Rigney. The glossary was based on a search through the manuscript for difficult words by Mrs. Alida Labrie. The publisher, F. Edward Peacock, was generous with time and money and his college editor, Tom LaMarre, was of constant and unfailing help.

But the greatest appreciation is due to the authors of the chapters. Not only does their work largely comprise the contents of the book, but, as one can see from the credits of the authors on pages xi-xiv, they are busy and important people. Nevertheless, they agreed to common guidelines governing what to say and how much to say and in what order to say it.

Finally, this long, demanding, and exhausting task is over. It called for dealing with a half hundred people, handling 1.5 thousand sheets of paper, and making thousands of decisions, small and large. This volume may not be the perfect book that had been envisaged, but it is certainly an adequate representation of the most important areas in personality theorizing. Hopefully, it will help advance understanding of human nature, and it will lead to newer, more encompassing and more useful theories of personality.

Raymond J. Corsini

Authors

ANSBACHER, HEINZ L., Ph.D.
Emeritus professor, University of Vermont
Fulbright lecturer, University of Kiel, Germany
Former president, Division 24 (Philosophical Psychology), American Psychological Association
> *The Individual Psychology of Alfred Adler,* 1956
> *Journal of Individual Psychology,* 1957–1973
> *Suicide: The Adlerian Point of View (Farberow and Shneidman, The Cry for Help),* 1961
> *Superiority and Social Interest,* 1964
> *Individual Psychology (Arieti, American Handbook of Psychiatry),* 1974

CORSINI, RAYMOND J., Ph.D.
Private practice, clinical psychology, Honolulu
Senior counselor, Family Education Centers of Hawaii
Formerly associate professor, University of California (Berkeley)
> *Methods of Group Psychotherapy,* 1957
> *Critical Incidents in Psychotherapy,* 1959
> *Roleplaying in Psychotherapy,* 1966
> *Current Psychotherapies,* 1973
> *The Practical Parent,* 1975

GIOVACCHINI, PETER L., M.D.
Private practice, psychoanalysis, Chicago
Clinical professor, University of Illinois Medical School
Co-editor, *Adolescent Psychiatry,* 1971–1974
> *Psychoanalytic Treatment of Schizophrenia and Characterological Disorders,* 1967
> *Tactics and Techniques of Psychoanalytic Therapy,* 1971
> *Psychoanalysis of Character Disorders,* 1975
> *Tactics and Techniques of Psychoanalytic Therapy—Contratransference,* 1975
> *Psychoanalysis of Primitive Mental States,* 1976

HOLDSTOCK, T. L., Ph.D.
Visiting fellow, Center for the Studies of the Person, La Jolla, Cal.
Senior lecturer, Department of Psychology, University of Witwatersrand, South Africa

KOBASA, SUZANNE C., Ph.D.
Lecturer, University of Chicago
Formerly psychiatric clinician, Connecticut Mental Health Center, New Haven, Conn.

LUNDIN, ROBERT W., Ph.D.
Professor and chairman, Department of Psychology, The University of the South, Sewanee, Tennessee
Associate editor, *The Psychological Record*
Formerly associate professor, Hamilton College
> *Personality: An Experimental Approach*, 1961
> *Principles of Psychopathology*, 1965
> *An Objective Psychology of Music*, 1967
> *Theories and Systems of Psychology*, 1972
> *Personality: A Behavioral Analysis*, 1974

MADDI, SALVATORE R., Ph.D.
Professor, psychology and social sciences, University of Chicago
Private practice, clinical psychology
Formerly visiting professor, Harvard University, 1969–1970
> *Functions of Varied Experience*, 1961
> *Perspectives on Personality: A Comparative Approach*, 1971
> *Humanism in Personology, Allport, Maslow, Murray*, 1972
> *Personality Theories: A Comparative Analysis*, 1976

MADURO, RENALDO J., Ph.D.
Private practice, clinical psychology, San Francisco
Research psychologist, Langley Porter Neuropsychiatric Institute
Formerly lecturer, Neuropsychiatric Institute, Banaras Hindu University, India
> *Artistic Creativity in a Brahmin Painter Community*, 1976

PEDERSEN, PAUL B., Ph.D.
Associate professor, University of Minnesota
Senior fellow, East-West Center, University of Hawaii
Formerly U.S. Director of Research, Japan–U.S. Intercultural Communication Institute
> *Batak Blood and Protestant Soul*, 1970
> *Counseling Across Cultures*, 1975
> *Culture and Mental Health*, 1975
> *Ethnicity in Indonesia*, 1975

ROGERS, CARL R., Ph.D.
Resident fellow, Center for the Study of the Person, La Jolla, Cal.
Formerly professor, Universities of Chicago and Wisconsin
Formerly president, American Psychological Association

> *Client-Centered Therapy*, 1951
> *On Becoming a Person*, 1961
> *Freedom to Learn*, 1969
> *Carl Rogers on Encounter Groups*, 1970
> *Becoming Partners: Marriage and Its Alternatives*, 1972

SAHAKIAN, WILLIAM S., Ph.D.
Professor, Suffolk University, Massachusetts
Advisory editor, Rand McNally Publishing Co.
Formerly lecturer, Northeastern University, Massachusetts

> *Psychology of Personality*, 1965/1974
> *Psychotherapy and Counseling*, 1969/1976
> *Systematic Social Psychology*, 1974
> *History and Systems of Psychology*, 1975
> *Introduction to the Psychology of Learning*, 1976

SECHREST, LEE, Ph.D.
Professor, Florida State University
Formerly professor, Northwestern University

> *Unobtrusive Measures*, 1966
> *Psychotherapy and the Psychology of Behavior Change*, 1966
> *Psychology and Human Problems*, 1967
> *Psychological Foundations of Education*, 1970
> *The Nature and Study of Psychology*, 1973

SHONTZ, FRANKLIN C., Ph.D.
Professor, University of Kansas
President, Division 22 (Rehabilitation Psychology), American
  Psychological Association, 1975–1976
Formerly chief psychologist, Cuyahoga County Hospital, Cleve-
  land, Ohio

> *Research Methods in Personality*, 1976
> *Perceptual and Cognitive Aspects of Body Experience*, 1969
> *Psychology in Progress*, 1971
> *The Psychological Aspects of Physical Illness and Disability*,
>   1975

STRAUSS, ANSELM, Ph.D

Chairman, graduate program in sociology, University of California, San Francisco

Formerly research director, Social Science Laboratory, Psychosomatic and Psychiatric Institute, Michael Reese Hospital, Chicago

> *Time for Dying*, 1967
> *Mirror and Masks: The Search for Identity*, 1970
> *Where Medicine Fails*, 1970
> *Chronic Illness and the Quality of Life*, 1973
> *Social Psychology*, 1975

WHEELWRIGHT, JOSEPH B., M.D.

Professor emeritus, clinical psychiatry, University of California Medical School

Senior analyst, Society of Jungian Analysts of Northern California, San Francisco

Formerly president, International Association of Analytical Psychology, 1965–1971

> *Sex and the College Student*, 1966
> *Reality of the Psyche*, 1968
> *Analytic Process, Aims, Analysis, Training*, 1968
> *Jung's Psychological Types*, 1973

ZIFERSTEIN, ISIDORE, M.D.

Private practice, psychiatry, Los Angeles

Associate clinical professor, psychiatry, University of California, Los Angeles

Formerly research fellow, Foundations' Fund for Research in Psychiatry, 1963–1965

> *Psychological Habituation to War: A Sociopsychological Case Study*, 1967
> *Soviet Psychiatry: Past, Present, Future*, 1969

No topic is more interesting to people than people. Biographies, auto-biographies, histories, novels, plays, and newspapers are about people. Short stories, poems, movies, television commercials and children's books are about people. Peter Rabbit, Br'er Fox, Mickey Mouse and the Little Engine That Could are humans in animal or machine disguise. Of all courses in college, the most popular are those that deal with people. Our interest about ourselves and others is boundless and endless. And yet, despite this enormous and constant interest, despite the novels and plays and books about people, at this point in history there still is no generally accepted, comprehensive, uniform understanding of human nature.

Introduction

Raymond J. Corsini

There are many personality theories, some extremely complex and complicated, some simple and clear, some old and some new, each intending to explain how we develop our unique personalities and how we maintain them.

The curious layman learns of the theories of the original big three, Sigmund Freud, Alfred Adler, and Carl Jung, and reads about the modern theories of Carl Rogers, Gordon Allport, B. F. Skinner, and George Kelly. He or she wonders about constitutional theories, existential theories, sociological theories, Asian theories, and Soviet theories about the nature of man. It is logical to ask: Why are there so many theories? Why can't they come to some agreements about human nature?

This book will help answer these questions. Probably you will be at first overwhelmed and confused by all the answers given, and then, hopefully, you will be able to see the entire spectrum of theories in a unified and comprehensive manner and begin to understand personality formation and maintenance—how we become and remain ourselves —and why we have so many theories about personality.

Toward a Definition of Personality

Allport (1937), who collected no fewer than 50 definitions of personality, divided them into five types:

1. *Omnibus.* Any definition that says "sum total" is an omnibus definition.
2. *Arrangement.* A second type of definition arranges personality traits in some orderly manner.
3. *Hierarchical.* This kind of definition views traits as stages of development, appearing in a fixed order.
4. *Adjustment.* Another definition type views the individual as struggling to find his identity, trying to adjust to the world.
5. *Distinctiveness.* This kind of definition stresses the individual's uniqueness.

Allport defined personality as follows:

Personality is the dynamic organization within the individual of those psychophysical systems that determine his unique adjustment to the world.

What are these psychophysical systems? To give "something" a name generates the idea that what is named actually exists. For example, in the statement, "Jim has a good deal of intelligence," the word *intelligence* tends to be conceived as something, that is as some *thing*, otherwise how could one have "a good deal" of it? We hear it in the same way we would hear this sentence: "Jim has a good deal of money." This process whereby abstract words gain meaning is known as reification or hypostatization: making a concept real through naming it. We shall soon give names to a number of concepts and then in a circular manner use them to explain behavior.

Concepts intended to explain something or assumed to exist as entities are known as *constructs.* They are imaginary and are used on an "as if " basis—*as if* they were real. The word *intelligence* thus represents a construct to explain why some people learn more quickly than others: *because they have a high intelligence.* While it is necessary in personality theory to create and to give names to various concepts, you should always keep in mind that constructs are hypothecated entities but are not real in the sense that

your arm or your nose is real.

Below is a partial list of hypothecated psychophysical systems within the individual, elements which make up what we call personality.

1. *Temperament.* A temperament is a biologically-based, physiological function. Thus, a "temperamental" person may be sensitive, nervous, fast-moving, irritable, and tense because he was "born that way." Some new-born infants are placid, while others are squirmy. We say that the first group has an even temperament, and the second is temperamental. In short, the basic concept of temperament is that it is biologically based.

2. *Trait.* A trait represents a constant or persistent way of behaving. Thus, if an individual tells the truth always, this is an indicator of his trait of honesty.

3. *Character.* The semantic problem of personality theory is illustrated by this word. Character can mean about the same as personality, but it can also mean about the same as trait, and it can mean "personality evaluated," as in "He has a good character." Generally, in personality theory, it has this third denotation, and it is used evaluatively, such as "She has a character defect," meaning that she tends to act unethically in certain circumstances.

4. *Mood.* This word represents a general, overriding, sometimes constant and sometimes temporary, emotional state. People who are generally sad or happy, optimistic or pessimistic, have these particular moods. The word "state" more or less means the same as mood. "He is in a bad mood" means that he behaves in an angry, emotional, touchy manner.

5. *Disposition.* This term has a similar meaning to the word *set* in general psychology. It means the tendency of an individual to act in a particular manner. A person who has a happy disposition is likely to see things in a pleasant way; a person with a mean disposition is likely to be cruel or punitive.

6. *Trend.* This term indicates direction. Thus a person may have a tendency to go one way or another. Disposition and trend fit together in the sense that one may be disposed (set) to go in a particular direction (trend).

7. *Habit.* This refers to a persistent mode of behavior generally fixed, constant and automatic.

8. *Attitude.* This term encompasses opinions, views and dispositions representing a generalized set of values toward classes of objects.

Personality and Values

Psychology is neutral, but psychologists are not. As a science, psychology is not concerned with good or bad, but as a profession, it is certainly tied up with values. This position is quite common for all sciences. A physician who examines under a microscope a parasite that may be harming his patient has no animosity to that particular creature, even though he may prescribe medicine as a cure, thereby killing the parasite. The term *normal* is used in one way by the psychologist-as-scientist (normal = average) and in a different way by the psychologist-as-therapist (normal = desirable). The same is true for other evaluative terms about personality, such as good, desirable, pleasant, strong, or impressive. These terms are employed by people who like or dislike certain aspects of certain people, but they do not have constant meanings. In personality theory we will not be concerned about "good" and "bad" personalities and not even about "normality" and "abnormality." We will be simply concerned with how people develop and maintain their personality.

Perspectives

Any individual can be viewed from three perspectives:

1. *Subjectively*—as the person sees himself.
2. *Objectively*—as seen by others.
3. *Veridically*—as one really is.

We all strive for veridicality, but no one can ever know if this state of absolute truth is ever reached.

To illustrate, let us take the person about whom more biographies have been written than anyone else: Napoleon Bonaparte. Suppose that Napoleon himself, his wife Josephine, and his Austrian opponent Metternich were asked to use the most appropriate word to describe him relative to the seven characteristics listed at the left of Table 1-1.

The table shows three different perspectives on one man. Napoleon probably saw his own lifestyle as cautious, while Josephine saw him as daring and Metternich as being secretive. Which view is the more accurate? Not only do we not know, but the answer is never knowable. When we talk about personality of any person, we are always dealing with opinions—not facts. It is not a fact that Napoleon was smart or kind or brave or ambitious or wily, even though everyone might have so agreed. It is not a fact that Lincoln was compassionate or that Washington was truthful or that Roosevelt was energetic.

Imagine the consequences when two sets of personality concepts clash. This explains many conflicts between husbands and wives, children and parents, employees and employers. It explains racial and religious prejudices when personalities of groups of people are identified.

Issues in Personality Theory

Personality theories take up many disputed issues—some going back to the very beginnings of concern about human nature, none of them ever settled.

Below are some important issues:

Responsibility. Suppose someone breaks the law, to what degree is he responsible? In most of our states the McNaghten rule applies: People are not responsible for their behavior if they are considered insane, but otherwise they are responsible and if they break the law, they deserve punishment.

Table 1-1: Hypothetical Judgments About Napoleon Bonaparte

Characteristics	NAPOLEON	JOSEPHINE	METTERNICH
LIFESTYLE	Cautious	Daring	Secretive
INTELLIGENCE	Foresighted	Clever	Shrewd
STABILITY	Self-controlled	Jealous	Suspicious
DOMINANCE	Independent	Aggressive	Stubborn
ACTIVITY	Active	Quick	Hasty
SENSITIVITY	Appreciative	Sensitive	Sarcastic
MOOD	Worrying	Excitable	Emotional

Personality theorists assume a variety of attitudes on this issue of responsibility. Some say that the person is completely determined by the environment; he has no choice about his behavior. Others take the biological deterministic position that from the instance of conception the individual's personality is established by heredity, and, consequently, he has no choice. Another deterministic attitude is that the individual's behavior is controlled by environment and heredity —but again he cannot be considered responsible. He has no choice.

These three points of view of the individual's powerlessness are rejected in the real world by everyone, including the strictest of theoreticians. One can visualize a professor who accepts theoretically the inability of the individual to make real decisions or to be responsible nevertheless telling a student: "You'd better make up your mind to do some studying, otherwise you'll fail my course."

A fourth general position relative to this issue of responsibility is "soft determinism," which holds that a person does have freedom to make judgments and decisions, and he is responsible, but his thinking and his behaving are affected and limited by both heredity and environment. A fifth position, generally assumed by the law and by some religions, is that regardless of heredity or environment, each not-insane individual is fully responsible for his own behavior, and we all have free will.

Proof. Another important issue in personality theory has to do with proof. There are three general ways of trying to prove any issue. The first is by logic. One may start with what appears to be a valid statement, such as Descartes's famous "I think, therefore I am", and having made this point can go on to further theorizing. So-called armchair philosophers often assume that how they think and feel and act is similar to how all others operate, and so they project themselves as representatives of mankind.

A second general way of getting proof is to depend on observations of a number of individuals taken one at a time. This clinical method is known technically as the idiographic method. Freud is an example of an idiographic therapist who came to general nomothetic conclusions about human nature. He would study an individual thoroughly, and on the basis of all the evidence he had would come to conclusions not only about that person but about people in general. His conclusions would be backed also by his own experiences, knowledge of other patients, and readings. Generally speaking, the understandings of human nature given by clinicians such as Freud and Rogers and Albert Ellis come from close attention to individual patients dealt with over a long time.

The third way of getting proof about personality theories is by experimentation. In this procedure many people are observed or tested and conclusions are based on group norms. Allport and Skinner are examples of theorists who validate their contentions on the basis of the nomothetic method.

Time. Theorists differs relative to time emphasis. There are three general positions. Some, such as Freud, generally emphasize the importance of the *past*: one's heredity, one's childhood. Others, such as Ludwig Binswanger, emphasize the importance of the *present*, the immediate moment, the now. Still others, such as Alfred Adler, emphasize the importance of the future, holding that expectation of attainment of goals explains behavior.

An eclectic position might be that a person makes decisions in the *present* in terms of his expectations for the *future,* affected by his experiences in the *past,* so that the past, the present, and the future are involved to some degree at all times.

Consciousness. There are three points of view about consciousness. One is that consciousness is a private matter and so is meaningless and valueless. People should simply be evaluated objectively in terms of behavior, without consideration of what may be in their heads. A second point of view states that personality is really one's consciousness: How one thinks and feels is what personality is all about, since behavior is a consequence of one's thoughts and emotions. A third point of view states that the unconscious is what is really important and that consciousness is only the tip of the personality iceberg.

For a behaviorist such as B. F. Skinner, the concept of consciousness is unimportant in understanding personality; for a commonsense theorist such as Rogers, one's consciousness and self-awareness explain personality; and for a depth theorist such as Jung, the real understanding of personality depends on the unconscious.

Integrity. Some personality theorists see the individual as an indissolvable, single unity. A person is mind-body and not body and mind. Those who assume such unity are monists. Those who assume the existence of mind and body are dualists. A pluralist might add "soul" and sees the individual as having a body and a mind and a soul.

Learning. One difference between theorists often has to do with how much learning, under what conditions, and what kinds of learning occur, rather than with whether one learns or not. Personality is usually considered by all theorists as modifiable, some in terms of autochthonous processes and some by environmental processes, and some by both internal and external processes.

The Mind. A monist who believes there is only body is impatient with any discussion about "mind." Behaviorists following the original notions of John B. Watson may not deny their own phenomenology or that others have thought and feelings, but they believe that psychology should be the science of behavior; any concern with subjective awareness leads to a dead end and so should simply be disregarded.

Those who do take the mind-body position have a variety of views. One of them is *interactionism,* namely that the body affects the mind and the mind affects the body. Psychosomatic medicine, for example, is interactionism. Another point of view is *parallelism,* that the mind and body operate in a synchronous manner but do not directly affect one another.

Functions of the Mind. If we accept the existence of mental processes, then it should be possible to make some sort of divisions of the mind. The most common separation is in two parts: cognition and affection. Cognitive or "thinking" functions are remembering, planning, creating, imagining, and so on, and affective or "emotional" functions are feeling, suffering, worrying, and so on.

Balance. Another important concept is whether the person generally tends to inertia or to change. There are a number of terms relative to this issue. Conation (an old name for will-want-volition-desire) is the tendency for an individual to move forward, change, modify, develop.

Some people see the person as constantly in motion towards goals. Adler and Karen Horney are examples of theorists who feature this aspect. The contrasting position is homeostasis, the ultimate tendency of the individual to remain at rest, to be in balance, to achieve quietude, harmony, equilibrium.

Viewpoint. By viewpoint is meant whether the theorist starts from the "top" or from the "bottom," whether he is inductive or deductive in approach. An inductive theorist is generally a reductionist and takes a mechanistic, elementarist view: The individual is composed of parts—organs which, fitted together, make the person. The deductive theorist takes a molar, holistic, Gestalt type of view about the person, seeing him as an indivisible unit operating on the basis of some organizing principle.

Zeitgeist. It is possible that personality theories are a function of the dominant philosophical-political position of one's society, the Zeitgeist. Pastore (1949) has shown that psychologists' theories are related to their politicosocial views. The theorist is not necessarily free of the influences of his own environment. He is quite likely to be biased by his sociopolitical views and to present to the world something which he believes to be objectively true but which nonetheless is a distorted personal view.

This social issue has important consequences. All our interactions with people are based on certain conceptualizations of the nature of people. A school staffed and directed by Adlerians would be quite different from one directed by Sheldonites. A prison operating on the basis of the theory of Allport would be different from one run by Jungians.

In Pastore's research, hereditarians were generally politically conservative, while environmentalists were politically liberal. Those in the hereditarian camp are more likely to espouse a eugenic point of view, while those in the environmental camp will likely take a euthenic stance on social issues.

Summary

Semantics. One of the major problems of personality theory is the issue of language. There are many difficulties in communication. Here are some of them. (1) *Translations.* Since some of the more important theories, including the first three in this book, were originally written in foreign languages and then translated into English, the issue of proper translation is important. The fact is that in some cases the translation was improper (as for example Freud's *Trieb*, by which he meant *drive* but was translated as *instinct*); in some cases an apparently proper translation gives a wrong impression (*Individuale Psychologie* translated into English as *Individual Psychology* gives a completely incorrect impression that Adler's system is about individuals, when the word *Individuale* as used by Adler meant *unitary* or *indivisible*); or in some cases there just is no accurate translation (Adler's term *Gemeinschaftsgefühl* which literally means "a feeling for community" is best, but still inadequately, translated as *social interest*.) (2) *Duplications.* Different theorists may mean the same thing and yet used different words. An example is Freud's *defense mechanism* and Adler's *safeguarding tendency*. (3) *Varying denotations.* The same word may be used by different theorists to have somewhat different meanings. *Transference* to a psychoanalyst means a displacement of affect from one person to another but to an eclectic therapist it may simply mean a strong emotional reaction or attachment by the therapist to patient or vice versa. (4) *Unrecognized commonalities.* In many theories there is implicit the notion of innate growth, or inherited propensity for perfection, or drive to perfection, etc., but this and other concepts are not generally made explicit.

As an examination of the glossary starting on page 433 shows, the special language of personality theory is rather extensive.

Personal factors. The question asked earlier: "Why are there so many theories?" may be answered simply by saying that personality theorists project their own personalities into their views about human nature. In an earlier publication (Corsini, 1956) the observation was made that the system of therapy and the manifest personalities of Freud, Rogers and Moreno were correlated. Having met and having gotten to know a number of the theorists in this book: Alfred Adler, Albert Ellis, Erik Erikson, Harold Greenwald, Karen Horney, Abraham Maslow, J. L. Moreno, Frederick Perls and Carl Rogers, it appears to me that the same can be said about theorists and personality theory: personality theories often seem to be a reflection of the theorist's own personality. Regardless of how much a theorist attempts to be impartial and objective, to verify hypotheses and to be cautious in suggesting theories, most probably there is some kind of bias which distorts perception. But this is what theories are all about: means for individuals to express opinions based on observations and contemplation.

Every theorist in this book has conducted clinical research and/or objective experimental research and is convinced of the validity of his or her views. One possible explanation for differences in views is that they do not necessarily contradict one another but simply represent different experiences, different awarenesses, different perceptions and finally different conclusions from others.

Metrics. In the history of science, advances often have been a function of metrics: instruments, tools, techniques. The telescope advanced astronomy, the microscope advanced medicine, and the weighing balance advanced chemistry. Also, in the history of science, advances have been a function of classifications. Mendeleev's periodic law and Linnaeus's biological structure permitted students of chemistry and zoology to cooperate in systematic study. Personality researchers and theoreticians badly need objectives, valid and reliable instruments and meaningful matrixes to measure accurately and to planfully evaluate.

Extensive work in this area has been done by Raymond B. Cattell (1965, 1967) and a number of other researchers in this field, including Hans J. Eysenck, J. P. Guilford, and Frederick Thorne. Cattell has been producing prodigious amounts of information in the two important areas of charting the basic traits of personality and in providing objective instruments for the measurement of facets of personality through multivariate research studies.

Our intention in this first half of the Introduction is to raise questions, to consider issues, to help you realize that personality theories have important personal and social consequences. They are not "just theories." The theory that you personally will accept is highly likely to be one that fits in with your own world-view.

While it is extremely difficult not to take sides and to find some theories more sensible than others, in reading the theories in this book you should be alert to the strong possibility of only reinforcing your present biases. For your personal development and for the sake of science, you should be as neutral and as open-minded as possible and for as long as possible, especially as regards those views you are likely to reject if they contradict your own position philosophically, socially, or politically.

We have by no means touched on all the important issues involved in personality theories. We could discuss personality theories in relation to religion, to social movements, to history, to science, to politics, to individual growth and still be legitimately within our area of discussion. However, limitations of space and the constraints of the purpose of this book do not make this possible.

Construction of the Book

Now I will part the curtains, as it were, and take you backstage to tell you something about how this book was planned and developed. If you participate vicariously in the process of editing this book, you may become more sensitive to some of the issues in personality theory, and thus you will be more involved and more motivated to understand this complex and fascinating subject.

All substantive chapters in this book have a common outline. The reason for this uniformity originally came from my own study of personality theory. Everyone seemed to be trying to "sell" me something, to convince me of the correctness of one point of view. And just as I agreed to something, someone else would get me to agree to something else, but they didn't seem to be discussing the same sorts of things. This general tendency among writers about personality theory for each to go his own merry way did not seem to me to be a proper method of science or of teaching. I vowed if I would ever do a book on personality theories, it would, if possible, provide for direct comparisons.

To achieve this end, I gathered terms such as *teleology, instincts, unconscious, constructs, emotions, determinism, cognition* (some of which you will find in the Glossary) and then categorized them. Eventually, these terms led to the creation of the outline of the book, which was sent to authors of the chapters with an explanatory manual.

The authors were asked to discuss these various concepts in the several sections of their chapters. Each chapter was to begin with a short abstract, to provide a quick understanding of that particular personality theory. Consequently, if you want a rapid overall view of the first 12 theories, you should read the first section of each chapter. Every chapter also includes the following sections:

1. *Introduction.* This part for each chapter is intended to show the need for the particular theory, by discussing it in terms of history, politics, religion, social movements, logical necessity, science, and so on.

2. *History.* This section provides an understanding of the *precursors* of each theory, the story of its *beginnings* and its *current status*. In addition, the authors were asked to discuss *similar theories*.

3. *Assertions.* This section is the heart of each chapter. It is divided into two parts: *development* (of personality) and *maintenance* (of personality). Each author was asked to make a number of short statements summarizing what the theory he discussed is all about and then to comment on these assertions. The goal was to achieve short, simple sentences about the essence of the various theories.

4. *Applications.* Since a theory not used is not of much value, the practical applications of the various theories are considered—how they are used in *assessment*, in *treatment*, and in *institutions*. The authors were asked to speak to the readers directly about the issue of *self:* What does that theory say of practical use about life, success, happiness, goodness? I believe this to be an innovation in a personality textbook.

5. *Validation.* To give proof of the correctness of their theories, the authors were asked first for *evidence*, hard facts, and then for critical *comparisons* with other theories. This was a difficult chore for some authors, who did not want to discuss other theories critically but preferred to discuss only their own. The authors' manual on this issue read:

Comparisons. This is a hot potato. You are to criticize (*ad verbum*, not *ad hominem*) other systems.

Try to mention as many systems as you feel comfortable with. Purpose: The whole book is seen as an exposition of a unified system of personality theory—and each of us is seeking to give our opinions about what is true and what is false. We now want to attack errors and mistakes in our own system as well as other systems. But essentially, this division attacks other systems.

Some authors were not as critical as they could have been. Nevertheless, in this book you will find authorities on a particular system taking pot shots at other theories, and this is unusual in books on personality theory.

Why this aggressive destructiveness? Science develops in two ways: through creators, who build up theories; and critics, who destroy theories. Both are equally useful. A critical confrontation—with some authors "selling" their theories and other authors "criticizing" them—can provide a lively sense of the competition in personality theory.

6. *Prospect.* Pyschologists generally assume the viewpoint that personality theory is science rather than philosophy. If it is a science, there can be an eventual convergence of all theories into one final theory of human nature. The present situation is similar to that of the blind men describing the elephant: Each theorist sees the truth, but not the whole truth.

This notion underlies every chapter and section of this book but is most appropriately seen in the prospect sections, in which the authors look into the future for their theories, other theories, and personality theory in general.

7. *Annotated Bibliography.* Some of the theories presented in this book should interest you enough to make you want to explore them further, and therefore each author has suggested a half dozen or so major titles for further investigation. These are accompanied by comments to indicate their particular nature and value.

Selection of Theories

Once an outline for the chapters on personality theory had been established, the next problem was to select the theories to be discussed. The usual method textbook writers and editors seem to use is to select theories in terms of their familiarity with them or their estimates of their importance. Deciding to operate somewhat differently, I gathered the names of a large number of personality theorists, as listed in Table 1-2, and read from the original and secondary literature about those with which I was not too familiar. Then I evaluated these theories in terms of the criteria listed below:

1. Is the individual seen as determined (unresponsible) or indetermined (responsible)?
2. What kind of proof is sought for: clinical or experimental?
3. Where is the time emphasis: past, present, future?
4. Is the individual seen as mostly conscious or unconscious?
5. Is the person seen as a whole or as a sum of parts?
6. How important is learning in the theory, in comparison to instincts?
7. What is the nature of the role of the body to the mind?
8. Is the individual seen primarily as cognitive or affective?
9. Does the individual seek for inertia or for movement?
10. Is the system of the inductive or the deductive type?
11. Is the system "conservative" or "radical" sociopolitically?

In terms of my perceptions of the maturity of the systems which developed in replying to these questions, I selected 35 theories for further consideration. I then went through a number of steps (discussed below) to reduce these 35 selections to 10.

The Selection Process

Step 1. The names of the screened theorists and the names of the major theories were put on 35 cards. These cards were presented to several advisers, with the following instructions:

A. Group these cards in terms of their similarity as types.
B. Now that you have separated them into clusters, select the one theory in each cluster you believe to be the most representative (or the most important) of that type.

As a result 10 clear-cut clusters were identified.

Step 2. Each of the 35 theories was then evaluated independently in terms of the 11 cri-

TABLE 1-2: A Partial List of Current Personality Theories

Abelson, R. P.	Least effort	Jung, Carl	Analytical psychology
Adler, Alfred	Individual psychology	Kelly, Charles	Neo-Reichian theory
Allport, G. W.	Personalism	Kelly, George A.	Personal constructs
Angyll, Andreas	Organismic theory	Kohlberg, Lawrence	Moral developmental theory
Assiogoli, Roberto	Psychosynthesis	Korsybski, Alfred	General semantics
Bandura, Albert	Social learning theory	Lecky, P.	Self-consistency
Berne, Eric	Transactional analysis	Lewin, Kurt	Topological psychology
Binswanger, Ludwig	Daseinsanalysis	Low, A. A.	Semantic theory
Blake, R. R.	Grid theory	Lowen, Alexander	Bio-energetics
Branden, Nathaniel	Biocentrism	Maltz, Albert	Psychocybernetics
Burrow, Trigant	Phyloanalysis	Maslow, Abraham	Self-actualization
Buhler, Charlotte	Humanistic psychology	May, Rollo	Existentialism
Buhler, Karl	Funktionslust	Mead, G. H.	Social interaction
Boss, Medard	Daseinsanalysis	Meyer, Adolf	Psychobiological theory
Cattell, Raymond B.	Multivariate exper-	Miller, Neal	Learning theory
	imental theory	Moreno, J. L.	Sociometry
Combs, Arthur	Phenomenology	Mowrer, O. H.	Two-factor theory
Dollard, John	Learning theory	Murphy, Gardner	Biosocial theory
Ellis, Albert	Rational-emotive theory	Murray, H. A.	Need-press theory
Erikson, Erik	Developmental theory	Osgood, Charles	Congruity theory
Eysenck, Hans	Factor theory	Perls, Frederick	Gestalt therapy theory
Feldenkreis, Moishe	Body awareness	Piaget, Jean	Developmental theory
Festinger, Leon	Cognitive dissonance	Rank, Otto	Will theory
Fisher, Seymour	Body image theory	Reich, Wilhelm	Character analysis
Frankl, Viktor	Logotherapy	Rogers, Carl	Person-centered theory
Freud, Sigmund	Psychoanalysis	Rolf, Ida	Structural integration
Fromm, Erich	Humanistic psychoanalysis		theory
Gendlin, Eugene	Experiential theory	Rotter, Julian	Social learning
Glasser, William	Reality theory	Sarbin, Theodore	Role theory
Goldstein, Kurt	Organismic theory	Schutz, William	Open encounter
Greenwald, Harold	Direct decision theory	Sheldon, William H.	Morphological theory
Guilford, J. P.	Factor theory	Skinner, B. F.	Operant conditioning
Harvey, O. J.	Conceptual systems	Snygg, Donald	Phenomenology
Heider, F.	Balance theory	Sullivan, H. S.	Interpersonal theory
Horney, Karen	Sociopsychological theory	Thorne, Frederick	Eclecticism
Hubbard, H. Ron	Scientology	Thurstone, L. L.	Experimental theory
Jackins, Harvey	Reevaluation counseling	Van Kaam, Adrian	Transpersonal psychology
Jackson, Don	Systems theory	Walters, Bernard	Observational learning
Janov, Arthur	Primal theory	Werner, Heinz	Developmental psychology
Jourard, Sydney	Transparency theory	Wolpe, Joseph	Behavior theory

teria defined above. Dr. Milton Bloombaum of the University of Hawaii grouped the theories mathematically, using the Guttmann Multidimensional Scalogram Analysis Method. This was an independent validation of Step 1. The results obtained were about the same as the findings of the clinical clusterings made by the advisers.

Step 3. I made my selections using the first two steps as guides.

As you can see, the book does not concentrate on ten theories but on a dozen. The other theories were added after discussing the outline of the book with advisers. Dr. Laurence Jacobs suggested that this was *not* a book on current personality theories; rather it was about Occidental personality theories. As a result, another chapter, on Asian theories, was added. Then Dr. Heinz L. Ansbacher insisted that Soviet personality theo-

ry must be included, and this twelfth chapter was added.

But this was not to be the end. In discussing the book with various individuals, many showed surprise and shock that certain theories had been left out. Therefore Chapter 14 was added to briefly summarize 12 additional personality theories.

As a result, the book got to be considerably larger than originally planned. I believe it now truly deserves its title, however.

Dimensions of Personality Theory

If the study of personality theories is to be scientific, then the scientific method must be applied. This means operational definitions,

clear-cut categorizations, consensual valida-
tions, replicable experiments—the usual scientific procedures which call for precision and which
lead to hard data.

It might seem impossible to apply the scientific method to such complex, diffuse, contradictory, and vague phenomena as theories of personality. How can one measure intangibles? How
can one categorize a theory with millions of
words? How can one find meaningful dimensions
that will permit comparison between theories?

The usual procedure throughout the centuries
has been to make arbitrary judgments; such armchair theorizing is quite common in this field.
Anyone can endlessly subdivide personality
theories in different ways. However, it does not
advance personality theory as a science to operate on the basis of solitary opinions. To make
meaningful comparisons, what is needed is a
firm delineation of the dimensions of personality
theory. Such information does exist, but unfortunately, I learned about it only after I had made
my initial selections.

Coan and Zagona (1962) located 142 psychological theorists and then had them rated by experts. Eventually, they isolated 54 important
theorists. Later Coan (1968) developed a series
of 34 variables in four categories relative to personality theories. The four categories and some
of the variables are listed in Table 1-3.

Coan now had 54 important theorists and 34
crucial variables. Each variable was put on a
five-point scale. He then located 232 presumably
qualified experts, mostly psychologists, who were
asked to rate theorists they were familiar with on
these 34 variables. This resulted in a 54 x 34 matrix. Correlations were made between the variables, and the resulting mass of data was analyzed
mathematically through a procedure known as
factor analysis to yield what Coan was looking
for—relatively independent factors or dimensions of personality theory.

Thus, there is now available a method of categorizing the independent factors of personality
theory, based on the consensus of judgments of a
considerable group of individuals, and objectively evaluated via mathematical procedures. This
pattern of factors can be replicated for consistency of findings.

In Table 1-4 the theories featured in this book
are evaluated in terms of six of Coan's dimensions plus four of the criteria I used in selecting
the theories. Careful study of this table will give
you an overall understanding of the theories in
comparison to one another. (See Table 1-4 on
page 12.)

Why Study Personality Theory?

There are three main reasons why you should
learn personality theory.

For Its Own Sake

Any subject—be it curtain stretchers, wrestling,
the trajectory of missiles, the love life of the
wombat, Chinese culture, or lottery systems—is
a legitimate subject of study in its own right.
Personality theory is a topic well worth understanding for its own sake. It is complex, interpe-
netrated with literature, culture, politics,
science, art, religion, and history, and innately
fascinating because of the enormous variety of
personalities and the sometimes peculiar behavior of individuals.

For the Sake of Personal Adjustment

You live in a world of people who affect your life;
they can make you happy or they can make you
unhappy. But you have to live the rest of your
life with yourself. If you understand yourself and
others, you are more likely to become successful

Table 1-3: Representative Items of Variables Used by
Coan (1968)

Content Emphasis:
  1. Learning
  2. Motivation
  3. Emotion
Methodological Emphasis:
  19. Statistical analysis
  20. "Armchair" theorizing
Basic Assumptions:
  23. Determinism
  24. Finalism—teleology
Modes of Conceptualization:
  26. Operational definitions of concepts
  34. Use of analogies based on physical systems

Note: The numbers are those employed by
Coan (1968)

and to feel part of the world. You can do better in your family, on your job, or in society if you understand yourself and others, and it is more likely that you will be able to achieve your potential.

Most individuals succeed in life by using their givens wisely and applying ways that work in their dealings with people. While understanding personality theories does not necessarily mean that you can or will apply what you learn, it is possible that your intellectual comprehension of personality will help you to put some of these ideas into successful practice.

The summaries of these two dozen theories have at least the potential of helping some people understand themselves and others better. Since knowledge is power, people reading this book may gain some power over themselves and their environment.

For the Sake of Idealism

I believe most people want a safe and happy world in which everyone lives together cooperatively. Most college students are idealistic and look forward to a better world—one without strife, discrimination, hatred, or tension. While the history of mankind has been a bloody one in which wars and revolutions and violence seem to have been constantly in existence, it is the hope of all people of goodwill that perhaps someday, somehow, we will really learn how to get along with one another. Religions and governments seem to have failed to make a better world for all. Perhaps, through science, we may learn how to live in peace and prosperity, free of fear from other humans. Then undoubtedly, personality theories will be important in leading to a better world.

Therefore, for the sake of studying the topic for its own interest, to satisfy our own personal needs, or for idealistic reasons, personality theories are a valuable topic for study.

References

Allport, G. W. *Personality: A psychological interpretation.* New York: Holt, Rinehart & Winston, 1937.

Cattell, R. B. *The scientific analysis of personality.* Baltimore: Penguin Books, 1965.

Cattell, R. B. *Objective personality and motivation tests.* Urbana: University of Illinois Press, 1967.

Coan, R. W. Dimensions of psychological theory. *American Psychologist,* 1968, *23,* 715–722.

Coan, R. W., & Zagona, S. V. Contemporary ratings of psychological theorists. *Psychological Record,* 1962, *12,* 315–322.

Corsini, R. J. Freud, Rogers and Moreno. *Group Psychotherapy,* 1956, *9,* 274–281.

McGuire, W. (Ed.) *The Freud-Jung letters: Correspondence between Sigmund Freud and C. G. Jung.* Princeton. N.J.: Princeton University Press, 1974.

Pastore, N. *The nature-nurture controversy.* New York: King's Crown, 1949.

Table 1-4: Ratings on Some Theories of Personality on Ten Dimensions

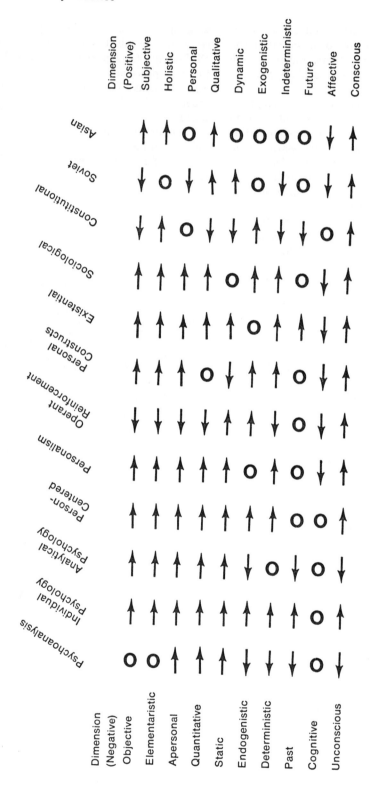

This table attempts to summarize ten dimensions of the 12 principal theories. The first six dimensions come from Coan (1968), and the remaining four are the editor's. An arrow pointing to the right means that the theory is considered to be positive with respect to the particular dimension. (Positive and negative are arbitrary designations.) A zero may mean that the dimension is unimportant to the theory, or is unknown, or that the theory encompasses both poles or is in between the two. In terms of this chart, Kelly's personal construct theory is seen as subjective, holistic, personal, static, exogenistic, indeterministic, cognitive, and conscious, but neither dynamic nor static, and neither past nor future-oriented. Zeros in the time dimension ordinarily mean that the theory is oriented to the present, e.g., Rogers' person-centered theory is oriented to the present rather than to the past or the future.

The meanings of the dimensions used in Table 1-4 are as follows:

1. *Objective–subjective.* Objective theories feature explicit, observable, unequivocal behavior that can be counted and numbered. Subjective theories are concerned with the inner personal life of an individual—his ineffable self—and are of the introspective type.

2. *Elementaristic–holistic.* Elementaristic theory sees the person as composed of parts: organs, units, elements put together to make the whole. Holistic theories see the person as having a central unity, and the parts as aspects of the total entity. The individual is seen as indivisible.

3. *Apersonal–personal.* Apersonal theories are impersonal, statistically based, and consider generalities rather than individualities. They are based on group norms. Personal theories deal with the single individual, or are idiographic.

4. *Quantitative–qualitative.* A quantitative theory makes it possible to measure units of behavior. A qualitative theory does not see behavior as able to be measured exactly, holding that behavior is too complex for such dealings.

5. *Static–dynamic.* Static theory sees the individual as a unit reactor, not a learner; filled with instincts, and based on generalizations preestablished by heredity. Dynamic theory is concerned with the individual as a learner, with interactions between behavior and consciousness and between consciousness and unconsciousness.

6. *Endogenistic–exogenistic.* Endogenous theories view the person as biologically based. They are constitutional theories. Exogenistic theories are social learning theories.

The remaining four dimensions are based on my own judgment of additional important factors involved in theories. These probably overlap to some degree with Coan's factor-based dimensions.

7. *Deterministic–indeterministic.* Deterministic theories in effect see the individual as not responsible for his behavior, as being the pawn of society, heredity, or both. Indeterministic theories put emphasis on self-direction of the individual. Control is within the person, and prediction is never completely possible.

8. *Past–future.* Some theories see the individual in terms of what he has inherited or learned in the past, and others see the individual as explained by his anticipation of future goals.

9. *Cognitive–affective.* Cognitive theories are the so-called ego theories which see man as essentially rational, with the emotions subserving the intellect. Conversely, affective theories see man as operating on an emotional basis, and with the intellect at the service of the emotions.

10. *Unconsciousness–consciousness.* Theories that stress the unconscious see the person as having considerable investment below the level of awareness. Consciousness refers to awareness, and such theories see the individual as rational.

Psychoanalysis began as a conceptual system designed to explain certain types of psychopathology. It later developed into a technique of treatment and finally expanded to a theory of personality of both normal and disturbed individuals. It has not, however, achieved the ultimate goal of being a comprehensive general psychology.

Originally developed by Sigmund Freud (1856–1939), psychoanalysis for many years had him as its only proponent. As a result, the theory still has many of his biases. Nevertheless, although still controversial, psychoanalysis is the oldest and most influential of all personality theories.

Psychoanalysis

Peter L. Giovacchini

Psychoanalysis, a depth psychology, views the mind as an entity containing primitive and sophisticated elements, hierarchically ordered. The primitive end of the spectrum has biologically based instincts (known as *id*) striving for expression against more structured reality-based elements (known as *ego*), which strive to make instinctual gratification consonant with internalized moral standards (known as *super-ego*).

Since psychoanalytic theory views psychopathology as a clash of forces within the mind, it is dynamic. Based upon deterministic principles, its foundation depends upon strict causality. The clashing forces within the personality are, for the most part, unconscious but nevertheless have effects on conscious feelings and behavior. An unconscious having effects on conscious (higher) levels of the personality is known as a dynamic unconscious and represents the most fundamental unique hypothesis of psychoanalytic theory.

Psychoanalytic treatment essentially is based upon interpretation by the analyst of unconscious motivations. Because the patient is allowed to verbalize freely (free association), he ascribes certain attributes of infantile feelings and relationships onto the therapist (transference). The classical analyst confines his therapy to the interpretation of the transference.

Today the psychoanalytic method, by focusing upon the structure of the psychic apparatus, in addition to instinctual impulses (Freud considered instincts differently than zoologists and ethologists do), permits a wider range of emotional disorders to be treated psychoanalytically than was the case originally.

Other than the immutability of a few fundamental concepts—such as the dynamic unconscious and working within the transference context—psychoanalysis is far from static. This is due to a unique interplay between learning and research activities and therapeutic application. One augments the other. This interplay not only sheds light upon man's most precious possession, his mind, it also leads to therapeutic innovations aimed at alleviating the misery of many apparently hopeless patients.

SIGMUND FREUD

Introduction

In the last century, the fundamental goal of medicine advanced from ameliorating symptoms to extinguishing diseases by eradicating causes. With the introduction of the germ theory of Louis Pasteur and Robert Koch and the discoveries in pathology by such giants as Rudolph Virchow, doctors became hopeful that eventually all diseases would be conquered. Such ideals were founded on a purely organic, physicochemical, materialistic approach.

Patients suffering from emotional problems tended to upset this idyllic outlook, but most investigators did not question the feasibility of searching for organic causes for emotional disturbances. They attributed their lack of knowledge about these disturbances to the fact that adequate methods to discover fundamental physiological causes had not yet been developed. In the late 1800s psychiatrists, then known as alienists, contented themselves for the most part with describing and classifying abnormal behavior. Most were inclined to think in terms of organic, neurological causes for disturbed behavior. This approach was useful for the understanding of certain dementias, but it did lead to insights about the neuroses and psychoses.

An extremely important discovery set dynamic psychiatry back many years. Just when many scientists were beginning to consider emotional problems in terms of intrapsychic factors, Hideyo Noguchi discovered (in 1904) that general paresis, a relatively common disease often characterized by states of grandiosity associated with insanity, was caused by bacteria. What was beginning to be looked upon as a functional psychosis turned out to be syphilis of the brain.

It is interesting to note that the only psychiatrist who ever received a Nobel prize was Julius von Wagner-Juaregg for his fever treatment of this same general paresis. These discoveries reinforced the hope that all mental diseases could be explained on a similar basis.

However, very little further has been discovered since then regarding organic etiology or treatment of emotional disorders. As a consequence, some investigators in the late 1800s and early 1900s returned to a psychological approach.

In such an environment, Freud discovered psychoanalysis. Psychoanalysis thus emerged because of clinical necessity. Those clinicians consumed by an unrelenting need to understand what was happening within a person's mind rather than just simply controlling behavior needed a conceptual system to restore order to the chaotic confusion that patients presented. This is where Freud entered the picture. He generated order where patients had been viewed as exhibiting meaningless behavior or outright shamming.

Although some analysts have modified Freud's superstructure and some of his metapsychological concepts, such as the energic hypothesis, the fundamental postulates of psychoanalysis remain unchanged today. Psychoanalysis is a science because it stems from observations made within a consistent frame of reference.

History

Precursors

Abnormal psychology goes back to Hippocrates. We shall not go into great detail regarding the forerunners of psychoanalysis since this topic has been admirably done by others, including Alexander and Selesnick (1966), Zilboorg and Henry (1941) and, in particular, Ellenberger's (1970) scholarly treatise.

Man has always been fascinated by mental aberrations and has usually concocted some remedy or explained mental phenomena whenever possible. Madness holds a particular fascination for people as do "mental" situations, such as dreams. One need only refer to the Bible or to Herodotus (1952) for examples of explanations of such phenomena.

Psychoanalysis is a pragmatic therapeutic procedure as well as a conceptual system. It joins early historical attempts aimed at restoring sanity. Some of these early therapies had rationales. Treatment was aimed at eliminating what were regarded as noxious causes. Most primitive therapies were based on the exorcism of internalized devils. Even though these orientations prevailed centuries ago, one cannot help being reminded of a best seller of the 1970s, *The Exorcist,* which was not universally considered a work of fiction.

Any therapy based upon restoring psychic equilibrium by eliminating causes can be considered a precursor of psychoanalysis. Methods used to achieve such resolutions have varied from primitive brain surgery (trephining) to torture. Others before Freud used free association, the principal tool of psychoanalysis. Freud apparently was quite familiar with Ludwig Börne, who recommended that one who wished to become a writer should put every thought that occurred to him on paper for three days, without any regard for coherence or relevance (see Jones, 1953). There is an interesting episode in one of Aristophanes' comedies (Aristophanes, 1955) where Socrates instructs a merchant to lie on a couch and uninhibitedly tell him what came to his mind. This episode seems very much like free association. In addition, the concept of the unconscious mind has been known for centuries. Reaching into the hidden depths of man's soul preoccupied poets, philosophers, and physicians, as well as the clergy. Nietzsche (1937) and Spinoza (1952), for example, gave descriptions of the unconscious similar to Freud's, and he openly acknowledged his debt to them.

In spite of similarities of various earlier procedures and systems of thought, Freud's resolution of causal factors, development of free association, and recognition of unconscious forces were combined in the unique fashion that unequivocally makes him the discoverer of psychoanalysis.

Beginnings

The construction of psychoanalysis, therefore, is the work of a single man, Sigmund Freud. In most other sciences it is usually possible to trace a continuum of development from antiquity to the present, punctuated with moments of deceleration (as in the Dark Ages) or acceleration (as in the 17th century). But Freud's achievement was discontinuous with what had preceded him; in terms of modern physics, it can be considered a quantum jump. Since he did not fit into any preexisting tradition, Freud worked alone, isolated for many years during a period which he referred to as his "splendid isolation" (Freud, 1914a).

Any great discovery creates opposition, since it disturbs established ways of thought. Freud (1914a) compared the reactions to his work with those experienced by Copernicus and Darwin. He noted that Copernicus's demolition of the geocentric theory threatened man's omnipotence regarding his central position in the universe, and Darwin's theory of evolution shook man's belief in his uniqueness of being specially created by God. Now psychoanalysis postulated that man was not even in control of his mind, because unknown forces within him ruled his behavior.

Freud is so important to psychoanalysis that some of his background is sketched below, to help account for the various movements within psychoanalysis. He was born in 1856 in Moravia (now part of Czechoslovakia), but when he was very young his family moved to Vienna. He did very well in school and was repeatedly the first in his class. He showed a great interest for the humanities: history, classical literature, and languages. Some of his early letters are truly remarkable for their erudition and sophistication (Freud, 1969). Nevertheless, he turned to science. It is interesting that at the tender age of 21 the future discoverer of castration anxiety wrote in his first article about his discovery of the testes of a particular species of eel, an animal whose genitals had not been previously located (see Freud, 1877).

After having graduated with honors from the gymnasium, Freud entered medical school. He was not particularly interested in treating patients (Freud, 1925, 1964); his main interest was in research. After graduation he postponed his final clinical training and spent eight years working under the renowned neurophysiologist Ernst Brücke.

His work in Brücke's laboratory was successful, and it seems that if he had remained, he might have achieved fame as a neurologist or neurophysiologist. In those days, research scientists were often gentlemen of means who did not rely upon their work for their income. Science was not sullied by pecuniary considerations, but Freud had to support his family. He had fallen in love and wanted to get married, so following Brücke's advice, he decided to leave the laboratory and make a living by the clinical practice of neurology. The majority of patients who came to a neurologist's office then usually turned out to be psychoneurotics. Because of his scientific background, and perhaps the natural bent of his mind, Freud was not content with the superficial therapies of the time—hydrotherapy, massage, and Faradic (electric) stimulation. There was considerable ambivalence about hypnosis, stemming from the ways Mesmer had employed it (Ellenberger, 1970). Freud, in his late twenties, had learned that the great Jean-Martin Charcot was using hypnosis to do marvelous things with hysterical patients in Paris. In his eagerness to learn more about their treatment, Freud spent nearly a year in Paris, attending Charcot's lectures and demonstrations and visiting and watching Hippolyte Bernheim hypnotize subjects. These experiences made a profound impression upon him.

The principal fact Freud learned from his Paris experience, mainly from Bernheim's experiments on posthypnotic suggestion, was that there is a part of the mind, largely unknown to consciousness, which nevertheless has effects upon feelings and behavior. In other words, he formulated the concept of the dynamic unconscious. The concept of the unconscious mind which influences feeling and behavior and can create symptoms is Freud's unique discovery. He now had a basis upon which he could begin to understand what, up to this time, had seemed totally irrational.

Returning to Vienna, Freud met considerable opposition from his colleagues when he tried to make them view hysterical patients from the viewpoint of a dynamic unconscious. Unfortunately for Freud, he presented his ideas in terms of unconscious sexual feelings which are capable of producing anxiety (Freud, 1895a, 1895b, 1898). The world was not ready for this viewpoint, and the combination of outraged morality and wounded narcissism which resulted from being told that there were forces within persons over which they had little control created considerable opposition. Freud therefore had to develop psychoanalysis mostly on his own. Ellenberger (1970) points out that the medical community was not particularly hostile to Freud. Freud found a sympathetic ear in Josef Breuer, a successful, well-respected Viennese internist who took a somewhat paternal interest in him. More important was the fact that Breuer was treating a patient by hypnosis. Charcot would suggest symptoms away, but Breuer regressed his patient back to a traumatic moment when the symptoms had begun and then, through catharsis (relieving tension by talking freely) and abreaction (emoting), was able to eliminate the symptom.

Freud collaborated extensively with Breuer, and together they produced *Studies on Hysteria* (Breuer & Freud, 1895), which Freud believed represented the beginnings of psychoanalysis, a discovery which at first he generously granted to Breuer but later withdrew (Freud, 1914a)—as he should have, since quite clearly the psychoanalytic aspects of this early book were written exclusively by Freud. In any case, after several years, Breuer was glad to dissociate himself from the movement (Jones, 1953).

Current Status

The current acceptance of psychoanalysis varies from country to country, and there have been considerable changes in astonishingly short periods of time. Psychoanalysis is practically nonexistent in Iron Curtain countries. In Vienna, Freud's birthplace, it was virtually ignored and has only recently become respectable. It received an enthusiastic early reception in England, and after World War II the United States became its strongest bastion. It has also achieved great popularity in Mexico and South America, although the situation is fluid, and rapid changes keep occurring.

After World War II, there was a rush of candidates in the United States to psychoanalytic institutes, and interest in psychoanalysis almost followed a geometric progression. In the 1960s a slow decline in the interest in psychoanalysis began to be noted, as encounter and sensitivity groups emerged and the drug culture developed.

Treatment Perspectives and Applications. Psychoanalysis as a treatment technique has encompassed a wider range of clinical conditions than the early practitioners anticipated. In addition to treating psychoneuroses, the only clinical entity that Freud finally concluded was amenable to analysis, the psychoanalytic method has been expanded to include the treatment of patients suffering from characterological disorders and some psychoses (Boyer & Giovacchini, 1967; Giovacchini, 1975, 1977).

Freud's model was based upon unconscious forces clashing with higher levels of the personality. His theory was dynamic in that it focused upon conflicting forces which led the ego to defenses against unacceptable feelings and impulses. This process results in symptoms which define the neurosis. This approach has been referred to as id-psychology in contrast to ego-psychology, which emphasizes defects in the structure of the psychic apparatus due to emotional maldevelopment. Id-psychology and ego-psychology complement rather than replace each other.

In view of the recent shift of interest toward the group or the community, psychoanalysis represents a return to concern for the individual. It stresses autonomy rather than adjustment or conformity. It belongs neither to the establishment nor to those who rebel against the establishment. Its aim is to widen a person's range of choice, rather than to dictate choice.

However, in spite of the accent on autonomy, psychoanalysts have not remained impervious to the surrounding culture, even those elements of the culture antithetical to it. Some analysts believe that the forces underlying movements concerned with the fate of the world should be their concern, rather than the individual. The Chicago Institute for Psychoanalysis has recently opened up a center for psychohistory specifically designed to study national and international problems in terms of psychoanalytic constructs.

The involvement of psychoanalysis in areas other than the treatment of individual patients is prevalent today. This is undoubtedly due to the world we live in, but it began with Freud, who had a wider viewpoint than the clinical one. He speculated about the development of man from the primeval horde (Freud, 1913a), the evolution of civilization (Freud, 1930), and the origins and delusional qualities of religion (Freud, 1927). He also did psychoanalytic studies on great men of the past, as well as a variety of papers on myths (Freud, 1922), fairy tales (Freud, 1913a) and literary themes (Freud, 1907, 1913b). His monograph on Moses (Freud, 1939) has attracted considerable attention and controversy.

Freud quite likely envisioned psychoanalysis as a much more encompassing discipline than just a clinical specialty. Today we have patho-biography and psychohistory. Freud contributed to the former, which attempts to explain how certain men—Leonardo da Vinci (Freud, 1910), Dostoyevsky (Freud, 1928)—functioned, in terms of their character structure and unconscious motivation. Psychohistory attempts to explain history in terms of psychoanalytic theory and then to apply such insights to current national or worldwide problems.

Psychoanalysis evolved in a very specific fashion (see the Assertions section in this chapter). Its theoretical system is based upon the concept of the unconscious motivation of the individual, how the mind develops, and the specific modalities a person uses to deal with the external world. How useful the knowledge of such mental processes is for the understanding of global phenomena or groups (see Freud, 1921) is debatable. This does not mean that there might not be some possibilities, but such an interaction is at this time only in an embryonic phase, and to take seriously those analysts who have suggested solutions of world problems would be to mistake the mutterings of an infant for oracular wisdom. As it stands today, the psychoanalyst, because of his background and training, has no more expertise in world affairs than any other person with a comparable general education.

Similar Theories

Although there are many systems of psychotherapy, and many of them deal with individual patients, none is really similar to psychoanalysis. Transactional analysis, Gestalt therapy, behavioral modification, and the existential and client-centered approaches have very little, if anything, in common with psychoanalysis.

The psychoanalyst's exclusive interest is in intrapsychic processes, how the patient's mind works. He does not manipulate the environment or evaluate behavior. He does not intrude his viewpoints or standards; he restricts his activity to interpretation within the transference context.

All the above-mentioned therapies, and many others as well, control patients' behavior. In some instances there is no recognition whatsoever of intrapsychic processes, particularly in the behavioral modification approaches, and some therapies even lack a coherent theoretical system to support their manipulations. It is important to recognize that these other systems are self-contained and separate and distinct from psychoanalysis, in spite of an occasional superficial resemblance.

Considering other approaches from a historical perspective, Carl Jung and Alfred Adler formed the first and most enduring systems. Their theoretical differences with psychoanalysis were so great that they have to be considered in their own right, apart from and independent of psychoanalysis.

Others have attempted to remain within the psychoanalytic frame of reference, but with modifications. Ferenczi and Rank (1924) devised a method of treatment which they referred to as "active therapy." Alexander & French (1946) attempted to shorten the length of treatment by being active. Erikson (1950) attempted to view sociocultural phenomena in a psychoanalytic perspective. He constructed his own developmental scheme based upon such variables as trust, mutuality, and commitment, rather than on biological factors. However, his ideas do not, in essence, contradict basic psychoanalytic principles; rather, they purport to introduce other dimensions, sociological and anthropological.

Another group has been referred to as neo-Freudians. Many members of this group were originally psychoanalysts in the classical tradition. For a variety of reasons, they became dissatisfied with some aspect of psychoanalysis, and as a consequence they set up their own system. Some of these analysts have become very prominent and influential.

Karen Horney (1937) is one of the leaders of the neo-Freudians. Initially she was opposed to Freud's views of female sexuality insofar as he stressed a predetermined biological sequence. She believed that cultural factors should be stressed, and gradually her formulations gave them primary importance in determining both normal emotional development and psychopathology. She has tended to focus her attention on interpersonal relations and has concentrated on causative factors in the environment rather than on early childhood experiences and traumas.

Erich Fromm (1955) has written extensively in a similar fashion. His emphasis is even further away from a biological orientation than Horney's is. In addition, he has made more concerted efforts to understand cultural changes and shifts from a psychoanalytic perspective. His focus has moved from the clinical dyadic relationship to more global considerations which deal with groups and societies.

Harry Stack Sullivan (1939) has also laid great stress on interpersonal factors, but he has managed to remain in the clinical setting rather than becoming involved with wider issues. His conceptual system very closely follows conventional psychoanalytic principles even if, on the surface, it seems different. Sullivan constructed a new terminology, some of which would be compatible with some elements of modern information and communication theory. By so doing, Sullivan believed he was stressing various personality systems that are more involved with a person's relations with other persons rather than simply between parts of the self. His followers continue to be active, but as time goes by the differences between them and the main body of psychoanalysis seem to be mitigated, as terminological differences fade in importance.

Melanie Klein (1948) has created a system which, in contrast to the above schools or systems, focuses with even greater emphasis than traditional psychoanalysis does upon mental operations, almost to the total exclusion of environmental factors. Klein attributes rather complex fantasies to the recently born infant and believes these are involved in psychic development and psychopathology. She has been accused of attributing qualities to the child that are far too complex for his immature and unformed psyche. Nevertheless, she has had a large following in Great Britain, and her writings determine the prevailing orientation in South America and Mexico. In spite of the bizarreness of some of her formulations, she has made important contributions to our understanding of primitive mental mechanisms.

Assertions

Since from the very beginning the chief focus of psychoanalysis has been on patients suffering from emotional disturbances, the mind is studied mainly in the context of psychopathology. To paraphrase Freud, psychoanalysis is "first and foremost" a clinical discipline.

Development
Metapsychology is a term Freud coined in a book dealing with normal behavioral phenomena (Freud, 1901). He was attempting to construct a comprehensive psychology applicable to all mental states. Metapsychology is defined as a system of psychology that views the mind and its development from several different frames of refer-

ence simultaneously. Originally, they were topographical, psychodynamic, and psychoeconomic. Today several others have been added, such as, the structural, adaptive, and genetic hypotheses.

1. THE TOPOGRAPHICAL HYPOTHESIS VIEWS THE MIND IN TERMS OF THREE SYSTEMS.

Freud (1900, 1915d) initially conceptualized the mind as consisting of three systems, the *unconscious*, the *preconscious*, and the *conscious*. The unconscious contains elements which cannot become conscious by volition. They cannot ascend to the level of awareness without special efforts. By contrast, the preconscious, although also unconscious, contains elements (some of which are referred to as memory traces) which can easily become conscious by simply directing attention toward them. Consciousness is the agent of the mind which perceives both inner and outer stimuli.

This model simplified and clarified various phenomena. Viewing the unconscious both as an area of the mind and as a quality of mental processes, Freud was able to distinguish between forces easily accessible to conscious control and those rigidly defended against (see psychodynamic hypothesis, below). To summarize briefly, the topographical hypothesis postulates a tripartite organization where the unconscious and preconscious, both having the attribute of being unconscious, are compared to consciousness. The pathway to consciousness is blocked for the unconscious but remains open (to be more precise, partially open) for the preconscious.

These ideas were quite useful clinically, especially when the clinician's interest was chiefly focused upon the effects of the unconscious system. However, Freud noted some inconsistencies as he made further clinical discoveries. He noted that certain impulses were prevented from reaching consciousness. He referred to this act of exclusion as repression and located the repressive process in the higher levels of the mind, those that are conscious or close to consciousness. But one is not able to bring the act of repression into conscious awareness. Thus one is faced with the dilemma of a process being unconscious and incapable of becoming conscious being located in an area (preconscious or conscious) where it should have access to consciousness. In a similar vein, Freud discovered the existence of an unconscious sense of guilt in some patients. Guilt is a feeling which, in order to be experienced, requires the type of organization characteristic of the preconscious and conscious (the unconscious presumably is an inchoate, disorganized system which does not follow the usual rules of logic).

2. THE MIND IS COMPOSED OF THE ID, EGO, AND SUPEREGO.

To resolve these contradictions, Freud (1923a) constructed another system known as the *structural hypothesis*. Here again, he dealt with a tripartite model. He divided the mind into the now familiar *id*, *ego*, and *superego*. The id corresponds to the unconscious of the topographical hypothesis, and the ego includes the preconscious and conscious. The superego is located within the ego, although it dips into the id and makes judgments as to what aspects of the id should be admitted into ego territory.

The principal advantage of the structural hypothesis is that the ego has unconscious as well as conscious attributes. The structural hypothesis also gives greater emphasis to the higher levels of the personality, such as the ego, which can now be conceptualized as a group of subsystems. The topographical hypothesis is in a sense linear, whereas the structural hypothesis allows room for expansion and breadth.

Both systems are compatible with hierarchal structuring of the psychic apparatus. In the structural hypothesis, however, it is easier to visualize how the ego or superego "dip" into the id. It must be emphasized that these are descriptions of a model, a way of looking at things. The structural model is an abstraction, but too often it has been looked at in a concrete fashion. The ego and id have been considered actual entities, with specific brain locations (Brenner, 1957). The metaphors of id demons and superego watchmen have even been taken literally (Waelder, 1960).

3. THE MIND IS A DYNAMIC BATTLEGROUND.

One of the aims of psychoanalysis is to explain emotional disturbances. Freud found it useful to view his patients' psyches in terms of clashing forces between various parts of their minds. At first, conflicts were described as struggles between the unconscious and conscious. The concept of the dynamic unconscious as a psychic state which cannot easily become conscious and yet can have effects upon consciousness makes it natural for the adoption of the *psychodynamic* viewpoint, which stresses opposing or conflicting vectors.

Something unconscious, usually referred to as an *impulse, need, drive* or *instinct*, seeks access to consciousness. Inasmuch as the conscious part of the personality (ego) finds this aspect of the unconscious objectionable, it will strive against permitting the impulse to gain its objective. The ego has to serve three masters, according to Freud (1923a)—the id, the superego, and reality.

The structural hypothesis adds dimensions to psychodynamic formulations in this manner. If an unconscious impulse seeking expression offends the psyche's morality by being unacceptable to the superego, which is the site of moral judgments, then it must be defended against. It must be similarly excluded from motility or conscious expression if it is at variance with the demands of the external world.

Basically, the psychodynamic hypothesis views the mental apparatus as a series of interacting forces. The id and the ego conflict with each other when id elements are either not acceptable to the superego or are at variance with reality. Since the psychic apparatus is also conceptualized as consisting of various levels with different degrees of complexity—one end of the spectrum being considered primitive and the other end sophisticated and reality attuned—it would seem inevitable that forces emanating from one level would conflict with forces derived from other levels.

4. THE MIND SEEKS HOMEOSTASIS AND REQUIRES ENERGY.

A model of the psychic apparatus requires concepts that will account for movements within it. Some vitalizing principle must be elucidated to make a conceptual system that deals with living processes comprehensible. Borrowing from Claude Bernard (1949) and thermodynamic theory, Freud postulated a constant low level of energy as the ultimate optimal state of balance for the mind. High energy levels experienced as tension states are painful, according to Freud (1911a). Pleasure results from changing a high energy state to a low energy state, although later,

Freud (1920) added that it was the change itself that accounted for pleasure, rather than the low energy level.

The id is the mind's energy reservoir (Freud, 1915d). Instincts reside in the id and, when activated by biological needs such as hunger, push forward toward consciousness. They possess a quantum of energy known as *cathexis*. Inasmuch as instincts have energy, they are referred to as being *cathected*; the greater the cathexis, the more they are energized. The energy of the sexual instincts is called *libido*, although the term has gained a more general connotation and often refers to energy levels in general. There is some confusion here intrinsic to the *psychoeconomic hypothesis*, because Freud did not elaborate on differences in types of energy.

Instincts reach a certain level of cathexis which, if sustained, is experienced as unpleasure or painful. At this point the instinct requires gratification; that is, the need which the instinct represents has to be satisfied. The process of satisfaction is accompanied by a discharge of tension, which also means that the instinct loses its cathexis; it is *decathected*. In essence, Freud's energic theory is a tension-discharge hypothesis, and it was in context with the prevailing hydrodynamic orientation of the physics of his day.

Today, many analysts believe that the psychoeconomic hypothesis is imprecise, not in accord with biological data, and anachronistic. It is considered to be the weakest part of the psychoanalytic theoretical edifice, and many think it should be eliminated. However, rather than weakening the conceptual system by discarding it, some theoreticians believe that modifications will strengthen Freud's model.

5. A PERSON'S PAST AFFECTS HIS PRESENT ADAPTATIONS.

Later hypotheses were formulated after Freud, but some certainly were suggested by him. Hartmann (1964), Rapaport (1966), and Erikson (1950) are prominent among those analysts who have contributed extensions of metapsychology.

The *genetic hypothesis* represents an orientation which evaluates the influence of the past upon a person's current adjustment. Although psychoanalytic theory from the very beginning has stressed the importance of infantile experiences, only relatively recently has there been an increased interest in the early years of life. This is due to research projects that collect their data from direct observation of the mother-child relationship rather than from the psychoanalytic treatment of patients which had previously been the chief source of information. In such *longitudinal studies* the child's emotional development is usually followed for years.

How the individual reacts and adjusts to his environment represents a frame of reference called the *adaptive hypothesis*, which is primarily concerned with various systems within the ego responsible for meeting needs in a fashion acceptable to reality. This point of view has become prominent recently because patients today have problems related to defects in these systems or, at least, such defects are more readily recognizable today than in Freud's time.

6. FUNDAMENTAL MOTIVES ARE
    INSTINCTUAL.

Instincts are the basic motivating forces of the psyche, according to psychoanalytic theory. However, the concept of instinct here is different from the one commonly accepted by biologists and ethologists. Freud did not actually use the word *instinct*. He employed the word *Trieb*, which translators of Freud's work reproduced as *instinct*. In German *Instinkt* corresponds more closely to our similar word in English, whereas *Trieb* is more closely related to the word *drive*. Freud was referring to an impetus, an impelling force within the mind which has effects on both psychic equilibrium and development. Freud (1915a) defined instinct (*Trieb*) as a borderline concept between the somatic and the psychic, characterized by its (1) source, (2) aim, and (3) object.

The *source* of instincts emphasizes their organic origin. It consists of the organ system responsible for the excitation that sets the process of forming an instinct in motion. For example, when an organism needs food, certain physiological changes occur. The stomach muscles periodically contract, and these contractions are felt as hunger pangs by the perceptual elements of the mind. The whole organism is driven to gratify its need for food and can be considered as being propelled by an oral drive or instinct. One can draw similar conclusions about the sexual drive, locating the inciting factors in the gonads.

The *aim* of the instinct is to achieve gratification, the fulfillment of a need. According to the psychoeconomic hypothesis, an instinct causes tension, which means it raises the energy level. The organism seeks to lower the energy level to maintain psychic equilibrium, or homeostasis. This process is conceptualized as *instinctual discharge*, that is, the tension created by instinctual forces has to be dissipated by gratifying the instinct. These concepts have been briefly criticized above and will be elaborated upon further.

The *object* of the instinct is simply the product that fulfills the need which the instinct expresses. Food, the breast, the nurturing person can all be considered objects of the oral instinct. Those situations or objects that lead to sexual release are the objects of the sexual instinct. Unlike the biologist's static concept of instinct, Freud's view of instincts considers them as undergoing development. Some instincts are more primitive than others. He (Freud 1905b) postulated a continuum, a progressively structured hierarchy, which describes the course of emotional development.

7. ALL INSTINCTS ARE BASICALLY SEXUAL.

Since Freud believed that all instincts are basically sexual, although his concept of sex extended far beyond genital sexuality, this continuum is known as *psychosexual development*. At the very beginning of life, there is very little psychic organization. The mind consists simply of the id, which is considered an undifferentiated mass (Freud, 1900, 1917a, 1920, 1926a). The id reacts to contacts with the outer world as impingements and constructs a protective outer core (*Reizschutz*) against potentially disruptive stimulation. The progressive structuralization of this core leads to the formation of the ego.

During this early phase, before the construction of the ego, instincts are (as Freud designated) *autoerotic*. They stem from various sources, known as *erogenous zones,* and achieve their gratification through their own body. For example, the need to suck is stimulated by physiological tension in the mouth (oral mucosa being the source) and satisfied by sucking of the thumb. These erogenous zones, which involve the mouth, skin, genitals, and thermal and equilibratory systems, are poorly coordinated during the neonatal stages. In a relative sense, they act independently, as if they did not know of the existence of one another. As the psyche gains structure and unity, these autoerotic instincts become subordinated to the *genital zone*. As Freud (1905b) stated, they undergo confluence.

When autoerotic instincts act separately, they are known as part instincts. On their road to genitality, or as psychoanalysts would say toward the state of genital dominance, they traverse through several stages. During the autoerotic phase, there is as yet no ego. Once the ego begins to form, the autoerotic instincts, instead of going directly to the part of the body which gives gratification, now aim themselves toward the ego. This stage is known as *primary narcissism* (Freud, 1914b).

With greater differentiation of the psychic apparatus, the mind begins to have some dawning awareness of the existence of an outer world. This permits distinctions to be made between the inner and outer world. Instincts now can momentarily direct themselves toward the outer world, but since the perception and acceptance of the outer world is still tenuous, they easily retreat back into the ego. Freud (1914b) compared this interaction to the pseudopodia of an amoeba which tentatively extrudes into the environment to seek particles of food and then withdraws back into the cell body. This phenomenon is analogous to what is known as *secondary narcissism*.

8. INSTINCTUAL DEVELOPMENT AND EARLY SEXUALITY ARE INTIMATELY RELATED.

As noted above, Freud (1911b, 1914b) postulated three early phases of instinctual development.

1. *Autoerotism*, a stage of partial instincts achieving gratification through the body before ego structure has been consolidated.

2. *Primary narcissism*, a stage where there is a rudimentary ego toward which the instincts direct themselves.

3. *Secondary narcissism*, a stage where distinctions are beginning to be made between the psyche and the outer world, and instincts transiently reach into the external world, only to be pulled back into the ego.

It is germane before proceeding to clarify some issues regarding the role of sexuality in instinct theory. Instinct theory is often referred to as *libido theory*, and this has led many people to believe that Freud was obsessed with the idea of sex. True, Freud did stress sexual factors as being primary causes for the neuroses. From the very beginning, he viewed psychopathology in terms of sexual trauma occurring early in childhood (Breuer & Freud, 1895; Freud, 1896). However, he did not limit sex to just genital excitation. All the component instincts already discussed and those about to be discussed yield pleasure when gratified, and Freud viewed all this pleasure as erotic. Hunger and sex are basic needs, the former being associated with individual survival and the latter with survival of the species. What goes beyond survival involves erotic pleasure. Thus, Freud called the energy of the sexual instincts *libido*, but he had no corresponding term for the instincts of self-preservation.

Freud has been accused of being a pan-sexualist. He argued this against his opponents, but inasmuch as he stressed sexual factors and considered early infantile activity as erotic, there seems to be some merit to the arguments of his adversaries. Later Freud was careful to point out that he was describing *pregenital* sexuality and, in essence, he was emphasizing that there are other types of strivings beyond simply seeking to satisfy basic survival needs. He carefully described the sequential progression of methods of obtaining gratification and linked them with various bodily zones. Insofar as the body and pleasure are involved, he preferred to regard these activities as sexual in a pregenital sense.

9. INSTINCTUAL DEVELOPMENT IS PERCEIVED AS A SERIES OF PSYCHOSEXUAL STAGES.

Freud (1905a) postulated the existence of an oral sexual phase following the narcissistic stage. The outside world is perceived in terms of *oral satisfaction*. From autoerotic pleasure, the infant begins to recognize the mother's breast as a source of gratification. Oral instincts are the only instincts connected with both survival and erotic pleasure. Sucking is a pleasure in itself and not simply part of an activity that seeks food. Abraham (1921) elaborated upon Freud's descriptions and divided the oral stage into two subphases. The first is a passive phase where the infant just lies back, so to speak, and expects to be fed. This he called the *passive-dependent phase*. It is followed by a phase where the infant aggressively seeks satisfaction of oral needs. The second phase usually occurs around six months of age, at the time of dentition, and is accompanied by aggressive biting. Abraham called this phase the *oral cannibalistic phase*.

The next phase that Freud postulated is the *anal phase*, which is related to toilet training, occurring usually around 12–16 months. Gratification now refers to sphincter control. Previously certain impulses could not be subjected to conscious volition. During this phase, the child begins to control the retention and the expulsion of his feces. Freud felt that the child was becoming preoccupied with preservation and destruction, so he referred to this stage as the *sadistic-anal phase* and called the corresponding instincts anal-sadistic. Freud (1926a) raised the question as to whether these were also sexual instincts and finally concluded that parts of them were. Abraham (1924) also subdivided this stage of psychosexual development into two subphases. He divided the anal phase into passive and aggressive components, the former being concerned with retention and the latter with forcible expulsion.

Following the anal phase comes the *phallic phase*, a relatively later addition to the psychosexual scheme of development (Freud, 1923b). The male child attaches pride to the penis, an organ which becomes treasured and idealized. Phallic instincts are concerned with ambition and the acquisition of power. This phase created difficulties when considered a stage of normal development, since it is difficult to see where the female fits in this phase. Previous phases were concerned with the gratification of impulses and the maintenance of control. Now, at the genital phase, the child is preoccupied with conflicting feelings *within* his psyche. Although during some pregenital phases the child was also concerned with conflicts, these conflicts were between an instinctual wish and a prohibition from the outer world.

10. CHILDREN DEVELOP LIBIDINAL ATTITUDES TOWARD PARENTS.

The child's dependence upon his mother acquires additional qualities. He begins to feel possessive and wants her exclusively. This attitude may have been reinforced by earlier experiences which stimulated rivalry, such as the birth of a sibling. The boy's chief rival is the father, and now we have the famous *Oedipus complex*. The child's possessiveness acquires incestuous overtones. The child has ambivalent feelings toward his father. He is dependent upon him for support and as a source of identification, and so he loves him. But he also fears and hates his father because he stands in his way of possessing his mother. Since the penis is the organ of sexual activity and since his fears of the father's retribution are related to incestuous feelings, the child fears his father will punish him by castrating him. Thus, we have the concept of *castration anxiety*.

11. THE CONSCIENCE DEVELOPS IN REACTION TO THE OEDIPUS COMPLEX.

This situation seems similar to others seen during earlier stages of psychosexual development in that there is an instinctual wish, this time a genital rather than an oral or anal wish, and an external prohibition, in the form of a castrating father. Now the situation changes. Whereas in previous phases the child defended himself against an external prohibition, during the genital phase the child defends himself against an *internal prohibition*. The child incorporates various elements of his father's personality as he perceives them. These elements have the qualities of moral imperatives and, as an internalized set of rules emphasizing what is forbidden, come to represent what is commonly called conscience, or in freudian terms, *superego*.

Incestuous wishes are repressed at the behest of the superego. Although the child is deprived of a desired relationship with his mother, he is spared the terror of the threat of castration. More accurately, he is spared the pangs and torments of guilt, the reactions to a superego whose harshness would become manifest if incestuous wishes were to emerge from repression.

There are advantages to obeying the superego besides protection from anxiety or guilt. The superego has two faces: "thou shalt" and "thou shalt not." The latter has received primary emphasis, but the former, "thou shalt," becomes the basis of the child's identification with the father. That part of him which admires his father will want to emulate him, and his attitudes about masculinity will be based upon the model his father presents.

Freud (1923a) repeatedly stated that the superego which arises about age four is the heir to the Oedipus complex. The Oedipus complex is then buried and the next several years are designated as the *latency phase*, when the child is seemingly unpreoccupied with sexual matters. During earlier stages prior to the latency period the child's sexual curiosity is intense, reaching a peak around the phallic phase, and his behavior displays this erotic orientation. Infantile masturbation is common. During the latency phase, all elements of infantile sexuality seem to be repressed. The latency phase has been divided into two subphases, early and late. During the former, the child is still grappling with oedipal problems and repressive defenses, and during the latter he concerns himself with adjustments forced upon him because of the biological changes of puberty and the social demands of adolescence (see Bornstein, 1951).

Some analysts (Fenichel, 1945) do not believe the latency period is at all sexually quiescent. They consider that the repression Freud described is far from complete. Undoubtedly social and cultural factors play a significant role in this. The forces which supported repression in Freud's mid-Victorian milieu have been considerably modified. Still, when compared to the next phase, puberty, whatever happens sexually in the latency phase is mild.

12. PUBERTY IS A PHASE OF SWEEPING READJUSTMENTS.

The next phase, *puberty*, is often, but not always, stormy. Due to hormonal and physiological factors, repressed sexual feelings become greatly intensified. Previous defenses are no longer adequate, and sweeping readjustments are required. These become further complicated because the adolescent cannot regress to earlier dependent infantile states, as might occur during the early latency period. The reactions to these stresses are varied and range from flagrant, rebellious, antisocial and promiscuous behavior to the seeking of ascetic ideals and the pursuit of a monastic life.

Erikson (1950) extends psychosexual development into adulthood and old age. He and others tend to stress cultural factors more than the primarily biological orientation of Freud.

Freud's scheme has been criticized (Horney,

1937) because it overemphasizes biology and minimizes interaction with the environment. Freud has been accused of being a male chauvinist (Ellenberger, 1970), and as one scrutinizes some of his concepts of psychosexual development, such as the phallic phase and the passing of the Oedipus complex in girls (Freud, 1924), there seems to be some merit to the argument. The little girl feels castrated from the beginning, so castration anxiety cannot be the motivating factor which represses incestuous feelings.

13. FREUD POSTULATES A DEATH INSTINCT.

A preceding section described the development of instincts considered sexual. However, Freud always viewed the mind in terms of polarities and so maintained a fundamental dualism. Consequently he had to bring another group of instincts into either apposition or opposition to the sexual instincts. His first instinct theory postulated two classes of instincts, the *ego instincts*, which are self-preservative, and the *sexual instincts*. After much analysis and consideration, he eventually came to his final statement about instincts, in which he posited a *life instinct* (Eros) and a *death instinct* (Thanatos), a duality and polarity which finally contented him. While this concept is intuitively appealing and certainly all-embracing, modern analysts for the most part have been unwilling to go along with it.

Maintenance

Nosology. The various developmental processes discussed above must be placed in a proper perspective to be clinically useful. The deviations and distortions that occur throughout the course of emotional maturation are varied in form and have different outcomes.

Although psychoanalysts are more interested in psychic processes than in classification, a diagnostic system had to be erected which went beyond simple description. In the past, clusters of behavioral phenomena and symptoms had been given specific names. Diagnosis was purely descriptive. In underplaying behavioral categorization, psychoanalysis offers the clinician a different method to reach a diagnosis.

Freud had to begin at the beginning because he wanted to use his insights to classify patients. Still, he tried to use well-known labels whenever possible. His excursions into the field of diagnostic formulations were still imprecise; he believed that psychoanalytic treatment could be used for many conditions, even for paranoid patients (see Freud, 1896). Later, he became more discriminative and reserved his method only for psychoneurotic patients.

14. SOME PATIENTS DO NOT HAVE PSYCHOLOGICAL PROBLEMS.

The first group of patients other than hysterics to be subjected to analytic scrutiny were not considered to have purely psychological problems. They were viewed in terms of dammed-up tension which manifested itself in symptoms but which did not achieve mental representation. These were known as the *actual neuroses*. In German, *Aktuell* means topical, in the sense of current. These neuroses, precipitated by events in the outside world, were not due to internal psychological conflicts but were what we now call *situational neuroses*. Freud distinguished between patients with periodic physiological needs that were either being constantly gratified, or that could not be gratified. The former he labeled *neurasthenia*, and the latter *anxiety neurosis*. These two entities were distinguished from the *psychoneuroses*.

Neurasthenics suffered from fatigue, weakness, and headaches, in general symptoms that characterize a depleted person. Freud believed that these patients practiced excessive masturbation and that they were drained of energy, since they were discharging sexual energy faster than physiology could build it up. Anxiety neurosis, on the other hand, was considered due to dammed-up accumulated sexual energy which, because of external circumstances, could not be discharged directly. Freud (1895a) thought the periodicity of anxiety attacks was based upon the cyclical buildup of sexual tension. He also postulated that persons who experience enforced sexual abstinence or incomplete sexual satisfaction were likely to develop this neurosis.

Pent-up sexual feelings are transformed into anxiety without reaching higher levels of mentation. This means that the libido does not energize (cathect) memories of sexual gratification which would impel the person to repeat the experience with an appropriate partner. Instead, sexual feelings are discharged by episodic anxiety attacks.

15. THE PSYCHONEUROSES ARE DIVIDED INTO THE TRANSFERENCE AND NARCISSISTIC NEUROSES.

Freud's clinical experience caused him to subdivide the psychoneuroses further, on the basis of his judgment as to which patients would be amenable to psychoanalytic treatment. He divided the psychoneuroses into the transference neuroses and the narcissistic neuroses (Freud, 1915a).

The *transference neuroses* are characterized by their capacity to form transferences, that is, to project infantile feelings onto the psychoanalyst. These patients usually can be analyzed, because transference is the most important and indispensable therapeutic vehicle in psychoanalytic treatment. The transference neuroses are generally considered to be hysteria, phobic states, and obsessive-compulsive neuroses (Freud, 1914b). There have been other classifications included in the transference neuroses, but the above three are always found in diagnostic handbooks.

The *narcissistic neuroses* consist of two entities, depression and the psychoses. Freud did not make major distinctions between the psychoneuroses and the psychoses, and he was inclined to group the depressions into the same category as the psychoses. He first called the latter paraphrenias, and he did not particularly distinguish between schizophrenia, paranoia, or what in recent times have been called borderline states and characterological disorders. Persons with these conditions, according to Freud, did not form transferences and therefore were untreatable by the psychoanalytic method. The patient's libido was fixated onto his own ego and could not be directed sufficiently toward the analyst, so that a transference could be established. Further experience, however, has proven that even these patients can, indeed, develop transferences (Giovacchini, 1972, 1975).

16. THE CONCEPTUAL CLARIFICATION OF ANXIETY IS CRUCIAL TO PSYCHOANALYTIC THEORY.

Anxiety Theory. The concept of anxiety is fundamental and central in psychoanalytic theory. Freud's concept of anxiety underwent major changes throughout the years. It is easy to group his ideas into two categories referred to as the first and second anxiety theories. The *first anxi-*

ety theory, sometimes known as the toxic or surplus theory, was formulated in 1895 (Freud, 1895a). Anxiety was simply considered deflected libido. Freud believed that sexual tension builds up because of internal hormonal accumulation and by external erotic stimuli. If such feelings are not gratified, they overflow and are discharged as anxiety. Thus anxiety originates in the deeper levels of the personality, the id. Sexual feelings, instead of being perceived by the ego, are directly transformed into anxiety.

In 1926 (Freud, 1926a) anxiety theory was markedly revised. Instead of originating in the id, the origin of anxiety was located in the ego. When an unacceptable instinctual impulse threatens to break into the sphere of the ego, the ego becomes aware of impending danger. Since the danger is internal, the ego cannot flee from it as from an external danger. Instead, it generates anxiety, which acts as a signal to inform the psyche it is being threatened. Anxiety sets in motion various psychic mechanisms designed to protect the ego. These mechanisms, known as defenses, repress the aberrant impulse. This is the *second anxiety theory,* which is also known as the *signal theory.*

Anxiety is distinguished from fear by its consequences, since from a subjective viewpoint both emotions are identical. Fear disappears when one flees from external danger, but one cannot physically escape from anxiety, an internal danger.

17. THE PSYCHE EMPLOYS A VARIETY OF DEFENSES.

Defenses and Symptoms. The ego may use many methods to defend itself against internal dangers. The ultimate aim of all defenses is to achieve repression.

Repression is a mental mechanism which keeps certain impulses and feelings from becoming conscious. A repressed impulse cannot be brought to the surface by conscious effort. *Suppression* of an impulse, on the other hand, means that the impulse can easily be made conscious. A suppressed impulse is deliberately withheld.

Freud (1915c) described two types of repression, primal repression and repression proper. *Primal repression* is the most archaic of the two types. Freud postulated that there are elements within the id that can never reach consciousness.

He traced these elements back to the prehistory of mankind and believed that something our ancestors repressed still resides in a state of primal repression in the id of modern man. There is considerable similarity between these ideas and Jung's primitive archetypes and collective unconscious. The primally repressed core within the id attracts ego elements that are in some ways (associatively) similar to it. This attraction from within can be compared to a magnet.

By contrast, *secondary repression* is more like a pressure from the outside, an "afterpressure" (*Nachdrängen*), as Freud described it. The impulsion to repression originates in the ego, and the objectionable feeling or impulse is pushed back into the id. If it is associatively related to other repressed elements in the id, then there is a combination of afterpressure and the attraction exerted by primal repression.

Secondary repression, a useful clinical concept, helps explain many otherwise incomprehensible phenomena. The concept of primal repression is only of historical interest; it is untestable, inasmuch as it postulates the existence of elements that have never been conscious and never can be conscious. Therefore it is of limited interest scientifically.

Repression has been discussed here first because it is a central concept to the theory of defenses. It is both a defense and the aim of defenses. Defenses are mental mechanisms set in motion by anxiety which, in turn, is a response to internal danger. Defenses protect the psyche from being overwhelmed by unconscious impulses perceived as dangerous. The aim of a defense is to rerepress the aberrant impulse which had been repressed and now threatens to reemerge. A defense is a mechanism, an abstract concept. Behavioral manifestations of this postulated mechanism can be observed and are known as character traits or symptoms.

18. DEFENSES CAN BE ARRANGED IN A HIERARCHY.

Although there are differences of opinion among psychoanalysts regarding the significance of various defenses relative to each other, practically everyone agrees that, as with everything else in psychoanalysis, defenses can be arranged along a hierarchal continuum. There may be some disagreement as to exactly where a particular defense belongs on this continuum, but the principle of a hierarchy is firmly established. There is also some variation as to precisely what the defense mechanisms are. The list in Figure 2-1, therefore, includes only those widely accepted by a majority of clinicians. They are also listed, with the principle of hierarchy in mind, so that the more sophisticated defenses characteristic of a well-structured ego are at the top. Further down the list, the defenses are more primitive and are characteristic of early developmental phases.

1. Rationalization
2. Repression
3. Displacement
4. Identification
5. Conversion
6. Isolation or intellectualization
7. Reaction formation or overcompensation
8. Undoing
9. Introjection
10. Projection
11. Denial

FIGURE 2-1: Defenses Arranged in a Hierarchal Continuum

Other authors have listed many more defenses, but these are probably the most readily accepted ones (Waelder, 1960). The problem is further complicated because many of these defenses subsume other more elemental processes. For example, in order to project, the psyche has had to use splitting mechanisms first. That is, in a regressive fashion, a significant person referred to as an object is split into good and bad objects. The bad object is then projected into the outside world. The study of defenses deals with the interplay between observable data and the preconceived conceptual system. The latter has to be consistent with the data. In this instance, the data fit well with a conceptual system first established in another frame of reference, the stages of psychosexual development.

The most important criterion which determines whether a defense is relatively sophisticated or primitive is the amount of reality testing the defense retains. Rationalization, at the top end of the spectrum, distorts reality only minimally, whereas denial, at the bottom end, totally disavows reality. A person who uses *rationaliza-tion* explains his behavior in a socially acceptable manner to maintain his self-esteem. For example, a student fails an examination. He rationalizes that too many responsibilities did not give him adequate time to study. It could well be that the student was, indeed, overburdened in the fashion he described, so he is dealing with reality elements. His distortion may be slight: He may be magnifying the significance of his responsibilities in bringing about his failure. There also may be other more important reasons for his poor performance. He may have been lazy, or the material may have been too difficult for his ability. He may have felt inadequate to compete with his classmates. There may have been many reasons for his failure, but none was acceptable to him. He chose the least threatening one, and rationalized.

By contrast, *denial* involves a blotting out of reality. The patient who uses this defense does not acknowledge a sector of reality. A mother may continue nursing her dead baby as if he were still alive, or a rejected bridegroom may keep the wedding table intact for years, as occurs in one of Dickens's novels. In not perceiving a segment of reality, gross reality distortion occurs, and for that reason denial is placed at the bottom of the hierarchal list.

Different levels of emotional development are associated with specific defenses. Although psychosexual theory was not constructed with the concept of defense in the foreground, it is conceptually consistent that the more primitive levels of development would have the least developed reality-testing functions. The rationale for the psychosexual theory of development is strengthened when empirically observed defenses can be arranged in a hierarchal continuum on the basis of their reality-testing properties, and this hierarchy is found to be parallel to the developmental hierarchy.

Since defense presupposes conflict, developmental stages must be considered in terms of psychopathological distortions. The hierarchy of defenses can be easily juxtaposed with the hierarchy of psychopathology. Briefly, rationalization is found in a more-or-less normal psyche; repression, displacement, and conversion are typical of hysteria; isolation, reaction formation, and undoing characterize the obsessive-compulsive neurosis; and introjection, depression, projection, and denial characterize paranoid and other psychotic states.

This does not mean that certain defenses are only associated with particular conditions. To allay the anxiety some readers may have, it can be emphasized that everyone uses all of these defenses at some time or other. One is not necessarily paranoid just because one uses projection on occasion.

Different psychopathological states are characterized by the preponderant use of particular defenses. If a particular defense has become the chief modality by which a person maintains a balance between the inner world of his psyche and the external world, then it is possible to diagnose a specific type of emotional disorder. Ordinarily, defenses are human attributes called occasionally into play under appropriate circumstances.

Brief descriptions of the other types of defenses and their symptomatic expression follow. To repeat, a defense is simply a mechanism, an abstraction which has no meaning unless considered together with its behavioral manifestations. Various constellations of behavior can be conceptualized in terms of these mechanisms.

Repression has been described first (see Assertion 17) because of its special position as a defense as well as the aim of all defenses. In repression, the unacceptable impulse is pushed out of the ego, and this self-protecting process may involve special mechanisms which cover the whole gamut of defenses. In hysteria, repression can occur without the further aid of defensive portions of the ego. The impulse is simply shut out, a process normally seen when something meaningful or sought after is forgotten, through a lapse of memory. This obliteration of feelings and impulses is less reality oriented than the socially acceptable reasons chosen by a person who rationalizes, and in spite of the fact that the aim of all defenses is to achieve repression, the defense of repression is nevertheless lower on the hierarchal list than rationalization.

Displacement refers to replacing the object of the impulse (usually the person capable of gratifying the impulse) by a substitute object.

Identification is part of normal development as well as a defense. Anna Freud (1936) described how a person takes the character traits of another person and makes them his own. He in- corporates someone else's personality to defend himself against unacceptable, usually destructive, feelings toward a particular person, as well as fear of retaliation, which often takes the form of castration anxiety. Anna Freud described the special instance of *identification with the aggressor*. In a situation where one feels a potential victim of another person's aggression, he may identify with that person and behave like the aggressor, to master the terror of his passive helplessness. Anna Freud referred to instances of this sort in concentration camps.

Conversion was one of the first defenses Freud described. Today, examples of conversion are rare, but this defense illustrates qualities characteristic of all defenses. A conflict between a sexual impulse and opposing forces is converted into a somatic dysfunction, a situation typically found in the psychoneurotic entity, conversion hysteria. Thus, conversion refers to the transformation of a psychical impulse into a somatic disturbance. The latter, a symptom, may take many forms, such as paralysis of a limb, areas of anesthesia, blindness, and deafness. The symptom is a symbolic expression of a compromise between the unacceptable impulse and the forces that oppose it. Defenses in general incorporate the very elements being defended against, and this is reflected in the symptom. For example, a hysterical paralysis of the arm may be a symbolic compromise between the wish to masturbate and the prohibition against that wish. The wish, itself, is to some extent gratified by the attention the arm receives from both physicians and the patient. It is manipulated, stroked, examined; it receives considerable attention. To the patient, the arm unconsciously represents the penis. The substitution of the arm for the penis is called an *upward displacement*. This is an example of how a symptom may represent more than one defense—in the above example, conversion and displacement.

19.   ISOLATION, REACTION FORMATION, AND
         UNDOING ARE CHARACTERISTICS OF
         OBSESSIVE COMPULSIVE NEUROSES.

In *isolation*, the impulse reaches consciousness but it is deprived of its feelings. As psychoanalysts would say, it is decathected, since it loses its cathexis. Without its affect the unacceptable impulse, say a sadistic impulse, is rendered harmless. A defensive maneuver, isolation (often referred to as intellectualization) is an important aspect of normal thinking, but it accounts for the obsessional patient's propensity to deal with seemingly violent or disturbing thoughts in a calm, detached fashion.

Reaction formation, or overcompensation, leads to the repression of the forbidden impulse by replacing it with its opposite. Repressed cruelty is converted into kindness. Like conversion, overcompensation is another example of how the defense incorporates what is being defended against. Frequently, even casual observers recognize intuitively what overcompensating people are defending themselves against. The cloying sweetness of some do-gooders can be devastating and infuriating, because the recipient of such "kindness" can sense the murderous underlying rage. "Killed with kindness" is an apt expression of the situation where a destructive feeling is portrayed by its opposite.

Undoing is another example of a mental mechanism involving the expression of an unacceptable impulse and prohibiting forces. There is a temporal separation between the two. The unacceptable impulse is expressed or acted out by some action, and the prohibitive forces make up or "undo" the previously intended destruction. The latter usually takes the form of a ritual of atonement or expiation. Both the hostile act and the atonement for it may be symbolically disguised. Freud (1909b) offers the following example. His patient, while walking down a country road, kicks a stone onto the middle of the road. He then reflects that when his beloved's carriage comes down the road it will hit this stone, overturn, and kill her. To undo this potential murder, he now kicks the stone off the road. On reflecting further, he decides this is all very silly, and so he kicks the stone back to the center of the road. He repeats this sequence endlessly.

20. INTROJECTION AND PROJECTION POSITION FEELINGS IN THE INTERNAL AND EXTERNAL WORLDS.

Introjection is in some ways similar to identification. Some aspect of the outer world is internalized for defensive purposes. It differs from identification, however, in that the psyche does not structure the whole personality according to someone else's attributes. Rather, a portion of the external world, usually an ambivalently perceived person, remains circumscribed within the psyche, rather than being amalgamated into various ego systems, as occurs with identification. Freud (1917b) conceptualized such a mechanism when he studied mourning reactions and depressions, conditions in which the loss of a beloved is defended against by preserving and reacting to the memory of that person, who is tenaciously preserved in the psyche.

Projection is the counterpart of introjection; introjective-projective processes are often discussed. Something unacceptable within the self is attributed to, that is, is projected onto, someone else. This is the familiar paranoid orientation where all goodness stays inside and all badness emanates from outside forces and persons.

21. SUBLIMATION HAS BEEN CONSIDERED A DEFENSE, BUT IT IS NOT.

No discussion of defenses would be complete without considering *sublimation*. Sublimation is not included in the list of defenses because it is not considered a defense. It is an adjustive socializing process, but inasmuch as it does not lead to repression, it is neither defensive nor psychopathological. Sublimation involves the transformation of a sexual instinct into something nonsexual. This process converts what may initially have been antisocial into socially acceptable behavior. The instinctual impulse, although transformed, is nevertheless gratified, or discharged, according to Freud. This does not occur to any significant extent with defenses. The commonly given example of sublimation is that of the artist who sublimates anal impulses to smear feces to painting with a brush and producing beautiful paintings. Sublimation is included in this section because even though technically different from defenses, it resembles reaction formation to the point that there is no sharp line of demarcation between them. It is doubtful whether a sexual instinct can really be gratified by nonsexual activity. Consequently, some analysts (Waelder, 1960) believe that true sublimations do not exist: What seems to be sublimatory behavior is probably reaction formation.

22. THE CHOICE OF NEUROSES IS STILL UNKNOWN.

Neurosogenesis refers to the processes involved in the causation of neuroses. The *choice of neurosis* remains as baffling a puzzle as it was in the early days of psychoanalysis. Undoubtedly, to a larger or smaller degree, there is an interplay of constitutional and environmental factors at the bottom of every neurosis or emotional disturbance. Psychoanalysis limits itself to the environmental aspect and how it affects the development and the stability of the mind. The differences between the various neuroses have been discussed briefly above; now they will be focused upon. It will be noted that a neurosis is defined by the chief defenses it utilizes and the level of psychosexual development that has been reached.

23. THE NEUROSES ARE REGRESSIVE PHENOMENA.

Before proceeding, a few words of explanation are in order about the level of psychosexual development characteristic of the various neuroses. This brings us to the concepts of *fixation* and *regression*.

Presumably, in the psychoneuroses the patient has already reached the phallic level of development. Difficulties are encountered when the patient attempts to resolve the Oedipus complex. Inasmuch as oedipal feelings are traumatically conflicted, the patient regresses to a previous stage of emotional development. In terms of psychic development, he returns to a stage where he was relatively comfortable.

Fixation Point. The fixation point is well described by Freud's analogy of an advancing army. As the army proceeds it captures various garrisons on the way to its final objective. The harder the battle, the more soldiers are required to hold their position. This weakens the advancing army, and if it encounters intense opposition, it retreats back to the position where it left the greatest number of troops behind.

In hysteria, considered the most "advanced" neurosis, the person has practically reached the genital level of development. The conflict is oedipal, and the patient regresses only slightly. This description is purposely tentative because many analysts (Giovacchini, 1972, 1975) believe that this picture is incomplete. In any case, the hysterical patient uses such defenses as repression, identification, displacement, and conversion.

The *obsessive-compulsive person* has regressed to the anal phase and employs isolation, reaction formation, and undoing as chief defensive modalities. The *depressed individual* is regressed to the oral phase and is characterized by introjective defenses. More severely disturbed people—paranoids, schizophrenics, borderline states and those with character disorders—regress to early narcissistic phases and use such primitive defenses as projection, denial, and splitting.

24. DREAMS HAVE MEANING AND PURPOSE.

Dream theory has always been a cornerstone of the psychoanalytic conceptual framework. Psychoanalysts believe that dreams have a rationale and are not simply the breakdown products of a disordered or fatigued mind. The dream's function is to *preserve sleep,* and each dream represents the *fulfillment of an unconscious wish.*

A dream is formed in the following fashion. Something during the day, usually some incompleted thought or action, is retained in memory. Usually this element is an indifferent or trivial element and is known as the *day residue.* During sleep, due to a lowering of defenses, an unconscious impulse threatens to break through into consciousness and awaken the dreamer. This often occurs with nightmares. The day residue, however, usually has some associative connection with the unconscious impulses; thus, the latter attaches itself to it and, through a variety of mechanisms, becomes transformed into a dream.

The operations of the unconscious are called *primary processes* and are characterized by (1) displacement, (2) condensation or overdetermination and (3) symbolization. These account for the bizarre qualities of many dreams. *Displacement* occurs when the unconscious impulse attaches itself to the day residue. The energy of one is transferred (displaced) to the other. *Condensation* or *overdetermination* refers to several impulses being represented by a single dream element, and *symbolization* calls attention to the use of symbols in dreams.

Dreams are divided into two levels: the *latent dream* refers to the unconscious wish, and the *manifest content* refers to what is remembered or what the dreamer reports. For the dream to progress from the latent to manifest dream stage it must undergo what Freud (1900) called *secondary revision*: the unconscious, turbulent elements of the latent dream have to be pulled together in a sufficiently rational, coherent fashion so that it can be put in a visual and sometimes auditory form. Recent dream research, acccording to some investigators, seems to contradict some of Freud's assertions and strengthen others. Freud himself discussed certain situations, such as punishment and traumatic dreams, which he believed contradicted some aspects of his thesis.

25. THE EGO HAS BECOME THE CENTRAL
     FOCUS OF OUR CLINICAL CONCERNS.

The type of patients found in the consultation rooms of current psychoanalysts have little resemblance to the patients described by the pioneers of psychoanalysis. Instead of presenting clear-cut symptoms that can be conceptualized in terms of clashing forces within the mind, they speak of vague dissatisfactions and frequently ruminate about where they fit in society and the purpose of their existence. Consequently, certain aspects of psychoanalytic theory have required further emphasis and development. Since the ego is the organ of the mind which adapts to both the external and internal world and which defines the sense of identity, it had to be examined further. Several schools of ego psychology have developed, but essentially only two have remained effective.

Heinz Hartmann (1964) and his co-workers Ernst Kris and Rudolph Lowenstein, as well as others (mainly in New York), postulated an ego psychology which retained Freud's dualistic instinct theory and energic hypothesis. Hartmann compartmentalized the ego into an *autonomous* part, independent of instinctual forces, and a part that is the outgrowth of instincts. He retained the energic hypothesis and added *neutralized energy* to libidinal and aggressive energy as an extension of Freud's hypothesis that sexual energy is sublimated into nonsexual energy. According to Hartmann, aggressive energy is neutralized into nonaggressive, or neutral, energy.

Winnicott (1958) modified many of Klein's (1948) concepts and combined them with his own. Winnicott has had a substantial following in Great Britain, but an ever-increasing number of analysts in the United States, such as Boyer (Boyer & Giovacchini, 1967), Ekstein (1966), Giovacchini (1972, 1975), Lindon (1967), and Searles (1965) is integrating his views with their own. Basically these analysts regard the ego in terms of various subsystems, principally focusing upon the identity system (often known as the self-representation), the integrative system (a coordinating system), and the executive apparatus, which interacts with the outer world. No specific energic hypothesis is required for these concepts. A consequence of this theoretical orientation is that it enables psychoanalysts to treat a wider range of patients than had previously been thought possible.

Applications

Assessment

Methods of evaluating potential patients for psychoanalytic treatment vary. Once Freud had consolidated his treatment approach and technique, he adopted a nondirective attitude. He did not advocate systematic history taking but took a wait-and-see attitude following the patient's verbal material, without preconceived judgments regarding psychopathology or treatability. This established an atmosphere in which the patient experienced maximum freedom to express himself as uninhibitedly as possible.

Today, some psychoanalysts, in conformance with the medical model, resort to a more structured approach. They usually see patients for two to four interviews and take an extensive history. The history of the present problem is chronologically ordered, with special emphasis on life circumstances that can be associated with the exacerbation or remission of symptoms. Then the analyst inquires about the patient's emotional development, paying particular attention to childhood events. Finally, a family history is elicited, with special relevance being given to the personalities and possible emotional disorders of parents. Sibling relationships are also emphasized.

At the same time the psychoanalyst does a mental status examination, noting the patient's appearance, orientation to time and space, appropriateness of affect, and characteristics of stream of thought, as well as the appearance of any special symptoms, such as delusions and hallucinations. This assessment is to determine whether the patient has sufficient ego strength to undergo analysis. The analyst may also interview other members of the family, although this is seldom done with adults. It is frequently done with adolescents and is practically standard procedure with children.

If the analyst still has doubts about the feasibility of conducting analysis with a particular patient, he may ask for psychological testing—usually projective tests, especially the Rorschach examination. If the patient seeks psychoanalysis in a clinic or institute, a routine social history is done by a social worker, and the analyst has this information at his disposal before he sees the patient.

The analyst with medical training is especially sensitive to the possibility that organic factors may cause or contribute to the clinical picture. He may ask for an independent medical examination to check the possibility of a neurological disorder. Many analysts without medical degrees insist upon a routine physical work-up, and sometimes they consult with a physician when they suspect their patient may be developing symptoms that cannot be explained on a psychological basis.

After having obtained the above information, the analyst will ordinarily conduct a trial analysis. The analyst asks the patient to lie down and begin free associating. He listens to the patient for about two weeks, seeing him four to five times a week to determine whether it is wise to continue.

Freud initially advocated a trial analysis, without such involved examinations. He believed that such an analysis could serve as a therapeutic test to determine whether the patient is analyzable. Today, some analysts (Giovacchini, 1972, 1975, 1976) believe that the complicated investigations outlined above are not only unnecessary but a hindrance to analysis as well. They advocate little history taking and starting analysis as soon as possible. The patient is not told that this is a trial analysis, since the analyst wants to avoid giving the patient the impression that he is on trial. The patient's psychopathology does not have to meet any standards to be treated by the psychoanalytic method. Treatment is simply instituted, and the patient determines whether he wishes to continue.

Treatment

The essence and chief focus of psychoanalysis is the treatment relationship. Its most meaningful discoveries have been in this area. Some superficial aspects of the psychoanalytic interview have undergone modification, but the principles underlying therapeutic strategy have remained remarkably constant.

Psychoanalytic therapy began with hypnosis. Breuer (Breuer & Freud, 1895) hypnotized his famous patient, Anna O., and had her relive the traumatic moments that reputedly were responsible for her symptoms. Inasmuch as the patient discharged pent-up tension and anxiety, this procedure was referred to as *abreaction*, or "chimney sweeping". This was the beginning of the talking cure.

Freud (Breuer & Freud, 1895) replaced hypnosis by pressing his finger on the reclining patient's forehead and having him say anything that came to mind associated with the period of time when his symptoms originated. Through this experience Freud discovered *resistance*. The patient who at one level was anxious to cooperate with the therapist because of his tormenting symptoms would nevertheless withhold material in direct defiance of the instructions he had been given.

Almost simultaneously with the discovery of resistance, Freud recognized another phenomenon which he called *transference*. He noted that patients, especially female patients, formed rather intense positive feelings toward him. Some professed being in love with him. Freud, rather than accepting this as a reaction to his irresistible charm, looked at himself in the mirror and, always the scientist, asked what factors could account for his patients' reactions. He considered such situations as phenomena worthy of study rather than a natural consequence not requiring further explanation.

The patient gradually attributes to the analyst qualities that once belonged to a significant person of his infantile past. Thus, some of his feelings toward the analyst become irrational in view of present-day realities. The ability of the patient to distinguish between this childish orientation and the actual analytic relationship becomes the main therapeutic vehicle. The patient relives his childhood conflicts in the here and now of the analytic interaction, and the recognition by the patient (through the analyst's interpretations) of how his infantile orientation influences his behavior and thinking permits him a greater freedom of choice in his reactions and relations with both the inner world of his psyche and reality.

Transference is the most important therapeutic vehicle as well as the chief obstacle to cure (Freud, 1905, 1912, 1915b). If the patient's negative transference is too intense, he will attack and defy the analyst, refusing to cooperate. Interpretations will be of no avail, and the patient will cling to his anger, stubbornly resisting any acknowledgment of its infantile origin or transference implications. Erotic transference has a similarly disruptive effect. The patient wants to be loved by the analyst and loses sight of the therapeutic task (Freud, 1915b). The modern therapeutic task can be defined as making the unconscious conscious through the use of transference interpretations. The analyst uncovers unconscious feelings as the patient allows himself to be fully aware of transference feelings. Gradually the patient begins to recognize how he is distorting his image of the analyst according to needs that originated in childhood.

Psychoanalytic Procedure. The patient is asked to lie down on the couch and to put all of his feelings or thoughts into words. He must not choose what he will say or omit anything because he believes it is trivial, irrelevant, nonsensical, painful, or embarrassing. This is about the only demand the analyst makes of the patient. It is known as the *fundamental rule (Gründregel).* This process is called *free association.*

Rational behavior and thinking are governed by what psychoanalysts refer to as the *secondary process.* Irrelevant and distracting thoughts are excluded, and behavior is determined by an assessment of needs and of the available and acceptable methods that will satisfy such needs. This is known as *reality testing,* an important aspect of the secondary process, based upon logical principles and organization and realistic judgments.

In psychoanalytic treatment, the patient is asked to give up secondary-process thinking. He is supposed to let what is called the *primary process* dominate, suspending logical operations as much as possible so that his thinking will follow a more primitive course than it previously did. By practicing free association, the patient relives infantile feelings in the transference. These are now subjected to logical scrutiny and reality testing, mediated by higher psychic systems which previously had no influence over such impulses as they remained hidden in the unconscious. In a preceding section this latter process was referred to as maintaining repression through defenses.

The analyst provides a setting where the patient can reveal the most frightening aspects of himself. He does this in a nonanxious atmosphere. Instead of viewing the patient's revelations as frightening human tragedies, the analyst calmly accepts the fact of their occurrence and views them as topics of extreme interest and worthy of inquiry. The patient gradually shares the analyst's perspective and becomes further involved with the infantile within himself, rather than feeling overwhelmed by it. The analytic setting permits the patient to regress with some degree of comfort.

Because of a somewhat relaxed regression (although its manifestations may from time to time be stormy), and the concomitant bringing to the surface of infantile elements, primitive forces within the self are no longer as oppressive or constrictive as previously. Furthermore, often the patient regresses to an ego state which precedes the formation of pathological psychic structures. Having reached such a regressed state, the patient has another chance to develop, this time without the constricting and distorting influences that plagued his initial development.

The knowledge gained about primitive mental states from the study of regressed states has led to a more extensive application of psychoanalytic treatment. Many analysts no longer confine psychoanalytic technique to the treatment of psychoneuroses. Patients suffering more severe emotional conditions, even some psychoses, are now being treated by the psychoanalytic method.

Institutional

Psychoanalysis loses some of its character once it strays outside the consultation room. However, in spite of the opposition it has encountered, its principles have overtly or covertly guided various types of institutions. Three types in particular can be emphasized: (1) child-rearing practices, (2) education, and (3) therapeutic institutions.

Child-Rearing Practices. In many ways, child-rearing has become institutionalized. There are certain principles and traditions which cannot be ignored if the goal is the approval of society and presumably if optimal results in producing a happy, healthy adult are desired.

The psychoanalytic orientation stood in marked contrast to the rigid behavioristic approach advocated by John B. Watson, and practiced primarily in the twenties. The behaviorist arranged everything on a rigid schedule, to introduce the child to order and discipline. A certain amount of frustration was considered to be in the child's best interest. The psychoanalytic approach stresses relating to the child's needs and abandoning any preconceived adult notions about schedules and delay. More specifically, it maintains that the adult should not force the child to move on to a higher developmental position; the child is to proceed at his own pace. The psychoanalytic position is permissive.

Education. Psychoanalysis stresses that the child focuses upon various activities at specific stages. His behavior is phase specific. There are appropriate ages for introducing certain learning experiences. Because of attributes characteristic of a particular developmental phase, the child of any given age may be better able to incorporate some aspects of the external world than others. Some teachers have used these ideas in setting up educational programs. Psychoanalysis also stresses autonomy, and educators have tried to integrate this focus in their formats. Usually this has led to less rigid curricula and a tendency toward a permissive outlook.

How successful these attempts have been is an open question. Psychoanalysis does not have a comprehensive learning theory, and until this lack is remedied it seems unlikely that much will be accomplished by psychoanalytic insights in furthering the educational process.

Therapeutic Institutions. One might expect that psychoanalysis would be influential in mental hospitals. Actually, it has received a mixed reception there. From the psychoanalyst's viewpoint, hospitalization is not a treatment issue. A patient is hospitalized generally for the benefit of the relatives who can no longer stand him. If he is not able to care for himself and requires that someone look after him, hospitalization is custodial rather than psychotherapeutic.

How can the patient's hospitalization be turned to best advantage? Is the hospital simply a place to contain the patient between analytic hours? Bettelheim (1974) constructed a total therapeutic milieu based on psychoanalytic principles at the Orthogenic School of the University of Chicago. Basically, he created a setting tailored as much as possible to the child's needs, reacting to the child's unconscious requests as well as being sensitive to nonverbal communications. Chestnut Lodge in Maryland has a similar philosophy and is probably the only psychoanalytic hospital in the world today. The Menninger Clinic has also hospitalized some patients for psychoanalytic treatment.

Drugs and somatic approaches such as shock therapy are often employed in hospitals. This emphasizes the medical model. The doctor and other staff decide what should be corrected, and then they institute methods to achieve desired changes. In this regard, the patient is not really consulted and remains the passive recipient of authoritative caretaking.

Psychoanalysis in a hospital setting retains some elements of the medical medical model, inasmuch as it is concerned with total person. In contrast to the medical world it attempts also to foster maximal autonomy. This combination often stimulates considerable resistance among mental health professionals.

Self

Psychoanalysis focuses upon the workings of the mind. The Socratic motto "Know thyself" would be the most appropriate end point of analysis. The world is looked at in terms of subtle and often hidden motivations.

The psychoanalytic frame of reference is empathic. This does not mean that the analyzed person should go around analyzing others, in what is derisively called parlor analysis. To look at and interpret someone else's behavior in terms of unconscious motivation is not the hallmark of a successful analysis. It represents the clumsy fumbling of the insecure amateur.

Analysis should not foster arrogance. There

have been analysts and analysands who adopt a superior attitude because they believe they now know all the secrets of the human mind and feel they belong to an exclusive cult. This was especially true during the early days of psychoanalysis, when analysts banded together and isolated themselves, presumably for mutual protection. Their behavior probably was an overcompensation for an experienced vulnerability. Today the situation is much different. Ecclesiastic and esoteric seclusion is not part of the analytic scene. If such accusations, on specific occasions, seem justified, then one is attacking a particular analyst or group and not analysis. These are grotesque distortions of analysis. If anything, analysis should promote tolerance and acceptance, recognizing every man's right to construct his own reality and to choose a lifestyle consonant with his private world. His world may be different, but it is worthy of being respected and understood. The analytic perspective does not seek to manage another's life. It is the polar opposite of those philosophies and therapies designed to control behavior.

In addition to being a theoretical system and a therapeutic technique, psychoanalysis is also a philosophy, a *Weltanschauung*. One's personal psychoanalysis never ends. The analysand may terminate the ritual of analysis by stopping his appointments, but the process continues.

Should everyone be analyzed? This frequently asked question is antianalytic. The essence of analysis is autonomy. Can autonomy be imposed? Obviously, this is a contradiction. One has to choose for oneself. Some people have made comfortable adjustments to life and seek no further. Some are not curious and do not care to look inward. There are many others whose minds are restless and are admirably suited for the mutually explorative activity that characterizes the patient-analyst relationship.

Validation

Evidence

Psychoanalysis has been attacked as being unscientific (Nagel, 1959), since its theories and hypotheses are not based upon experiments and controlled studies. Its theoretical edifice is considered empty and speculative by some opponents.

Science is a formal way of looking at things. According to Max Planck, it is based upon two assumptions: (1) there is a real world, and (2) it is knowable (see D'Abro, 1951). Hypotheses are constructed so that parts of the universe which seem chaotic can be understood in a more orderly fashion. Science is based upon a series of abstractions that help explain apparently unrelated data. A better hypothesis applies to a wider range of data. Then, previous hypotheses recede into the background.

Opponents of psychoanalysis point out that psychoanalysis is not based upon controlled experiments (Nagel, 1959). They question the validity of obtaining data from treating patients or relying upon observations. If these factors disqualify psychoanalysis as a science, then astronomy and geology would find themselves in similar straits.

Nagel once criticized psychoanalysis because he believed that its hypotheses were not capable of being disproven. He cited the Oedipus complex as an example and did not elaborate what he meant by disproof. In his classic textbook (Cohen & Nagel, 1934), Nagel stated that if a body of data could be better explained by a new hypothesis, then older ones, for pragmatic purposes, were disproven. If the child's feelings toward his parents as manifested through dreams and behavior or if the fantasies of patients can be better explained by other hypotheses, then the oedipal hypothesis can be considered no longer useful. Psychoanalysis, as a part of science, is nonjudgmental. It does not deal with right or wrong. Some hypotheses are better than others only if they are more useful (Giovacchini, 1967).

The fundamental hypothesis of psychoanalysis is the *dynamic unconscious*. Other hypotheses can be considered extensions or superstructures of the dynamic unconscious. These secondary hypotheses can be modified or discarded without threatening psychoanalysis. If, however, the concept of the dynamic unconscious were proven invalid, then psychoanalysis would crumble. But the demise of psychoanalysis is highly improbable, since the evidence that supports the concept of the dynamic unconscious stems from more frames of reference than those validating the existence of electricity.

Before enumerating these frames of reference,

it is germane to consider again the dynamic unconscious, which postulates the existence of mental processes that cannot spontaneously become conscious. These unconscious elements, Freud claimed, have effects upon conscious behavior without the person being aware of it. This latter aspect is novel. Unconscious mental elements were well known since antiquity, but that they could affect so-called rational behavior is Freud's unique discovery and constitutes the essence of psychoanalysis.

The following frames of reference, listed in order of decreasing probability, support the concept of the dynamic unconscious: (1) posthypnotic phenomena, (2) parapraxes, (3) symptoms, and (4) dreams.

Posthypnotic Phenomena. Posthypnotic suggestion furnishes the most elegant evidence to support the validity of the dynamic unconscious. A patient in hypnosis can be given suggestions to behave in a particular manner later, when he is no longer in a trance. He can be told that he will have no conscious recall of such suggestions. Under hypnosis a person may be told that when awake he is to turn off a lamp when the hypnotist coughs. Following hypnosis, the subject will not consciously know of any connection between the cough and his turning off the light. He may not even be aware that the hypnotist coughed. He may deny that he turned off the light or may rationalize his behavior. When the hypnotist explains that the subject was instructed to behave in the way he did during hypnosis, there may be no recall. It is obvious that the subject responds to a situation of which he consciously knows nothing. This is an example of the dynamic unconscious at work.

Parapraxes. The slips of the tongue, unusual lapses of memory such as forgetting familiar names, and other common, inexplicable aberrations of behavior which can be considered the psychopathology of ordinary life are called parapraxes (Freud, 1901). They are also often called "freudian slips." Such behavior often seems irrational, and it is plausible to assume that it emanates from forces within the self of which the person has no conscious awareness. Forgetting something "well known," if that something is later recalled, almost defines the unconscious. The bursting forth of an unintended insult is evidence that something relegated to the unconscious can affect one's behavior, in spite of efforts to control revealing such feelings. The assumption made about such slips is that what breaks through is a derivative of some element which remains in the unconscious.

Symptoms. From a rational viewpoint, symptoms make very little sense. During the course of psychoanalytic treatment, the analyst may discover their meaning. Insofar as the patient was not aware of the rationale behind his symptomatic behavior, the motivating forces behind such behavior must reside in the unconscious. The symptom can be understood as a compromise between an unconscious impulse and the defense against that impulse.

Dreams. In the same way as symptoms, dreams also have a rationale which can be discovered through free association. Unconscious impulses and defenses against such impulses are regularly encountered in analyzing dreams. In dreams, however, the unconscious wish is more often discernible than in symptomatic behavior, because of the partial relaxation of defenses occurring during sleep. In some dreams, however, distorting forces may make it difficult to arrive at their meaning. The same assumptions are made about dreams as are made about symptoms.

Comparisons

Psychoanalytic theory and treatment are fundamentally different from any other system of psychotherapy. The differences are particularly noteworthy when the objectives of treatment are examined. Most systems of treatment make the assumption that the therapist's reality is better than the patient's. Consequently, their efforts are directed toward altering the patient's behavior to conform to a preestablished reality model. How this is achieved varies with the type of treatment.

Behavioral modification achieves its goals by a system of rewards and punishments. This is fundamentally the same conditioning principle that Ivan Pavlov elucidated at the beginning of the century. This approach, concrete and mechanistic, totally ignores deeper, inner causes. The person's autonomy is considered a hindrance, because the essence of the behavior modification approach is to manipulate a person into conforming. Some behaviorists apparently do not like the word *conform* and point out they attempt to change behavior that the client wants to change. This implies that the person has freedom of choice. What is ignored is the unconscious. The person's decision is neither spontaneous nor free. He has been coerced into making it because society or his conscience is at variance with his symptomatic behavior. His true motivations are subtle and complex and cannot simply be disposed of by signing a contract, or whatever manipulation the behavioral modification approach contrives.

Transactional analysis has goals similar to behavioral modifications; only the method is different. It takes into account psychoanalytic principles, those concerned with the dynamics of various interpersonal relationships. Beyond this point it parts company with psychoanalysis, because the transactional analyst becomes involved in role playing. He pretends to be the mother or father or whatever and then somehow gets the patient to work out some conflict. The method of transactional analysis is as far removed from psychoanalysis as is behavioral modification. It is concerned with reenactment, and even though it is aimed at bringing to the fore infantile relationships, transference, which refers to viewing the analyst in terms of an emotionally significant person of the past, is essentially ignored. The nature of the interaction as a game strategy is stressed, and it is believed this understanding should lead to corrections at the behavioral level. The correction of the transference distortion, however, is impossible because the therapist has adopted a role rather than reflected what the patient has projected onto him.

Client-centered therapy, supposedly nonintrusive, is designed to give the client insight by reflecting back to him what he has said. The fact that expressions such as "reflecting back" are metaphors is unfortunately forgotten. In client-centered therapy the process underlying the metaphor is not even considered, so in a sense this is a therapy primarily based upon a model defined by the idea of mirroring the client's verbal statements and not upon a conceptual system, since client-centered therapy really has no theory. In fact, the use of a conceptual system is decried.

New therapies are springing up every day, involving groups and individuals. To some extent, most of them utilize some psychoanalytic principles. However, *allowing transference to develop, with the aim of increasing the patient's autonomy by extending control over inner primitive forces, is unique to psychoanalysis.*

Psychoanalysis developed from medicine and has retained some superficial elements of the medical model. Some psychoanalysts admit that certain aspects of the medical model are inappropriate to their ultimate goal of enhancing autonomy (Freud, 1926b).

The background of the therapist is important in determining his orientation. The medical psychoanalyst has the most rigorous and lengthiest training of any profession. He must attend medical school and then put in one year of internship, usually three years of psychiatric residency, and, on the average, five years of analysis and supervised training in a psychoanalytic institute.

Many therapists, in rejecting the medical model, argue that medical education is unnecessary for the practice of psychoanalysis (Freud, 1926b). Quite a few analysts agree, but most would like to retain some medical training in a much modified and abbreviated form. In some cities arguments about training have led to absurd consequences. In rejecting the present arduous process of training for psychotherapy, many persons have rejected all training. In New York City, for example, quite a sizable number of persons start practicing psychotherapy with little more than a course in undergraduate psychology. In some instances, they do not even have that. Frequently, they have been in treatment with someone who represents some school of psychotherapy. The therapist treats him and then trains him. Such trainees band together, and a new movement is born.

Obviously, standards of training and competence in psychotherapy have to be established. This is taking place, but it is a slow process.

Prospect

From time to time, as in response to a questionnaire by several analysts from the Chicago Psychoanalytic Society, the opinion is stated that psychoanalysis is dead. The course of psychoanalysis has been stormy since its very beginning, but it has survived.

One must expect dissent when dealing with a

topic as sensitive as basic motivations. To learn there are forces within your mind over which you do not have complete control and to place yourself in the hands of someone who implicitly claims he knows more about you than you do must be threatening. Opposition led to counter-reactions; analysts defended themselves by withdrawing from their contemporaries. In Freud's day, this meant separation from the psychiatric group. As analysts isolated themselves, they overcompensated by acting as if they were an elite cult. As the years passed, others began recognizing some of the exciting ideas in psychoanalytic theory and became intrigued with the analytic method and philosophy. Gradually, psychoanalysis became more popular and accepted. The influx of students seeking training after World War II made psychoanalysts less secretive and esoteric.

Today there are several issues which affect psychoanalysis and which may determine its future course. Rapid and immense changes have occurred in our society, and psychoanalysis has been caught in the swirl. Many previous standards and mores have been discarded. What had been considered psychopathology, such as homosexuality, is now called alternate lifestyles.

Psychoanalysis has been attacked because it has been viewed as a representative of the establishment. Psychoanalysis originated in a mid-Victorian, highly structured conformist culture and was rejected because it was too much at variance with traditional beliefs. Today, its role has been reversed; it is called reactionary and traditional.

Psychoanalysis is said to advocate conformity by a culture that considers itself anticonformist. In truth, psychoanalysis stresses autonomy in a culture that wants to equalize everything and is really frightened of autonomy.

This confusion has led to the emergence of many schools of psychotherapy which, on the surface, seem to be against conformity but which, by manipulating behavior, sometimes takes on an Orwellian, big-brother grotesqueness. There are other motives behind these movements, such as seeking the prestige and economic advantages that psychoanalysts have acquired without the training and sacrifices they underwent.

As psychoanalysts come out of seclusion, they may no longer provoke mystical awe and it may then be possible to make progressive changes that will put psychoanalysis where it belongs, among the other clinical disciplines. The trend is toward moving away from a strict medical model, and this will be reflected in educational practices. Psychoanalytic education will become more available, and present-day institutes will upgrade and modify entrance requirements and curricula.

Psychologists and social workers are now beginning to be given the clinical training formerly reserved only for physicians. The question of a medical background will have to be reevaluated, and perhaps it will prove to be an anachronism—as Freud himself indicated (Freud, 1926b). It is possible that special programs which include some exposure to clinical medicine will be instituted for the training of future lay analysts.

As psychoanalysis becomes less parochial, general attitudes about it should become more relaxed. Then it can be appreciated for what it is. Psychoanalysis is not a religion, a cult, or a fantasy; it is a scientific theory and a clinical technique which attempts to alleviate misery and suffering and to accentuate and bring out the dignity and nobility inherent in every man.

Annotated Bibliography

Primary Source

Freud, Sigmund: *The Complete Psychological Works of Sigmund Freud.* Standard edition. London: Hogarth Press, 1952–1974 (24 volumes).

This magnificent collection of all of Freud's psychological papers, books, lectures, and monographs is an absolute essential for any person who wishes to understand psychoanalysis in depth. This is a scholarly, annotated collection, each article being preceded by an introduction which places it in its proper perspective and in the context of the development of Freud's ideas. The 24th volume is a comprehensive index which contains considerably more than just the standard subject-author index.

Secondary Sources

Fenichel, Otto. *The Psychoanalytic Theory of Neuroses.* New York: Norton, 1945.

This relatively long textbook has been a standard reference for many years. Classical psychoanalysis is systematically and accurately represented, and up until the time of its publication, most of the relevant literature is reviewed. This book is being revised to bring it up to date.

Brenner, Charles. *An Elementary Textbook of Psychoanalysis.* New York: International Universities Press, 1957.

This is a short, concise, excellent textbook for the student who does not want the detailed expositions found in the above works. In spite of its brevity, this book is remarkably lucid.

Giovacchini, Peter L. *Psychoanalysis of Character Disorders.* New York: Jason Aronson Press, 1975.

This book consists of a collection of articles dealing with the theory and treatment of patients suffering from severe psychopathology, a focus which is becoming increasingly prevalent in modern analysis.

Waelder, Robert. *Basic Theory of Psychoanalysis.* New York: International Universities Press, 1960.

This is another relatively short, excellent textbook. In addition to examining the technical aspects of psychoanalysis, it briefly concerns itself with some philosophical issues.

Winnicott, Donald W. *Collected Papers: Through Pediatrics to Psychoanalysis.* New York: Basic Books, 1958.

This book contains many of the major articles of a prominent leader of the British school. His ideas about psychopathology and treatment are more in accord with present-day psychoanalysts whose focus is mainly ego psychological.

References

Abraham, K. The influence of oral erotism on character formation. In *Selected Papers on Psycho-Analysis* (pp. 370–393). London: Hogarth Press, 1948. (Originally published, 1921.)

Abraham, K. A short study of the development of the libido, viewed in the light of mental disorders. In *Selected Papers on Psycho-Analysis* (pp. 418–480). London: Hogarth Press, 1948. (Originally published, 1924.)

Alexander, F., & French, T. *Psychoanalytic Therapy.* New York: Ronald Press, 1946.

Alexander, F., & Selesnick, S. *The history of psychiatry.* New York: Alfred A. Knopf, 1966.

Aristophanes. The plays of Aristophanes. In *Great Books of the Western World.* Chicago: Encyclopaedia Britannica, Inc., 1955.

Bernard, C. *An introduction to the study of experimental medicine.* Henry Schuman, 1949.

Bettelheim, B. *A home for the heart.* New York: Alfred A. Knopf, 1974.

Blos, P. *On adolescence.* New York: Free Press, 1962.

Bornstein, B. On latency. *Psychoanalytic Study of the Child* (Vol. 6, pp. 279–285). New York: International Universities Press, 1951.

Boyer, L. B. & Giovacchini, P. L. *The psychoanalytic treatment of characterological and schizophrenic disorders.* New York: International Science Press, 1967.

Brenner, C. *An elementary textbook of psychoanalysis.* New York: International Universities Press, 1957.

Breuer, J. & Freud, S. *Studies on hysteria.* Standard edition *The Complete Works of Sigmund Freud* (Vol. 2). London: Hogarth Press, 1955. (Originally published, 1895.)

Cohen, M. & Nagel, E. *An introduction to logic and scientific method.* New York: Harcourt, Brace, 1934.

D'Abro, A. *The rise of the new physics.* New York: Dover Publications, 1951.

Ekstein, R. *Children of time and space of action and impulse.* New York: Appleton-Century-Crofts, 1966.

Ellenberger, H. *The discovery of the unconscious.* New York: Basic Books, 1970.

Erikson, E. H. *Childhood and society.* New York; W. W. Norton, 1950.

Fenichel, O. *The psychoanalytic theory of neuroses.* New York: Norton, 1945.

Ferenczi, S. & Rank, O. *The development of psychoanalysis.* Baltimore: Williams & Wilkins, 1924.

Freud, A. *The ego and the mechanisms of defense.* New York: International Universities Press, 1946. (Originally published, 1936.)

Freud, S. Beobactungen über Gestaltung und feineren Bau der als Hoden beschriebenen Lappenorgane des Als, S. B. *Akad. Wiss.,* Wien, 1877 III Abt., 75, 15.

Freud, S. *On the grounds for detaching a particular syndrome from neurasthenia under the description "anxiety neurosis."* Standard edition (Vol. 3, pp. 85–119). London: Hogarth Press, 1962. (Originally published, 1895.) (a)

Note: Standard edition refers to the Standard edition of *The Complete Psychological Works of Sigmund Freud*, which consists of 24 volumes. See the Annotated Bibliography above.

Freud, S. *A reply to criticisms of my paper on anxiety neurosis.* Standard edition (Vol. 3, pp. 119–141). London: Hogarth Press, 1962. (Originally published, 1895.) (b)

Freud, S. *Further remarks on the neuro-psychoses of defense.* Standard edition (Vol. 3, pp. 157–187). London: Hogarth Press, 1962. (Originally published, 1896.)

Freud, S. *Sexuality in the aetiology of the neuroses.* Standard edition (Vol. 3, pp. 259–287). London: Hogarth Press, 1962. (Originally published, 1898.)

Freud, S. *The interpretation of dreams.* Standard edition (Vols. 4 and 5). London: Hogarth Press, 1953. (Originally published, 1900.)

Freud, S. *The psychopathology of everyday life.* Standard Edition (Vol. 6). London: Hogarth Press, 1966. (Originally published, 1901.)

Freud, S. *Fragments of an analysis of a case of hysteria.* Standard edition (Vol. 7, pp. 1–123). London: Hogarth Press, 1953. (Originally published, 1905.) (a)

Freud, S. *Three essays on the theory of sexuality.* Standard edition (Vol. 7, pp. 123–247). London: Hogarth Press, 1953. (Originally published, 1905.) (b)

Freud, S. *Delusions and dreams in "Jensen's Gravida."* Standard edition (Vol. 9, pp. 1–97). London: Hogarth Press, 1959. (Originally published, 1907.)

Freud, S. *Five lectures on psycho-analysis.* Standard edition (Vol. 11). London: Hogarth Press, 1957. (Originally published, 1909.) (a)

Freud, S. *Notes upon a case of obsessional neurosis.* Standard edition (Vol. 10, pp. 151–319). London: Hogarth Press, 1955. (Originally published, 1909.) (b)

Freud, S. *Leonardo da Vinci and a memory of his childhood.* Standard edition (Vol. 11). London: Hogarth Press, 1957. (Originally published, 1910.)

Freud, S. *Formulations on the two principles of mental functioning.* Standard edition (Vol. 12, pp. 213–227). London: Hogarth Press, 1958. (Originally published, 1911.) (a)

Freud, S. *Psycho-analytic notes on an autobiographical account of a case of paranoia.* Standard edition (Vol. 12, pp. 1–85). London: Hogarth Press, 1958. (Originally published, 1911.) (b)

Freud, S. *The dynamics of transference.* Standard edition (Vol. 12, pp. 97–109). London: Hogarth Press, 1958. (Originally published, 1912.)

Freud, S. *The occurrence in dreams of material from fairy tales.* Standard edition (Vol. 12, pp. 279–289). London: Hogarth Press, 1958. (Originally published, 1913.) (a)

Freud, S. *The theme of three caskets.* Standard edition (Vol. 12, pp. 289–303). London: Hogarth Press, 1958. (Originally published, 1913.) (b)

Freud, S. *Totem and taboo.* Standard edition (Vol. 13). London: Hogarth Press, 1955. (Originally published, 1913.) (c)

Freud, S. *On the history of the psycho-analytic movement.* Standard edition (Vol. 14, pp. 1–67). London: Hogarth Press, 1957. (Originally published, 1914.) (a)

Freud, S. *On narcissism: an introduction.* Standard edition (Vol. 14, pp. 67–105). London: Hogarth Press, 1957. (Originally published, 1914.) (b)

Freud, S. *Instincts and their vicissitudes.* Standard edition (Vol. 14, pp. 109–141.) London: Hogarth Press, 1957. (Originally published, 1915.) (a)

Freud, S. *Observations on transference love.* Standard edition (Vol. 12, pp. 157–172). London: Hogarth Press, 1958. (Originally published, 1915.) (b)

Freud, S. *Repression.* Standard edition (Vol. 14, pp. 141–159). London: Hogarth Press, 1957. (Originally published, 1915.) (c)

Freud, S. *The unconscious.* Standard edition (Vol. 14, pp. 159–217). London: Hogarth Press, 1957. (Originally published, 1915.) (d)

Freud, S. *Introductory lectures on psycho-analysis.* Standard edition (Vols. 15 and 16). London: Hogarth Press, 1963. (Originally published, 1917.) (a)

Freud, S. *Mourning and melancholia.* Standard edition (Vol. 14, pp. 237–259). London: Hogarth Press, 1957. (Originally published, 1917.) (b)

Freud, S. *Beyond the pleasure principle.* Standard edition (Vol. 18). London: Hogarth Press, 1955. (Originally published, 1920.)

Freud, S. *Group psychology and analysis of the self.* Standard edition (Vol. 18). London: Hogarth Press, 1955. (Originally published, 1921.)

Freud, S. *Medusa's head.* Standard edition (Vol. 18, pp. 173–178). London: Hogarth Press, 1955. (Originally published, 1922.)

Freud, S. *The ego and the id.* Standard edition (Vol. 19). London: Hogarth Press, 1961. (Originally published, 1923.) (a)

Freud, S. *The infantile genital organization: An interpolation into the theory of sexuality.* Standard edition (Vol. 19, pp. 141–149). London: Hogarth Press, 1961. (Originally published, 1923.) (b)

Freud, S. *The dissolution of the Oedipus complex.* Standard edition (Vol. 19, pp. 173–183). London: Hogarth Press, 1961. (Originally published, 1924.)

Freud, S. *An autobiographical study.* Standard edition (Vol. 20). London: Hogarth Press, 1959. (Originally published, 1925.)

Freud, S. *Inhibitions, symptoms and anxiety.* Standard edition (Vol. 20, pp. 75–173). London: Hogarth Press, 1959. (Originally published, 1926.) (a)

Freud, S. *The question of lay analysis.* Standard edition (Vol. 20). London: Hogarth Press, 1959. (Originally published, 1926.) (b)

Freud, S. *The future of an illusion.* Standard edition (Vol. 21). London: Hogarth Press, 1961. (Originally published, 1927.) (b)

Freud, S. *Dostoevsky and parricide.* Standard edition (Vol. 21, pp. 173–195). London: Hogarth Press, 1961. (Originally published, 1928.)

Freud, S. *Civilization and its discontents.* Standard edition (Vol. 21). London: Hogarth Press, 1961. (Originally published, 1930.)

Freud, S. *Analysis, terminable and interminable.* Standard edition (Vol. 23, pp. 209–255). London: Hogarth Press, 1964. (Originally published, 1937.)

Freud, S. *Moses and monotheism.* Standard edition (Vol. 23). London: Hogarth Press, 1964. (Originally published, 1939.)

Freud, S. *The origins of psychoanalysis* (M. Bonaparte, A. Freud, & E. Kris, Eds.). New York: Basic Books, 1964.

Freud, S. Some early unpublished letters of Sigmund Freud. *International Journal of Psycho-Analysis,* 1969, *50,* 419–426.

Fromm, E. *The sane society.* New York: Holt, Rinehart & Winston, 1955.

Giovacchini, P. L. Transference, incorporation and synthesis. *International Journal of Psycho-Analysis,* 1965, *46,* 287–296.

Giovacchini, P. L. Methodological aspects of psychoanalytic critique. *Bulletin of the Philadelphia Association for Psychoanalysis,* 1967, *17,* 10–26.

Giovacchini, P. L. *Tactics and techniques in psychoanalytic treatment, I.* New York: Science House, 1972.

Giovacchini, P. L. Character development and the adolescent process. In S. Feinstein and P. Giovacchini (Eds.), *Adolescent Psychiatry* (Vol. 2, pp. 402–415). New York: Basic Books, 1973.

Giovacchini, P. L. *Psychoanalysis of character disorders.* New York: Jason Aronson Press, 1975.

Giovacchini, P. L. *Psychoanalysis of primitive mental states.* New York: Jason Aronson Press, 1977.

Hartmann, H. *Essays on ego psychology.* New York: International Universities Press, 1964.

Herodotus. *The history of Herodotus.* In *Great Books of the Western World.* Chicago: Encyclopaedia Britannica, Inc., 1952.

Horney, K. *The neurotic personality of our time.* New York: Norton, 1937.

Jones, E. *The life and works of Sigmund Freud, I.* New York: Basic Books, 1953.

Klein, M. *Contributions to psycho-analysis, 1921–1945.* London: Hogarth Press, 1948.

Lindon, J. (Ed.). Panel on regression. *Psychoanalytic Forum,* 1967, *12,* 295–317.

Nagel, E. Methodological issues in psychoanalytic treatment. In S. Hooke (Ed.), *Psychoanalysis, Scientific Method and Philosophy* (pp. 38–57). New York: New York University Press, 1959.

Nietzsche, F. *The philosophy of Nietzsche* (W. Wright, Ed.) New York: Random House, 1937.

Rapaport, D. The structure of psychoanalytic theory. *Psychological Issues,* 5 (2 and 3), 1966.

Schur, M. *Freud, living and dying.* New York: International Universities Press, 1972.

Searles, H. S. *Collected papers on schizophrenia and related subjects.* New York: International Universities Press, 1965.

Spinoza, B. *The chief works of Benedict de Spinoza.* New York: Dover Publishing Co., 1952.

Sullivan, H. *Conceptions of modern psychiatry.* New York: Norton, 1953. (Originally published, 1939.)

Waelder, R. *Basic theory of psychoanalysis.* New York: International Universities Press, 1960.

Winnicott, D. *Collected papers: Through pediatrics to psychoanalysis.* New York: Basic Books, 1958.

Zilboorg, G. & Henry, G. *A history of medical psychology.* New York: Norton, 1941.

Individual Psychology is the name Alfred Adler (1870–1937) gave to the personality theory he developed when, after a nine-year association with Sigmund Freud, from 1902 to 1911, he broke with him and established his own school of thought. Adler began lecturing in 1926 in the United States, where he made his home after 1934. He published some 300 books and articles, gave countless public lectures, founded a journal, and headed an organization to further his theory and its applications. Individual Psychology is thus one of the oldest among the modern schools of personality. After a period of relative neglect following Adler's death and World War II, Individual Psychology has since found increasing interest and support.

Unique among personality theories, Individual Psychology has inherent in it a philosophy of humanism, best seen through the essential concept of social interest, which states in effect that human well-being and progress are a function of cooperative behavior. Despite its name, Individual Psychology is a social psychology which considers the concept of an isolated human being to be a meaningless abstraction.

Adler's psychology is

1. *Holistic*, viewing the individual as an indivisible entity.
2. *Phenomenological*, seeing the person from his unique point of view.
3. *Teleological*, viewing man as pulled by the subjective future rather than pushed by the objective past, creatively striving for goals rather than reacting automatically to events.
4. *Field-theoretical*, considering a person's actions, thoughts, and feelings as transactions with his surrounding world.
5. *Socially oriented*, viewing the individual as not only reacting to society, but also as being a contributing active participant.
6. *Operational* in methodology.

Adlerian psychology stresses consciousness and cognition, responsibility, meanings, and values. It is optimistic in that it considers man as creator and essentially captain of his soul and believes he can overcome obstacles. Both behavior and emotions subserve the individual's purpose, of which he may, however, be quite unaware. Behavior follows from cognitive constructs in a logical manner, characterized in the normal individual by reasonableness and in the mentally disturbed, by "private intelligence" or "private logic."

Adler's psychology presents itself as a complete and full method of understanding people, and it is used in counseling, psychotherapy, education, and other aspects of human behavior. The Adlerian movement is numerically not particularly impressive, although since 1952, when the American Society of Adlerian Psychology was founded, it has enjoyed a steady growth. Yet, Adlerian theory, developed as an alternative to Freud's theories, stands today validated and can be considered a prototype of most present-day theories of personality and psychotherapy.

Individual Psychology

Heinz L. Ansbacher

ALFRED ADLER

Introduction

When Alfred Adler presented his system of personality and psychopathology he named it Individual Psychology. The name presented difficulties from the start because it is easily mistaken for individualistic psychology, whereas it means nearly the opposite.

Meaning of the Name

Adler chose the term *individual* in its Latin meaning of indivisible, for he regarded the person as an indivisible organic unit, in contrast to the view that a person can be meaningfully analyzed into parts. Furthermore, Adler (1912) described the individual as "a unified community in which all parts cooperate for a common purpose" (p. iv, translation modified from the original), suggesting that Individual Psychology is a socially oriented teleological psychology.

This description is a quotation from Rudolf Virchow (1862), the great 19th-century German physician and founder of German social medicine. It is from an essay, "Atoms and Individuals," in which Virchow contrasts the inorganic with the organic world and shows, in opposition to the dominant physicalism of his time, that living phenomena cannot appropriately be reduced to physicochemical principles. It turns out that indivisibility is not the most important meaning of *individual*, since this is shared with the term *atom*. The more important meaning is that which differentiates the individual from the atom, namely that the individual is a unified biological *community*, *cooperating* for a *common purpose*. If these characteristics are intrinsic to the biological unit, then it should be "natural" for man, the highest form of biology, to realize his biological properties in his social living.

The term *individual*, so understood—as the polar opposite not of *society* but of *atom*—embodies the entire conception of an organismic, humanistic, and teleological approach, in contrast to a mechanistic, reductionistic, and causalistic approach. In this light the name Individual Psychology would appear to have been a most thoughtful choice by Adler to express the complete antithesis from the scientific standpoint of Freud's psychoanalysis.

Purpose of the Theory

Adler realized, without stating it in so many words, that a theory is not a replication of reality but a human construction, a tool, to be used for a purpose. The purposes of a personality theory may be to conceptualize the development of man in general, to construct a number of postulates to stimulate research in the field of personality, to demonstrate how man's behavior is controlled by internal and external forces as other events in the natural sciences are, and so on.

Adler's primary concern was to construct a theory useful not only to the helping professions but to the largest possible number of people in their process of living. Adler (1927a) wrote: "Only the understanding of human nature by every human being can be the proper goal for the science of human nature" (p. 15). "The understanding of human nature seems to us indispensable to every man" (p. 224). Adler believed he had come close to this goal when he wrote: "There may be more venerable theories of an older academic science. There may be newer, more sophisticated theories. But there is certainly no theory which could bring greater gain to all people" (1964, p. 364 n).

Following this general program, Adler introduced only a minumum of technical terms and constructed his theory in adaptation to what one finds and must deal with in everyday living, while taking into account all the established facts. His criteria were applicability and usefulness.

Philosophy of Science

Accordingly, in matters of the philosophy of science—concerned with the scientific ground rules, so to speak, where basic issues are still being debated—Adler consistently selected the alternative which would facilitate the improvement of man and which expressed confidence in man—the more optimistic alternative. On the issue of *determinism versus free will* Adler took the position that man has at least sufficient options to make all the difference in the world. As to the *ethical nature of man*, Adler held that man by nature is neither good nor evil but has the potentiality for either. On the *mind-body issue*, he emphasized the ultimate importance of the mind; on the *past-present issue*, the importance of the present, including in the present the conception of the future; and on the *nature-nurture issue*, the importance of nurture, plus, however, man's own creativity, Adler's concept for man's relative indeterminism.

From his aim that his theory should be practically applicable to life situations, and from his view that life in its sociocultural aspects is continuously evolving, it follows that Adler (1930) was satisfied if his theory was applicable to present conditions. "Individual Psychology claims not more for itself than to be taken as a theory which does justice to the present conditions of civilization, and to our present knowledge of man and his psychological condition, and which does so better than other theories" (p. 47).

History

Precursors

Adler's personality theory is essentially a conceptualization of the nature of man. Of course, man has, throughout the ages, been concerned in philosophy and in literature with constructing the most useful and satisfactory concept of himself to serve as a guiding principle for his conduct. Since Adler's orientation was humanistic rather than mechanistic and physicalistic, he could freely acknowledge his indebtedness to some of these earlier developments. In a general sense he acknowledged his indebtedness to the Bible, the Stoics, and great authors such as Shakespeare, Goethe, and Dostoevsky. In particular, he recognized the following:

Marx. As a young student Adler became interested in socialism and Karl Marx—not the economic and political but the psychological and philosophical aspects. This is reflected in Adler's emphasis on the social nature of man, his creativity, and his ability to influence his circumstances while at the same time being influenced by them. Adler's main dynamics, striving to overcome felt inferiorities, is related to Marx, as is Adler's conviction of the necessity for attaining equal rights for women.

Nietzsche. Adler's inferiority-superiority dynamics in particular was most likely inspired by the dialectics of Nietzsche. Adler (1913) consi-

dered him "one of the soaring pillars of our art" (p. 123). "Among all great philosophers ...Nietzsche is closest to our way of thinking" (Nunberg & Federn, 1962, p. 358). The great difference—one that makes, practically speaking, all the difference in the world—is that Nietzsche's ideal was Superman, whereas Adler's ideal was Fellowman.

Vaihinger. The idea of thought constructs as tools for coping with the problems of life Adler found confirmed in the work of the German pragmatic philosopher Hans Vaihinger. Adler (1912) wrote: "A fortunate circumstance made me acquainted with Vaihinger's ingenious *Philosophy of 'As If'*, a work in which I found the trains of thought suggested to me by the neurosis set forth as valid for general scientific thought" (p. 30).

Bergson. The particular idea of memory as purposeful Adler found in the works of the French pragmatist Henri Bergson. Adler (1912) noted in connection with "apperceiving memory" (p. 55), "I have to call attention here to Bergson's fundamental teachings" (p. 56 n). In writing about the goal orientation of the "stream of life," Adler (1920a) added, "I consider it a special honor that in discussing these psychological phenomena I can cite the fundamental theories of Vaihinger and Bergson, in addition to my own findings and views" (p. 245).

Kant. Adler referred to Immanuel Kant for his own important conception that "reason is inseparably connected with social interest" (1956, p. 149). Furthermore, Adler's notion of "common sense" as a criterion of sanity, in contrast to "private intelligence" as one of insanity, can be traced to Kant (Ansbacher, 1965a).

Others. Still other influences on Adler were Ludwig Klages for the importance of nonverbal communication, and Pierre Janet for the concept of neurosis as based on a feeling of insufficiency. Adler also saw certain parallels between his own views and those of G. Stanley Hall, John Dewey, and William James. For some of his organismic concepts he referred to the early anthropological social psychologists Moritz Lazarus and Heymann Steinthal.

Beginnings

Adler was born in 1870 in Vienna, the son of a Jewish merchant. After receiving his M.D. degree from the university there in 1895, he became a practising physician. In 1902 he was invited by Freud, with three others to form the original circle which became the Vienna Psychoanalytic Society. He became president in 1910 but resigned from the society a year later. Freud claimed Adler as a disciple who had subsequently defected. Adler (1956) strongly denied this, conceding however, that he learned a great deal from Freud, although in a negative sense: "I profited by his mistakes" (p. 358).

Early Recognition in the United States. Adler's major work, *The Neurotic Constitution,* appeared in 1912, and his first volume of collected papers, *Heilen und Bilden,* edited with Carl Furtmüller, in 1914. Adler's subsequent acceptance in the United States by important individuals who were also friendly toward Freud was astoundingly rapid.

Among psychiatrists, William Alanson White and Smith Ely Jelliffe, at that time editors and publishers of the new *Psychoanalytic Review,* became interested in Adler. White wrote an introduction to *The Neurotic Constitution* which appeared in English translation in 1917, and Jelliffe supplied a translation of Adler's (1907) earlier monograph on organ inferiority which also appeared in 1917. That year also Adler's (1917) original essay on homosexuality was published in English, simultaneously with its German publication.

Among psychologists, G. Stanley Hall, who had invited Freud to the United States in 1909, took an immediate interest in Adler's books and studied them in seminars with his students. This led to an invitation to Adler to give a lecture series in the United States; however, it never took place, undoubtedly due to the outbreak of World War I in August 1914 (Ansbacher, 1971a).

After such early successes, how is the subsequent unquestionable gradual decline of Adler, which today in turn is being followed by a renaissance of interest, to be explained? Our hypothesis is that Adler's early acclaim rested on an inadequate understanding of his work, due to two factors:

1. Adler was then at the mere beginning of his development of his ideas, whereas the present-day renaissance rests largely on the later writings of Adler (1964) and the practical work of the followers he eventually acquired.

2. Adler's psychology was understandably, yet erroneously, taken as a supplement or corrective of psychoanalysis.

Within this framework, Freud's (1914) accusation that Adler's theory "is actually nothing else but psychoanalytic knowledge, which the author . . . has now labelled as his own by changing the terminology of it" (p. 342), eventually had its impact.

Events in Europe. After the separation from Freud, Adler (1912) introduced the name Individual Psychology and founded the Society for Individual Psychology, at first named Society for Free Psychoanalytic Research. In 1914 he founded the *Zeitschrift für Individualpsychologie.* During World War I Adler served in the Austrian Army as a neuropsychiatrist. Directly after the war he created a series of child guidance clinics in the Vienna public schools, with the consent of the authorities but on a completely voluntary basis. They were conceived as training seminars for teachers and other interested persons (parents, physicians, social workers, students) and were thus conducted generally before 30 to 50 such persons. By 1927 there were 22 such clinics in Vienna and 20 in the rest of Europe (Freudenberg, 1928). When the Vienna clinics were closed in 1934 by a new reactionary government, there were over 30 of them.

The year 1930 represented a peak, with the Fifth International Congress of Individual Psychology in Berlin. The congress was attended by over 2,000 participants and was reported at length in a leading psychiatric journal (Kankeleit, 1931). The honorary congress committee included Kurt Lewin and Bruno Klopfer. There were then also some 33 local Individual Psychology organizations, 15 in Germany, 16 in various European countries, and one each in Palestine and the United States.

Later Years. From 1926 on Adler spent increasing portions of the fall and winter in the United States, primarily lecturing but also conducting clinics and a private practice. Among the numerous institutions he lectured at were Columbia University, the New School for Social Research, Harvard University, Wayne University, and the City College of New York. Two years after Adler was appointed visiting professor of medical psychology at Long Island College of Medicine in 1932, he and his wife Raissa took up residence in New York, and in 1935 the *International Journal of Individual Psychology* was founded, with Sydney Roth as publisher. Adler died on a lecture tour in Aberdeen, Scotland, on May 28, 1937, leaving his wife, a son, and two daughters, a third daughter having died before him. His daughter Alexandra and son Kurt are practicing Adlerian psychiatrists in New York City.

There are essentially five biographies of Adler available in English. These are by Hertha Orgler (1963), psychotherapist and enthusiastic early follower of Adler; Phyllis Bottome (1957), novelist and good friend; Carl Furtmüller (1964), earliest co-worker and friend; Henri F. Ellenberger (1970), psychiatrist and historian, who gives the most scholarly account; and Manes Sperber (1974), novelist and early protégé of Adler, who appraises him quite critically.

Early Disciples. As a founder of societies, periodicals, and guidance centers, and a believer in carrying psychology to the people, Adler had a large number of significant early disciples. We can name only some of these here; for their writings, consult the bibliography of Mosak and Mosak (1975).

Rudolf Dreikurs continued (in Chicago) Adler's method of counseling before a group, systematized the technology of Adlerian counseling and psychotherapy, and succeeded in creating a new generation of Adlerian practitioners. Alexandra Adler and Danica Deutsch founded the first mental hygiene clinic and training institute in New York. Lydia Sicher introduced Adlerian methods at the West Coast. Sofie Lazarsfeld originated Adlerian sexual and marital counseling and wrote several books on the subject. Carl Furtmüller was Adler's original collaborator, even from before the time when they both participated in the Freudian circle. Oskar Spiel and Ferdinand Birnbaum were instrumental in establishing an Adlerian experimental school in Vienna. Erwin Wexberg wrote an early textbook and did some important editing. Herbert Schaffer and Eric Weissmann became the deans of Adlerian psychology in France and England, respectively.

Adler was quite determined that Individual Psychology should not be identified with any religion or political party. On these grounds he separated from Fritz Künkel, Rudolf Allers, and Viktor Frankl on the one side, and Otto Rühle, Alice Rühle-Gerstel, and Manes Sperber, on the other. A third category continued functioning in Germany under National Socialism; outstanding among these are Leonhard Seif, founder of the Munich group, who trained a large number of Adlerian psychologists, and Johannes Neumann.

Current Status

To consider the current status of Adlerian psychology, one must distinguish between the Adlerian movement, the validation of Adler's theories, and the recognition of Adler by the profession and the world at large.

The Adlerian Movement. The Adlerian movement today numbers several thousand members in the United States, Canada, and European countries, especially Germany. It is composed of psychiatrists, psychologists, social workers, counselors, and educators, as well as lay people who accept the theory and apply the method of Adlerian psychology to family life and personal development. The lay movement received its strongest boost through the work of Dreikurs (1957, 1964).

Organizationally, the movement consists of numerous local societies and many study groups. In the United States the central organization is the American Society of Adlerian Psychology, which holds annual meetings and publishes as its main organ the *Journal of Individual Psychology*, devoted primarily to theoretical and research papers. There are Adlerian training institutes in New York, Chicago, Minneapolis, and other cities. Numerous courses and summer institutes at various colleges and universities are also given. Internationally, there is the International Association of Individual Psychology, founded in Adler's day, which meets every three years. One independent summer institute which has been meeting for several years in Europe and Israel has drawn hundreds of participants from many countries. The movement has in recent years enjoyed a steady growth.

Validation of Adler's Theories. The importance and soundness of Adler's theories have been established beyond a doubt by those, Adlerian and non-Adlerian alike, who know him and who care to express themselves. This will be dealt with at some length in the validation section below.

Recognition of Adler. The recognition of Adler is small in proportion to the validation of his theories. Although in books dealing specifically with personality theories he usually receives adequate consideration, in books on personality in general and other relevant topics he may not be mentioned. Yet his concepts are being used widely, although in most cases without proper attribution. To mention only a few, concepts introduced by Adler include: inferiority feelings, striving for self-esteem, goal orientation, dependency, overprotection, avoidance of responsibility, life style, achievement striving.

This discrepancy between the acceptance and wide use of Adlerian concepts and the prevailing relative lack of recognition of Adler is a paradox which will be dealt with in the last section of this chapter, Prospect.

Similar Theories

Adler's system was originally mistaken for a derivative of and a deviation from Freudian psychoanalysis. Despite continued efforts to correct this error, it is still quite prevalent. The explanation is that Adler participated for nine years as a "charter member" in the Freudian circle and with Freud was interested in similar problems. But he differed fundamentally in purpose and philosophy of science. Freud wanted to be a natural scientist in the positivistic sense, hoping to discover what really is and using what Rychlak (1968) has called the "demonstrative approach" (p. 456). Accordingly, Freud was a physiological reductionist who adhered to a strictly analytical, elementaristic, physicalistic concept of man (Holt, 1965; Lowry, 1967).

Adler, on the other hand, wanted to be a helper of mankind. As a practicing physician he was a pragmatist and an artist who adhered to a holistic, organismic, humanistic concept of man. He saw psychology as a social science built on an organismic foundation. We shall briefly discuss here various personality theories which share this outlook, confining ourselves to personalism, Gestalt psychology, psychological existentialism, and others included under humanistic or third-force psychology in general.

Personalism. Adler was most in sympathy with the personalism of William Stern, which Stern (1938) defined as "the science of the person having experience." Experience is to be identified and interpreted "in terms of . . . the unitary, goal-directed person" (p. vii). Adler felt indebted to Stern "for his great contribution of a philosophical foundation for finalism" (1956, p. 10).

Among more recent psychologists, Gordon W. Allport was closely related to Stern, and consequently to Adler. Comparing Adler and Allport, Long (1952–1953) summarized: "Both can be called holistic and organismic, . . . [both] opposed the pansexuality theory and denied the pleasure principle. . . . Both could be roughly classified as purposivists . . . and had little use for typologies . . . Both manifest hope and optimism in their description of man" (p. 43).

Gestalt Psychology. From his emphasis on the holistic approach follows the close affinity of Adler to the Gestalt psychology of Max Wertheimer, Wolfgang Köhler, and Kurt Koffka. Bruno Klopfer (1925) wrote that Individual Psychology was "the most vigorous and consistent application of the Gestalt theory." The two systems complement each other quite naturally, Gestalt being concerned with mental processes per se (primarily perception), and Adler with the individual. When Gestalt theory reached over into the field of personality, the conclusions were often amazingly "Adlerian," as in Wertheimer's (1959) *Productive Thinking.* We find there observations supplementing and strengthening Adler's concept of social interest: e.g., "When self-centering is extreme, it becomes a well-known symptom . . . Self-centering is not . . . the natural attitude, as some influential views of our time would have us believe" (p. 183).

The outstanding current exponent of Gestalt psychology, Wolfgang Metzger, is also the outstanding academic representative of Individual Psychology in Germany and the editor of a new edition of all of Adler's books in paperback.

Existential Psychology. As we have stated, Adler drew on Vaihinger and Nietzsche. Since Vaihinger recognized similarities of his own with Nietzsche, and Nietzsche is often considered a fountainhead of existentialism, it is not surprising that several authors, such as Ford and Urban (1963) and Maddi (1968), have placed Adler in a category with existential psychology. Harold Kelman (1962) stated: "Of existentialism there is least in Freud, somewhat more in Jung and Rank, and the most in Adler and Ferenczi"

(p. 120). Quite similar to Adler is Paul Sartre (A. Stern, 1967). Similarities to Albert Camus and to Ludwig Binswanger and Medard Boss have been pointed out by Rom (1960) and Van Dusen (1959), and to Viktor Frankl and Rollo May by Birnbaum (1961) and R. R. Ansbacher (1970).

Existential psychology shares with Adler the basic assumptions that man lives in interaction with his world, that he is goal- and future-oriented, that his problems arise from his freedom to choose his goals and projects, and that he is concerned with the meaning of his life.

Humanistic Psychology. To cover other trends similar to that set by Adler, it seems convenient to regard those that Maslow (1968) included in his "third force" or "humanistic psychology" grouping. They all were opposed to "the two comprehensive theories of human nature most influencing psychology until recently ... the Freudian and the experimental-positivistic-behavioristic" or as Maslow reworded it later "to objectivistic, behavioristic (mechanomorphic) psychology and to orthodox Freudianism" (p. iii).

Among those Maslow included in the third force were first "the Adlerians" and then representatives of the three orientations discussed above: personalism, the original Gestalt school, and existentialism. Additionally Maslow listed the neo-Freudians, including Franz Alexander, Erich Fromm, Karen Horney, H. S. Sullivan, and Clara Thompson; the post-Freudians; and such psychiatrists as Judd Marmor and Thomas Szasz. Among psychologists he listed the phenomenologists and the Rogerians, as well as George A. Kelly.

These groups are united by six basic premises of humanistic psychology derived by Ansbacher (1971b) from a paper by Matson (1969). They are the assumptions of:

1. Man's creative power as a crucial force, in addition to heredity and environment.
2. An anthropomorphic instead of a mechanomorphic model of man.
3. Purpose, rather than cause, as the decisive dynamic.
4. The holistic approach as more adequate than the elementaristic one.
5. The necessity of taking man's subjectivity, his opinions and viewpoints, conscious and unconscious, fully into account.
6. Psychotherapy as essentially based on a good human relationship.

Other Systematic Similarities. Further systematic similarities are indicated by the way in which Adler has been classified by various authors. Hall and Lindzey (1957) named Adler "the ancestral figure of the 'new social psychological look' " (p. 115) which is shared with Horney, Fromm, and Sullivan. Sundberg and Tyler (1962) described Adler as probably the first among the cognitive change theorists of psychotherapy, among whom they include Albert Ellis, Adolf Meyer, Frederick Thorne, George Kelly, E. L. Phillips, Rollo May, Viktor Frankl, and O. H. Mowrer. To Ford and Urban (1963) Adler, together with Rank, Rogers and the existentialists, represented a "pilot" view of man in contrast to a "robot" view (pp. 595–598). Maddi (1968) places Adler under "fulfillment model of personality: perfection version," together with Robert W. White, G. W. Allport, Fromm, and existential psychologists.

Assertions

Due to the holistic and purposive-dynamic nature of the theory of Individual Psychology, its assertions do not readily lend themselves to a distinction between processes of development (becoming) and processes of maintenance (being). However, to abide by the requirements of this book, the distinction is made (although with some reluctance) as follows: Of the 17 assertions, the first 5 are placed under the development heading and the remainder under maintenance. The last assertion is actually developmental in nature, however.

Development

1. MAN, LIKE ALL FORMS OF LIFE, IS A UNIFIED ORGANISM.

This is the most fundamental assertion of Adler. As a unified organism man differs basically from a mechanism. A mechanism consists of a number of separate parts assembled. An organism starts from one fertilized ovum, and all the parts grow and develop from the original cell.

The individual is not divided against himself. He is not the battleground of conflicting forces. What sometimes appears as inner conflicts are really alternatives of choice presented by a given situation derived from man's self-determination. This includes the freedom to make mistakes. Says Adler (1929b): "Rightly understood, the whole of this mental process ... is not ambivalence but a dynamic unity. Only if it is not understood as a whole do we see it as two contradictory and warring entities" (p. 87).

Another important consequence of this understanding is that the opposition between conscious and unconscious is done away with. "The conscious and the unconscious [are] not separate and conflicting entities, but complementary and cooperating parts of one and the same reality" (Adler, 1929b, p. 29).

This unity is to be understood also longitudinally, over time. Adler (1912) stated, "We must regard each single life manifestation as if traces of the past, the present and the future, together with the superordinated guiding idea, were present in it at the same time" (p. iv, translation modified).

To regard the individual as a unity has the practical advantage that this corresponds to the way in which one encounters another person in actual life, in friendship, in an employment situation, or in psychotherapy. No matter under what circumstances, all we have before us and all we can deal with is one individual and what he tells us or what we can see that he does. Even when he talks about his past, his present, or his future—it all comes from the present individual and is channeled through and directed from his highest nervous centers. It is all channeled through the individual and expresses his totality, his life style.

2. ALL LIFE IS MOVEMENT, DIRECTED TOWARD GROWTH AND EXPANSION.

While a mechanism is inert and needs a driving force to set it in motion, the living organism is always in motion: heart beat, blood circulation, breathing, brain waves (EEG). The entire metabolism consists of movements which go on without interruption from birth to death. The main dynamic problem thus is understanding not various drives or motives, but the direction and form of the ongoing movement, a view which

was also advanced by George Kelly (1955, pp. 34–39). To quote from Adler:

> The most important characteristic of life is motion. ... The chief characteristic of a movement is ... direction and, therefore in a psychic movement, a goal. ... Striving towards a goal. ... we find everywhere in life. Everything grows "as if" it were striving to overcome all imperfections and achieve perfection. This urge toward perfection we call the goal of overcoming, that is, the striving to overcome. (1964, pp. 85–86)

3. MAN IS ENDOWED WITH CREATIVITY AND THUS IS SELF-DETERMINED, WITHIN LIMITS.

Adler sees the human being as active and as initiator of actions, not as a passive S-R mechanism. Man actively interprets and uses presented stimulus material for his own purposes. In this sense everybody is creative. The criterion is the capacity to formulate, consciously or most often unconsciously, a goal of success for one's endeavors and to develop planful procedures for attaining the goal. Only in the truly feeble-minded is such purposeful creative power absent (Adler, 1964, pp. 46–47).

The presupposition is that man is not completely determined by heredity and environment, but that, once he has come into existence, he develops the capacity of influencing and creating events, as witnessed by the cultural products all around us, beginning with language, which are all human creations.

> The important thing is not what one is born with, but what use one makes of the equipment. ... As to the influence of the environment, who would claim that the same influences are ... responded to by any two individuals in the same way? Thus we find it necessary to assume the existence of still another force: the creative power of the individual. (Adler, 1964, pp. 86–87)

The individual's uniqueness ultimately rests in this creative power. Objective biological and social conditions, past and present, provide probabilities, opportunities, and limitations. But they are not directly causal factors in the individual. These are the individual's self-determined goals and purposes.

4. HUMAN MOVEMENT IS GUIDED BY
SUBJECTIVE GOALS POINTING TO THE
FUTURE.

Adler's basic disagreement with Freud was over
his mechanistic and zoomorphic approach to human dynamics. Adler found that many psychologists, like Freud, "present their dogmas disguised in mechanistic or physical similes.... a
pump handle ... a magnet ... a sadly harassed
animal struggling for the satisfaction of its elementary needs" (1956, p. 92). But human dynamics can be adequately presented and approached only if we make central the fact that
man is guided in his actions by his future as he
anticipates it and as he wants to effect it. Thus
Adler's dynamics became one of final causes
rather than efficient causes. Adler expressed his
position most forcefully in the following:

> The most important question of the healthy and
> the diseased mental life is not whence? but, whither?
> Only when we know the effective, direction-giving
> goal of a person may we try to understand his
> movements... In this whither? the cause is con-
> tained. (1956, p. 91).
> Individual Psychology insists on the indispensabil-
> ity of finalism for the understanding of all psychol-
> ogical phenomena. Causes, powers, instincts, impul-
> ses, and the like cannot serve as explanatory princi-
> ples. The final goal alone can. Experiences, trauma-
> ta, sexual development mechanisms cannot yield an
> explanation, but the perspective in which these are
> regarded ... which subordinates all life to the final
> goal, can do so. (1956, p. 92)

5. HUMAN DYNAMICS INVOLVE A GOAL AND A
STARTING POINT—A DIALECTICAL
CONCEPTION.

Adler's original dynamic conception was: (1) Inferiority feelings, (2) Goal of superiority, (3)
Compensatory movement.—a bipolar, dialectical
conception, with compensation being an effort to
resolve the antithesis. When Adler (Adler &
Furtmüller, 1914) soon afterward introduced the
concept of "masculine protest," he specified
these three factors as follows: "(a) traits evaluated as feminine, (b) wanting to be a real man,
(c) compromise formation between *a* and *b*"
(p. 90).

Adler gave up the concept of drive in favor of
"masculine protest" and striving, because he did
not want to express himself in terms of a
mechanistic natural science, but rather in social
science terms. *Drive* is a mechanistic concept:
machines are driven, have drives (overdrives,
drive shafts, etc.). But *protest*, as well as *striving*, are human concepts; machines neither protest nor strive.

Typical for a mechanistic concept, a drive is
unipolar, that is, it is simply an applied force
and nothing else. It is a *demonstrative*, positivistic conception. On the other hand, a protest is a
solemn declaration of opinion, usually of dissent
or objection, although it may also be an assertion. It is a *bipolar, dialectical* conception
regarding which Rychlak (1968) states: "Dialectical terminology presents us with the *most accurate* picture of the fundamental human condition" (p. 255). Instead of "human condition," we
would say "how man operates." While Adler
soon gave up the broad usage of the terms *feminine, masculine,* and *masculine protest,* he retained the dialectical structure and meaning.

This dynamic is expressed by Adler particularly well in the following, where it is also tied in
with the concept of the past and the future.

> The future is tied up with our striving and with
> our goal, while the past represents the state of inferi-
> ority or inadequacy which we are trying to overcome.
> This is why ... we should not be astonished if in the
> cases where we see an inferiority complex we find a
> superiority complex more or less hidden. On the
> other hand, if we inquire into a superiority
> complex.... we can always find a more or less hid-
> den inferiority complex.... If we look at things this
> way, it takes away the apparent paradox of two con-
> tradictory tendencies... existing in the same
> individual.... The striving for superiority and the
> feeling of inferiority are naturally complementary.
> We should not strive to be superior and to succeed if
> we did not feel a certain lack in our present
> condition.... The striving for superiority never
> ceases. It constitutes in fact the mind, the psyche of
> the individual. (1929c, pp. 27-28)

The naming of the two poles—inferiority feeling and superiority—is, however, meant to convey a more general concept. Adler (1912) illustrated this in the diagram shown in Figure 3-1,
which he described as "a preliminary, certainly
incomplete schema which corresponds more to
the psyche of the neurotic which is given more to
abstractions, than to the structure of the sound
psyche" (p. 73, translation modified).

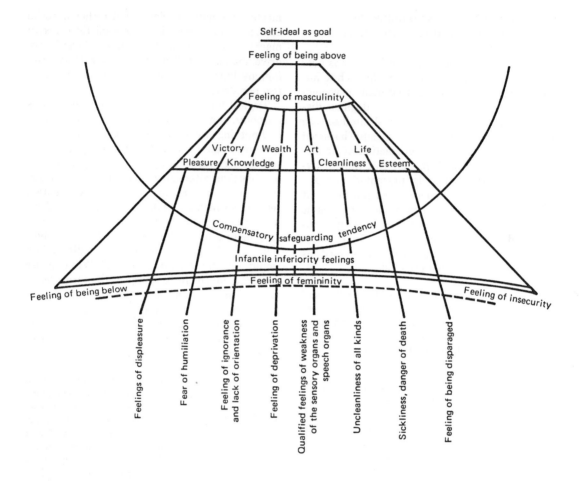

FIGURE 3-1: The Inferiority-Superiority Dynamics

It is instructive to tabulate the pairs of opposites given in this diagram, to render a more complete picture of what Adler understood by his bipolar dynamics. Table 3–1 is arranged in the order in which the terms appear in Figure 3–1, starting at the bottom and going from left to right.

Over the years Adler found still other names to describe the general aspired goal of people, such as striving to be a real man, striving for power, or striving for a goal of superiority, success, perfection, or completion—all as subjectively understood. Superiority was the most frequently used description. "It runs parallel to

TABLE 3-1: Adler's Dynamic Pairs of Opposites

Starting point *Feelings of:*	Goal point *Feelings of:*
Displeasure	Pleasure
Humiliation	Victory
Ignorance	Knowledge
Deprivation	Wealth
Weakness of sensory organs and of speech	Art
Uncleanliness	Cleanliness
Sickliness, mortal danger	Life
Disparagement	Esteem
Being below	Being above
Femininity (stereotype)	Masculinity
Insecurity	Safeguards
Infantile inferiority	Self-ideal

physical growth and is an intrinsic necessity of life itself.... All our functions follow its direction. They strive for conquest, security, increase, either in the right or in the wrong direction" (Adler, 1956, p. 103).

Since the striving is so often in the wrong direction, that is, without social interest (see below), the terms *power* or *superiority* have generally acquired the meaning of power or superiority over others, and the neutral meanings of these terms, such as mastery, competence, and superiority over difficulties in general, have been mostly forgotten. This being the case, we prefer Adler's neutral designation of the two poles as simply – and +, as in,

> The impetus from minus to plus never ends.... The history of the human race points in the same direction.... All [functions] betoken the essence of this eternal melody.... Even if anyone wanted to escape... he would still find himself in the general system, striving upward from below. This not only states a fundamental category of thought, a thought construct, but what is more, it represents the fundamental fact of our life. (Adler, 1956, p. 103)

The table of opposites (Table 3–1) indicates some of the particular concrete contents which the minus-to-plus dynamics may take on.

Maintenance

6. MAN LIVES INEXTRICABLY IN A SOCIAL WORLD.

In a holistic theory such as Adler's, man is seen not only as a whole but also as a part of larger wholes. A unified organism, he is also part of social organizations—his family, community, humanity—in the larger context in which he lives. In other words, man as a system is also part of larger systems.

Adler opposed Freud's argument that society is based on individual repression with the question: Which came first, the individual or society? After all, society is formed by individuals, and the individual is unthinkable without cooperation among individuals. The concrete reality is the existence of individuals, while society is an abstraction. The culture into which we are born is the precipitate of the creativity, the contribution, the work of countless thousands of individuals just like ourselves, over thousands of years,

all striving from a minus to a plus situation, thus enabling human progress.

The outstanding example of the unity of the individual and the social world is language. On this point Adler (1956) says: "Language . . . a miracle which distinguishes man from all other creatures . . . reckons with the social life of man, is its product and, at the same time, its cement." (p. 130). Only by the acquisition of language through social interaction does the growing infant become a person. The self or the lifestyle develop as the individual acquires the ability to communicate and to form concepts with the aid of language.

7. MAN'S IMPORTANT LIFE PROBLEMS — BEHAVIOR TOWARD OTHERS, OCCUPATION, LOVE—ARE SOCIAL PROBLEMS.

The important problems of human beings are not drive satisfaction. Drives do not exist to any degree of purity in human beings. They become soon merged with cultural conceptions and regulations, and the individual's own ideas as to how a specific need should be met to satisfy his striving for success. Take, for example, hunger. There is an infinite variety of ways, quantitatively and qualitatively, in which various cultures and individuals have met this need. These arbitrary ways of satisfying hunger become so compelling that they appear to the individual as the only natural and correct way. The satisfaction of hunger becomes socially and individually determined.

The sexual problem is not so important from the viewpoint of the satisfaction of a physiological need which, after all, can be met by masturbation. It becomes a great problem precisely because it is additionally and most importantly a social problem: the situation of two people of different sexes intimately living and working together demands greater cooperation than almost any other situation. The successful solution of this problem is not only of concern for the two individuals involved directly, but through the procreative function it becomes of general social concern. The sexual problem is posited by nature through the phenomenon of sexual dimorphism, since the species is created in two sexes.

Occupation is set as a problem by the fact that we have to gain our livelihood on this earth, and it has become an immensely social problem through the phenomenon of the division of labor.

Adler (1956) describes the general social problem as a continuous necessity "to reckon with others, to adopt ourselves to others, and to interest ourselves in them" (p. 132). Finally, these three problems are interrelated. "None . . . can be solved separately. Each demands a successful approach to the other two" (p. 131).

8.   MAN HAS AN INNATE APTITUDE FOR SOCIAL INTEREST WHICH MUST BE CONSCIOUSLY DEVELOPED.

Every system of psychology must deal with the fact that the individual lives in society, is socialized, as well as the problem of human nature in relation to society. Asch (1952, pp. 324–349) has shown that there are essentially three views possible about this relationship.

The first view is that man is, by his original nature, entirely selfish. These selfish tendencies are opposed by society, so that intrinsically a state of conflict exists between individual and society. A favorable resolution requires repression of the primary tendencies and their sublimation into secondary, socially acceptable tendencies. Asch calls this the " 'private profit' notion of social relations" (p. 326): The individual engages in social action to be better able to pursue his individual ends.

This is the original behavioristic and Freudian view. Miller and Dollard (1941) considered social interests a "facade behind which the functions of the underlying innate drives are hidden" (p. 14). Freud (1921) stated: "What appears . . . in the shape of *Gemeingeist, esprit de corps,* group spirit, etc., does not belie its derivation from what was originally envy. . . . Social justice means that we deny ourselves many things so that others may have to do without them as well" (pp. 87–88).

While from the start Adler did not accept Freud's *concept* of repression, he nevertheless at first expressed himself similarly as far as *structure* was concerned. Considering at that time that inferior organs have important dynamic attributes, Adler (1907) stated that the inferior organ "has to bow under *the yoke of civilization.* . . . In this process, organic instincts are changed, ennobled, psychically molded, and often transformed to their polar opposites—occurrences which are grouped by Freud as 'organic repression' " (p. 57). This position was, of course, completely given up by Adler, although he never renounced it specifically.

The second possible view is that man harbors within himself both innate selfish and social drives whose dominance alternates, depending on the circumstances. Charles Darwin, William McDougall, and W. Trotter are the representatives of such a theory. Man would be in conflict with himself, a struggle between bad and good, the prototype of the dual personality. This view is today quite outdated.

Adler accepted this view briefly in a second stage of his development, writing then of a guiding fiction "of overcoming others" and of a counter-fiction which "forces considerations upon the guiding fiction, takes social and ethical demands of the future in account. . . . The harmony of these two fictions . . . is the sign of mental health" (1956, pp. 143–144). In the same vein he wrote somewhat later, "An overstimulated striving for power either finds its limits in the demands of society and in the admonitions of social interest, which is physiologically and socially founded, . . . or goes astray" (1956, p. 144). He also spoke of a "blending of social interest with the striving for personal superiority" (1956, pp. 144–145).

The third view, rejecting the first two, leaves man with a unitary dynamic force toward growth plus a positive interest in interacting with the surrounding world, a social interest. This view is shared with Adler by the Gestalt psychologist Solomon Asch. In Asch's (1952) version,

> Social tendencies are an expression of our most basic orientation to the world. . . . We seek the company of others for the same general reason that we seek for the company of things, because we strive to relate ourselves meaningfully to the surroundings. Social interest is an intrinsic part of our extending interest in the surroundings. (p. 334)

Whereas for Asch social interest is apparently wholly innate, in Adler's (1956) final formulation, "Social interest is not inborn, but is an innate potentiality which has to be consciously developed" (p. 134). By this formulation Adler accomplished several things:

1.   The assumption of an innate positive factor for social living is straightforward and logical, considering that all culture has been cre-

ated by people spontaneously interacting and cooperating with one another.

2. By conceiving of the social factor initially as a potentiality or aptitude, Adler took it out of the dynamic or conative realm and into the cognitive realm. This is required by an organismic, holistic theory which can recognize only one dynamic force, certainly no conflict among opposing forces.

3. By saying the social disposition must be trained, Adler could account for the observation that under unfavorable conditions it is most often underdeveloped.

Additionally, as we shall see below, social interest is characterized by its usefulness. Usefulness in turn is defined by Adler (1929b) as "in the interests of mankind generally" (p. 78). Thus, social interest actually means not merely an interest in others, but an *interest in the interests of others*. This distinction is important because the first could be merely for the sake of exploiting others, as a slave holder may be interested in his slaves or a confidence man in his prey. This is also how Ralph Barton Perry (1954) defined social interest; he wrote that it is an "interest of one person in the interest or interests of a second person" (p. 81), the crucial part being that we are not merely interested "in a second individual where [his] interests are disregarded" (p. 81). The second person can, of course, be extended into a group and the whole of society.

The original term for social interest, *Gemeinschaftsgefühl*, has offered difficulties to the translators. The following translations have been used: social feeling, community feeling, communal feeling, fellow feeling, sense of solidarity, social sense, communal intuition, community interest, and, finally, social interest. Some have thought the term cannot be translated.

But the difficulty is with the term itself—in any language. It has, in any language, two components: *interest*, referring to a psychological process and its development; and *social*, referring to objects in the outside world toward which the process is directed. The difficulty is that both components denote entire dimensions rather than single referents. Under the next two assertions—based on Ansbacher (1965b, 1968)—we aim to clarify these dimensions and thereby to clarify the meaning of the term.

9. THE SOCIAL INTEREST CONCEPT COMPRISES VARIOUS PSYCHOLOGICAL PROCESSES.

Adler refers to three different processes which can be arranged into three developmental steps in forming the social interest concept.

1. *Aptitude*. Social interest is an assumed aptitude for cooperation and social living which can be developed through training.

2. *Ability*. When this aptitude has been developed it will find expression in objective abilities or skills of cooperating and contributing, as well as in understanding others and empathizing with them.

3. *Secondary dynamic characteristics*. The developed social aptitude is likely to acquire secondary dynamic characteristics, as abilities generally may do in the form of attitudes and interests. In this form social interest would influence the direction of the basic striving, by becoming part of the goal of success, but be no more in conflict with it than any other interest.

In Table 3–2 the term *social interest* has been analyzed according to its implied developmental sequences and corresponding attributes assigned to them by Adler. These sequences could be shown to exist also for such skills as reading or skiing: Initially aptitudes, they can be developed into skills, and can acquire secondary motivational characteristics.

10. THE SOCIAL INTEREST CONCEPT COMPRISES A WIDE RANGE OF "OBJECTS."

Extension in Space. By "social" Adler refers developmentally to ever-widening circles of actual persons.

> After the mother has succeeded in connecting the child with herself, her next task is to spread his interest towards his father, ... the other children of the family, to friends, relatives. ... She must give the child his first experience of a trustworthy fellow being and then ... spread this trust and friendship until it includes the whole of our human society. (1956, p. 373)

But Adler extended the meaning of *Gemeinschaft*, the "social" in social interest, to a variety of other "objects," way beyond what one would expect. *Gemeinschaft* is not limited to the com-

TABLE 3-2. Analysis of Term *Social Interest* According to Implied Developmental Steps, and Corresponding Attributes

Developmental Steps	Corresponding Attributes*
1. Aptitude	Innate potentiality or substratum of social interest (p. 134), for cooperation (p. 135), for contact feeling (p. 295)
2. Ability	
a. Behaviorally	Ability to cooperate (p. 136), relating to others in a useful way (p. 139), contributing to common welfare (p. 155), behaving as part of mankind (p. 156), true compensation for all weaknesses (p. 154)
b. Intellectually	Understanding others (p. 137), empathy (p. 136), reason (p. 149), common sense vs. private intelligence (p. 149)
3. Secondary dynamic characteristics	
a. Attitudinally	Evaluative attitude toward life (p. 185), of harmony with the universe (p. 136), feeling at home on this earth (pp. 136 & 155), identification with others (p. 136), feeling of belongingness (p. 138)
b. Motivationally	Interest in others (p. 140), interest in community *sub specie aeternitatis* (p. 142), striving for an ideal community (p. 142), making spontaneous social effort (p. 134)†

*Attributes assigned to developmental steps in social interest by Adler (1956). Page numbers refer to this source.

†These last attributes sharply distinguish social interest from social conformity. They allow for the striving for general betterment which implies changing existing norms rather than conforming to them. Mere conformity "would be nothing other than an exploitation of the accomplishments of the striving of others" (Adler, 1956, p. 107).

munity of men but means general connectedness. Thus Adler stated that "Social interest may extend beyond these boundaries and express itself toward animals, plants, lifeless objects, or finally towards the whole cosmos" (1927a, p 46). "Social feeling is actually a cosmic feeling, a reflection of the coherence of everything cosmic, which lives in us, which we cannot dismiss entirely, and which gives us the ability to empathize with things which lie outside our body" (1927a, p. 60, new translation). Another time Adler simply equated social interest with "being in harmony with the universe" (1964, p. 43).

Extension in Time. With the concept of social interest serving as a guiding principle in making choices, the ultimate criterion is an ideal society of the future. By the *community* in "community feeling" Adler did not mean "a private circle of our time, or a larger circle which one should join."

> Social interest means . . . *feeling with the whole, sub specie aeternitatis,* under the aspect of eternity. It means a striving for a form of community . . . as it could be thought of if mankind had reached the goal

of perfection. It is never a present-day community or society, nor a political or religious form. Rather the goal . . . would have to be a goal which signifies the ideal community of all humanity, the ultimate fulfillment of evolution. (1964, pp. 34–35)

This consideration removes behavior imbued with social interest from mere conformity, or mere "adjustment" to a presently existing group and present standards. Such an adjustment would actually freeze the evolution, the progress, the becoming. It would limit the individual, whereas social interest liberates him from the inadequacies of the present society in his efforts for a better society of the future.

"An adaptation to immediate reality," on the contrary, "would be nothing other than an exploitation of the accomplishments of the striving of others, as the picture of the world of the pampered child demands" (Adler, 1956, p. 107). But the great cooperation and social culture which man needs demand "spontaneous social effort" (Adler, 1929b, p. 31).

Through extension into the future, the concept of social interest not only provides a place

58

for the independent spirit, the nonconformist who contributes to the advancement of mankind; it also makes him the ideally normal man. The criterion is whether the nonconformity is in the ultimate interest of mankind, or whether it is merely a rebellion for personal, private reasons.

11. SOCIAL INTEREST IS THE CRITERION OF MENTAL HEALTH.

For Adler the degree of social interest was "the main characteristic of each person" and "involved in all his actions" (1937, p. 774). Furthermore, all desirable traits were subordinated to social interest and nearly all undesirable traits to its lack. Adler said:

> It is almost impossible to exaggerate the value of an increase in social feeling. The mind improves, for intelligence is a communal function. The feeling of worth and value is heightened, giving courage and an optimistic view, and there is a sense of acquiescence in the common advantages and drawbacks of our lot. The individual feels at home in life and feels his existence to be worthwhile just so far as he is useful to others and is overcoming common, instead of private, feelings of inferiority. Not only the ethical nature, but the right attitude in aesthetics, the best understanding of the beautiful and the ugly, will always be founded upon the truest social feeling. (1956, p. 155)

Thus social interest becomes Adler's criterion for mental health. "Social interest is the barometer of the child's normality. The criterion which needs to be watched ... is the degree of social interest which the child or the individual manifests" (1956, p. 154).

The idea of social interest and its relationship to mental health, especially in advancing age, had been expressed by John Stuart Mill, with whom Adler had also other important ideas in common (see Ansbacher, 1968, p. 140 n.). But Adler was not aware of any of this. Mill (1863) wrote:

> When people who are tolerably fortunate in their outward lot do not find in life sufficient enjoyment to make it valuable to them, the cause generally is, caring for nobody but themselves. To those who have neither public nor private affections, the excitements of life are much curtailed, and in any case dwindle in value as the time approaches when all selfish interests must be terminated by death: while

those who leave after them objects of personal affection, and especially those who have also cultivated a *fellow-feeling with the collective interests of mankind*, retain as lively an interest in life on the eve of death as in the vigor of youth and health. (pp. 16–17; italics ours)

12. OPERATIONALLY, SOCIAL INTEREST IS STRIVING ON THE SOCIALLY USEFUL SIDE.

Adler (1927b) introduced the concept of social usefulness with the comment:

> A person ... who does not have a true social feeling ... stops, hesitates, fights, escapes, when he comes in a new situation such as kindergarten, school, marriage, friendship. All these are social situations and require social feeling. It is this type that become the criminals, problem children, neurotics and suicides. Striving for superiority [like everybody] and lacking in courage [defined as activity plus social feeling or social interest] they turn from the useful to the useless side. (p. 119)

This was illustrated by Adler with an informal diagram similar to Figure 3-2.

It is noteworthy that socially useless behavior is described in terms of making a choice in the face of a critical situation, a quite operational definition. In explanation of the choice, Adler asserted:

> There is only one reason for an individual to sidestep to the useless side: the fear of a defeat on the useful side.... Since all problems of life require a well-developed social interest and the patient is lacking this in his style of life, he is in a certain sense right to make a detour. (1956, pp. 157–159)

At the same time Adler published a much more sophisticated version of this diagram, stating that it comprised his entire system. "More than twenty years of work ... are reflected in it" (1956, p. 157). This diagram is shown in Figure 3-3, where the lines and loops represent movements of individuals; the circles, life problems. The small circles stand for children's preliminary problems—friendship, school, relationship to the other sex. The larger circles stand for the three life problems of adulthood—social relations, occupation, and love and marriage. The loops below the small circles stand for turning away from the respective problems and seeking

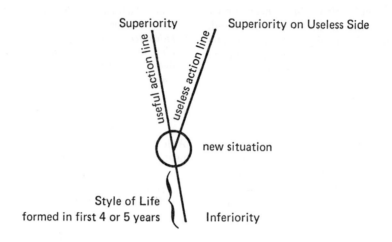

FIGURE 3-2: Deviating To The Useless Side In Face Of A New Situation

distance. This will occur when the individual, due to underdeveloped social interest, is unprepared for meeting the problem. From lack of courage he will detour and continue his striving on the socially useless side. The horizontal lines from left to right indicate the detouring at the adult level. The striving on the left side is for a commonly useful goal of perfection; that on the right side, for an exaggerated private goal of personal superiority. Such persons are the failures in life.

Artists were for Adler a special case of people who, while retreating from life problems, eventually become eminently useful for humanity through their work. Scholarly activity could probably also be included here.

But no one's choices are always on one side or the other. Hence, in a concrete case it is decisive where a person stands on balance: "The path of the neurotic, etc., and of the problem child runs on both sides of life, although in different degrees" (Adler 1929a, p. 123). This is equally true for the normal person.

13.   BY THEIR FRUITS YE SHALL KNOW THEM.
To serve as a criterion of mental health in a given case, social interest must be empirically validated. Adler's psychology is not only subjective or phenomenological; it is also pragmatic and empirical. When there is a discrepancy between word and deed, the latter counts. Adler held, with the Bible and William James: "By their fruits ye shall know them" (1964, p. 64). Accordingly, socially useful action, that is, action that others may recognize as being in the general interest, is more important than professed social interest. Adler (1926) expressed this very strongly in stating: "It is quite insignificant what a person thinks, feels, or wants by his performance. Only the accord of his action with the requirements of evolution can vindicate him. He creates for the community and for posterity, even if in so doing he considers only his own well-being" (pp. 363–364). Adler (1929c) expressed the same thought again in the following: "The normal man is an individual who lives in society and whose mode of life is so adapted that, *whether he wants it or not*, society derives a certain advantage from his work" (p. 41, italics added).

The neurotic, on the other hand, while he "expects a contribution from the group in which he lives" (Adler, 1956, p. 114), often has the most lofty social and ethical ideals and daydreams, which may be considered a means of gaining feelings of superiority over others. Adler warned: "We must not be confused by the fact that some neurotics seem to be benevolent and wish to reform the whole world" (1964, p. 60).

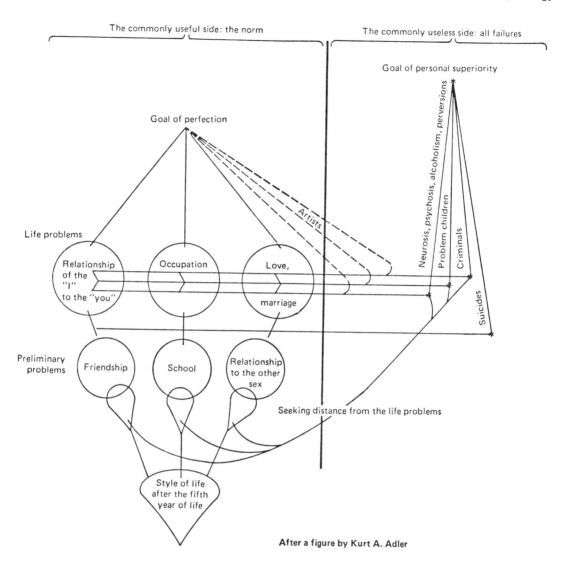

FIGURE 3-3: Outline Of The Dynamics Of The Norm And Of The Failures

The really important difference of conduct is ... that of usefulness and uselessness. By useful I mean in the interests of mankind generally. The most sensible estimate of the value of any activity is its helpfulness to all mankind, present and future, a criterion that applies not only to that which sub-serves the immediate preservation of life, but also to higher activities such as religion, science, and art. It is true that we cannot always decide what is strictly worth while from this point of view. But [the more]

we are guided by the impulse to act usefully ... the nearer we approach to true perception. (Adler, 1929b, p. 78)

14. ACTIVITY IS, AFTER SOCIAL INTEREST, THE SECOND MOST IMPORTANT PERSONALITY TRAIT.

As the physicist describes movement it involves two variables—space (or direction), and time (or speed), which depends on energy. When the psychologist uses the concept of movement he should logically also account for these two variables.

Adler acknowledged the first variable by the dimension of social usefulness–social uselessness, the *direction* of movement. "As in physics we cannot measure any movement without relating it toward another space, so in Individual Psychology this other space is the social organization of mankind and its supposedly eternal demands" (1956, p. 163). The preceding two assertions have dealt with this dimension.

The second dimension, *energy,* was acknowledged by Adler a few years later through the concept of activity. One would expect degree of activity to be related to the individual's physiological make-up. And indeed Adler notes: "Hereditary and environmental factors play a part" (1964, p. 60). But, as always in Adler, this is modified by the personality, the style of life. It is not a matter of straight causality, but of "probability."

To explain what he means by activity Adler stated, "A child who runs away from his parents, or a boy who starts a fight in the street, must be credited with a higher degree of activity than a child who likes to sit at home and read a book" (1964, p. 60). Degree of activity is relatively constant throughout life, "corresponding entirely to the constancy of the individual law of movement, i.e., the style of life" (p. 60). Adler believed the recognition of this second personality dimension "opens an entirely new and valuable perspective for psychiatric treatment, education, and prophylaxis" (p. 61).

15. SOCIAL INTEREST AND ACTIVITY IMPLY A TWO-DIMENSIONAL PERSONALITY THEORY WITH A FOURFOLD TYPOLOGY.

With the two movement variables—social interest or usefulness, and activity—Adler advanced a two-dimensional theory of personality structure. Such a conception leads to four personality types when the two dimensions are dichotomized. Adler described the four personality types as follows:

> The first type consists of individuals whose approach to reality shows . . . a more or less dominant or "ruling" attitude (the "ruling" type). . . .

> A second type—surely the most frequent—expects everything from others and leans on others. I might call it the "getting" type.

> A third type is inclined to feel successful by avoiding the solution of problems, . . . tries to "side-step" problems in an effort thereby to avoid defeat (the "avoiding" type).

> The fourth type struggles, to a greater or lesser degree, for a solution of these problems in a way which is useful to others. (1964, p. 68).

As Adler did not name this type we shall name it —the socially useful type. Adler continues:

> In the fourth type . . . we can always find a certain amount of activity . . . used for the benefit of others. . . . The first type also has activity, but not enough social interest . . . this type acts in an unsocial way. . . . They become delinquents, tyrants, sadists. . . . To this type also belong suicides, drug addicts, and alcoholics, whose lesser degree of activity causes them to attack others indirectly. They make attacks upon themselves to hurt others. The second and third types shown even less activity and not much social interest. . . . Their shock results are neuroses and psychoses. (1964, p. 69–70)

This description led us to construct a fourfold table, the results of which are shown in Table 3-3. Only Adler's second, the "getting" type, does not quite fit. But then Adler had the least to say about this type, although he described it as "surely the most frequent."

The process of constructing this table gave rise to two syntheses within Adler's writings which are now incorporated in the table.

1. *The four temperaments.* A few years before describing his activity–social interest typology, Adler discussed the four temperaments of Hippocrates (1956, pp. 169–171). These are so similar in behavioral content to the four types that we have added them—the sanguine matching the socially useful type; the choleric, the ruling type; the melancholic, the avoiding type; and the phlegmatic, the getting or leaning type.

2. *Opinion of the self and the world.* Individual Psychology is behavioral (objective), as well as phenomenological (subjective). The dimensions of activity and social usefulness are objective, with the first referring to the individual and the second to his objective relationship to the world around him. But Adler expressed also a purely phenomenological conception of these two di-

TABLE 3-3: Social Interest—Activity Typology

Objectively (Behaviorally) and Subjectively (Phenomenologically)

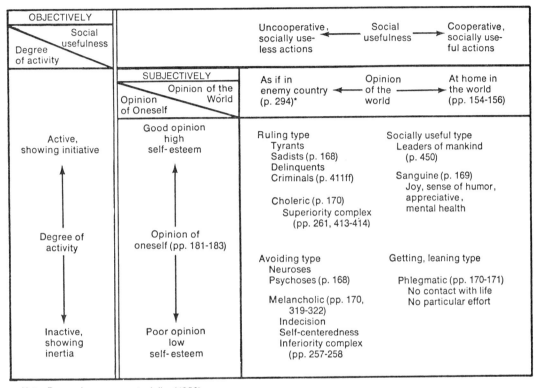

Note: Page references are to Adler (1956).

mensions, "the individual's opinion of himself and of the environment with which he has to cope" (1964, p. 24). Connected with a person's law of movement is a specific apperception, "the way in which man looks at himself and the external world" (Adler, 1956, p. 182). "For me there can be no doubt that everyone conducts himself in life from the very beginning of his action as if he had a definite opinion of his strength and his abilities and a clear conception of the difficulty or ease of a problem at hand" (1956, p. 182), "without his understanding it or giving himself an account of it" (1956, p. 195).

In Table 3-3 we have plotted "opinion of oneself" along with "degree of activity" on the left side of the table, the y axis, and "opinion of the world" and "social usefulness" across the top, the x axis.

Adler frequently indicated that activity and opinion of oneself are positively related, as is shown in Table 3-3. Criminals are active and display a good opinion of themselves, "a cheap superiority complex" (1956, pp. 413–414). At the other extreme, "Every neurotic has an inferiority complex" (1956, p. 257) and is also low in activity.

Regarding social usefulness and opinion of the world reflecting one another, we can cite: "Feeling-at-home is an immediate part of social interest" (Adler, 1956, p. 155), which in turn is evaluated by social usefulness. Among the requirements of a good leader are "a strongly developed social interest" and "an optimistic outlook" (1956, p. 450). On the other hand, the criminals who are active on "the useless side of life" are in conflict with what they consider "this hostile world" (1956, p. 413). In melancholia, or depression in more modern language, Adler sees an "aggressive nature" and a perception that "the preponderant majority of men are hostile" (1956, p. 319). These examples may suffice to make the point.

16. ALL HUMAN FUNCTIONS SERVE THE INDIVIDUAL'S "LAW OF MOVEMENT," HIS LIFESTYLE.

The unit to be studied in psychology is the individual person and his way of living. All the general processes one can observe among people, such as drives, emotions, and cultural experiences, must be understood as subordinated to the individual's unique organization, "his law of movement," his style of life. Upon entering life, a child

> ... is more or less dependent on his own creative power and ability to divine a path.... Thus he arrives at his law of movement which aids him after a certain amount of training to attain a style of life, in accordance with which we see the individual thinking, feeling, and acting throughout his whole life. (Adler, 1956, pp. 187–188)

Organic as well as psychological functions are subordinated to the style of life, although both were originally factors in its formation.

> The organic functions are dominated by the style of life. This is notably the case with the lungs, the heart, the stomach, the organs of excretion and the sexual organs. The disturbance of these functions expresses the direction which an individual is taking to attain his goal. I have called these disturbances the organ dialect, or organ jargon, since the organs are revealing in their own most expressive language the intention of the individual totality. (1956, p. 156)
>
> The dialect of the sexual organs is especially expressive. (1956, p. 156)

My questioners often ... believe that the sexual impulse is the central motive.... Our experience is that the sexual components cannot even be correctly estimated except in relation to the individual's style of life. (1956, p. 46)

We are far from disputing that every mental and bodily function is necessarily conditioned by inherited material, but what we see in all psychic activity is the *use which is made* of this material to attain a certain goal. (1956, p. 30)

Such a functional dynamic psychology Adler called "psychology of use," in contrast to a "psychology of possession." In the former all functions as well as all hereditary and environmental influences become "building blocks" for the lifestyle.

17. CERTAIN DEVELOPMENTAL CONDITIONS PROVIDE PROBABILITIES FOR PERSONALITY FORMATION.

A holistic theory of personality has little use for developmental stages, in that they artificially divide the individual life cycle into discrete steps, raising self-fulfilling expectations for the various stages as described. Instead, personality, that is the lifestyle, is seen by Adler (1929b) as emerging gradually, uniquely, and as a whole: "In the first four or five years the child builds up its own prototype ... and lays the irrevocable foundation of his style of life" (p. 31). Since Adler stresses man's "free creative power," all influences on the child function only as probabilities, not as "causes."

The great positive factor is a mother, or her equivalent, who fills "the two-fold function of motherhood: to give the child the completest possible experience of human fellowship, and then to widen it into a life-attitude towards others" (Adler, 1956, p. 372).

Three negative factors threatening the child's development of self-esteem and social interest are:

1. *Organ inferiorities and childhood diseases.* "Such children may easily become self-centered, lose hope of playing a useful part in our common life, and consider themselves humiliated by the world" (1956, p. 368).
2. *Pampering.* A pampered child "has been trained to receive without giving.... He has lost his independence and does not know that he can do things for himself" (1956, p. 369).

His social interest and ultimately his self-esteem are low, which combination makes him prone to failure.

3. *Neglect.* The neglected, hated, or unwanted child "has found society cold to him. . . . He will be suspicious of others and unable to trust himself. . . . Many failures in life come from orphans or illegitimate children" (1956, pp. 370–371). Such a child strives "to escape and to get at a safe distance from others" (Adler, 1929b, p. 36).

Under all three of these circumstances, the child is more likely to develop a "pampered style of life" (Adler, 1956, pp. 241–242), the actual predisposing condition for failure in life. It is characterized by expecting from others, pressing them into one's service, evading responsibility, blaming circumstances for one's shortcomings, while actually feeling incompetent and insecure. It is, however, not to be attributed to the circumstances. Rather, "the pampered style of life as a living phenomenon is the creation of the child, though its formation is frequently aided by others" (1956, p. 242).

For other aspects of lifestyle development, the person's family constellation provides important probabilities. This will be dealt with in the Assessment section below.

Applications

Assessment

Adler's methods of personality assessment were aimed at obtaining a conceptualization of the whole person, his lifestyle. Since personality is a unified whole, in theory any judicial sampling of behavior would suffice. Adler asserted: "We can begin wherever we choose: every expression will lead us in the same direction—towards the one motive, the one melody, around which the personality is built. We are provided with a vast store of material. Every word, thought, feeling, or gesture contributes to our understanding" (1956, p. 332). Adler and his followers developed three specific methods of lifestyle assessment: the interpretation of (1) early recollections, (2) the family constellation, and (3) dreams.

Early Recollections. It is a paradox that with a conception of man as largely self-determined and future-oriented, Adler should go into the past to ask for early recollections. The answer is that the Adlerian is not primarily interested in what happened to the individual in the recollection, but how he chose to respond to the situation which he described. The recollection itself is understood as of his choosing. Adler stated categorically:

> There are no chance memories. Out of the incalculable number of impressions which meet an individual, he chooses to remember only those which he feels, however darkly, to have a bearing on his situation. Thus his memories represent his "Story of my life"; a story he repeats to himself to warn him or comfort him, to keep him concentrated on his goal, and to prepare him by means of past experiences, so that he will meet the future with an already tested style of action. (1956, p. 351)

From this viewpoint, it is not important whether or not a given recollection corresponds to the objective facts.

Two early recollections serve as illustrations. Marilyn Monroe, the sensationally successful film star and "sex symbol," always described herself as a poor waif and a victim of circumstances. Eventually she put her career in jeopardy, after three divorces lived a lonely life, and finally committed suicide. She reported the following incident from the age of one, at her grandmother's: "I remember waking up from my nap fighting for my life. Something was pressed against my face. It could have been a pillow. I fought with all my strength" (Ansbacher, 1974b, p. 129).

By contrast, Betty Ford, the cheerful, outspoken wife of President Gerald Ford and the mother of an apparently happy family, reports:

> I was either 2 or 3, in my mother's arms on the front porch of our summer cottage by a lake in Michigan. A summer storm was approaching, and my mother— I can still "see" her doing this—pressed me closer to her while saying, over and over again, how nice it was going to be, how beautiful the storm was going to be. To this day I like an approaching storm and dark water and the thunder and lightning. My mother was, of course, terrified of storms, but didn't want me to be, and I'm not. (Agel, 1975)

Family Constellation. Adler (1929c) made certain inferences from a person's birth order as to how he was most likely to have reacted to his ordinal position. A firstborn is for a while like an only child and is then dethroned from that position. Thus oldest children are often conservatives, who feel that those in power should remain there. The second child, on the other hand, "wants to equal" the first. "He does not recognize power, but wants the power to change hands" (p. 91). The youngest child "is in an advantageous position since he can never be dethroned." Regarding such and many further observations on birth order, Adler, however, warned that these are only "tendencies" and that "there is no necessity about them" (p. 92).

As an aid to such investigation, Dreikurs (1967, pp. 87–94) devised an interview guide with the questions: "Who was most different from you? In what respect? Who was most like you? In what respect? What kind of child were you?" This is followed by asking the person to describe other siblings and to identify the highest and lowest ranking sibling on each of 21 attributes. If the person does not include himself in a ranking he is asked to which of the two siblings he is most similar. The attributes include intelligence, school grades, rebelliousness, pleasingness, gregariousness, to name a few. In rationale this method is similar to Kelly's (1955, pp. 219–266) Role Construct Repertory Test, although much simpler.

Dream Interpretation. Adler's method of dream interpretation differs basically from that of Freud who considered dreams a disguise for alien thoughts deeply buried in the unconscious. One may think that for Freud the dream represented a wish, while for Adler the dream was an intention, a kind of rehearsal, and so had premonitory qualities. For Adler (1956, pp. 357–365) the dream is a metaphorical expression, as in poetry, of thoughts, referring to some actual problem to be faced. The dream metaphors and metaphorical solutions are in line with the person's lifestyle and support it. Adlerian dream interpretation has been well presented by Shulman (1969).

The following account by Ansbacher (1974c, p. 802) may serve as a brief example of Adlerian interpretation. William D. Dement, dream physiologist, reported: "One subject in our laboratory in a single night ran the gamut from being with 'two hippopotamuses in a millpond' through a 'taffy pull in the Soviet Embassy' to 'hearing Handel's *Messiah* sung by a thousand-voice chorus in this beautiful cathedral,' back to 'writing at my desk.'" Dement gave this as an example of "the wildly unpredictable nature of dream content" the "fundamental determinants" of which "remain cloaked in obscurity." However, while specific dream content is unpredictable, due to the dreamer's creativity, it is not unintelligible. In the dreams described above the common denominator is bigness, strength, activity, and a pleasant feeling tone. From this we infer that the dreamer in waking life shows great activity, buoyancy, and optimism, with perhaps some grandiosity and manic traits. He is also a cultured person and interested in music. The dreams sustained his confidence and optimism for the next day's work. When this interpretation was given to Dement he replied: "The individual in question is essentially as you describe him."

Treatment

Adler's conceptualization of mental disorders followed the educational model which considers mental disorders not a disease to be cured, but rather an erroneous way of living, a mistaken lifestyle with mistaken opinions of self and the world and mistaken goals of success, all strongly connected with underdeveloped social interest. Through these mistakes the patient is a "failure" in solving his life problems. That is his disorder.

The purpose of assessment in treatment is to gain a clear conception of the patient's particular mistakes and convey this to the patient so that he may then avoid these mistakes. It is as in sport instruction. In swimming, tennis, or skiing, the pupil does not know why he is not doing better. But the instructor can see exactly the mistakes the pupil makes, in breathing, leg position, or distribution of weight. The instructor makes him aware of his mistakes so that he may avoid them and replace them by the "correct" movements. Adler's (1929b) aim was "to replace the great mistakes by small ones. ... Big mistakes can produce neuroses, but little mistakes a nearly normal person" (p. 62).

Psychopathology Theory. In a general way the patient's mistake is that he is striving on the socially useless side, and in a way that makes only "private sense," contrary to "common sense" (Adler, 1956, pp. 150, 253–254). This is usually based on a high goal of personal superiority, compensating for strong inferiority feelings, which precludes the development of social interest. "The striving for personal superiority and the nondevelopment of social interest . . . are one and the same mistake" (1956, pp. 240–241). In consequence, the individual will have difficulty in meeting his life's problems, which in turn makes him fear failure which would "injure his vanity and interfere with his striving for personal superiority" (1956, pp. 293–294). This constellation is the "neurotic disposition," later called the "pampered lifestyle" (discussed above).

The symptoms are the patient's "arrangements" to serve as excuses for not meeting his life problems, and to protect his self-esteem.

> The life plan of the neurotic demands categorically that if he fails, it should be through someone else's fault and that he should be freed from personal responsibility. . . . When the individual helps along with his devices, then the entire content of life is permeated by the reassuring, anesthetizing stream of the life-lie which safeguards the self-esteem. (Adler, 1956, p. 271)

Later, Adler replaced the term life-lie by self-deception. Adler adds the important principle, "Every neurotic is partly right" (1956, p. 334), in that he met with "traumas" and "frustrations," which can easily be construed as adverse "causes." But he is only "partly right" in that he is not obligated to construe his life in this manner. Others with similar experiences have responded differently.

An individual with a mistaken lifestyle may still go through life without coming to a crisis, as long as his circumstances are so favorable that he is spared any test. For a crisis to develop there must be such a test or a task—"the exogenous factor, the proximity of a task that demands cooperation and fellowship" (1956, p. 297).

Individual Therapy. Four phases of Adlerian psychotherapy have been variously described. These are, however, only conceptual categories which in practice may and do freely run into one another and may also be condensed. The phases are:

1. *Establishment and maintenance of a good relationship with the patient.* The therapist presents himself as a trustworthy person and extends social interest to the patient to awaken and develop the patient's social interest. Thereby the therapist also raises the patient's self-esteem and encourages him. "Psychotherapy is an exercise in cooperation and a test of cooperation" (Adler, 1956, p. 340). To this Dreikurs (1967) adds: "Therapeutic cooperation requires an alignment of goals. . . . What appears as 'resistance' constitutes a discrepancy between the goals of the therapist and those of the patient" (p. 7). An important way to win the patient is to make him feel understood, whereby one also wins his respect. To maintain cooperation one must be tactful and avoid dogmatic statements. Dreikurs offers interpretations with such phrases as, "Would you like me to tell you?" or "Could it be?" (p. 60).

2. *Psychological exploration.* The methods presented in the preceding section on assessment are to enable the therapist to gain an understanding of the patient's hidden and presumably erroneous goal and purposes of which the patient may be quite unaware, and thus to conceptualize the patient's lifestyle.

3. *Conveying the therapist's understanding to the patient.* This may also be called giving insight, which is accomplished through interpreting the patient's statements and actions to him. This is what Watzlawick, Weakland, and Fisch (1974) have called reframing, giving the patient a new frame of reference. As to the content of interpretation, the therapist listens dialectically, that is, he asks himself what opposite could be paired with a certain statement. This is in accord with the assumed self-deception of the patient. "While he regards one point, we must look at the other. He looks at his obstacles; we must look at his attempt to protect his fictive superiority and rescue his ambition" (Adler, 1964, p. 199). When the patient speaks of his generosity, the therapist may understand an accusation of stinginess against others. The question, "What would you do if you were well?" (Adler, 1956, p. 332) leads to the interpretation that this may be the exact activity from which the patient is excusing himself by his symptoms.

4. *Reorientation and reeducation.* This is the most important phase in psychotherapy. It uses various forms of confrontations and directives. For example, when a middle-aged man who had been in psychoanalytic treatment brought up his unresolved Oedipus complex, Adler would say:

"Look here, what do you want of the old lady?" (Ansbacher, 1965b, p. 347). As mentioned, Adler was a pragmatist. Thus insight on the part of the patient is less important than change in behavior. The criterion of success of treatment is objective: "As soon as the patient can connect himself with his fellow men on an equal and co-operative footing, he is cured" (Adler, 1956, p. 347).

Group Processes and Approaches. Adlerian theory is so keyed to group process that it brings this even into individual therapy, in that "The therapist appears as the representative for the human community" (Dreikurs, 1967, p. 32), the "common sense."

Within the framework of social interest Adlerians have used any form of therapy beyond the one-to-one dyadic mode: multiple psychotherapy, family therapy, out-patient treatment and therapeutic social clubs, psychodrama and action therapy, milieu therapy, conventional group therapy, as well as educational group counseling. For references see Ansbacher (1974c, p. 804). But as Papanek (1961) pointed out, it is understood that the group "be based on healthy social values," else it would merely encourage "socially shared autisms" (p. 188).

Adler originated in his child guidance clinics a form of group approach in which children were treated before a group of observers, the children coming in with, or shortly after, their parents or teachers. The group was at first primarily a training seminar for teachers, but was soon recognized as actually facilitating therapy. By their mere presence and occasional comments, the observers embodied the common sense, as "witnesses" so to speak.

Today this type of treatment is carried on in numerous Family Education Centers. The technique, which has been described by Dreikurs, Corsini, Lowe, and Sonstegard (1959), has become particularly teachable through videotapes of counseling demonstration sessions by Dreikurs (1969, 1971).

Counseling. Any distinction between counseling and psychotherapy is quite arbitrary in Adlerian theory. Dreikurs (1967) talks about the same four phases or steps in counseling as in psychotherapy, but considers counseling "concerned mainly with the acute situation and the solution of immediate problems," while psychotherapy aims more at "a complete re-organization of the individual's life" (p. 258).

Institutional

Of the ten applications discussed under this heading, the first six are practical, while the other four are more conceptual or theoretical. The first two, school and family, greatly outdistance the remainder as far as the number of people actually involved is concerned.

School. As early as 1931, Oskar Spiel (1962), together with Ferdinand Birnbaum, applied Adlerian principles in the classroom. The difficult child was considered to be one who himself suffers difficulties. He must be given insight into his goals and mistaken ways of achieving them and led to correct his misconceptions of himself and the world around him. Part of the method was class discussions aimed at self-government, at mutual academic aid among class members, and at understanding the reasons for misbehavior of classmates so as to encourage them and to elicit their cooperation.

Dreikurs (1957, pp. 12–17) advanced this approach by classifying children's problems according to four goals of disturbing behavior and developing ways of identifying these goals and dealing with them.

Family. Adlerian parent education is again best represented by Dreikurs (1964), in a book particularly useful for parent study groups. Averaging 14 members, such groups meet under lay leadership for about 10 sessions, discussing the book's "practical steps in a new direction" (p. viii). The spread of these groups has been phenomenal. One of the techniques recommended is the family council (Dreikurs, Gould, Corsini, 1974). This is a deliberative body composed of all family members, meeting regularly for the purpose of arriving at a consensus on family problems. Everyone must abide by a decision once it has been reached by consensus. The functions of chairman and secretary rotate among all family members.

Social Work. Although Adlerian psychology has not yet found its place in American social work as it has in educational guidance and parent education, it would, according to Harold Werner (1967), "provide a theoretical rationale that completely supports the traditions and beliefs of social work" (p. 16). In pre-Hitler Germany, Individual Psychology was apparently widely applied in social work. Hilde Ottenheimer (1959) explains in her review, "Since in social work we are mostly dealing with persons who have lost their community ties, the Adlerian theory was ready-made to determine the remedial measures" (p. 849).

Crime and Delinquency. Adler (1964) was particularly interested in the rehabilitation of criminals. He was, according to Ellenberger (1970), "among the great pioneers of dynamic psychiatry . . . the only one who wrote something on criminals from his direct experience" (p. 618). Adler hired an ex-convict as his gardener and won in him a lifelong devoted friend (Bottome, 1957, pp. 191–193; Orgler, 1963, pp. 227–239). A follower of Adler, Ernst Papanek, who was director of the Wiltwyck School for Boys, was immortalized by Claude Brown (1965, pp. 84–88, 124–128) through his description of how Papanek brought him back to a useful life.

Work, Industrial Morale, Old Age. If the striving to overcome difficulties, the striving for success, is basic, it is to be expected that, everything else being equal, people's morale would be higher when they are working than when idle. Industrial morale studies have amply confirmed this hypothesis. At the same time, according to Willard Beecher (1955), the principal job of management should be "to set up and maintain conditions that lead to *teamwork,* just as a good therapist would do . . . where everyone . . . regards all others as equal," and where "the job is our only boss" (p. 128). The mental hardship in both unemployment and old age is that the person is prevented from contributing and exercising his skills and thus feels useless and diminished in his sense of well-being.

Leadership, Group Morale. A main component of group morale is a common purpose, and a main function of the leader is to formulate the goal and give the group a sense that it can be attained. The question of the personal requirements of leadership was answered by Adler in the following:

A strongly developed social interest is the first. An optimistic outlook and sufficient self-confidence are just as necessary. The leader must be capable of quick action; . . . he must have ease in making contact with people; and he must possess tact so as not to frustrate the assent of others. . . . He must, in a word, be a real human being who possesses courage and skills. In him becomes realized what other men dream about. (1956, p. 450)

Social Movements. Adler considered racial and other prejudices a form of depreciation tendency, boosting one's own self-esteem by depreciating others. Prejudice as scapegoating provides excuses for one's own inadequacies. Kenneth B. Clark (1967), well-known black psychologist, found that in his work and struggles "the most significant and persistent influence . . . had been the social dynamic theories of Alfred Adler" (p. 181). Frantz Fanon (1967), a black revolutionary who had studied psychiatry, believed that "Adler will help us to understand the conception of the world held by the man of color" (p. 62).

The prejudice of woman's inferiority takes the same form as other prejudices. Adler (Adler & Furtmüller, 1914) strongly advocated equal rights of the sexes, deploring masculine supremacy as "one of the deepest wounds of our social life" (p. 133). Equality must, however, be "fitted into the natural scheme of things" (Adler, 1929c, p. 67). *Machismo* has for some time been explained in Adlerian terms (Batt, 1969; Ramos, 1962).

Religion. For Adler the idea of God is a concretization of a goal of perfection and greatness in which an entire culture can share. Adler contended that "an unpremised mechanistic position" is "an illusion, inasmuch as it is without goal and direction, . . . after all, the essence of life" (1956, p. 461). In this respect he considered the religious view far ahead, pointing out, however, that "God cannot be proven scientifically," but "is a gift of faith." The applicability of Adlerian theory to religious concerns was the object of a small symposium (Ansbacher, 1971c).

Literary Criticism. "Every individual," Adler stated, "represents both a unity of personality and the individual fashioning of that unity. . . . But as an artist . . . he is . . . an imperfect human being" (1956, p. 177). If real and fictional persons are artistic creations, they both can be similarly approached. The task of Adlerian literary criticism is to understand a given character in his unique style of life, including his goal of success, through seeking the coherence of all his thinking and acting. Adler (1920b) admired the writer's synthesis, "whereas analysis profanes and desecrates" (p. 268, translation modified), and he validated his own thinking against great literary works. Some recent Adlerian studies have dealt with Camus (Rom, 1960); *Hamlet* (Mairet, 1969); Somerset Maugham, (Burt, 1970); and *The Catcher in the Rye* (Irving, 1976). The numerous studies of an earlier period are included in Kiell (1963) and Mosak and Mosak (1975).

Psychohistory and Psychobiography. One may well say with Jacob Bronowski that all of man's history is a record of the *Ascent of Man,* revealing his incessant striving from a minus to a plus situation, for competence, overcoming difficulties, power. Cruelties were in every case based on the misapplication of power in the interest of personal, ethnic, or class superiority over others; blessings, on its application in the common, the social interest. Although Freudian ideas still dominate psychohistory, as they do literary criticism, the historian Mazlish (1974) notes that since the work of Harold D. Lasswell "Adler's influence . . . has continued to inspire political scientists and, to a lesser degree, historians as well" (p. 1037). Mazlish refers to the "exemplary" study of Woodrow Wilson by Alexander L. and Juliette George (1956). According to A. L. George (1968), Lasswell's Adlerian-based hypothesis, "power . . . to overcome low estimates of the self," has had some influence on five studies of political leadership, and "the fruitfulness of Adler's theories . . . is now widely recognized" (p. 29). Youngdale (1975) presented a "new perspective" on American populism which is "closely linked with . . . the outlook of Alfred Adler" (p. 45), who stresses "the goal-directed and social quality of human life" (p. 13). Adler himself wrote "On the psychology of Marxism," "Danton, Marat, Robespierre," and gave an interview on Mussolini (Adler, 1964, pp. 313, 405, 320). Other studies are on the Schreber case (Shulman, 1959), the assassins of American presidents (Chaplin, 1970), Ben Franklin (McLaughlin and Ansbacher, 1971), Hitler (Brink, 1975), and Marilyn Monroe (Ansbacher, 1974b, pp. 124–138).

Self

As we have stated, Adler constructed his theory with the intent that every human being should be able to understand it and profit by it. With this in mind he clad his theory mostly in everyday language and selected, from among still-debated basic issues regarding the nature of man, those alternatives that hold the greater promise for man, the more optimistic alternative. Such a theory should certainly be suited for self-help and self-improvement of the more "normal" person, although the more neurotic would still require outside help. The large and continuous sale of Adler's *Understanding Human Nature* (1927a), translated in some dozen languages, and others of his books would seem to reflect this self-help aspect.

Self-application among College Students. Some specific information as to what a person may find useful in Adler comes from an informal inquiry among a class of undergraduate students, conducted some time ago by the present writer. The students had taken a course entitled "Personality," with Adler (1956) as text. After the final examination the students ($N = 60$) were asked to write on: "What have you learned in this course which should be of direct help to you in daily life?" They were assured that they would not be graded on their replies. From this three basic assumptions of the theory emerged as particularly helpful: (a) human self-determination, (b) goal orientation, and (c) innate capacity for social interest. These were helpful in supporting existing optimistic views, in providing new encouragement, and in giving meaning to life. A sundry category is made up of such statements as:

> I can attempt to avoid . . . oversensitivity.
> Striving on the useful side will, I hope, guide many of my actions.
> I hope to employ the principle that more interest in the partner than the self is the only way to have a happy marriage.
> I will understand my role as a teacher more fully . . . try to prevent any child from being discouraged.

An Early Self-Help Group. Rühle-Gerstel (1930) recognized three pre-conditions of therapy: a need for help, insight, and encouragement. Insight may be attained through lectures and books, but courage to change is achieved very rarely by oneself. Here a study group can take the place of the therapist. She reported on a study group which, under her tutelage, read books by Adler and from which she was often absent months at a time. In this group, encouragement was provided in the following ways: "Everybody came to experience his mistakes as average, without a particularly tragic note.... He also experienced much comradeship and sincere effort on his behalf and thereby learned to extend these toward others" (p. 60). "Thus they learned ... gradually to laugh at themselves and like themselves. They found the right method not to be hard toward themselves nor to pity themselves, but to be pleasant, helpful and considerate" (p. 61).

Present-Day Study Groups. The numerous study groups mentioned in the preceding section generally meet under lay leadership, as noted. Thus they can rightfully be noted also in the present section on self-help.

Validation

Three papers have reviewed validation of Adlerian theories. Ansbacher (1947) dealt with the areas of perception, memory, intelligence, mother-child relationship, compensation, organ inferiority, crime and delinquency, the consistency of personality, and human dynamics. Ansbacher (1964) reviewed consensual validation or acknowledgments of Adler's importance in general personality theory, existential psychology and psychiatry, neo-Freudian psychoanalysis, Freudian psychoanalysis, theory of mental health, and anthropology. Ferguson (1968) was concerned with trends in contemporary academic psychology toward Adlerian theory. Her categories were: the active organism, stimulus selection, feedback process, central processes, and expectancy-purpose. This section, sampling the current scene, carries these reviews further with only a minimum of duplication.

Evidence: Consensual Validation

Father of Modern Psychotherapy. Adler's principles are being reiterated by increasing numbers of academic and clinical psychologists, mostly without reference to Adler. Yet this phenomenon represents in fact a far-flung consensual validation. It was best described by Albert Ellis (1970), founder of Rational-Emotive Psychotherapy, in the following:

Alfred Adler, more even than Freud, is probably the true father of modern psychotherapy. Some of the reasons are: He founded ego psychology, which Freudians only recently rediscovered. He was one of the first humanistic psychologists.... He stressed holism, goal-seeking, and the enormous importance of values in human thinking, emoting, and acting. He correctly saw that sexual drives and behavior, while having great importance in human affairs, are largely the result rather than the cause of man's nonsexual philosophies.

For these and other reasons Adler strongly influenced the work of Sullivan, Horney, Fromm, Rogers, May, Maslow and many other writers on psychotherapy, some of whom are often wrongly called neo-Freudians, when they more correctly could be called neo-Adlerians.

My own system of rational-emotive psychotherapy was profoundly influenced by Adler; and the public demonstrations of psychotherapy which are so often given today by Moreno, the late Perls, Schutz, Dreikurs, Ackerman, myself, and many other therapists also owe much to Adler's pioneering methods.

It is difficult to find any leading therapist today who in some respect does not owe a great debt to the Individual Psychology of Alfred Adler. (pp. 11–12)

Floyd W. Matson (1964), political scientist and humanist, made a similarly strong statement when he wrote:

The influence of Adler ... seems in retrospect to have been scarcely less extensive than that of Freud ... It might even be argued (with conscious heresy) that it was the turn first taken by Adler some fifty years ago which has come to be the "mainstream" of the psychoanalytic movement—and that taken by Freud which has been in fact the "deviation." (p. 194)

Judd Marmor (1972), former president of the American Psychiatric Association, wrote:

Adler truly deserves to be recognized as one of the most original, creative, and progressive thinkers in the history of modern psychiatry. He must be credited with being the first of the ego-psychologists, and the first psychoanalyst to conceive of human psychology in holistic terms. (p. 153)

Viktor E. Frankl (1970), founder of Logotherapy, says about Adler that what he achieved in opposing Freud

> ... was no less than a Copernican switch. No longer could man be considered as the product, pawn and victim of drives and instincts; on the contrary, drives and instincts form the material that serves man in expression and in action. Beyond this, Alfred Adler may well be regarded as an existential thinker and as a fore-runner of the existential-psychiatric movement. (p. 12)

H. L. Minton (1968) comments particularly on Adler's concept of power having found validation. "Several contemporary approaches appear to parallel Adler's final conceptualizations regarding power and social interest" (p. 47), that is, power in the sense of success, effectance, or competence. These are the approaches of R. W. White, Minton, Kurt Lewin, Fritz Heider, Thibaut and Kelley, and Rotter.

Maslow (1970), founder of modern humanistic psychology, sums up briefly in stating, "For me Alfred Adler becomes more and more correct year by year. As the facts come in, they give stronger and stronger support to his image of man." He adds, "In one respect especially the times have not yet caught up with him. I refer to his holistic emphasis." (p. 13)

The Breadth of Adler's System. Adler always endeavored to show that "Individual Psychology is the heir to all great movements whose aim is the welfare of mankind. Although its scientific foundation obligates it to a certain intransigence, it is eager to receive stimulation from all fields of knowledge and experience, and to return the stimulation" (1956, p. 463). In the same vein Adler (1935) also wanted "every student of Individual Psychology to acquire as full a knowledge of other psychological systems as possible.... Any unprejudiced critic must admit that introspectionism, psychoanalysis, functionalism, behaviorism, purposivism, reflexology, and Gestalt psychology have made valuable contributions. But the same must be said of Individual Psychology" (pp. 3–4, translation modified).

This approaches a broad eclecticism from a definite point of view. That Adler realized this can be seen from his immediately following disclaimer: "Thereby we are by no means advocating the weakly *(schwächlich)* eclecticism" (1935, p. 4).

This breadth of Adler's system has best been recognized and supported by Frederick Thorne (1970). Thorne wrote: "The ultimate clinical validation of any theoretical viewpoint ... is a function of breadth of phenomena which the system is able to clarify and explain ... Adler ... receives increasing recognition because more and more of his concepts are found to be relevant and clinically valid" (p. 142). Thorne finds that Adler was concerned "with a much wider range of behavior than Freud, and [was] much more pragmatic than Jung's mysticism" (p. 135). "Adlerian psychology is the only system to have some practical relevance in case handling with mental defectives, social misfits, felons, and maladjusted normals" (p. 142). "Historically it is important to keep the record straight by giving Adler credit for his pioneering in broadening the spectrum of psychological theorizing" (p. 143).

Thus Thorne considers Adler

> ... one of the earliest eclectics, being concerned with everything from psychobiology, in his concept of organ inferiority, to existentialism, in his preoccupation with the social meaning of life. Adler saw the need for a global theory that would describe global behaviors.... His social ideology was modeled after biological truth in such breadth as only an eclectic viewpoint could encompass. (Thorne, 1970, pp. 135–136)

Adler's broadness was also pointed out by Ernest Becker (1963), social scientist, who, going beyond clinical psychology, compared Adler to Dewey in this respect, and believed they both suffered just on that account. "Adler, like Dewey in a sense, suffered both from narrow popularization and from his own broadness: he was either cheapened in the common understanding, or ignored because the reach of his ideas led too far" (p. 83). Becker (1970) praised Adler for setting "a standard for breadth of mind and moral courage without which the science of psychology will remain an idle pastime" (p. 169).

Evidence: Empirical Validation

Comprehensiveness of Theory. Two studies may be offered as empirical validation of sorts of the comprehensiveness of Adler's system.

Farberow and Shneidman (1961, pp. 306–313)

asked clinicians of various orientations to appraise in writing one case of attempted suicide from the summary of interviews of the case by a psychiatrist. Subsequently they asked the clinicians to Q-sort into nine normally distributed categories 76 cards, each with a statement to be judged for applicability to the case. The Q-sorts from the six participating clinicians were then subjected to a conventional factor analysis reported by Kelly (1963). The Adlerian judgments showed the highest communality, $h^2 = .74$; followed by the Kellian, .71; the Sullivanian, .51; the Rogerian, .46; the Freudian, .43; and the Jungian, .39. This would indicate that the Adlerian judgments expressed the consensus of all the judgments better than any of the others.

Taft (1958) submitted the ratings by Hall and Lindzey (1957) of 17 personality theories on 18 dimensions to a cluster analysis. Among other results he found that with regard to "most similarity in factors to the 16 other theories," Adler's theory came first, followed closely by the theories of Freud and H. A. Murray. From this Taft concluded that these three theories "are either very eclectic ... or have had a major influence on other theories. Let the reader decide for himself."

Two-dimensional Personality Theory. Adler's two-dimensional personality theory has been validated through extensive factor-analytic studies—by J. B. Guilford, R. B. Cattell, H. J. Eysenck and others—of questionnaire returns and ratings. According to Eysenck and Rachman (1965), these studies have led to "almost universal agreement" regarding a two-dimensional theory (pp. 18–22). Although the authors named the two dimensions "emotionality" and "introversion-extraversion," these may be reconciled with Adler's dimensions of social interest and activity.

The Eysenck-Rachman typology is presented in Table 3-4. A comparison with Table 3-3 above will show how closely it resembles the Adler typology. Both typologies also embody the four temperaments.

Self-Determination and Mental Health. Freud (1917) prided himself on having shown that "man is not even master in his own house ... his own mind" (p. 252). According to Adler, man "is and wants to be the master of his fate" (1956, p. 156). Only the neurotic seeks freedom from personal responsibility (1956, pp. 270–271), blaming all sorts of "objective causes" not under his control for his difficulties, and it is the discouraged individual who has lost "faith in his own mental and physical powers" (1956, p. 400).

Adler's understanding has been validated by a massive body of research on "internal versus external control," initiated by J. B. Rotter (1966) and discussed by H. M. Lefcourt (1966). This has established that it is indeed the disadvantaged and discouraged of all sorts who tend to perceive events as being beyond their personal control, while the others do perceive "events as being a consequence of one's own actions, and thereby, under personal control" (Lefcourt, p. 186). This applies to retardates and schizophrenics compared to normal peers, to persons with lower mental age compared to those with higher mental age, to delinquents who did not learn information useful for obtaining parole compared to those who did, to Negroes and American Indians compared to whites, to lower-class compared to middle-class persons, and to Negroes not willing to participate in social action compared to those

TABLE 3-4. Emotionality and Extraversion-Introversion Typology (Eysenck & Rachman 1965)

	Unstable ⟵————————— Emotionality ————————⟶ Stable	
Extraversion ↑	*Choleric*: active, impulsive, aggressive; psychopaths, delinquents; truants; rude, egocentric	*Sanguine*: leadership; carefree, responsive, outgoing, sociable
↓ *Introversion*	*Melancholic*: Depressed, anxious, quiet, unsociable, rigid, inferiority feelings, nervousness, obsessive	*Phlegmatic*: passive, careful, thoughtful, controlled, even-tempered, calm

willing (Lefcourt, p. 189). All this validates Adler's assertion of "normal" as self-determined within limits. According to D. L. Mosher (1968), Adler's influence on Rotter "was heuristically powerful and pervasive" (p. 33).

Seeking Success—Avoiding Failure. Adler considered "the striving for success ... inherent in the structure of life" (1964, p. 102). While in discouraged individuals this principle is still valid, success is redefined as avoidance of further failure and defeat. "It is the fear of defeat . . . which occasions the outbreak of the so-called neurotic symptoms. . . . Psychoses . . . appear when the patient feels absolutely checkmated, with no hope of going on" (Adler, 1929b, p. 13).

This is supported by research of McReynolds and Guevara, as reported by McReynolds (1968). Schizophrenics, and to a lesser degree neurotics, were indeed found to be "more highly motivated to avoid failure and less strongly motivated to attain success" (p. 157) than normal individuals. The studies by J. W. Atkinson on achievement motivation, as well as the earlier work of Kurt Lewin, both quoted by McReynolds, point in the same direction.

Depreciation Tendency. Adler described the phenomenon of undervaluation of others to raise one's own self-esteem as one of the characteristics of the neurotic striving for success (1956, p. 55). He called this the "depreciation tendency, a tendency analogous to the fable of 'The fox and the sour grapes' " (p. 68). Similar dynamics are expressed in what J. Haley (1963) has humorously termed "oneupmanship," which he defined as "the art of placing a person 'one-down' " (p. 192).

Research studies relevant to this hypothesis, reviewed by M. R. Goldfried (1963), have led him to conclude: "(a) In general, there is a positive relationship between one's attitude toward self and one's attitudes toward others. (b) Individuals who are maladjusted [presumably have low self-esteem] tend to have more negative attitudes toward others" (p. 44).

More recently, Teichman and Foa (1972) reported a study specifically designed to test Adler's hypothesis that "the neurotic, to a greater extent than the normal, employs depreciation and accusation of significant others to safeguard his self-esteem" (p. 49). They found the hypothesis confirmed in the United States and in India

with regard to one's parents.

Antithetical Thinking. Adler noted: "The neurotically disposed individual has a sharply schematizing, strongly abstracting mode of apperception. Thus he groups ... events according to a strictly antithetical schema ... and admits no degree in between" (1956, p. 248). This hypothesis has been supported from several sides.

Neuringer (1974) found this hypothesis amply validated in cases of suicide, and acknowledged that Adler saw clearly that "a certain cognitive style determined certain outcomes in a much more powerful way than the experiences themselves" (p. 63). Ryle and Breen (1972) found that neurotics generally "tend to extreme judgments." Teichman (1971) concluded from his data that neurotics "will differentiate among family members more than well-adjusted controls" (p. 75). Berger (1964) observed, in underachieving college students, that they engage indeed in the kind of sharply categorizing thinking which Adler had described as "I must have this or nothing" (1956, p. 190).

Sex-Role Identification. For Adler, "uncertainty of one's sexual role and of one's masculinity" was first among "the typical occasions for the onset of a neurosis and psychosis" (1964, pp. 296-297). Supporting this hypothesis, H. B. Biller (1973) found in his studies that sex-role uncertainty is indeed "a very basic determinant of psychopathology." He praises Adler's astuteness in listing it first among "developmental precursors to psychopathology."

Mother's Influence on Attitude toward Father. Adler described the mother as the child's "bridge to social life" (1956, p. 372), the focal agent in developing his social interest. "After she has succeeded in connecting the child with herself, her next task is to spread his interest towards the father, and this task will prove almost impossible if she herself is not interested in the father" (p. 373). From this, Baxter, Horton, and Wiley (1964) developed the hypothesis that "father identification should be adversely affected by interparental conflict" (p. 167). They found this hypothesis confirmed in a study of 180 male and female college students. More specifically, while males identified significantly more with the father than females, in harmonious homes both sexes identified significantly more with the father than in conflictful homes.

This second finding particularly would never have been predicted from a Freudian hypothesis.

Personality of the Criminal. Chaplin (1970), reporting on a study of American presidential assassins, noted that all nine cases fitted Adler's description of the criminal personality. They all were zealots; were socially and physically disadvantaged; had ideas of grandiosity; were loners, unmarried, or failures in marriage; and were unable to work steadily. "Even the cases of the two exceptions ... can be understood in terms of these dynamics. Thus the salient characteristics developed and described ... independently of Adlerian theory, confirm it strikingly" (p. 212).

Rebelliousness of the Second Born. Adler advanced a number of hypotheses on the effect of birth order on personality (p. 46). Research in this area has taken on enormous dimensions, amounting to some 400 publications between 1963 and 1971 (Vockell, Felker, & Miley, 1973). We shall mention here only two studies referring to the hypothesis of Adler (1956, pp. 376–382) that second-borns are likely to be rebellious and not to recognize power or authority. Taintor (1970) found among 323 psychiatric diagnoses of Army recruits that 35% of the firstborns were diagnosed as neurotic and 37% as personality disorders, whereas among second-borns only 10% were found to be neurotic and 54%, personality disorders. Adler's hypothesis was also supported by LeMay (1968) with college girls referred for misconduct, among whom second-borns were found overrepresented and firstborns underrepresented.

Early Recollections. While early recollections are widely used by Adlerian practitioners in personality appraisal, validating research is still limited. Taylor (1975) reviewed six studies done between 1957 and 1965 and found the evidence in support of early recollections as a clinical tool "far from conclusive, but ... encouraging" (p. 218). Manaster and King (1973) found that in accordance with Adlerian theory in at least one out of three or four early recollections of male homosexuals, there is a woman seen in a negative light. And Manaster and Perryman (1974) found that a number of early recollection variables differentiated between students in different occupational areas.

Comparisons

In discussing similar systems above, we began by establishing the contrast to Freud's system as an alternative to which Adler's system developed. We shall presently pursue this comparison further by presenting judgments of the relative soundness of the two systems. This will be followed by comparisons with other systems.

Adler's Optimism and Soundness. Shortly after Adler's separation from him, Freud (1914) noted: Based on aggression, "there is no room in the Adlerian system for love ..., a cheerless view of life" (p. 347). Ironically, further development proved exactly the opposite to be the case; Freud augmented his system with the death instinct or instinct of destruction, while Adler added to his system social interest, which does indeed include love. Today Adler generally is recognized as the optimist, Freud as the pessimist. In the words of Hall and Lindzey (1957), "Adler restored to man a sense of dignity and worth that psychoanalysis had pretty largely destroyed" (p. 125).

More importantly, many recent judgments refer to Adler's greater soundness. Maddi (1968), comparing three models of personality—the psychosocial conflict model (Freud), the actualization fulfillment model (Rogers), and the perfection fulfillment model (Adler)—concludes that "the Adlerian view is the most sound" and, given a choice among the three, "I would cheerfully choose the latter" (p. 160). Mowrer (1959) wrote: "Adler was probably not so gifted as Freud and was nothing like as brilliant a writer; but he was, it now appears, *sounder.*" Ashley Montagu (1970) also stressed Adler's soundness: "When we come to evaluate the overall view of human nature and of man's future, there can, in my opinion, be no doubt of the far greater soundness and hopefulness of Adler's view than of Freud's" (p. 19). And finally a judgment by R. W. White (1957): "Unlike Freud, who struggled relentlessly ... to secure immortality for his concepts, Adler struggled to secure immortality for his practical wisdom. ... Now Adler's ideas have gone into the stream of contemporary thought and have become the accepted clinical common sense of our time" (p. 4).

Freud's Unsoundness. Freud's greater unsoundness is founded in his "metapsychology." Adler's original critique referred to Freud's sexual instinct or libido theory, including the concepts of repression and pleasure principle; his mechanistic, elementaristic and reductionistic approach; and the reifications which all this suggests. After Adler's separation, Freud worked these and similar additional concepts into his metapsychology, which consists of (1) the "topography" of id, ego, and superego, and the distinction between unconscious, preconscious, and conscious; (2) the instinct theory, including the psychosexual stages of development; and (3) the pleasure principle and repetition compulsion. Today, even many who consider themselves followers of Freud reject these basic assumptions, thereby implicitly validating Adler. We shall give three examples of such rejections.

According to George S. Klein (1973), the Freudian system actually contains two separate and conflicting theories. The first is Freud's metapsychology, which is positivistic, deterministic, reductionistic, and mechanistic. Klein found this incompatible with and "irrelevant" to psychoanalytic practice, where one meets and interprets in terms of "purpose, function, accomplishment," intention, and meaning. This implies a second, teleological rather than causalistic theory, according to which Klein would reconstruct psychoanalysis while completely abandoning the first theory. Ansbacher (1974a) has shown that Klein's arguments are point for point restatements of Adler's original critique of Freud.

Marmor (1973) rejects Freud's sexual theories as not having withstood the test of time. "The postulate of a fluid-like energy coursing through the body...and capable of 'repression' or discharge, simply does not jibe with modern neurophysiology" (p. 86); "Oedipus complex and incest guilt...prove...to be no explanation at all" (p. 88); infantile "incestuous" wishes may be considered as merely "a metaphorical ...description" (p. 87). This is exactly what Adler had maintained: the Oedipus complex "must be taken symbolically" (1956, p. 69), as "a figure of speech" (p. 375) of the "pampered child who does not want to give up his mother" (p. 185).

Leon J. Saul (1972) rejects Freud's metapsychology because those who stress it tend to describe patients in mere generalities. He cites a case of guilt feelings in whom two years of

psychoanalysis achieved only the interpretation that the guilt "was from masturbation as a child" (p. 11). Saul's new approach "quickly revealed that the guilt stemmed from hostility...derived from...(a) *feelings of inferiority*...because he had been...consistently *overprotected*...and (b) *protest* against all the *responsibility* which he now carried in adult life" (pp. 11–12, italics added). The new interpretation uses entirely Adlerian concepts: inferiority feelings; overprotection, corresponding to Adler's "pampering"; protest, as in "masculine protest"; and avoidance of responsibility, of which Adler had noted: "The neurotic vehemently resists being removed from his freedom of responsibility" (1956, p. 271).

Other Systems. Compared to the various similar systems described initially, it is to be noted in general that Adler's system was created not by an academic psychologist or a philosopher but by a practitioner with a shrewd sense for the theoretical essentials that would facilitate treatment. Further, it was kept, in terminology and structure, as simple as possible to make it accessible to nonprofessional persons, yet it is in fact most comprehensive, as shown above. Additionally, we want to make two further specific comparisons.

Regarding present-day *humanistic psychology*, it must be noted that with its encounter groups and emphasis on self-actualization it is less rational and cognitive and less socially oriented than Adler's humanism. Kurt Adler (1970) commented on this, "These groups foster mainly catharsis...and very often...overt depreciation of others" (p. 116). O'Connell (1971) found that a poorly led sensitivity group "reinforces the neurotic behavior of the self-centered person" (p. 67, while Papanek (1961) noted the danger of "socially shared autisms" (p. 188) as mentioned above.

On the other hand there are important methodological similarities with modern *behaviorism*, while differences in the concept of man also seem to be diminishing. O'Connell (1973), comparing Adler and Skinner, summarized:

Both see the movements of an individual toward his goal as the basic psychological reality; both see these movements taking place in a social environment as transactions influenced by the consequences they generate...Both distrust reified terms and emphasize concrete data. Adler's concept of encouragement is a close parallel to reinforcement...Both put feelings in a place of secondary importance,...are favorably disposed to religion,...committed to bringing about a better social order. (p. 93)

There are also numerous systems of psychotherapy bearing considerable similarity to Adler's approach, such as William Glasser's Reality Therapy, Eric Berne's Transactional Analysis, Frederick Perls' Gestalt Therapy, and family therapy as represented by Virginia Satire. But they generally do not have a personality theory of their own.

Prospect

The future of Individual Psychology is difficult to predict, for we are confronted with the paradoxical situation mentioned earlier. On the one hand there is the general agreement among those who know Adler—Adlerian or non-Adlerian—that Adler's ideas have been most widely accepted. On the other hand there is equal agreement that Adler's ideas have made their way anonymously without due credit to their originator. Munroe (1955) noted that "Adler's fate is like that of Heine, whose little masterpiece *The Lorelei* attained such prompt popularity that when he himself asked a group of people singing it for the name of the author, he was told, 'Why, nobody wrote it—it's a folk song' " (p. 335). Fifteen years later, Ellenberger (1970) still found this story applicable to Adler, in a version referring to Franz Schubert and his *Lieder* (p. 646).

With Adler this situation is extreme. Ellenberger describes in some detail the extent to which Adler has influenced the neo-Freudians, from Edward Kempf to H. S. Sullivan, Karen Horney, Erich Fromm, Thomas French, Clara Thompson, Sandor Rado, Theodore Reik, and Abraham Kardiner; as well as the existentialists Frankl, Binswanger and Sartre; and still others, including Freud (Ellenberger, 1970, pp. 637–645). Ellenberger notes "a collective denial of Adler's work and the systematic attribution of anything coined by him to other authors. We have numerous instances of psychoanalysts picking up some of Adler's most original findings and asserting that they were implicitly contained in Freud's writings, or neglected aspects of Freud's thinking" (p. 645). Rotter (1960) also noted: "Theorists for the last 20 years have been writing books re-expressing many of Adler's concepts without reference to Adler, although sometimes twisting and turning considerably in order to prove that these ideas were accepted by Freud" (p. 383), often "invoking 'neglected aspects' of Freud's writing" (p. 384).

Ellenberger calls this "wide-scale, quiet plagiarism" (1970, p. 646), and believes, "It would not be easy to find another author from whom so much has been borrowed from all sides without acknowledgment than Alfred Adler" (p. 645). Meerloo (1970) admitted, with regard to Adler, that "we are all plagiarists, though we hate to confess it" (p. 14).

When *The Individual Psychology of Alfred Adler,* in which nearly all of Adler's thoughts are recorded with detailed references to the sources, appeared, White (1957) believed, "It will hereafter count as fair play in reviews and criticism to point out that an author's supposedly new ideas come straight from Adler" (p. 3). But this hopeful prediction has not come to pass. Nor has the appearance of Ellenberger's work brought any change. The vigorous Adlerian movement of which we wrote earlier, being essentially on the practical level, has also had little influence on the general literature, although it has undoubtedly been a factor in bringing all of Adler's books into print again, in English as well as in German. Thus it is still not uncommon today that an otherwise well-trained psychologist or psychiatrist will admit he knows little of Adler and never read him in the original, although numerous textbooks on personality theories, specifically, deal with Adler at length and quite adequately.

Ellenberger (1970) attempts to explain this Adler paradox, in comparison to the recognition and prestige conceded to Freud, partly on the basis of their respective personalities. Freud was imposing, well-groomed, lived in the best residential quarter, kept several servants, acquired university titles, was a master of

German prose, and the founder of "a science bent on discovering the mysteries of the soul." Adler was unassuming, lived in a more bourgeois residential area with only one servant, was refused a university title, wrote in ordinary style, and promoted a rational, commonsense psychology with immediate practical application (p. 647).

Will the situation continue as it is, or will there be a change toward adequate general recognition of Adler? Opinions differ. Interestingly, Adler (1933) was inclined toward the first alternative. He wrote: "Individual Psychology is born of this age and will have a lasting influence on the thought, poetry and dreams of humanity. It will win many adherents who clearly understand its value, and still more who will hardly know the names of its pioneers."

The second alternative, growing recognition of Adler in the future, is taken by Gardner Murphy (1970). He believes that "There will be more and more recognition and application of the basic Adlerian conception of the need of the living individual to fulfill and complete itself in an environment which can be less competitive and less hostile; less impersonal; more and more genuine and socially meaningful." This view is shared by Sahakian (1970), who believes, "The psychology of Adler is due for a . . . resurgence, owing to a renewed appreciation of the viability of its profundity and originality" (p. 15). Finally, there is the word by Wilder (1970): "The chapter 'Alfred Adler' is not closed yet in the history of mankind" (p. 460).

Our hope is with these last three predictions. A full recognition of Adler would greatly facilitate an understanding of all personality theory and psychotherapy, in addition to what his theory still has to offer on its own, and would thus be of great benefit to all.

Annotated Bibliography

Primary Sources

Adler, A. *The Neurotic Constitution: Outlines of a Comparative Individualistic Psychology and Psychotherapy* (1912). Translated by B. Glueck and J. E. Lind. New York: Moffat, Yard, 1917.

This is Adler's most important book, and the only one not based on a series of lectures or a collection of separate papers. In it he developed his inferiority-superiority dynamics, striving for enhancement of self-esteem which in the neurotic takes the form of an exaggerated "masculine protest," where "I want to be a real man," striving for personal power, becomes the guiding fiction. In contrast to the normal guiding fiction, that of the patient is based on an accentuated and dogmatized antithetical mode of apperception. Unfortunately, the translation is poor, beginning with the title, the correct translation of which would be: "The Nervous Character: Principles of a Comparative Individual Psychology and Psychotherapy."

Adler, A. *The Individual Psychology of Alfred Adler: A Systematic Presentation in Selections from His Writings.* Edited by H. L. and R. R. Ansbacher. New York: Basic Books, 1956.

This is an anthology of all of Adler's writings from 1907 to 1937, designed to make his contributions to theory and practice available in a systematic and authentic form. The first two chapters present Adler's writings between 1907 and 1911, most of which are to date not available anywhere else in English. The six following chapters present Adler's personality theory proper. Chapters 9 to 14 deal with psychopathology, psychotherapy, and personality appraisal; Chapters 15 and 16, with developmental psychology and treatment of the problem child; Chapter 17, with crime and related disorders; Chapter 18, with general life problems; and Chapter 19, with problems of social psychology. The Introduction by the editors compares Adler's theory with other theories.

Adler, A. *Superiority and Social Interest: A Collection of Later Writings.* Edited by H. L. and R. R. Ansbacher. Evanston, Ill.: Northwestern University Press, 1964.

This second anthology, supplementing the first, presents Adler's significant later writings which had heretofore not appeared in book form. It contains 21 papers by Adler, with 17 dating between 1931 and 1937 and 9 being original translations. Part I deals with general assumptions and principles, Part II with theory of neurosis, Part III with case discussions and techniques of treatment, and Part IV with various psychological disturbances. Part V consists of Adler's essay on religion. Part VI is a biographical essay on Adler by Carl Furtmüller. Part VII is the complete bibliography of Adler's writings.

Adler, A. *The Practice and Theory of Individual Psychology* (1920). Translated by P. Radin. Totowa, N.J.: Littlefield, Adams & Co., 1968.

A collection of 28 papers published between 1909 and 1920 covering all important aspects of Adler's theories up to that time. Included are important articles on homosexuality, compulsion neurosis, dream interpretation, the unconscious, depression, prostitution, and wayward children.

Adler, A. *Understanding Human Nature* (1927). Translated by W. B. Wolfe. New York: Fawcett Premier Books, 1969.

Adler's best-selling book; addressed to the general reader, based on popular lectures, and widely translated.

Adler, A. *Problems of Neurosis: A Book of Case Histories* (1929). Edited by Philip Mairet. New York: Harper & Row, 1964.

A collection of 37 case discussions interwoven with important theoretical considerations. The book has an introduction by H. L. Ansbacher.

Adler, A. *Social Interest: A Challenge to Mankind* (1933). Translated by John Linton and Richard Vaughan. New York: Capricorn Books, 1964.

This is Adler's last book, presenting his most advanced thinking. Social interest has become the most important concept, and life style has replaced life plan. The German title is *Der Sinn des Lebens,* the translation of which is "The meaning of life." But this could not be used since previously a series of lectures had been published in English entitled *What Life Should Mean to You* (Adler, 1931), which, although very good, has incidentally never been translated into German.

Secondary Source

Mosak, H., & Mosak, B. *A Bibliography for Adlerian Psychology.* New York: Wiley, 1975.

This is a listing of references for Adlerian psychology in the broadest possible sense. It includes, from Adlerian writers, even their smallest contributions in newsletters and reviews, as well as their papers on non-Adlerian topics, and from non-Adlerian writers, their contributions on topics of Adlerian interest. An item by several authors is entered under each name. In all there are nearly 10,000 entries. These are provided with a subject index of 38 pages.

References

Adler, A. *Study of organ inferiority and its psychical compensation: A contribution to clinical medicine.* (S. E. Jeliffe, trans.). New York: Nervous and Mental Disease Publication Co., 1917. (Originally published, 1907.)

Adler, A. Der Aggressionstrieb. In A. Adler, C. Furtmüller, & E. Wexberg (Eds.), *Heilen und Bilden* (2nd ed., pp. 18–25). Munich: Bergmann, 1922. (Originally published, 1908.)

Adler, A. *The neurotic constitution* (B. Glueck & J. E. Lind, trans.). Introduction by William A. White. Freeport, N.Y.: Books for Libraries, 1972. (Originally published, 1912.)

Adler, A. Der nervöse Charakter. In A. Adler & C.

Furtmüller (Eds.), *Heilen und Bilden* (W. Metzger, Ed.; pp. 123–133). Frankfurt am Main: Fischer Taschenbuch, 1973. (Originally published, 1913.)

Adler, A. The homosexual problem. *Alienist and Neurologist,* 1917, *38,* 268–287.

Adler, A. *Praxis und Theorie der Individualpsychologie.* Frankfurt am Main: Fischer Taschenbuch, 1974. (We are referring to the German edition for material not included in the English edition.) (Originally published, 1920.) (a)

Adler, A. *The practice and theory of Individual Psychology.* Totowa, N. J.: Littlefield, Adams, 1969. (Originally published, 1920.) (b)

Adler, A. Marriage as a task. In H. Keyserling (Ed.), *The book of marriage: A new introduction by twenty-four leaders of contemporary thought.* New York: Harcourt, Brace, 1926.

Adler, A. *Understanding human nature.* New York: Fawcett Premier Books, 1969. (Originally published, 1927.) (a)

Adler, A. Individual Psychology. *Journal of Abnormal and Social Psychology,* 1927, *22,* 116–122. (b)

Adler, A. *Individualpsychologie in der Schule.* Frankfurt am Main: Fischer Taschenbuch, 1973. (Originally published, 1929.) (a)

Adler, A. *Problems of neurosis.* New York: Harper & Row, 1964. (Originally published, 1929.) (b)

Adler, A. *The science of living.* Garden City, N.Y.: Doubleday Anchor Books, 1969. (Originally published, 1929.) (c)

Adler, A. Fundamentals of Individual Psychology. *Journal of Individual Psychology,* 1970, *26,* 36–49. (Originally published, 1930.)

Adler, A. *What life should mean to you.* (Originally published, 1931.) New York: Capricorn Books, 1958.

Adler, A. Vorrede. In R. Dreikurs (Ed.), *Einführung in die Individualpsychologie.* Leipzig: Hirzel, 1933.

Adler, A. Prevention of neurosis. *International Journal of Individual Psychology,* 1935, *14,* 3–12.

Adler, A. Psychiatric aspects regarding individual and social disorganization. *American Journal of Sociology,* 1937, *42,* 773–780.

Adler, A. *The Individual Psychology of Alfred Adler: A systematic presentation in selections from his writings* (H. L. & R. R. Ansbacher, Eds.). New York: Basic Books, 1956.

Adler, A. *Superiority and social interest: A collection of later writings* (H.L. & Rowena R. Ansbacher, Eds.). Evanston, Ill.: Northwestern University Press, 1964.

Adler, A., & Furtmüller, C. (Eds.). *Heilen und Bilden.* Frankfurt am Main: Fischer Taschenbuch, 1973. (Originally published, 1914.)

Adler, K. A. Adlerian view of the present-day scene. *Journal of Individual Psychology,* 1970, *26,* 113–121.

Agel, J. First memory. *New York Times Magazine,* October 26, 1975, p. 111.

Ansbacher, H. L. Alfred Adler's place in psychology today. *Internationale Zeitschrift für Individualpsychologie,* 1947, *16,* 97–111.

Ansbacher, H. L. The increasing recognition of Adler.

In A. Adler, *Superiority and social interest* (pp. 3–19). (H. L. & R. R. Ansbacher, Eds.). Evanston, Ill.: Northwestern University Press, 1964.

Ansbacher, H. L. Sensus privatus versus sensus communis. *Journal of Individual Psychology*, 1965, *21*, 48–50. (a)

Ansbacher, H. L. The structure of Individual Psychology. In B. B. Wolman (Ed.), *Scientific psychology* (pp. 340–364). New York: Basic Books, 1965. (b)

Ansbacher, H. L. The concept of social interest. *Journal of Individual Psychology*, 1968, *24*, 131–149.

Ansbacher, H. L. Alfred Adler and humanistic psychology. *Journal of Humanistic Psychology*, 1971, *11*, 53–63. (a)

Ansbacher, H. L. Alfred Adler and G. Stanley Hall: Correspondence and general relationship. *Journal of the History of the Behavioral Sciences*, 1971, *7*, 337–352. (b)

Ansbacher, H. L. (Ed.). Religion and Individual Psychology. *Journal of Individual Psychology*, 1971, *27*, 3–49. (c)

Ansbacher, H. L. The first critique of Freud's metapsychology: An extension of George S. Klein's "Two theories or one?" *Bulletin of the Menninger Clinic*, 1974, *38*, 78–84. (a)

Ansbacher, H. L. Goal-oriented Individual Psychology: Alfred Adler's theory. In A. Burton (Ed.), *Operational theories of personality* (pp. 99–142). New York: Brunner/Mazel, 1974. (b)

Ansbacher, H. L. Individual Psychology. In S. Arieti, (Ed.), *American handbook of psychiatry* (2nd ed.), Vol. 1 (pp. 789–808). New York: Basic Books, 1974. (c)

Ansbacher, R. R. Intentionality and care (Review of *Love and Will* by Rollo May). *Journal of Individual Psychology*, 1970, *26*, 230–233.

Asch, S. E. *Social psychology*. New York: Prentice-Hall, 1952.

Batt, C. E. Mexican character: An Adlerian interpretation. *Journal of Individual Psychology*, 1969, *25*, 183–201.

Baxter, J. C., Horton, D. L., & Wiley, R. E. Father identification as a function of mother-father relationship. *Journal of Individual Psychology*, 1964, *20*, 167–171.

Becker, E. Adler and the modern world (Review of *Adler's place in psychology* by L. Way). *Journal of Individual Psychology*, 1963, *19*, 83–89.

Becker, E. Tribute to Alfred Adler. *Journal of Individual Psychology*, 1970, *26*, 169.

Beecher, W. Industrial relations in the light of Individual Psychology. *American Journal of Individual Psychology*, 1955, *11*, 123–130.

Berger, E. M. Antithetical thinking in personality problems. *Journal of Individual Psychology*, 1964, *20*, 32–37.

Biller, H. B. Sex-role uncertainty and psychopathology. *Journal of Individual Psychology*, 1973, *29*, 24–25.

Birnbaum, F. Frankl's existential psychology from the viewpoint of Individual Psychology. *Journal of Individual Psychology*, 1961, *17*, 162–166.

Bottome, P. *Alfred Adler: Portrait from life*. New York: Vanguard, 1957.

Brink, T. L. The case of Hitler: an Adlerian perspective on psychohistory. *Journal of Individual Psychology*, 1975, *31*, 23–31.

Bronowski, J. *The ascent of man*. Boston: Little, Brown, 1973.

Brown, C. *Manchild in the promised land*. New York: New American Library, Signet, 1971. (Originally published, 1965.)

Burt, F. D. William Somerset Maugham: An Adlerian interpretation. *Journal of Individual Psychology*, 1970, *26*, 64–82.

Chaplin, J. P. The presidential assassins: A confirmation of Adlerian theory. *Journal of Individual Psychology*, 1970, *26*, 205–212.

Clark, K. B. Implications of Adlerian theory for an understanding of civil rights problems and action. *Journal of Individual Psychology*, 1967, *23*, 181–190.

Dreikurs, R. *Psychology in the classroom*. New York: Harper, 1957.

Dreikurs, R. (with Vicki Soltz). *Children: The challenge*. New York: Duell, Sloan and Pearce, 1964.

Dreikurs, R. *Psychodynamics, psychotherapy, and counseling*. Chicago: Alfred Adler Institute, 1973. (Originally published, 1967.)

Dreikurs, R. *Understanding your children: Study guidebook*. (J. A. & N. M. Peterson, Eds.). Burlington, Vt.: Vermont Educational Television, University of Vermont, 1969.

Dreikurs, R. *Counseling the adolescent: Guidebook*. (J. A. & N. M. Peterson, Eds.). Burlington, Vt.: Vermont Educational Television, University of Vermont, 1971.

Dreikurs, R., Corsini, R. J., Lowe, R., & Sonstegard, M. *Adlerian family counseling: A manual for counseling centers*. Eugene: University of Oregon Press, 1959.

Dreikurs, R., Gould, S., & Corsini, R. J. *Family council*. Chicago: Regnery, 1974.

Ellenberger, H. F. Alfred Adler and Individual Psychology. In *The discovery of the unconscious* (pp. 571–656). New York: Basic Books, 1970.

Ellis, A. Tribute to Alfred Adler. *Journal of Individual Psychology*, 1970, *26*, 11–12.

Eysenck, H. J., & Rachman, S. *The causes and cures of neurosis: An introduction to modern behavior therapy*. London: Routledge and Kegan Paul; San Diego: Knapp, 1965.

Fanon, F. *Black skin; white masks*. New York: Grove Press, 1967.

Farberow, N. L., & Shneidman, E. S. (Eds.). *The cry for help*. New York: McGraw-Hill, 1961.

Ferguson, E. D. Adlerian concepts in contemporary psychology: The changing scene. *Journal of Individual Psychology*, 1968, *24*, 150–156.

Ford, D. H., & Urban, H. B. *Systems of psychotherapy*. New York: Wiley, 1963.

Frankl, V. E. Tribute to Alfred Adler. *Journal of Individual Psychology*, 1970, *26*, 12.

Freud, S. On the history of the psychoanalytic movement. In *Collected Papers*. Vol. 1 (pp. 287–359). London: Hogarth, 1953. (Originally published, 1914.)

Freud, S. *A general introduction to psychoanalysis*. Garden City, N. Y.: Garden City Publishers, 1943. (Originally published, 1917.)

Freud, S. *Group psychology and the analysis of the ego*. New York: Liveright, 1949. (Originally published, 1921.)

Freudenberg, S. *Erziehungs-und Heilpädagogische Beratungsstellen*. Leipzig: Hirzel, 1928.

Furtmüller, C. Alfred Adler: A biographical essay. In A. Adler, *Superiority and social interest* (pp. 311–393). Evanston, Ill.: Northwestern University Press, 1964.

George, A. L. Power as a compensatory value for political leaders. *Journal of Social Issues*, 1968, *24*, 29–49.

George, A. L., & George, J. L. *Woodrow Wilson and Colonel House*. New York: John Day, 1956.

Goldfried, M. R. Feelings of inferiority and the depreciation of others: A research review and theoretical reformulation. *Journal of Individual Psychology*, 1963, *19*, 27–48.

Haley, J. *Strategies of psychotherapy*. New York: Grune & Stratton, 1963.

Hall, C. S., & Lindzey, G. *Theories of personality*. New York: Wiley, 1957.

Holt, R. R. A review of some of Freud's biological assumptions and their influence on his theories. In N. S. Greenfield & W. C. Lewis (Eds.), *Psychoanalysis and current biological thought* (pp. 93–124). Madison: University of Wisconsin Press, 1965.

Irving, J. *The Catcher in the Rye*: An Adlerian interpretation. *Journal of Individual Psychology*, 1976, *32*, 81–92.

Kankeleit, O. 5. Internationaler Kongress für Individualpsychologie in Berlin, vom 26. bis 28. September 1930. *Archiv für Psychiatrie und Nervenkrankheiten*, 1931, *93*, 261–336.

Kelly, G. A. *The psychology of personal constructs* (Vol. 1). New York: Norton, 1955.

Kelly, G. A. Nonparametric factor analysis of personality theories. *Journal of Individual Psychology*, 1963, *19*, 115–147.

Kelman, H. Psychoanalysis and existentialism. In L. Salzman & J. H. Masserman (Eds.), *Modern concepts of psychoanalysis* (pp. 115–126). New York: Philosophical Library, 1962.

Kiell, N. (Ed.). *Psychoanalysis, psychology and literature: A bibliography*. Madison: University of Wisconsin Press, 1963.

Klein, G. S. Two theories or one? *Bulletin of the Menninger Clinic*, 1973, *37*, 102–132.

Klopfer, B. Individualpsychologie, Wissenschaft und Weltanschauung. *Internationale Zeitschrift für Individualpsychologie*, 1925, *3*, 340. (Abstract)

Lasswell, H. D. *Power and personality*. New York: Norton, 1948.

Lefcourt, H. M. Belief in personal control: research and implications. *Journal of Individual Psychology*. 1966, *22*, 185–195.

LeMay, M. L. Birth order and college misconduct. *Journal of Individual Psychology*, 1968, *24*, 167–169.

Long, L. M. K. Alfred Adler and Gordon W. Allport: A comparison on certain topics in personality theory. *American Journal of Individual Psychology*, 1952–1953, *10*, 43–53.

Lowry, R. Psychoanalysis and the philosophy of physicalism. *Journal of the History of the Behavioral Sciences*, 1967, *3*, 156–167.

Maddi, S. R. *Personality theories: A comparative analysis*. Homewood, Ill.: Dorsey Press, 1968.

Mairet, P. Hamlet as a study in Individual Psychology. *Journal of Individual Psychology*, 1969, *25*, 71–88.

Manaster, G. J., & King, M. Early recollections of male homosexuals. *Journal of Individual Psychology*, 1973, *29*, 26–33.

Manaster, G. J., & Perryman, T. B. Early recollections and occupational choice. *Journal of Individual Psychology*, 1974, *30*, 232–237.

Marmor, J. Holistic conception, and points of mild issue. *Journal of Individual Psychology*, 1972, *28*, 153–154.

Marmor, J. Freud's sexual theories 70 years later. *Medical World News, Psychiatry*, 1973, 86–88.

Maslow, A. H. *Toward a psychology of being* (2nd ed.). Princeton, N. J.: Van Nostrand, 1968.

Maslow, A. H. Tribute to Alfred Adler. *Journal of Individual Psychology*, 1970, *26*, 13.

Matson, F. W. *The broken image: Man, science and society*. Garden City, N. Y.: Doubleday-Anchor, 1966. (Originally published, 1964.)

Matson, F. W. What ever became of the Third Force? *American Association of Humanistic Psychology, Newsletter*, 1969, *6*(1), 1 & 14–15.

Mazlish, B. Psychiatry and history. In S. Arieti (Ed.), *American handbook of psychiatry* (2nd ed. Vol. 1, pp. 1034–1045). New York: Basic Books, 1974.

McLaughlin, J. J., & Ansbacher, R. R. Sane Ben Franklin. An Adlerian view of his autobiography. *Journal of Individual Psychology*, 1971, *27*, 189–207.

McReynolds, P. The motives to attain success and to avoid failure: Historical note. *Journal of Individual Psychology*, 1968, *24*, 157–161.

Meerloo, J. A. M. Tribute to Alfred Adler. *Journal of Individual Psychology*, 1970, *26*, 14.

Mill, J. S. Utilitarianism. In *Utilitarianism, liberty, and representative government* (pp. 1–80). New York: Dutton, 1951. (Originally published, 1863.)

Miller, N. E., & Dollard, J. *Social learning and imitation*. New Haven, Conn.: Yale University Press, 1941.

Minton, H. L. Contemporary concepts of power and Adler's views. *Journal of Individual Psychology*, 1968, *24*, 46–55.

Montagu, A. Social interest and aggression as potentialities. *Journal of Individual Psychology*, 1970, *26*, 17–31.

Mosak, H. H., & Mosak, B. *A bibliography for Adlerian psychology*. New York: Wiley, 1975.

Mosher, D. L. The influence of Adler on Rotter's social

learning theory of personality. *Journal of Individual Psychology*, 1968, *24*, 33–45.

Mowrer, O. H. Comments on Trude Weiss-Rosmarin's "Adler's psychology and the Jewish tradition." *Journal of Individual Psychology*, 1959, *15*, 128–129.

Munroe, R. L. *Schools of psychoanalytic thought*. New York: Dryden, 1955.

Murphy, G. Tribute to Alfred Adler. *Journal of Individual Psychology*, 1970, *26*, 14–15.

Neuringer, C. Validation of the cognitive aspects of Adler's theory of suicide. *Journal of Individual Psychology*, 1974, *30*, 59–64.

Nunberg, H., & Federn, E. (Eds.) *Minutes of the Vienna Psychoanalytic Society, Vol. 1, 1906–1908*. New York: International Universities Press, 1962.

O'Connell, W. E. Sensitivity training and Adlerian theory. *Journal of Individual Psychology*, 1971, *27*, 65–72.

O'Connell, W. E. Social interest in an operant world. *Journal of Individual Psychology*, 1973, *29*, 93. (Abstract)

Orgler, H. *Alfred Adler: The man and his work*. New York: Mentor, 1963.

Ottenheimer, H. Soziale Arbeit. In S. Kaznelson (Ed.), *Juden im Deutschen Kulturbereich* (2nd ed.; pp. 825–857). Berlin: Jüdischer Verlag, 1959. Quoted by H. L. & R. R. Ansbacher, Editorial review, *Journal of Individual Psychology*, 1973, *29*, 204–209.

Papanek, H. Psychotherapy without insight: Group therapy as milieu therapy. *Journal of Individual Psychology*, 1961, *17*, 184–192.

Perry, R. B. *Realms of value: A critique of human civilization*. Cambridge, Mass.: Harvard University Press, 1954.

Ramos, S. *Profile of man and culture in Mexico*. Austin: University of Texas Press, 1962.

Rom, P. The notion of solidarity in the work of Albert Camus. *Journal of Individual Psychology*, 1960, *16*, 146–150.

Rotter, J. B. Psychotherapy. *Annual Review of Psychology*, 1960, *11*, 381–414.

Rotter, J. B. Generalized expectancies for internal versus external control of reinforcement. *Psychological Monographs*, 1966, *80* (1) Whole No. 609.

Rühle-Gerstel, A. Individualpsychologische Autodidaktik. *Internationale Zeitschrift für Individualpsychologie*, 1930, *8*, 52–61.

Rychlak, J. R. *A philosophy of science for personality theory*. Boston: Houghton Mifflin, 1968.

Ryle, A., & Breen, D. Some differences in the personal constructs of neurotics and normal subjects. *British Journal of Psychiatry*, 1972, *120*, 483–489.

Sahakian, W. S. Tribute to Alfred Adler. *Journal of Individual Psychology*, 1970, *26*, 15.

Saul, L. J. *Psychodynamically based psychotherapy*. New York: Science House, 1972.

Shulman, B. H. An Adlerian view of the Schreber case. *Journal of Individual Psychology*, 1959, *15*, 180–192.

Shulman, B. H. An Adlerian view. In M. Kramer et al. (Eds.), *Dream psychology and the new biology of dreaming* (pp. 117–137). Springfield, Ill.: Thomas, 1969.

Sperber, M. *Masks of loneliness: Alfred Adler in perspective* (Krishna Winston, trans.). New York: Macmillan, 1974.

Spiel, O. *Discipline without punishment: An account of a school in action*. London: Faber & Faber, 1962.

Stern, A. *Sartre: His philosophy and existential psychoanalysis* (2nd ed.). New York: Dell, Delta Books, 1967.

Stern, W. *General psychology from the personalistic standpoint*. New York: Macmillan, 1938.

Sundberg, N. D., & Tyler, L. E. *Clinical psychology*. New York: Appleton-Century-Crofts, 1962.

Taft, R. A cluster analysis for Hall and Lindzey. *Contemporary Psychology*, 1958, *3*, 143–144.

Taintor, Z. Birth order and psychiatric problems in boot camp. *American Journal of Psychiatry*, 1970, *126*, 1604–1610.

Taylor, J. A. Early recollections as a projective technique: A review of some recent validation studies. *Journal of Individual Psychology*, 1975, *31*, 213–218.

Teichman, M. Antithetical apperception of family members by neurotics. *Journal of Individual Psychology*, 1971, *27*, 73–75.

Teichman, M., & Foa, U. G. Depreciation and accusation tendencies: Empirical support. *Journal of Individual Psychology*, 1972, *28*, 45–50.

Thorne, F. C. Adler's broad-spectrum concept of man, self-consistency, and unification. *Journal of Individual Psychology*, 1970, *26*, 135–143.

Van Dusen, W. Adler and existence analysis. *Journal of Individual Psychology*, 1959, *15*, 100–111.

Virchow, R. Atoms and individuals. In (Ed.) L. J. Rather. *Disease, life, and man: Selected essays*. Stanford, Calif.: Stanford University Press, 1958. Pp. 120–141. (Originally published, 1862).

Vockell, E. L., Felker, D. W., & Miley, C. H. Birth order literature 1967–1971: Bibliography and index. *Journal of Individual Psychology*, 1973, *29*, 39–53.

Watzlawick, P., Weakland, J., & Fisch, R. *Change: Principles of problem formation and problem resolution*. New York: Norton, 1974.

Werner, H. D. Adler, Freud, and American social work. *Journal of Individual Psychology*, 1967, *23*, 11–18.

Wertheimer, M. *Productive thinking* (Enlarged ed.; Michael Wertheimer, Ed.). New York: Harper, 1959.

White, R. W. Is Alfred Adler alive today? (Review of *The Individual Psychology of Alfred Adler*, H. L. & R. R. Ansbacher, Eds.). *Contemporary Psychology*, 1957, *2*, 1–4.

Wilder, J. Alfred Adler in historical perspective. *American Journal of Psychotherapy*, 1970, *24*, 450–460.

Youngdale, J. M. *Populism: A psychohistorical perspective*. Port Washington, N.Y.: Kennikat Press, 1975.

Analytical psychology, a major school of psychoanalytic thought and clinical practice, seeks to understand the structure, psychodynamics, and unfolding of the human psyche. Founded in 1914 by Carl Jung (1875–1961) as a development from, as well as a reaction against, Freud's position, it widens and deepens orthodox Freudian theory.

Current Jungian theory can be seen from three historical perspectives: (1) the point of view of Dr. Jung's original formulations, (2) how classical concepts which distinguish current Jungians from members of other analytical schools have been modified, amplified, or remained unchanged, and (3) the judgments of relatively objective observers in the field of personality studies. In this chapter, each of these three perspectives will be taken into consideration.

We shall discuss nine important emphases of Jungian personality theory:

Analytical Psychology

**Renaldo J. Maduro and
Joseph B. Wheelwright**

1. Jung's relatively introverted perspective on unconscious mental processes: his lesser attention to external reality per se than to intrapsychic reality, the complicated interaction of internal objects, archetypal images, complexes, and unconscious fantasies.

2. Jung's discovery and elucidation of the importance of an archetypal or transpersonal layer of the psyche—the collective unconscious.

3. Jung's teleological emphasis on the psyche's spontaneous striving *toward* psychological wholeness and self-realization. This life process is purposive and implies active dialogue between ego-consciousness and a *psychodynamic self.*

4. Jung's concept of a self-regulating psyche in which the principle of creative unconscious compensation is at work, often through the polarization and union of symbolic opposites.

5. Analytical psychology's broad definition of psychic energy which does not reduce all of man's instinctual life to only sex or aggression but includes many other instincts, such as creativity.

6. Jung's stress on personality development throughout normal stages of the lifecycle, and on an innate potential or religious instinct for intensified self-actualization in later life, beginning typically with a midlife crisis.

7. Jungian psychology's greater concern for central preoedipal experiences and anxieties involving freedom from the images of the personal and transpersonal mother, than for later developmental issues related to oedipal strivings.

8. Jung's emphasis on the adaptive significance of regression.

9. Jung's discovery and classification of different psychological types — ego attitudes and functions.

CARL JUNG

Introduction

Importance of Theories

Man is distinguished from other primates by his unique capacity to symbolize. Intrinsic to the emergence of *homo symbolicus* is his capacity to organize and give meaning to complex symbolic experiences. From time immemorial, all cultures and individuals have created and maintained belief systems or theories about how, why, and when individuals and groups behave as they do. Anthropologists use the terms *world view* and *ethos* in reference to how diverse peoples think and feel reality is actually or logically constructed.

Every personality theory, like any culture, has its own world view and ethos: a fundamental character or spirit, an underlying sentiment which characterizes the beliefs, customs, or practices of a group of adherents, and an integrative set of dominant assumptions which order and classify experiences. For example, a personality theory may or may not highly value the concept of free will. The existence of an ethos or world view lends psychological security, meaning, and coherence to everyday life and its activities.

Personality theories are assumptions and hypotheses that seek to explain the natural order of things in terms of the extremes of human behavior and individual differences, but also of typical and universal patterns. Useful theories attempt to construct a reality of the psyche which takes both intrapersonal and interpersonal dynamics into account.

The Unconscious

Underlying theoretical suppositions or premises are not always explicit or conscious. They are often unconscious and exist as predispositions to behave in certain consistent and predictable ways over a long period of time. Thus the concept of motivation, conscious and unconscious, assumes great importance. A comprehensive theory of personality considers unconscious, irrational inner promptings important. The study of personality should not attend only to overt behavior, or what is consciously known; it also should investigate covert or implicit culture. It does not overlook vital consideration of powerful unconscious motivating forces. Personality theories differ in the extent to which they are open to

and value unconscious aspects of personality structure, development, and psychodynamics. One may rightly question the validity of any theory which refuses to take the subjective elements of experience into account.

Theories are not necessarily facts. They are abstract speculations and by definition tentative, often innovative. A personality theory has heuristic and orienting value but should never be considered final or closed. If it is to be holistic, practical, and able constantly to generate new hypotheses, it must deal with the following dimensions of human existence: (1) the psychological, conscious and unconscious, (2) the physiological, biological, and constitutional, and (3) the sociocultural context in which personalities develop, grow, and behave.

The Personal Equation

Theoretical systems in psychology cannot escape the elements of a founder's own personal psychology. In this sense, every theory is a personal confession. It reflects a subjective bias, even in the very questions it selects to ask and how it sets out to answer them. If acknowledged openly and taken seriously into account, this personal bias may prove to be a scientific asset rather than a liability.

Jung, for example, derived his theoretical structure from many sources, not the least of which was his own inner life and self-analysis. He wrote from his own conflictual depths, from his own self-healing process, but also from his extensive work with neurotic, borderline, and psychotic patients. For him the existence and manifestation of the deep unconscious was central to everything he wrote or did. His work was characterized by scholarly empiricism, drawing objectively on the observation of dreams and other clinical phenomena. Yet the modern science of analytical psychology, as put forth by Jung, may also be said to respect the irrational, the intuitive, the teleological, and the parapsychological dimensions of human existence.

History

Precursors

Jung's intellectual ties and philosophical foundations are more firmly rooted in what Ellenberger

(1970) calls "psychiatric Romanticism and philosophy of nature" (p. 657), rather than in the period of the Enlightenment. Jung's thought is related to classical Greek and Latin philosophers, to Protestant theological tradition, and to Asian philosophies. More specifically, it is related to Europeans such as Immanuel Kant, Johann Schiller, Friedrich Nietzsche, Sören Kierkegaard, Johann Wolfgang Goethe, and to certain phenomenologists such as Edward Husserl and Martin Heidegger.

Jung was educated in Basel, a city famous for its humanistic tradition, and was familiar with the works of the anthropologist Johann Bachofen and the philosopher Jakob Burkhardt. Bachofen studied symbolism cross-culturally, especially as he thought it reflected the social evolution of mankind. He thought that the earliest stage of human development was matriarchal and that a patriarchal system of social organization evolved later to overthrow an original matriarchy. Jung's psychology (cf. Giegerich, 1975; Neumann, 1954) translates many of Bachofen's social ideas into psychological or symbolic terms relevant to individual ego development.

In addition to Bachofen, Jung's extended readings included the works of two noted German cultural anthropologists, Adolf Bastian and Leo Frobenius. Bastian promoted the idea that the psychic unity of mankind could explain the occurrence of the same rites, myths, and symbols all over the world better than the concept of diffusion could. Bastian's "elementary ideas" in many ways foreshadow what Jung would later call the "archetypes" and what modern anthropologists would return to study as "natural symbols," once the limitations and fallacies of unilinear social evolutionary theory were put aside. In connection with Jung's lifelong interests in cross-cultural studies, the Romantic Georg Friedrich Creuzer deserves mention. Creuzer's work explored symbolism among so-called primitive peoples, giving special psychological attention to the interpretation of complex myths and folktales.

Among Romantic philosophers, who constituted a counterpoint to the Enlightenment's enthronement of reason over emotion, E. T. A. Hoffman, Gotthilf von Schubert, Ignaz Troxler, and Friedrich Scheeling were important precursors of Jung. Four of Jung's predecessors are particularly important as philosophers of the unconscious: (1) Gottfried Leibnitz, who postulated the concept of an irrational unconscious in the 18th century, (2) Carl Gustav Carus, who distinguished three levels of the unconscious, including a "general" universal one that had creative, compensatory, self-healing functions, (3) Arthur Schopenhauer, who in the 1880s emphasized irrational forces at work in man, principally blind sexual forces that are often repressed, and (4) Eduard von Hartmann, who described three levels of unconscious functioning, including an absolute or universal source of images.

Jung matured intellectually at a time when great changes were taking place in psychiatry and neurology. Many of his contemporaries were innovators, and he benefited from them by personal contacts as well as reading. In addition to Eugen Bleuler, Pierre Janet had great influence on Jung. What Janet studied as "psychological automatism," dual personalities, the "function of synthesis," and "subconscious fixed ideas," Jung later called *complexes*. Theodore Flournoy's study of parapsychology aided Jung in similar scholarly endeavors, and it inspired Jung's early interest in the phenomenon of cryptomnesia. Alfred Binet's two types of intelligence became an integral part of Jung's work on introverted and extraverted types. Finally, Jung incorporated much from Alphonse Maeder's work on the teleological function of dreams. Throughout his own work, Jung credits and acknowledges his debt to these and many other men who form the backdrop for his intellectual growth and development, including later influences from Sigmund Freud and Alfred Adler.

Beginnings

Jungian psychology can best be understood through an appreciation of the founder's personal background, especially his childhood experiences, which Jung himself felt were decisive in forming his basic character, scientific attitudes, and psychological interests. From early childhood, Jung was an introvert. In his autobiography (1961) he describes himself as solitary, intellectual, and fascinated by the questions which philosophy, psychology, and theology normally pose.

Because the development of Jung's thought sunk deep roots in philosophical-humanistic soil, the symbolic was just as real to him as the physical. Natural science or rationalism were never enough for him. Jung's fundamental approach to the psyche, based on a coherent humanistic world view, stands at the center of his work throughout his long life, in sharp contrast to Freud's pessimism. Moreover, this difference existed before they collaborated. Jung's relative lack of concern for materialistic and strictly rational interpretations is reflected as early as November 28, 1896, in a talk he gave to fellow medical students at the University of Basel entitled "On the Limits of the Exact Sciences." Concepts drawn from the physical sciences were not ignored by Jung, but as we shall see, he much preferred to emphasize "psychological reality," and he dealt with questions which belonged traditionally to comparative religion, philosophy (e.g., Nietzsche's struggle with the nature of good and evil), and humanistic psychology.

Carl Gustav Jung was born on July 26, 1875, in the small village of Kesswil, Switzerland. He was named after an illustrious and unconventional paternal grandfather, a physician who was interested in mental health, philosophy, classical studies, and poetry. Jung's maternal grandparents were renowned Hebrew scholars, theologians of distinction, and interested in parapsychology. Thus many of Jung's later interests, including creativity in old age, were reflected in his kinship identifications.

Jung's father, a poor country pastor of the Swiss Reformed Church, was devoted to intellectual pursuits and the care of his parishioners. Although Jung experienced him as religiously conventional, he was a classical and oriental scholar, and much of the son's erudition and appreciation for these subjects can no doubt be traced to early contact with his father. Jung experienced his father as irritable, ineffectual, and distant, and his childhood was marked by religious conflicts with his father which persisted into adolescence. These disputes usually ended acrimoniously. It is as though Jung wrestled to come to terms with his father's views versus his own personal discovery of a truly religious attitude toward life for most of his career.

Jung's mother was in many ways a more influential person in his life—perhaps ultimately the source of his emphasis on a creative unconscious and man's universal need to free himself from the potentially engulfing "world of the Mothers." In his autobiography (1961), Jung recalls that his mother was perceived as very strong but also as emotionally ambivalent ("dual") and at times weak, disturbed, and depressed.

Jung reports a singularly lonely and often unhappy childhood in which he had to cope with the severe marital problems of his parents. He would often retreat to the attic or some other solitary place to be alone. He was the oldest child and only son, and intimate relationships with a younger sister do not seem to have figured prominently in his life or to have provided much satisfaction.

After completing secondary school studies, Jung chose to study medicine at the University of Basel. This was made possible by a scholarship which his father, soon to pass away, helped his son secure. Jung was a medical student from 1895 to 1901. During that time he distinguished himself academically among fellow students and decided to specialize in psychiatry. To this end he received a position under the tutelage of the famous psychiatrist Eugen Bleuler at the well-known Burghölzli Psychiatric Hospital in Zurich. Soon after this important and creative relationship began, Jung published his medical dissertation in 1902 entitled, "On the Psychology of So-called Occult Phenomena." This first publication demonstrates originality and insight. In this earliest paper can be found the seeds of central concepts which would later, when more highly developed, cost him his "orthodox" psychoanalytic standing.

Jung took a leave of absence to study hypnosis with Janet in Paris during the winter of 1902. Upon his return he married, was appointed lecturer in psychiatry at the University of Zurich and, under the influence of Bleuler, resumed his work with patients at Burghölzli, developing psychological tests and measurements, principally his Word Association Test. These experiments added to his rapidly growing fame. Prior to meeting Freud, Jung's position as one of Europe's leading psychiatrists was secure, his private practice was flourishing, and he had already impressed his colleagues as being unusually brilliant.

In 1906 Jung first corresponded with Freud and thereafter took up the cause of psychoanalysis with outstanding vigor. This meant defending Freud and his theories against public and professional outcry, as well as teaching and promulgating the particular orientation of the Zurich school, which always differed somewhat from that of the Viennese inner circle. In the same year Jung visited Freud for the first time in Vienna, his well-known psychoanalytic interpretation of schizophrenic process was published as the *Psychology of Dementia Praecox* (1907). A copy was presented to Freud, who was extremely impressed by it.

The first Freud-Jung meeting ushered in six years of close collaboration in the discovery and development of psychoanalysis. Jung never relinquished his profound admiration for Freud as a person and for his discoveries. The enthusiasm was mutual: Freud considered Jung his "successor" for life and a "crown prince." The nature of this relationship has until recently been known mainly through Freudian accounts, as a result of which Jung's break with Freud was generally viewed as heresy. With the publication of the Freud-Jung letters, the father-son nature of the relationship (Freud was 19 years older than Jung) has been clarified, as well as the fact that Jung had already developed a clear independent orientation to the unconscious which differed significantly from Freud's, even before they met (Adler, 1973; McGuire, 1974).

By 1909 Jung had achieved an international reputation. With Freud, he traveled to the United States to lecture on the controversial science of psychoanalysis at Clark University. Jung was so devoted to the psychoanalytic movement that he gave up his post at Burghölzli, and from 1909 to 1913 involved himself deeply in organizational affairs. Jung was the first president of the International Psychoanalytic Association and managing editor of the very first psychoanalytic journal, the *Jahrbuch*. He lectured extensively on psychoanalysis and taught courses at the University of Zurich.

Although this period is characterized by Jung's leadership, passionate involvement, and constant defense of and devotion to Freud, there was from the very start a fundamental misunderstanding. Ellenberger (1970) writes: "Freud wanted disciples who would accept his doctrine without reservation. Bleuler and Jung saw their relationship as a collaboration that left both sides free" (p. 669).

For a time divergencies between Jung and Freud remained unchecked, and Jung continued to champion Freud. However, with Jung's *Symbols of Transformation* (1911) there was a decisive break. In the same year Jung went to New York to lecture on psychoanalysis, declaring that his own version of psychoanalysis was a further development of Freud's ideas. The rift grew wider as Freud's suspicions and anger grew, and when the International Association met in Munich in October of 1913, Jung resigned as president and as editor of the *Jahrbuch*.

There followed six years (1913–19) during which Jung suffered profoundly. Jung describes this obscure period of introversion or creative illness in his autobiography (1961). After this period of intense mental turmoil and self-analysis, Jung emerged with increased strength and creative vigor.

The end of this period is marked by the publication in 1921 of what some consider his most important work, *Psychological Types.*

After 1914, Jung became the founder and leader of his own psychoanalytic school of thought, which he called Analytical Psychology. For the rest of his life he devoted himself to teaching, study, and to his family of five children and a wife, Emma, who became an analyst in her own right. He was a dedicated psychotherapist with a huge practice. Although his later life was characterized by increased interiority, he also took delight and scholarly interest in travel to England, America (the Pueblo Indians), black Africa, and Asia.

Before his death Jung experienced increased world recognition for his creative experimental genius and his courageous pursuit of knowledge in previously unexplained areas of the mind. Jung died in his home at Küsnacht, Zurich, on June 6, 1961, at the age of 85.

Current Status

Jung may be considered one of the most revolutionary and creative thinkers of modern time concerning psychoanalytic theory and related subjects. Although a small group of Jung's students constituted a Psychology Club in Zurich as early as 1916, Jung himself was not quick to encourage formal Jungian institutions. Until 1946 he remained ambivalent and reluctant about founding training institutes. In the light of an accelerating rediscovery of Jung and his analytic theories today, the increasing number of such organizations reflects greater structure and activity in this area since his death.

The number of Jungian analysts has remained relatively small. In 1976 about 400 certified Jungian analysts belonged to the International Association of Analytical Psychology. At present 14 autonomous Jungian analytic training institutes function in England, France, Germany, Israel, Italy, Switzerland, and the United States. Additional certified analysts belong to smaller societies or are individual members of the international association in at least 20 additional countries, including Australia, Belgium, Brazil, Canada, Finland, India, Japan, Korea, the Netherlands, Sweden, and Venezuela. Training institutes in the United States have joined the National Accreditation Association for Psychoanalysis. Some Jungians belong to the liberal, all-inclusive American Academy of Psychoanalysis, which includes followers of Erich Fromm, Karen Horney, Harry S. Sullivan, and others who share a belief in the validity and importance of the unconscious.

Although training procedures vary widely, the heart of Jungian analytic training everywhere is a lengthy personal-training analysis, plus years (usually four) of didactic seminars, written and oral examinations, controlled case supervision, tutorial work, and, in most places, a clinical dissertation.

Jungian institutes traditionally train duly recognized clinicians at the doctoral level in medicine or clinical psychology (M.D. or Ph.D.), although, as with other schools, clinical social workers and exceptional others complete the trainee picture. From beginning to end, the average length of time invested by an individual in Jungian training amounts to six to eight years. Candidates at various stages of the training process may join the International Association of Jungian Trainees and Newly Qualified Analysts which meets once a year in a different part of the world.

Although Jungian psychology has been taught in major colleges and universities for many years, not until recently does the world seem to have caught up with Jung. Some contemporary interest in Jung is superficial and stems from so-called occult or mystical notions which get confused with Jung's concept of experiences of the self. More significant is the serious attention being given to Jung's ideas which were so ahead of his time and which are being rediscovered by psychoanalysts of many schools. In many scientific quarters, the shift has been from Freud to include Jung (cf. Frey-Rohn, 1975).

Particular theoretical *emphases* characterize Jungian analytical theory. This chapter draws attention to particular aspects of modern depth psychology which seem, in our view, to relate most cogently to selected theoretical emphases or assertions stressed early by Jung and his students. Given the great areas of overlap with basic psychoanalytic theory as developed by pioneers in this field, a comparative approach may prove useful to the student considering an approach to unconscious mental processes which differs, in some respects radically, from so-called "orthodox" analytical theory. Readers interested in greater in-depth understanding of analytical psychology are referred to the 19 volumes of *The Collected Works of C. G. Jung*; his autobiography, *Memories, Dreams, Reflections*; *The Library of Analytical Psychology*; the *Journal of Analytical Psychology*; *Spring, An Annual of Archetypal Thought*; *Psychological Perspectives*; and other publications dealing with the modern science of analytical psychology available to the scholarly public. The items in the Annotated Bibliography at the end of this chapter are also recommended.

Similar Theories

Jungian theory cannot be discussed without reference to basic Freudian hypotheses, since there are obvious links to a body of cornerstone assumptions, especially in relation to psychopathology, from which Jungians differ little if at all (e.g., the unconscious, resistance, defenses, transference-countertransference, dream analysis, and so on). In important ways, however, Jung went beyond Freud, and his psychology differs starkly from core psychoanalytic assumptions. For instance, while both schools agree that dream analysis is central to the analytic process, the Jungian position on dream interpretation is extremely different from the Freudian wish-fulfillment theory (cf. Jung, 1916a, 1934b, 1945a). It follows logically, therefore, that techniques for dream analysis would also differ significantly (Alex, 1971; Maduro & Martinez, 1974; Zinkin, 1969).

Among other schools or theorists, the ideas of Erich Fromm, Carl Rogers, Abraham Maslow, Melanie Klein, Erik Erikson, and Harry S. Sullivan come closest to rephrasing, and at times creatively extending, original Jungian formulations. Adler's stress on future-oriented life "goals"—on the importance of teleological processes in the psyche—is a view strongly supported and held in common by Jungians. Jungian theory is also in basic harmony with the developmental theories of Erikson and other ego psychologists, to the extent to which they are willing to accept the Jungian idea of the dynamic emergence of ego consciousness out of the unconscious, and to address themselves to health as well as psychopathology.

As is true of concepts in other analytical schools, "classical" Jungian theory has undergone constant revision and change (Adler, 1967). This occurred with Jung during his lifetime, and later among neo-Jungians working with other schools, in particular the Kleinian school in Britain and neo-Freudian ego-psychology in the United States. Over the past 30 years, aspects of Kleinian theory have become indistinguishable from neo-Jungian psychology. These concepts (discussed later) include projective identification, the depressive position, part-object psychology in the first year of life, internal object relations, and the functions of a death instinct. New lines of direction have continued to expand theoretical horizons—to synthesize and differentiate where points of theory, technique, and clinical practice converge to provide contexts for creative and fruitful dialogue. This process has been one of complementary articulation. Neo-Freudian, Frommian, and Kleinian schools in particular have come to agree with many of Jung's original formulations which, until recently, have been misinterpreted or have seemed alien to them. The situation was not helped by the facts that Jung himself often presented his theories abstrusely, and many of his introverted students have chosen not to enter the mainstream of psychoanalysis or to define their positions.

Assertions

Development

1. PERSONALITY IS INFLUENCED BY THE EXISTENCE AND POTENTIAL ACTIVATION OF A COLLECTIVE TRANSPERSONAL UNCONSCIOUS.

Jung's general concept of a collective unconscious in which archetypes exist as potential symbols grew out of his practicing the classical psychoanalytic method. In day-to-day analytic work, gradually, his awareness of a deeper transpersonal level of the psyche was sharpened and further corroborated by personal experiences in self-analysis. His understanding of the collective unconscious was rounded out by many years of scholarly research into the basic underlying structures and functions of geographically widespread myths and symbolic motifs. As a result of his own confrontations with unconscious mental processes, distinct part-personalities or categories of human experience which could not be reduced to personal sexual causes presented themselves. He discovered motifs which could not be attributed to individual experiences alone. In Jungian theory, therefore, a critical topographical and structural distinction is made between the personal and the collective unconscious, for purposes of exposition but not necessarily in practice. Before proceeding to a discussion of psychodynamic maturational processes from a modern Jungian perspective, we will first say something about the structure of the psyche.

Jung's structural model includes four main entities: (1) a psychodynamic self which includes activities of a personal and a collective unconscious, (2) complexes, (3) the ego, and (4) archetypes. They are defined in the Glossary, and during the course of our discussion they will be clarified further.

2. UNCONSCIOUS ELEMENTS UNACCEPTABLE TO THE EGO ARE LOCATED IN THE PERSONAL UNCONSCIOUS.

The personal unconscious may be equated roughly with the Freudian "repressed unconscious." Although Jungians do not want to be limited to this concept of the unconscious, Jung's theory locates painful experiences, anxiety-laden fantasies, feelings, and thoughts unacceptable to the ego and the superego in the personal unconscious. Here they remain repressed, suppressed, isolated, denied, "forgotten," split off, and dangerously unrecognized by ego-consciousness. Experiences which have never been strong enough to make a significant impression on the ego also exist in this region of the mind, but, like the contents of Freud's preconscious region, they are accessible to consciousness. During deep analysis, they are remembered, repeated, and can be integrated or worked through, so that large portions of this material may be assimilated and made conscious through confrontation and synthesis. Jung calls this area of the mind the *shadow,* a global term with both personal and transpersonal connotations. In addition to standing for the denied or projected "otherness," the shadow can be considered the archetype of primary evil or moral "badness." The concept of the shadow, however, need not be restricted to evil or to fantasies contrary to superego demands (repressed for the sake of ego ideals); it can refer simply to whatever natural potentials are undeveloped and relatively undifferentiated in the psyche. In this sense the shadow has great value. Here *complexes* located in the personal unconscious assume great importance.

3. COMPLEXES ARE STRUCTURED AND ENERGIZED OVER TIME AROUND AN ACTIVATED ARCHETYPAL IMAGE.

Jung's free association experiments after the turn of the century drew heavily on the scientific methodology of his day. He had first impressed Freud with his discovery of unconscious affect-toned "complexes" which belong essentially to the personal unconscious. Later in his analytic career, however, he extended this concept to include the archetype as the "nuclear element" or energy center of any given complex. Complexes may be seen, therefore, as containing archetypal cores (affect-images) which, when activated, draw personal experiences to them. The ego is in constant "dialogue" with the unconscious via its encounters with this inner world of interrelated complexes. Because this dialogue involves fantasy transactions between the ego and complexes which are personal *but rooted in the archetypal psyche,* it is only partially accurate to equate Jung's "personal unconscious" with Freud's repressed unconscious.

The ego is either strengthened or weakened by contact with the unconscious in its encounters with the complexes. The ego may relate to a complex in four different ways: (1) by remaining completely *unconscious* of it, (2) by *identification* or "possession," (3) by *projection,* and (4) by *confrontation* which alone leads to assimilation and growth.

Complexes are always *bipolar* in two senses. First they have both a "negative" and a "positive" valence and are always potentially growth restricting or growth fostering when activated. Second, when activated, a complex always relates structurally to another complex. Complexes are not randomly dispersed in the unconscious. In terms of inner-world relations, for example, the mother complex is paired and interacts with a daughter or son (child) complex, father complex, and so on (Perry, 1970). If a mother complex is predominantly negative, when activated ("tapped") it may overwhelm the ego. The goal of Jungian psychoanalysis would be, in this case, to weaken or depotentiate the negative effect of complexes through analysis of transference and the internalization of a "corrective emotional experience" with a "good" mother-person. During development, the child or adult is constantly "taking in" (introjecting) experiences from contact with significant others, referred to in Jungian theory as "external objects." The individual, simultaneously, puts out (projects) the state of his inner world, his cast of characters, the "internal objects" who inhabit him. External objects taken in and added to an ever-changing sense of inner-world reality, however, are not totally accurate perceptions of external reality. On the contrary, introjections and identifications are altered or colored to some extent by the individual's preexisting complexes, internal objects, archetypal images, and instinctual needs. The structuring (internalization) of an inner world is therefore intricate and subtle, utilizing complicated projective-introjective processes assumed to be operative at birth.

The dominant role of complexes as feeling-toned groups of internal objects or representations in the unconscious is a central part of Jungian theory. An understanding of how unconscious complexes are structured, internalized, energized (cathected), activated, built up, and developed over time has been greatly augmented by developments in modern internal-object relations theory. The central position given to complexes by Jung has changed little with time. In Jung's words: "The individual representations are combined according to the different laws of association (similarity, coexistence, etc.), but are selected and grouped into larger combinations [fields of interaction] by an affect" (1907, p. 40).

Complexes belong to the basic structure and psychic energy distribution system of the psyche which functions on the principle of energic balance or homeostasis. Jungian analysis seeks to make conscious and then to integrate energy contained in the complexes—especially those that promote dissociation and impair the unity of the psyche. A complex can remain autonomous, either because it is totally unconscious and therefore not known to the ego, even by the symptoms it causes, or because even though it is "known" intellectually, resistances are still great enough to prevent assimilation into consciousness of the disturbing affects associated with the complex and its core, an archetypal image. Complexes, therefore, can remain independent, split off from the integrating ego, and be harmful. Jacobi (1959) describes how simple conscious knowledge of a complex's existence may be futile: "the complex's harmful action will continue until we succeed in 'discharging' it, or until the excess of psychic energy stored up in it is transferred to another gradient, i.e., until we succeed in assimilating it emotionally" (p. 10).

In therapy, growth-inhibiting complexes must be weakened. The first step in the treatment process is to make complexes conscious and therefore accessible to the synthetic functions of the ego. It is not enough to know about them intellectually; they must be experienced and lived through in the transference during analysis. In such a setting the infantile roots, the genetic development, and the bipolarity of the positive or negative aspects of complexes are thrown into clear relief, worked through, and understood in relation to the analyst, who may be said to "incarnate" the archetypal image. Once brought to conscious attention, a complex and its historical development can be understood. This usually occurs only after the analysis of defenses and resistances to such insights has been sufficiently dealt with. Such understanding makes a complex less autonomous, uncontrollable, and compulsive. Correction, disidentification of the ego with

a complex, new adaptive behaviors, and transformation are possible once a person is in dialogue with the internal figures that inhabit him. In connection with this process, dream analysis and the helpful collaboration of the analyst are central.

Any general understanding of the archetypes of the collective unconscious begins with an appreciation of the *indivisibility* of the personal and collective aspects of the psyche (cf. Neumann, 1959; Williams, 1963). This indivisibility is perhaps conceptualized most lucidly in terms of how personal-transpersonal elements come together in the formation, building up, activation, or weakening of innumerable complexes in the personal unconscious during the course of normal development.

From another point of view, the personal unconscious is closer structurally to the ego in the psyche than to the collective unconscious. The latter may be seen as an extension of the personal unconscious and outside the comprehension of the ego much of the time. The ego itself, on the border (so to speak) between the personal unconscious and external reality, is the center of consciousness, although important portions of the ego are also unconscious. The ego is not made up only of conscious perceptions, feelings, thoughts, and memories—especially when unconscious material related to the developmentally early "body ego" is activated during analysis and psychotherapy (cf. Jung, 1951), and when normal or pathological unconscious ego defense mechanisms are called into play (Stein, 1962).

4. THE EGO MEDIATES BETWEEN THE UNCONSCIOUS AND THE OUTSIDE WORLD.

The ego represents the vantage point of consciousness, the complex factor to which all conscious contents are related. It is located conceptually between the unconscious inner world and the external world, and it mediates, partakes of, and copes with unknown stimuli from each of these areas. Jungian theory asserts that a strong, well-structured ego is the result of ideal normal development. A strong ego encounters the archetypes as they enter into the structural arrangement of complexes located in the personal unconscious.

A person with a healthy, strong sense of *ego identity* experiences himself as having continuity, sameness, individuality, and autonomy over time; likewise he experiences a sense of firm inner and outer ego boundaries which are flexible and relatively permeable when appropriate, and he has a feeling that he can contain and locate what is "inside" *as distinct from* what exists separately "outside." At birth the newborn perceives only sensations originating within his body. Only gradually does he turn from inner stimuli to outer perception, from fusion to dialogue.

As the conscious point of reference in the psyche as a whole, the ego rests on both somatic and psychic beginnings. In the earliest nondifferentiated stage of life, the ego is not separate from the self. In a global, total sense, the baby does not distinguish what is "I" from what is "not-I," the ego from the self, let alone any precise perceptions of his environment (Tate, 1961). In early life only fragments of ego-consciousness exist. In the first few weeks and months of life the infant remains in a state of what Jung has variously called "primitive identity" or "participation mystique" with the mother, or with parts of her body (i.e., the breast or nipple, a *"part-object"*). This part-object state of ego boundary fusion is called *projective identification*. Gradually, as an individual separates out of this nursing couple, projective identification states change to include gradual perception of the mother as a whole person (simultaneously good *and* bad), rather than as a part-object experienced as a split "all or nothing" person (idealized *or* persecuting). These "all or nothing" primitive affects of love and hate in relation to images of the inner and outer personal mother integrate substantially as development proceeds. As this occurs, the infant is said to have achieved what Melanie Klein (Segal, 1973) first called the *depressive position* in the first year of life (M. Fordham, 1969a). The depressive position starts in the fourth or fifth month of life and reaches a peak at about seven months. Separation of the ego out of the original state of unconscious identity with the self-mother-breast has taken place. Ego fragments then form a more coherent and organized island around which a vast sea of personal and collective unconscious material exists (cf. Plaut, 1959, 1966, 1974).

In connection with the earliest stages of life, Michael Fordham (1957, 1963, 1965, 1969a,

1971a, 1971b), building on Jung's foundation, has extended Jungian theory. Fordham's seminal work on the complicated processes involving "deintegration" of an innate "primary self" constitutes a major advance not only in Jungian theory but in psychoanalytic theories of the self-concept in general. Fordham's major contributions relate to the ego and its dynamic relationship to the self during infancy and childhood (1976). His focus on "defenses of the self" (1974a) is highly original. His concept of the *primary self*, however, must be cited, *since it is generally assumed in Jungian developmental theory that an integrated self system is primary. It exists in the very beginning. Consequently the infant or fetus is looked on as a unitary self or basic psychosomatic unity out of which the archetypes and the ego are derived. The self, in the sense of a basic undivided wholeness, is precursor of the ego.* Fordham (1961) explains:

> The theory of the original self grew first of all from the empirical observation. Self images could be observed in childhood and could be conjectured in infancy; the conjectures were supported, amongst other indirect evidence, by statistical studies made by Gesell on the appearance of the word "I" in childhood. The theoretical source derived from Jung's idea that the self lies behind ego development, a conception which, applied to infancy and childhood, led me to postulate an original state of the self prior to the appearance of the ego. This would explain the observed phenomena and made it possible to postulate an initial wholeness. The original state was assumed to be a simple integrate without other manifestations than its wholeness. It could be compared with the zygote before it begins to divide. (p. 78)

5. THE SELF REPRESENTS WHOLENESS, AND
    IS AN ORGANIZING ARCHETYPE.

Jung's views of the *self* embrace two fundamental ideas: (1) innate potential wholeness of man, and (2) an ordering, integrating, and organizing archetype. According to the first view, the self system includes not only the ego but also the archetypes; various symbolic forms (e.g., mandala) represent this orginal state of wholeness and integration. Following Jung, until recently, analytical psychologists tended to conceive of the self as a stabilizing, centralizing, and even closed system (Redfearn, 1969). However, Fordham (1972) reflects neo-Jungian theoretical advances when he writes that "exclusive emphasis on stability and organization is not suitable when applied to developing periods of infancy and early childhood" (p. 463). Rather, it is assumed that a dynamic relationship between the self and the ego exists; this relationship, viewed in developmental perspective, involves fluctuating periods throughout the life cycle of integration-deintegration of the primary self. Life-crises states of deintegration are characterized by the spontaneous release of archetypal activity, and the activation of archetypal potential during important developmental phases. (Fordham, 1967).

6.   ARCHETYPES FUNCTION AS ORGANS OF
      THE COLLECTIVE UNCONSCIOUS PSYCHE.

Jung initially used a variety of words, such as *primordial image*, to describe an early and relatively undifferentiated formulation of the archetypal dimension of the psyche, but the word *archetype* appeared in 1919 for the first time. For the remainder of his life, the major focus of his theoretical work and clinical practice was devoted to the serious exploration and elucidation of the role of the collective unconscious, or what he later came to call the *objective psyche* in human development.

From the very beginning Jung widened and deepened Freud's position, which he did not so much dispute, reject, or supplant as go beyond. Jung felt his colleague's views were correct but not comprehensive enough to adequately describe the complicated workings of the mind. He could not accept Freud's exclusive emphasis on sexuality and personal psychobiological determinism.

In the light of Jung's balanced approach to the psyche, a relevant remark made by the anthropologist Clyde Kluckhohn is paraphrased here: *Every man is in certain respects like all other men, like some other men, like no other man.* This statement is particularly helpful to put Jungian psychology and the concept of the archetype into proper perspective. Although Jung never denied the importance of culture and strictly personal life history variables in the development of an individual, he contributed most richly to psychoanalysis by addressing himself to the psyche's phylogenetic heritage and to the psychic unity of mankind. It was Jung's holistic contention that the psyche and the unconscious

cannot be understood without a consideration of the interpenetration of sociocultural, personal, and archetypal (transpersonal) forces. With Jung's approach in mind, Kettner (1967) refers to Kluckhohn and puts it well: "That, in a nutshell, is how an archetype works—a basic theme, recognizable patterns of variation, and the unique individual twist taken in a specific case" (p. 34–35).

Having touched briefly on how, when, and why Jung discovered the importance of the transpersonal psyche, we shall now turn more specifically to questions related to what an archetype is, and when it functions as it does.

Jungian theory holds that the mind is not a *tabula rasa* at birth but that there is an archetypal ground plan built into the structure of the human brain. It would take us too far afield here to discuss modern biology in relation to the theory of archetypes. Such a focus would have to include research on the limbic system and on right-left hemispheres of the brain, modern behavioral genetics, and how natural selection and the mutation of germ plasm are viewed by modern scientists (cf. M. Fordham, 1957; Osterman, 1968). These studies would clearly indicate, moreover, that there need be nothing "mystical" about archetypes, which are inherited predispositions to apperceive typical or nearly universal *situations and figures*. The archetype can further be described as a "system of readiness" to respond to environmental cues, a dynamic nucleus of concentrated psychic energy ready to be actualized, as an affect-image and as an *autonomous*, numinous structual element outside the comprehension of the ego. Fordham (1969a) sheds further light on the problem of defining archetypes.

> Though most studied in their complex symbolic forms, i.e., in dreams, fantasies, mythology, folklore and religion, the essential core that emerges from Jung's work is that an archetype is a psychosomatic entity having two aspects: the one is linked closely with physical organs, the other with unconscious and potential psychic structures. The physical component is the source of libidinal and aggressive "drives"; the psychic one, the origin of those fantasy forms through which the archetype reaches incomplete representation in consciousness. (p. 96)

Although at first Jung considered mainly archetypal images, he later considered patterns of emotions and predispositions to species-specific behavior as well. Jung's concept of the archetype, as developed and refined (cf. Jacobi, 1959), provides for two essential distinctions: (1) *the archetype as such,* and (2) *the archetypal image.* It is important to keep these two distinctions in mind, since Jung's contributions have been greatly misunderstood and misrepresented by confusing these theoretical issues. Misinformed opinion would have it, for example, that actual ideational content is inherited. Although Jung never ruled out such a possibility, he could never accept Freud's strictly Lamarckian concept of a "racial memory."

The Archetype As Such. Archetypes are not inherited ideas or images but are a priori possibilities.

For Jung the "primordial image" or "archetype as such" belonging to the deepest unconscious is an a priori, phylogenetically transmitted predisposition or "readiness" to apperceive a universal, emotional core human experience, myth, or thought-image-fantasy. This "archetype as such" can never be exactly pinpointed or apprehended because it exists in such a primitive formal state. Jung (1947) summarizes his views:

> The archetypal representations (images and ideas) mediated to us by the unconscious should not be confused with the archetype as such. They are very varied structures which all point back to one essentially "irrepresentable" basic form. The latter is characterized by certain formal elements and by certain fundamental meanings, although these can be grasped only approximately. The archetype as such is a psychoid factor that belongs, as it were, to the invisible, ultra-violet end of the psychic spectrum.... It seems to me probable that the real nature of the archetype is not capable of being made conscious, that it is transcendent, on which account I call it psychoid (quasi-psychic). (p. 213)

The Archetypal Image. There is a dynamic relationship between environmental situations and archetypal response. Unlike the archetype as such, the image is a representation already perceived by at least a portion of ego-consciousness: "A primordial image is determined as to its contents only when it becomes conscious and is therefore filled out with the material of con-

scious experience" (Jung, 1938a, p. 79).

Jung's theory stresses the role of culture in activating and symbolically structuring ("clothing") archetypal activity arising from the deep conscious. It follows that the same environmental experience may evoke different archetypal responses and that various environmental factors may evoke the same or similar archetypal responses. To turn again to Jung (1936a): "There are as many archetypes as there are typical situations in life. Endless repetition has engraved these experiences into our psychic constitution, not in the forms of images filled with content, but at first only as *forms without content,* representing merely the possibility of a certain type of perception and action" (p. 48).

The passage above, indicates that Jung considers the archetypes to be innumerable. Yet certain archetypal images, situations, and experiences are more commonly encountered than others during a personal analysis, in the course of individual human development, or in everyday life. They are found in dreams, literature, religious mythologies, art forms, symptoms, and so on. Several examples are presented below.

Symbolic Death and Renewal. A common archetypal situation experienced cross-culturally relates to Jung's emphasis on potentiality in the human psyche for symbolic transformation involving reconstitutive experiences of death and rebirth, and on his extremely positive evaluation of therapeutic regression. For Jung it is clearly the birth of the ego, or part of the ego, which renews the sense of self (feeling centered and whole). Ego-consciousness is reborn, experiences growth, is expanded; it emerges dynamically from a state of projective identification or fusion with a primordial state of unconsciousness (non-ego). This healthy process in later life repeats the earliest separation of the ego from identification and containment in the primary self. The ego feels threatened by death and experiences (perceives) rebirth (Perry, 1961).

The concept of symbolic death and rebirth, as an archetypal/transpersonal motif, came to characterize Jung's overall theoretical approach to man's unconscious, psychological growth during analysis (Jung, 1911, 1940a), as well as patterns of initiation or *rites de passage* (Henderson, 1967). While there are no specific *contents* common to the death-rebirth motif in all cultures, the mythological *form* may be seen as an important archetypal given.

The Child. The symbol of an infant or child is an example of a common archetypal *figure*. It can foreshadow or accompany forward movement and progression through creative regression leading to symbolic death and renewal in the psyche (cf. Jung, 1940b; Maduro, 1976; Maduro, in press; von Franz, 1970).

The meaning of the child symbol is highly overdetermined. In addition to all the personal (e.g., a sibling) and biological (e.g., child-penis-breast) associations, the archetypal dimension can at times assume great importance. The appearance of a child in dreams may signify a turning point in one's life or analysis; it may also indicate a good prognosis. The image of the "divine child" is found in many cultures and can stand for new life and direction, the free playful child in oneself, new awakenings, new beginnings, new symbolic identities, futurity, creativity, potential, and growth (the good internalized breast or fecundating phallus). The child image may stand for the self, the process of individuation or self-actualization, and symbolic rebirth. The child may also be infernal, monstrous, and sadistic.

Children in fantasy life may stand for potentiality and creativity, because they are always on their way to developing into something else. Babies stand for wholly new ideas born out of the unconscious and therefore not yet known, as against the mere juggling of old ideas into forming what appear to be new ones. But original ideas are growths, not constructions. They gestate and, when ready, are born, and this is the difference between creativity and imitation.

It is easy to see that this particular archetypal figure, when analyzed, takes on an added future-oriented significance. Narrow causal-reductive (personal) explanations alone cannot account for its full symbolic meaning. Jungian theory posits the appearance of this particular symbol (the child) at different phases of human development and asserts that it is more a question of symbolic transformation requiring teleological explanation than one of simple causalities. The true symbol, according to Jung, looks not only backward in time but also forward. It may accompany positive or negative transformations.

Anima-Animus. Two part-personalities frequently encountered in dreams, visions, literature, male-female interaction, analytical treatment, and myth are the contrasexual archetypes of the anima and animus: the inherited potential carried by a man to experience the image of woman (his anima), and in a woman the experience of man (her animus).

The unconscious of a man contains a complementary feminine component which takes the image of a woman: "An inherited collective image of woman exists in a man's unconscious, with the help of which he apprehends the nature of woman" (Jung, 1928e, p. 190). When a man has repressed his feminine nature, undervalued feminine qualities with contempt and neglect, or conversely has identified with his anima image, he is cut off from his own creativity and wholeness. The anima performs a mediating role to the creative unconscious and can stand for the whole unconscious in general (Jung, 1936a).

The anima is expressed in projection upon women and in creative process involving fantasies. With regard to the anima and the mother who first carries this projection for a man, Frieda Fordham (1953) writes:

> The image only becomes conscious and tangible through the actual contacts with woman that a man makes during the course of his life. The first and most important experience of a woman comes to him through his mother, and is most powerful in shaping and influencing him: there are men who never succeed in freeing themselves from her fascinating power. But the child's experience has a marked subjective character and it is not only how the mother behaves, but how he *feels* she behaves that is significant. The image of his mother that occurs in each child is not an accurate picture of her, but is formed and colored by the innate capacity to produce an image of woman—the anima. (p. 53)

Likewise, the personal father first embodies the animus image for a girl.

Thus, in addition to parental figures who first activate and symbolically structure the contrasexual images in culturally patterned ways, anima and animus are derived from the inherited collective images of man and woman, as well as the latent masculine and feminine principles found in all individuals who are, according to psychoanalytic theories, assumed to be fundamentally bisexual.

7. PSYCHIC REALITY, THE UNCONSCIOUS
INNER WORLD, IS AS IMPORTANT AS THE
EXTERNAL WORLD.

With the fundamental role of external (sociocultural) reality in mind, Jung (1945b) notes: "Try as we may to concentrate on the most personal of personal problems, our therapy nevertheless stands or falls with the question: 'What sort of world does our patient come from and to what sort of world has he to adapt himself?' " (p. 95).

At times Jung demonstrates an astute awareness of interpersonal processes and external influences on the development of personality. We have already noted that personal and outer events activate innate unconscious potential, the archetype. Jung stresses, however, an inner realm, the deepest layers of the psyche, as being equally significant to outer reality. His major orientation gives *far greater attention to unconscious dynamic structures as motivating forces* than do other analytical models, with one exception: Melanie Klein's concept of an inner world which differs significantly from classical and neo-Freudian theories, coming close enough to original Jungian formulations to warrant the term "Klein-Jungian hybrid" (cf. Jackson, 1961b, 1963a, 1963b; Plaut, 1962).

Jung was personally most comfortable exploring the inner world. He opens his autobiography (Jung, 1961) with a consideration of an inner dialogue between ego and self, stating that "outward events" are no more real to him than "inner experiences." He writes: "I can understand myself only in the light of inner happenings. It is these that make up the singularity of my life, and with these my autobiography deals" (p. 5). So also Jung's psychology—and that of Klein (Maduro, 1974b).

Jung's theory of personality development posits intrapsychic potential for altering external reality, its perception, and reintrojection. Fantasies are not purely escape and defense against internal and external realities, although they may serve these ends too; they are also natural mental expressions of "the instincts." In line with his assertion that the unconscious is not just a repressed unconscious and that there are creative unconscious contents which have never been conscious and subsequently have been repressed, Jung writes (1921): "The psyche creates reality everyday. The only expression I can use for this activity is *fantasy*. . . . Fantasy, therefore, seems to me the clearest expression of the specific activity of the psyche" (p. 52). Put differently, development and maturation of the individual take place through natural, spontaneous fantasy as the psyche "reaches out" for what it needs to grow and to further integrate inner and outer experiences. Innate developmental potential for individuation exists throughout the life cycle; Jung places great emphasis on phylogenetically determined autonomous forms, events, and broad developmental themes which are emergent entities in their own right. For example, Jung (1928a) asserts that, "From a consideration of the claims of the inner and outer worlds, or rather, from the conflict between them, the possible and the necessary follows" (p. 205). The life process or development is, to all intents and purposes, the result of energy freed from the counterplay of inner and outer world tensions. For this reason, Jung (1929a) adds: "We must be able to let things happen in the psyche" (p. 16).

Jung (1913) claimed that, "We must never forget that the world is, in the first place, a subjective phenomenon. The impressions we receive from these accidental happenings are also our own doing. It is not true that the impressions are forced on us unconditionally; our own predisposition [i.e., psychic reality] conditions the impression" (p. 177). Personal experiences, like a key, may be said to unlock developmental potential (Neumann, 1959). The following remarks made by Jung (1943b) in setting forth this basic viewpoint make his position on the primary importance of innate, endopsychic developmental potential clear: "Our consciousness does not create itself—it wells up from unknown depths. In childhood it awakens gradually, and all through life it wakes each morning out of the depths of sleep from an unconscious condition" (pp. 569–570).

8. JUNG'S PSYCHOLOGY CONCERNS ITSELF
MORE WITH CENTRAL PREOEDIPAL
EXPERIENCES, ANXIETIES, AND DEFENSES
THAN WITH OEDIPAL CONFLICTS.

Although Jung himself never systematically developed a comprehensive and clear theoretical statement on the intricacies of child development, he thoroughly appreciated the importance of childhood and infancy. Where the analysis of infantile fixations and complexes in adults was indicated, he most often encouraged classical reductive methods and techniques, in addition to his own "constructive" or synthetic approach (cf. Adler, 1967; Whitmont, 1969; Whitmont & Kaufmann, 1973), which may be said to take into account both growth and repair.

Jung took no special interest in child analysis as such, although he supported his students who built on his theories to include a full appreciation of how conflicts in a child may be understood in terms of unconscious processes in parents (Wickes, 1927), as well as archetypal activity and individuation processes in childhood (M. Fordham, 1969a, 1971a). For an analyst more attuned to the developmental complexities of later life, Jung nevertheless made significant contributions to child psychology.

The first contribution is the accentuation of early developmental tasks as belonging to the preoedipal period. As the first major psychoanalytic theorist to place the mother *imago* in the center of the field for study, Jung was one of the first, if not the first, object relations theorists. He was ahead of his time in focusing on the original relationship between mother and child and on the psychological problems related to disturbances during this period. Jungian theory has never given the singular attention to later oedipal strivings (conflicts between father and son) that characterize Freudian approaches. Jung's revised and broadened understanding of the Oedipus complex (discussed below) relied heavily—at times unwittingly—on the elucidation of predisposing earlier developmental tasks and antecedents.

Classical theory and clinical practice emphasize the triangular (three-person) oedipal situation or "family romance." Jungian theory, in contrast, underlines normal and pathological issues related to an earlier *dyadic* (infant-mother pair) situation. An analyst's handling of an intense transference neurosis would differ greatly, depending upon whether the analyst accepts and highlights a three-person or a two-person model of interaction.

Fordham's explorations into early infancy and childhood elaborate Jung's concept of the self and stress maturational processes in the first year of life. The ego develops out of the unconscious matrix in stages, following alternating phases of deintegration-integration of the primary self—the *spontaneous* division of the self into parts, after which ego fragments are formed. The self is precursor of the ego and embraces it.

Jung reformulated Freud's incest theory in terms of preoedipal fantasies which focus on "a return to the mother's body"—the "original state of nondifferentiation" or "unconscious identity"—a tendency from which mankind is compelled by archetypal forces to free itself. In such a state of projective identification, the primitive ego exists in a primordial fusion state characterized by the lack of separate ego boundaries. This is a state of part-object relatedness, not a truly mutual relatedness. In other words, the ego experiences no "other" except as a narcissistic extension of its own that exists to meet or not meet its "all or nothing" needs. People and situations are then experienced as either all good or all bad. Such an ego becomes inflated, through symbiotic attachment, to omnipotently control and manipulate in a way characteristic of overly dependent adults who pathetically resort to this kind of magical thinking in later life, if mother-infant separation has not adequately taken place.

In focusing on the central role of the mother, Jung did not deny the universality of the well-known oedipal struggle. Jung accepted the idea that a later Oedipus complex is an archetypally determined phase of normal development, but he did not accept Freud's literal concrete "biological" explanation as sufficient. For Jung the unconscious aim is not so much the longing for actual coitus with the forbidden mother in a genital sense, but rather a seeking for a return to her body and the omnipotent infant fusion states which occur in connection with this. Of great importance to Jungian theory is the point that this return may be negatively regressive or it may be adaptive (progressive), and so it may result in positive experiences of symbolic death and rebirth. In any case, Jung's accent is not so much on sexual aim and object as it is on the universal longing to reenter the mother's body, which may represent a childish refusal to grow up and change. Thus Jung pushes the "incest taboo" back in time and stresses its early roots, its social meanings, as well as the human need to "grow beyond oneself" by such a symbolic (archetypal) entry into the mother's womb for rebirth and contact with the archetypal realm of the psyche, which he sees as "prenatal." To quote Jung (1911):

> The real point is that the regression goes back to the deeper layer of the nutritive function, which is anterior to sexuality, and there clothes itself in the experiences of infancy. In other words, the sexual language of regression changes, on retreating still further back, into metaphors derived from the nutritive and digestive functions.... The so-called Oedipus complex with its famous incest tendency changes at this level into a "Jonah-and-the-Whale" complex, which has any number of variants, for instance, the witch who eats children, the wolf, the ogre, the dragon, and so on. Fear of incest turns into fear of being devoured by the mother. The regressing libido apparently desexualizes itself by retreating back step by step to the presexual stage of earliest infancy. *Even there it does not make a halt, but in a manner of speaking continues right back to the intra-uterine, prenatal condition and, leaving the sphere of personal psychology altogether, irrupts into the collective where Jonah saw the "mysteries"...in the whale's belly. The libido...may easily stick fast. But it can also tear itself loose from the maternal embrace and return to the surface with new possibilities of life* (pp. 419–420, emphasis added).

Jung's archetypal psychology leaves a special place for the importance of early object relations and part-object relations in development, because it is through these that the archetypes are expressed as the psyche or primary self unfolds. Therefore, many of Jung's ideas relative to development, such as the archetypal image of the breast, can be linked to concepts studied clinically and theoretically refined by Kleinian analysts (Segal, 1973). Modified Kleinian theory has richly contributed to our general understanding of early object relations and archetypal activity in the first two years of life. The so-called achievement of the depression position in the first year of life, for example, is no less archetypally grounded (cf. Jaques, 1965) than the Oedipus complex. Overlapping developmental sequences involving perception of a bipolar archetypal "dual mother," split ambivalently into "good" and "bad" aspects in need of eventual integration; "separation from the mother" and from a state of projective identification (Gordon, 1965) or primary identity with her body (breast);

and the lifelong yearning to reconnect with that blissful fusion state in times of stress—all these are emphases which characterize Jungian thinking on early development. Although Jung made no special claims to revolutionary revisions of theory in child development, he understood the significance of these earliest stages of the life cycle and made original contributions to this specialized field of analytic endeavor.

9. PERSONALITY GROWTH OCCURS THROUGHOUT THE ENTIRE LIFE CYCLE AND CAN BE ACCELERATED BY THE "INDIVIDUATION" PROCESS IN LATER LIFE.

Although individuating processes occur throughout infancy and childhood, a distinction is made between these and what might be called individuation proper in adulthood: a challenge typically encountered in middle age in relation to life crises. If accepted, individuation may proceed at an accelerated pace and lead to increased inner growth and transformation. This is an *active* life process in which arduous self-exploration and the scanning of inner resources take place. It is a period of creative introversion of libido in which what has heretofore remained unconscious seems to "push" forward or "press" toward greater self-realization as part of the psyche's natural tendency to achieve total integration (F. Fordham, 1969).

Beginning often with a midlife crisis, thought by many to be innately archetypally determined (cf. Jaques, 1965; Jung, 1925), growth and expansion, facilitated by the organizing functions of the ego, may play a crucial role in the development of enhanced creative potential which has remained dormant in the psyche. Middle age may also be a period, as in adolescence, when universal developmental themes encountered earlier (e.g., the depressive position) are reactivated, looked at again, and reexperienced. Yet developmental aims—closely related to the teleology intrinsic to the psyche—may be qualitatively very different after midlife, even if nuclear questions or conflicts seem to repeat themselves.

Jung (1930) outlined "the normal stages of life," stressing a psychological transition, conflict, or crisis in middle age that could, under growth-fostering conditions, lead to intensified striving toward self-actualization. Jung's autobiography is a testimony to what he called "the work" of later life: an active struggle for increased psychic differentiation and synthesis. One of Jung's major contributions to depth psychology was that he first included a total life-cycle perspective. His theories of self-development in later life anticipated Erikson's (1950) attempts to correct the limitations and inadequacies of classical Freudian theory relative to adult personality formation. Jung was optimistic about the potential for growth and change in older people and actually preferred to work with people in the second half of life.

Jung recognized early that perhaps the most important developmental task in the second half of life is to let the ego go, to give its satisfactions less exclusive emphasis in relation to the demands of the larger self. We have noted that the original primary self divides into parts through deintegration. This gives rise to the ego complex, causing a state of ego-self estrangement for much of adulthood until middle age. At that point a "return" to a qualitatively different kind of relationship with the self ensues, and an ego-self axis exists. The individual may need to experience a degree of disintegration (ego boundary diffuseness) to acquire a more well-rounded perspective and an ability to tolerate *nonrational* inner promptings. During the first half of life, according to Jung, a person has been busy winning freedom from the mother, giving up childhood, being assimilated to adult society, and forming a strong, well-integrated ego identity with a "rational" orientation to life. But with the transitional midlife introversion-crisis, a reluctance to let youth and ego strivings and defenses go becomes the central problem. Only a strong ego can confront the demands of the self in this way. For this reason, so-called mystical states should not be confused with Jung's concept of experiences of the self. In a mystical experience, the ego abdicates and fuses oceanically; when the ego encounters the self it does not abdicate but is strong and participates in integrative processes.

Jung observed that the conscious portion of the ego complex assists in the growing integration and manifestation of the total psyche or self. This occurs as a psychodynamic process, involving fluid inner and outer ego boundaries around a strong organizing core or nucleus. It involves an adaptive capacity to endure flux and nonclo-

sure—the expansion and contraction of boundaries to further synthesis, individuation (cf. Maduro, 1974a). Individuation in later life is the process of centering or reestablishing the ego-self axis, a connection which exists in earliest infancy, but as an unconscious identity, not a dialogue (cf. Neumann, 1966). In a most trenchant and elaborate discussion of the ego-self axis, Edinger (1972) writes:

> Clinical observation leads one to the conclusion that the integrity and stability of the ego depend in all stages of development on a living connection with the self. . . . Thus ego and self have a close structural and dynamic affinity. . . . The ego-self axis represents a vital connection between ego and self that must be relatively intact if the ego is to survive stress and grow. This axis is the gateway or path of communication between the conscious personality and the archetypal psyche. Damage to the ego-self axis impairs or destroys the connection between conscious and unconscious, leading to alienation of the ego from its origin and foundation. (pp. 37–38)

Maintenance

Personality is both developed and maintained by how the psyche handles conflict which arises from various intrapsychic or ectopsychic sources. Opposition and conflict are basic to encounters between the ego and the archetypes via the complexes. As an overall "relatively closed" energy system (cf. Jung, 1928c, p. 7), the psyche includes all conscious and unconscious processes. Anything coming into association with the ego will partake of consciousness and its attributes, to some extent (cf. Jung, 1926b, p. 323). Everything else outside the purview of ego-consciousness is unconscious.

With this hypothetical energy system in mind, Jung's model assumes systemic tendencies toward balance and homeostasis. Systems of personality interact and affect each other through the principles of (1) *compensation*, (2) *opposition*, and (3) *unification*. The following concepts in Jungian theory relate to or utilize these three principles and are, therefore, important to the maintenance of personality:

1. The self-regulating and compensatory nature of prospective unconscious processes.
2. Ego mechanisms of defense.
3. The spontaneous self-actualizing tendency within the psyche.

4. Symbolic processes of transformation in periods of deep therapeutic regression.
5. The nature of psychic energy.
6. Jung's notion of psychological types.

10. THE PSYCHE, A SELF-REGULATING
SYSTEM, UTILIZES THE PRINCIPLE
OF CONSTRUCTIVE UNCONSCIOUS
COMPENSATION.

Jung contended that consciousness and the unconscious exist in a reciprocal, complementary relationship. Dreamwork is a good example of the interaction of different systems of the personality. Although dreams at times disguise repressed negative or painful instinctual wishes and fears, Jung insisted that the dream's major function is not to conceal but to reveal.

A dream arising from the unconscious part of the psyche complements or completes consciousness by presenting feelings, attitudes, identifications, and images outside conscious awareness. What is within the comprehension of the ego is only a tiny portion of the total psyche or self. Often healing symbols, synthesizing various aspects of a conflict and pointing toward potential resolution, arise where discrepancies between conscious and unconscious attitudes are severe, sharp, and growth-restricting. Limited one-sided consciousness is compensated for in dreams by what is felt and observed in the unconscious. In other words, the dream is richer and more complete than conscious awareness.

Regarding the nature of dreams and the principle of compensation, Jung (1934b) wrote: "The relation between conscious and unconscious is compensatory. This is one of the best proven rules of dream interpretation. When we set out to interpret a dream, it is always helpful to ask: What conscious attitude does it compensate?" (p. 153). And in 1916 Jung wrote:

> I should like to distinguish between the *prospective* function of dreams and their *compensatory* function. The latter means that the unconscious, considered as relative to consciousness, adds to the conscious situation all those elements from the previous day which remained subliminal because of repression or because they are simply too feeble to reach consciousness. This compensation, in the sense of being a self-regulation of the psychic organism, must be called purposive (Jung, 1916a, p. 255).

Dreams have adaptive, healing, and synthesizing functions. The Jungian approach stresses the natural and spontaneous attributes of dream, myth, and artistic vision. Jungians see the unconscious not only as the repository of unacceptable garbage but also as a dynamic, creative unconscious: lifegiving as well as death-dealing. It is a natural creative function of the psyche to produce symbols—not fundamentally a disease process. Dreams are like an X ray of the human psyche, a view of one's psychic reality or inner world, at any given time. Jung (1934a) wrote: "The dream shows the inner truth and reality of the patient as it really is: not as I conjecture it to be, and not as he would like it to be, but *as it is*" (p. 142).

Dreams may also be looked at for unrecognized cultural stresses, sources of social support, and hidden creative potential, outside conscious awareness. Jung's teleological viewpoint frees the dream from being relegated automatically to only classical causal-reductive analysis, to psychopathology, and to symptom formation or substitute instinct gratification.

Art, myth, and dream all express the natural creative spontaneity of the psyche, available to all who will make the most of the lifelong process of individuation. In addition to the neurotic and negative, a person's dreams also reveal his positive side, the creative potentialities which lie dormant in his unconscious. Jungians assert that often the brightest, most creative side of a personality is repressed, undeveloped. Interpretations by an analyst seek to develop an awareness of these potential lines of development in the patient, as well as the causes of neurotic anxieties. Projections of positive and negative potential reflected in dreams also constitute extremely important elements in the transference.

Growth potential is commonly realized and maintained by an uncrippled capacity for ego participation in the *symbolic process*. If unimpaired, this process involves the containment and experiencing of symbolic opposites from which new life and direction eventually arise. Psychic energy made available to the human psyche for creative symbolic, expressive behavior comes through the union of opposites, or more precisely, from the tension caused by the polarization of psychic opposites contained *simultaneously* in the mind.

Throughout his life Jung was fascinated by

symbolic process, as well as content, especially in relation to the growth and maintenance of personality (cf. Gordon, 1967). As early as 1916, he refers to the process as the "transcendent function" (Jung, 1916a). In later work he referred to the hidden third quality born out of the unconscious (i.e., a new awareness of greater importance than the two opposites from which it has sprung) as the uniting or reconciling function of the symbol, or "uniting symbols" (Jung, 1940b). The child symbol (discussed earlier) is one of the most common of these.

Symbols of polarity are well known in every art form and mythology the world over: male-female, light-dark, good-bad, right-left, thinking-feeling, father-mother, heaven-earth, and so on. In Jungian theory the contrasexual components (anima and animus archetypes) are never left out or discarded for a strictly patriarchal model of human consciousness and personality dynamics. Nor is the satanic (Jung's "shadow") dismissed as simply unwanted and valueless. The shadow is given some positive value, even nobility in terms of its ability to activate oppositional tensions that facilitate growth through the symbolic process which aims at achieving ultimate integration and wholeness: completeness, not perfection.

Ego Functions. If the ego matures, it is strengthened by contact with good educational experiences with parental figures who mirror parts of the child's self and its integrating functions. We may then speak appropriately of various *functions of the ego complex*, once they are acquired and take on significance for the maintenance of healthy personality during development. For Jungians many of these differ little, if at all, from current Freudian concepts (cf. A. Freud, 1936). Only those ego functions related to how Jungian theory differs from other schools in emphases, therefore, will be elaborated here.

Reality Testing. Adaptation to both external reality and a *sense of inner psychic reality* requires adjustment to things, persons, and situations. The well-functioning ego can accurately scan and assess the external world and its shared symbolic meanings, as well as encounter its internal resources.

Regulation and Control of Drives. The healthy ego tolerates strong affects such as *depressive anxiety*, postponement of satisfactions, and instinctual wishes, without inappropriately giving way to compulsive urges.

Capacity for Object Relations. The ego has a capacity to form and maintain intimate, close affectionate attachments to other people, without being overwhelmed by forces of hate, i.e., destructive feelings of hostility such as envy and greed which militate against experiences of interpersonal warmth, empathy, and sustained love.

Ego-Self Polarity. Jungians may appear to place relatively little emphasis on the executive functions of the ego. The Jungian concern is not so much with ego capacity for control "from the top down," as a classical Freudian ego-id (instinctual antiego) dichotomy would imply, as with how, in what ways, and under which specific circumstances the ego complex assists in the self-actualization of the total psyche. Moreover, it is important in some situations, such as in creative process or in later life, for the ego to give way to a larger aim or sense of meaning associated with increased interiority, and in accord with the importance given to the self as the center of the personality, rather than the ego (Edinger, 1972; Maduro, 1974a).

Perceptive Processes. The ability to think in terms of categories, classifications, the future, similarities, and differences is important for day-to-day living. This ego function includes good judgment, concentration, and a capacity to sort out what is important from a welter of internal and external stimuli, so that one can make sound conclusions.

Autonomous Functions. These include intelligence, perception, motility, speech, thinking, and language. They develop relatively independently of instinctual demands.

Synthetic Functions. Jungian theory places most emphasis on the integrating activities intrinsic to the ego. The ego organizes, assimilates, and integrates material arising from the unconscious. This activity is at times a response to external needs and situations, but the process is a natural, autonomous, healthy one which is assumed to arise intrapsychically as well. It is a striving toward wholeness and self-realization, an instinctual process *sui generis* of becoming, in which the ego assists. Dreams are a good example, according to Jungian theory, of the psyche's natural tendency toward growth—its push toward greater consciousness and awareness. Although he recognized the central role of resistance and the need to come to terms with it if growth is to occur at all, Jung's theory tends to stress the ego's synthesizing capacity and lines of future development more than any other psychoanalytic school. This difference makes Jung one of the major precursors of contemporary humanistic psychology.

11. NORMAL AND PATHOLOGICAL EGO DEFENSES ARE BASIC OPPOSITIONAL FORCES TO HANDLE CONFLICT IN A SELF REGULATING PSYCHE.

Defense Mechanisms. The ego must defend itself against anxiety of a depressive and persecutory character, generated by impulses unacceptable or alien to it. These maneuvers are unconscious attempts to keep various wishes, thoughts, feelings, and unconscious fantasies from awareness, and therefore they feature prominently in any deep Jungian analysis. Defenses are oppositional forces which constitute an essential part of the psyche's self-regulating functions, without which there could be no balance (or imbalance). This is the case because ego development is closely linked to the formation of characteristic defensive organizations in the psyche and social masks—what Jung called the *persona* (cf. Jung, 1928a, 1928d: Whitmont, 1969).

Ego defenses are normal and help maintain personality. They have been investigated phylogenetically, and it is easy to see that without them a human being would be overwhelmed by inordinate and unmanageable amounts of guilt and anxiety. As with everything, however, there is a psychopathology of defenses too.

Jung clearly recognized defenses as being both necessary and pathological. In stressing that every encounter with an archetype involves a moral or ethical problem, Jung recognized that the avoidance of the moral or ethical dimension (superego) would be an avoidance of an encounter between ego and archetype. Although necessary, typical defenses (e.g., denial, repression, projection, reaction formation, undoing, isolation, and others) can also be destructive. Therefore they need to be analyzed to facilitate ego encounters with the archetypal psyche. Of the various defenses, projective identification (inflation), introjection, splitting, primitive idealization, deni-

al, devaluation, and the manic defenses against depressive anxieties are perhaps most highlighted in Jungian personality theory, since they are acquired early and reflect Jungian psychology's preoedipal developmental bias.

12. THE PSYCHE SPONTANEOUSLY STRIVES TOWARD PSYCHOLOGICAL WHOLENESS, INTEGRATION OF CONSCIOUS AND UNCONSCIOUS MATERIALS, AND SELF-HEALING.

What has been said of dreams applies also to "symptoms" and other projective data. Jung's attention to the growth factor intrinsic to all psychopathological states appears in his earliest work. One of his finest contributions to the entire psychoanalytic movement is the point that symbols look not only backward in time but also forward. In 1902, Jung wrote:

> It is, therefore, conceivable that the phenomena of double consciousness are simply *new character formations, or attempts of the future personality to break through,* and that in consequence of special difficulties (unfavorable circumstances, psychopathic disposition of the nervous system, etc.) they get bound up with peculiar disturbances of consciousness. In view of the difficulties which oppose the *future character,* the somnambulisms *sometimes have an eminently teleological significance,* in that they give the individual who would otherwise inevitably succumb, the means of victory. (p. 79, emphasis added)

This early evidence for the prospective (forward-looking) function of unconscious mental contents provided an empirical foundation for much of what Jung and his followers would formulate and study phenomenologically in the future. Jung's characteristic point of view that the psyche strives towards self-realization is perhaps most lucidly reflected in another observation made later, in 1917, in *Two Essays on Analytical Psychology:*

> The symptoms of a neurosis are not simply the effects of long-past causes, whether "infantile sexuality" or the infantile urge to power; they are also attempts at a new synthesis of life—unsuccessful attempts, let it be added in the same breath, yet attempts nevertheless, with a core of value and meaning. They are seeds that fail to sprout owing to the

inclement conditions of an inner and outer nature. (Jung, 1917b, p. 46)

Even before their association, Jung held views which were radically different from Freud in relation to the nature of unconscious processes and symbolism. This is especially clear now that many of Jung's letters have been published (cf. Adler, 1973; McGuire, 1974). In a letter dated April 2, 1909, Jung tells Freud: "I had the feeling that under it all there must be some quite special complex, a universal one having to do with the prospective tendencies in man. If there is a 'psychoanalysis' there must also be a 'psychosynthesis' which creates future events according to the same law." (Adler, 1973, p. 4).

The classical Jungian position is clear: Neurotic phenomena are regarded as positive events offering new life and direction under growth-fostering circumstances. Jung never lost sight of this theoretical perspective: the notion that conflict, compensation, and unification are basic to future growth and the maintenance of a healthy personality. Because Jung saw creative potential in the unconscious, he was the first psychoanalyst to stress the adaptive significance of regression, a concept which remains central to his school in both theory and clinical practice.

13. REGRESSION MAY HAVE ADAPTIVE SIGNIFICANCE AND TAKE PLACE "IN THE SERVICE OF THE EGO," AND "IN THE SERVICE OF THE SELF."

In *Symbols of Transformation* (1911) Jung underlined the positive value of regression of ego-consciousness, in contrast to then current Freudian theory. Early in his psychiatric career, Jung stressed the teleological function of symbolic interpretation *in addition* to causal-reductive analyses. He felt that growth during analysis was possible only through regression of the ego to the very deepest levels of the unconscious psyche. Here powerful integrative forces urged not only compulsive repetition of previously experienced personal conflicts but future-oriented self-actualization as well. This was a major difference between the two greatest pioneers of psychoanalysis from the very beginning. Jung (1911) writes:

As against this [i.e., the "one-sided 'biological' orientation of the Freudian school"], *therapy must*

support the regression, and continue to do this until the "prenatal" stage is reached. It must be remembered that the "mother" is really an imago, a psychic image merely, which has in it a number of different but very important unconscious contents. The "mother," as the first incarnation of the anima archetype, personifies in fact the whole unconscious. Hence the regression leads back only apparently to the mother; in reality she is the gateway into the unconscious, into the "realm of the Mothers." Whoever sets foot in this realm submits his *conscious ego personality to the controlling influence of the unconscious,* or if he feels that he has got caught by mistake, or that somebody has tricked him into it, he will defend himself desperately, though his resistance will not turn out to his advantage. For regression, if let undisturbed, does not stop short at the "mother" but goes back beyond her to the prenatal realm of the "Eternal Feminine," to the immemorial world of archetypal possibilities where, "thronged round with images of all creation," slumbers the "divine child," patiently awaiting his conscious realization. This son is the germ of wholeness, and he is characterized as such by his specific symbols. (pp. 329–330)

Clearly, Jung's very early stand in 1911 on the need for regression to archaic object relationships and to innate primordial modalities of the autonomous, unconscious psyche outside the comprehension of the ego relate directly to his emphasis on growth *and* repair (i.e., an analytic method which is both reductive-reconstructive and synthetic). The central issue raised above turns on Jung's general definition of libido or psychic energy—on his acceptance, in particular, of a separate creative instinct which is *sui generis.*

14. PSYCHIC ENERGY (LIBIDO) IS A GENERAL HYPOTHETICAL ENERGIC FORCE THAT INVESTS MENTAL PROCESSES AND REPRESENTATIONS.

In contrast to Freud and Adler, it is an essential feature of Jungian theory that libido is not automatically committed to purely sexual, aggressive, or will-to-power ends. Jung insisted that psychic energy may take many forms which satisfy many different drives, all of which are as deeply rooted in the human psyche. Thus the end of art can be power, sexual gratification, symbolic death and renewal, release of destructive-aggressive impulses, or creativity, as well as to fill social, "religious," or other aims. There are many different possibilities, paths, or "myths" libido can take. Only in the analytic theory of Jung do we find creativity (play) elevated to the status of a separate instinct in its own right, subject to the same vicissitudes and transformations as any other instinct. Creativity may not be reduced simply to something psychosexual.

Jung's concept of psychic energy is monistic in that it is a pure, "sheer," or general force which charges all psychic contents or mental representations of the instincts (i.e., archetypal images) with intensity. Jung's concept is related to the polarities, of which psychic and physical reality are one example and out of which the union of opposites, the symbol, is born. Jung (1917b) writes that, "It seems to me simpler to define libido as an inclusive term for psychic intensities, and consequently as sheer psychic energy" (p. 53). Thus he rejected a strictly dualistic model in which dynamic processes are conceived exclusively in terms of play between the life (Eros) and death (Thanatos) instincts.

At another level of abstraction and interpretation, however, Jung is strictly dualistic, or pluralistic. In referring to Freud's concept of the death instinct, Jung (1917a) states: "What Freud probably means is the essential fact that every process is a phenomenon of energy, and that all energy can only proceed from the tension of opposites" (p. 29). Jung's dualism stresses that there is no energy unless there is tension of opposites in the psyche. Gordon (1961) clarifies this issue:

> Ultimately eros and thanatos are only parts of the general life process, just as anabolism and catabolism are interdependent functions of the metabolic process. And though Jung may reject an over-riding dualism in terms of two principal and opposed instincts, he is in fact very much alive to the essential conflict which is at the root of all behavior and experience. (p. 131)

Jung accounts for destructive-aggressive impulses and negative violent phenomena in terms of Eros-Phobos (fear) opposites rather than Eros-Thanatos (death) (Jung, 1917b, p. 53). The Jungian counterpart of the death instinct is found in the love-hate, or Eros-Phobos, opposites which exist *as a pair among pairs of opposites*. The Phobos aspect of the pair can be seen

as fundamentally based on anxiety, fears of intimacy, instinctual excitement, and the wish to destroy.

Jung's concept of psychic energy also assumes purpose and forward-moving aims or roughly predetermined goals. In "On Psychic Energy" Jung (1928c) explains:

> The energic point of view ... is in essence final; the event is traced back from effect or cause on the assumption that some kind of energy underlies the changes in phenomena, that it maintains itself as a constant throughout these changes and finally leads to entropy, a condition of general equilibrium. The flow of energy has a definite direction (goal) in that it follows the gradient of potential in a way that cannot be reversed. (p. 4)

Jung's concept of a "religious instinct"—the instinct for individuation and goal-oriented self-actualization—has been particularly controversial. Jungians differ from other analysts in their appreciation and understanding of this "spiritual" instinctual force as being separate from sex or aggression. This powerful "drive" to individuate is thought to emanate from the self, not the ego. Perhaps more than most Jungian concepts, it has generated misunderstanding and acerbic criticism. If we assume the existence of psychic-physical polarities (opposites) and a transitional phase of development in which the infant separates out from primary identity with the mother, moving from part to whole object relations, as well as the essential bipolarity of archetypes, there need be no incompatibility between what Jung spoke of as a "religious instinct" and modern object relations theory. Religious forms and all other "higher" cultural achievements would arise from and take on form and meaning in the transitional period (M. Fordham, 1969a; Winnicott, 1951) when *the first true symbol—the transitional object—is formed through play*. Early self-representations are the transitional objects and the body image.

The concept of *value* is important in Jung's understanding of psychic energy. By this he means that "The amount of psychic energy in an element of the personality is called the value of that element. Value is a measure of intensity" (Hall & Lindzey, 1957, p. 91). It relates to how much power a particular idea or feeling may have as a motivating force in the psyche and can also be thought of in terms of degree of cathexis, or the extent to which a force with potential to instigate behavior is "invested" with available psychic energy. To the extent that energy is intensively deployed in one part of the psyche, it will be diminished in another, although the psyche is not strictly a closed system. Jung (1928a) explains his view of the principle of equivalence and the transformation of psychic energy:

> The disappearance of a given quantum of libido is followed by the appearance of an equivalent value in another form ... for a given quantity of energy expended or consumed in bringing about a certain condition, an equal quantity of the same or another form of energy will appear elsewhere. (pp. 18–19).

15. INDIVIDUATION PROCESSES PROCEED THROUGHOUT LIFE IN RELATION TO ONE'S "PSYCHOLOGICAL TYPE."

The two basic ego attitudes toward life are *extraversion* and *introversion*. The extravert's libido (or psychic energy, or interest) flows outward to the object; objective facts or external happenings are the most important factors of life for him. People, things, and events are endlessly interesting to him, and he adapts himself easily and well to his environment. His interest is held and his mind stimulated by the external object; he reacts to it on a specific basis and does not tend to either generalize or introspect from it. He talks fluently, makes friends readily, and is in general a useful and appreciated member of society.

The libido of the introvert is directed predominantly inward, not outward. For the introverted person the significance of the internal object lies not in itself but in how it relates to his own psychology. It is not the situation objectively considered, but the situation as he reacts to it, that is the dominating factor. The introvert is never completely at home in the external world of men and things but prefers his own inner life, where he is quite at ease. He can not only endure solitude to a degree which would break the extravert; he must have a considerable amount of it for his mental health. Outer activities may be difficult for him, but he has a richly differentiated inner world where he feels at home. The normal introvert also cultivates friends but tends to limit them in number. It might be said that he forms vertical (depth) relationships as opposed to the horizontal (breadth) relationships of the extraverted person.

The two modes of perception are *sensation* and *intuition*. These two alternatives are nonrational functions, not because they are contrary to reason but because they are outside the province of reason and therefore not established by it.

The term *sensation* as used here refers to sense perception through the five senses. The sensation type perceives mostly through his senses; outer and inner spontaneously sensed convictions constitute reality for him. He perceives these realities as they exist now, in the present.

The intuitive's psychological function transmits perceptions via the unconscious of the other person. Intuition is an immediate awareness of the whole configuration, without a real comprehension of the details of the contents. It concerns itself with inner or outer phenomena. The focus is on possibilities.

Whereas the sensation type is interested in things as they are now, the intuitive type sees things as they may be. The solid inner or outer facts of the sensation type tend to be uninteresting to the intuitive, and the possibilities which are so full of life to him have little meaning for the sensation type. The intuitive tends to live in the future or the past, the sensation type in the present. The sensation type depends on concrete data for reaction; the intuitive finds himself hampered by such inflexible matters. The sensation type can't see the woods for the trees; the intuitive can't see the trees for the woods.

Thinking and *feeling* are the two functions used in an assessing or judging capacity. They are termed rational functions.

Jung considered the thinking individual as one whose every important action proceeds from intellectually considered motives. He meets a situation with logical thought, shaping his actions by its conclusions. Thinking often takes into account the known rules of human experience. Thinking must always be concerned with content, whether inner or outer. It classifies, clarifies, and names; it can be impersonal.

Feeling involves an appreciation or depreciation of inner or outer realities. Feeling imparts to the content a definite value in the sense of acceptance or rejection. The feeling function judges by an evaluation of the time, the place, and the person. The feeling function is personal;

it represents the individual's acceptance or rejection of something based on his own values, but it is also related to its intrinsic worth. The feeling function is chiefly concerned with values and morality—although not necessarily related to conventional attitudes.

It should be stressed that every individual utilizes both ego attitudes—extraversion and introversion—and all four functions—sensation, intuition, thinking, and feeling. One of these attitudes and several relatively more developed functions, however, generally predominate and characterize a person's typical way of relating to inner and outer life.

Applications

Assessment

Jung's ideas have had a profound impact on techniques of personality assessment and research within academic psychology. MacKinnon's (1962, 1963, 1965) important work on creativity is one example. In psychometrics, this is especially true of the so-called projective techniques which as the term implies, rely heavily on the Jungian assumption that *everything* unconscious—psychic reality—tends to get projected into ambiguous external stimuli.

Carl Jung was the first psychiatrist to apply the scientific method in studying disturbed patients. In developing his Word Association Test, he produced the first experimental data on unconscious processes. Jung thus constructed the very first projective test, which became a part of routine testing in mental hospitals and inspired others to construct tests and to conduct research. McCully (1971) notes that,

> As progenitor of the [projective test] movement, Jung's word association technique earns him the title of father of the indirect way of activating subjective processes, as a means to understanding individuals. Some of the major pioneers worked with Jung personally or knew him. Others were influenced by reading his works. Among these are Bruno Klopfer, Henry A. Murray, [Florence] Miale and [James] Holsopple, and Hermann Rorschach himself. He trained and influenced some of the major thinkers in the existential approach to symbol interpretation, including Ludwig Binswanger and Medard Boss (p. 2).

Word Association Tests. Jung's word association experiments at the turn of this century located feeling-toned complexes, thus corroborating the existence of an unconscious realm of the psyche which Freud and others had been exploring. These experiments laid the foundation for all later attempts to assess, by word association, free association, biofeedback techniques, or sentence completion, the structural and dynamic dimensions of personality, both qualitatively and quantitatively. These highly original scientific works (1904) now comprise over 600 pages of Volume 2 of Jung's *Collected Works*.

Rorschach Test. Hermann Rorschach, a Swiss psychiatrist, closely followed Jung's work and relied heavily on basic Jungian concepts, such as introversion and extraversion, in the development of what is perhaps the most respected projective technique in clinical psychology, the Rorschach Psychodiagnostic Inkblot Test. Like Jung, Rorschach was a student of Bleuler; he also attended two lecture courses given by Jung at the University of Zurich and, according to Ellenberger (1954), used Jung's techniques prior to learning about Freud's methods and psychoanalysis. In another work Ellenberger (1970) sheds historical light on the subject: "Hermann Rorschach . . . . followed the development of Jung's typology with keen interest, integrated the notions of introversion and extraversion into the framework of a psychological theory linked with the invention of a new and original projective test" (p. 840).

Bruno Klopfer, a Jungian analyst, made major advances in Rorschach technique (Klopfer, 1955; Klopfer & Kelley, 1942; Klopfer, Ainsworth, Klopfer, & Holt, 1954). Klopfer is well known for developing a widely used Rorschach scoring system, and he was also interested in Jung's psychological types, ego development, personality growth in later life, and complex symbolic interpretation. Moreover, Klopfer's sphere of influence outside clinical psychology was wide indeed, and many psychological anthropologists (e.g., I. Hallowell) and psychoanalysts of other schools (e.g., B. Boyer) learned Rorschach methods and techniques from him.

In addition to Klopfer, other Jungians have made significant contributions to Rorschach theory and technique (Brawer & Spiegelman, 1964; McCully, 1971; Mindness, 1955). McCully has been particularly prolific and innovative. His book *Rorschach Theory and Symbolism: A Jungian Approach to Clinical Material* (1971) provides original and convincing data for archetypal analyses of Rorschach responses.

Thematic Apperception Test. The TAT, a widely used projective technique, was designed by Henry Murray, who spent time with Jung in Zurich, helped found the first Jungian training institute, and was strongly influenced by Jungian analysis and psychology (cf. Murray, 1962).

Tests of Psychological Types. A second major Jungian contribution to personality assessment and research stems from Jung's typology as outlined above (cf. Hinkle, 1922; Meier, 1971). At present two valid and reliable tests are available and widely in use: the Gray-Wheelwright Questionnaire (Gray & Wheelwright, 1946), and the Myers-Briggs Type Indicator (Myers, 1962). Bradway (1964) has reviewed both tests and notes that:

> Despite the fact that Jung presented his theory of psychological types nearly half a century ago (Jung, 1921) American psychology has continued to classify individual differences in personality, almost exclusively, according to psychological theories based upon a normal distribution of personality traits from none to much. This is in contrast to Jung's concept of a pair of opposing attitudes: introversion and extraversion; a pair of opposing perception functions: sensation and intuition; and a pair of opposing judgment functions: thinking and feeling. (p. 129).

Bradway's study found the Gray-Wheelwright test more useful in discriminating between the thinking-feeling classification than the Myers-Briggs. The Gray-Wheelwright has been applied to many areas of Jungian psychological interest (Gray, 1949b; Gray & Wheelwright, 1945), including marriage (Gray, 1949b; Gray & Wheelwright, 1944), the aging process (Gray & Wheelwright, 1947), and type differences between Freud and Jung (Gray, 1949a).

In experimental psychology, a wide range of studies by or based upon the work of Raymond Cattell, J. P. Guilford, and Hans Eysenck have all indicated strong evidence for the existence of an introversion-extraversion factor (cf. Dicks-Mireaux, 1964). These studies and others support Jung's original ideas and complement the

results of the Gray-Wheelwright studies which assess dichotomous typologies.

In psychotherapy or analysis, a theoretical understanding of psychological types and ways to assess ego functions and attitudes may be crucial and can assume great practical significance. Wheelwright (Henderson & Wheelwright, 1974) notes that:

> It is enormously helpful to the therapist to be able to estimate the abilities and limitations of his patients, in terms of their possible behavior and adaptation. And it is essential that he speaks to them in a language that they understand. To talk intuitively to a factual man, or intellectually to a woman who lives through feelings, is a waste of breath. (p. 813).

Treatment

Theoretical models of personality development and maintenance lead inevitably to considerations and questions of appropriate treatment situations and techniques. Jungian psychotherapy or analysis, in many respects, does not differ at all from basic psychoanalytic practice. Several observations on treatment, nevertheless, are required, due to the uniqueness or distinctiveness of Jungian theory.

Stages of Psychotherapy. Jung's equal theoretical attention to a variety of instincts and to a collective unconscious, in addition to personal and social demands, always presupposed the inclusion of other relevant techniques, notably those of Sigmund Freud and Alfred Adler. Gerhard Adler (1967) a Jungian analyst, summarized Jung's point of view on four overlapping phases of treatment, each requiring a special technical approach:

> ... the first stage of "confession" (or the cathartic method); the second stage of "elucidation" or "interpretation" (in particular the interpretation of the transference, thus being very near to the "Freudian" approach); the third stage of "education" (the adaptation of social demands and needs, thus most nearly expressing the standpoint of Alfred Adler); and finally what he calls the stage of "transformation" (or "individuation"), in which the patient discovers and develops his unique individual pattern, the stage of "Jungian" analysis proper. ...
>
> These stages are not meant to represent either consecutive or mutually exclusive stages of treatment, but different aspects of it, which interpene-

trate and vary according to the needs of the particular patient and the therapeutic situation. Thus, treatment has to be undogmatic, flexible, and adjusted to the needs of the individual patient, and this specification is one of the main tenets of analytical psychology. (p. 338)

Believing that theories are indispensable for sound, day-to-day analytical work, Jung remained skeptical of holding to any one general theory for every individual. His flexibility in analytical technique anticipated new developments in other psychoanalytic schools by many years (Zinkin, 1969). For example, Jung (1926a) wrote: "This means that the method of treatment is determined primarily by the nature of the case.... The real and effective treatment of neurosis is always individual, and for this reason the stubborn application of a particular theory or method must be characterized as basically wrong" (p. 113). Jung took a dim view of dogmatism but not of theoretical consistency and orientation toward any given individual patient.

Jung's great concern for enhanced individuation in later life and his fruitful researches into the phenomenology of this creative life process have always inspired many Jungians to treat older persons. The Jungian emphasis on growth throughout the life cycle stands in sharp distinction to analysts of most other schools. The Jungian approach to older patients who seek analytical treatment is, therefore, radically different in its optimism (Dunn, 1961).

Creative Regression. Jung's early positive emphasis on the adaptive significance of regression has led to the use of at least the following treatment modalities among contemporary Jungians:

1. Greater frequency of interviews per week and use of the couch, chiefly in England, to facilitate active imagination (Jackson, 1961a, 1963a), the analysis of infancy and childhood, and creative regression within the transference situation, to activate "prenatal" archetypal potentialities.
2. The treatment of schizophrenics in residential settings. They are allowed to become deeply regressed, often without medication, in an effort to promote self-healing and natural reconstitutive processes which might otherwise

remain dormant in the unconscious (Perry, 1961, 1974).

3. The use of sandtray therapy with both children and adults to activate archaic, waking fantasies, memories, and other playful states of awareness. This technique may accompany artistic efforts at painting, drawing, clay modeling, or dance.
4. The analytical treatment of severely damaged and regressed borderline and schizophrenic patients who are often considered by non-Jungian analysts to be unreachable by analytic techniques (F. Fordham, 1964).

Therapy as a Dialectical Process. Because Jung viewed the psyche as self-regulating, Jungian analysis and psychotherapy both seek to establish dialogue between ego-consciousness and an activated, dynamic, integrating self. The compensatory or reciprocal relationship between conscious and unconscious is assumed, and the analyst is a participant-observer in this process. He brings his total personality (conscious and unconscious) to the treatment context, using the countertransference (his own thoughts, fantasies, and feelings) creatively, interactively, in ways that provide for a dialectical relationship in which his interpretations and confrontations compensate for what is unconscious in his patient. To work effectively, the analyst must be in touch with his own feelings and have developed access to his own unconscious processes. The idea that every psychoanalyst should undergo a personal-training analysis began with Jung.

Jung (1939) wrote: "Psychotherapy is at bottom a dialectical relationship between doctor and patient. It is an encounter, a discussion between two psychic wholes, in which knowledge is used only as a tool" (p. 554). Although Jung made a distinction between analysis and psychotherapy, seeing them as two psychotherapeutic modalities among many, the goal of treatment is in both cases self-realization. The inevitable entering into the process of the reality of an interacting therapist means growth for both analyst and analysand, and Jung's early attention to this working alliance (1913, 1921) constitutes yet another of his unique contributions to psychoanalysis (cf. M. Fordham, 1969b, 1974b).

The Jungian analyst is an *activator of potential,* since the unconscious is not thought of only in pathological terms. Because Jungian theory holds that attributes of the most creative and positive side of a personality may be repressed, including never-before-awakened archetypal activity, the task is to facilitate regression and to activate potential by providing a facilitating environment. Jung uses an alchemical term, *temenos*, to describe the analytical container in which transformations and integrations of personality take place and exist *in potentia*. Following current Jungian emphasis on early object relations (cf. Davidson, 1965; Edwards, 1972; Newton, 1965, 1975; Plaut, 1966, 1974), *the treatment situation may be described in terms of both structure (= containing, holding), and dynamics (= growth,* repair, transformation). Moreover, Jungian analysts today would tend to view the entire analytical process as a series of ever-recurring, guided experiences of symbolic death and rebirth.

The Archetypal Transference. The extremely complicated and controversial concept of transference as the fulcrum of analysis is central to all psychoanalytic schools. It is no less so for Jung (1946), who held in theory that the whole success or failure of long-term analytical treatment depends on the successful resolution of the dependent transference neurosis (cf. M. Fordham, 1969b; Gordon, 1968; Henderson, 1955; Plaut, 1956). Yet Jung's point of view differs in emphasis from other schools in that he highlighted:

1. The reality-based personal therapeutic alliance between two collaborating people and the importance of the analyst's own personality in the work (Lambert, 1974).
2. The archetypal aspect of transference projections, which may be positive or negative and represent repressed positive potential as well as repressed "shadow" material unacceptable to the ego.
3. The cultural importance of transference in psychohistorical perspective.

Thus, in addition to the analysis of transference projections derived essentially from unconscious personal complexes (e.g., parental, sibling) or from culturally patterned unconscious fantasies, feelings, and thoughts related to racial and ethnic identity issues (Maduro, 1975), the analyst also captures or is the inevitable recipient of transpersonal (archetypal) affects and images

(cf. Adler, 1955, 1967; M. Fordham, 1974b; Plaut, 1956). In any deep analysis, the analyst also carries the archetypal images projected into him.

Two further considerations on the archetypal nature of transference emerge clearly from Jung's work. First, the real relation to the analyst occurs naturally, as all the stages of the individuation process are reflected in the transference, and as the personal projections are simultaneously dealt with analytically, reductively, and reconstructively (Lambert, 1970). Only then may the real relation to the analyst genuinely emerge, as self-realization increases and the possibility for what Henderson (1955) calls the "symbolic friendship" ripens naturally—as the fruit of a process begun long ago in the unconscious.

Second, the archetypal elements of the transference are intensely evoked and may be dramatically observed and lived through in the deepest states of therapeutic regression and active imagination, where a "delusional transference" is contained and allowed to flower, in contrast to more personal and superficial "illusion" states (cf. Campbell, 1967; Cannon, 1968; Davidson, 1966; Jackson, 1963a). Jung's work contributes the concept that there is an inherent evolution in the transference in the direction of individuation, or a relative shift in emphasis away from strictly personal or culturally patterned contents and meanings to a living connection with the archetypal psyche.

Institutional

Many of Jung's ideas can be applied to institutional settings, although this research domain remains relatively undeveloped at this time.

Education. All institutions that highlight self-actualization and creative expression as primary goals of the educational process are, generally speaking, in basic agreement with Jung's humanistic perspective (Jung, 1926a, 1928b, 1928f, 1934a, 1943a). This may mean the accentuation of at least the following purposes:

1. To activate hidden potential, outside conscious awareness, in children.
2. To teach children to respect and value the inner promptings of the unconscious and its symbolic fantasy productions (e.g., dreams).
3. To provide a facilitating environment in

which the idea of wholeness or completeness is presented as a viable alternative to rigid social adaptation, one-sided intellectual development, or strivings for perfection.

4. To insist on teacher attention to unconscious processes in themselves which may communicate messages just as strongly as conscious intents (i.e., transference-countertransference issues).

5. To encourage free play, so that innate natural growth processes are released.

In connection with the fifth point, Jung was always quick to insist that children should not be expected to act like adults at too early an age. He felt, in general, that they should not have their fantasy worlds destroyed by adult "rational" explanations before they have had enough time to "play through" normal developmental conflicts. Jung (1910) wrote:

> As a result of this and similar observations, I have been left wondering whether the fantastic or mythological explanation preferred by the child might not, for that very reason, be more suitable than a "scientific" one, which, although factually correct, threatens to clamp down the latch on fantasy for good. . . . The fact that the fantasy activity simply ignored the right explanation seems, in my view, to be an important indication that all freely developing thought has an irresistible need to emancipate itself from the realism of fact and to create a world of its own. (pp. 33–34).

Jung's attitudes toward children and therapeutic aspects of regression are reflected (although usually not acknowledged as Jungian ideas) in diverse settings, especially in progressive preschools, kindergartens, and other learning contexts such as mental hospitals, where art and play therapy techniques are encouraged and employed with both child and adult patients.

Group Psychology. Although Jung placed great emphasis on individuality (individuation), he thought of it always in relationship to larger social groups. For example, in 1921 he wrote: "The psychology of the individual can never be exhaustively explained from him alone: a clear recognition is needed of the way it is also conditioned by historical and environmental circumstances. His individual psychology is not merely a physiological, biological, or personal problem; it is also a contemporary problem" (p. 431).

Jung's concept of the "shadow" is closely related to contemporary scapegoat theories. In group therapy, as well as in society at large, individuals and ethnic or racial minorities (e.g., blacks, Chicanos, Jews) are apt to capture the archetypal shadow projection. People in every culture must locate or identify feelings of "badness" somewhere. All too often these feelings are not consciously accepted or owned as a part of oneself or one's own society; thus badness gets disowned or projected into another individual or group singled out for this unconscious purpose. One may then disown destructive impulses, have the pleasure of attacking them somewhere "out there" in projection, and feel safe and self-righteous about it. In considering these sociopsychological mechanisms, Jung's ideas concerning the need for individuals and groups to come to terms with the nature of good and evil by wrestling with what he called the "shadow" have great social meaning (cf. Frey-Rohn, 1967; Progoff, 1953; von Franz, 1974).

At times whole nations or social institutions may be seized by negative archetypal forces. For example, Jung anticipated and warned against the Nazi holocaust. He viewed Hitler as possessed by the mythological figure, Wotan, who, when in control of the ego complex, could produce what Jung called "the psychosis of the German nation." Moreover, more recent cold war conflicts as in Vietnam may be considered in terms of one nation's inability to come to terms with its own internal "shadow" problems. Adding conscious insight to the phenomenon of scapegoating decreases the likelihood that unconscious prejudicial attitudes and feelings will be blindly acted out.

Self

Jung's ideas touch on numerous aspects of everyday life, from "slips" of the tongue or pen to creative activities of all kinds, and thus may be of special interest to students who are psychologically minded.

Students willing to accept the living reality of the unconscious mind as central to all thought and behavior may wish to undertake Jungian analysis or psychotherapy. Such an undertaking would hold the possibility of greater consciousness, psychological wholeness, and self-understanding. Through self-understanding, one also comes to perceive others more clearly: this occurs as a multitude of unconscious projections into others are recognized and withdrawn. Only then is one free to experience friends and family members more as they really are than what one internally needs them to be. The analytical process fosters more successful living, through a greater sense of reality (inner and outer) and less of a feeling of being crippled by anxieties related to infantile fixations and complexes.

To experience growth and a creative relationship to unconscious processes, courage and self-criticism are needed, since owning up to one's own darkest side is certainly never a pleasant or easy undertaking. Analytical therapy requires a willingness to suffer defects and to sacrifice identification with false personas. "The persona," wrote Jung (1928a), "is a complicated system of relations between individual consciousness and society, fittingly enough a kind of mask, designed on the one hand to make a definite impression upon others, and, on the other, to conceal the true nature of the individual" (p. 192).

Although personas may be as necessary to normal daily life as ego defenses, they too can become maladaptive. As artificial, superficial personalities, personas are those masks which in reality one is not—false selves. Nevertheless, confrontation with oneself offers hope of greater internal freedom, interpersonal warmth, and the activation of repressed positive potential. It also introduces the analysand to a lifelong process of working with the unconscious which can be carried on outside, or after the analysis has ended. One may, for example, continue to self-analyze dreams, using new skills and attitudes acquired in analysis.

Greater consciousness adds to the quality of the individual's life in many ways. He learns to accept greater responsibility for his own life and also for the unconscious choices he makes to repeat or not to repeat the painful past in the present. In short, consciousness favors dissolution of repetition compulsions. One may come also to accept oneself in a nonpunitive way, with enhanced awareness of both strengths and limitations. Finally, although Jungian analysis and psychotherapy do not provide any magical answers to the universal problems of life, they can promote growth and lead to the acquisition of new values, a fresh approach to life, a new gra-

dient. Several examples clarify what is meant by insight into unconscious motivations.

Workaholism. Jungian theory asserts that life and health call for the rounding out of personality, that the notion of balance and harmony of the mind-body must be taken into consideration. Executives and academicians, to cite two examples, often lack a balance or integration of feeling and thinking. It is a self delusion to suppose that the mind is only rational and that irrational, unconscious, instinctual, and emotional factors may be neglected. Jung's psychology emphasizes the well-known fact that the tree of knowledge (thinking) may become the tree of spiritual or psychological death, without any connection to life (people and feelings). Jung (1938b) expresses this archetypal metaphor concisely: "The educated man tries to repress the inferior man in himself, not realizing that by so doing he forces the latter into revolt" (p. 79). This in turn produces emotion.

Jung's theories place high value on hidden emotional life, intuition, and openness to the irrational or spiritual dimension of human existence. The person who would employ a manic defense against underlying depressive anxiety, through becoming a work addict or workaholic, could by means of self-understanding come to accept unwanted destructive impulses as part of his wholeness. This in turn could release unrecognized feeling and lead to a balanced devotion to business or intellectual pursuits that would not be experienced as anxious, compulsive addiction to work.

Individuality. Jungian psychotherapists are likely to place greater emphasis on intrapsychic adjustment than on adaptation to external conventional morality. The goal of psychotherapeutic work is individuation or development—dialogue with constructive creative unconscious processes—and not, strictly speaking, "cure," mere rational understanding, or symptom removal. For these and other reasons, many creative artists and inner-directed (introverted) persons have often preferred Jungian psychotherapy and analysis to other systems of psychotherapy.

Jung took an extremely strong position in favor of individuality, even to the point of insisting that individuals have the creative prerogative to remain "abnormal." In support of the individual,

Jung (1921) writes: "It is obvious that a social group consisting of stunted individuals can not be a healthy and viable institution; only a society that can preserve its internal cohesion and collective values, while at the same time granting the individual the greatest possible freedom, has any prospect of enduring vitality" (p. 448).

Although individuality involves arriving at a truly symbolic or "religious" attitude toward life (conscious and unconscious), Jungian theory refers more to the acquisition of a system of personal ethics than to religion in any conventional sense.

Changing Male-Female Roles. Jung's theory of the fundamental bisexuality of human beings —both physiologically and psychologically— frees men and women to experience both the masculine and feminine components of their personalities. The masculine or the feminine is each incomplete, relative, and one half of the same whole (cf. the Chinese Yin-Yang premise). Jung's theory that the difference between man and woman is qualitative stands in sharp opposition to Freud (Whitehead, 1975), who took the natural inferiority of women for granted (e.g., an assumed intellectual inferiority because of stronger sexual repression in women, and a masochism and passivity Freud felt was natural to women). Jung held that the difference is not of inferiority and superiority, and that the sexes are psychologically complementary to each other (his theory of the anima in man and the animus in woman).

In this regard, Jung's theory has strong ties to views held by Alfred Adler, Karen Horney, and Erich Fromm. Contemporary interest in Jungian theory and the "women's movement" reflect, in part, yet another way in which Jung's genius was far ahead of his time. As we have seen, Jung never could accept Freud's overestimation of maleness, the phallus, and the phallic phase of psychosexual development characteristically marked by the activation of the Oedipus complex.

Marital Relationships. Many vexing marriage situations revolve around the business of psychological types. Research using the Gray-Wheelwright Questionnaire (Gray & Wheelwright, 1944) demonstrated that in a series of over a thousand subjects, the overwhelming majority have married their polar opposites, although for friends the same subjects tend to pick similar types. It is a little startling to think of most of us marrying people whom we would never pick as friends.

An understanding of Jung's theory of types encourages the development of tolerance toward others who differ from us. Type theory allows us to imagine standing in the other person's shoes and to appreciate the variety of equally valid responses to any given situation.

Jung's idea of individuation is closely related to types. As long as we are content, in a marriage, to let somebody else carry our introverted side or our feeling, we remain relatively unconscious and undeveloped. Growth involves a constant increase in consciousness—that is, the incorporation into our conscious personalities of aspects of our psyche that have hitherto lain in the unconscious. Marriage inhibits growth processes in individuals when it is not viewed as a psychological relationship (Jung, 1925), and when the willingness to accept a partner's inherent differentness or to develop one's own least developed psychological functions is absent.

Validation

Evidence

The discovery of the dynamic unconscious gave rise to modern depth psychology (Ellenberger, 1970). Although at the turn of this century the new science of psychoanalysis contained much that was rooted in the intellectual tradition of the 19th century, it nevertheless constituted a threat and an expansion of the earlier psychology, which had been severely limited in scope to the study of conscious mental processes and observable behavior.

Jung sought to prove the existence of unconscious processes by examining hysterical symptoms, dreams, and free association. He studied hypnosis in France and was inspired by the work of Jean Charcot, Hippolyte Bernheim, and Pierre Janet in their attempts to show that repression is a major factor in mental malfunctioning, and it could be removed by "talking cures" or hypnotic suggestion.

At the end of the 19th century, hypnosis was the chief method of access to unconscious processes. Hypnosis could retrieve apparently forgotten memories and subliminal perceptions. Freud's early work, in particular, showed that some physical symptoms stand symbolically for underlying, repressed, unconscious conflicts which, when brought to awareness and to insight into their symbolic meanings, lead to remission of the symptoms. Hypnosis demonstrated that motivations existed outside consciousness.

Jung's early experimental research on word association, somnambulism, and mediumistic trance states complemented and corroborated Freud's attempts to prove the existence of an unconscious realm. Jung's methodology and techniques continue to be used and empirically validated today by criminologists, biofeedback therapists, and others who use galvanic skin responses to monitor a wide variety of subjective processes occurring in the mind-body.

Archetypes of a Collective Unconscious. Nothing has caused more misunderstanding between Jungians and students of other schools of personality theories than Jung's concepts of the archetypes and a collective unconscious (i.e., the importance of heredity and constitutional factors in a broad sense). At such an early time in the history of depth psychology, it took courage for Jung to explore these areas of the mind and to report his findings (cf. Jung, 1919, 1929b). He often met with resistance, misinterpretation, rejection, and ridicule. He continued, nevertheless, to explore assiduously, to report on the analysis of dreams and other symbolic systems (e.g., alchemy), and to refute the impressions that he was a "mystic," something he denied throughout his long life.

Today, oddly enough, what Jung and his followers have said concerning archetypal activity in the psyche can be related to recent scientific findings in other fields, where controlled studies by eminent researchers postulate and provide very convincing evidence for the presence of basic, a priori structures in the mind. Personal experiences are necessary but not sufficient conditions for their actualization. These studies confirm much of what Jung had to say. We can note, for example:

1. Psychedelic drug experiences which, for better or worse, plunge individuals into transpersonal layers of the psyche.
2. Levi-Strauss's structural theories in modern anthropology ("binary oppositions").
3. The ethological work done by Konrad Lorenz and many others ("innate releaser mechanism").
4. Jean Piaget's innate "schemata."
5. Rene Spitz's "innate organizers."
6. Melanie Klein's "unconscious phantasy" or "unconscious knowledge."
7. Michael Balint's "pre-object" or "object-Anlage."
8. Noam Chomsky's rules for transformational grammar in linguistics.
9. Modern ego psychology, whereby archetypes in action are described as the unfolding of the genetically social character in response to an average, expectable environment.

Jung's original ideas have become the focus of serious study in many scientific quarters, without being labeled mystical. That Jung's contributions have so long been relatively unacknowledged is remarkable, to say the least; but the validity of his theoretical work is corroborated independently by scientists in other fields.

Innate Ego. The ego is one basic structure of the mind that has been the focus of much recent attention. It is important to note Jung's reference to the ego as a *complex.* This implies that such a psychic structure has an innate archetypal core or nucleus around which personal associations are formed as maturation proceeds.

Outside the limitations of classical drive theory, modern ego psychologists now recognize the importance of an "innate ego" or an ego present at birth, which to all intents and purposes is as far back as we can go, even though recent advances in embryology promise to shed light on these issues. Here, too, modern Jungian theory differs in emphasis and is corroborated by research and clinical inference (e.g., Call, 1964). Until recently the idea that ego exists with a *capacity to initiate* activity and to be object-related very early in infancy (i.e., part-object relatedness) has not been acknowledged widely or given much importance in models of development. Students of Jung, Klein, and Sullivan have given great attention to the ego's capacity for primitive albeit absolutely fundamental states of relatedness in earliest infancy.

Current Jungian theory, in other words, does not accept the concept of "primary narcissism" which remains basic to Freudian developmental theory and which implies that a baby must be coaxed out of a pool of narcissism by the mother (cf. M. Fordham, 1971a). Much more ego exists from the beginning than Freud or Jung recognized. *Neo-Jungians therefore place great emphasis on the normal development and management of part-objects.* Fordham (1971a) clarifies this as follows:

> Deintegration was conceived as the active contribution by the infant in bringing about states from which it was previously assumed he passively began. Thus the idea that mother, infant togetherness is created by the mother alone is done away with and attention is focussed on what the baby does to help bring this about. The idea that the self deintegrates, rather than splits or disintegrates, grew out of this line of thought. (p. 86)

Evidence suggests that object relations begin very early. Much more observation and experiment are needed to shed light on postulated unconscious (archetypal) processes working behind perceptual development.

Comparisons

A great deal of what has already been said about Jungian theory implies comparison with classical or orthodox Freudian psychoanalysis. A number of more specific issues concerning the work of Freudian, Jungian, and Kleinian analysts will now be highlighted.

Ego Psychology. Controversies among analysts of diverse schools involve a wide variety of mutual misunderstandings and the different use of language. Although words such as *ego, symbol,* or *self* are commonly used, they may carry different meanings. We are indebted both to the Freudian school for major advances in the field of ego psychology and to the Jungian school for its consistent, theoretical emphasis on a psychodynamic self.

Providing an overview of contemporary Freudian psychotherapy, Fine (1973) remarks: "Since 1923 all of psychoanalysis has been ego psychology" (p. 4). In accord with this point of view, Fenichel (1945) refers to the Freudian model: "All neurotic phenomena are based on insufficiencies of the normal control apparatus" (p. 19). This position stands in sharp contrast to the Jungian emphasis on a psychodynamic self in relationship to differentiating and synthesizing ego processes. Thus Jung (1925) writes:

A dissociation is not healed by being split off, but by more complete disintegration [cf. therapeutic regression, the delusional transference, guided psychosis, etc.]. All the powers that strive for unity, all healthy desire for selfhood, will resist the disintegration, and in this way he will become conscious of the possibility of an inner integration, which before he has always sought outside himself. He will then find his reward in an undivided self. (pp. 196–197)

Jung's use of the word *self* differs from current Freudian usage, since his concept is not interchangeable with the term ego or thought of as a representation within the ego. In 1921, Jung wrote:

> Inasmuch as the ego is only the centrum of my field of consciousness, it is not identical with the totality of my psyche, being merely a complex among other complexes. Hence I discriminate between the ego and the self, since the ego is only the subject of my consciousness, while the self is the subject of my totality; hence it also includes the unconscious psyche. (p. 590)

Later, in 1939, he wrote: "For this reason I have elected to call it the 'self,' by which I understand a psychic totality and at the same time a centre, neither of which coincides with the ego but includes it, just as a larger circle encloses a smaller one" (p. 142).

While both Jung and Freud were concerned with the central importance of ego strength, Freudian psychology stresses ego "control" and Jungian psychology creative "dialogue" between the ego and the dynamic unconscious. Moreover, the Jungian emphasis on the inner reality of the psyche may at times make modern Freudian ego-psychology, with its exclusive emphasis on adaptation to the external world, seem inordinately mechanistic, limited, one-sided, and overly abstract for students of Jung. In this connection, it is telling that contemporary Freudians still find it necessary to refer to the inner world or psychic reality as metapsychology, when for Jungians it is simple plain psychology. Again, we are talking about a matter of emphasis, since Jung places great importance on the personal evocation of the transpersonal.

In contrast to Jung's fundamentally introverted position vis-à-vis the unconscious, Anna Freud (1926) sums up the Freudian orientation with this position statement: "In working with an adult we have to confine ourselves entirely to helping him to adapt himself to his environment" (p. 61). Her remark obviously posits quite a different intellectual slant on a "psychic apparatus" and on the relative weight given in therapy to intrapsychic dynamic structures as motivating forces in the unconscious, in comparison to outer interpersonal reality. Thus the emphasis of Freudian theory with regard to developmental factors differs radically from that of Jung. Jungians may accept the orthodox Freudian view as being true but extremely limited to the elucidation of psychopathology (e.g., the depreciation of primary process per se), rational ego control, and adaptation to the external world. In comparison, Jung's model would stress the *whole human personality in the process of growth and repair,* an ego-self polarity.

Symbols or Signs. When Freudian views blur distinctions between the ego and self, psychoanalytic interpretations and analyses can seem excessively reductionistic, too heavily weighted in favor of psychic determinism (causality). Lacking any appreciation of the constructive, creative, or natural symbolic functions of the psyche as a self-regulating teleological system, which Jung's model adds, the scope of Freudian theory appears to be narrow indeed. Any idea of a creative self which seeks unfolding and would add meaning to life is neglected for a systemic man-as-machine model. While such a model may bind the analyst's anxiety by seeming to create tight and neatly packaged categories or systems within the psyche, it ignores the positive attributes of a tolerance for ambiguity from which new syntheses, symbolic representations, and theoretical constructions flow. Jungian enthusiasts, on the other hand, must guard against the unconscious defense of idealization of all unconscious processes—remembering that the unconscious is both life-giving (creative) *and* death-dealing (destructive).

Moreover, the psychological or symbolic point of view which Jungian theory contributes is ignored when Freudian analyses reduce everything to concrete, literal body parts—when they might equally well talk of *signs* or *substitutions* (known, conventional) rather than emerging dynamic living *symbols* (ambiguous, transforming, with no fixed meanings).

The tree, for example, may be an elongated phallic symbol, as Freudian theory rightly posits. To reduce it to this level of concrete biological reality alone, however, would be a grave error, from a Jungian perspective. The tree may also stand for the father as something old rooted in tradition; it may be a mother symbol par excellence, as something which bears fruit and is nurturing (lays down shade, protects and harbors birds). It may stand for psychological differentiation (the many branches) and wholeness. Because it loses its leaves, dies in the winter, and seemingly comes to life again in the spring, it may stand for the process of symbolic death and rebirth. Finally, the tree may stand for the connection between heaven and earth, the *axis mundi,* a link between the polarity of matter (mother earth) and spirit (father sky) which transcends each alone by combining or unifying both.

These are only some of the richer symbolic dimensions of the tree symbol; many more could be added. Which facet or combination of facets would be important to a particular dreamer and his unique life history and present circumstances would be the question. From a Jungian point of view it would be wrong to simplistically equate the tree *literally* with a phallus, simply because it is an elongated object. This illustration should help the student see that from a Jungian point of view Freudian analyses often appear to deal with signs rather than symbols (cf. Stein, 1957).

Freud's "Racial Memory." It is of interest to note that although Freud and his followers have almost completely neglected the archetypal nature of the psyche, Freud in this respect was not in basic disagreement with Jung. Sigmund Freud (1918) asserts: "I fully agree with Jung in recognizing the existence of this phylogenetic heritage" (p. 97). In contrast to what is generally acceptable in Jungian psychology, however, Freud held that actual ideational contents, "racial memories," are transmitted. Near the end of his life, for example, Freud (1939) wrote, in *Moses and Monotheism:* "The archaic heritage of mankind includes not only dispositions, but also ideational contents, memory traces, the experiences of former generations" (p. 98). Jung (1928e), on the other hand, stresses the innate capacities and potentials for all human beings sharing the same brain structure to be moved by the power of the archetypes and complexes associated with many of them: "The universal similarity of the brain yields the universal possibility of a similar mental functioning. This functioning is the collective psyche" (p. 147).

Eschewing a strictly Lamarckian stand, Jung underlines archetypal potentialities available to all members of the human species. Freud's notion that something could happen only once in the human race and be forever passed on phylogenetically in terms of specific ideational content (cf. S. Freud's highly speculative primal horde theory in *Totem and Taboo,* 1913) is equally untenable for Jungians, as well as for modern anthropologists concerned with the importance of culture. Jung is very clear on this point, and the following passage, written in 1938, should dispel the mistaken interpretation that archetypal analysis precludes the concept of culture and societal forces:

> *Again and again I encounter the mistaken notion that an archetype is determined in regard to its content,* in other words that it is a kind of unconscious idea (if such an expression be admissible). It is necessary to point out once more that archetypes are not determined as regards their content, but only as regards their form and then only to a very limited degree. A primordial image is determined as to its content only when it has become conscious and is therefore *filled out with the material of conscious experience.* Its form, however, as I have explained elsewhere, might perhaps be compared to the axial structure of a crystal, which, as it were, preforms the crystalline structure in the mother liquid, although it has no material existence of its own. This first appears according to the specific way in which the ions and molecules aggregate. *The archetype in itself is empty and purely formal, nothing but a facultas praeformandi, a possibility of representation which is given a priori. The representations themselves are not inherited,* only the forms, and in that respect they correspond in every way to the instincts, which are also determined in form only (Jung, 1938a, p. 79 —emphasis added).

Phallocentrism. That Jung should have made the mother so central a figure in understanding the psychodynamics of normal personality development at a time when Freud emphasized the role of the father (i.e., castration anxiety in oedipal dynamics) is an important distinction between them, no less so as Freudian

theory moves closer and closer toward acceptance of the original Jungian position. Jung's early insight is today axiomatic. Indeed this theoretical difference was a major cause of the split between Freud and Jung in 1913; when Jung wrote *Symbols of Transformation* (1911), he went his own way. In this landmark work he writes about the heroic ego's task of separating from the mother complex as if he were discussing adolescence; it is unclear whether Jung was completely aware of all the implications of his work for early object relations. Nevertheless he describes separation from symbiotic attachment to the mother, important features of splitting in part-object relations, and developmental hurdles related to working through what Klein later called the depressive position (cf. Segal, 1973; Winnicott, 1954).

Jung's emphasis on the mother imago, in contrast to Freud, takes the feminine principle and preoedipal dynamics seriously into account. Unlike Freudian patriarchal formulations, Jungian perspectives—at least in theory—are not as permeated by unconscious resistances to the analysis of early conflicts and anxieties associated with the mother, a developmental level deeper than the oedipal complex. Freud's theories treat both the feminine genitalia and vital feminine aspects of secure male identity (cf. Jung's anima in males) with severe patriarchal contempt. Such a hypermasculine pose may well mask male insecurities in relation to conflicted attributes of femininity, passivity, orality, and breast-womb envy.

Klein's emphasis modifies Jung's but also seems to represent a rather extreme position, inasmuch as masculine aspects of identity are often devalued in favor of an overemphasis on the female breast. Man is seen as merely the extension of the nipple (Whitehead, 1975). Moreover, Klein's conceptual formulation of an inner world, although very similar to Jung's, differs significantly in that Klein's is, according to Plaut (1962), "first and foremost a hostile murderous place where aggression and anxiety, greed and sadism abound" (p. 6). Jung's inner world does not overly stress anxiety and disease to the exclusion of healthy aspects of personality. It is a much less pathological place—a both friendly and hostile territory.

In reaction to the Victorian era, Jung's theoretical stance with regard to the masculine and feminine components of the personality is truly remarkable for its balanced and relatively unbiased assertions, in comparison to either Freud or Klein. Jungian theory provides a starting point that can synthesize the best of Freud and Klein to meet the feminist challenge of our time. Jung's work needs to be further extended and modified so that an even more objective and accurate psychology of women may evolve. There is a special need to elucidate developmental issues where personal experiences and archetypal patterns closely interrelate. It is particularly important to move on to the position that women can relate to life directly and not only through men.

Prospect

Despite the many challenges ahead, the future of Jungian psychology appears secure. Jung's contributions are increasingly hard to ignore, as interest in his psychology grows and as scientific validation of his ideas comes from many quarters, including modern biology and atomic physics. It is probable that current superficial fascination with popularized Jungian concepts will diminish, and Jungian piety and the need to idealize and mysticize Jung will be further distinguished from the theory and practice of Jung's analytical psychology. The concepts central to Jung will remain vital and continue to form foci around which serious investigation can take place.

Predictions about what will happen to the Jungian school can be viewed in the light of three perspectives: (1) other psychoanalytic schools, (2) other personality theories of a nonanalytic nature, and (3) the social and behavioral sciences.

Other Psychoanalytic Schools.
Although various other individuals have made extremely original contributions to psychoanalysis over the years, all schools ultimately derive from the theoretical emphases of the first three great pioneers: Sigmund Freud, Carl Jung, and Alfred Adler. A great deal of what passes today for "neo"-Freudian theory (e.g., "regression

in the service of the ego") turns out, upon investigation of the historical development of the psychoanalytic movement, to be recently *rediscovered*, extended, or modified Jung and Adler.

At present, creative dialogue among schools is on the increase, and gaps are being narrowed. There is no reason to expect that this trend will reverse itself. Moreover, psychoanalysts of all schools are being forced into closer association and collaboration because of the rather recent development of an "antianalytic" climate among psychotherapists in general.

The time is ripe for a greater integration of psychoanalytic theories. Each school has its own particular strengths and limitations; in emphasizing one theme, others have been sacrificed. Today fewer "purists" exist than when the three pioneers were still alive. It is reasonable to expect that the number of Jungian analysts will continue to increase, and that these will choose to enter into the mainstream of psychoanalysis more than their predecessors did.

More specifically, this trend will affect diverse perspectives within Jungian circles, where analysts practicing today can be thought of as orthodox-classical, moderate, or neo-Jungian in orientation. Among Jungians there is increased cognizance that one theory alone is not sufficient. There is a general shift, for example, toward a more serious reevaluation of Freud's theory of infantile sexuality. Greater attention in the analytic situation is being given to the reconstruction of infancy and childhood as it unfolds within the analysis of the transference neurosis. Jung certainly thought this was in most cases indispensable, yet perhaps because two thirds of his patients were in the second half of life—and because childhood simply interested Jung less than later life—he did not write a great deal about the earliest stages of development. Analytical psychologists after Jung concentrate in a more balanced way on a method which is simultaneously *both* reductive and constructive (growth *and* repair). Freud's theories of infantile sexuality were never abandoned by Jungians, but among contemporary students they appear to receive more of the emphasis Jung always said they deserved.

Finally, contact with the sociopsychoanalytic theories of Adler, Fromm, Sullivan, and Horney can only enrich Jungian psychology and add to its attempts at understanding the psyche comprehensively, holistically.

Other, Nonanalytic Theories.

Interaction with nonanalytic theories of personality affects the practice of Jungian psychotherapy and analysis more than the underlying theories do. By knowing behaviorist theories, the analyst may become more accurately aware of his own reinforcing behaviors within the analytic context. The Jungian analyst may also recognize much of what he does, particularly in brief psychotherapy, in the reported work of Eric Berne on "games," the Gestalt techniques of Fritz Perls, or the self-actualizing theory of Carl Rogers.

As a result of accelerating contact with other theories, Jungians can refine techniques, especially those applicable to working with larger numbers of individuals than is usually the case in traditional analytical therapy. Combined with Jung's emphases on the state of the relationship between patient and doctor in the "here and now" and on the link between neurosis and a patient's present life circumstances, many Gestalt approaches could perhaps be usefully incorporated under the analytical technique commonly referred to as confrontation. Moreover, Jung's techniques of active imagination and dream analysis—where part-personalities (complexes) of one's total self enter into dialogue or interact with each other and an observing ego—seem closely related, at least in theory, to Gestalt exercises of "talking to" various parts of one's dream, and to "waking fantasies."

Jungian psychology will remain open to diverse technical approaches espoused by other psychotherapies. This receptivity will undoubtedly increase in the future, as Jungians engage more actively than ever in applying Jung's theories to group analysis and to conjoint marital and family therapy.

The Social and Behavioral Sciences.

The sociocultural has been a relatively neglected area of concern among Jungians; if analytical psychology is to survive and thrive it will have to consider interpersonal issues and make itself socially relevant to a changing world.

In the future modern anthropology promises to play an important role in the development and validation of Jungian theory. More recent interests among anthropologists in "symbolic anthropology" (the analysis of rituals, myths, and symbols of transformation), and in so-called primitive mentality share links to core Jungian hypotheses. It is significant that in some parts of the United States and Great Britain anthropologists and sociologists are now as likely to have a Jungian analysis and training as they are to have been exposed to traditional Freudian views. In addition to the analysis of symbolic content and process, Jung's influence will continue to grow within the social and behavioral sciences in the following teaching and research domains: (1) art and culture, (2) human development and aging, (3) medical anthropology, (4) folklore studies, and (5) clinical psychology.

Annotated Bibliography

Primary Sources

Jung, C. *The Collected Works of C. G. Jung* (20 vols.). Princeton, N. J.: Princeton University Press, 1954–1972. (Vol. 9 is in two parts; vols. 18 and 19 have not yet appeared.) See especially:

Jung, Carl. *Two Essays on Analytical Psychology. Collected Works* (Vol. 7).
This clearly written work defines Jung's central concepts and is the best place to begin reading the *Collected Works*. "On the Psychology of the Unconscious" (1917) and "The Relations between the Ego and the Unconscious" (1928) contribute richly to an understanding of the structure and function of the unconscious, the early history of depth psychology, descriptions of method and technique, and definitions of concepts, such as Jung's unique contribution—"The Synthetic or Constructive Method" (1917).

Jung, Carl. *The Practice of Psychotherapy. Collected Works* (Vol. 16).
Jung's papers on psychotherapy are divided into two parts. The first deals with general issues and therefore is aimed at a wide audience. Here Jung discusses his point of divergence from Freud and Adler, making clear his own position with regard to the general aims of psychotherapy and distinguishing between the needs of younger patients and those in the second half of life. Part two contains more specific material on the therapeutic value of abreaction and on elementary principles of dream analysis. The final essay, "The Psychology of the Transference" (1946), is long; this was Jung's final statement on the central role of transference in analytical work. This essay is difficult to comprehend, and students are advised to read only its introduc-

tion carefully. This volume is especially useful to psychotherapists and others in contact with clinical material.

Jung, Carl, et al. *Man and His Symbols*. New York: Doubleday, 1964.

This work, published posthumously, is not part of Jung's *Collected Works*. It was the only attempt he ever made to popularize his work, and it provides a good introductory approach to his scholarly researches. Chapters by Henderson on initiation and by Von Franz on individuation are interesting and set forth fundamental principles of Jungian psychoanalytic theory.

Secondary Sources

Adler, Gerhard. *Studies in Analytical Psychology.* New York: G. P. Putnam's Sons, 1969.

The revised edition of this book is fundamental reading. It includes a comparison of Jungian method and technique with other schools, an in-depth study of a dream, important thoughts on Jung's psychological approach to religion, and his early attention to ego processes in relation to the lifecycle. Foreword by C. G. Jung.

Fordham, Frieda. *An Introduction to Jung's Psychology*. Baltimore: Penguin Books, 1953.

A brief and good, if slightly outdated, introduction to classical Jung. Foreword by C. G. Jung.

Fordham, Michael. *Children as Individuals.* New York: G. P. Putnam's Sons, 1969.

This study of child development is an essential introduction to modern Jungian theory. Fordham lucidly discusses play, dreams, and picture drawing as part of child-analytical treatment procedures aimed at facilitating the release of maturational processes. He provides convincing clinical evidence to complement theoretical advances, focusing on the child as an individual who functions in relation to wider family and societal settings. Chapter 5, "The Conceptual Model," and Chapter 6, "Maturation," are particularly crucial.

Fordham, Michael, et al. *Technique in Jungian Analysis. The Library of Analytical Psychology* (Vol. 2). London: William Heinemann Medical Books Ltd., 1974.

This fine collection of articles on technique is indispensable for students and analysts alike, since it brings together important papers in an area that is relatively neglected by Jungians. Moreover, there is a healthy complementary articulation between theory and clinical practice; thoughts on management, flexibility in analytic technique, interpretation, reconstruction, the symbolic attitude, and termination are related to practical, everyday treatment concerns of transference and countertransference issues. This book is one of a kind.

Whitmont, Edward. *The Symbolic Quest.* New York: G. P. Putnam's Sons, 1969.

This text is the most comprehensive, clear, and contemporary overview of traditional Jungian concepts. Both classical and neo-Jungian theories are discussed in life-cycle perspective, although vital contributions of analytical psychologists who extend traditional Jung are relatively untouched. The book frankly sidesteps any systematic consideration of analytic technique and related issues (the transference neurosis, defenses, countertransference, resistance, etc.), but it does provide abundant illustrative material. The author discusses archetypal themes as they commonly emerge in the analytical situation (persona, shadow, anima-animus, self), and as they relate to the structure, dynamics, and development of personality.

References

Adler, G. On the archetypal content of transference. In *Report of the International Congress of Psychotherapy, Zurich, 1954*. Basel/New York: Karger, 1955.

Adler, G. Methods of treatment in analytical psychology. In B. Wolman (Ed.), *Psychoanalytic techniques* (pp. 338–378). New York: Basic Books, 1967.

Adler, G. (Ed.). *C. G. Jung letters, I: 1906–1950.* Princeton, N. J.: Princeton University Press, 1973.

Alex, W. *Dreams, the unconscious, and analytical therapy*. San Francisco: C. G. Jung Institute, 1971.

Bradway, K. Jung's psychological types: Classification by test versus classification by self. *Journal of Analytical Psychology*, 1964, 9(2), 129–136.

Brawer, F., & Spiegelman, J. M. Rorschach and Jung: A study of introversion-extraversion. *Journal of Analytical Psychology*, 1964, 9(2), 137–150.

Call, J. D. Newborn approach behavior and early ego development. *International Journal of Psycho-Analysis*, 1964, 45(2–3), 286–295.

Campbell, R. The management of the countertransference evoked by violence in the delusional transference. *Journal of Analytical Psychology*, 1967, 12(2), 161–174.

Cannon, A. Transference as creative illusion. *Journal of Analytical Psychology*, 1968, 13(2) 95–108.

Davidson, D. A problem of identity in relation to an image of a damaged mother. *Journal of Analytical Psychology*, 1965, 10(1), 67–76.

Davidson, D. Transference as a form of active imagination. *Journal of Analytical Psychology*, 1966, 11(2), 135–146.

Dicks-Mireaux, M. J. Extraversion-introversion in experimental psychology: Examples of experimental evidence and their theoretical implications. *Journal of Analytical Psychology*, 1964, 9(2), 117–128.

Dunn, J. Analysis of patients who meet the problems of the first half of life in the second. *Journal of Analytical Psychology*, 1961, 6(1), 55–67.

Edinger, E. *Ego and archetype*. New York: G. P. Putnam's Sons, 1972.

Edwards, A. Fantasy and early phases of self-representation. *Journal of Analytical Psychology*, 1972, 17(1), 17–30.

Ellenberger, H. F. Hermann Rorschach, M.D., 1884–1922. *Bulletin of the Menninger Clinic*, 1954, *18*, 173–219.

Ellenberger, H. F. *The discovery of the unconscious.* New York: Basic Books, 1970.

Erikson, E. *Childhood and society.* New York: W. W. Norton, 1950.

Fenichel, O. *The psychoanalytic theory of neurosis.* New York: Norton, 1945.

Fine, R. Psychoanalysis. In R. J. Corsini (Ed.), *Current psychotherapies* (pp. 1–33). Itasca, Ill.: F. E. Peacock, 1973.

Fordham, F. *An introduction to Jung's psychology.* Baltimore: Penguin Books, 1953.

Fordham, F. The care of regressed patients and the child archetype. *Journal of Analytical Psychology*, 1964, *9*(1), 61–74.

Fordham, F. Some views on individuation. *Journal of Analytical Psychology*, 1969, *14*(1), 1–12.

Fordham, M. *New developments in analytical psychology.* London: Routledge & Kegan Paul, 1957.

Fordham, M. Comment on the theory of the original self. *Journal of Analytical Psychology*, 1961, *6*(1), 78–79.

Fordham, M. The empirical foundation and theories of the self in Jung's works. *Journal of Analytical Psychology*, 1963, *8*(1), 1–24.

Fordham, M. The importance of analysing childhood for assimilation of the shadow. *Journal of Analytical Psychology*, 1965, *10*(1), 33–48.

Fordham, M. Active imagination—deintegration or disintegration? *Journal of Analytical Psychology*, 1967, *12*(1), 51–66.

Fordham, M. *Children as individuals.* New York: G. P. Putnam's Sons, 1969. (a)

Fordham, M. Technique and countertransference. *Journal of Analytical Psychology*, 1969, *14*(2), 95–118. (b)

Fordham, M. Maturation of ego and self in infancy. In *Analytical psychology: A modern science*, Library of Analytical Psychology (Vol. 1, pp. 83–94). London: William Heinemann Medical Books, 1973. (Originally published, 1971). (a)

Fordham, M. Primary self, primary narcissism and related concepts. *Journal of Analytical Psychology*, 1971, *16*(2), 168–187. (b)

Fordham, M. A theory of maturation. In B. Wolman (Ed.), *Handbook of child psychoanalysis* (pp. 461–500). New York: Van Nostrand Reinhold, 1972.

Fordham, M. Defences of the self. *Journal of Analytical Psychology*, 1974, *19*(2), 192–199. (a).

Fordham, M. Jung's conception of transference. *Journal of Analytical Psychology*, 1974 *19*(1), 1–21. (b).

Fordham, Michael. *The Self and Autism. Library of Analytical Psychology* (vol. 3). London: William Heinemann Medical Books, 1976.

Freud, A. *The psychoanalytical treatment of children.* New York: Schocken Books, 1964. (Originally published, 1926.)

Freud, A. The ego and the mechanisms of defense. *The writings of Anna Freud* (Vol. 2). New York: International Universities Press, 1966. (Originally published, 1936.)

Freud, S. *Totem and taboo.* In *Standard edition of the complete psychological works of Sigmund Freud* (Vol. 13, pp. 1–162). London: Hogarth Press, 1953. (Originally published, 1913.)

Freud, S. From the history of an infantile neurosis. In *Standard edition of the complete psychological works of Sigmund Freud* (Vol. 17, pp. 1–104). London: Hogarth Press, 1955. (Originally published, 1918.)

Freud, S. Moses and monotheism. In *Standard edition of the complete psychological works of Sigmund Freud* (Vol. 13, pp. 1–132). London: Hogarth Press, 1964. (Originally published, 1918.)

Frey-Rohn, L. Evil from the psychological point of view. In *Evil* (pp. 151–200). Evanston, Ill.: Northwestern University Press, 1967.

Frey-Rohn, L. *From Freud to Jung: A comparative study of the psychology of the unconscious.* New York: G. P. Putnam's, 1975.

Giegerich, W. Ontogeny-Phylogeny? A fundamental critique of Erich Neumann's analytical psychology. *Spring: An Annual of Archetypal Psychology and Jungian Thought*, 1975, pp. 110–129.

Gordon, R. The death instinct and its relation to the self. *Journal of Analytical Psychology*, 1961, *6*(2), 119–136.

Gordon, R. The concept of projective identification: An evaluation. *Journal of Analytical Psychology*, 1965, *10*(2), 127–150.

Gordon, R. Symbols: Content and process. *Journal of Analytical Psychology*, 1967, *12*(1), 23–34.

Gordon, R. Transference as a fulcrum of analysis. *Journal of Analytical Psychology*, 1968, *13*(2), 109–117.

Gray, H. Jung's psychological types and changes with age. *Journal of Clinical Psychology*, 1947, *3*(3): 273–277.

Gray, H. Freud and Jung: Their contrasting psychological types. *Psychoanalytic Review*, 1949, *36*(1): 22–44. (a)

Gray, H. Psychological types in married people. *Journal of Social Psychology*, 1949, *29*: 189–200. (b)

Gray, H., & Wheelwright, J. Jung's psychological types and marriage. *Stanford Medical Bulletin*, 1944, *2*(1): 37–39.

Gray, H., & Wheelwright, J. Jung's psychological types, including the four functions. *Journal of Genetic Psychology*, 1945, *33*: 265–284.

Gray, H., & Wheelwright, J. Jung's psychological types, their frequency and occurrence. *Journal of General Psychology*, 1946, *34*: 3–17.

Hall, C., & Lindzey, G. *Theories of personality.* New York: Wiley, 1957.

Henderson, J. Resolution of the transference in the light of C. G. Jung's psychology. *Report of the International Congress of Psychotherapy, Zurich, 1954* (pp. 75–91). Basel/New York: Karger, 1955.

Henderson, J. *Thresholds of initiation.* Middletown, Conn.: Wesleyan University Press, 1967.

Henderson, J., & Wheelwright, J. Analytical Psychology. In *The American handbook of psychiatry* (Vol. 2; S. Arieti, Ed.). New York: Basic Books, 1974.

Hinkle, B. A study of psychological types. *Psychoanalytic Review*, 1922, *9*, 107–197.

Jackson, M. Chair, couch, and counter-transference. *Journal of Analytical Psychology*, 1961, *6*(1), 35–43. (a)

Jackson, M. Jung's "archetype": Clarity or confusion? *British Journal of Medical Psychology*, 1961, *33*, 83–94. (b)

Jackson, M. Symbol formation and the delusional transference. *Journal of Analytical Psychology*, 1963, *8*(2), 145–164. (a)

Jackson, M. Technique and procedure in analytic practice with special reference to schizoid states. *Journal of Analytical Psychology*, 1963, *8*(1) 51–64. (b)

Jacobi, J. *Complex/archetype/symbol in the psychology of C. G. Jung.* Princeton, N. J.: Princeton University Press, 1959.

Jaques, E. Death and the mid-life crisis. *International Journal of Psychoanalysis*, 1965, *46*, 502–514.

Jung, C. On the psychology and pathology of so-called occult phenomena. In *Psychiatric studies,* Collected works (Vol. 1, pp. 1–88). Princeton, N. J.: Princeton University Press, 1957. (Originally published, 1902.)

Jung, C. Studies in word association. In *Experimental researches,* Collected works (Vol. 2). Princeton, N. J.: Princeton University Press, 1973. (Originally published, 1904.)

Jung, C. The psychology of dementia praecox. In *The psychogenesis of mental disease,* Collected works (Vol. 3, pp. 1–152). Princeton, N. J.: Princeton University Press, 1960. (Originally published, 1907.)

Jung, C. Psychic conflicts in a child. In *The development of personality,* Collected works (Vol. 17, pp. 1–36). Princeton, N. J.: Princeton University Press, 1954. (Originally published, 1910.)

Jung, C. *Symbols of transformation,* Collected works (Vol. 5). Princeton, N. J.: Princeton University Press, 1956. (Originally published, 1911).

Jung, C. The theory of psychoanalysis. In *Freud and psychoanalysis,* Collected works (Vol. 4, pp. 83–226). Princeton, N. J.: Princeton University Press, 1961. (Originally published, 1913.)

Jung, C. General aspects of dream psychology. In *The structure and dynamics of the psyche,* Collected works (Vol. 8, pp. 235–280). Princeton, N. J.: Princeton University Press, 1960. (Originally published, 1916.) (a)

Jung, C. The transcendent function. In *The structure and dynamics of the psyche,* Collected works (Vol. 8, pp. 67–91). Princeton, N. J.: Princeton University Press, 1960. (Originally published, 1916.) (b)

Jung, C. The eros theory. In *Two essays on analytical psychology,* Collected works (Vol. 7, pp. 19–29).

Princeton, N. J.: Princeton University Press, 1953. (Originally published, 1917.) (a)

Jung, C. The problem of the attitude-type. In *Two essays on analytical psychology,* Collected works (Vol. 7, pp. 41–63). Princeton, N. J.: Princeton University Press, 1953. (Originally published, 1917.) (b)

Jung, C. Instinct and the unconscious. In *The structure and dynamics of the psyche,* Collected works (Vol. 8, pp. 129–138). Princeton, N. J.: Princeton University Press, 1960. (Originally published, 1919.)

Jung, C. *Psychological types,* Collected works (Vol. 6). Princeton, N. J.: Princeton University Press, 1971. (Originally published, 1921.)

Jung, C. Marriage as a psychological relationship. In *The development of personality,* Collected works (Vol. 17, pp. 187–204). Princeton, N. J.: Princeton University Press, 1954. (Originally published, 1925.)

Jung, C. Analytical psychology and education. In *The development of personality,* Collected works (Vol. 17, pp. 63–132). Princeton, N. J.: Princeton University Press, 1954. (Originally published, 1926.) (a)

Jung, C. Spirit and life. In *The structure and dynamics of the psyche,* Collected works (Vol. 8, pp. 319–337). Princeton, N. J.: Princeton University Press, 1960. (Originally published, 1926.) (b)

Jung, C. Anima and Animus. In *Two essays on analytical psychology,* Collected works (Vol. 7, pp. 188–211). Princeton, N. J.: Princeton University Press, 1953. (Originally published, 1928.) (a)

Jung, C. Child development and education. In *The development of personality,* Collected works (Vol. 17, pp. 47–62). Princeton, N. J.: Princeton University Press, 1954. (Originally published, 1928.) (b)

Jung, C. On psychic energy. In *The structure and dynamics of the psyche,* Collected works (Vol. 8, pp. 3–66). Princeton, N. J.: Princeton University Press, 1960. (Originally published, 1928.) (c)

Jung, C. The persona as a segment of the collective psyche. In *Two essays on analytical psychology,* Collected works (Vol. 7, pp. 156–162). Princeton, N. J.: Princeton University Press, 1953. (Originally published, 1928.) (d)

Jung, C. The relations between the ego and the unconscious. In *Two essays on analytical psychology,* Collected works (Vol. 7, pp. 123–244). Princeton, N. J.: Princeton University Press, 1953. (Originally published, 1928.) (e)

Jung, C. The significance of the unconscious in individual education. In *The development of personality,* Collected works (Vol. 17, pp. 149–164). Princeton, N. J.: Princeton University Press, 1954. (Originally published, 1928.) (f)

Jung, C. Commentary on "The secret of the golden flower." In *Alchemical studies,* Collected works (Vol. 13, pp. 1–56). Princeton, N. J.: Princeton University Press, 1967. (Originally published, 1929.) (a)

Jung, C. The significance of constitution and heredity in psychology. In *The structure and dynamics of the psyche,* Collected works (Vol. 8, pp. 107–113). Princeton, N. J.: Princeton University Press, 1960. (Originally published, 1929.) (b)

Jung, C.   The stages of life. In *The structure and dynamics of the psyche,* Collected works (Vol. 8, pp. 387–404). Princeton, N. J.: Princeton University Press, 1960. (Originally published, 1930.)

Jung, C.   The development of personality. In *The development of personality,* Collected works (Vol. 17, pp. 165–186). Princeton, N. J.: Princeton University Press, 1954. (Originally published, 1934.) (a)

Jung, C.   The practical use of dream analysis. In *The practice of psychotherapy,* Collected works (Vol. 16, pp. 139–161). Princeton, N. J.: Princeton University Press, 1954. (Originally published, 1934.) (b)

Jung, C.   Concerning the archetypes, with special reference to the anima concept. In *The archetypes and the collective unconscious,* Collected works (Vol. 9, part I, pp. 54–74). Princeton, N. J.: Princeton University Press, 1959. (Originally published, 1936.) (a)

Jung, C.   The concept of the collective unconscious. In *The archetypes and the collective unconscious,* Collected works (Vol. 9, Part I, pp. 42–53). Princeton, N. J.: Princeton University Press, 1959. (Originally published, 1936.) (b)

Jung, C.   Psychological aspects of the mother archetype. In *The archetypes and the collective unconscious,* Collected works (Vol. 9, Part I, pp. 73–110). Princeton, N. J.: Princeton University Press, 1959. (Originally published, 1938.) (a)

Jung, C.   Psychology and religion. In *Psychology and religion: West and east,* Collected works (Vol. 11, pp. 3–106). Princeton, N. J.: Princeton University Press, 1958. (Originally published, 1938.) (b)

Jung, C.   Foreward to Suzuki's "Introduction to Zen Buddhism." In *Psychology and religion: West and east,* Collected works (Vol. 11, pp. 538–557). Princeton, N. J.: Princeton University Press, 1957. (Originally published, 1939.)

Jung, C.   Concerning rebirth. In *The archetypes and the collective unconscious,* Collected works (Vol. 9, Part I, pp. 113–150) Princeton, N. J.: Princeton University Press, 1959. (Originally published, 1940.) (a)

Jung, C.   The psychology of the child archetype. In *The archetypes and the collective unconscious,* Collected works (Vol. 9, Part I, pp. 151–181). Princeton, N. J.: Princeton University Press, 1959. (Originally published, 1940.) (b)

Jung, C.   The gifted child. In *The development of personality,* Collected works (Vol. 17, pp. 133–148). Princeton, N. J.: Princeton University Press, 1954. (Originally published, 1943.) (a)

Jung, C.   The psychology of eastern meditation. In *Psychology and religion: west and east,* Collected works (Vol. 11, pp. 558–575). Princeton, N. J.: Princeton University Press, 1958. (Originally published, 1943.) (b)

Jung, C.   On the nature of dreams. In *The structure and dynamics of the psyche,* Collected works (Vol. 8, pp. 281–297). Princeton, N. J.: Princeton Univer-

sity Press, 1960. (Originally published, 1945.) (a)

Jung, C.   Psychotherapy today. In *The practice of psychotherapy,* Collected works (Vol. 16, pp. 94–125). Princeton, N. J.: Princeton University Press, 1954. (Originally published, 1945.) (b)

Jung, C.   The psychology of the transference. In *The practice of psychotherapy,* Collected works (Vol. 16, pp. 163–322). Princeton, N. J.: Princeton University Press, 1954. (Originally published, 1946.)

Jung, C.   On the nature of the psyche. In *The structure and dynamics of the psyche,* Collected works (Vol. 8, pp. 159–234). Princeton, N. J.: Princeton University Press, 1960. (Originally published, 1947.)

Jung, C.   The ego. In *Aion, researches into the phenomenology of the self,* Collected works (Vol. 9, Part II, pp. 3–7). Princeton, N. J.: Princeton University Press, 1959. (Originally published, 1951.)

Jung, C.   *Memories, dreams, reflections.* New York: Random House, 1961.

Kettner, M.   Some archetypal themes in homosexuality. *Proceedings of the fifteenth annual joint meeting of the Northern and Southern California Societies of Jungian Analysts* (pp. 33–58). San Francisco: C. G. Jung Institute, 1967.

Klopfer, B.   Editorial dedication honoring Jung's eightieth birthday. *Journal of Projective Techniques,* 1955, *19*(3): 225.

Klopfer, B., & Kelley, D.   *The Rorschach technique.* New York: World Book Co., 1942.

Klopfer, B., Ainsworth, M. D., Klopfer, W. G., & Holt, R. R. (Eds.).   *Developments in the Rorschach technique* (Vol. I, *Technique and theory*). New York: Harcourt, Brace & World, 1954.

Lambert, K.   Some notes on the process of reconstruction. *The Journal of Analytical Psychology,* 1970, *15*(1), 42–58.

Lambert, K.   The personality of the analyst in interpretation and therapy. In *Technique in Jungian analysis.* Library of Analytical Psychology (Vol. 2, pp. 18–44). London: William Heinemann Medical Books, 1974.

McCully, R.   *Rorschach theory and symbolism: A Jungian approach to clinical material.* Baltimore: Williams & Williams, 1971.

McGuire, W. (Ed.).   *The Freud-Jung letters: The correspondence between Sigmund Freud and C. G. Jung.* Princeton, N. J.: Princeton University Press, 1974.

MacKinnon, D.   The nature and nurture of creative talent. *American Psychologist,* 1962, *17*(7), 484–495.

MacKinnon, D.   Creativity and images of the self. In R. W. White (Ed.), *The study of lives.* New York: Prentice-Hall, 1963.

MacKinnon, D.   Personality and realization of creative potential. *American Psychologist,* 1965, *20*(4), 273–281.

Maduro, R.   Artistic creativity and aging in India. *International Journal of Aging and Human Development,* 1974, *5*(4), 303–329. (a)

Maduro, R.   Notes on the adaptive significance of regression in analytical psychology. In R. Davidson and R. Day (Eds.), *Symbol and realization: A contribution to the study of magic and healing* (pp. 116–131). Berkeley: University of California, Center for South and Southeast Asia Studies, 1974. (b)

Maduro, R. Hoodoo possession in San Francisco: Notes on therapeutic aspects of regression. *Ethos*, 1975, *3*(3), 426–447.

Maduro, R. *Artistic creativity in a Brahmin painter community.* Research Monograph No. 14. Berkeley: University of California Center for South and Southeast Asian Studies, 1976.

Maduro, R. Symbolic motifs in creative process: A Jungian Contribution. In N. Graburn (Ed.), *Art and culture: Approaches to process and change.* Albuquerque: University of New Mexico Press, in press.

Maduro, R. & Martinez, C. Latino dream analysis: Opportunity for confrontation. *Social Casework*, 1974, *55*(8), 461–469.

Meier, C. A. Psychological types and individuation: A plea for a more scientific approach in Jungian psychology. In J. Wheelwright (Ed.), *The analytic process: Aims, analysis, training* (pp. 276–289). New York: G. P. Putnam's Sons, 1971.

Mindness, H. Analytical psychology and the Rorschach test. *Journal of Projective Techniques*, 1955, *19*, 243–252.

Murray, H. A. In *Carl Gustav Jung, 1875–1961: A Memorial Meeting* (pp. 17–22). New York: Analytical Psychology Club of New York, 1962.

Myers, I. *The Meyers-Briggs Type Indicator.* Princeton, N. J.: Educational Testing Service, 1962.

Neumann, E. *The origins and history of consciousness.* Princeton, N. J.: Princeton University Press, 1954.

Neumann, E. The significance of the genetic aspect for analytical psychology. *The Journal of Analytical Psychology*, 1959, *4*(2), 125–138.

Neumann, E. Narcissism, normal self formation and the primary relationship to the mother. *Spring: Contributions to Jungian Thought.* (Analytical Psychology Club of New York), 1966, pp. 81–106.

Newton, K. Mediation of the image of infant-mother togetherness. *Journal of Analytical Psychology*, 1965, *10*(2), 151–162.

Newton, K. Separation and pre-oedipal guilt. *Journal of Analytical Psychology*, 1975, *20*(2), 183–193.

Osterman, E. The tendency toward patterning and order in matter and in the psyche. In J. Wheelwright (Ed.), *The reality of the psyche* (pp. 14–27). New York: G. P. Putnam's Sons, 1968.

Perry, J. Reconstitutive process in the psychopathology of the self. *Annals of the New York Academy of Sciences*, 1961, *96*, 853–876.

Perry, J. Emotions and object relations. *Journal of Analytical Psychology*, 1970, *15*(1), 1–12.

Perry, J. *The far side of madness.* Englewood Cliffs, N. J.: Prentice-Hall, 1974.

Plaut, A. The transference in analytical psychology. In *The Library of Analytical Psychology, Technique in Jungian Analysis* (Vol. 2). London: William Heinemann Medical Books, 1974, pp. 152–160.

Plaut, A. Hungry patients, reflections on ego structure. *The Journal of Analytical Psychology*, 1959, *4*(2), 153–160.

Plaut, A. *Some reflections on the Klein-Jungian hybrid.* Paper presented to The Society of Analytical Psychology, London, May, 1962.

Plaut, A. Reflections about not being able to imagine. *Journal of Analytical Psychology*, 1966, *11*(2), 113–134.

Plaut, A. Part-object relations and Jung's "luminosities." *Journal of Analytical Psychology*, 1974, *19*(2), 165–181.

Progoff, I. *Jung's psychology and its social meaning.* New York: Julian Press, 1953.

Redfearn, J. Several views of the self. *Journal of Analytical Psychology*, 1969, *14*(1), pp. 13–25.

Segal, H. *Introduction to the work of Melanie Klein* (Enlarged ed.). New York: Basic Books, 1973.

Stein, L. What is a symbol supposed to be? *Journal of Analytical Psychology*, 1957, *2*(1), 73–84.

Stein, L. An entity named ego. *Journal of Analytical Psychology*, 1962, *7*(1), 41–54.

Tate, D. Invasion and separation. *Journal of Analytical Psychology*, 1961, *6*(1), 45–53.

Von Franz, M. L. *The problem of the Puer Aeternus.* New York: Spring Publications, 1970.

Von Franz, M. L. *The shadow and evil in fairytales.* New York: Spring Publications, 1974.

Whitehead, C. Additional aspects of the Freudian-Kleinian controversy: Towards a "psychoanalysis" of psychoanalysis. *International Journal of Psycho-Analysis*, 1975, *56*(4), 383–396.

Whitmont, E. *The symbolic quest.* New York: G. P. Putnam's, 1969.

Whitmont, E. & Kaufmann, Y. Analytical psychotherapy. In R. J. Corsini (Ed.), *Current psychotherapies* (pp. 85–117). Itasca, Ill.: F. E. Peacock, 1973.

Wickes, F. G. *The inner world of childhood.* New York: Appleton-Century-Crofts, 1927.

Williams, M. The indivisibility of the personal and collective unconscious. *Journal of Analytical Psychology*, 1963, *8*(1), 45–50.

Winnicott, D. Transitional objects and transitional phenomena. In *Through paediatrics to psycho-analysis* (pp. 229–242). London: Hogarth Press, 1975. (Originally published, 1951.)

Winnicott, D. The depressive position in normal emotional development. In *Through paediatrics to psycho-analysis* (pp. 262–277). London: Hogarth Press, 1975. (Originally published, 1954.)

Zinkin, L. Flexibility in analytic technique. *Journal of Analytical Psychology*, 1969, *14*(2), 119–132.

Person-centered personality theory, formerly known as *nondirective* (Rogers, 1942) and later as *client-centered* (Rogers, 1951), had its origin around 1940 in the growing dissatisfaction of Carl R. Rogers, a psychologist, with the theories and the methodologies then current in the treatment of emotional and behavioral "problems." His basic conception, held from the beginning to the present, is that the proper focus for any theory of personality or method of treatment is the person.

The latest name change accentuates this. The person is recognized as a gestalt of thoughts, feelings, actions, perceptions, and complex biological processes, always in relation to time, as well as to the world of people, objects, and events around him. The present shift in emphasis to person-centered highlights the social outreach of the theory. Although Rogers's theory has grown out of psychotherapy and is still developing as a means of growth and change, the principles underlying the theory are believed to be relevant to almost every aspect of man's behavior.

A distinctive feature of person-centered theory is and has been its continued stress on the self-actualizing and self-directing quality of people. This apparently simple notion of "empowering the person," trusting that he or she can know the proper direction of movement in his or her own actualizing process, is one of the most revolutionary aspects of the theory, cutting it loose from the materialistic determinism of some other systems.

Self-actualization occurs when one's own experience becomes more important than the values of others in maintaining one's self-concept. Experiencing means to be aware how one attends, perceives, processes, and integrates information of one's internal, visceral world and one's external, interpersonal, and physical world. Openness to full organismic sensing comes when one experiences realness, caring, and sensitive, nonjudgmental understanding in relation with others.

These principles apply to all people, irrespective of age and adjustment, and they represent a total theory of humanness. In the special situation of therapy it is important that the therapist be real, caring, and trusting, and that he or she be seen as such. The person-centered therapist meets the client in a moment-to-moment encounter, continually focusing on the phenomenal world of the client.

The historical roots of person-centered theory reach across many cultures and many centuries, and it has considerable commonality with many present-day approaches within the perceptual-phenomenological and existential frameworks. In addition, person-centered theory has consistently attempted to validate its hypotheses through research.

Person-Centered Theory

T. L. Holdstock and Carl R. Rogers

CARL R. ROGERS

Introduction

Our fascination with ourselves is seen by the varieties of myths about our creation and also by the very large number of theories and attitudes about human beings in general and about individual persons in particular. Over the millennia a number of general positions have been taken about these and other issues, relative to who we are, how we got to be what we are, and what to do about ourselves and, others, especially those who do not act the way we want them to act. Even today, there exist dozens of more or less formal theories—and new ones crop up periodically.

Such personality theories are important, since they help organize people to cooperate, and, if the theories are valid, they help people to deal with one another in helpful ways. If it is possible to apply the advances of science to such theorizing, then it is possible for us to take a great step toward the age-long dream of a happy and peaceful world. We may also help accomplish the aim of alleviating human misery of the kind that to normal people seems so unnecessary, those states of misery called *delinquencies, neuroses,* and *psychoses.*

In philosophy, the direct ancestor of our present personality theories, a number of problems, still unsolved, were taken up. One has to do with the nature of the person. *Is the person exclusively body? Does something control that body?* These issues have not been settled. Some people take the monist position that there is only the body; while others implicitly or explicitly take the dualistic position that there are body and mind, or body and soul. Is the individual free or a slave? Is behavior determined, or does the person have a capacity for creative and independent judgment and decision? This issue of freedom versus determinism also is still with us. Are human beings rational, following the dictates of a kind of moral calculus, doing what is in their apparent best interests, or are they directed by feelings and emotions, conscious or unconscious? Here, too, modern personality theorists cannot come to agreement.

Many other positions have been taken in the attempt to understand human beings. Some come from religion, some from tradition, some from armchair theorizing, and some from experimentation. No fewer than 40 more or less scientifically oriented theories of personality are in existence at the present time, some wide and all embracing in nature, and some narrow and specialized. But all are in pursuit of truth, hoping to see us as we truly are.

In this chapter we will discuss a theory of personality formation and maintenance which, although started through clinical experience, has over some 30 years developed and expanded while going through a variety of changes, as has also been true of other mature personality theories. Person-centered theory is validated in a number of ways: through clinical experience, through a large amount of research, through analogy, and through the latest knowledge about basic neurophysiology. It represents, in our judgment, not only a total and complete veridical picture of man and woman's nature, but also a philosophy of life which can help us realize the centuries-old dream of peace and harmony in this unstable world.

History

Precursors

To place person-centered theory in a historical perspective is easy, since the core aspects of the theory have been a central concern of humanity for many thousands of years. But it is also difficult, because it is not possible to determine specific occurrences as definite precursors of the theory.

The person-centered belief in the unique potential of each individual has religious overtones. It is conceivable that Rogers has given the concept of God new meaning, due to his unfailing belief in the worth of each person. The Hebrew word for God (*Yahweh asher Ychweh*) means *I am* or *I am what I am; I am who I am; I am as I am.* Further indications of the centrality accorded the person in biblical times are the command-

Note: This chapter has essentially been written by Dr. Holdstock. He has enriched it with his special knowledge in neurophysiology and cognitive psychology. I have served as consultant, editor, and author of certain sections. I add my name as co-author to indicate that I have been involved and am fully in accord with the final product.—C.R.R.

ments: Love thy neighbor as thyself, and love thy God as thyself.

Other central concepts of the person-centered approach have ancient ethical counterparts. Congruence, empathy, and unconditional positive regard have been key concepts in religion through the ages. Oden (1972) demonstrated that important antecedents of current encounter group processes can be found in the life and literature of Protestant and Jewish pietism. The universality of the concerns of the person-centered approach is evident in the fact that its roots can also be traced to Oriental philosophies such as Zen and Yoga. Zen holds that each person must find the answers to life within him/herself. The importance placed by Yoga on the physical and physiological aspects of the body closely resembles the importance attached to organismic experiencing by person-centered theory. Krishnamurti, for instance, said that the body has its own intelligence and that life is here and now, but if you are fearful you cannot live.

The philosophies which culminated in the existential movement (Patterson, 1973) have close ties to the person-centered approach. Edmund Husserl postulated that the real world can only be inferred on the basis of perceptions. Existential philosophy, originating in the work of Sören Kierkegaard and Karl Jaspers, is concerned with the nature of humans, their existence and involvement in the world, and with the meaning of existence for the individual. Aspects of existentialism are key concepts in person-centered theory: (1) being conscious of self and being able to choose at every moment; (2) the idea that man/woman is *being*, thus constantly becoming, evolving; (3) the notion that each person has the capacity to transcend the self and the physical world. The person-centered approach, like existentialism, is an attitude, an approach to life.

Since Afred Adler has been considered to fall within the existential framework (Mosak & Dreikurs, 1973), it is not surprising to find close affinities between Individual Psychology and person-centered theory. Individual Psychology "views man holistically as a creative, responsible, 'becoming' individual moving toward fictional goals within his phenomenal field" (Mosak & Dreikurs, p. 35). The similarity between certain core concepts of the two approaches is striking.

Even the titles bear close resemblance, with the emphasis being on the individual, or the person, in both cases. Rogers could have written: "We must be able to see with his eyes and hear with his ears" (Adler, 1958).

Thomas Hanna (1970) accords Sigmund Freud a special place in making us aware of the significance of our bodies. In this sense Freud can be regarded as a precursor to person-centered theory. Ever since Rogers (1959b) suggested that experiences are valued in terms of satisfactions organismically experienced, this concept of bodily felt sensing has become increasingly important, culminating in the Experiential Psychotherapy of Eugene Gendlin (Gendlin, 1973). We can move one step up the ladder of theory construction by conceptualizing the unconscious in terms of organismic processes.

Like Kierkegaard or Freud, Rogers must also be seen as reacting against the prevailing zeitgeist of his time. The questions raised by wars, the materialism and competitiveness of American society, heavy reliance on modern technology, the rigid adherence of academic psychology to logical positivism as the only approach to scientific truth—all these served to sharpen Rogers's focus on the essence and dignity of human beings. Consequently, such global situations contributed to the development of the person-centered theory. The individualism of the American frontier, the belief in self-reliance, and the conviction that the individual could learn and do whatever was necessary probably also contributed to Rogers's development of the person-centered approach, according to Meador (Meador & Rogers, 1973).

The widespread root system of person-centered theory seems to indicate that a collective unconsciousness in involved. It is conceivable that Rogers, in actually *being* the principles of person-centered theory, in tuning in and utilizing all of himself, made explicit some basic collective truths. He did so at a time when and in a language to which a great many people were receptive. Thus, there is yet another root to the person-centered plant, the root that grew from Jungian soil. However, the plant is vastly more than the sum of its roots. It is also much more than the sum of all its leaves, branches, and flowers. It is a growing, living thing, responsive to the conditions in which it grows.

Beginnings

In light of the centrality of religious concepts in person-centered theory, it is not surprising to find that Rogers grew up in a family "where hard work and a highly conservative (almost fundamentalist) Protestant Christianity were about equally revered" (Rogers, 1959b). His parents raised their children in a firm, gentle way; definite orders were seldom given, as with Rogers as a therapist. Although he rejected the family view of religion, he spent two years as a graduate student at the Union Theological Seminary. The freedom of philosophical thought and respect for honest attempts at resolving meaningful problems which Rogers encountered at the seminary gave him a taste of unconditional positive regard. He also experienced the same spirit of tolerance when he attended the World Federation of Christian Students in Peking during his third year at the university. His contact with Oriental philosophies was a moving and exciting experience for him.

As a child, Rogers loved solitude, preferring to work independently and alone on the farm. Luckily, from high school through graduate school he encountered several teachers who encouraged him to be original in his academic work. He spent two years studying medieval history and two years studying philosophy and religion before he began to study psychology. Besides Union Theological Seminary, he attended the University of Wisconsin and Teachers College at Columbia University and did his psychological internship at the Institute for Child Guidance in New York in 1927–28. After completing his doctorate in 1931, he was a clinician for 12 years at the Child Study Department of a Rochester social agency. In January 1940, Rogers accepted a position as professor in the Department of Psychology at Ohio State University, and in 1945 he moved to the University of Chicago, where he organized the Counseling Center. His next appointment, at the University of Wisconsin in 1957, was in the departments of psychology and psychiatry. In 1964 he moved to the Western Behavioral Sciences Institute and in 1968 was one of a group forming the Center for Studies of the Person.

Some of the main ideas, concepts, and people Rogers came in contact with at these places can be subsumed under general categories of history, scientific agriculture, philosophy and religion, education, and academic and applied psychology. In the educational field the emphasis John Dewey placed on the project method and on the importance of the phenomenal world of the student in the educational process was certainly meaningful to Rogers. As a student at Teachers College, Rogers encountered not only Dewey's ideas but psychology as it was developing in the United States, with emphasis on the control and manipulation of operationally defined variables.

In the applied field, Rogers had extensive contact with major personality theory orientations. Only the approach of Otto Rank, however, directly affected the development of the person-centered concept. The relationship of person-centered theory with psychoanalysis during the early and later phases of its development was more congenial than during the middle phase. Rogers was at variance not only with psychoanalysis but also with many of the concepts held by nonmedical practitioners who believed in the medical-diagnostic model of counseling and therapy. His acquaintanceship with behavior modification, at least with its "theoretical underpinnings," is one of longstanding disagreement.

Although these other theories in applied areas did not contribute to the development of person-centered theory, they certainly had their influence. Constantly assessing and defining his view of man in relation to the philosophies implicit in these approaches helped Rogers to clarify his own conceptions. At Rochester, Rogers's ideas about therapy began to take shape. He "began to sense the orderliness inherent in the experience of therapy, an orderliness which emerged from the therapeutic relationship, not one which was imposed from the outside" (Meador & Rogers, 1973, p. 121). He also discovered the value of listening attentively to the client in therapy. A social worker with a background of Rankian therapy made him aware of the importance of listening for the feelings behind the client's words. "I believe she was the one who suggested that the best response was to 'reflect' these feelings back to the client" (Rogers, 1975c).

His contact with the ideas of Rank through social workers at Rochester and through the writings of Jessie Taft confirmed Rogers in the direction he was taking. It also encouraged him to continue exploring the orderliness which he sensed to be similar to what Rank regarded as the essence of psychotherapy. Rank believed that the individual client has within him the potential to grow. He believed that the therapist can best guide the client toward self-understanding and acceptance by relying on human qualities rather than on technical skills.

To recapitulate, although several stages characterize the development of person-centered theory throughout its development, the core idea of trust in the individual's capacity has remained unchanged.

The Precursor Stage. The period before and during the full-time involvement of Rogers in counseling at Rochester can be considered as the precursor stage (Meador & Rogers, 1973). Through his experience in therapy, contact with the ideas of Rank and earlier contact with the ideas of Dewey, his view of the person as self-directing began to take shape (Rogers, 1973).

The Nondirective Stage. Rogers pinpoints December 11, 1940, as the day on which person-centered theory was born. On that day he gave a talk at the University of Minnesota entitled "Newer Concepts in Psychotherapy," and the reaction to this paper made him realize that he was saying something new which came from him (Rogers, 1974c). "Reflection of feelings" and "nondirective techniques" became the trademarks of this period. His main publication during this time was *Counseling and Psychotherapy* (1942).

The Client-Centered Stage. The name change from *nondirective counseling* to *client-centered counseling* was introduced by the publication of *Client-Centered Therapy* in 1951. During this time Rogers developed his theory of personality and psychotherapy (see Rogers, 1959b). Client-centered theory stressed that the person seeking help was not to be treated as a dependent patient but rather as a responsible client.

The Experiential Stage. During this stage the counselor became free. Organismic experience became as important a referent in guiding the therapist's behavior as it was for the client. Full humanization and mutuality of the professional relationship between psychotherapist and client paved the way for widespread applicability of the theory which began during this time.

Current Status

The Person-Centered Stage. The current status of the theory is best portrayed by the change in emphasis from *client*-centered *therapy* to a *person*-centered *approach*. This change indicates that the theory is conceived to have much wider applicability than simply in the arena of helping relationships. When the theory was extended to education, it was known as student-centered teaching. But as it has moved into a wide variety of fields, far from its point of origin, it seems best to adopt as broad a term as possible. Rogers has helped to initiate and develop what might be called a person-centered approach, not only in counseling, psychotherapy, and education, but also in marriage and family relationships, in intensive groups, and, to a lesser extent, in administration, the problems of minority groups, and interracial, intercultural, and even international relationships. The principles underlying the theory are indeed of relevance in every aspect of the behavior of human beings.

The shift in emphasis to person-centered points out more than the widespread applicability of the theory. It attempts to emphasize that it is as *person*, as *I am*, as *being*, and not just in terms of some role identity as client, student, teacher, or therapist that the individual is the unit of all interactions. The name change conveys the full complexity of each person; it indicates that each individual is more than the sum of the parts that make the person.

It also focuses renewed attention on the importance of actualizing the full potential of each individual and on the meaning of concepts such as experiencing, organismic valuing, and organismic sensing which the theory holds to be of crucial importance in fulfilling that unique potential. Earlier, experiencing had been regarded largely in terms of awareness of the richness of subjective feelings (Rogers, 1961). However, explaining experiencing in terms of inward references to feelings and bodily processes only represents at best a single aspect of the full human potential. Experiencing is more than just sensing visceral and feeling states. It involves being aware of the way one attends, perceives, processes, and integrates information of the internal visceral and external interpersonal and physical world.

Regarding experiencing in terms of the ability

to perceive, process, and organize information is in line with the thinking of Wexler and several other person-centered theorists (Wexler & Rice, 1974). These theorists regard experiencing primarily as something created cognitively by the person. Since disappointment has been expressed recently about the lack of real understanding of the essence of person-centered theory (Gendlin, 1974; Farson, 1974), recasting the theory in terms of the language and concepts of cognitive psychology and information-processing theory may help to make the principles of the theory more readily available to more people.

Rogers has consistently resisted continuing efforts to make him into a "guru, an idol, the leader of a movement." He is able "to let go of ideas, to share them, to prevent them from being dogmatized and identified solely with him" (Farson, 1974). These characteristics of Rogers are very much in keeping with person-centered theory. He demonstrates by his behavior his solid belief that each person has to discover those principles that are experientially meaningful to him or her. Thus there are no exclusive societies, institutions, or journals which are mostly devoted to the person-centered point of view. The very nature of the theory as an approach, a way of life, an attitude makes compartmentalization into exclusivity impossible. The theory is operative wherever and whenever people accept the different realities of each other in a spirit of separate togetherness. Any approach to the theory which treats it in compartmentalized form fails to do justice to the potential of the theory. As in all aspects of living, however, the theory is only as good as it is implemented, and its implementation is not as easy as it would seem at first. In fact, person-centered theory is deceptively simple. In the final analysis it boils down to one's ability to live one's potential in terms of self and others; and such actualization is not restricted to any group of people, organization, or institution.

Person-centered theory continues to be vigorously researched. As the theory reached further afield, so did research related to the theory. For example, Dr. Reinhard Tausch, in a talk given at the University of California, San Diego, in February 1975, stated that at his university, the University of Hamburg in West Germany, 120 masters' theses and nine doctoral dissertations exploring person-centered psychotherapy had been completed in the preceding six years. In addition to this spread of research in psychotherapy, the effectiveness of a person-centered approach has perhaps been most strikingly demonstrated by a decade of work by D. N. Aspy, F. N. Roebuck, and their colleagues in the field of education (Aspy & Roebuck, 1974).

Similar Theories
Person-centered theory overlaps with many other theories, but at the same time it maintains its own character. In this respect the theory symbolizes what its central holistic concern, the person, is all about. One way to indicate the generality of the person-centered approach is to consider possible alternative labels for person-centered theory.

Various descriptions in terms of a *perceptual-phenomenological* framework capture the essential nature of the theory. *Field theory* emphasizes the interrelationships of all systems within the total field, so that change in one affects all the others. The total field cannot be subdivided except for analytical purposes. Field theory stresses the importance of the past and present social, cultural, economic, and ethnic environments of the people interacting. Other headings in the perceptual framework closely related to field theory also describe person-centered theory as *transactional* and *Gestalt*. Although R. R. Grinker's transactional approach is not a theory of personality, the assumptions on which his psychotherapy is based have much in common with the process and feedback nature of personality defined in the person-centered way (Grinker, 1961).

The similarity in assumptions between Gestalt and person-centered theory has been mentioned earlier. Like the person-centered approach, Gestalt theory holds that the person functions as a whole and continually strives toward integration of balance of body, mind, and soul. Its concept of figure and ground also emphasizes the interdependence of man and his environment. The Gestalt approach, like the person-centered one, is phenomenological. The person creates a world according to individual interests and needs. One example will suffice. "To recognize man as a process is a beginning. To see him as a composite of processes in an endless universe of processes is to define him" (Kempler, 1973, p. 255).

The work of Combs and Snygg (1959) must be mentioned, not only to point out the similarity to the person-centered approach but to acknowledge its influence on development of Rogers's theory. Patterson (1973) questions whether phenomenology is consistent with the person-centered theory of personality, however. Combs and Snygg argued that all behavior is completely determined by the person's perceptual field. Rogers, on the other hand, believes in freedom and choice (see Patterson, 1973, for the development of this argument). Combs and Snygg (1959) are in general agreement with Rogers about assuming a basic integrative motive to explain behavior: "From birth to death the maintenance of the phenomenal self is the most pressing, the most crucial, if not the only task of existence. . . . Man seeks not merely the maintenance of the self. . . . Man seeks both to maintain and enhance his perceived self." However, Rogers has never been in full agreement with this view. The organism is maintaining and enhancing itself, and thus maintaining and enhancing the self-concept, but sometimes the latter task is not consistent with the former. Angyal (1941) and Lecky (1945) similarly arrived at a unified concept of self-consistency as the motivating force in our lives, stressing such notions as self-expansion, self-determination, self-realization, and increased autonomy.

The holistic nature of person-centered theory also suggests some kinship with *eclectic* approaches to personality. "Thorne contends that the Person is the basic datum and the only proper subject in the global unit of the 'person-running-the-business-of-his-life-in-the-world' " (Thorne, 1973, p. 455). This short statement indicates the shared optimism of the approaches of Thorne and Rogers. The routes by which these end products have been reached are, however, different. Thorne's eclecticism identifies and integrates meaningful elements from diverse, even incompatible sources into a consistent whole which facilitates understanding of behavior. The person-centered degree of eclecticism, on the other hand, can be said to have grown from within, utilizing the potential of a single individual as model rather than the ideas of several approaches. The meaningfulness of integrating seemingly diverse elements has been experienced

emotionally as well as cognitively in the Rogers model, whereas Thorne's approach appears more rational in nature.

Another broad classification of theories with which the person-centered approach shows intimate kinship is the *existential*. The relationship is so close that the person-centered theory might well have been presented under an existential heading. Not much more can be done in this section than to mention the names of some existential theorists showing kinship with Rogers. Among these Ludwig Binswanger, Medard Boss, Ronald Laing, James Bugenthal, and Rollo May are perhaps the foremost. Gendlin's approach of experiential philosophy is of special interest, not only because of his argument for creating an experiential base for existential concepts but also, as has already been stated, because he helped to return the focus to organismic sensing as an ongoing process (Gendlin, 1973). Although Gordon Allport and Abraham Maslow cannot be regarded strictly as existential thinkers, their view of humankind as being in the process of becoming blends with that of Rogers.

While it has been mentioned previously, the relation between person-centered theory and the Individual Psychology of Adler should be pointed out in this section as well. Person-centered theory could just as well have been called a *self* or *individual* theory, to emphasize the centrality of the person.

The unifying theme of all these approaches with that of Rogers is the concept of the person as an ever-growing, self-enhancing being. "The organism has one basic tendency and striving—to actualize, maintain, and enhance the experiencing organism" (Rogers, 1951).

Assertions

Development

Throughout the development of person-centered theory, the main concern has always been with dynamic aspects of the person, such as communication, relationships, and ability to change, rather than with the static structure of the person, such as personality. Personality is not conceived of as something one has. It is "a living, holistic entity, with goals, purposes, needs and meanings" (Burton, 1974).

Person-centered theory has grown out of continuing experience in therapy, with a broadening range of clients, rather than out of armchair or laboratory formulation. It was not only the experiences of the clients as perceived by Rogers that was important in formulation of the theory, but also Rogers's awareness of his own experiences which provided the materials for building the theory.

Some of the tentative, though important, conclusions arrived at over the years have to do with the basic nature of the individual.

1. EACH PERSON HAS AN INHERENT TENDENCY TO ACTUALIZE UNIQUE POTENTIAL.

Like all other living organisms, each person is born with "an inherent tendency to develop all his/her capacities in ways that serve to maintain or enhance the organism" (Rogers, 1975a). This growth force is part of the genetic makeup of all organisms. Human beings differ from other organisms only in that they are more complex. Thus, besides the fulfillment of basic biological potentials, human beings also have uniquely human and psychological potentials to be actualized. Each person, furthermore, is unique in the sense that the biological and psychological potentials of no two persons are the same. The physical, social, and cultural environment each one is born into can facilitate the actualization of our psychological and biological potentials to a greater or lesser extent. In both realms the tendency to growth is strong enough to overcome considerable hardships. One needs only to think of the many ways in which we behave irresponsibly toward our children, without destroying their ability to be accepting, understanding, and to love.

2. EACH PERSON IS BORN WITH AN INHERENT BODILY WISDOM WHICH ENABLES DIFFERENTIATION BETWEEN EXPERIENCES THAT ACTUALIZE AND THOSE THAT DO NOT ACTUALIZE POTENTIAL

From the moment of birth the baby knows what feels good and what does not. He or she knows this organismically and not consciously. The baby trusts organismically. This trust in one's own body goes a long way to make oneself known. Organismic valuing is not an elementary process. It is not only continually differentiating unpleasantness from pleasant bodily states but also monitoring varying degrees of pleasantness and unpleasantness involving many different functions of the body. It is clearly directed from within and based on a complex feedback system.

In the life span of the individual there are a number of critical developmental periods. These are not only periods of genetically determined biological changes (completion of neuron development, maturation of muscles), but also some periods which have been socially determined (such as starting school).

3. IT IS CRUCIALLY IMPORTANT TO BE FULLY OPEN TO ALL OUR EXPERIENCES.

The continuous use of bodily sensing is necessary for full development as a human. Use of our senses after birth seems to be necessary in several respects. First, receptor cells will atrophy if not stimulated. This is true for those modalities receptive to external sources of stimulation, such as the rods and cones in the retina of the eye. Investigators have shown that depriving animals of the use of their visual modality from birth is as deleterious as physically damaging the eye would be.

It is more difficult to demonstrate physical atrophy of cells responsive to internal sources of stimulation. However, it is conceivable that the same atrophying process will occur with disuse, since the receptor cells of the different sense modalities employ similar principles of operation. Continuous use of sense modalities is necessary to ensure their development, not only at peripheral levels (e.g., in the skin and muscles), but also at the level of the central nervous system. If no neural impulses are forthcoming from the receptor level, atrophy sets in at the different relay stations along the pathways to the brain and in the areas of representation in the brain.

4. SIGNIFICANT OTHERS ARE IMPORTANT IN HELPING US TO EXPERIENCE FULLY.

As the infant grows older it becomes increasingly important that it differentiate between its various bodily sensings and learn to identify each appropriately. The mother is of greatest significance in helping the child differentiate between and identify each bodily sensing, such as being tired, cold, and hungry, as well as the degree of tiredness, coldness, or hunger.

The process of bodily identification can be interfered with, not only by the proverbial "bad" mother, but also by the too-careful mother. Such a mother dresses the child too warmly in summer or not warmly enough in winter; forces the child to eat at mealtimes, whether hungry or not; punishes the child for wetting his pants, and so on. An overly careful mother may interfere with development of the organismic valuing process by not letting the child learn and by anticipating the child's needs to such an extent that the child never experiences a full range of organismic states, like never being cold or seldom being hungry.

Significant others, thus, can help a child focus attention on and symbolize his own organismic sensings appropriately. They can also be of help by not providing stimuli which interfere with the organismic sensings of the child, e.g., spanking or scolding the child for wetting. In Assertion 7, under the topic of conditions of worth, this aspect is touched on again, while it is discussed in greater detail in the section of validation.

5. EXPERIENCING BECOMES MORE THAN BODILY SENSING AS THE CHILD GROWS OLDER.

The organismic valuing process is based on the organism's potential available for that purpose at any moment in time. It develops as the child develops. It starts out purely as a sensing of bodily states, but the child's potential to process information becomes more differentiated over time. When that happens integration of one's developing faculties is necessary for optimal organismic sensing. An example is the integration of cognitive abilities with bodily awareness. Integration can perhaps be described as awareness of the relative contribution of each of the components of an experience to that experience. As the individual grows older, his life space, especially his contact and interactions with other people, also becomes more differentiated. Full realization of the organismic valuing process requires these external experiences to be integrated with the information which the person obtains from his body.

6. THROUGH COMPLEX INTERACTIONS WITH ONE'S OWN BODY AND WITH OTHER PERSONS, EACH INDIVIDUAL DEVELOPS A CONCEPT OF SELF.

The complex configuration of the self-concept begins when the individual experiences his or her physical self as separate from the environment. The infant at times bites its toys and at other times bites its fingers. The respective sensations are quite different, and on the basis of such experiences an awareness develops that the finger is "me" and the toy is "not me." At about the same time that the physical self is being differentiated from the environment, the social self emerges as part of the physical self. Thus, as the infant grows older he slowly builds up an increasingly differentiated field of experiences, called *self-experiences*, which become further elaborated through interactions with significant others into a *self-concept*. Once the self-concept is formed, a *need for positive regard* from others develops. Rogers believes this need is universal. We all need love—to be touched, literally and figuratively. In light of what happens to rhesus monkeys deprived of the companionship of others, it is clear that the need for contact, symbolic and physical, is of the utmost importance for the optimal development of a person's full potential (Harlow & Suomi, 1970). The need for positive regard, for love, influences perceptions, and perceptions in turn have a significant effect on self-concept. Since the individual's need for positive regard can only be satisfied by others, self-concept is increasingly differentiated in terms of others.

7. ONE CAN SACRIFICE THE WISDOM OF ONE'S OWN EXPERIENCING TO GAIN ANOTHER'S LOVE.

To the extent to which the individual perceives the need for positive regard from others to have been met, he or she develops self-regard. Both the need for positive regard from others and the *need for self-regard* are social manifestations of the actualizing tendency. It is important, first, to be liked by others, but eventually to like oneself, so that one's self-regard or self-worth is not always based on the regard of others.

Positive regard from others can be provided unconditionally (unconditional positive regard) or conditionally, i.e., *conditions of worth* which are attached to others' positive regarding of a person. If an individual receives unconditional regard from another, he will regard himself positively and will continue to evaluate experiences in terms of the organismic valuing process. However, conditional regard from others is more or less consistently the rule in life. Very early in life the child experiences that in some respects he is valued by significant others and in other respects he is not. However, many experiences satisfying to the individual may not receive positive regard from significant others. And since the regard of significant others is so important, the individual comes to disregard personal experiencing and adopts the view which significant others have of the experiences.

> This means that some behaviors are regarded positively which are not actually experienced organismically as satisfying. Other behaviors are regarded negatively which are not actually experienced as unsatisfying. It is when he behaves in accordance with these introjected values that he may be said to have acquired conditions of worth. He cannot regard himself positively, as having worth, unless he lives in terms of these conditions (Rogers, 1959b).

However, such a sequence in not theoretically necessary. If the child is allowed to retain its own organismic evaluation of each experience, even though some behaviors have to be inhibited, life would become a balancing of these satisfactions. There is little chance this will occur in the lives of most children raised in Western cultures.

A common example of not allowing a child organismic experiences occurs when it has been hurt. Our first response to the crying child is usually something like, "Now, now, it is not so bad," if we are irritated with the crying and want it to stop. The child then is faced with two unpleasant stimuli, one originating within its own body and one from a significant other. Whichever stimulus is more important to the child will tend to inhibit awareness of the other. This is the way the nervous system operates, as will be seen in a later section. Due to the importance of significant others for the child's survival and the need for self-regard, the child is likely to pay more attention to stimuli emanating from significant others and so comes to ignore self-actualization in terms of organismic experiences. Thus

the child may, for example, become an adult who denies the existence of pain or the painful systoms of an illness.

Summary. Each person needs to actualize his or her own self. The fullest extent of actualization is to love and to be loved. Love provides the climate for optimal functioning of our organismic valuing process, which makes possible the full actualization of our unique potential. Unfortunately, the fulfillment of our potential is fraught with dangers, the greatest of which is sacrificing the self for another's love. The next section deals with this aspect.

Maintenance

Person-centered theory does not believe that development of personality is ever completed. The foregoing discussion can be regarded as developmental in the sense that it introduced the elements and interplay between elements of importance in shaping and reshaping that complex process we call personality. This section on maintenance, therefore, logically continues where the previous section left off.

8.   A RIFT CAN DEVELOP BETWEEN WHAT IS ACTUALLY EXPERIENCED AND THE CONCEPT OF SELF.

When conditional regard takes the place of the organismic valuing process, the individual loses touch with organismic potential, and self-alienation begins. To maintain the existing self-concept, experiences inconsistent with conditions of worth, internalized into the self-concept, are perceived selectively and distortedly or denied to awareness completely or partly. Experiences in accord with the self, as defined in terms of others, are perceived and symbolized accurately in awareness. Thus the self-concept becomes increasingly inaccurate, unrealistic, and rigid over time. For the sake of positive regard from others, the individual comes to falsify some of the values experienced and to perceive them only in terms based upon their value to others. The person ceases to function as a unity as he or she did as an infant.

It is easy to lose contact with oneself, as demonstrated by the words of a well adjusted wife and mother of three.

I have an overwhelming sense of sadness—that I am unable to let others be. The problems of each individual making me bury myself in the morass—my doing, not theirs! A negation of myself where I become a myriad tentacled meddler trying to be responsible for all but myself, because the me is not there. I am carried away by feelings that are not always my own. Have I lost the key to my own being? Did I ever have it?

A while later she says:

Surely I should have learned that nonbeing can only be when I cease to exist in terms of my own consciousness. Why is it so hard for me to grow this way? I find I am repeatedly failing in trying to fight against this annelidic creature. To understand my own feelings and to recognize them is most important at present.

On another occasion this woman says: "I share with you this need for affirmation, and yet, if one has to lose oneself in the process, is it worth it? No and again NO!" She is experiencing the gap between her own experiencing, and the way of being she has taken on from others.

9. WHEN THE RIFT BETWEEN EXPERIENCING AND SELF IS TOO GREAT, ANXIETY OR DISORGANIZED BEHAVIOR RESULTS.

Experiencing new events enhances the likelihood of incongruence between the experiences of these events and the self-concept. If experiences highly discrepant with the self-concept are symbolized in awareness, the integrated balance of the self-concept would be broken, and anxiety or disorganized behavior may result.

Rogers (1974b) discussed the case of Ellen West as an illustration of self-estrangement. Ellen West was made to feel, in some of the most significant moments of her life, that her own experiencing was invalid, erroneous, and unsound, and that she should be feeling something quite different. She surrendered her capacity for valuing experience and substituted the opinions of her parents and later of her psychiatrists. Twice she fell in love with a man, and on both occasions she surrendered her love in favor of her father's wishes against it. Tragically, not only did she give up, but she came to mistrust her inner experiences. Rogers puts her feelings schematically. "I thought my feelings meant that I was in love. I

felt I was doing the positive and meaningful thing to get engaged. But my experience cannot be trusted. I was not in love."

10. VALIDATING EXPERIENCING IN TERMS OF OTHERS CAN NEVER BE COMPLETED.

Contemporary men and women are faced with an additional dilemma. They often distrust and ignore their own experiencing in order to be accepted, respected, and loved by others, but then they find that adopting the norm of significant others still does not guarantee them that acceptance. The person of today is faced with a bewildering array of beliefs and meanings, so that it is impossible to take on a generally approved self.

Incongruence, thus, exists between one's social experience and one's self-concept, but also between the self-concept based on the value of some groups of significant others and the values of still other groups. It would therefore seem wise, if self-concept is defined in terms of the values of others, to maintain contact with a unified and strongly supportive set of beliefs and meanings. This is perhaps the life-saving "wisdom" behind many religious sects, various schools of psychology, and, within various schools, subschools.

11. ALL MALADJUSTMENT, OF WHATEVER DEGREE, COMES ABOUT THROUGH DENIAL OF EXPERIENCES DISCREPANT WITH THE SELF-CONCEPT.

Adjustment problems represent only part of a continuum of human behavior, ranging from disorganized behavior to highly self-actualizing behavior, with defensive and normal behavior falling in between. Person-centered theory conceives behavior to differ not in kind but only in degree of incongruence between one's self-concept and one's experiences.

Incongruence between self and experience exists whenever an individual's perception of his or her experience is distorted or denied, whenever he or she fails to integrate such experiences into the self-concept. Experiences which are not in accord with the concept a person has of himself are regarded as a threat in that, if such experiences were accurately symbolized in awareness, they would disturb the organization of the self-concept by being contrary to the conditions of worth which the individual has incorporated.

Thus, such experiences create anxiety in the person and arouse defense mechanisms which either distort or deny such experiences, thereby maintaining the individual's consistent perception of self.

The continuing estrangement between self-concept and experience leads to increasingly rigid perceptions and behavior. If experiences are extremely incongruent with the self-concept, the defense system may be inadequate to prevent the experiences from intruding into and overwhelming the self-concept. When this happens the self-concept will break down, resulting in disorganization of behavior. This is conventionally classed as psychosis when the disorganization is considerable. During such a state of disorganization the person will at times behave in ways consistent with experiences which have hitherto been distorted or denied to awareness. At other times the person will behave in terms of the self-concept or will experience such conflict and anxiety that no action is possible.

Rogers's classification of behavior along a continuum denies the conception of neurosis and psychosis as discrete entities. Defensive behaviors include rationalization, fantasy, compensation, projection, and paranoid ideas. Incongruence between self ("I am intelligent") and experience ("I failed the exam") is handled by distorted perceptions of experience or behavior ("If I had only studied," or "The teacher dislikes me"). When defensive behaviors are unsuccessful, denied aspects of experience contradictory to the self-conception of the person come to the fore and overwhelm the individual. Acute psychotic and irrational behaviors fall into this category. After a period of disorganization, a process of defense sets in to protect the organism against the exceedingly painful awareness of incongruence, but the self-concept now incorporates the idea of being sick and has even less trust in its own worth than before. However, considering the continuum of incongruence, these labels have little useful meaning, especially since Rogers does not have the slightest investment in diagnosis, symptomatology, and forms of treatment specifically designed for a particular dysfunction.

12. PERHAPS THE MOST PERSISTENT DENIAL OF OURSELVES IS BY COMPENSATION.

The incongruence between a self-concept of worthwhileness—others like me—and the experience of not really being liked, of not being worthwhile, is handled by defining the self in terms of some role definition. Instead of "I am," the core identity of the person now becomes "I am teacher," "I am student," "I am male," "I am female," "I am a Hell's Angel." By adopting an identity in terms of some clearly defined role, we are buying a ticket into a relationship with someone else. Although such a relationship most likely precludes meaningful communication, it at least allows contact with others. However, the core of all relationships must rest on that which we have in common with all other people, on being, on "I am."

Two members of an encounter group spoke eloquently and meaningfully on their decisions on who they wanted to be. One said: "After overhearing a conversation where I was referred to as a 'nice Jewish girl' I realized the absolute futility of trying to please all with whom I came in contact, for I became a no one. I would hate to be a somebody, but I do strive to be *a* someone (not someone)." It is difficult in our society to be *a* someone without being a somebody. Another member said: "To be somebody needs only willingness to barter—to be someone requires unconditional unvaluing interaction."

13. TO BE ACCEPTED BY OTHERS IN TERMS OF ONE'S OWN REALITY RATHER THAN THE REALITIES OF OTHERS FACILITATES ACCEPTANCE OF ONE'S REALITIES.

So far in this section a great deal has been said about the conditions responsible for incongruence between self and experiencing. Perhaps the other side of the coin needs to be stated. We have a good idea about which conditions facilitate congruence between self and experiencing. One of the principal ingredients is an interpersonal relationship or relationships in which a person experiences unconditional regard and respect, where each person feels accepted in terms of his or her reality, and not another's. Such acceptance is a basic necessity for each person to accept his reality, all of his experiencing, the good as well as the bad. Other aspects on interpersonal relationships which facilitate congruence are discussed in the Treatment section below.

Applications

Assessment

It is a goal of scientific psychology to assess phenomena as reliably as possible, in a consistent manner, so that different measures of the same thing will agree. Also, of course, there is the aim to measure these phenomena accurately or validly. Psychologists have been very clever in devising all sorts of measurement methods. However, within the person-centered theory, certain forms of assessment have seemed more meaningful than others. Since in this theory, life is seen as process rather than as content, static concepts such as *intelligence* or terms such as *insane* are of little merit; of much more concern is measuring movement, assessing dynamics or estimating strivings. It is not as important where one is as it is whether one is moving. In addition, person-centered theorists are interested in the here and now, attempting to be with the person in the moment of his being.

Accordingly, we will discuss two major assessment methods used by person-centered researchers:

1. The Q-sort, a technique refined by William Stephenson (1953), a colleague with Carl Rogers at the University of Chicago in the early 1950s, which was employed extensively in a number of research studies reported in Rogers and Dymond (1954).
2. A process scale (Rogers & Rablen, 1958) which offers a kind of measuring stick to determine the level of psychological functioning of any person at any time in terms of analysis of verbal productions.

The Q-Sort. Rogers used Stephenson's Q-sort technique in an attempt to give operational definition to the self-concept as well as to evaluate the relationship of inner phenomenological changes occurring during psychotherapy to externally perceived diagnostic changes. The Q-sort consists of a series of statements regarding the self, such as "I am an attractive person," which the individual has to sort to present himself or herself as of the present. The Q-sort is a flexible approach; items can be constructed to serve a variety of purposes. In this sense it is similar to Osgood's semantic differential technique.

A popular use of the Q-sort is to obtain a measure, not only of the concept of self but also of a person's concept of his or her ideal self. The discrepancy between real and ideal self is believed to provide an index of a person's adjustment. For instance, several researchers reported an increase in self–ideal self congruence as coinciding with successful psychotherapy. Individuals who know a person well can also be asked to complete a Q-sort of the same self-referent items to get a fairly "objective description" of another person. However, Hart (1970) questioned whether congruence of self and ideal represented congruence between self-structure and experience, which Rogers regards as the basis for adjustment.

The Process Continuum. In the late 1950s Rogers wanted to obtain a much more detailed view of the process of personality change. As he listened to a great many recorded interviews, he noted those points at which therapists agreed that change had taken place. He conceptualized a process continuum which gave both a microscopic view of the minute elements of change and a picture of the continuous flow inherent in change. Finally he evolved a process scale (Rogers & Rablen, 1958) in which seven stages were described. This scale involves recorded examples from therapy, rated as to their place on the scale. New samples of therapeutic interaction can be compared with these examples to indicate the state of process a client is in.

The low end of the scale describes rigid, static, unfeeling, undifferentiated, superficial functioning. The upper end of the scale is marked by personal fluidity, openness to change, richly differentiated reactions, personal feelings experienced in the immediate moment which are owned and accepted.

The scale can best be understood by some examples. Here is a client statement from Stage 2:

Disorganization keeps cropping up in my life.

Note that the problem is not owned but is described as external. No responsibility is taken for it. The statement is impersonal, remote from subjective experiencing. Self resembles an object.

The following client statement is rated as Stage 3.

I felt guilty for so much of my young life that I expect I felt I deserved to be punished most of the time anyway. If I didn't feel I deserved it for one thing I felt I deserved it for another.

This is typical of Stage 3 in that feelings are *described*, not expressed. They are in the past, not present. They are seen as bad. There is a freer flow of expression about self as an object. Personal constructs tend to be rigid, as the guilt is in this example. There is at times a beginning recognition that problems exist in the individual rather than externally.

An example from Stage 5, from a client in the middle of the change process, contrasts with the prior two examples:

I'm still having a little trouble trying to figure out what this sadness—and the weepiness—means. I just know I feel it when I get close to a certain kind of feeling—and usually when I do get weepy, it helps me to kinda break through a wall I've set up because of things that have happened. I feel hurt about something and then automatically this kind of shields things up and then I feel like I really can't touch or feel anything very much . . . . and if I'd be able to feel, or could let myself feel the instantaneous feeling when I'm hurt, I'd immediately start being weepy right then, but I can't.

Here we find a different relationship between the individual's feelings and personal meanings. Feelings are freely expressed in the moment of their occurrence. They are experienced in awareness and recognized as a contradiction existing in the self. The client is communicating his or her self in a highly differentiated way; personal constructs are fluid and open to question. The client's relationship to problems is one of self-responsibility.

An example from Stage 6 will give a sense of a high level on the process scale:

I could even conceive of it as a possibility that I could have a kind of tender concern for me . . . how could *I* be tender, be concerned for *myself*, when they're one and the same thing? But yet I can *feel* it so clearly . . . .You know, like taking care of a child. You want to give it this and give it that . . . . I can kind of clearly see the purposes for somebody else . . . but I can never see them for . . . myself, that I could do this for me, you know. Is it possible that I can really want to take care of myself, and make that

a major purpose of my life? That means I'd have to deal with the whole world as if I were guardian of the most cherished and most wanted possession, that this *I* was between this precious *me* that I wanted to take care of and the whole world. . . . It's almost as if I *loved* myself—you know—that's strange—but it's true.

Here feelings previously denied to experience are felt, expressed, owned, and accepted. The experiencing is vivid and releasing for the individual. Incongruence is experienced and dissolved. Self, at any given moment, *is* the experiencing which is going on. Personal constructs are dissolved, and the individual feels "shaky." Problems are no longer objects. There is much more trust in relationships.

The process scale contributes to personality theory as well as to an understanding of therapy. It constitutes essentially a step-by-step description of the manner in which the fully functioning person evolves (Rogers, 1959a).

Treatment

"It began to occur to me that unless I had a need to demonstrate my own cleverness and learning, I would do better to rely upon the client for the direction of movement in the process" (Rogers, 1967). This statement, at the heart of person-centered therapy, is deceptively simple. Defining the activity of the therapist in terms of trust in the self-actualizing tendency of the individual, someone not functioning adequately, requires a great deal more from the therapist than would at first appear.

Therapist Attitudes. Attitudes most important for releasing the potential toward growth appear, on the basis of research findings, to be: (1) a sensitive and accurately empathic understanding of the client, (2) the therapist's complete acceptance of, or unconditional positive regard for, the client, and (3) the therapist's genuineness, or congruence.

The relative importance of these attitudes or conditions has been a matter of a good deal of research and discussion. Until recently Rogers and others considered genuineness to be most basic (Rogers, 1975a). J. K. Wood, however, regards unconditional regard as most basic (Rogers & Wood, 1974).

Rogers (1975c) now considers the three attitudes to be differentially important, depending on the life situation a person is in. Congruence seems to be most important in ordinary, everyday interactions. In certain other special situations, such as between parent and infant, or between therapist and "out of touch" psychotic, caring or prizing may turn out to be the most significant.

Several authors concur with Rogers in restoring empathic responding as the crucial ingredient in helping relationships (Wexler, 1974; Raskin, 1974). N. J. Raskin found that psychotherapists from many different orientations agreed that their ideal therapist would first of all be empathic. Therapy appears to be most effective when all three attitudes are present to a high degree.

Accurate Empathic Understanding. The most important aspect of the therapist's "work" is to try to understand what the other person (the client) is experiencing, thinking, and feeling, and how the other perceives his or her behavior. This requires more than merely understanding the client's words. It involves being sensitive, moment to moment, to the changing felt meanings which flow in this other person, to the fear or rage or tenderness or confusion or whatever the other is experiencing. It means temporarily living in the client's life, moving about in it delicately without making judgments, sensing meanings of which the client is scarcely aware but not trying to uncover feelings of which he or she is totally unaware, since this would be too threatening.

The therapist must also communicate his or her sensings of the client's world, frequently checking with the client as to their accuracy and being guided by the responses received. By pointing to the possible meanings in the flow of the client's experiencing, the therapist helps the client to focus on this useful type of referent, to experience meanings more fully, and to move forward in the experiencing.

To be with another in this way means that for the time being the therapist lays aside his or her own views and values to enter another's world without prejudice. In some sense, laying aside one's self in this way can only be done by those secure enough in themselves that they know they will not get lost in what may turn out to be the strange or bizarre world of others, and they can

comfortably return to their own world when they wish (Rogers, 1975c).

Wexler (1974) considers empathy to be more than an attitude. He sees it as a consistent pattern of overt behaviors, an attempt by the therapist to organize the information presented by the client so that the *meaning* of the information stands out more clearly and accurately to the client.

Only if the client's *attention* is focused on important facets of meaning in the flow of experiencing can his nervous system process such information so that it stands out clearly in awareness. The more competing information is focused on by the client or introduced by the therapist, the less likely it is that experientially significant material will be processed.

Empathy is not sympathy. A person who is sympathetic negates himself and by an osmotic process is both absorbed and absorbing. With empathy there is an inner strength which can alienate the giver from the receiver, unless the person being confronted is prepared to stifle initial emotion and "feel" only after chewing the feedback, swallowing it, and then deciding whether to regurgitate it or not. Thus an intellectualizing process must be put into motion.

Caring or Unconditional Positive Regard. Understanding, or even just sincerely trying to understand, another person from the other's perspective contributes a great deal to fulfilling the second condition for psychotherapy, caring for the client. Caring means that the psychotherapist accepts the client as he or she is—contrary, aggressive, or vulnerable, yet with potentialities for growth. It means valuing the client as a person, independent of the client's behavior or thoughts.

Acceptance of the client as a fallible but basically trustworthy human being is blended with an empathic understanding. These two therapeutic attitudes do not exist as separate entities. Respect without empathy is of little value, since the client may view such respect as indiscriminate. "If you knew the real me you wouldn't respect me," or "You like everybody, so there is nothing special about your liking me."

The person-centered approach to therapy and Rogers's own behavior as therapist have often been conceptualized as being purely a commitment in verbal terms. It should be pointed out that Rogers's expressions of concern through behavioral acts is perhaps one of the least appreciated aspects of his work as therapist and of his theory.

Genuineness or Congruence. The third condition of therapy as described by Rogers in responding fully to another, interacting and accepting the person regardless of his or her role definition as client, as neurotic, as psychotic, and so on, can only be fulfilled if the therapist responds as a full human person and not just in terms of the role of therapist. Being real in a relationship is risky. However, it is precisely the fact that one is prepared to take the risk of being a fallible human being, of being a someone rather than a somebody, that indicates to the other person that he or she is cared for, regardless of status or lack of status. Thus, in being transparent to the other person, in being open to the feelings and attitudes flowing at any moment, the therapist fulfills the essential prerequisite for empathic understanding of another.

Congruence can be considered as a precondition for being real in the fullest sense of the term. It requires that what one is feeling at an experiential or visceral level is clearly present in awareness and available for direct communication to another person when appropriate. *Genuineness* is not burdening the client or another person with one's own problems or feelings; it is not impulsive blurting out of feelings. For example, a therapist who is bored during the therapy hour does not express this boredom to the client before considering his or her own responsibility in feeling bored. However, if such feelings persist in the relationship, genuineness means willingness to express such feelings.

In general terms, the process of change can be described as a sequence of experiences by which the client gradually comes to have the same regard for self as the therapist does. Someone really listening helps the client, little by little, to become sensitive and aware of communications and feelings from within. When the client can express feelings never before dared to be expressed and still experiences the unshaken regard of the therapist, it becomes easier to adopt that same attitude and to find self-acceptance just as one is.

When this happens the client is able to differentiate more accurately between the various components of experiencing: bodily state, perceptions, social situation, and the way the information from all these sources is integrated. In so doing the person is able to symbolize experiences more accurately in awareness.

In the process of growth, the self-concept the person has keeps changing, as previously denied experiences are assimilated. The individual also comes to realize personal responsibility for the meanings given to these experiences. Thus, the concept of self becomes more internally based, more congruent with immediate experiencing. And since experiencing is ever changing, the self-concept also becomes more fluid and changing. The increasing congruence between self and experience reflects the improved psychological adjustment.

Institutional

Richard Farson (1974), who regards Rogers as "one of the most important social revolutionaries of our time", considers the core of person-centered theory, empowering the person, to be the forerunner of such "political" developments as students' rights movements, the use of paraprofessionals, self-help groups in health and welfare, participative management in industry, and new concepts of children's rights. In the same sense the insistence of Rogers on the dignity and worth of the individual can be related to the dissent with American participation in the war in Southeast Asia of the 1960's and 1970s and large-scale draft evasion by American youth. In a manuscript entitled *"Empowering the Person: A Quiet Revolution,"* which Rogers is working on at present (1976), he is reassessing the "political" effects of all that he and his colleagues throughout the world have done and are doing.

The extent of the social outreach and subtle political implications of person-centered principles is nowhere more clear than in the encounter group movement. It has been estimated that an encounter experience has been part of the lives of perhaps as many as 10 million Americans. Not only in North America but in Europe and other countries, the encounter experience has had considerable influence. One encounter group (filmed) was used to endeavor to bring together the warring factions in Northern Ireland. A considerable number of interracial group sesions have been conducted in the United States. People from various racial groups in South Africa—black, white, and Indian—have also joined in basic encounter groups.

Education. At the present time, the spread of person-centered principles in education is of special significance and is evident in many respects. It is being realized that the basic concepts, theory, and even the methods of the person-centered approach have a clear relevance to education at all levels.

The publication of *Freedom to Learn* (Rogers, 1969) contributed to the widespread dissemination of person-centered principles in education. The teacher is regarded as a facilitator of learning, not only of cognitive learning but of emotional learning as well. The task of the teacher is to provide a psychological climate conducive to self-directed learning and to be the provider of resources necessary for full exploration by the student of his or her interests, curiosity, and creativity. Galileo said it long ago: "You cannot teach a man anything, you can only help him discover it within himself."

Person-centered education is committed to learning by the whole person, to the inseparable unity of ideas and feelings, and to educating the total person, not just his cognitive faculties. Rogers believes these goals can be achieved best if teachers trust and respect students as being able to, and indeed desirous of, actualizing their fullest potential. Teachers who accept students as "incomplete" at the moment and who care enough to involve themselves in an open, expressive, mutual relationship with students can also learn.

Though the whole Winter 1974 issue of *Education* documented the influence of Rogers on education, it still did not cover the full range of his involvement in that field, especially his theoretical contributions to academic psychology and education, or his thinking on the nature of knowledge and the philosophy of science (Rogers & Coulson, 1968). Rogers has emphasized his belief that the real challenge to education, institutional as well as general, is not blind commitment to a point of view but acceptance that there are as many realities as there are persons, and that open-minded exploration of these differing realities is the most promising resource for learning (Rogers, 1974a).

Social Responsibility. The emphasis Rogers places on separate realities does not mean social irresponsibility. It does not mean self-indulgence or self-centeredness; or that each one does his or her thing without regard for others.

As far back as 1951 Rogers considered that enhancement of the self in the long run "inevitably involves the enhancement of other selves as well .... The self-actualization of the organism appears to be in the direction of socialization, broadly defined" (Rogers, 1951). Without social responsibility and social action, human life will atrophy (Gendlin, 1973). Maslow considered social interest as one of the characteristics of self-actualizing people, but even he failed to capture the very essence of social interest, which is the need to belong. Adler's concept of *Gemeinshaftsgefühl*, portrayed by this saying, comes close to describing this most basic of human motivations.

> I sought my soul, I sought my God; but neither could I see.
> But then I sought my brother, and then I found all three.

Community. Although the emphasis of person-centered theory has shifted toward greater social awareness, the focus is still on individual personal growth. The time seems to be ripe for the application of person-centered principles to more fundamental changes in community and social structures, as has been the case in two school systems reported on by Foster and Back (1974) and Rogers (1974d).

The powerful advent of community psychology raises the distinct possibility that strategies of social change can have a far broader effect on optimal development of human lives and relationships than even encounter group procedures can have. William Rogers (1974) gives such an account of the South End Urban Renewal Project of Boston. The project started with an analysis of the identity and the decay of the South End community, noting, for example, the decreasing population and playground facilities and the increasing concentration of liquor stores. Various groups in the community were interested in reversing the trend. They coordinated their efforts and, in the best sense of the belief that the population with the problem has the greatest knowledge for solving that problem, they managed to contribute significantly to reversing the decay of the Boston South End. Their efforts ranged from the construction of housing units and new businesses to the development of improved educational facilities and the awakening of greater community awareness. The trust in and releasing of the capacities of the individuals in the community and of the community itself is a good example of person-centeredness in community development.

Other Applications. Even more important than the contribution of person-centered theory to psychotherapy is the ethical base it provides for people to be with one another. This base has influenced some restructuring of almost every field of human endeavor. Areas other than those mentioned above in which the influence of the theory is acknowledged to a greater or lesser extent include religion, nursing, medicine, psychiatry, dentistry, law enforcement, race and cultural relations, social work, industry, and organizational development.

Of special significance is the impact of person-centeredness on marriage and family life (Rogers, 1972). These areas of interaction are so basic to the lives of all, and yet there is considerable floundering in this regard. It is safe to assume that being married and raising a family is much more complex than has been assumed heretofore.

A profound description of the complexity of marriage was given by a woman in an encounter group:

Marriage is not voice and echo, but too often becomes two very definite and distinct voices wanting to be heard together, without harmony. It is to achieve the harmony that usually takes a lifetime of concentrated effort. But when the effort is too deliberate, conscious, the trying is more obvious than the result.

It is obvious that most people lack the skills to cope with such complexity. For these reasons Rogers urges that serious consideration be given to exploring the person's involvement with marriage and family life. Rogers's views on marriage are that neither the success nor the failure of a relationship is to be sought in the format, the institution of marriage as a partnership. More likely the answer is to be found in the commitment of each person to the *process* of living together in

harmony, in realizing what the woman quoted above said about her marriage: "In living with limitations there is a challenge and disciplined variety which builds resilience in adversity."

Self

Since most readers of this book are likely to be students, this section deals primarily with the student and the student's relation to the educational institution, and it addresses the student directly.

Person-centered theory believes wholeheartedly in something basically simple. *KNOW* yourself—*BE* yourself. By being yourself you can actualize the very best in you. You are like no one else in the world. Simply being ourselves is our greatest potential. We do not have to be great artists or scientists and contribute something worthwhile to *be* worthwhile. By tapping our individuality, each one of us can contribute as no one else can.

It sounds so easy. But, as it has been said so truly, "To be nobody but yourself in a world which is doing its best, night and day, to make you everybody else, means to fight the hardest battle which any human being can fight, and never stops fighting." Being yourself requires, first of all, *trust* in your own worthwhileness. And trust is not something that can be obtained from somewhere. Each of us has to experience our worthwhileness before we can know what it feels like. The opportunity for such an experience is all too rare in an educational and societal structure which consistently bombards you with the message that you are not worthwhile unless you behave in ways which others consider are important for you to follow. In the typical school situation, this means to learn facts. Others choose what you are to study and how you must study.

Person-centered theory maintains that you should have an integral part in deciding the content of your education and the manner in which you are to study that content. How many students have this opportunity? Person-centered theory also holds that the most meaningful way to learn about anything is to be actively, experientially involved with it. This means involvement not only with the theoretical nature of the subject matter but also with the practical aspects of the area you are interested in. In the case of studying personality, it is basic to be involved with people in a climate conducive to exploration of who you are, discovering slowly, through interaction with others, just who and what the forces are which go into the making of a person, into the making of you. How many students of personality theory have such an opportunity to learn about the person-centered theory in an affective-experiential way and not just theoretically?

Do you find it meaningful to do the course work required to learn about all the theories in this book? Do you want to go about it the way the teacher of the course does? This can be doubted. Yet your alienation from your studies is not over until you are evaluated. Will this be done in ways meaningful to you? External criteria are usually imposed on the already "foreign" evaluation. Your worthwhileness is dependent on achieving a certain level of performance on the examination of the subject matter, which may have some (but more likely than not will have little) significance to your real interests, to what your life is really about. Will the evaluation, like so many others, be only of your memory capacity? Yet will your whole person feel evaluated? Will you *allow* your whole person to feel evaluated?

To discover yourself you have to differentiate the components making up your experience. Recognize the demands of the institution, group, and society you are in for what they are, as having more or less meaning to what your life and the great gestalt of things are about. Listen to what you are saying to yourself, to the way you interpret these external pressures. What feelings are evoked by your interpretation of these pressures and your reaction to them?

Do you accept responsibility for the subjectivity of your interpretations? Do you accept that your eyes and ears and brain select, perceive, and process information differently from anyone else? This is your greatest strength, but it can also be your greatest weakness. While you are using your own emotional and cognitive experiencing as a referent for your behavior, you have to be sensitively in interaction with others and at the same time must allow them the opportunity to actualize their own unique potentials. You have to be responsibly independent, separately together. It is the belief of person-centered theo-ry that in being yourself fully, you will come closer to, rather than more alienated from, others. In being yourself, you will discover your need of and kinship with other human beings.

In your interaction with the present institutional system, you have constantly to define and redefine who and what you are through your choices, perceptions, decisions, and commitments. In fact, you *are* your choices, perceptions, and interpretations. The better you are able to symbolize your experiences of internal and external processes in awareness, the clearer will be the various alternatives among which you can choose.

Validation

Evidence

Most of this section will be devoted to work in other disciplines and areas of psychology which has a bearing on elements of the person-centered theory of personality, especially the concept of experiencing.

Experiencing. Experiencing emerged as a key concept in person-centered theory (Rogers, 1959b). It is variously referred to as organismic sensing, ongoing psychophysiological flow, or organismic experiencing. At the heart of Gendlin's Experiential Psychotherapy (Gendlin, 1973)—considered by Hart (1970) to represent the development of person-centered theory during the 1960s—it is the referent to which the individual can turn for guidance in understanding himself and in directing his behavior. Experiencing or organismic sensing has been defined above. Briefly, it represents utilization of all the person's faculties. It is an awareness by the person of the way he or she attends, perceives, processes, and integrates information of the environment internal and external to the body.

Each aspect of experiencing exists in relation to all other aspects. It is important to be aware of what is going on in the body—in touch with visceral activity—as well as to have knowledge of events occurring outside the body. It is also important to realize how the individual interprets the relationship between bodily and external events. Change in any aspect of experiencing influences the total experience. Work done in the areas of perception and sensory neurophysiology, brain research, cognitive psychology, and psychobiological approaches to social behavior have direct relevance to an understanding of the concept of organismic experiencing. A common thread which runs through all these disciplines is the importance of the information-processing capabilities of the organism.

Neurophysiology of Sensing Modalities and Perception. One aspect of experiencing or organismic sensing can be conceptualized as heightened sensory awareness. Or, stated differently, the average person is dead to the body and needs to be awakened to the world inside his or her skin. Paradoxically, to become more aware of bodily processes, the person has to pay less attention to stimulation emanating from the external world, for the nervous system processes sources of stimulation relative to one another (Rosenblith, 1961). This is true within each sensory system and also between different sensory systems (von Békésy, 1969).

We constantly have to decide what we want to pay attention to. Thus, we really cannot be open to *all* of our experience at any one moment in time. However, there is a consolation prize. Although we have to focus our attention selectively for our perceptions to stand out clearly in awareness, the choice of what we want to focus on is very much ours. We restrict our attention to those physical cues that we find meaningful and relevant. We also choose the modality with which we respond. How, when, and where we look, listen, touch, taste, and smell are important factors in determining what we will perceive. For instance, such a simple act as turning our heads away from a sound diminishes the intensity of the sound just that much to allow further inhibition at neural level to occur. You are likely to close your eyes when you listen intently to what is being said.

The impulses controlling the activity of sensory neurons and pathways usually originate in the neocortex of the brain, which represents consciousness. However, it is not only in the brain that impulses controlling sensory activity originate. The body has a wisdom of its own by which it determines what is to be perceived. On many occasions the activity of the brain is "controlled" by visceral reflexes. A dramatic example of such control is provided by the way reflexes arising in the tendons of the muscle control messages sent to it from the brain, thereby preventing the muscle from reaching dangerous states of tension (Cranit, 1955).

Research in the controversial area of subliminal perception also has a bearing on organismic sensing. One of the most clear-cut examples of subception, or, in the present context, organismic experiencing, is Helson's (1964) demonstration that a subthreshold electrical stimulus to the skin influences the perceived intensity of subsequent shocks of differing intensities. The same phenomenon has been established on other modalities as well.

The tonic-sensory theory of perception of Werner and Wapner (Allport, 1955), and the research evidence related to their theory, demonstrates quite convincingly that organismic states are part and parcel of the perceptual process. Although we can seldom claim awareness of the activity of our proprioceptors and interoceptors, the effect of such activity on our perception is nevertheless marked.

Very few individuals are aware of the control they exert over their perceptions by attending with some and not other modalities. The extent of the sensory awareness we are capable of is just now being realized. It is possible to use our sense modalities in nontraditional ways.

The current wave of interest in biofeedback, yoga, and various forms of meditation has great promise in helping the person-centered dream of trust in one's ability come true. Indeed, it is irrelevant whether or not biofeedback control over physiological functions and other altered states of consciousness are achieved through mediation of such physiological mechanisms as respiration and muscular control. Large numbers of people in the Western world are beginning to realize some of their organismic potential by trusting the ability they have to control their own bodies.

Brain Research and Organismic Experiencing. Organismic sensing can be considered not only in terms of receptor cell activity but also in terms of the activity of those areas of the brain, the so-called limbic system, which serve as the repository for phyletically significant instinctual behaviors. The limbic system organizes such behaviors as eating, drinking, renal activity, basal metabolism, digestion, temperature regulation, aggression, and sexual and maternal responses. In obesity, for instance, the ventromedial nucleus of the hypothalamus may be underactive due to the lack of attention being paid to the viscera. It is generally accepted that babies who are stuffed with food by their mothers have a good chance to become obese. They learn to ignore messages not only from the viscera but from the hypothalamic nuclei as well.

There is no disagreement that memories accumulated within the lifetime of an individual are stored in the brain. How it is done is still an open question. Although the genetic code has been broken, it is thought to be primarily a memory in terms of physical characteristics. Is it not conceivable, however, that the limbic system, for instance, also harbors archetypes along Jungian lines? Work on the transfer of memory from one animal to another and from one species to another indicates such a possibility. An uneducated flatworm or laboratory rat can apparently get an education by digesting educated flatworms or the brains of rats trained to do things. (Domagk, Laufenberg & Kuebler, 1976)

The integration of the functions of the left and right hemispheres of the brain has been of special interest during the past decade, with evidence emerging that the psychological natures of the functions of the two hemispheres differ. Psychological functions of the right hemisphere have been described as preverbal, prelogical, subjective, intuitive, global, synthetic, and diffuse, compared to the linear, logical, rational nature of the functions of the left hemisphere.

Thus, organismic sensing or experiencing is more than heightened sensory awareness of internal bodily states and of limbic system activity. It is the integration of this awareness with awareness of those functions represented by the neocortex. It is also the integration of the activities of the left and right cortices. Interpretation of organismic sensing along these lines is analogous to the way R. W. Sperry (1969) considers consciousness to be more than the activity of millions of neurons.

Psychobiological Approaches to Social Behavior, Cognition, and Organismic Sensing. The ingenious demonstrations of Stanley Schachter indicated the importance of physiological arousal and of awareness of such arousal in being emotionally alive during everyday living (Schachter, 1965). However, Schachter also demonstrated that although the pattern of physiological activation is necessary to experience feeling, it does not determine the nature of the emotion. Thus persons injected with adrenalin, if not told about its effects, experience anger or joy depending on the "behavior" of the stooge with whom they are placed.

Trying to find a one-to-one correlation between physiological activation and emotional experience has been one of the great wild-goose chases of psychophysiological research (see Sternbach, 1966). The specific nature of the emotion is dependent on the way we interpret the social situation in which we find ourselves. Thus, the perception of the social situation provides the label to the emotional experience. A woman cries when she is happy and when she is sad. She interprets the same physiological event quite differently, depending on circumstances.

Schachter's theory of emotion has been called a jukebox theory; although the electrical mechanism is all-important in the playing of a record, it does not determine which record is being played. That depends on which button is pressed. Social situations can be likened to the array of selector buttons.

In his cognitive theory of experiencing, self-actualization, and therapy, Wexler (1974) acknowledges but underplays the importance of physiological activation. Schachter (1965), however, has shown that physiological underarousal, such as that following chlorpromazine injections, causes flattening of the emotional response to situations with emotional-evoking potential. Schachter has also related psychopathic behavior and crimes committed against people to lowered levels or lowered awareness of physiological arousal. In his more recent work he has indicated how obese people are much more responsive to external stimuli than nonobese persons and, by inference, less responsive to stimuli originating within their own bodies (Schachter & Rodin, 1974). A major implication of much of his work is that greater awareness of internal bodily states can have far-reaching consequences for many, if not all, aspects of living.

Schachter's views are of direct relevance to the state of "being high" following the taking of drugs. It is clear from his work, and from many other studies, that the state of being high resides not in the drug but in the cognitive interpretation by the person of the change in the pattern of physiological activity caused by the drug. Thus, if drugs are to be used as a means to achieve altered states of consciousness, it must be done with full awareness of all the interactive elements involved in the experience.

Experiencing consists of many components, ranging from possible representation and utilization of Jungian-like archetypes in the molecules of the brain to human beings' most vivid cognitive abilities. What constitutes the differential proportions for optimal integration of these elements, however, is certain to remain a mystery for a long time to come.

Quantification of the concept of experiencing will have to assess the extent to which a person is aware of and utilizes the different facets of experience, especially perceptions pertaining to the body and to the prevailing situation. It will also assess the extent to which a person is able to integrate the different components making up the raw data of experience.

Research. This section will not attempt to present an overview of research in the area. Several such reviews are in existence (Cartwright, 1957; Seeman & Raskin, 1953; Shlien & Zimring, 1970; Truax & Mitchell, 1971).

It has repeatedly been shown that clients whose therapists offered high levels of positive regard, genuineness, and empathy evidenced significant positive personality and behavior change, while clients whose therapists offered low levels of these core conditions evidenced no change, or even exhibited deterioration in personality and behavioral functioning. These relationships held over a number of conditions, such as the theoretical or practical orientation of the therapist, the "type" of client, whether in an individual or group setting or in a therapeutic setting at all, and time of follow-up (as long as nine years).

In view of the importance of empathy as perhaps the most significant of the three basic therapist attitudes (see the section on treatment above), the following summary statements of the research reviewed in a recent article by Rogers (1975c) on empathy should be considered:

1. A large number of therapists of all persuasions agree that the ideal therapist is first of all empathic.
2. Empathy is correlated with self-explora-

tion and process movement.
3. Empathy early in the relationship predicts later success.
4. The client comes to perceive more empathy in successful cases.
5. Empathy is provided by the therapist, not drawn from him or her.
6. The more experienced the therapist, the more likely he or she is to be empathic.
7. Empathy is a special quality in a relationship, and therapists offer more of it than helpful friends do.
8. The better integrated the therapist is within himself, the higher the degree of empathy he exhibits.
9. Even experienced therapists often fall far short of being empathic.
10. Clients are often better judges of the degree of empathy than are therapists.
11. Brilliance and diagnostic perceptiveness are unrelated to empathy.
12. An empathic way of being can be learned from empathic persons.

Variables relating to the client have also been found to be of considerable importance to the outcome of therapy. The level of involvement of the client in the therapy process from the very beginning is an important predictor of improvement. If the client's level of functioning is too low initially, little improvement will result. The other variable which should be mentioned relates to the client's perception of the core conditions as being present in the relationship.

The research described in this section has been in the field of psychotherapy. But the effectiveness of a person-centered approach has perhaps been most strikingly demonstrated by a decade of work by Aspy, Roebuck, and their colleagues in the field of education (Aspy & Roebuck, 1974). They recorded over 3,500 hours of classroom interaction, involving 550 elementary and high school teachers in various parts of this country and abroad. They studied many variables of teacher behavior, based on ratings of these classroom hours, and measured numerous achievement and behavioral outcomes in the students involved. They consistently found that the teacher's empathy—her or his attempt to understand the *meaning* of the school experience to the student—was the factor *most* conducive to constructive educational outcomes. When taken together with positive regard (respect for the student) and congruence or genuineness, the results were most confirming. These three facilitative conditions correlated clearly with academic achievement, more positive self-concepts in the students, decreased discipline problems and truancy, and higher morale. Students who had teachers with "high" levels of these conditions were more creative and more effective at problem solving.

The full implications of this series of studies has yet to be felt, for the findings are just now being disseminated. But the totality of the research adds up to the statement: It *pays*—in countless ways—to be person-centered in the classroom.

The recent trend to view person-centered principles from an information-processing and cognitive framework may add an additional impetus to research in the area. Attempts are made to translate the concepts of the theory into overt behavior (Wexler, 1974). Also, the language used may be more congruent with the Zeitgeist and thus may make it easier for people who trust their cognitive faculties to understand and utilize the theory.

Comparisons

This section compares the person-centered approach with other theories and therapies generally and then with two specific approaches to personality with which it has experienced the greatest degree of conflict. In contrast to the person-centered approach these two approaches believe that the basic nature of man is reactive.

Relation to Theories in General. It has already been stated that person-centered theory is an approach, a way of life, upon which can be superimposed various specific techniques or theories. In a sense, then, the manner in which a theory is presented is more distinctive than the specific theory.

Person-centered theory attempts to look at the person as completely as it can. On the one hand it recognizes the importance of the microscopically small biochemical structure of the body. It considers the possibility that the genetic structure encapsulates even greater "wisdom" than generally recognized, in the form of primordial images of behavior patterns serving mankind. On the other hand, it views man ma-croscopically, with each person being inseparably related to the others. Person-centered theory recognizes the unique individuality of each person as well as the relatedness of each person to the other—the necessity of community.

Traditionally, the theory has been regarded as stressing primarily the emotional-experiential component of being. Emphasizing the emotional aspect has been necessary to complement the imbalanced view of man which has emerged from the scientific views of this century. But perhaps that point has been made, and the interactive and gestalt nature of the theory can be stressed. Like its view of man as a being in the process of becoming, an integral aspect of person-centered theory is that it too is constantly in process, constantly becoming.

Viewed from such a perspective, person-centered theory is distinguishable from those theories that deal only with certain aspects of the person. But since the person is an infinitely complex organism, it is highly likely that each theory, emphasizing a particular aspect of behavior, has value. Intellectual, perceptual, experiential, and other limitations have made it necessary to split investigations of the person into various fields and perspectives, such as physiological, political, spiritual, sociological, verbal, nonverbal, or past, present, or future oriented. However, the artificial barriers erected between different approaches should not blind us to the basic unity of the processes underlying the organismic functions. The life processes continue inexorably on their course, whether they are approached from the viewpoint of a behaviorist, psychoanalyst, Rolfian, or Rogerian. The person does not have a separate set of phenomena for each theorist. But the same phenomenon looks quite different when its different aspects are viewed from different approaches, methods, and preconceptions.

Relation to Psychotherapy in General. It is clear, then, that person-centered theory acknowledges the value of multiple perspectives and reacts against any compartmentalized approach which claims to be more than it is. The same is true with regard to other psychotherapeutic procedures. In contrast to most other methods of psychotherapy, the person-centered approach does not rely primarily on the technical training or skills of the therapist for therapeutic success. A fact seldom appreciated, however, is that the person-centered approach does not exclude such expertise from therapy, as long as it is made available to and not forced on the client. The person-centered approach is not a technique but a philosophy of life, more specifically an *attitude* toward interpersonal relationships, which when lived allows for variation in the concrete transactions of a relationship, in the specific symbols used in communication. How therapy is done is more important than what therapy consists of—the medium is the message. The melody remains the same, irrespective of whether the tune is played on a piano or violin or is sung.

Making the contributions of various techniques, such as Gestalt, transactional analysis, and behavior modification, available to the client actually is very much in keeping with the rationale behind the person-centered approach. It acknowledges that people perceive and are differentially receptive to various symbols. Some individuals may be particularly receptive to therapies working with the body. Others may find techniques dealing with skills in interpersonal behavior useful or may prefer to deal with situational and behavioral aspects, or with the existential and spiritual dimensions of their existence.

It is not only the idiosyncratic needs of the individual client which are catered to by making a variety of procedures available for exploring him or her. Such a procedure also allows the facilitator to contribute that skill or technique most congruent with his or her own level of experiencing.

Behavior Theory. Diehard behaviorism sees man as a biological organism at the mercy of stimuli from his environment. Rogers (1974c) describes this view as follows: "The universe was at some point wound up like a great clock and has been ticking off its inexorable way ever since. Thus, what we think are our decisions, choices, and values are all illusion." According to strict determinism you have been destined to read these very words which we have been destined to write ever since time immemorial.

However, behavior theory, or at least some learning theorists, are moving away from such a deterministic viewpoint. They seem to be realizing more and more, that awareness and cognitive

processes form part of behavior theory. In his presidential address to the American Psychological Association in 1974, Albert Bandura, for instance, stated that by representing foreseeable outcomes symbolically, future consequences can be converted into current motivators of behavior.

In yet another sense certain learning theorists have become more open to the full complexity of living in their thinking and practice of therapy. These individuals even allow feeling states and the actual expression of such feelings to enter into transactions with their clients. Reading Lazarus (1971) is a good example of the discovery by a learning theorist of the kinds of things Rogers has been talking about for decades.

Much can be said about the controversy surrounding the philosophical viewpoints of person-centered and behavior theory. However, only one last statement ought to be made. Person-centered theory has never disclaimed the importance of the principles of behavior theory in the lives of each and every one of us; neither does it disclaim the value of the methodological procedures of behaviorism in science. In fact, person-centered theory has all along acknowledged the importance of the environment to such an extent that it perhaps overemphasizes individualism—in the same way that it accentuates the emotional-experiential aspect—to counteract the increasingly pervasive and dominant role social situations and institutions play in alienating the person from himself.

Psychoanalytic Theory. Psychoanalysis also views the person as reactive. Rather than being a victim of the environment, each individual is seen as a victim of innate drives, motives, and needs, influenced by past frustrations and satisfactions. Person-centered theory, however, holds that the behavior of man and woman is exquisitely rational, even when the individual is not aware of that rationality.

In contrast to the view of the person as reacting solely to forces or stimuli, in the one case from without and in the other from within, person-centered theory regards the person as both reacting and acting, a being in the process of becoming, personal, conscious, and future oriented.

Many distinctions between person-centered and the two theories discussed above—behaviorism and psychoanalysis—as well as other theories have not even been touched upon. The main reason is that each theory probably has a great deal of merit and a great deal of meaningfulness for its adherents. In the person-centered framework the person is the theory; thus the other theories all contribute in the sense that they reflect what is meaningful for each person. Although what is meaningful for one theorist may not have the same significance for another, the theory of each represents a stage of conceptual-experiential development at that moment in time. It cannot be more, it cannot be less. Only in being that stage of theoretical and personal development as fully as possible in relation to others can there be movement and change. Only if the various theorists, learning theorists included, accept the different realities of one another, in a climate of trust, care, and respect, will there be optimal development in the area.

Prospect

In several recent papers Rogers has emerged as an outspoken prophet of the future.

In all candor I must say that I believe that the humanistic view will in the long run take precedence. I believe that we are, as a people, beginning to refuse to allow technology to dominate our lives. Our culture, increasingly based on the conquest of nature and the control of man, is in decline. Emerging through the ruins is the new person, highly aware, self-directing, an explorer of inner, perhaps more than outer space, scornful of the conformity of institutions and the dogma of authority. He does not believe in being behaviorally shaped, or in shaping the behavior of others. He is most assuredly humanistic rather than technological. In my judgment he has a high probability of survival. (Rogers, 1974c)

Rogers goes on to describe the emerging person as someone who hates phoniness, who is opposed to all rigidly structured institutions, who desires intimacy, closeness, and community. Such a person is willing to live by new and relative moral and ethical standards, is open to his own and other's feelings, is spontaneous, and is determined to translate his ideals into reality (Rogers, 1972).

Eventually this emerging person would foster a culture which would move toward nondefensive openness in all interpersonal relationships, toward exploration of the self as a unity of mind and body, toward prizing of the person as she or he *is*. This culture would seek greater respect and balance with the natural world, deemphasis on and the more equal distribution of material goods, a society more interested in human needs than rigid adherence to structure. It would value leadership based on competence for meeting specific needs, greater care for those who need help, a more human view of science, and creativity in all aspects of living (Rogers, 1975b).

Annotated Bibliography

Hart, J. T., and Tomlinson, T. M. (Eds.). *New Directions in Client-Centered Therapy*. Boston: Houghton Mifflin, 1970.

An easily digested book which presents a good account of person-centered theory as it developed up to and during the 1960s. The bulk of the book is devoted to principles in psychotherapy, process scales, client-therapist interaction variables, developmental theory, group experience, and phenomenological and experimental methodologies.

Rogers, C. R. *Client-Centered Therapy*. Boston: Houghton Mifflin, 1951.

This book introduced the name change from *nondirective counseling* to *client-centered*. The change was not merely semantic. It indicated a shift in emphasis from the negative, narrower statement, *nondirective*, to a positive focus on the growth-producing factors in the individual client.

Rogers, C. R. "A Theory of Therapy, Personality and Interpersonal Relationships as Developed in the Client-Centered Framework." In S. Koch (Ed.), *Psychology: A Study of a Science*. Vol. 3, *Formulations of the Person and the Social Context*. New York: McGraw-Hill, 1959.

Though written two decades ago, this article is still brand new. It is a classic, but the full extent of the experiential and cognitive wisdom portrayed in it remains to be discovered, even by adherents of the person-centered theory. Rogers presents his theory of personality, psychotherapy, and interpersonal relationships.

Rogers, C. R. *On Becoming a Person*. Boston: Houghton Mifflin, 1961.

This book has changed the lives of many individuals and may influence your life as well. Rogers shares his experiences as a person, a man, a husband, a father, and a professional in terms of what he sees as their relevance for personal living in a perplexing world.

Rogers, C. R. *Freedom to Learn: A View of What Edu-*

cation Might Become. Columbus, Ohio: Charles E. Merrill, 1969.

Rogers presents a design of what education might become, what its full potential involves. This is a book to help you maintain your sanity while you are receiving an "education" and also, like all Rogers's writing, to help you maintain faith in the great gestalt of things.

Wexler, D. A., and Rice, L. N. (Eds.). *Innovations in Client-Centered Therapy.* New York: Wiley, 1974.

A stimulating and scholarly work. Some of the chapters certainly represent a fresh and invigorating approach to person-centered theory.

Client-centered therapy. Film No. 1 in E. Shostrom (Ed.), *Three Approaches to Psychotherapy.* Sound film in color, 50 minutes (1965). Psychological Films, 105 West 20th Street, Santa Ana, California.

A therapeutic interview with explanatory comments.

References

Adler, A. *What life should mean to you.* New York: Capricorn Books, 1958.

Allport, F. H. *Theories of perception and the concept of structure.* New York: Wiley, 1955.

Angyal, A. *Foundations for the science of personality.* New York: Commonwealth Fund, 1941.

Aspy, D. N., & Roebuck, F. N. From humane ideas to humane technology and back again many times. *Education,* 1974, *95,* 163–171.

Burton, A. The nature of personality theory. In A. Burton (Ed.), *Operational theories of personality.* New York: Brunner/ Mazel, 1974.

Cartwright, D. Annotated bibliography of research and theory construction in client-centered therapy. *Journal of Counseling Psychology,* 1957, *4,* 82–100.

Combs, A. W., & Snygg, D. *Individual behavior: A perceptual approach to behavior* (Rev. ed.). New York: Harper & Row, 1959.

Cranit, R. *Receptors and sensory perception.* New Haven, Conn.: Yale University Press, 1955.

Domagk, G. F., Laufenberg, G. & Kuebler, G. Chemical transfer of acquired information in mice. *The Journal of Biological Psychology,* 1975, *13,* 13–17.

Farson, R. Carl Rogers, quiet revolutionary. *Education,* 1974, *95,* 197–203.

Foster, C. M., & Back, J. A neighborhood school board: Its infancy, its crises, its growth. *Education,* 1974, *95,* 145–162.

Gendlin, E. Experiential psychotherapy. In R. J. Corsini (Ed.), *Current psychotherapies.* Itasca, Ill.: F. E. Peacock, 1973.

Gendlin, E. Client-centered and experiential psychotherapy. In D. A. Wexler & L. N. Rice (Eds.), *Innovations in client-centered therapy.* New York: Wiley, 1974.

Grinker, R. R. A transactional model for psychothera-

py. In M. I. Stein (Ed.), *Contemporary psychotherapies.* New York: Free Press, 1961.

Hanna, T. *Bodies in revolt.* New York: Holt, Rinehart & Winston, 1970.

Harlow, H. F., & Suomi, S. I. Nature of love—simplified. *American Psychologist,* 1970, *25,* 161–168.

Hart, J. T. The development of client-centered therapy. In J. T. Hart & T. M. Tomlinson (Eds.), *New directions in client-centered therapy.* Boston: Houghton Mifflin, 1970.

Helson, H. Current trends and issues in adaptation level theory. *American Psychologist,* 1964, *19,* 16–38.

Kempler, W. Gestalt therapy. In R. J. Corsini (Ed.), *Current psychotherapies.* Itasca, Ill.: F. E. Peacock, 1973.

Lazarus, A. *Behavior therapy and beyond.* New York: McGraw-Hill, 1971.

Lecky, P. *Self-consistency: A theory of personality.* New York: Island Press, 1945.

Meador, B. D., & Rogers, C. R. Client-centered therapy. In R. J. Corsini (Ed.), *Current psychotherapies.* Itasca, Ill.: F. E. Peacock, 1973.

Mosak, H. H., & Dreikurs, R. Adlerian psychotherapy. In R. J. Corsini (Ed.), *Current psychotherapies.* Itasca, Ill.: F. E. Peacock, 1973.

Oden, T. C. The new pietism. *Journal of Humanistic Psychology,* 1972, *12,* 24–41.

Patterson, C. H. *Theories of counseling and psychotherapy.* New York: Harper & Row, 1973.

Raskin, N. J. Studies of psychotherapeutic orientation: Ideology and practice. *American Academy of Psychotherapists Research Monograph,* 1974 (No. 1).

Rogers, C. R. *Counseling and psychotherapy.* Boston: Houghton Mifflin, 1942.

Rogers, C. R. *Client-centered therapy.* Boston: Houghton Mifflin, 1951.

Rogers, C. R. A tentative scale for the measurement of process in psychotherapy. In E. Rubinstein (Ed.), *Research in psychotherapy.* Washington, D.C.: American Psychological Association, 1959. (a)

Rogers, C. R. A theory of therapy, personality, and interpersonal relationships, as developed in the client-centered framework. In S. Koch (Ed.), *Psychology: A study of a science* (Vol. 3, *Formulations of the person and the social context*). New York: McGraw-Hill, 1959. (b)

Rogers, C. R. *On becoming a person.* Boston: Houghton Mifflin, 1961.

Rogers, C. R. Autobiography. In E. G. Boring & G. Lindzey (Eds.), *A history of psychology in autobiography* (Vol. 5). New York: Naiburg Publishing, 1967.

Rogers, C. R. *Freedom to learn.* Columbus, Ohio: Charles E. Merrill, 1969.

Rogers, C. R. *Becoming partners: marriage and its alternatives.* New York: Delacorte Press, 1972.

Rogers, C. R. My philosophy of interpersonal relationships and how it grew. *Journal of Humanistic Psychology,* 1973, *13,* 3–15.

Rogers, C. R. *Do we need "a" reality?* Unpublished manuscript, 1974. (a)

Rogers, C. R. *Ellen West—and loneliness.* Unpublished manuscript, 1974. (b)

Rogers, C. R. In retrospect: Forty-six years. *American Psychologist,* 1974, *29,* 115–123. (c)

Rogers, C. R. The project at Immaculate Heart: An experiment in self-directed change. *Education,* 1974, *95,* 172–189. (d)

Rogers, C. R. Remarks on the future of client-centered therapy. In D. A. Wexler & L. N. Rice (Eds.), *Innovations in client-centered therapy.* New York: Wiley, 1974. (e)

Rogers, C. R. Client-centered psychotherapy. In A. M. Freedman, H. I. Kaplan, & B. J. Sadock (Eds.), *Comprehensive textbook of psychiatry II.* Baltimore: Williams & Wilkins, 1975. (a)

Rogers, C. R. The emerging person: A new revolution. In R. I. Evans, *Carl Rogers: The man and his ideas.* New York: E. P. Dutton, 1975. (b)

Rogers, C. R. Empathic: An unappreciated way of being. *The Counseling Psychologist,* 1975, *5,* 2–10. (c)

Rogers, C. R., & Coulson, W. R. (Eds.). *Man and the science of man.* Columbus, Ohio: Charles E. Merrill, 1968.

Rogers, C. R., & Dymond, R. F. (Eds.). *Psychotherapy and personality change.* Chicago: University of Chicago Press, 1954.

Rogers, C. R., & Rablen, R. A. *A scale of process in psychotherapy.* Unpublished manuscript, Center for Studies of the Person, La Jolla, Calif., 1958.

Rogers, C. R., & Wood, J. K. Client-centered theory: Carl R. Rogers. In A. Burton (Ed.), *Operational theories of personality.* New York: Brunner/Mazel, 1974.

Rogers, C. R. Client-centered and symbolic perspectives on social change: A schematic model. In D. A. Wexler & L. N. Rice (Eds.), *Innovations in client-centered therapy.* New York: Wiley, 1974.

Rosenblith, W. A. (Ed.) *Sensory communication.* Cambridge, Mass.: MIT Press, 1961.

Schachter, S. The interaction of cognitive and physiological determinants of emotional state. In P. H. Leiderman & D. Shapiro (Eds.), *Psychobiological approaches to social behavior.* London: Tavistock, 1965.

Schachter, S., & Rodin, J. *Obese humans and rats.* New York: Wiley, 1974.

Seeman, J., & Raskin, N. J. Research perspectives in client-centered therapy. In O. H. Mowrer (Ed.), *Psychotherapy: Theory and research.* New York: Ronald Press, 1953.

Shlien, J. M., & Zimring, F. M. Research directives and methods in client-centered therapy. In J. T. Hart & T. M. Tomlinson (Eds.), *New directions in client-centered therapy.* Boston: Houghton Mifflin, 1970.

Sperry, R. W. A modified concept of consciousness. *Psychological Review,* 1969, *76,* 532–536.

Stephenson, W. *The study of behavior: Q-technique and its methodology.* Chicago: University of Chicago Press, 1953.

Sternbach, R. *Principles of psychophysiology.* New York: Academic Press, 1966.

Thorne, F. C. Eclectic psychotherapy. In R. J. Corsini (Ed.), *Current psychotherapies.* Itasca, Ill.: F. E. Peacock, 1973.

Truax, C. B., & Mitchell, K. M. Research on certain therapist interpersonal skills in relation to process and outcome. In A. E. Bergin & S. L. Garfield (Eds.), *Handbook of psychotherapy and behavior change.* New York: Wiley, 1971.

Von Békésy, G. Similarities of inhibition in the different sense organs. *American Psychologist,* 1969, *24,* 707–719.

Wexler, D. A. A cognitive theory of experiencing, self-actualization, and therapeutic process. In D. A. Wexler & L. N. Rice (Eds.), *Innovations in client-centered therapy.* New York: Wiley, 1974.

Wexler, D. A., & Rice, L. N. (Eds.). *Innovations in client-centered therapy.* New York: Wiley, 1974.

Personalism is at the same time a class of personality theories and a specific theory; its general analog to psychology as a whole is functionalism. Personalism, a pervasive point of view of general eclecticism about personality, embraces a number of other specific systems, such as the theories of Viktor E. Frankl, Abraham H. Maslow, Gardner Murphy, Henry A. Murray, and Carl R. Rogers. However, personalism is most closely identified with the work of Gordon W. Allport (1897–1967), which evolves from the general psychological principles established by William Stern. It is also closely related to the British psychologist James Ward and the Americans William James and Mary W. Calkins.

Personalism is not easily defined, as is also the case with functionalism. While it is relatively eclectic, it is nonetheless specific. In the discussion in this chapter, paradoxes will be noticeable, as suggested by its most specific definition, *unitas multiplex*—a unity of multiples. The individual is seen as a unified *person* who is an organization of diverse *elements*: the recrudescence of billions of cells and millions of experiences, all fused into a single whole. Conceptual analogs to personalism in psychology are Gestalt and holism.

In the final analysis, all functions of the individual, all aspects and explanations concerning him, devolve on the self—the indivisible unity that makes a particular individual different from all others, consistently and peculiarly himself. This, the essence of individuality, is the reference point from which all psychological explanations are oriented. Accordingly, adaptation signifies the adaptation of the self; functioning means the functions of a person; adjustment pertains to the adjustment of an individual—and each element is identical.

In Allport's formulation, personalism is the uniqueness of the total physical-psychological system dynamically organized to cope with the world, inside and out, in an internally congruent manner.

Personalism

William S. Sahakian

GORDON W. ALLPORT

Introduction

Human knowledge, scientific or otherwise, would be impossible without the ability to theorize. In psychology, theories play a vital role, not only in personality, where courses are specifically entitled as concerning "personality" theory, but in other areas, such as the psychology of learning, where a number of books have been designated as concerning "learning theory." Kurt Lewin, a Gestalt psychologist, went so far as to assert that "nothing is so practical as a good theory." Other psychologists, among them the distinguished experimentalist Clark L. Hull, who influenced many notable psychologists, have found that it is necessary to begin with a good theory or hypothesis if one is to engage in meaningful experiments. To emphasize this theoretical characteristic, he termed his psychological methodology the "hypothetico-deductive method."

There are psychologists, however, who are adverse to theories. The history of the antitheoretical stance stems from the early part of the 20th century, when psychological views were espoused without adequate experimental substantiation, but this is not the case at present, for experimentation abounds in every field of psychological endeavor. Nevertheless, some psychologists continue to feel that the less that is left to theorizing, the less is the chance of error.

One of the current psychologists who has been less receptive than most to the acceptance of theories is B. F. Skinner. Skinner's earlier attitude toward the role of theory in psychology was quite negative, but in later years he has been less adamant. Like most behaviorists or neobehaviorists, he prefers to deal with observable, objective data rather than subjective theory. Yet, in the last analysis, he, too, had to resort to theory. Thus theory not only plays an important role in psychology, especially the psychology of personality, it retains an indispensable place.

In effect, theoretical knowledge is personal, for it exists in persons as an attribute of personality. Some psychological positions shy away from theoretical knowledge because it lacks objectivity. Nevertheless, it is a personal quality and a vital characteristic of a human personality. Psychologists must reckon with theoretical knowledge if they are to deal adequately with the personality of a human being. It is in this respect that personalism as a personality theory has the advantage over other systems, because it not only allows for human or theoretical knowledge but emphasizes it, along with any other human characteristic, whether or not it is subject to objectivity or observation in the usual sense of the term.

History

Precursors

Although self-psychology or personalistic psychology finds its earliest beginnings in the views of Socrates and Plato, its modern development begins in the preceding century. During the last quarter of the 19th century, psychologists such as William James rebelled against the elemental psychology of Wilhelm Wundt and interminable analysis of the data of sensation, feeling, and images. James, who sought to underscore the person, or the self, proclaimed that:

1. Every "state" tends to be part of a personal consciousness.
2. Within each personal consciousness, states are always changing.
3. Each personal consciousness is sensibly continuous.
4. It [the consciousness] is interested in some parts of its objects to the exclusion of others. (1892, p. 152)

James saw the person as a "stream of thought" or a "stream of consciousness" that belongs to a "common self."

The momentum of James was perpetuated by his student, Mary Whiton Calkins (1900, 1909), whose definition of psychology as a "science of selves" was intended as a repudiation of the elementalism of Wundt and his associates. She insisted that implicit in the concept of consciousness is a person or self, "a somebody-being-consciousness." Divorced from a perceiving self, perceptions are meaningless. Who, for example, can conceive of thinking without a person? Thoughts without persons obviously do not exist.

Although Gordon Allport received his doctorate from Harvard when it was steeped in the tradition of William James, his attraction toward personalism derives mainly from German psychologists, the line stemming from Wilhelm Dilthey, Eduard Spranger, and William Stern. According to Dilthey, it is a person who does the knowing, has the feelings, and then proceeds to will. Cognitive, affective, and conative processes are the contents of one's consciousness. A "uniformity of psychic life" derives from mental processes, resulting in a *unitas compositionis*, a unity of composition. This functional unity is a *sui generis* (unique) functional entity consisting of irreducible elements of a nonfunctional character. As a fundamental reality, the unity of life is basic; whatever psychological processes exist must occur within the person or *unitas compositionis*.

It was Dilthey's student, Eduard Spranger, however, who exerted a direct influence on Allport as well as on Eric Fromm, Karen Horney, and Kurt Lewin, with his publication of *Types of Men* (1928). The book, predicated on Dilthey's *understanding psychology*, contained Spranger's typological theory of personality. Spranger stated that meaningful human activity motivates one to goals and values because a meaningful act is not only goal directed but also is seen as worthwhile. Valued, meaningful, human activity extends beyond mere self-preservation or reproduction of the species; it encompasses all values. From this goal-directed or meaningful human activity concept, an integrated psychology of values was developed by Spranger. Spranger spoke of "types of men", and so designated his influential work in psychology. The six value attitudes producing six personality types are: (1) the theoretic attitude (knowledge-seeking type), (2) economic attitude (the practical type), (3) aesthetic attitude (the artistic type), (4) social attitude (the sympathetic type), (5) political attitude (the managerial type), and (6) religious attitude (the religious type). Every person cannot be completely designated by one of these types, for many persons are characterized by more than a single attitude or type. Nevertheless, most people lean heavily toward one of these six attitudes or traits.

The influence Spranger exerted upon Allport is particularly evident in *A Study of Values* (with P. E. Vernon, 1931; revised, with G. Lindzey, 1951, 1960). This book contains the Allport-Vernon Study of Values test which was popular for a number of years. Allport (1968b) was even more influenced by William Stern, whose per-

sonalistic psychology is explained in his three-volume *Person und Sache* (*Person and Thing*, 1906, 1918, 1924) and *General Psychology from the Personalistic Standpoint*, 1938).

Seeking to reconcile a world of value with a world of fact, and mechanism with teleology, Stern found a synthesis possible in a personalistic psychology. In the person, he said, one finds many parts unified into an integrated whole, a *unitas multiplex*. Unity, value, and purpose are found only within persons. Accordingly, he defined a person as "a living whole, individual, unique, striving toward goals, self-contained and yet open to the world around him; he is capable of having experience" (Stern, 1938, p. 70). A person actively engages in his environment, for it is partially self-selected. A person's relation with his environment transpires on three dimensions: (1) the biological (nutrition), (2) the psychological (conscious experience), and (3) valuational. Psychology is concerned with the acts of an individual, his enduring dispositions, the unitary person, and a value system.

Beginnings

The humanistic orientation in Allport's personalistic psychology has deep roots. Allport's father, a physician, turned his home into a virtual hospital, in which the son attended to patients' needs. Allport credited this experience for his abiding interest in human welfare and his humanistic outlook in psychology. Owing to his deep concern for people, he sought out those areas of psychology that were conducive to enhancement of the human lot. Throughout his life, his experiments and research were people oriented (rather than animal oriented). But Gordon Allport's interest was not only in people but in normal humans. Convinced that clinical psychologists dealing with troubled patients derived a distorted view of what the human being truly was, he sought to research qualities indicative of a wholesome personality.

In this, Allport shared views with Abraham Maslow. Both were concerned with healthy people. For the most part his students, such as Gardner Lindzey, Jerome Bruner, Hadley Cantril, Leo Postman, Brewster Smith and Thomas Pettigrew, also followed along this general path.

Allport became a key figure in establishing the Social Relations Department at Harvard, thus separating humanistic psychology from experimental or animal psychology. His humanistic interest evident in his personalistic psychology is also demonstrated in the titles of his five books on personality, which spanned over three dozen years (Allport, 1937, 1950a, 1954, 1955, 1961) as well as a sixth posthumous volume containing selected papers on personality (Allport, 1964). Gordon Allport also served as editor of the *Journal of Abnormal and Social Psychology* from 1937 to 1949 and was president of the American Psychological Association in 1939.

A pleasant person, Allport readily made warm and lasting friendships. Even his telephone voice and manner gave the feeling that establishing a durable relationship with this distinguished psychologist would be effortless. Friendships with Allport were not made at the cost of one's mental integrity or at the expense of making concessions to him, for he honored the independent thinking of not only his colleagues but his students as well.

Allport was born in Montezuma, Indiana, in 1897, but he was reared in Cleveland in a home of "plain Protestant piety." The humanitarian disposition acquired during the early boyhood years was to play a major role in his choice of career and the motivation of his activities. Allport always regarded the practice of medicine as a humanitarian calling. Consequently, it pleased him when he saw his son enter the profession.

Gordon Allport followed in the footsteps of his older brother Floyd, who distinguished himself in the field of social psychology, having written one of the early texts in that discipline, *Social Psychology* (1924). At the behest of Floyd, who had been graduated from Harvard in 1913 and was pursuing graduate work there, Gordon Allport applied for admission to Harvard, entered in 1915 and graduated in 1919. Allport's doctorate, conferred in 1922 when he was only 24 years old, centered on personality theory. His maiden publication, with Floyd Allport, was "Personality Traits: Their Classification and Measurement" (Allport & Allport, 1921).

The first course ever taught in the United States on personality was offered by Gordon W. Allport at Harvard University in 1924 as "Personality: Its Psychological and Social Aspects." Thus began Allport's professional career at Harvard, which was to last throughout his life except

for a four-year appointment at Dartmouth College from 1926 to 1930.

Personalism became even more deeply imbedded in Allport's psychological system when he cultivated associations with the philosopher-psychologists at Boston University, across the Charles River from Harvard. Boston University, a traditional stronghold of personalism in philosophy and psychology, afforded Allport congenial spirits with whom to discuss his personalistic psychology. One in particular whom Allport met in the 1940s was Peter A. Bertocci, who later became Borden Parker Bowne Professor of Philosophy at Boston University.

While at Dartmouth College, Allport enlisted some able students in psychology, among them Hadley Cantril and Leonard Doob, who followed him to Harvard and later distinguished themselves in social psychology. In 1928 Edwin Boring, then chairing the department at Harvard, offered Allport a position on the faculty, but Allport remained at Dartmouth two more years before returning to Harvard, where he stayed for the remainder of his life. "It is obvious to the reader," wrote Allport in his "Autobiography," "that I had from 1915 a deep attachment to Harvard—an infatuation that has continued to this day" (1967, p. 14).

Current Status

The current status of personalism, Allport's theory of personality, can best be appreciated by the development of his thinking as it proceeded from book to book. It could be said that every one of his major findings has become an established part of an integrated, eclectic knowledge about personality, its causes and its aspects. Consequently, in reviewing his various books and their main themes, we are not so much expressing a summary of historical findings as we are stating the current status of personalism.

By 1930 Allport had returned to Harvard, and by 1937 his thoughts were crystallized in his classic *Personality: A Psychological Interpretation* (1937b). In this book he stressed the notion of each person being a unique individual entity, as well as his important concept of functional autonomy.

As an outgrowth of his interest in personality theory, Allport was led to a study of religious values. The end product of this research was *The*

Individual and His Religion (1950a), initially delivered as the Lowell Lectures in Boston and the Merrick Lectures at Ohio Wesleyan University. Notwithstanding the fact that major religious leaders promote brotherhood, Allport found—to the amazement of many—that the average church-goer is more prejudiced than the average person.

The various findings of Gordon Allport and of his many students which fit under the general heading of the unorganized school of thought that is called personalism have been incorporated into general psychology and, often without identification, have been accepted as information of which everyone is cognizant. This is probably just what Allport would have wanted. A modest man, he had no intention of generating a personal school of thought or of developing disciples. The sorry record of alliances and enmities so characteristic of schools of dynamic psychology devoted to attempts to understand abnormal individuals, and the evident attempts at self-glorification by leaders of such schools, were completely foreign to his thinking. His main thought was to find the truth, to help people, to share with the world his knowledge—not to establish any sort of personal monument to himself. Consequently, this most unassuming man did not become identified with any of the evident signs of a system or a school; yet perhaps in the long run he may be more influential than others who are much better known in the field of personality theory.

Having researched religion, it was quite a natural course for Allport to proceed to prejudice (*The Nature of Prejudice*, 1954). Defining prejudice as "being down on something you're not up on" (1971, p. 58), Allport held that there is no single, simple cause of prejudice. He found up to 20 different distinguishable factors causing prejudice.

Allport's next statement on the development of his personality theory came with *Becoming: Basic Considerations for a Psychology of Personality* (1955), delivered as the Terry Lectures at Yale University in 1954. Here his contention was that inasmuch as personality develops in a continuous manner, it does not lend itself to divisions or segmental stages, such as Sigmund Freud, Erik Erikson, Jean Piaget, and a number of other psychologists had attempted. Personality, he claimed, cannot be locked into watertight compartments, for, as William James would say, human psychology is a psychology of constant becoming. In this respect Allport is also in accord with Abraham H. Maslow and Kurt Goldstein.

Allport's final major statement on his personality theory was *Pattern and Growth in Personality* (1961). It served both as his definitive statement and as his revision to his magnum opus, *Personality: A Psychological Interpretation* (1937b). From his first book to his last one, the theme of personality never lost central interest for Allport.

Similar Theories

Personality theories consonant with Gordon Allport's personalism include Abraham Maslow's humanism, Henry Murray's personology, and Viktor Frankl's logotherapy. All four psychologists are humanistic in their approach, belonging to what is currently termed *third-force psychology*. Each of them shows a disaffection for reductionistic behaviorism. Murray eschewed behaviorism as peripheralistic, Maslow as atomistic-reductionistic, Allport as Lockean, and Frankl as reductionistic. While three of these show respect for Freud, they developed personality systems independent of psychoanalysis. However, Allport held Freud and psychoanalysis in low esteem, if not near disdain, probably owing to an unpleasant personal encounter he had with that celebrated psychologist. At least three of the four (Allport, Frankl, and Maslow) were friends and visited one another on occasion.

Their conceptions of personality reflected their holistic and humanistic orientation. While Frankl defined the human being "as unity in spite of multiplicity" (1969, p. 22), Murray "supposed that personality is at all times an integral whole—that the constituent processes are functionally inseparable" (1938, p. x). Maslow spoke of "personality syndrome" to emphasize that personality is "a structured, organized complex of apparently diverse specificities (behaviors, thoughts, impulses to action, perceptions, etc.) which . . . . are found to have a common unity (1970, p. 303). The concept of personality to which Allport clung throughout the years is as follows: "Personality is the dynamic organization within the individual of those psychophysical systems that determine his unique adjustments to his environment" (1937b, p. 48).

Although Allport was more emphatic than the others in his insistence on the uniqueness of each person, Maslow, Frankl, and Murray also regarded every human being as an individual. Asserted Allport:

> Man alone has the capacity to vary his biological needs extensively and to add to them countless psychogenic needs reflecting in part his culture (no other creature has a culture), and in part his own style of life (no other creature worries about his life-style).
>
> Hence the individuality of man extends infinitely beyond the puny individuality of plants and animals. (1955, p. 22)

These four humanistic psychologists also are in accord with respect to the person being oriented toward the future. More than merely beings-for-the-present, people are beings-for-the-future. Future attainments as well as future states of being are of value and are motivating. While psychoanalysis, regarding "the child as the father of the man," finds the explanation of personality in one's past and present motivations in past experiences, these third-force psychologists view the individual in a state of becoming, as ever changing, rather than as tied to or victimized by his past. Allport even entitled one of his books *Becoming* (1955). Maslow referred to motivation by futural events as growth motives, in contrast to deficit motives. Long-range purposes, ideals, and values are instances of the future motivating an individual's present state of behavior.

Unlike Freudian psychologists, these psychologists maintained that healthy personalities are not incessantly motivated by tension reduction or the restoration of homeostatic equilibrium. On the contrary, healthy people often are stimulated by tensions, greatly enjoying those tensions that lead to self-actualization, often actually perpetuating them rather than eliminating them. Maslow spoke of self-actualizing tensions as pleasurable.

Still another point on which these humanistic psychologists agree pertains to psychology being socially relevant. Each held the individual responsible for his behavior, not only as an individual but as a social being. Frankl is fond of recommending that Americans should place a statue of responsibility on the Pacific shore to complement the majestic one on the Atlantic shore which symbolizes liberty.

Many of the humanistic views expressed in this section are also pertinent to Alfred Adler and Carl R. Rogers. Inasmuch as these two are treated in this book in separate chapters devoted to their systems, they are not discussed here.

Assertions

The assertions that can be extracted from Allport's writings are of two types: the developmental class, which relates to how people acquire their personalities, and a maintenance group, which deals with how people adjust, adapt, and cope. In Allport's system, which abhors sharp divisions, these two categories overlap to a considerable extent. They will be demarcated here to meet the conditions of this book, even though, as will be evident from a close scrutiny, the separation is indeed arbitrary.

Development

1. THE FUNDAMENTAL TENET OF PERSONALISM IS THAT "EVERY MENTAL FUNCTION IS EMBEDDED IN A PERSONAL LIFE."

This statement from Allport (1937b, p. 18) is one with which all personalistic psychologists will concur, since the individual person is central to psychological investigation. A person is more than a patterned entity toward which all valid psychology gravitates, for a person is a coordinating concept, a unity in the midst of multiplicity, that is, a multiple unity. Allport claimed:

> Without the coordinating concept of *person* (or some equivalent, such as *self* or *ego*), it is impossible to account for the interaction of psychological processes. Memory affects perception, desire influences meaning, meaning determines action, and action shapes memory; and so on indefinitely. This constant interpenetration takes place within some *boundary,* and the boundary is the person. The flow occurs for some purpose, and the purpose can be stated only in terms of service to the person. (1961, p. 553)

Psychological processes are not self-organized, nor do mental states carry on an independent existence. They are constituents of a whole, of a larger arrangement that is the person. To speak of adaptation, function, use, and the like devoid of persons is meaningless, because if adjustment occurs, it is the adjustment of a person, to and for something. Mental states are engulfed in a superior totality, that totality being the person.

Personalistic psychologists contend that the task of psychology—investigating the whole of behavior—necessitates the postulation of a person who is the originator, regulator, and carrier of the states and processes researched by the psychologist. For example, explained Allport, "There can be no adjustment without someone to adjust, no organization without an organizer, no perception without a perceiver, no memory without self-continuity, no learning without a change in the person, no valuing without some-one possessed of desires and a capacity to evaluate" (1961, p. 554). It is as William James claimed—all mental operations are found in some "personal form." Accordingly, from the orientation of personalistic psychology, the person must be regarded as the psychologist's point of departure.

This contention of the personalistic psychologist can be well illustrated by William Stern's treatment of space. Whereas traditionally psychologists have spoken of visual space and of auditory space, Stern repudiated them as fabricated abstractions arising out of psychological laboratories, for the only space that exists is *my space*, which is one space rather than one dissected into fragments. A person seated beside you on an airplane may strike you as being quite distant, while a cherished friend you will meet at the airport (though a thousand miles away) will feel quite close. Similarly, the psychology of time is comparable to space in being a quite personal matter. A segment of life lived ten years ago may seem closer in time than a segment only a few years behind. Temporal distance is highly personal, when viewed in a psychological light. A person's space perception and time perception blend.

Ask a personalistic psychologist what kind of creature a human being is, and his reply will be: The human is a creative unity, a purposive being, and a growing individual rather than a dismembered reactor reacting to stimuli. The se-cret of the human will be found not in analyzing

being but in coherently tracking the course of a person's *becoming*.

2. "PERSONALITY IS MANY THINGS IN ONE —A *UNITAS MULTIPLEX*" (Allport 1961, p. 376).

The tenet of the unity of personality permeates personalistic psychologies, and Allport's is no exception. The very concept of *self*, claimed Allport (1961), implies unity. Unity, however, is an achievement, for one must strive to attain it. The unification of personality as an achievement was also a focal point in the psychology of Carl Jung. According to Jung, a self is not something that the individual possesses; rather, a lifetime is spent in an endeavor to achieve it. Once it is achieved, however, fuller unity is realized. The self, therefore, confers unity.

Unification of personality is acquired by pursuing one major goal, with lesser goals in their rightful place of priority in a hierarchal order. A number of major goals affect the unification of the self, segmenting it and thereby making it lose its identity. Furthermore, they can affect a unified self-image adversely. A unified self-image is more than what a person is; it includes what he wants to be or what he ought to be. The more formative goals are the least attainable ones, yet unification is a product of striving, pursuing the fundamental goals of life which configurate it.

Since a unity or pattern is never quite complete, a personality cannot be wholly unified. The best, therefore, that a person can hope to aspire to achieve is a degree of congruence more or less in accordance with his direction of development.

3. PERSONALITY IS "THE DYNAMIC ORGANIZATION WITHIN THE INDIVIDUAL OF THOSE PSYCHOPHYSICAL SYSTEMS THAT DETERMINE HIS CHARACTERISTIC BEHAVIOR AND THOUGHT" (Allport, 1961, p. 28).

Earlier, Allport had defined personality as "the dynamic organization within the individual of those psychophysical systems that determine his unique adjustments to his environment" (1937b, p. 48). The principal difference between the two definitions indicates that Allport moved away from an evolutionary or adjustmental view of personality to one somewhat more consonant with a trait theory of personality.

By *dynamic organization* is meant the formation of organized patterns which results in hierarchies among the habits and ideas responsible for directing a person's activity. The term *organization* more than implies integration; it intimates the possibility of disorganization of personality, that is, abnormality.

Allport insisted on the term *psychophysical systems* to emphasize that human personality is neither restricted to nor reducible to the solely physical or the solely mental. Rather than being exclusively neural or mental, personality is an inextricable unity of both the functioning of the mind and neural activity. Psychophysical systems include habits, attitudes, sentiments, and all other orders of dispositions which can be subsumed under a theory of traits.

Note that Allport speaks of psychophysical *systems*. System pertains to traits, or preferably, a group of traits, regardless of whether the traits are latent or active. Systems, potentials for activity, are comprised of habits, sentiments, conceptual outlook, or a behavior style. Consequently, a habit, trait, concept, sentiment, or style of behavior is a system.

Another key term in Allport's definition of personality is *determine*. Not only *is* personality something, it also *does* something. Psychophysical systems are motivating. As motivators of the personality, they prompt or influence the individual to specific thought activity or behavioral action. Thus the systems are more than influential; they are directive, with their exertions on adjustive behavior and expressive activity of the individual. The personality, by such activity, comes to be characterized and known.

By *characteristic,* Allport means any behavior or thought distinguishing the person as an individual, as a unique personality. Although a number of mental concepts and behavioral activities are shared with others, they are essentially and fundamentally both individual and unique. Each personal concept and act possesses its own personal flavor, notwithstanding the fact that some concepts and acts are more idiosyncratic than others.

"*Behavior* and *thought,*" the final words in Allport's definition of personality, are all-inclusive terms referring to whatever the individual does by way of behavioral or mental activity. While an individual's behavior is adjustmentally oriented, mental reflection is necessary for effective action. Survival is not the only objective of behavior and thought; growth too is their paramount concern. The environmental situation in which a person finds himself plays a major role with respect to an individual's behavior and thought activity.

Although animals may be said to possess a personality, it is in a rudimentary form. As far as animal thought activity is concerned, our knowledge of comparative psychology is virtually nil in this respect. Animal investigations fail to provide facts that can be extrapolated for understanding human personality. Personality differences between two animals, such as rats, for example, are quite small compared to two humans. One warrant for this assertion is the immense complexity of the brain of a human being, as contrasted to the more simple brain of animals.

Note the term *individual* in Allport's definition. Along with *trait*, this word best characterizes Allport's personality theory, with the possible exception of *personalism*.

4.   CHARACTER IS PERSONALITY EVALUATED. Although many people employ the terms *personality* and *character* interchangeably, Allport delineates sharply between them. Whereas character is personality evaluated, personality is character devaluated; that is, once values are ascribed to a person, then the discussion has shifted from personality to character. When personality is considered in terms of good or bad, beautiful or ugly, and the like, the topic has moved from the psychology of personality to the philosophy of character. Character, then, is a question of moral values. To discuss character is to moralize, while to describe personality is to be engaged in the objective science of psychology.

Because character is commonly used clinically in the evaluation of personality, it need not be entirely dispensed with because of its etymological meaning. Etymologically, character means engraving. This connotation of an indelibly etched feature can be useful in the psychology of personality. It is in this latter sense that character is utilized by Allport.

Whereas *type* might be used in personality

theories of other psychologists, Allport would find the term *character* preferable. Typing individuals did not appeal to Allport, who stressed the individuality of each person. Allport, the essentialist, regarded personality as what an individual really is.

5. TEMPERAMENT, PHYSIQUE, AND INTELLIGENCE ARE THE RAW MATERIALS FROM WHICH PERSONALITY IS CONSTRUCTED.

Because infants possess physique, temperament, and intelligence, this does not necessarily mean that they have personalities; they only have a potentiality for acquiring them. If infants are outgoing, their parents might be prompted to describe them as having a "good" personality. For the psychologist, however, a good personality need not be outgoing. Both extraverts and introverts are merely personality types, neither necessarily good nor bad. It would therefore be more accurate to speak of infants just entering the world as "psychological things," rather than referring to them as persons.

People are born with intelligence, temperament, and physique, the materials from which their personalities are fashioned. Despite their being inborn, these three elements are nevertheless changeable, but any attempt to change them is restricted within the limits of one's potentiality.

By *temperament* Allport meant

> ... the characteristic phenomena of an individual's emotional nature, including his susceptibility to emotional stimulation, his customary strength and speed of response, the quality of his prevailing mood, and all peculiarities of fluctuation and tensity in mood, these phenomena being regarded as dependent upon constitutional make-up, and therefore largely hereditary in origin. (1961, p. 34)

Within certain limits, the temperament of an individual is alterable; it alters with the evolvement of personality. Nevertheless, as a biological endowment, temperament is fairly well prescribed from the time of birth, owing to one's constitutional, metabolic, chemical, and neural makeup.

Finding considerable difficulty in defining *intelligence*, Allport noted that most psychologists identify it "as the innate potential of a person for making appropriate judgments, for profiting from experience, or for meeting adequately new problems and conditions of life" (1961, p. 63). While one cannot be quite specific in delineating intelligence, it is obvious that geniuses differ considerably from idiots with respect to general intelligence. Yet, an exceedingly stupid person generally can possess a limited area of remarkable ability, such as is found in the idiot savant. On the other hand, some people with IQs considerably higher than average may lack a sense of direction, becoming lost rather easily when away from the familiar surroundings.

Although a person's intellectual capacity is for the major part inherited, his intelligence pattern is idiographic, that is, basically unique. One reason for this is that one's inherited potentials become enmeshed and affected by the personality as a whole. Both heredity and environment play important roles; that is, personality, including its subsystems (trait, habit, sentiment, etc.), is the function of heredity multiplied by environment:

$$\text{Personality} = f(\text{heredity x environment}).$$

Note that the causal factors (heredity and environment) are not added but rather are multiplied. The significance is that if either factor, heredity or environment, were at zero value (absent or too weak to have any effect), then it would be impossible for personality to come into existence. If the two were added together, then personality would emerge even if only heredity or environment were present. Allport stated the matter succinctly when he wrote:

> A geneticist once said, "Human personality is 100 percent genetic," meaning that no feature or act is without some genetic influence. But equally correct is the statement, "Human personality is 100 percent environmental," meaning that surrounding influences and learning enter into every feature and act. Researches, however, help us to decide that genetic influences weigh heavily in the endowments of physique, temperament, intelligence. (1961, p. 82)

Viewing personality from a biological perspective, Allport holds that *physique* plays as an important role as the raw material from which personality develops. While personality is fashioned by training and experience, the materials they work on and form are those of one's physique, temperament, and intelligence. Despite the early start that biology had as a science, our knowledge of the mechanics of genetics and the neurology of learning is quite meager compared with knowledge of the psychology of learning. It remains for the future to tell whether biological models of personality will ever parallel or surpass the psychological ones.

Biologically defined, personality is a "mode of adjustment or survival that results from the interaction of his organic needs with an environment both friendly and hostile to these needs, through the intermediation of a plastic and modifiable central nervous system" (Allport, 1961, p. 74). Personality, in the light of this definition, is depicted as the executive of the organism, its function being the assurance of the organism's survival.

The personality is viewed as sort of a "troubleshooter," confronted by the tyranny of the autonomic nervous system, on the one hand, and the environment, on the other. This scheme, to be sure, is oversimplified, for many human cravings, such as curiosity and ideals, derive from the intellectual component of the organism.

6.   PERSONALITY DEVELOPMENT IS
        ESSENTIALLY A MATTER OF LEARNING.
We must turn to the psychology of learning to ascertain precisely how personality develops. The problem is complicated further because every theory of learning is predicated on a philosophy of the human being, that is, what is conceived to be the nature of the human organism. Is the human a machine, or does a person possess freedom of choice? Is the human pushed by physiological forces, or is one pulled by ideals and values?

In personalism, psychological principles encountered in learning, such as conditioning, reinforcement, generalization, and the like, are utilized to explain personality development. They are however, valid only to a limited extent, being more applicable to infants and animals than to adults. To explain advanced stages of personality development, it is more profitable to resort to cognitive approaches to supplement or even supplant stimulus-response explanations of the learning process. Cognitive principles of learning include insight, learning sets, imitation, and subsidiation; stimulus-response principles include

reinforcement, conditioning, discrimination, and generalization. Participation, attentiveness, and biographical learning also can supplement cognitive and stimulus-response principles of learning.

7.   THE PROPRIUM ENGULFS "THOSE
        FUNCTIONS THAT MAKE FOR THE PECULIAR
        UNITY AND DISTINCTIVENESS OF
        PERSONALITY, AND AT THE SAME TIME
        SEEM TO THE KNOWING FUNCTION TO BE
        SUBJECTIVELY INTIMATE AND
        IMPORTANT" (Allport, 1955, p. 61).
Proprium, a term coined by Allport, must not be regarded as a thing to be separated from the person as a whole. It is Allport's version of *ego* or self. Personality includes more than propriate functions, for the person is an individual with the ability to perform propriate functions, among them the function of knowing.

The proprium is not, however, synonymous with the self, for the proprium is not a given element at birth but the personality's evolving aspect. Rather than a static entity, it is always in process, developing over time. To speak of psychological growth, then, is to be concerned with propriate functions. Citing the fundamental quality of propriate striving, Allport, noting that its goals are unattainable, stated: "Propriate striving confers unity upon personality, but it is never the unity of fulfillment, of repose, or of reduced tension" (1955, p. 67). Although the proprium is not in reality central to a person's sense of existence, it nevertheless includes "all aspects of personality that make for inward unity" (1955, p. 40).

8.   THE PROPRIUM HAS EIGHT ASPECTS:
        (1) BODILY SELF, (2) SELF-IDENTITY, (3) SELF-
        ESTEEM, (4) SELF-EXTENSION, (5) SELF-
        IMAGE, (6) SELF AS RATIONAL COPER, (7)
        PROPRIATE STRIVING, AND (8) SELF AS
        KNOWER.
These eight facets, or functions, of the proprium evolve in successive stages of life. They are experienced as peculiarly one's own whenever one senses one's self as present. The proprium unifies these various aspects into an integrated whole, a *unitas multiplex.* Accordingly, the proprium is the evolving perception of self as the person undergoes various stages of development.

It is not something of which one is aware of initially, despite its being the central core of one's existence.

The first aspect of the self, or proprium, arises as a *bodily me* or *self*. The experience of a "bodily me" is the first sense of selfhood, the initial experience of a proprium. To experience a rapid pulse or a sense of nervousness as "butterflies in the stomach" is *coenesthesis,* or a sense of oneself as physical. Illustrating the bodily sense, Allport offered the following experiment: ·

> How very intimate (propriate) the bodily sense is can be seen by performing a little experiment in your imagination. Think first of swallowing the saliva in your mouth, or do so. Then imagine expectorating it into a tumbler and drinking it! What seemed natural and "mine" suddenly becomes disgusting and alien. Or picture yourself sucking blood from a prick in your finger; then imagine sucking blood from a bandage around your finger! What I perceive as belonging intimately to my body is warm and welcome; what I perceive as separate from my body becomes, in the twinkling of an eye, cold and foreign. (1955, p. 43)

The bodily sense, to be sure, is not one's entire self, as is evidenced by those who have suffered torture and who report that the pain happens to the body rather than to the "me." Hence they sense a feeling of detachment. It follows, therefore, that there is more to a person's proprium than the bodily self.

The second stage of development of the proprium is *self-identity*. A person becomes keenly aware of his self-identity through memory. Because of this retentive capacity, there gradually grows a sense of self-identity. The phenomenon of self-identity continues, notwithstanding the fact that the individual is in the process of continual change. "Every experience we have modifies our brain, so it is impossible for the identical experience to occur a second time. For this reason every thought, every act is altered with time. Yet self-identity continues, even though we know that the rest of our personality has changed" (Allport, 1961, p. 115). Allport believes that the sense of self-identity begins with one's second year of life and continues throughout one's entire existence.

Ego-enhancement (later designated *self-esteem* by Allport) is the self-seeking aspect of the proprium, a kind of selfishness. It is closely related to self-preservation and egoism, with phenomenal manifestations of pride, narcissism, and humiliation. Despite these prominent manifestations of ego-enhancement, self-love does not necessarily reign sovereign in the proprium, for the proprium has other functions.

During the second or third year of life, children become acutely aware of themselves as selves and of their need for autonomy. This phenomenological outlook on life becomes a hallmark of selfhood. The child wants to make his own decisions with an air of independence, without the interference of adults. By the time children reach the age of six or seven their sense of self-esteem additionally acquires an element of competitiveness. Their unabashed egoism craves praise.

A sense of bodily self, self-identity, and self-esteem are the earliest developments of the proprium, all evolving by the time the child is three. The next two aspects of the proprium to be discussed—self-extension and self-image—emerge between ages four to six.

Self-extension or ego-extension, the fourth aspect of the developing proprium, arises in consequence of learning and the acquisition of possessions. The child develops a high regard for material objects and people whom he has come to love. With a sense of possessiveness, he proudly announces: "This bike is *mine; I* own a ball; that is *my* daddy; this is *my* house." Such objects are sensed as a part of himself, an extension of the self or ego. Thus the proprium acquires a new aspect, self-extension or ego-extension.

Related to self-extension is the self-image, which begins to develop as the child learns that his parents want him to be good and refrain from being naughty. Self-image is evidence of a sense of moral responsiveness, goal intentions, and self-knowledge. The two aspects of the self-image include the way in which a person "regards his present abilities, status, and roles; and what he would like to become, his *aspirations* for himself " (Allport, 1955, p. 47). It is comparable to the idealized self-image in Horney's personality theory. As the imaginative facet of the proprium, the ideal self-image charts the course of propriate progress, as well as coordinating the future with the present.

Between 6 and 12 years of age, an aspect of

selfhood develops in the proprium in which the person comes to know the self as thinker. This function Allport termed the *self as rational coper*. The proprium finds itself coping rationally with the social and physical environment. Sometimes referred to as the *rational agent* of the proprium, Allport's "self as coper" compares with Freud's ego as the conscious executor of the personality, with its task of coping the best it can with reality, and if necessary, rationalizing and inventing plausible excuses to preserve self-esteem.

It is not that the child does not think before the age of 6; rather, from 6 to 12 the child is thinking about thinking. At these ages the child may feign solutions to the problems that confront him, scheme, invent ways to avoid unpleasant experiences, or even deny the existence of obstacles he must face.

During adolescence the proprium develops another aspect: *propriate striving,* or the self as motivator. By the propriate-striving aspect of selfhood, Allport had in mind William James's definition of the self as a "fighter for ends." During adolescence long-range planning for goals and remote purposes such as the choice of a career occur. "The possession of long-range goals, regarded as central to one's personal existence, distinguishes the human being from the animal, the adult from the child, and in many cases the healthy personality from the sick" (Allport, 1955, p. 51). Propriate striving always refers to the future. Unlike other forms of motivation, propriate striving effects a unification of the personality, despite its being beset by conflicts. Furthermore, propriate striving, unlike animal striving, does not necessarily seek tension reduction or the maintenance of equilibrium, for often it maintains and even produces tension to realize its objectives.

Propriate striving, then, is comparable to Maslow's (1968) growth motives, rather than to Clark Hull's (1943) drive-reduction motivation. Borrowing Maslow's concepts of deficit and growth motivation, Allport pointed out that:

> ... deficit motives do, in fact call for the reduction of tension and restoration of equilibrium. Growth motives, on the other hand, maintain tension in the interest of distant and often unattainable goals. As such they distinguish human from animal becoming

and adult from infant becoming. By growth motives we refer to the hold that ideals gain upon the process of development. Long-range purposes, subjective values, comprehensive systems of interest are all of this order. (Allport, 1955, p. 68)

Although it is true that some people drift into adulthood devoid of any sense of purpose, they have failed to mature, and their selfhood is in a state of arrested development.

The cognizing self or the *self as knower* presented a difficult issue for Allport, who did not want to admit that a substantive self existed, other than the sum total of an individual's experiences. Accordingly, it was difficult for him to admit the self as knower. He finally concluded:

> We not only know *things,* but we know (i.e., are acquainted with) the empirical features of our own proprium. It is I who have bodily sensations, I who recognize my self-identity from day to day; I who note and reflect upon my self assertion, self-extension, my own rationalizations, as well as upon my interests and strivings. When I thus think about my own propriate functions I am likely to perceive their essential togetherness, and feel them intimately bound in some way to the knowing function itself.
>
> Since such knowing is, beyond any shadow of doubt, a state that is peculiarly ours, we admit it as the eighth clear function of the proprium. (Allport, 1955, p. 53)

By the eighth function of the proprium, Allport, of course, means an aspect of the self or ego. The "knower" is often regarded as the self per se, rather than merely an aspect of the self. The proprium engulfs the self as an object of knowledge as well as the knower.

The various aspects of the proprium together comprise the self or "me" as felt by me and known by me. Each aspect is a state of self-relevance, subjectively felt. While each aspect of the self is phenomenologically different from any other aspect, together they are united under the overarching concept *proprium*. Either *self* or *ego* would have served well instead of *proprium* had they been sufficiently encompassing, but these other terms are suitable for only a few of the aspects or facets of the proprium as discussed here. While the proprium is often conscious, there are many occasions when propriate striving functions on an unconscious level. Regarding the proprium as an operational construct, Allport defined it phenomenologically as "part of the personality which seems to be warm and central to the person, involving matters that are of importance in this life over and above the mere matters of fact in it" (1971, p. 42). The propriate functions provide the personality with unity.

Maintenance

9.　FUNCTIONAL AUTONOMY ACCOUNTS FOR UNIQUENESS IN PERSONAL MOTIVATION.

Functional autonomy is Allport's (1973b) theory of motivation. It does not purport to explain all forms of motivation, only contemporaneous motives. Pertaining to adults, functional autonomy views the motives of an adult "as varied, and as self-sustaining, contemporary systems, growing out of antecedent systems, but functionally independent of them" (Allport, 1961, p. 227). Defined more technically, functional autonomy "refers to any acquired system of motivation in which the tensions involved are not of the same kind as the antecedent tensions from which the acquired system developed" (1961, p. 229).

Holding that a vast difference exists between the motives of children and adults, Allport accounted for transformational change from juvenile to adult motives in terms of functional autonomy, that is, an acquired network of motivation developed from antecedent tensions rather than current tensions. Early tensions initially responsible for motivation may cease to exist, yet the motivation nevertheless functions on its own, autonomously.

For example, a castaway may seek refuge on an island, having abandoned a sinking ship. To survive, he fishes. Months later he is rescued. His work is that of an executive, and he is no longer required to fish to live. The original motivation for fishing no longer exists, yet this man may have acquired something new—an irresistible compulsion to fish and joy in fishing. Fishing has become functionally autonomous for this person. Allport, as did William James in discussing habits, illustrated functional autonomy by citing an ex-sailor's craving for the sea.

Now, the sailor may have first acquired his love for the sea as an incident in his struggle to earn a living. The sea was merely a conditioned stimulus associated with satisfaction of his "nutritional craving." But now the ex-sailor is perhaps a wealthy banker; the original motive is destroyed; and yet the hunger for the sea persists unabated, even increases in intensity as it becomes more remote from the "nutritional segment." (Allport, 1950b, p. 80)

Regarding motivation as contemporary, Allport held that functionally autonomous motivation can be central to a person's principal trends in life, and therefore it can be involved in propriate development. Functional autonomy as perseverative means that it is a local and self-sustaining system. While some functional autonomous transformations occur abruptly, others are gradual. An instance of perseverative functional autonomy is seen in the rat that runs a maze correctly when hungry to receive food, but when fully fed will run the maze anyway just "for the fun of it"—an example of what Karl Bühler (1927) called "function pleasure."

10.　PERSONALITY IS DEFINABLE IN TERMS OF COMMON TRAITS.

Traits, the common denominator by which the personality of one individual can be compared with another, are dispositions, which are more general and less restricted than habits or attitudes. The term *trait* as employed in the personalistic psychology of Allport (1931, 1965b, 1966) compares with the terms *dimension* in Hans J. Eysenck's personality theory, *factor* in Raymond B. Cattell's system of psychology, or *variable* in the psychology of other personality theorists. Allport viewed a trait as "a neuropsychic structure having the capacity to render many stimuli functionally equivalent, and to initiate and guide equivalent (meaningfully consistent) forms of adaptive and expressive behavior" (Allport, 1961, p. 347).

While traits, habits, and attitudes are all determining tendencies, each is distinguishable from the other. Habits relate to narrow and restricted modes of determining tendencies, such as brushing one's teeth regularly, whereas traits, as the more generalized forms of habits, would in this context extend to the removal of any sort of uncleanliness from one's person. As such, general self-cleanliness is a trait rather than a habit, such as brushing teeth after meals or removing dirt from one's clothing.

Traits can also be distinguished from attitudes. While attitudes have an object of reference and are pro or con in nature (favorable or unfavorable), traits are neutral. Furthermore, a trait relates to the structure of personality and thus is a useful concept in the psychology of personality. Attitudes, on the other hand, relate to the orientation of people toward their social and physical environment, and hence they are a valuable concept for social psychologists.

Relative to *common traits,* Allport regarded them as possessing extraordinary breadth and inclusiveness. In other systems of psychology, such as Jungian psychology, common traits are called empirical types. But Allport, seeing no special advantage in the concept of type, was reticent in allowing it a place in his psychology of personality. To apply a certain type to a particular individual is to do violence to him by forcing him into a pseudo category. Allport stated that a common trait is:

> ... a category for classifying functionally equivalent forms of behavior in a general population of people. Though influenced by nominal and artifactual considerations, a common trait to some extent reflects veridical and comparable dispositions in many personalities who, because of a common human nature and common culture, develop similar modes of adjusting to their environments, though to varying degrees. (Allport, 1961, p. 349)

When Carl G. Jung, Ernst Kretschmer, and others spoke of personality types, they had in mind two to four main types, whereas Allport believed there exist between four to five thousand permanent, distinguishable psychological traits. The best trait names, for Allport, were not specific but were range names, such as *aggressive, alert, ambitious.* Consequently, asserting that two people are aggressive identifies their aggressiveness not as being identical in kind but as belonging to a general class.

Allport also sought to distinguish between common traits and personal dispositions, the former being couched in one's common culture and the latter in "nature's own cleavages." Technically, a *personal disposition* is defined by Allport as "a generalized neuropsychic structure (peculiar to the individual), with the capacity to render many stimuli functionally equivalent, and to initiate and guide consistent (equivalent) forms of adaptive and stylistic behavior" (1961,

p. 373). Both traits and dispositions constitute a *modus vivendi* (manner of living). They derive their importance from the role they assume in enhancing an individual's adjustment to and mastery of his personal world. Traits and dispositions related to values, interests, sentiments, complexes, ambitions, and the like are motivational. Both traits and dispositions are constructs, that is, they are not directly observable but can be theoretically inferred from empirical data.

11. A PERSON MAY HAVE A CARDINAL TRAIT
    AND SECONDARY TRAITS, AS WELL AS
    COMMON TRAITS.

While personality is analyzed or summarized in terms of common traits, rare individuals can be found who are dominated by a single, overriding *cardinal trait,* with subsidiary dispositions being ancillary to this trait. A cardinal trait, being pervasive and outstanding, is regarded as a ruling passion, or the master sentiment of an individual's life. Notwithstanding its pivotal position in the personality and its pervasiveness, a cardinal trait should not be identified as one and the same with personality, for it is an aspect of personality rather than coincident with it.

Few people can be found with a cardinal trait dominating their personality, for most persons possess a small number of central traits. If you were writing a letter of recommendation for a person, the probability is that you would call to mind a smaller number of common traits characteristic of the individual in question, rather than a single cardinal trait.

In addition to cardinal and common traits, there are secondary traits, the less conspicuous identifying features of a person. Allport identified these secondary traits as "less generalized, less consistent, and less often called into play than central traits. They are aroused by a narrower range of equivalent stimuli and they issue into a narrower range of equivalent responses" (1937b, p. 338). These traits tend to be noticed only by close acquaintances.

Applications

Assessment

In Allport's personalism, personal documents

provide a major method for the assessment of individuals—for evaluating and describing the uniqueness of individuals. Allport described the procedure in a work prepared for the Committee on Appraisal of Research of the Social Science Research Council *(The Use of Personal Documents in Psychological Science,* 1942).

The personal document is an instrument which enables the researcher to learn what transpires in another's mind. Modern use of this procedure began with the work of W. I. Thomas and Florian Znaniecki, *The Polish Peasant in Europe and America* (1918, 1919, 1920). Defining the personal document, Allport called it "any self-revealing record that intentionally or unintentionally yields information regarding the structure, dynamics, and functioning of the author's mental life" (1942, p. xii). This technique peaked with the publication of Allport's *Letters from Jenny* (1965a), which "comprised intimate letters, gushing forth from raw personal experience" (p. v). The record or personal document can consist of: (1) an individual's report of his personal experiences; (2) a person's deliberate attempt at self-scrutiny or self-description; or (3) an unconscious or incidental self-revelation. Thus, it embodies one type of case study material.

The value of the personal document or human document, as Allport saw it, is its spontaneity, candor, and other phenomenological characteristics. "As a self-revealing record of experience and conduct," explained Allport,

> ... the personal document is usually, though not always, produced spontaneously, recorded by the subject himself, and intended only for confidential use. Its themes naturally revolve around the life of the writer, its manner of approach is naturally subjective (phenomenological). Such documents vary greatly in candor, scope, authenticity, and psychological value. Sometimes they are deceptive and trivial; but sometimes they represent distillations of the most profound and significant experiences of human life. And always they are interesting to the psychologist who must ask even of the deceptive and trivial documents why they were written and, further, why they are dull or deceptive. (Allport, 1942, p. xiii)

The use of personal documents did not originate with Gordon Allport, nor did they originally derive from Thomas and Znaniecki, for William James had employed them extensively in his *The Varieties of Religious Experience* (1902), G. Stanley Hall in his *Adolescence* (1904), and Freud in a number of his writings. The psychotherapeutic situation lends itself to the use and analysis of personal documents, and they also serve as an excellent vehicle for autoanalysis.

There are a variety of sources for personal documents: diaries, letters, autobiographies, questionnaires, verbatim recordings (such as confessions, interviews, etc.), and expressive and projective documents (literature, automatic writing, art forms, compositions, projective productions, and the like). The validity of personal documents as acceptable data in psychology lies in their ability "to enhance understanding, power of prediction, and power of control, above the level which man can achieve through his own unaided common sense" (Allport, 1942, p. 185). Properly utilized, the personal-documents method meets the three criteria of scientific method: understanding, prediction, and control.

Treatment

Most, if not all, forms of psychotherapy must become warmly personal if they are to be effective forms of intervention. This statement is not merely the contention of personalistic psychologists, it is readily admitted by many other major leaders and schools of psychotherapy, and it becomes a point of emphasis in several psychotherapeutic systems. This is tantamount to saying that personalism is an important ingredient of many schools of psychotherapy, even though a school may not in its entirety be designated as embracing personalism. For example, the *interpersonal theory of psychiatry* of Harry Stack Sullivan is decidedly personalistic. Not only is the term *personal* in the title of his school of thought, but the basic therapeutic relationship is so highly personal that he coined a special word, *empathy,* to depict that personal experience. Empathic is also a vital concept in the personalistic client-centered therapy of Carl R. Rogers. Jung, too, noted that the personalistic relationship between the psychotherapist and patient is so uniquely personal that the therapist can find himself acquiring the problems of his client.

There is an increasing realization among psychotherapists that if therapy is to be effective, it must become highly personalistic, so much so that the existential psychotherapists hold that the therapist must get into the phenomenological world of the patient. Nor did psychoanalysis escape personalism, for here too is found the personalistic relationship deeply imbedded in the transference relationship. In the last analysis, therefore, a psychotherapeutic system must become or acquire characteristics of personalistic psychology if it is to be effective.

Institutional

Allport's contributions to institutional thinking can be divided into his research on religion, rumor, and prejudice. While operating mostly from an idiographic point of view, he came to nomothetic conclusions.

Religion. Eager to apply his personality theory to the field of psychology of religion, Allport reported his findings in *The Individual and His Religion: A Psychological Interpretation* (1950a). His self-imposed task was to understand the character of the religious sentiment and its functioning and to ascertain the place subjective religion holds in the personality structure.

Unlike Freud, whose psychology of religion derived from the investigation of neurotic personalities, Allport was concerned with the psychology of religious experience in mature, normal personalities. Hence while Freud studied the psychopathology of religion, Allport dealt with the psychology of religion. Declared Allport:

> The neurotic function of religious belief, its aid as an "escape from freedom," is indeed commonly encountered, so commonly that opponents of religion see only this function and declare it to dominate any life that harbors a religious sentiment. With this view I disagree. Many personalities attain a religious view of life without suffering arrested development and without self-deception. Indeed it is by virtue of their religious outlook upon life—expanding as experience expands—that they are able to build and maintain a mature and well-integrated edifice of personality. The conclusions they reach and the sentiments they hold are various, as unique as is personality itself. (Allport, p. viii, 1950a)

In making this statement, Allport concurred with William James's thesis as enunciated in the latter's *The Varieties of Religious Experience* (1902).

While consensus among psychologists does not support the existence of a single emotion uniquely religious in character, evidence does warrant the postulation of a religious sentiment. The characterizing fact of the religious sentiment is not the particular nature of the experience per se but the intentional and regular focusing of experience. According to William McDougall (1908), there is no common pattern of content in subjective experience which makes it characteristically religious, nor is there any common point of origin of the religious sentiment. Even the emotion of reverence is not a simple common denominator, for reverence can be quite complex, entailing admiration, gratitude, and fear. Admiration, according to McDougall, itself is a compound of wonder and negative self-feeling, while gratitude is a fusion of tender emotion with a negative self-feeling. Allport endorsed McDougall's findings.

Although the roots of religion grounded in temperament are poorly understood, Allport suggested that subjective religion arises from inherent psychogenic desires. The values for which a person longs—truth, goodness, beauty—are objectified by being located externally to the self. Furthermore, their significance is distinctively human. Restoration and conservation of values is ordinarily sought through religion. Allport concluded that subjective religious experience is so varied that "there are as many varieties of religious experience as there are religiously inclined mortals upon the earth" (1950a, p. 27).

The Psychology of Rumor. During the 1940s Allport became interested in the relationship of personality to rumor, the fruit of his research being published as *The Psychology of Rumor* (Allport & Postman, 1947). In the "Rumor Clinic," a syndicated daily column in the *Boston Traveler*, Allport especially addressed his attention to damaging wartime rumors. He trichotomized rumors into "bogies," "pipe dreams," and "wedge-drivers." The last type, the severest, was said to arise from prejudice and group antagonism.

Allport and Postman defined rumor as "a specific (or topical) proposition for belief, passed along from person to person, usually by word of mouth, without secure standards of evidence being present" (1947, p. ix). Rather than being idle gossip, rumors are quite purposive, as well as catering significantly to emotional ends. The ends, however, ordinarily cannot be articulated by the two parties of the rumor—the one who perpetuates the rumor, as well as the one who is willing to listen. The force of the rumor is its importance to the parties involved, for in some cryptic manner it appears to diminish the parties' state of anxiety and doubt.

During periods of crisis, rumors escalate to major proportions. False reports grow virulently during stressful events in society. In wartime rumors not only peak, they harm morale, evoke extravagant hopes, and menace the safety of a nation through the spread of unnecessary alarm. While the usual transmission of rumors is by word of mouth, they may also be found in other media, such as newspapers, magazines, or radio. Since rumors for the most part are topical and specific, they are of only temporary interest. Virtually all rumors have personal victims who are explicitly identified. One tends to become rumor prone in areas where one lacks expertise, for one is not in a position to verify the rumor as fact or fancy.

Self

Personalism is not only a theory of personality; it is also a philosophy of life, and Allport, as we have described him, may well have been said to have been an exemplary of his theory and philosophy, in terms of his gracious warmth, his nondemanding but helpful personality, and his sincere regard for the individual. A personalist holds every person, regardless of his station in life, as of extreme importance as a human being.

This point of view holds for those in the so-called third-force psychologies and is seen clearly in the client-centered theory of Carl Rogers, who believes that the therapist's nondemanding acceptance of the patient, his unconditional regard, is essential in facilitating the mental health of clients. It is also seen in Alfred Adler's horizontal view of humanity, with all considered equal, in contrast to the vertical view of superior and inferior beings.

What does this all mean to you, the reader, in a personal sense? How can this point of view affect your behavior? What meaning can it have for how you regard others? How can you use the insights of personalists in your daily life?

Here is where theory and philosophy touch, where science and values come to terms with one

another and finally converge. The answers lie in nothing but an expression of the age-old principle of reciprocity which is known generally as the Golden Rule and which is a central aspect of all mature religions: Treat others as you would have them treat you.

This is the final message of personalism, to try to understand others, value them, and treat them fairly. Reaching out to help others be kind and altruistic is a further step along these lines. Pitirim Sorokin (1954), Allport's colleague at Harvard, gave evidence of the personal value of altruism.

A personalistic psychology which regards people as worthwhile helps one to elevate others' self-regard and augments well-being in others— but it does something else! It enhances the enhancer! If one regards one's acquaintances through the humanistic eyes of personalism, one becomes considerate and helpful, "a nice guy"— and, naturally, one becomes so regarded by others, who in turn behave appropriately.

To illustrate: in marriage, if one regards one's mate as a thing to be exploited rather than a person to be valued, then the relationship has little chance to grow and develop to mutual satisfaction. When one sees another human as a thing to be used, the other is reduced to an object—and when this attitude of superiority is apprehended, the other person regards this as an insult and returns the bad feelings.

In this world other people are the source of most pleasure—and most unhappiness. If a person is treated as a means rather than as an end, the inevitable result will be mutual dissatisfaction in the relationship. The absolute essence of personalism is concern for the dignity and value of others, regardless of any considerations of age or sex or color or position. This point of view, which is quite natural for some people and is expressed in most religions, is backed by the considerations, the theory, and the research of Allport's personalistic psychology.

Validation

Whereas most psychologists use only the nomothetic rather than the idiographic approach to the investigation of personality, Allport utilized both techniques. In the *nomothetic approach,* a psychologist attempts to extract general laws or principles to which all human beings respond. The *idiographic approach* regards each individual as a unique entity and is not concerned with general laws which refer to all people. Because he regarded each person as unique, Allport endorsed the idiographic approach, but not to the exclusion of the nomothetic. Personality, as viewed by Allport, "is distinctive and unique, as possessing strongly individualized motivational systems, and as representing an individual's style of adjustment and mastery within his behavioral environment" (Allport, 1937b, p. 238). Distinguishing between idiographic knowledge (knowledge of particular entities) and nomothetic knowledge (knowledge of universal principles or general laws of psychology), Allport wrote:

> Knowledge of general laws—including . . . the law of functional autonomy—quantitative assessments and correlational procedures are all helpful; but with this conceptual (nomothetic) knowledge must be blended a shrewd diagnosis of trends within an individual, an ability to transcend the isolated common variables obtained from current measuring devices and to estimate the ego-structure of the individual. Unless such idiographic (particular) knowledge is fused with nomothetic (universal) knowledge, we shall not achieve the *aims* of science, however closely we imitate the methods of the natural and mathematical sciences. (1960, p. 147).

Because so many people misspelled the word *idiographic*, Allport in his later years sought to replace it with *morphogenic*, a term he borrowed from biology. It is difficult to see the wisdom in exchanging the two terms, for people who experience difficulty in spelling idiographic will not find morphogenic much easier. The morphogenic problem, as Allport saw it, was that of explaining the uniqueness of a person as an individual.

> We have morphogenic and molecular biology, and I think the parallel represents the distinction I'm trying to make in psychology. Molecular biology takes common elements and finds that almost all of life is made up of the same basic elements. . . . The parallel dimension in psychology would be dimensional or differential or trait psychology. . . . In psychology . . . we're trying to explain the uniqueness of the person. That's what I call a morphogenic problem. (1971, p. 25).

Evidence

Expressive Movements. In the first half of the decade of the 1930s, Allport and Philip E. Vernon began research in *expressive behavior,* as well as propaganda, attitudes, and the psychology of radio, the last of which resulted in the publication of *The Psychology of Radio* (Cantril and Allport, 1935). The fruits of his research with Vernon produced *Studies in Expressive Movement* (1933) and *A Study of Values* (1931; revised with Gardner Lindzey, 1951 and 1960). *A Study of Values* sought to found on an empirical basis the six fundamental dimensions of personal values delineated in the then recently published book by Eduard Spranger, *Types of Men* (1928).

Defining expressive movement, Allport and Vernon stated that it pertains "to those aspects of movement which are distinctive enough to differentiate one individual from another" (1933, p. vii). The two researchers sought for a term which encompasses the individuality of expression with respect to motor activity as well as to emotion.

The issue selected for probing by Allport and Vernon was the hypothesis that:

> . . . the gestures or expressive movements of a person are consistent with one another. A man's style of writing is supposed to be harmonious with his manner of speaking, his facial movements with his posture, and his gesticulation with his gait. This belief undoubtedly derives from an underlying conviction that all the mobile features of the body are avenues for the expression of personality. If personality is self-consistent, it is reasoned, its expressions must in turn be consistent among themselves. (1933, p. 173)

The above statement assumes that an individual's personality is basically self-consistent, and that self-consistency is apparent in his behavior. Expressive acts, therefore, are assumed to be self-consistent. Allport and Vernon found that although no universal psychomotor factor exists which determines every act individuals express, neither is expressive behavior completely specific, that is, determined by independent and individual habits or by individual or particular situations in which the expressive acts or behavior occurs. The hypothesis favored by their results was that organized psychomotor dispositions or expressive traits do in fact exist. Furthermore, some of these traits are universal and scalable to some extent. While certain motor traits are scalable, others are singular or peculiar to the individual in question. Just as there are degrees of unity in personality, there are also degrees of unity in expressive movement or behavior.

Religion. Allport discovered that the religious experience of childhood fails to comport with that of youth. Whereas the former is egocentric, the latter departs from such narrowness. Nevertheless, there are more remnants of childhood in the religious life of the adult than in any other phase of his personality.

Defining the mature religious sentiment, Allport characterized it as "a disposition, built up through experience, to respond favorably, and in certain habitual ways, to conceptual objects and principles that the individual regards as of ultimate importance in his own life, and as having to do with what he regards as permanent or central in the nature of things" (1950a, p. 56). Elements characteristic of the mature religious sentiment are: fine differentiation; dynamic character; the generating of a consistent set of moral values; comprehensiveness; integrity; and a basic heuristic or investigatory quality. These characteristic elements of the mature religious sentiment serve at the same time as criteria of maturity of personality development.

Rumor. Gordon Allport's work on rumor, done under pressure, was his major contribution during World War II. At the same time he was writing his wartime newspaper column, which dispelled unfounded rumors, he and his students were attempting to determine the general conditions for the existence, maintenance, and propagation of rumors. He stipulated two basic conditions for the survival of a rumor: "first, the theme of the story must have some *importance* to the speaker and to the listener; second, the true facts must be shrouded in some kind of *ambiguity*" (Allport & Postman, 1947, p. 33). The ambiguity of the rumor is supported by absent, sketchy, conflicting, untrustworthy, or emotionally toned statements, leaving but a residual fragment of truth in the rumor.

Allport and Postman were able to formulate a generalization governing rumor: "The amount of rumor in circulation will vary with the importance of the subject to the individuals concerned *times* the ambiguity of the evidence pertaining to the topic at issue" (1947, p. 34). The formula states that the relationship of importance to the individuals in question and ambiguous evidence is a multiplicative one, so that if either one of the two is missing, rumor will fail to generate. Hence:

$$R = i \times a$$

(Rumor is a function of importance times ambiguous evidence.)

Note that rumor is more than a question of individual psychology, for in involving at least two persons, it is definitely a question of social psychology. At the same time, it is a problem for individual or personal psychology because the carrier of the rumor is merely the vehicle; the important event is what transpires in the mind of the individual entertaining the rumor. Is he or is he not receptive to the rumor?

While rumors begin with a "kernel of truth," Allport and Postman discovered that they undergo a basic pattern of distortion. Rumors are affected by mechanisms of distortion or change that have (1) leveling, (2) sharpening, and (3) assimilating functions. *Leveling* consists in omitting certain relevant facts that are contrary to the impression one wants to convey in a particular rumor. One's perception is adulterated with one's imaginations, valuations, and judgment. In *sharpening,* certain details are deleted in order to generate a clearer focus. *Assimilation* is the process of adapting one's perceptions to one's preconceived notions and biases, such as jumping to conclusions.

Prejudice. Allport moved from the psychology of rumor to the psychology of prejudice. In his book *ABC's of Scapegoating* (1948), he defined the topic of scapegoating as: "a phenomenon wherein some of the aggressive energies of a person or group are focused upon another individual, group or objects; the amount of aggression and blame being either partly or wholly unwarranted" (p. 13).

It should be noted that Allport, unlike other personality theorists generally, became involved in socially relevant issues; his intent was not only to discover general rules of psychology but also to work with issues of the day, with practical problems. We need no more than mention that at the time Allport was working on this issue of prejudice, scapegoating had mounted to the most incredible human horror in the gas ovens of Germany.

It was already well known that prejudice has a plural causation, involving such entities as economic exploitation, fear, social structure, sex conflict, mores, and a number of other cultural, historical, economic, and situational factors. In the last analysis, prejudice is basically a question of personality, one fostered by an individual. All the agents of prejudice will prove ineffective without the individual personality, who alone feels antagonism and practices discrimination.

Allport (1954) imputed universal validity to his theory of psychological dynamics of prejudice. Although prejudice manifests itself differently in varying cultures and countries, he said, its fundamental causes and correlates are basically identical. Prejudice and discrimination are rooted in the structure of the personality, but they also derive from the social structure.

The Nature of Prejudice. Allport's postwar researches (1946, with Kramer; 1948) sought to ascertain the roots of hostility to gain control over the destructiveness of prejudice. The results, published in his *The Nature of Prejudice* (1954), revealed that prejudice, contrary to popular opinion, is virtually unconnected with race. While the conception of race is only a little more than a century old, prejudice stems from antiquity.

> For the most part, prejudice and persecution have rested on other grounds, often on religion. Until the recent past Jews have been persecuted chiefly for their religion, not for their race. Negroes were enslaved primarily because they were economic assets, but the rationale took a racial form: they were pagans by nature, the presumed descendants of Noah's son Ham, and cursed by Noah to be forever "the servants of servants." The concept of race so popular today is in reality an anachronism. Even if it were once applicable, it is scarcely so any longer, owing to the endless dilution of human stocks through cross-mating. (Allport, 1954, p. xv)

The reason why race became an even more important issue in prejudice than religion is that religion's force declined, and consequently its tenacity in designating a particular religious group was diminished. Visibility or racial characteristics distinctly demarcated the victims of prejudice.

Comparisons

One chief advantage Allport's personality theory holds over a number of rival systems is that his personalism is based on and applies to normal human beings rather than to animals (as is the case with Skinnerian and some other theorists) or to abnormal people (as with psychoanalytically oriented theories such as those of Freud, Jung, Adler, Horney, Sullivan, or the theories of the existentialists or phenomenologists, such as Rogers).

Most personality theoreticians are deeply entrenched in clinical psychology, whereas Allport is one of a minority whose orientation is nonclinical. Thus the humanistic, nonclinical approach of personalism and the researching of subjects who are not psychopathological accord Allport's psychology an advantage over other theories. To derive a personality theory from neurotics and psychotics raises the question of whether a personality theory based on abnormality can be valid for all persons, both normal and abnormal. It is much too risky to assume that what is valid for the disturbed personality holds true for the normal.

Although in the later part of his career Allport was developing his personality theory in the direction of Abraham Maslow's third-force psychology, many of his basic ideas comport with the tradition of the factor theory of Charles Spearman and Cyril Burt. Two learning theorists in this tradition of the factor-theoretical approach, Hans J. Eysenck and Raymond B. Cattell, were deeply interested in traits or factors, as they referred to them following the lead of Spearman and Burt.

Allport shared with Maslow not only the humanistic approach of the third-force psychologies (as they are currently called), but also his views regarding psychological growth. He also shared Maslow's interest in and emphasis on healthy (rather than sick) personalities. Allport expressed displeasure at personality theorists who grounded their hypotheses "upon the behavior of sick and anxious people or upon the antics of captive and desperate rats." The two also shared the view of investigating the whole person rather than some fragmented aspect of the human being.

Prospect

What future is there for personalistic psychologies? How will personalistic psychologies fare in the competitive world of personality theories, where each is contending for an ascendant position? Happily, the future of personalism is assured, not merely or necessarily by differentiation from traditional personalistic psychologies but from other leading psychologies. Any psychology—such as the individual psychology of Adler, client-centered psychology of Rogers, existial psychology of Jean-Paul Sartre, or phenomenological psychology of Viktor E. Frankl— which shares personalistic characteristics assures the future of personalism in psychology.

Furthermore, given the premise that humans are essentially and genuinely persons rather than glorified animals, then personalism can never be eradicated from the psychology of personality. If the data of personalistic psychology are genuine facts, some psychologists might attempt to ignore them, but they cannot do so for long and expect to develop an adequate personality theory which accords with the facts of human experience.

There is a trend currently transpiring in psychology which will assure the future of personalism: what has come to be called the *third-force psychologies,* or more commonly, *humanistic psychology.* These psychologies, currently experiencing an upsurge, have not only reached the point of publishing their own journal (the *Journal of Humanistic Psychology),* but have gained sufficient force and numbers to establish a division of their own in the American Psychological Association, the Division of Humanistic Psychology. These third-force or humanistic psychologies are essentially personalistic in character. As long as their thrust is felt, the place of personalistic psychology in the future is assured. Thus the strength of personalistic psychology lies not merely in the vigor of traditional personalism but in all psychologies which accord singular characteristics to the human being, properties that are not shared with the animal kingdom.

Annotated Bibliography

Allport, G. W. *Personality: A Psychological Interpretation.* New York: Holt, 1937. Revised in 1961 under the title *Pattern and Growth in Personality.*

These two works, comprising the magnum opus of Allport, offer the most comprehensive and systematic development of his theory. The revised version provides virtually all of the important elements in Allport's system, including the theory of traits, the doctrine of functional autonomy, the nature and facets of the proprium, the hypothesis of the person as a *unitas multiplex,* and the definition of personality explained.

Allport, G. W. *The Nature of Personality: Selected Papers.* Cambridge, Mass.: Addison-Wesley, 1950.

This collection of previously published papers by Allport emphasizes a number of salient features of his personality theory as developed up to 1947.

Allport, G. W. *Becoming: Basic Considerations for a Psychology of Personality.* New Haven: Yale University Press, 1955.

Series of lectures emphasizes Allport's theory of growth and development of personality, uniqueness of the individual, the numerous facets of the proprium, as well as his psychology of becoming.

Allport, G. W. *Personality and Social Encounter: Selected Essays.* Boston: Beacon Press, 1960.

This volume updates the preceding collection of selected papers.

Allport, G. W. *The Person in Psychology: Selected essays.* Boston: Beacon Press, 1968.

This posthumously published volume contains the latest series of papers written by Allport.

Bischof, L. J. *Interpreting Personality Theories* (2nd ed.). New York: Harper & Row, 1970.

Not only does this book include a chapter which discusses Allport's personalistic psychology, it also provides an elaborate, extensive bibliography.

Ghougassian, J. P. *Gordon W. Allport's Ontopsychology of the Person.* New York: Philosophical Library, 1972.

This book is entirely devoted to Allport's personality theory.

Hall, C. S., and Lindzey, G. *Theories of Personality* (2nd ed.). New York: Wiley, 1970.

Contains a chapter devoted to Allport's personality theory written by one of his students.

Sahakian, W. S. *Psychology of Personality: Readings in Theory* (2nd ed.). Chicago: Rand McNally, 1974.

Original writings by Allport culled from various publications on the psychology of personality.

Sahakian, W. S. *History and systems of psychology.* New York: Wiley, 1975.

This book provides a discussion of Allport's place in the development of psychology, including his role in the founding of the Department of Social Relations at Harvard University.

References

Allport, F. H. *Social psychology.* Boston: Houghton Mifflin, 1924.

Allport, F. H., & Allport, G. W. Personality traits: Their classification and measurement. *Journal of Abnormal and Social Psychology,* 1921, *16*, 1–40.

Allport, G. W. *An experimental study of the traits of personality: With special reference to the problem of social diagnosis.* Unpublished doctoral dissertation, Harvard University, 1922.

Allport, G. W. What is a trait of personality? *Journal of Abnormal and Social Psychology,* 1931, *25*, 368–372.

Allport, G. W. The functional autonomy of motives. *American Journal of Psychology,* 1937, *50*, 141–156. (a)

Allport, G. W. *Personality: A psychological interpretation.* New York: Holt, 1937. (b)

Allport, G. W. Motivation in personality: Reply to Mr. Bertocci. *Psychological Review,* 1940, *47*, 533–554. (a)

Allport, G. W. The psychologist's frame of reference. *Psychological Bulletin,* 1940, *37*, 1–28.(b)

Allport, G. W. *The use of personal documents in psychological science.* New York: Social Science Research Council, 1942.

Allport, G. W. Personalistic psychology as science: A reply. *Psychological Review,* 1946, *53*, 132–135.

Allport, G. W. *ABC's of scapegoating* (Rev. ed.). New York: Anti-Defamation League of B'nai B'rith, 1948.

Allport, G. W. *The individual and his religion: A psychological interpretation.* New York: Macmillan, 1950. (a)

Allport, G. W. *The nature of personality: Selected papers.* Reading, Mass.: Addison-Wesley, 1950. (b)

Allport, G. W. *The nature of prejudice.* Reading, Mass.: Addison-Wesley, 1954.

Allport, G. W. *Becoming: Basic considerations for a psychology of personality.* New Haven: Yale University Press, 1955.

Allport, G. W. What units shall we employ? In G. Lindzey (Ed.), *Assessment of human motives.* New York: Rinehart, 1958.

Allport, G. W. Religion and prejudice. *The Crane Review,* 1959, *2*, 1–10.

Allport, G. W. *Pattern and growth in personality.* New York: Holt, Rinehart & Winston, 1961.

Allport, G. W. Peter Bertocci: Philosopher-psychologist. *Philosophical Forum,* 1963–1964, *21*, 3–7.

Allport, G. W. *Personality and social encounter: Selected essays* (Rev. ed.). Boston: Beacon Press, 1964.

Allport, G. W. *Letters from Jenny.* New York: Harcourt, Brace & World, 1965. (a)

Allport, G. W. Traits revisited. *Psychology Today, Journal of the Department of Psychology of the University of Newcastle on Tyne,* 1965, 57–76. (b)

Allport, G. W. Traits revisited. *American Psychologist,* 1966, *21*, 1–10.

Allport, G. W. Autobiography. In E. G. Boring & G. Lindzey (Eds.), *A history of psychology in autobiography* (pp. 3–25). New York: Appleton-Century-Crofts, 1967.

Allport, G. W. *The person in psychology: Selected essays.* Boston: Beacon Press, 1968. (a)

Allport, G. W. The personalistic psychology of William Stern. In B. B. Wolman (Ed.), *Historical roots of contemporary psychology* (pp. 321–337). New York: Harper & Row, 1968. (b)

Allport, G. W. *The man and his ideas.* New York: Dutton, 1971.

Allport, G. W., & Kramer, B. M. Some roots of prejudice. *Journal of Psychology,* 1946, *53*, 132–135.

Allport, G. W., & Postman, L. *The psychology of rumor.* New York: Henry Holt, 1947.

Allport, G. W., & Vernon, P. E. *A study of values,* 1931. Rev. ed. with G. Lindzey. Boston: Houghton Mifflin, 1951. 3rd ed., 1960.

Allport, G. W., & Vernon, P. E. *Studies in expressive movement.* New York: Hafner, 1967. (Originally published 1933.)

Bühler, K. *Die Krise der Psychologie.* Jena: Fischer, 1927.

Calkins, M. W. Psychology as a science of selves. *Philosophical Review,* 1900, *9*, 490–501.

Calkins, M. W. *A first book in psychology* (Rev. ed.). New York: Macmillan, 1914. (Originally published, 1909.)

Cantril, H., & Allport, G. W. *The psychology of radio.* New York: Harper, 1935.

Evans, R. I. *Gordon Allport: The man and his ideas.* New York: Dutton, 1970.

Frankl, V. E. *The will to meaning.* New York: World, 1969.

Hall, G. S. *Adolescence: Its psychology and its relation to physiology, anthropology, sociology, sex, crime, religion and education* (2 vols.). New York: Appleton, 1904.

Hull, C. L. *Principles of behavior.* New York: Appleton, 1943.

James, W. *Psychology: Briefer course.* New York: Henry Holt, 1892.

James, W. *The varieties of religious experience: A study in human nature.* New York: Longmans Green, 1902.

McDougall, W. *An introduction to social psychology.* London: Methuen, 1908.

Maddi, S. R., & Costa, P. T. *Humanism in personology: Allport, Maslow, and Murray.* Chicago: Aldine-Atherton, 1972.

Maslow, A. H. *Toward a psychology of being* (2nd ed.).

Princeton, N.J.: Van Nostrand, 1968.

Maslow, A. H. *Motivation and personality* (2nd ed.). New York: Harper & Row, 1970.

Maslow, A. H. *The farther reaches of human nature.* New York: Viking, 1971.

Murray, H. A. *Explorations in personality: A clinical and experimental study of fifty men of college age.* New York: Oxford University Press, 1938.

Sorokin, P. *Forms and techniques of altruistic and spiritual growth.* Boston: Beacon Press, 1954.

Spranger, E. *Types of men.* Halle: Max Niemeyer, 1928.

Stern, W. *Person und Sache* (3 vols.). Leipzig: Barth, 1906–1924.

Stern, W. *General psychology from the personalistic standpoint.* New York: Macmillan, 1938.

Thomas, W. I., & Znaniecki, F. *The Polish peasant in Europe and America* (2 -vol. ed.) New York: Knopf, 1927. (Originally published in 5 vols.; vols. 1 and 2, 1918; vol. 3, 1919; vols. 4 and 5, 1920.)

Behaviorism, in the widest sense of the word, is a point of view about psychology which is concerned with observable, measurable, operational behavior. Any conceptualization about what goes on "inside" the person, such as inner feelings, ideas, and the like, is considered unnecessary, redundant, and of no great value for understanding human beings. Its opponents refer to behaviorism as a "psychology of the empty organism."

The behaviorist's point of view is old; those who have championed it in the history of psychology assume there is no mind as such, but only body; reality is flesh and blood, rather than mind and soul. In the recent history of psychology as a science, among the major people who have accepted this view are the Russians V. M. Bechterev and I. P. Pavlov and the Americans John B. Watson, E. B. Holt, Karl Lashley, W. S. Hunter, and Clark Hull. Current personality theorists who are essentially behaviorists include O. Hobart Mowrer, John Dollard, Robert W. Lundin, Neal Miller, and Burrhus Frederick Skinner.

This chapter will concentrate on the work of B. F. Skinner (1904–   ), the best-known, most controversial, and most influential behaviorist alive, whose specific theory is known as *operant reinforcement*. Skinner believes that the aims of psychology are the prediction of *and* the control of behavior. Both are equally important, and we cannot have one without the other.

For Skinner all behavior is divided into two classes, operant and respondent. *Operant behavior,* the larger class, is so designated because organisms operate on their environment. The smaller class, *respondent behavior,* consists of simple unconditioned and conditioned reflexes.

Skinner's main stress is on the modification of behavior. With regard to personality, this emphasis has been intensively shown in the area of *behavior modification,* in which learning principles are applied to alter maladaptive behavior. In behavior modification, desired behavior is maintained and strengthened by positive reinforcers which follow given responses. Through the use of *selective* reinforcement, behavior may be altered by strengthening some responses and not others. Also, through selective reinforcement, discriminations essential to personality development are learned. Likewise, behavior can be altered when reinforcements are withdrawn (extinction). Without at least some intermittent reinforcement, specific learned behavior will eventually die out.

However, all prediction and control of behavior do not involve only positive reinforcement. Our environments contain many aversive stimuli which we try to escape from or avoid (bright lights, loud noises, nasty people). Other aversive stimuli involve infliction of punishment and so serve to create anxiety. Skinner strongly favors the use of positive reinforcement (rewards) as the best way to achieve a desirable culture with freedom and dignity. He would avoid aversive stimuli as used in punishment.

Behaviorism: Operant Reinforcement

Robert W. Lundin

B. F. SKINNER

Introduction

The Skinnerian approach to personality is probably the strongest departure from other theories represented in this book. In fact, some psychologists might not even consider it a personality theory as such. This chapter, therefore, amounts to an application of the basic principles of learning as employed by Skinner and his followers in experiments involving problems of human personality. Although early studies on operant reinforcement were done with animals, in later years more research has come from experiments and quasi experiments with human subjects.

One of the greatest departures from other theories is in the gathering of experimental data. Skinner's method of operant reinforcement is experimental in the strictest sense. It involves careful control of variables, with results presented quantitatively as often as possible. Introspection is generally rejected as a means of gathering information about a person.

A second major departure is Skinner's avoidance of mentalistic constructs. Such concepts as mind, mental apparatus, consciousness, inner experiences, and so forth, which are frequently used by many personality theorists today, are rejected on the grounds that they are not objectively verifiable and do not have direct reference to natural events. Thus Skinner's approach is monistic rather than dualistic, dealing only with living organisms operating in a natural world.

Traditionally, the behavioristic approach has been considered a form of S-R (stimulus-response) theory, in which the main events of study are the responses an organism makes to stimuli in its external environment. This is not the only S-R theory of personality current today, however. Others will be discussed in the next section, History.

Behavior is considered lawful and as such is subject to prediction and control. Were this not so, psychology and part of its scope, personality, could not be a branch of natural science. The task of the psychologist is to discover the laws of behavior, particularly through experimentation. Some Skinnerians feel that the simple discovery of these laws as they apply to any species or cross species is a sufficient task for psychology. Others who are concerned with human personality, including Skinner, believe that the laws should be discovered and then should be applied to the prediction and control of human behavior.

An individual's personality is a product of his genetic endowment *and* of his environmental stimulation (Skinner, 1971). Heredity does not cause behavior per se, but it does set limits. It also accounts for individual differences in physical appearance of which behavior is a function. Of much more importance for prediction and control are environmental stimuli, past and present. We are always under the control of these stimuli.

Skinner takes a strong deterministic view of human behavior: We may engage in self-control, but this must not be confused with free will. Man is the master of his own fate to the degree that he can manipulate the external stimuli which control him.

Personality is based on principles of learning. An understanding of personality comes from observations of how and under what conditions behavior has been learned. Because each of us has been subjected to different environmental conditions, each is a unique individual. Since each person has had a different conditioning history, each has learned different behaviors from different kinds of stimulation in the past.

Thus we can define personality "as that organization of unique behavior equipment an individual has acquired under the special conditions of his development" (Lundin, 1974, p. 7).

History

Precursors

A reinforcement theory of personality should begin with Ivan P. Pavlov and his work on the conditioned reflex. Initially, Pávlov, a Russian physiologist, discovered that a dog would salivate to an originally neutral stimulus if it were paired with a naturally eliciting stimulus such as food. It was Pavlov who first used the word *reinforcement* in referring to the food (Pavlov, 1927). The new reflex of salivation could be elicited when the conditioned stimulus (CS) alone was presented.

Of particular interest to the student of personality were Pavlov's investigations into what he called the experimental neuroses which could be produced when animals were forced beyond their discriminative capacity or subjected to excessively powerful stimulation. Dogs, for example, were taught to make appropriate discriminations by salivating at sight of a circle and not salivating when an oval was shown. As the figures were made increasingly similar, the dogs' ability to make discriminations broke down and they became extremely disorganized, wrestled in their harnesses, barked, urinated, defecated, and became generally agitated. Pavlov suggested personality types among dogs to account for such individual differences in their behavior. He explained the neurotic conditions basically in physiological terms, as an excessive strain on the nervous system due to traumatic conflict.

Like Pavlov, Edward Lee Thorndike began his initial studies with animals (Thorndike, 1898). He constructed a series of puzzle boxes in which his subjects—cats—had to perform some kind of operation to escape to get food. In one type of experiment the cat was placed in the box, and his problem was to press a pedal. When he made the desired response, the door of the box flew open, the cat got out, and it was given a piece of fish. On successive trials, the time taken to escape gradually decreased, although from one trial to the next time varied considerably. Eventually, however, the cat improved its performance so that when placed in the box it quickly performed the desired response. Thorndike called this trial-and-error learning, because initially it seemed so haphazard.

Thorndike, like Pavlov, explained learning on the basis of association. For Pavlov, the association was between the conditioned and the unconditioned stimuli paired together. For Thorndike, the cat associated the appropriate response with escaping and getting food; that the cat got food for making the desired response was important.

Out of these initial experiments, Thorndike formulated what he called the *law of effect*, stated as follows: "Of several responses made in the same situation, those which are accompanied or closely followed by satisfaction to the animal will, other things being equal, be more firmly connected with the situation" (Thorndike 1911, p. 244). Skinner later incorporated Thorndike's formulation into his *principle of reinforcement,* the learning tenet of his theory. Without reinforcement, learning does not occur.

In 1913 John B. Watson published an article in the *Psychological Review* entitled "Psychology as the Behaviorist Views It" (Watson, 1913). This article had considerable impact on the way psychology was to move in the future. Watson is generally credited as the founder of *behaviorism,* a movement to which Skinner and his followers adhere. Two points in Watson's article are worth noting. First, psychology, it was stated, is the study of behavior and not of mental events (consciousness, mind, and so forth). Watson declared introspection, then popular among other psychologists, to be an unreliable method of getting information. Another relevant point in this article was that the aims of psychology should be the prediction and control of behavior.

From a historical perspective, much of Watson's psychology was rather naive. However, what the modern behaviorist shares with Watson today is the concept that psychology should deal with the behavior of living organisms, not with mental phenomena. Watson, a determinist, stressed the extreme importance of the environmental position and more or less denied the importance of heredity, a position which Skinner has declared to be foolish (Skinner, 1974).

In his system Watson incorporated his conception of personality, which he considered to be a complex reaction system developed by training, including habits, abilities, emotions, remembering, and so forth. He also suggested that the way to change habits is by altering the environment in such a way that new habits could be learned (Watson, 1925). Impressed by Pavlov's work on the conditioned reflex, Watson used Pavlov's paradigm to experiment, with Rosalie Raynor (Watson & Raynor, 1920), on an eleven-month-old boy, Albert. They paired a white laboratory rat (CS) and the striking of a steel bar (US) behind the child's head. The loud sound evoked a "fear" reaction, the boy exhibiting violent movements and crying. Eventually the mere sight of the rat caused the boy to exhibit the "fear" response (CR). Generalization was also demonstrated; without any further conditioning, Albert exhibited "fear" to a dog, a fur coat, wool, and even a Santa Claus mask. Watson and Raynor had planned to extinguish the "fear" by later presenting the rat on successive trials without the loud noise. However, Albert's mother, who had been working at the hospital, left and took Albert with her.

Mary Cover Jones (Jones, 1924), a student of

Watson's, found a boy, Peter, who already had strong fears of furry animals. She presented a rabbit in a room where the boy was eating, each day moving the animal a little closer to the boy. Several repetitions of this procedure resulted in the elimination of the child's fear. After this extinction was completed, Peter's fear of other furry animals was also eliminated. Jones's experiment is significant, for it was the first practical demonstration of behavior therapy, a method of treatment widely used by behavior modifiers today.

Beginnings

Burrhus Frederick Skinner has had a long and distinguished career; his contributions to American psychology have been varied, and he has done much to alter its course. Born March 20, 1904 in Susquehanna, a small Pennsylvania town, he received his A.B. in 1926 from Hamilton College, Clinton N.Y.; earned his M.A. in 1930, and was awarded his Ph.D. in 1931 by Harvard. After several years of postdoctoral study he went to the University of Minnesota, where he remained from 1936 to 1945. He became chairman of the Department of Psychology at Indiana University in 1945 and in 1948 returned to Harvard, where he has remained up to the present time.

During the 1930s Skinner's efforts were devoted to research in the development of principles of learning, using white rats as subjects. He devised an apparatus, often called a Skinner Box—a term Skinner deplores, preferring that the apparatus be called an *operant conditioning chamber* (Skinner, 1932). In its original form the chamber consisted of a small box with a lever mounted on one side which the rat could press to receive a pellet of food as reinforcement. In the 1940s he adapted his apparatus for use with pigeons, for which the designated response was pecking a small disk mounted on the side of the cage to receive grain.

Skinner was appalled by the antiquated methods used in teaching and pioneered in the development of programmed learning. He devised a teaching machine which employed the principle of small steps each followed by positive reinforcements in the learning process. Through the use of programmed learning (Holland & Skinner, 1961), a child could proceed in small steps to master the material he was studying. (See the section, Applications, for a further discussion.)

Skinner's first major book was *The Behavior of Organisms* (1938), in which he described some of his early experiments. As early as 1948, Skinner had become interested in the application of his principles to human behavior. *Walden Two* (Skinner, 1948), a utopian novel, was the result. *Science and Human Behavior* (1953) furthered Skinner's studies and applied his principles to human behavior. In this book he applied his psychology to social issues, education, government, law, religion, and psychotherapy.

Skinner's interest in the study of language was demonstrated in *Verbal Behavior* (1957), in which language is seen as an aspect of human behavior for which the same kinds of analyses are appropriate as for other forms of behavior. This book has never met with much favor among traditional linguists. In the same year Skinner published, with Charles B. Ferster, *Schedules of Reinforcement* (Ferster & Skinner, 1957), a large volume of research explaining many different schedules or ways in which reinforcements may be delivered. (See Maintenance.)

Current Status

Skinner has devoted himself to social issues and to his own reinterpretation of such concepts as value, freedom, dignity, and personal control. *Beyond Freedom and Dignity* (1971) was for many months on the best seller list of nonfiction books, but by and large it received poor reviews from psychologists and others. His latest book, *About Behaviorism* (1974), tackles certain problems which have plagued behaviorists—concepts which other psychologists refer to as inner experience, self, knowledge, and so forth—and reinterprets them in behavioristic terms.

Skinner has been a controversial figure in psychology, but his efforts have not gone unappreciated or unrecognized. In 1951 an honorary doctor of science degree was conferred on him by his alma mater, Hamilton College. He received the American Psychological Association's Distinguished Contribution Award in 1958 and its Gold Medal Award in 1971. In 1968 he was given the National Medal of Science Award, the federal government's highest award for distinguished achievement in science, mathematics, or engineering. Only one other psychologist has received this award.

Skinner's followers are so numerous that it is difficult to single out the most important ones. Teodoro Ayllon, Nathan Azrin, Sidney Bijou, and Arthur Staats are important in the field of behavior modification and therapy. Charles B. Ferster, Richard Hernstein, Israel Goldiamond, and Donald S. Blough have dealt with rigorous experiments in psychology but have been concerned with applying behavior modification principles to human behavior. Robert W. Lundin has applied Skinner's principles to the field of personality.

Similar Theories

Two other currently popular theories make use of S-R concepts and reinforcement. John Dollard and Neal Miller have developed one and O. Hobart Mowrer the other.

Dollard and Miller's book, *Personality and Psychotherapy* (1950) presents a systematic formulation of a theory of personality within a learning theory context, based in part on the ideas of Clark Hull (1943). Mostly they have taken traditional psychoanalytic concepts and have translated them into learning theory terminology.

A number of key concepts are involved in their theory. The first is *habit,* behavior developed by association between a stimulus (cue) and a response. Personality, for them, consists primarily of complexes of habits. The nature of the habits depends on particular events to which the individual had been exposed.

A second concept is *drive,* basically an inner stimulus strong enough to cause an individual to engage in activity. Internal stimuli which become strong enough to compel activity are called innate or *primary drives.* These are usually linked to biological needs; examples are hunger, thirst, or sex. Derived or acquired drives are designated as secondary. *Acquired drives* represent an elaboration of the primary ones. In fact, in modern society, secondary drives often replace primary ones. For example, a person may not wait for the primary drive of hunger to appear before he starts to eat.

A third basic concept developed by Dollard and Miller is the *learning process,* which is crucial to personality development. Learning involves drives, cues, responses and reinforcement. Reinforcement works to reduce both primary and secondary drives.

Generalization is another important concept. With this process it is possible to explain appropriate response even when the cue stimuli are altered. An experimental illustration of this is a reinterpretation of the Freudian concept of displacement. Miller (1948b) placed two rats in a cage and shocked them; as a result, they tended to attack each other. Then one rat was removed and a white rubber doll was placed in the cage. When the shock was again delivered, the remaining rat attacked the doll. Miller accounted for this behavior in terms of generalization, since the rubber doll was similar in appearance to the original white rat and was thus dealt with in the same manner.

Dollard and Miller consider fear an important secondary drive. In one experiment (Miller, 1948a), a rat was given an electric shock in a white compartment and then allowed to escape into a black compartment in which there was no shock. After a number of trials, the white compartment (originally a neutral cue) came to evoke fear, so on succeeding trials, when the rat was placed in a white compartment without shock, he immediately escaped into the black one.

Another basic concept featured by Dollard and Miller is *conflict,* which is common to many other personality theories. Conflict occurs when an organism is placed in a situation where it is forced to make opposing choices. If a food-deprived rat is placed in a runway, and at the other end there are food and electric shock, this is an approach-avoidance situation. When given a signal, the animal leaves the start box and approaches the goal because he is hungry. He has also been previously conditioned so that to get food, he must also receive a shock. As he approaches the goal he stops and vacillates; this is the point of conflict. If the rat is very hungry, the point of conflict occurs near the goal. If the shock is excessively strong, the conflict will be farther away. Considerable research has been devoted to the study of other kinds of conflicts, along with approach and avoidance gradients. (For a more extended discussion, see Lundin, 1974.)

Although Dollard and Miller are no longer engaged in this kind of research and theorizing, their approach remains attractive to some students of personality. They and Mowrer were the first to develop an approach to personality based on learning theory.

Like Dollard and Miller, O. Hobart Mowrer has sometimes been classed as an S-R learning theorist. A student of Clark Hull, Mowrer emphasized the importance of reinforcement. However, he has given up total emphasis on reinforcement and substituted a two-factor learning theory. He believes that there are clinical, experimental, and commonsense reasons which suggest two fundamentally different learning processes: solution learning and sign learning. In *solution learning* a person acquires a tendency to respond appropriately by finding a solution to some problem, perhaps by the reduction of a primary or secondary drive. Here Mowrer is very close to the assertions of Dollard and Miller. In *sign learning* the individual acquires an *expectation, belief,* or *set.* This type of learning is characterized by autonomic nervous system involvement using stimulus substitution or associative shifting, whereas in solution learning the emphasis is more on the central nervous system. Another difference is that in sign learning the primary condition is association or contiguity, while in solution learning the primary condition is reinforcement (Mowrer 1950).

Thus Mowrer gave up a pure reinforcement theory in favor of one that depends on both reinforcement and contiguity. Later Mowrer shifted in the direction of many cognitive theorists, implying that learning is not so much a matter of forming S-R bonds as it is the development of "attitudes, meanings and expectations" (Mowrer, 1953).

Some specific examples might help clarify the distinctions between the two types of learning. Solution learning is problem solving and may involve drive reduction or pleasure giving. It requires rewards. Sign learning creates expectations, relates to contiguity, and does not necessarily require rewards, but it may involve classical or Pavlovian conditioning.

Mowrer (1953) has also applied his two-factor theory to neuroses and psychotherapy. Neuroses, he believes, are primarily the result of solution learning. The neurotic is using his problem-solving capacities defensively, engaging in actions that protect him against new learning and attitude changes which in the long run would be useful. At this point psychological dysfunctioning and abnormality begin. The neurosis is seen as an active problem-solving situation in which the person represses impulses he ought to acknowledge and satisfy. Repression, in Mowrer's context, is learning not to learn, and therapy should consist of a combination of fear deconditioning or extinction and the reinforcement of the habit of being "realistic," "facing reality," and acknowledging drives which have been denied expression.

Also related to the study of neurotic behavior is a concept which Mowrer calls the *neurotic paradox* (Mowrer 1948, 1950). He states that the behavior of the neurotic is self-perpetuating and self-defeating. For example, the compulsive hand washer continues to cleanse with strong soap even though endless time is wasted, and nothing is accomplished except getting sores on his hands. Mowrer's explanation for the paradox is that the neurotic is suffering from a learning deficit. At some point in the developmental process, the neurotic has gotten "stuck" or "bogged down." He cannot go forward on life's pathway, nor can he go backward, for to do so would be to become less human. Thus the neurotic lacks the ability to go forward toward more normal development.

In further revising his two-factor learning theory, Mowrer (1960) includes the idea of fear and hope within the organism as part of the development of habits. We gain the reward of hope, and we avoid pain. "In advancing a feedback conception of both responses, inhibition (punishment) and response facilitation (habit), we have emancipated behavior theory from what may be called the bondage of Thorndike's scheme and also liberated it from the crass reflexology of Pavlov" (Mowrer, 1960, p. 251).

One of Mowrer's early contributions to therapy was the development of a technique for treating enuresis (bedwetting) (Mowrer, 1938). The problem is not so much getting the child to control his elimination as it is to awaken him to the internal stimuli provided by the bladder tension, since these stimuli are relatively weak during sleep. Mowrer had the child sleep on a special pad containing two pieces of bronze screening between a heavy cotton fabric. When the urine struck the pad, it seeped through the fabric and penetrated the metal conductor, causing a bell to ring. This awakened the child and reminded him to go the the bathroom to finish urination. After conditioning, the child learned to awaken before wetting the bed, in response to small amounts of bladder tension which acted as the conditioned stimuli, according to the Pavlovian paradigm.

In *The Crisis in Psychiatry and Religion* (1961), Mowrer makes some distinctions between psychiatry and religion. Each, he says, must proceed towards its own aim. Among the many unrelated matters discussed, two are worth noting. The first is Mowrer's shift to a strong antipsychoanalytic position. "There is not a shred of evidence that psychoanalyzed individuals permanently benefit from the experience, and there are equally clear indications that psychoanalysis, as a common philosophy of life, is not only nontherapeutic but actively pernicious" (Mowrer, 1961, p. 161). A second point is that the pastoral counseling movement now prevalent in theological seminaries has taken over the more traditional psychotherapies. Various kinds of psychotherapies are now being practiced by ministers and priests. The study of theology as a basic subject to be taught in schools of religion has been set aside in favor of an emphasis on therapy.

Assertions

Development

1. THE BASIC AIMS OF PSYCHOLOGY AND
    THE STUDY OF PERSONALITY ARE THE
    PREDICTION AND CONTROL OF BEHAVIOR.
Like Watson (1913), Skinner (1953, 1971) has maintained that the two basic aims of psychology are the prediction and control of behavior. To achieve these aims, a functional relationship between antecedent conditions in the environment and the resulting behavior must be established. In this manner a science of psychology can be developed, and appropriate principles can be discovered.

The most desirable method whereby the principles can be discovered is through experimentation with proper experimental controls so that the antecedent condition (independent variable)

can be varied, and resulting changes in behavior (dependent variables) can be observed and measured. Thus, a functional relationship is established. This is also possible outside the laboratory. The adage, "You can lead a horse to water but you can't make him drink," assumes *no* knowledge of the antecedent conditions. If we know, for example, that a horse has been deprived of water (antecedent condition), we can predict with considerable certainty that when brought to the watering trough he *will drink* (resulting behavior). Therefore, we can control an animal's drinking behavior by either depriving it of, or satiating it with, water.

If prediction and control are possible, then we can presume that behavior is lawfully determined. Skinner (1953, 1971) believes strongly that behavior is neither capricious nor the result of whim. When we make a choice which seems to be other than the result of antecedent conditions and only of our own free will, the presumption is wrong. The choice is determined because of antecedent conditions.

> When all relevant variables have been arranged, an organism will or will not respond. If it does not, it can not. If it can, it will. To ask whether someone can turn a handspring, is merely to ask whether there are circumstances under which he will do so. A man who can avoid flinching at gun fire is a man who will not flinch under certain circumstances.... when all relevant variables have been taken into account it is not difficult to guarantee the result. (Skinner, 1953, p. 122)

What may appear to some to be evidence of the nondeterministic nature of behavior is the result of errors of prediction. However, an alternate and superior conclusion is that we do not know all relevant variables, or they are not under our control. In other circumstances our predictions would improve.

Skinner believes that both genetic endowment and environmental conditions must be taken into account (Skinner, 1971). This does not mean he believes in hereditary causes as such but rather that our genetic endowment limits the kinds of responses an organism can make or might eventually be able to make. We can compare two examples mentioned above. Skinner trained rats to press a lever to get food and later trained pigeons to peck a disk for food. In these two species the responses were quite different. It would be quite awkward for pigeons to press levers and for rats to peck at disks, since their genetic endowments are quite different. As mentioned earlier, the crucial events from which we predict and control behavior are environmental stimuli. These are what control our behavior and the source from which predictions are made. For example, if we know a man is greatly in need of money (antecedent condition) we can then predict that he is likely to accept a bribe (behavior).

In studying functional relationships, behaviorists have no need to appeal to causes inside the organism. Skinner has taken personality theorists to task for relying on internal causes such as Freud's mental apparatus to explain behavior. For example, Freud avers the superego punishes the ego to make it feel guilty. Skinner would prefer to look to a child's early environment to discover why he or she has been so conditioned in guilt.

2. BEHAVIOR CAN BE DIVIDED INTO TWO CLASSES, OPERANT AND RESPONDENT.

Skinner allows that some simple kinds of learning can take place according to the paradigm first developed by Pavlov. This simple kind of conditioning Skinner calls *respondent:* two stimuli, unconditioned and conditioned, are paired together, and eventually the organism will respond solely in the presence of the conditioned stimulus. The section on history mentioned Pavlov's work in which dogs were conditioned to salivate to the sound of a tone, as well as Watson and Raynor's (1920) experiment in conditioning "fear" in Albert. A practical example of respondent, or classical Pavlovian, conditioning can be found in the treatment of alcoholism. If a person is given a substance which produces nausea or vomiting, and if the sight or taste of alcohol is then paired with this substance, vomiting should eventually occur merely at the sight or taste of the drink. In humans, a number of unconditioned reflexes, such as coughing, sneezing, elimination, pupillary contraction, eye blink, and knee jerk, as well as internal reactions such as blood pressure and heart rate, can be conditioned to new stimuli.

Respondent behavior is so designated to indicate that the environment does something to the organism, which then responds. A piece of dirt in the eye causes blinking or tearing, or bright light causes pupils of eyes to contract. Respondent behavior, whether unconditioned or conditioned, constitutes only a small amount of total behavior.

For the most part, Skinner and his colleagues have emphasized *operant behavior,* so designated to indicate that the individual *operates on* the environment. We talk, walk to class, sit down at the dinner table, take a bath, play cards, read a book, and so on. In older psychologies, the distinction between operant and respondent was called voluntary and involuntary. However, since there is no behavior not under the control of environmental stimuli, the term *voluntary* is improper.

For the most part the rest of this chapter will be devoted to principles, examples, and experiments involving the acquisition, maintenance, or elimination of operant behavior. This distinction between operant and respondent behavior bears some resemblance to Mowrer's (1950) two-factor learning theory, since *respondent* roughly equates to *sign learning* and *operant* to *solution learning.* However, they are not exactly the same; Mowrer considers more kinds of behavior under sign learning and does not make as explicit a distinction between the two terms as does Skinner.

3. PERSONALITY IS ACQUIRED AND MAINTAINED THROUGH THE USE OF POSITIVE AND NEGATIVE REINFORCERS.

Skinner was much impressed with Thorndike's statement (1911) of the *Law of Effect* and has found it to be the most important principle in behavioral development. However, he took exception to Thorndike's use of the term *satisfying consequences* (Skinner, 1953). How can we know objectively that cats are "satisfied"? Since this is a subjective experience about which cats cannot tell us, a restatement is necessary for an objective psychology. Skinner substitutes the *principle of reinforcement* for *satisfying consequences.* To reinforce means to *strengthen,* as a package is reinforced with tape and twine or a wall is reinforced with concrete. Applied to behavior, reinforcement means that a behavior is strengthened or the probability of its occurrence is increased when reinforcement is applied.

In his early studies, Skinner (1932) found that

when a rat was placed in an operant conditioning chamber it would press the lever occasionally "by accident", but if food were presented following the response (positive reinforcement), the lever pressing increased to a steady rate of responding in which the animal continually pressed, taking time out only to eat the food pellets. For this reinforcement to operate, of course, the rat had to be food deprived. The presentation of food following a response is designated as a *primary* positive reinforcement. Other primary reinforcers include water and other drinks, sex, or other stimuli which might meet some biological need. They are designated as primary because their function to reinforce does not have to be learned.

Azrin and Lindsley (1956) have applied positive reinforcement to the training of cooperative behavior among young children. Twenty children aged 7 to 12 were matched into ten pairs. The two children in each pair were seated on opposite sides of a table, and in front of each child were three holes in the table and a stylus to be inserted in one of them. If the children happened to place their styli in the holes opposite each other (cooperative behavior), a red light flashed on and a single jelly bean was delivered, available to either child. Other arrangements were considered as uncooperative responses and yielded no reinforcement. All teams learned the cooperative response very quickly, in the absence of specific instructions. Almost immediately, eight of the teams divided the candy in some manner acceptable to both members.

In addition to the primary positive reinforcement discussed so far, there are also *conditioned* positive reinforcers which keep us going or help us acquire other behaviors which are not of direct biological significance. Such reinforcers as money (itself only paper or metal), diplomas, prizes, or the behavior of other people in granting praise, attention, or approval are conditioned reinforcers. They can serve as a powerful means of maintaining behavior.

Negative reinforcers can also strengthen behavior. A *negative reinforcer* is designated as a stimulus which *strengthens behavior when it is removed,* just as a positive reinforcer strengthens behavior when it is presented. Negative reinforcers can also be primary or conditioned. Some examples of primary negative reinforcement include putting on dark glasses to escape the glare of the sun, opening umbrellas to avoid getting wet, turning up the heat when it is cold, or turning on the air conditioning when the opposite holds. The removal of the aversive stimulus strengthens the behavior. With regard to conditioned negative reinforcers, we walk away from people who annoy us or slow down our car speed if we see police. Unfortunately, far too much of our behavior is controlled by negative reinforcement. Insurance companies ordinarily do not reward us for safe driving, but they do raise our rates when we have an accident. We pay heavy taxes only to avoid other penalties or be put in jail.

Reinforcement is necessary for personality development, since it is also necessary for learning to occur, and most of our behavior is learned.

4. Behavior may be altered or weakened by the withholding of reinforcements.

In Pavlov's early experiments, after he had conditioned dogs to salivate to the sound of a tone he found that if there were continuous sounding of the tones but no further food, the salivary response became weaker, until it died out completely. This process is called *extinction*. Likewise, operant behavior can be weakened by withholding the reinforcement following the response (Skinner, 1933). Gradually the rate of response slows down until it reaches a point of either no responding or the point where it was before reinforcements were applied. In many forms of personality development, both positive reinforcement and extinction must be applied. (See later Assertions below.)

Extinction is an effective means of getting rid of undesirable previously conditioned behavior. If a child throws a temper tantrum to get what he wants and we give in to his demands, we strengthen the temper tantrum behavior, but if we ignore the tantrums, they should eventually die out. If going to the movies has been positively reinforcing in the past and then later films are dull, movie-going behavior will occur less frequently. We can extinguish dull conversations by not paying attention or by failing to reply. Much of our verbal behavior needs rather regular reinforcing (Skinner, 1957). Sometimes extinction is a slow process, as the conversation of the bore may have had a long history of reinforcement.

A study by Williams (1959) illustrates the process of extinction in a 21-month-old boy who was exhibiting tyrannical screaming each time he was put to bed. If his parents did not remain in the room until he was asleep, he would scream wildly. Following medical assurance that he was in good health, it was decided to eliminate the tantrum behavior by discontinuing the reinforcement of the parents' remaining with the child. As instructed, the parents put him to bed quietly and in a relaxed fashion. They then left the room and closed the door, whereupon the child, as expected, began to scream and rage. The first night this lasted 45 minutes, but on the second occasion the boy did not cry at all. This was attributed (probably wrongly) to his extreme fatigue following the first session. By the tenth occasion (afternoon naps were also included), the tantrums had been eliminated. About a week later, however, the child exhibited the tantrums when put to bed by an aunt in his parents' absence. She reinforced the tantrums by remaining in the room until he was asleep. It then became necessary to extinguish the behavior all over again; this took nine more sessions. According to Williams, no further tantrums were exhibited in the next two years.

5.   OUT OF A GENERALIZATION OF RESPONDING, PERSONALITY DEVELOPS THROUGH A PROCESS OF DISCRIMINATION.

In our consideration of positive reinforcement, we have stressed that the event which follows the response increases the probability of that same response occurring again. Stimuli designated as *discriminative* precede the response. Discriminations are most crucial to personality development. An infant eventually discriminates the fist in the mouth from a nipple. We learn to discriminate colors, people, toys, sounds, acceptable and unacceptable behavior, and so on. The basic process in learning discriminations is that the response is reinforced in the presence of certain stimuli and not reinforced, or extinguished, in the presence of others (Skinner, 1933).

Consider a pigeon which learns to discriminate

a red disk from a green one. Once the bird has learned to peck a disk to get food, the color is unimportant; he will peck disks of any color presented. This is called *generalization.* In Watson and Raynor's study (1920), once Albert had been conditioned to fear the white rat, he also showed fear for other furry objects. In the development of color discrimination in the pigeon, the experimenter reinforced the bird with food whenever the red disk was presented and never reinforced when the green one appeared. Gradually, as soon as the red disk was presented, the pigeon would peck vigorously, and as the green disk appeared, he would peck only occasionally. Once the discrimination was firmly formed he would not peck the green disk at all. This simple example tells how discriminations develop. Discriminations are developed out of a process of *selective reinforcement.* In the presence of certain stimuli we are reinforced, and in the presence of others we are not.

As a child develops speech, every female figure he sees might be called "mommy." This illustrates some degree of generalization. Eventually, only one stimulus object, his mother, would be the source of saying "mommy." Eventually, other similar objects will be called by other names.

We always begin with generalization, that is, a person first responds to a variety of stimuli. Through selective reinforcement, discriminations are formed. We stop at red, go at green. In playing bridge we follow suit, play hearts instead of clubs. We distinguish men from women, cats from dogs, pick ripe strawberries and leave unripe green ones. We eventually learn to pull weeds from the garden instead of flowers.

As we continue to develop intellectually, concepts are formed which involve both generalization and discriminations. A concept may be defined as *generalization within a class of stimulus objects and discrimination between classes.* For example, a child learns to tell dogs, a class of objects, from a different class of objects called cats. This is where discrimination comes in: There are some basic differences between the two classes—size, behavior, and other physical characteristics. Yet generalization also takes place within classes: there are alley, Persian and Siamese cats, and big and small dogs with different colors and markings. This represents generalization within classes.

6.   OUT OF A VARIABILITY OF RESPONDING,
     PERSONALITY BECOMES SHAPED OR
     DIFFERENTIATED.

Even in tasks well learned, there is still some variability. We do not always do things in exactly the same way. In learning to talk, a baby utters a variety of sounds, and from this variability, words that can be understood are shaped.

In discussing discriminations, the emphasis was on the stimulus side; in dealing with differentiation, it is on the response side and includes the concepts of *stimulus discrimination* and *response differentiation*. Learning to walk, talk, eat, or perform simple or complex motor tasks involves *response differentiation*. Our first efforts to walk were random, unsteady, and variable, but as a result of biological maturation and differentiation we developed a coordinated, regular gait. Even so, there may be some variability, as when we trip or stumble.

Differentiation, like discriminations, also involves the process of selective reinforcement. Consider a child learning to say "Daddy." In the variable process of his early babbling he may utter the sounds "dadada" in the presence of his father, who reinforces him with affection. Other utterances go unreinforced. Out of this variability the child learns that the sound "daddy" gets reinforced, and thereby he learns to speak. Learning language involves a great deal of modeling, to be discussed as Assertion 7.

Complex skills such as athletic and musical abilities develop out of a long process of differentiation. Consider how many different kinds of golf strokes must be learned under a variety of conditions. First one has to learn to hit the ball; then more special responses are called for, as in driving, approach shots, putting, and so on. As differentiation takes place, we are reinforced in our game by making better shots. Practice constitutes an aspect of improvement, but it is not mere repetition that causes improvement. Repetition allows for variability, and out of this variability the more desired responses are reinforced and the poorer ones are extinguished.

Even in the most well-differentiated responses, there is still variability. The difference between well-executed skills and clumsy behavior is that in the former there is much less variability and greater uniformity, developed by careful shaping through selective reinforcement.

Differentiation and discrimination always go hand in hand. In golf, as well as differentiated golf shots there are also *discriminated stimuli:* the clubs (which ones are chosen for a shot), as well as the ball, greens, fairway, and so on. In learning to read, discrimination is foremost, while in writing differentiation is more important.

7.   MANY ASPECTS OF OUR PERSONALITY
     ARE DEVELOPED THROUGH MODELING.

Modeling means that we acquire behavior by watching or imitating others. If our behavior approximates the model, we are reinforced. A person brought up by a band of pirates would probably become a pirate, because in such a situation piratical behavior gets reinforced. The expressions "a chip off the old block" and "like father like son" illustrate the modeling of the father in the developing child. In teaching skills the teacher or coach exhibits behavior to be modeled, and if the learner's behavior approximates the model, reinforcement should occur.

Albert Bandura has studied modeling in children. In one study (Bandura, 1969) children were shown televised films in which models exhibited both verbal and physical aggression. In one group the children saw the models' aggressive behavior being positively reinforced; in a second group their aggressive behavior was punished, and in a third control group no particular consequences were observed. Following the films, the children were placed in a play situation where the degree of their aggression was rated (i.e., kicks Bobo doll, strikes it with a ball, shoots darts at toy animals). Those children who had seen the model punished in the film showed fewer aggressive responses than those who had seen aggression positively reinforced.

Later when the children were offered reinforcements for reproducing the model's behavior, all children showed greater modeling than when no particular reinforcements were involved.

O'Connor (1969) applied modeling to improve children's social behavior. Teachers were asked to select a group of socially isolated children to be shown a film which depicted other preschool children in social interaction, smiling, playing together, and gleefully tossing play equipment about the playroom. The experimental children were then returned to their classroom, and their social interactions were again rated. Their degree of social interaction increased as compared with a control group of equally socially isolated children who had not seen the film.

8. BESIDES POSITIVE REINFORCEMENT, PERSONALITY IS CONTROLLED BY AVERSIVE STIMULI WHICH CAN RESULT IN ESCAPE, AVOIDANCE, PUNISHMENT, OR ANXIETY.

In Assertion 2, reference was made to control by negative reinforcement, whereby the behavior is strengthened by the removal of an aversive stimulus. This is ordinarily referred to as *escape*. When an aversive stimulus is presented, the person does something to remove it. We go into the shade to escape the bright sun, or we remove a tight shoe. The stretching and squirming of an infant may represent its attempts to relieve irritating stimuli; perhaps it is too warm or too cold or has become caught in the blanket. Adults walk away from people who annoy them or turn off the TV when the program is boring. The threat of a spanking induces a child to behave.

Engaging in too much escape behavior can have marked effects on a person's personality development. Everyone is aware of others who are asocial, withdrawn, or seclusive. The withdrawn person, as a child, may have had considerable escape conditioning in running away from overdemanding adults. The removal of an aversive stimulus is reinforcing, and the person who continues to maintain escape behavior renders himself unavailable to the social behavior of others. When other people have become the aversive stimuli, normal social relationships are unobtainable. For many who continue to be withdrawn and seclusive, the causes are to be found in the multitude of aversive stimuli presented to them in their early conditioning history.

Out of escape, *avoidance* behavior may develop. Although similar to escape, there is a basic difference, and of the two, avoidance behavior may be more common. One can *escape* the rain by putting up one's umbrella as soon as it starts to rain, but one can *avoid* the rain by putting up the umbrella *before* going out into the rain. One can escape tight shoes by removing them, but one can avoid the pain by not putting on the shoes in the first place. In avoidance, a warning signal is ordinarily given. If one heeds the warning one avoids the more aversive stimulus which will follow. If the warning is ignored, the aversive stimulus is presented.

Unfortunately, government and law have depended almost entirely on avoidance as a means of control. We pay our taxes to avoid fines or being put in jail. We are given no positive reinforcement for obeying the law but may face imprisonment if we do not do so. Likewise, education has depended far too frequently on aversive control. Students are forced to go to dull classes or be flunked. Deans and discipline committees offer all kinds of threats to maintain student control, and if a student disobeys he may face expulsion. The church, too, has used the threat of hell and damnation to deter unrighteous behavior.

Ayllon and Michael (1959) studied two psychotic female patients who manifested eating problems. One of the patients ordinarily had to be forcibly taken to the dining hall, where she would permit a nurse to spoon-feed her; the other had to be spoon-fed in an adjacent room. Unlike many disturbed patients, both were extremely neat and clean. The experimenters used both escape and avoidance conditioning to alter the eating problems. The spoon-feeding was accompanied by slight food spilling as the aversive stimulus. The patients could avoid the food spilling by feeding themselves for the entire meal, and in both cases self-feeding was achieved.

Like excessive escape, too much avoidance conditioning can have adverse effects on personality development. The hazards are seen in the child who insulates himself from other people, possibly to avoid punishment. He may play "chronic invalid" or engage in excessive fantasy whereby he substitutes daydreams of positively reinforcing events for the real world, which has become something to avoid. Cameron (1947) has suggested three kinds of aversive conditions in the process of child rearing which lead to chronic avoidance: (1) long subjection to restrictive and excessive discipline, (2) excessive criticism for one's acts, and (3) inadequate occasions for social stimuli.

Punishment is the third popular means of aversive control: "Spare the rod and spoil the child." Punishment is widely used because its results are quickly noted. It can be thought of as a quick way of getting rid of undesirable behavior, but while punishment may suppress undesired behavior, unless it is continuous the suppressed behavior may return to its previous strength when the punishment has ceased. So punishment does not necessarily eliminate unwanted behavior.

In an early study, Skinner (1938) demonstrated this suppression effect in the animal laboratory. The control group was first conditioned until a steady rate had been established, and then nonreinforcement-extinction procedures were initiated. During extinction the behavior was maintained for a while and then gradually died out. The experimental group was also nonreinforced, and it was punished during the first ten minutes of extinction. Although the behavior showed initially greater suppression following the punishment, by the end of the second day of extinction the total number of responses of the punished group had recovered to the same level as the group that had received no punishment. So, punishment, overall, is not superior to simple nonreinforcement in extinguishing undesired behavior.

Besides not necessarily getting rid of unwanted behavior, punishment may lead to undesired consequences. First, it may lead to feelings of guilt or anxiety. The word *guilt* in this context merely refers to the fact that the behavior punished was of a moral or ethical sort. We may be punished for many things, some of which are described as "bad." The problem is that punishment generates anxiety (guilt is a form of anxiety) which accomplishes nothing except to upset the person. (An objective interpretation of anxiety is given below.)

A second unfortunate consequence of punishment is that it may lead to anger and aggression. Although aggression may be useful in warding off one's enemies, there are problems in that unnecessary aggression may impede social relationships, destroy or immobilize the punisher, or be directed against persons who were not responsible for the punishment (displaced aggression) (Azrin, 1966).

Another form of punishment not directly making use of aversive stimuli is called *time-out*, which involves removing a person from a situation which has been positively reinforcing into one which is not. Simple examples are sending a child to his room, the use of the penalty box for removing a player from a game such as ice hockey, or sending a man to prison.

Brown and Tyler (1969) report the use of time-out in treating an extremely aggressive delinquent boy of 16. It seemed that the boy was being strongly reinforced by bullying others, and he was informed that his aggressive behavior would result in social isolation from his peers. In being dethroned as the "duke" of the group, the reinforcement provided by the submission of those he bullied could be eliminated. The application of time-out, or being put in the "pokey," as he put it, had a marked effect not only in reducing his aggressive behavior but in improving his relations with his peers and the staff.

Anxiety is the fourth of the basic aversive conditions. Skinnerians interpret anxiety as behavior resulting from being placed in a situation in which escape or avoidance of the aversive stimuli are impossible. A warning signal is given, followed by some aversive stimulus. A child who has been naughty may be told that he will be punished when his father comes home; the waiting period constitutes the situation of anxiety.

In humans, anxiety has many manifestations, both in operant and respondent reactions. Among respondent reactions are changes in physiological functions (increased heart rate and blood pressure, perspiration, inclination to eliminate, shaking, and so on). On the operant side are feelings of nervousness, being upset, and fear, as well as increased inappropriate motor activity such as restlessness or heightened muscular rigidity.

Many personality theories, especially the psychoanalytic, find anxiety to be a condition which may lead to behavior disorders. Although the interpretations are different for behaviorists, both schools of thought tend to agree on the importance of anxiety. Too much early conditioning in anxiety can lead to later maladaptive behavior. Since neither escape nor avoidance is possible, there is no reinforcement. There is only the anticipation of punishment, and this anticipation may be more disruptive than the punishment. Excessive conditioning can lead to neurotic anxiety, in which the person feels chronically anxious and may have anxiety attacks in which he is overwhelmed with fear or panic.

Maintenance

9. BESIDES PRIMARY REINFORCEMENT,
   PERSONALITY IS MAINTAINED BY A
   SERIES OF CONDITIONED REINFORCERS.

In the Development section, we distinguished primary from conditioned reinforcers. Primary reinforcement is natural or unlearned; conditioned reinforcers are acquired. Such reinforcers start out as neutral stimuli, but by being paired with primary reinforcement they later strengthen behavior in their own right. However, just any pairing will not work. For a conditioned reinforcer to acquire its power, it must first become a discriminative stimulus. The better the discrimination, the more powerful it will be as a conditioned reinforcer. However, unlike primary reinforcers, conditioned reinforcers can lose their power unless occasionally paired with primary ones.

A demonstration from the animal laboratory illustrates this. A rat is conditioned to press a lever, and as a consequence of this behavior he receives food. But he only gets fed if light is present, and this condition becomes the discriminative stimulus. Eventually, a discrimination is formed; the animal presses in the presence of the light but not in its absence. Now a chain is placed in the cage. When the animal pulls it with his teeth he receives the light as the conditioned reinforcer. The rate of chain pulling will increase for a while, indicating that the conditioned reinforcer is working even if the animal is not otherwise rewarded by the primary reinforcer—the food.

Some of these conditioned reinforcers are specific to individuals, such as listening to music, or watching a football game. However, some classes of reinforcers are shared by many people. Skinner calls these *generalized reinforcers*; they include attention, approval, affection, submission of others, and tokens. (Skinner, 1953).

Attention can amount to a simple glance, a wave of the hand, a snap of a finger, or a verbal "hello." *Approval* is generally a powerful reinforcer; it includes verbal responses of praise, ("Thank you very much," "You did a fine job"), applause, cheering, nodding, smiling, and so on. *Affection* is even more powerful. Signs of affection include hugging, cuddling, shaking hands, and verbal endearments such as "darling" or "sweetheart."

An example of the *submission of others* as a reinforcer is illustrated in the previously cited study by Brown and Tyler (1969), in which the "duke," who had been powerfully reinforced by the submission of those he bullied, was dethroned. Superiors are reinforced by acquiescence. Giving in to a child's demands puts him in a superior position by strengthening his demanding behavior.

What we have considered so far as generalized reinforcers are specific behaviors on the part of other people. *Tokens* are even more specific, since they involve inanimate objects which have a constant stimulus value. Money is probably the most powerful and most common token reinforcer. The acquisition of its function can be easily understood in a child. In the beginning, money for the child may be nothing more than paper or "shiny stuff." As the child learns that money can be exchanged for such primary reinforcers as candy or ice cream cones, however, it begins to acquire its reinforcement function. Eventually, it is generalized to reinforce countless behaviors. Other tokens for children include trinkets and toys. Education employs many tokens, such as prizes, diplomas, Phi Beta Kappa keys or being named to the dean's list.

10. BEHAVIOR CAN BE MAINTAINED BY
    REINFORCERS DELIVERED REGULARLY OR
    INTERMITTENTLY.

Regular or continuous reinforcement means every response is followed by a reinforcement. This is not the usual case in everyday affairs, except possibly in the case of the spoiled child who gets everything he asks for or in some cases of verbal behavior in which a remark always receives some reply from another.

Ordinarily, behavior is reinforced on what are called schedules; that is, reinforcement is given intermittently. To reinforce on intermittent schedules develops stronger or more persistent behavior than if the reinforcement constantly follows the desired behavior (Ferster & Skinner, 1957).

There are four basic schedules: fixed interval, variable interval, fixed ratio and variable ratio. Others are variations of these.

In *fixed-interval schedules*, reinforcement is

delivered on a regular time basis. In a laboratory it could be once every 30 seconds, or every minute or two. The reinforcement is delivered by some outside agency according to a designated schedule, regardless of how many responses an organism makes in between, just so long as it makes the response at the time designated for the reinforcement or soon thereafter. In human affairs, being paid by the hour or week illustrates this kind of schedule. When we eat or sleep at regular hours or get mail at a designated time, we are working on a fixed-interval schedule.

In a *variable-interval schedule*, reinforcement is based on a time schedule which varies but averages out to a specified time. For example, if one responds on a variable-interval schedule of two minutes, reinforcements would be delivered on the average of once every two minutes, although at times a particular reinforcement might come after 45 seconds or three minutes. Frequently, our social life operates on some kind of variable-interval schedule. Some weeks we may be invited out several times, or we may go for weeks without being entertained.

In *fixed-ratio schedules*, the reinforcements are delivered on a basis of how many responses an individual makes, regardless of time. In a fixed-ratio schedule of ten, one would be reinforced after every tenth response. If one works fast, one receives more reinforcements than if one works more slowly. Being paid on a piecework or commission basis illustrates this schedule. The more cars a salesman sells, the more money he will make, providing he is working on commission.

Sometimes ratio and interval schedules can be combined. If one is paid an hourly wage but also receives extra commission for selling merchandise beyond a given amount, both ratio and interval schedules would be working.

The fourth basic schedule is the *variable-ratio schedule*. This is like the variable-interval one in that the reinforcements are delivered irregularly but average out to a given figure. A variable ratio of ten would mean that on the average of every tenth response, one will be reinforced. Many gambling devices, such as slot machines or roulette tables, work on this kind of schedule. When one is having a winning streak the reinforcements are close together, whereas in a losing streak they are few and far between.

11. MOTIVATION CONSISTS OF DEPRIVING OR
     SATIATING THE ORGANISM WITH REGARD
     TO SOME KIND OF REINFORCEMENT.

For behavior to be maintained, motivation must be present. In animal studies in which primary reinforcements are used, the reinforcement will not function if the organism is satiated with food —if food is being used as the reinforcing stimulus. The animal must, therefore, be food deprived for this primary reinforcement to function.

Some personality theories make use of complicated motivational principles such as instincts, drives, needs, and hypothetical or internal states. In the Skinnerian approach these are not necessary. The most acceptable motivational operations are the observable events of either depriving or satiating an organism with appropriate reinforcers.

Both operations can be applied to the practical control of behavior. We deprive a child of between-meal snacks so that he will eat enough at mealtime. When a child fails to eat his dinner, instead of coaxing or applying threats or other aversive stimuli, a better way to get him to eat, providing he is in good health, is to excuse him from the table. This increases his deprivation and also the probability he will eat properly at the next meal. Setting the time for a dinner party later than the guests' accustomed eating hour will ordinarily guarantee they will eat a hearty meal. If the goal is a short meeting, it should be scheduled just prior to normal eating time. Skinner (1953) has suggested if we want to make a man amenable to bribes, he should be encouraged to live beyond his means. The manipulation of deprivation of both primary and secondary reinforcers has been known as long as man has had a recorded history. Cutting off the lines of supply to opponents, for example, has been a basic military tactic.

Some advertisements aim at degrees of deprivation. They set up reinforcers, usually conditioned, as appeals for goods a person does not have. Owning a fancy sports car will bring on the conditioned reinforcements of attention and approval for some. Sales or bargains help to relieve financial deprivation by reducing normal prices. Small compact cars which provide fuel economy also reduce financial deprivation by saving on gas purchases and making more money available for other purposes.

Deprivation and satiation can be effective methods in altering undesirable behavior in psychiatric patients. Ayllon (1963) describes a patient who weighted 250 pounds. She not only ate the food given her but would steal food from other patients or pick up unauthorized food from the counter. To change her behavior, first she was assigned a table by herself in the dining room. Whenever she approached the tables of other patients or the counter, she was discharged from the dining room. This procedure eliminated the food stealing in two weeks. After she was limited to eating merely her own food, her weight was reduced from 250 to 180 pounds in the 14 months she was in the hospital. In being removed from the dining room when she took unauthorized food she experienced deprivation and learned that she could only eat the food allowed for her consumption.

Satiation has also been applied to the control of cigarette smoking. Marrone (1970) divided chronic cigarette smokers into three groups. The first group was instructed to chain smoke for 24 hours, the second to chain smoke for 10 hours, and the third to smoke as desired. After four months, a follow-up study was made. Of the first group, 6 out of 10 were not smoking; in the second group 2 out of 11 remained abstainers; and in the third group 9 out of 10 were still smoking.

Deprivation and satiation can also be applied with conditioned reinforcers. Gewitz and Baer (1958) used nursery school children in a game situation in which a child was to place a marble in one of two holes. Verbal approval—such as "good," "fine," or "Hm-hmmm"—was given for appropriate responses. Before playing the game, Group I was placed in social isolation for 20 minutes (deprivation of social reinforcers). Group II immediately played the game upon being led from the classroom. In Group III the children devoted 20 minutes to drawing and cutting out designs in which the experimenter maintained a stream of friendly conversation and approval. The results indicated that the reinforcement was most effective for the first group, who had been placed in social isolation. This was determined by the number of correct responses the children made in the game situation. Thus, effective reinforcement is partially a function of the degree of deprivation.

12. BEHAVIOR CAN BE MAINTAINED OR ALTERED BY MOTIVATION-LIKE OPERATIONS.

In motivation-like operations, something other than deprivation or satiation happens to the state of the organism which affects its behavior. Some of these operations include taking drugs, brain stimulation, pregnancy, fatigue, or illness. Skinner has suggested that we are now in an age of chemical control by drugs and that, for many, the normal daily life may be maintained or altered through their use (Skinner, 1953).

There is a vast literature on the effects of drugs on behavior. Tranquilizers such as librium or tranquizine tend to suppress anxiety. Other drugs, such as chlorpromazine or reserpine, are effective in controlling extremely aggressive behavior. The business man facing a tough sales meeting or the housewife overwhelmed with the tasks of raising a family and keeping house may find tranquilizers a means of getting through a problem situation. Other drugs, such as the amphetamines, tend to speed up activity.

From the dawn of history alcohol has not only reduced anxiety but has been a powerful positive reinforcer. Sometimes businessmen ply a customer with liquor to get his business or encourage him to let slip some unguarded information. Illicit drugs such as marijuana, "speed," or heroin are used in all branches of society for relaxation or escape from anxiety.

Another motivation-like operation is intercranial self-stimulation. Olds (1956) studied extensively the effect of this process in a variety of animal species. In a simple rat experiment, an electrode is implanted in a specific part of the brain (popularly called the pleasure center), and the rat is trained to press the lever to receive a slight electric shock. Because the lever pressing is maintained at a high rate, despite any deprivation of primary reinforcers, the shock is designated a positive reinforcer.

Other motivation-like operations, such as illness, pregnancy, or fatigue, are more difficult to study experimentally. Nevertheless, common observations indicate that they alter certain kinds of behavior. A pregnant woman finds getting around awkward and so restricts her activity, or a sick person takes to his bed or slows down his activity markedly.

These, then, are some of the basic assertions of

an operant reinforcement approach to personality. They are concerned with the development, maintenance, or alteration of many aspects of man's behavior. As principles which attempt to explain the basic nature of man as he behaves in a natural world, they are based on observable events and not hypothetical assumptions.

Applications

Assessment

Skinner's first attempt to apply the behavioral principles established in the laboratory to human life was in his Utopian novel *Walden Two* (Skinner, 1948). He describes a self-sustaining community with its own farm, dairy, livestock, medical care, symphony orchestra, and so on. The community is run by planners and managers. Work is appropriately shared through a system of "labor credits." Each member spends only about four hours a day in work, so there is ample time for recreation and creative activity. "Behavioral engineering" is the key term as to how the system works.

Skinner believes that other communes have failed because their members sought immediate ecstasy. The design of Walden Two provides alternatives for men of "goodwill," and it could act as a model for larger social systems.

Positive reinforcement is the principle on which Walden Two is based. Punishment does not exist. Fraser, one of the planners, explains how positive reinforcement works:

> "Now that we know how positive reinforcement works and negative doesn't", he [Fraser] said, at last, "We can be more deliberate and hence more successful in our cultural design. We can achieve a sort of control under which the controlled, though they are following a code more scrupulously than was the case under the old system, nevertheless feel free. They are doing what they want to do and not what they are forced to do. That's the source of the tremendous power of positive reinforcement. There's no restraint and no revolt. By a careful cultural design, we control not the final behavior, but the inclination to behavior—the motives, the desires and the wishes." (Skinner, 1948, p. 219)

Today a real community modeled after Walden Two exists in Virginia. Called Twin Oaks, at its inception in 1968 it contained only 23 people, but by 1973 the number had grown to 40. The community, located on a tobacco farm, consists of several frame structures. The money to run the community comes from its industry: hammock making and the fattening of calves. Unlike Walden Two, which was ideally self-sustaining, the members of Twin Oaks frequently have to go to neighboring communities to get temporary jobs. Although Twin Oaks farms its land, it has to go outside to buy products. The community does use the labor-credit system and a planner-manager system. All members must subscribe to a behavioral code which includes the sanctity of privacy, not talking behind another's back, abstinence from drugs, and giving up personal property.

Entertainment at Twin Oaks is much less elaborate than that described in Walden Two, consisting mainly of singing, guitar playing, and square dancing. One of the difficulties Twin Oaks has encountered is in turnover; members leave and new ones come in too frequently. Everyone who arrives does not have knowledge of Skinnerian principles, but those who stay are helped to learn the basic principles by classes in what is called behavioral psychology. In a recent book, *A Walden II Experiment: The First Five Years of Twin Oaks* (Kinkade, 1973), some of the problems and developments are described. Finding new members is no problem, but finding the right type of person is; there is no place for people who are irresponsible or lazy. The membership is subject to the typical human failings, however; there are encounter sessions (hardly a Skinnerian concept) in which they try to understand one another and improve their personal relations. Whether or not the experiment will succeed only time will tell.

In *Beyond Freedom and Dignity*, Skinner (1971) expanded some of his basic concepts. He has reinterpreted what he considers to be a number of outmoded notions on the nature of man, in the light of behavioristic psychology. Believing that man is a product of both his genetic endowment and the stimuli in his environment, he asserts that *man is not autonomous* but is always under the control of variables outside himself. He reiterates the strong determinism stated in his earlier works, which allows man to make decisions, but determined ones. To those who believe in man's free will to choose from his inner self or psyche, Skinner's assertions are considered inhuman. However, he interprets *freedom* to mean that man is no longer under the control of aversive stimuli which lead to escape, avoidance or punishment. In freedom, the control is positive reinforcement.

Concerning the design of a culture, Skinner writes:

> If the designer is an individualist, he will design a world in which he will be under minimal aversive control and will accept his own goods as the ultimate value. If he has been exposed to an appropriate environment, he will design for the good of others, possibly with a loss of personal goods. If he is concerned primarily with survival values, he will design a culture with an eye to whether it will work. (Skinner, 1971, p. 151)

Skinner has also been concerned with problems involved in *self-control*. If we accept the notion that we are under environmental control, does the possibility exist that we can engage in *self-control?* Goldiamond (1965) has suggested two kinds of procedures for developing self-control. The first involves instructing a person wishing to engage in self-control how to set up the procedures that will change his environment and will bring his own behavior under appropriate control. By exercising self-control, he is *reordering the environmental stimuli.* The second procedure involves training the person in the functional analysis of behavior (the principles outlined in the Assertions section) and then asking him to decide for himself the procedures he wishes to follow.

Treatment

In operant reinforcement theory, the basic methods of treating personality disorders are classed under the general heading of *behavior therapy,* to distinguish them from the more conventional therapies. What is significant in behavior therapy is the application of principles of respondent and operant conditioning in altering or eliminating inappropriate or undesirable behavior. This section will describe briefly some of the most popular methods used by behavior therapists.

Behavior therapy, in its various versions, differs markedly from methods used in psycho-analysis or nondirective therapy. First, a specific problem is identified. If the problem is complex, each aspect must be treated separately. Thus the target behavior—that is, what the change or outcome should be—is identified. The behavior therapist is not concerned with how the condition came about or what were its causes, but only with the treatment of the specific problems that will alter behavior for the better.

Systematic Desensitization or Reciprocal Inhibition. Dissatisfied with conventional therapies, Wolpe (1958, 1969) developed methods which make use of operant conditioning principles. In part his procedure involves training patients in progressive relaxation, whereby the patient is instructed to concentrate on the relaxation of specific muscle groups: face, chest, shoulders, arms, stomach, hips, thighs, and so on. After relaxation of the whole body is well established, the patient is asked to make a hierarchy of the things that trouble him. These are often anxiety-arousing events related to a particular problem, such as a fear of snakes. The subject is asked to imagine the least anxiety-arousing situation and then work through the group to the most severe. In some cases, as in snake or school phobias, it may only involve a single hierarchy, and in others there may be several sets of hierarchies for a given individual. When this hierarchy has been established, the process of desensitization begins. Wolpe suggests if a response antagonistic to anxiety, such as relaxation, can be developed in the presence of the anxiety-arousing stimulus, the result is suppression of the anxiety, and the bond between the stimulus which ordinarily provokes anxiety and anxiety responses will be weakened.

Reinforcement Therapy. A number of examples of reinforcement therapy have already been given in the Assertions section to show how positive reinforcement can modify undesirable behavior in a more adaptive direction. The basic principle involves the conditioning of new behavior through the process of differentiation (shaping) or reconditioning of more adaptive behavior in lieu of the persistent maladaptive responding. With ingenuity on the part of the therapist, reinforcement therapy can be applied to a wide variety of behavior problems in children as well as to neurotic and psychotic adults. The illustrations which follow are only a few of the hundreds of examples reported on the effectiveness of reinforcement therapy.

Isaacs, Thomas, and Goldiamond (1960) describe the differentiation or shaping of vocal responses in a catatonic schizophrenic who had been mute for 19 years. Shaping involved the following procedure. A piece of chewing gum was placed in front of the patient. If the patient noticed the gum it was given to him at first, but then the therapist waited until the patient made lip-moving responses before giving him the gum. As the gum was held up, the subject was instructed to say "gum," and obtaining the gum was contingent upon his making vocal responses which successfully approximated the word. Thereafter, other vocal responses were shaped out, and then vocal responses in the presence of other persons were requested. Eventually, the patient was trained in this manner to speak in group therapy sessions.

Wolf, Risley, and Mees (1964) used differentiation (shaping) to get an autistic boy three and one-half years old to wear glasses. Initially, when glasses were placed on his head he would tear them off and throw them to the ground. In the beginning of their treatment, they used a conditioned reinforcer by pairing the clicks of a toy noisemaker with a small bit of candy or fruit. The child was first reinforced for wearing merely the frames. Then a "roll bar" which would go over the top of the boy's head was added. Finally, lenses were added to the frame. The boy was required to wear the glasses during meals and snacks, on automobile rides and going out to play, all of which were positively reinforcing stimuli. At the time of his dismissal from the hospital, he had worn the glasses for a total of 600 hours.

Reinforcement therapy can be applied to more complex activities. Schwitzgebel (1967) gained therapeutic cooperation in a group of juvenile delinquents for a series of 20 interviews. The experimental group received positive reinforcement for statements of concern about other people and for prompt arrival at the sessions. Reinforcements included candy, cigarettes, money (25 cents to $1) for statements like "Joe is a good guy." The control group received no reinforcements. In a natural setting (a restaurant), the experimental group showed significant increase in such positive statements.

Sometimes *contracts* can improve behavior. The assumption in setting up a contract is that there will be a reciprocal exchange of reinforcement which depends upon specific behavior on the part of each party to the contract. Tooley and Pratt (1967) report a case where a husband agreed to cut down on his smoking in exchange for better housekeeping on the part of his wife. Thus the husband agreed to cut his smoking down to ten cigarettes a day in return for the living room being tidy when he came home from work. The technique was mutual cooperation

Aversion Therapy. In aversion therapy, based primarily on the principles of respondent conditioning, the conditioned stimulus (CS) is paired with an unconditioned stimulus (US) which is naturally aversive to the individual. It might be a nausea-producing substance or an electric shock. Prior to the conditioning the CS has had some positively reinforcing function, like alcohol for the alcoholic. When paired with the primary aversive stimulus (US), however, it takes on the function of being aversive.

The idea of treating alcoholics by associating a noxious stimulus with alcohol goes back to the ancient Roman practice of placing an eel in the wine jug and making the individual drink from it. Voegtlin (1940) and Voegtlin and Lemere (1942) used injections of an emetic, a substance which causes vomiting. The subjects were poured an ounce of whiskey and instructed to look, smell, and then taste and swallow it. Additional amounts of alcohol were given until the emetic took effect and the subject vomited. Ordinarily, the procedure was repeated at from four to seven sessions. Using a total of 4,096 subjects, they reported an average overall abstinence rate of 51% over a one- to ten-year follow-up period.

Aversion therapy has frequently been used in the treatment of sexual disorders. Raymond (1956) reports the case of a man who had a fetish for ladies' handbags and perambulators which brought him into frequent difficulties with the law. The treatment consisted of showing him a collection of handbags and perambulators, along with colored slides of the subjects, just before the onset of nausea produced by an injection of apomorphine. Not only was the fetish successfully eliminated, but the man showed improvement in his social and legal relationships. He was promoted in his job and no longer used fetish fantasies to have sexual intercourse.

Although the above examples made use of nausea-producing substances as the US, it should be noted that electric shock is also frequently so used. For examples, see Rachman and Teasdale, *Aversion Therapy* (1969).

Institutional

One of the most effective applications of operant conditioning principles in institutions has been the use of what is called *the token economy*. Ayllon and Azrin (1968) outlined a plan currently in use in mental hospitals as well as in schools. Basically, the idea is that the persons involved are given tokens for performing a variety of desired behaviors.

In mental institutions, tokens can be given for work done in the laundry, kitchen, waiting on tables, and so on. These tokens can be exchanged to buy privacy (a private room instead of the ward), sitting at more attractive tables in the dining room, or candy or cigarettes at the commissary. Through such a program, patients can be led to engage in more desirable activities and to acquire better social behavior, instead of just sitting around in the ward or being troublesome. As a necessary part of the system, ward assistants are trained to observe the behavior of the patients and are given direct responsibility for handing out the tokens. Generally, each attendant works with a small group.

In the use of the token economy in school or classroom situations, the teacher or an aide dispenses the tokens. The following two examples illustrate the use of the token economy, the first in a classroom and the second in a mental institution.

Chadwick and Day (1971) applied token economy to a group of underachieving elementary school children. The behaviors measured were percentage of time spent at work, work output per minute, and accuracy. The study was divided into three phases: (1) a base-line or prereinforcement period; (2) the treatment period, in which tokens and social reinforcements were given; and (3) a period in which only social reinforcements were used. The combination of tokens and social reinforcement increased all aspects of the behavior studied over that of the prereinforcement period. When only social reinforcements were used, the average time at work decreased as compared

to when tokens were applied, but the same degree of accuracy of work was maintained.

Schaefer and Martin (1966) used jobs for patients in a mental hospital as a basis for token reinforcement. The behavior of a dormitory cleaner was shaped out in specific steps until an entire chain was completed. To receive the tokens the sequence included: (1) pick up cleaning equipment, (2) dust partitions and sills, (3) mop entire floor except under beds, (4) shake out rag and dust mop outside the ward, (5) empty and clean water pail, (6) wash windows on Saturdays, and (7) turn in equipment. It should be noted that these behaviors were shaped separately with tokens before the entire sequence was accomplished.

Another application of operant conditioning principles in education has been the use of programmed learning (Skinner, 1968), a basic principle of which is that immediate reinforcement is given when the learner makes a correct response. As the first step in learning, the student makes a response to a given question, usually in writing. He or she then is given immediate knowledge of the result and moves to the next question (or frame, as it is frequently called). Skinner first thought that a machine was needed so the learner could not cheat by looking at the answer before he made his response, but it was later discovered that it was not necessary. Programs are now usually printed in book form, and a card can be used to cover answers while questions are being answered.

A course of carefully ordered small steps is followed in programmed learning, with each step (question) small enough that it can be easily accomplished. In this way the student works at his own rate and gradually gets closer to the target behavior, that is, the whole course of what is to be ultimately learned. If the steps are too large, the student may miss too many questions and become discouraged. Programs are designed for all educational levels, from children acquiring simple discriminations, to early school skills, to learning mathematics or how to do a simple task like making a bed properly, to the operation of complicated machinery.

Self

One who understands the basic principles of operant conditioning can control not only his own behavior but that of others. If it is known what positive reinforcements strengthen a particular person's behavior, they can be applied to the particular behavior to be shaped or strengthened. Undesirable behavior may be ignored, provided the intention is maintaining that behavior. Sometimes children engage in what is called *negative attention getting*, exhibiting obnoxious behavior just to get any kind of attention, even criticism or a spanking.

Children will be happier and more productive in school if the teacher uses positive reinforcement instead of punishment. This will facilitate learning and will lessen hostility in the classroom. However, time-out can be effective. While Skinnerians consider time-out a form of punishment, the behavior punished is not followed by an aversive stimulus.

A good coach applies shaping principles whether he realizes it or not. In learning an athletic skill, the novice needs some reinforcement even though his early efforts are clumsy. More effective responses will occur as selective reinforcement is applied until the skill has been mastered. The coach who never praises his team but only criticizes them will encourage poor morale and team spirit.

If certain discriminative stimuli are eliminated from the environment, it will be impossible to respond to them. One way to give up smoking is not to buy, borrow, or have cigarettes around. However, the problem is not that simple, because smoking is tied up with a variety of other stimuli besides cigarettes. We smoke when others around us do or while we are having a cup of coffee or a drink or after a meal. It is because smoking is involved in so many other contingencies that many people find it hard to quit. Of course, there are other stimuli, some aversive, which can help reduce smoking, such as the threat of lung cancer or heart disease or the high price of cigarettes.

Dieting is another exercise in self-control. A variety of positive reinforcements can help in losing weight: Our clothes are no longer tight, we look better in the mirror, and people tell us how our appearance has improved. We can weigh ourselves regularly to keep track of weight loss, count calories, and eliminate discriminative stimuli which quickly add pounds, such as candy and pasta.

Since we are all continually behaving organisms, correct behavioral principles are useful in all aspects of human existence, such as rearing a happy child or maintaining compatible marital relationships. We have gone a long way in understanding ourselves and others. The basic principles of operant reinforcement presented in the Assertions section suggest the great advantage of this personality theory: it is a practical system, easily understood. Any individual can try it for himself. Because the principles are not merely hypothetical constructs but have been derived from careful observations, we know we are on solid ground. This is one great advantage over other personality theories. Operant conditioning can be applied not only therapeutically but also to everyday living.

Validation

Evidence

Skinner's primary method of validation has been laboratory experimentation, although recent studies in what is referred to as *applied behavior analysis* have made use of studies in real-life situations such as classrooms, homes, and institutions for retarded and disturbed people.

In departing from traditional experimentation, Skinner and his followers have stressed the use of individual subjects, for it is believed that when proper controls are exercised, large numbers of subjects are not necessary. When large groups are used, whether animals or humans, the effects of environmental variables may be masked if appropriate controls are not applied. The traditional experimenter then uses sophisticated statistical procedures to get significant results. When proper controls are exercised, only a single subject or at most only a few are required, and complicated statistics are not necessary.

In many experiments in operant conditioning a base-line rate is established, the independent variable is imposed, and subsequent changes in behavior are observed and measured. This method, referred to as *using the subject as his own control*, eliminates the many possible uncontrolled variables involved when experimental and control groups are used, since under many circumstances the two groups cannot be properly matched.

Throughout this chapter reference has been made to experimental studies which have supported Skinner's assertions. These experiments, which have used animals and normal and disturbed children and adults in a variety of settings, have validated the system with a great deal of supporting evidence. Other examples can be cited from areas not discussed above.

One such area is *psychopharmacology*, the study of the effects of drugs on behavior. Many ethical drug companies are employing psychologists trained in Skinnerian methodology to test the effects of new drugs before placing them on the market. An example is a study by Boren (1960) in which rats were trained in an operant conditioning chamber to press a lever to receive food pellets as reinforcement. Once the base-line rate of lever pressing had been established, a drug, chlorpromazine, was administered, and results indicated that the rate was depressed. It is now known that this drug is an effective means of suppressing aggressive and extremely active behavior in severely disturbed psychiatric patients.

Another study, reported by Blough (1957), investigated the effects of LSD on the visual threshold in pigeons. A bird was presented with a visual stimulus panel illuminated by a spot of light which could be varied in intensity by the experimenter. The basic procedure was for the bird to indicate by pecking when it could or could not see. Two disks were used, and the bird was trained to peck at the first when it became visible and at the second when no light was visible. This is a more complicated version of the formation of a discrimination discussed in Assertion 5. When the pigeon pecked at the first disk the light intensity was lowered, and when it pecked at the second the intensity was raised. Thus the visual threshold was established, that is, a point where the bird "could just see" the light. Whenever the spot of light was no longer visible on the first disk, the bird stopped pecking and began to peck at the second. When the light on the second disk increased in intensity until the bird could see it, he stopped pecking and reverted to the first disk. After this initial training procedure had been established, LSD was administered. The findings indicated that the drug had the effect of lowering the visual threshold. This ingenious experimental procedure allows an experimenter to study sensation objectively without having to rely on subjective introspection.

Perhaps one of the most unique examples of the operant conditioning procedures was reported by Skinner (1960). This study, which involved an attempt to devise a method for controlling the flight of missiles, was carried on during World War II under the auspices of the U. S. government. The aim was to demonstrate whether pigeons placed in missiles could guide them to their targets. Pigeons were trained to respond by pecking at a stimulus which resembled the missile target. Since these birds have excellent visual discrimination, the stimuli could resemble any target—a ship, a part of a city, or a particular landscape. When the missile was on target the pigeon would peck in the center of the stimulus panel, directly at the pattern of the target. When the missile changed direction, deviating from the target, it would move to another display area, and an activity system which would change the course of the missile in the proper direction could be activated. If the target moved to the right, for example, the pigeon would peck an area to the right of center, and the missile would adjust accordingly. It was found that by using variable-interval schedules of reinforcement the pigeons would continue at their designated tasks for long periods, and satiation was no problem as it would have been if the birds were continuously reinforced. While this study was never put to practical use, pigeons could have been put in missiles for actual guidance.

We have already discussed the applications of behavior principles in the practical control of behavior. General principles can be applied outside the laboratory to everyday living conditions. Skinnerians do not typically rely on case histories, but some studies have reported the modification of behavior in more formal situations. Examples are Williams (1959), in the control of temper tantrums, and Tooley and Pratt (1967), in the development of contracts to reduce cigarette smoking by the husband in return for improved housekeeping by the wife.

Comparisons

Skinner's primary objection to most other personality theories is that they are dualistic, making use of mental events as distinct from purely physical ones. In the behavioristic tradition, Skinner has abandoned mental events, regardless of their sophistication. Other theories depend on hypothetical constructs and intervening variables such as "inner states" as causative explanations, instead of the clear data of the behaving organism operating in a natural environment. The methodology of self theories or existential theories depends almost entirely on introspection. Because it is phenomenological, it is unreliable and not subject to objective validation.

With regard to psychoanalysis, Skinner (1954) has leveled some specific criticisms. First, the nature of the act is never clarified. Such concepts as "libido," "cathexis," "instinctive tendencies," or psychic energy can hardly be quantified as objective events, because they lack any specific physical dimensions.

Second, Freud and the psychoanalysts have imposed a complicated mental structure (ego, superego, id) as an explanation for the causes of behavior. Instead of going back to the original environmental events, they accept the construct of these hypothecated mental events as an operating principle, which, in Skinner's thinking, is little more than fiction. In accepting such a hypothetical construct, little is left for behavior itself.

Third, in psychoanalysis there is a shift or transference from the physical to the mental event and vice versa, but how this happens is never explained. The psychic energy which runs man's personality is said to be derived from some kind of instinctual energy, presumably physical, but Freud never told us exactly how this transference occurs. Furthermore, the mental apparatus supposedly has some topological dimensions, as described in *The Ego and the Id* (Freud, 1923), but they are not exactly real.

Describing the evolution of psychoanalysis, Skinner says:

> One may take the line that metaphorical devices are inevitable in the early stages of any science and that although we may look with amusement upon "essences", "phlogistons" and "ethers" of the science of yesterday, these were necessary to the historical process.... However, if we have learned anything about the nature of scientific thinking ... it is possible to avoid some of the mistakes of adolescence. Whether Freud could have done so is past demonstrating, but whether we need similar constructs in the future prosecution of a science of behavior is a question worth considering. (Skinner, 1954, p. 301)

Skinner's objections to psychoanalysis would apply equally well to Individual and Analytical psychology, as well as to other neo-Freudian systems.

With regard to trait and type theories of personality, Skinner (1953) has further objections. He has suggested that prediction is more reliable on the basis of a single response than on the basis of a trait configuration. A trait is at best a measure of a variety of behaviors which appear to have some common descriptive characteristic, whereas a single response can be readily identified and measured. In traits, many behaviors originate in a variety of situations. It might be said that a person has a trait of *dominance*, but the situations in which such a person may or may not dominate are never specified. Traits, therefore, are not the causes of behavior but are mere verbal descriptions. The fewer traits are defined, the more generalized is the analysis and the less accurate are the predictions. Thus, a prediction will have to be made within a wide range of probability, and the chances of being right may often be only as good as the possibilities of being wrong.

Most personality theories depend too much on theory and too little on supporting data. When data are presented, they are frequently unreliable. For example, psychoanalysis, as well as Individual and Analytical psychology, relies on casual observations, things told the psychotherapist by clients, such as reports of dreams. This may lead to some interesting conjectures, but it can hardly be called science.

Prospect

In terms of the development of personality theorizing, the Skinnerian approach has arrived rather late on the scene. This was not the first personality theory based on S-R learning principles; other psychologists such as Dollard, Miller, and Mowrer, besides directing their efforts to many areas of psychology, have applied learning principles to the field of personality. Although Skinner began his work with animal experimentation, he and his followers have increasingly devoted their experiments and theorizing to problems of human behavior and to applications in the modification of deviant behavior. As early as the 1930s Skinner was recognized as an important learning theorist, and though he was not the first to recognize the importance of reinforcement, he did put it on operational grounds. It was Skinner's followers who applied operant conditioning principles more specifically to the field of personality.

If the course of development of thinking along the lines of operant conditioning is considered in a general way, the future looks bright. There is a division of the American Psychological Association devoted to this train of thought (Division 25, The Experimental Analysis of Behavior) and two journals reporting research using Skinnerian methodology: *The Journal of the Experimental Analysis of Behavior* and *The Journal of Applied Behavioral Analysis*. Other journals devoted to experimental psychology as well as behavior therapy also publish articles in which operant conditioning principles are applied, the *Psychological Record* and *Behavior Research and Therapy*, to name two.

The number of psychologists devoted to Skinner's ideas is rapidly increasing. Of course, they are not all concerned with problems of human behavior or personality. Skinner also has opponents who feel that his rigorous experimental and operational approach has dehumanized not only psychology but in particular the human personality.

Considering the varieties of personality theories mentioned in this book, it is unlikely that the Skinnerian approach is going to dominate the field. However, because of its many adherents and the vast amount of research being generated, even its most ardent opponents can hardly deny its impact on psychology.

Operant conditioning does not appear to be an approach that is on the wane or about to die out. The general scheme is attracting young, vigorous people who are devoted to the basic ideas Skinner has laid out. Certainly the movement Skinner represents is one of the dominant forces in psychology today.

Annotated Bibliography

Ferster, C. B., and Parrott, M. C. *Behavior Principles*. New York: Appleton-Century-Crofts, 1968.

A basic text for undergraduates on principles of Skinnerian psychology. Examples and experiments are cited which deal with both human and animal behavior.

Lundin, R. W. *Personality: A Behavioral Analysis*. 2nd ed. New York: Macmillan, 1974.

The latest attempt to apply operant conditioning techniques, using animal and human experimentation, to the area of human personality.

O'Leary, K. D., and Wilson, G. T. *Behavior Therapy: Applications and Outcomes*. Englewood Cliffs, N. J.: Prentice-Hall, 1975.

This book is outlined according to various behavior disorders: fears, autism, mental retardation, delinquent and sexual disorders, and so on. In each section various studies are cited showing how principles of behavior modification have been applied in treating the various disorders.

Rimm, D. C., and Masters, J. C. *Behavior Therapy: Techniques and Empirical Findings*. New York: Academic Press, 1974.

The organization of this book is by behavioral techniques, such as desensitization, aversion therapy, operant reinforcement, and extinction. Examples are given in each section of how these techniques can be applied to the treatment of behavior disorders.

Skinner, B. F. *The Behavior of Organisms: An Experimental Approach*. New York: Appleton-Century-Crofts, 1938.

Skinner's first major work presents his principles, based on experimentation with rats in an operant conditioning chamber.

Skinner, B. F. *Science and Human Behavior*. New York: Macmillan, 1953.

An application of behavioral principles to human conduct. Examples of control are treated as they apply to economics, government and law, education, religion, and psychotherapy.

Skinner, B. F. *Beyond Freedom and Dignity*. New York: Knopf, 1971.

This is an attempt to reinterpret in behavioral terms such concepts as freedom, dignity, value, and cultural design.

Staats, A. W., and Staats, C. K. *Complex Human Behavior*. New York: Holt, Rinehart & Winston, 1963.

As the title implies, the book is an application of operant conditioning principles to complex forms of human behavior such as language, reasoning, problem solving, and human motivation. Although not completely Skinnerian, the aim is definitely in that direction.

Ullmann, L. P., and Krasner, L. *Case Studies in Behavior Modification*. New York: Holt, Rinehart & Winston, 1965.

This is a collection of various studies using principles of behavior modification to alter neurotic and more severe disorders in children and adults. Some of the studies are reprinted from journal articles, others are presented for the first time in this book.

References

Ayllon, T. Intensive treatment of psychotic behavior by stimulus satiation and food reinforcement. *Behavior Research and Therapy*, 1963, *3*, 53–61.

Ayllon, T., & Azrin, N. H. *The token economy*. New York: Appleton-Century-Crofts, 1968.

Ayllon, T., & Michael, J. The psychiatric nurse as a behavioral engineer. *Journal of the Experimental Analysis of Behavior*, 1959, *2*, 232–334.

Azrin, N. H. Suggested effects of punishment. In T. Verhave (Ed.), *The experimental analysis of behavior*. New York: Appleton-Century-Crofts, 1966.

Azrin, N. H., & Lindsley, O. R. The reinforcement of cooperative behavior in children. *Journal of Abnormal and Social Psychology*, 1956, *52*, 100–102.

Bandura, A. *Principles of behavior modification*. New York: Holt, Rinehart & Winston, 1969.

Blough, D. S. Effects of lysergic acid diethylamide on absolute visual thresholds in the pigeon. *Science*, 1957, *126*, 304–305.

Boren, J. J. Some effects of chlorpromazine on several operant behaviors. *Psychopharmacologia*, 1960, *2*, 416–424.

Brown, C. D., & Tyler, V. O. Time out from reinforcement: A technique for dethroning the "duke" of an institutionalized delinquent group. *Journal of Child Psychology and Psychiatry*, 1969, *9*, 203–211.

Cameron, N. *The psychology of behavior disorders*. Boston: Houghton Mifflin, 1947.

Chadwick, B. A., & Day, R. C. Systematic reinforcement: Academic performance of underachieving students. *Journal of Applied Behavior Analysis*, 1971, *4*, 311–319.

Dollard, J., & Miller, N. E. *Personality and psychotherapy*. New York: McGraw-Hill, 1950.

Ferster, C. B., & Skinner, B. F. *Schedules of reinforcement*. New York: Appleton-Century-Crofts, 1957.

Freud, S. *The ego and the id*. London: Hogarth Press, 1947. (First German edition, 1923.)

Gewitz, J. L., & Baer, D. M. Deprivation and satiation of social reinforcers as drive conditions. *Journal of Abnormal and Social Psychology*, 1958, *57*, 165–172.

Goldiamond, I. Self-control procedures in personal behavior problems. *Psychological Reports*, 1965, *17*, 851–858.

Holland, J. G., & Skinner, B. F. *The analysis of behavior: A program of self instruction*. New York: McGraw-Hill, 1961.

Hull, C. L. *Principles of behavior*. New York: Appleton-Century-Crofts, 1943.

Isaacs, W., Thomas, J., & Goldiamond, I. Shaping vocal responses in mute catatonic schizophrenics. *Journal of Speech and Hearing Disorders*, 1960, *25*, 6–12.

Jones, M. C. A behavior study of fear: The case of Peter. *Journal of Genetic Psychology*. 1924, *31*, 508–515.

Kinkade, K. *A Walden II experiment: The first five years of Twin Oaks*. New York: William Morrow, 1973.

Lundin, R. W. *Personality: A behavioral analysis* (2nd. ed.). New York: Macmillan, 1974.

Marrone, R. I. M., Merksomer, A., & Saltzberg, P. M. A short term duration group treatment for smoking behavior by stimulus satiation. *Behavior Research and Therapy*, 1970, *9*, 347–352.

Miller, N. E. Studies of fear as an acquirable drive, I. Fear as motivation and fear reduction as reinforcement in the learning of new responses. *Journal of Experimental Psychology*, 1948, *38*, 89–101.(a)

Miller, N. E. Theory and experiment relating psychoanalytic displacement to stimulus-response generalization. *Journal of Abnormal and Social Psychology*, 1948, *43*, 155–178.(b)

Mowrer, O. H. Enuresis: A method for its study and treatment. *American Journal of Orthopsychiatry*, 1938, *8*, 436–459.

Mowrer, O. H. Learning theory and the neurotic paradox. *American Journal of Orthopsychiatry*, 1948, *18*, 571–610.

Mowrer, O. H. *Learning theory and personality dynamics*. New York: Ronald Press, 1950.

Mowrer, O. H. *Psychotherapy: Theory and research*. New York: Ronald Press, 1953.

Mowrer, O. H. *Learning theory and behavior*. New York: Wiley, 1960.

Mowrer, O. H. *The crisis in psychiatry and religion*. New York: Van Nostrand, 1961.

O' Connor, R. D. Modification of social withdrawal through symbolic modeling. *Journal of Applied Behavior Analysis*, 1969, *2*, 15–22.

Olds, J. Pleasure centers in the brain. *Scientific American*, 1956, *195*, 108–118.

Pavlov, I. P. *Conditioned reflexes* (G. V. Anrep, trans.). London: Oxford University Press, 1927.

Rachman, S., & Teasdale, J. *Aversion therapy and behavior disorders*. Coral Gables, Fla.: University of Miami Press, 1969.

Raymond, M. S. Case of fetishism treated by aversion therapy. *British Medical Journal*, 1956, *2*, 854–857.

Schaefer, H. H., & Martin, P. L. Behavior therapy for "apathy" in hospitalized schizophrenics. *Psychological Reports*, 1966, *19*, 1147–1158.

Schwitzgebel, R. Short term operant conditioning of adolescent offenders on socially relevant variables. *Journal of Abnormal Psychology*, 1967, *72*, 134–138.

Skinner, B. F. On the rate of formation of a conditioned reflex. *Journal of General Psychology*, 1932, *7*, 274–285.

Skinner, B. F. On the rate of extinction of a conditioned reflex. *Journal of General Psychology*, 1933, *8*, 51–60.

Skinner, B. F. *The behavior of organisms: An experimental analysis.* New York: Appleton-Century-Crofts, 1938.

Skinner, B. F. *Walden Two.* New York: Macmillan, 1948.

Skinner, B. F. *Science and human behavior.* New York: Macmillan, 1953.

Skinner, B. F. Critique of psychoanalytical concepts and theories. *Scientific Monthly*, 1954, *79*, 300–305.

Skinner, B. F. *Verbal behavior.* New York: Appleton-Century-Crofts, 1957.

Skinner, B. F. Pigeons in a Pelican. *American Psychologist*, 1960, *15*, 28–37.

Skinner, B. F. *The technology of teaching.* New York: Appleton-Century-Crofts, 1968.

Skinner, B. F. *Beyond freedom and dignity.* New York: Knopf, 1971.

Skinner, B. F. *About behaviorism.* New York: Knopf, 1974.

Thorndike, E. L. Animal intelligence: An experimental study of the associative process in animals. *Psychological Review: Monograph Supplement*, 1898 (No. 8).

Thorndike, E. L. *Animal intelligence: Experimental studies.* New York: Macmillan, 1911.

Tooley, J. T., & Pratt, S. An experimental procedure for the extinction of smoking behavior. *Psychological Record*, 1967, *17*, 209–218.

Voegtlin, W. L. The treatment of alcoholism by establishing a conditioned reflex. *American Journal of Medical Science*, 1940, *199*, 802–910.

Voegtlin, W. L., & Lemere, F. The treatment of alcoholic addiction. *Quarterly Journal of Studies in Alcohol*, 1942, *2*, 717–802.

Watson, J. B. Psychology as the behaviorist views it. *Psychological Review*, 1913, *20*, 158–177.

Watson, J. B. *Behaviorism.* New York: Norton, 1925.

Watson, J. B. & Raynor, R. Conditioned emotional reactions. *Journal of Experimental Psychology*, 1920, *3*, 1–14.

Williams, C. D. The elimination of tantrum behavior by extinction procedures. *Journal of Abnormal and Social Psychology*, 1959, *59*, 260.

Wolf, M. M., Risley, T., & Mees, H. L. Application of operant conditioning procedures to the behavior problems of an autistic child. *Behavior Research and Therapy*, 1964, *1*, 305–312.

Wolpe, J. *Psychotherapy by reciprocal inhibition.* Stanford, Calif.: Stanford University Press, 1958.

Wolpe, J. *The practice of behavior therapy.* Elmsford, N. J.: Pergamon Press, 1969.

George A. Kelly's theory of personal constructs is unique among personality theories, the most psychological of all theories in that it is "all in the head"—consisting almost entirely of a way of looking at how people construe life, meaning how they organize, perceive, evaluate, structure, and predict events. As such, it is almost entirely a cognitive theory and pays practically no attention to learning, emotions, motivations, needs, or even behavior, but at the same time it encompasses all of them, subsuming them as aspects or elements of the total personality controlled by these constructs of the individual. On top of this, Kelly's theory offers difficulty for anyone who likes to make orderly arrangements of theories in that it simply rejects as invalid or unimportant usual ways of seeing life. Kelly had his own unique ways of seeing things, and he used language in an idiosyncratic manner.

The psychology of personal constructs differs considerably from other theoretic constructions of personality, because of its indigenous origins in the heartland of America, by a man who was a clinical psychologist and who did not write much, and because it is not supported by an infrastructure of enthusiastic devoted followers, as well as because of its unique point of view.

CHAPTER 8

Personal Constructs Theory

Lee Sechrest

GEORGE A. KELLY

Introduction

Psychology is usually defined as the study of human behavior, and human behavior has two aspects: implicit and explicit. Implicit behavior ordinarily is known as phenomenology, the realm of the "mind," and often is divided into cognition and affection, that is, thinking and feeling processes. These also have been divided into awareness and unawareness, and so psychologists speak of consciousness and unconsciousness. It must be evident that there should be some relationship between behavior and phenomenology, and for the man in the street, the layman, how one behaves depends on one's thinking and feeling. But how one thinks or feels is a very great mystery, especially when people seem to act, as a result of their thinking processes, in unusual or peculiar ways. As a matter of fact, when we cannot understand a person's thinking, we call him mad.

Now one view toward understanding man is to see him as a scientist. The student of personality and his subject are both simultaneously trying to predict and control each other's behavior, establishing and testing hypotheses, maneuvering to attain desired results. How it came to pass that scientists studying other people should view their own activities as on a separate level from those of the people they are studying is an interesting question.

In an attempt to understand people, scientists have been seeking convergence, hoping to find a superordinate theory; that is, a final theory to explain all human behavior. An alternate point of view is that there is not necessarily one single correct theory but rather a multiplicity of correct theories, each having value for a variety of purposes. Theories are good if they help to attain desired ends, to make sense of a corner of the universe. No theory is likely to be correct for a wide range of purposes. A theory helpful in explaining man's aesthetic pleasures may not be helpful in understanding how to motivate people or explaining how investors behave in a declining market.

The preceding ideas may seem obvious, but they have profound implications (to be discussed later) which have not been grasped or even recognized by many theorists in the field. They are intended to set the stage for the personality theory of George A. Kelly, who asked and answered unusual questions in an unusual way. His theory is quite different from other theories in this book, since Kelly proposed entirely new ways of thinking about man[1]—what goes on in his head and about his behavior. He made little effort to deal with the traditional concerns of personality theory. Kelly explicitly stated the purpose of theory for him:

> A theory may be considered a way of binding together a multitude of facts so that one may comprehend them all at once. When the theory enables us to make reasonably precise predictions, one may call it scientific. . . . our anticipations of daily events, while not scientifically precise, nevertheless surround our lives with an aura of meaning. . . . A theory provides a basis for an active approach to life, not merely a comfortable armchair from which to contemplate its vicissitudes with detached complaisance. (1955, pp. 18–19).

Kelly made three fundamental assumptions about the world:
1. It is objectively real.
2. It has integrity with "all its imaginable parts having an exact relation to each other" (1955, p. 6).
3. The universe is an ongoing process which can only be understood in the perspective of time: time proves the ultimate bond in all relationships (1955, p. 6).

From this it may be evident that Kelly's theory covers cosmology as well as epistemology. It is, paradoxically, the narrowest and the broadest of all personality theories. It is an adventure into the mind of a great man to understand his thinking about man.

---

[1] George Kelly lived and wrote in a time preceding the increased consciousness of the many manifestations of sexism in our language and so used the literary masculine nouns and pronouns that were then thought adequate to represent statements pertinent to both sexes. The author of this chapter is confident that Kelly would have been quite sensitive to the nuances of sexism in language had it been any sort of issue in his time. However, because of the frequent quoting and paraphrasing of Kelly's work, he has adhered to the linguistic forms actually used by Kelly in the preparation of this chapter. *Man* and kindred terms should be taken to refer in the broadest sense to persons, with no disrespect intended.

At this point we should define our major term *construct* and the combination term *personal construct*, as well as the verb form *to construe*, since this is what Kelly's theory is all about.

To construe means roughly to interpret, to understand, to deduce, or to explain. It may be seen as a process of coming to a comprehension about something, such as finding out the answer to a problem. Just as a detective, given clues, may finally come to a reconstruction of a crime and develop a hypothesis to explain how the crime occurred and who is guilty, so too are ordinary people constantly in the process of trying to make sense out of their lives and out of events and people.

A simple example will make this clear. An individual may report to a therapist that he feels inadequate and unloved. The therapist may conclude that his client is indeed very capable and is highly regarded by many. We now have two constructions: the client's that he is inadequate and unloved, and the therapist's that the client has no reason for these constructions.

Thus, personal constructs are an individual's conclusions or interpretations or deductions about life. And Kelly's psychology of personal constructs relates then to one's cognition or private logic.

History

Precursors

Though it is difficult to determine the precise origins of the philosophical views at which he finally arrived, George A. Kelly dealt directly with several of the great issues presented by the classical philosophers. His universe was real and not the shadows on the walls of Plato's cave. A philosophical monist, with an avowed similarity to Spinoza, Kelly stated that for given purposes it might be desirable to think of the plural attributes of the monistic substance. Kelly's views about the importance of time have an obvious relationship to Henri Bergson's ideas, and he notes ways in which he tried to avoid the criticisms of Aristotelian thought. Kelly also specifically notes that his ideas about the anticipatory nature of behavior bear a resemblance to the thinking of John Dewey, stating that Dewey's philosophy and psychology can be read between many

of the lines of the psychology of personal constructs. Nevertheless, Kelly refers to Dewey in only three places, and then only fleetingly. There is also something of a similarity between Kelly's conception of man as gradually approximating but never, perhaps, achieving truth in his progression of thought and the dialectic of G. W. H. Hegel, a point which Kelly himself notes in one place. Kelly was known to have had a considerable collection of Hegel's works in his own library (Leon Levy, personal communication, 1975).

In the first, theoretical, volume of his major work, *The Psychology of Personal Constructs* (1955), Kelly cites 14 philosophers ranging from Empedocles and Heraclitus to William James and Percy Bridgman. However, only Aristotle, Dewey, and Auguste Comte are cited on more than one page, and for none of them is there more than passing reference. It might also be noted that Kelly cites only 28 psychologists, other than his own students, and four of them are merely mentioned as his teachers. Only 11 of the 28 are cited on more than one page, and, again, rarely is the citation more than a passing reference. Carl Rogers is cited in seven places, and Sigmund Freud in six. To complete the inventory, Kelly cites 16 additional "persons" ranging from Hamlet (four times) and Solomon to Darwin, Dickens, Shelley, and Nabokov. Five of these additional citations are, however, former teachers mentioned in passing.

The point of this inventorial paragraph is to show, in part, the rather wide acquaintance Kelly had with classical philosophy and, to a certain extent, classical literature. It is also intended to show that his work is a very personal *integration* of all the influences which came to bear upon him, and his theory is not a mere collection of ideas from here and there or even some synthesis of his readings. Rather, the psychology of personal constructs is an *invention* of George Kelly, for which he borrowed bits and pieces here and there. But even his borrowing is only of a very general sort, and one can detect only similarities to the work of others, not direct influences.

Beginnings

George Alexander Kelly was born on April 28, 1905, and died in March 1967. The firstborn, he was the only child of devoutly religious parents.

His father had been a Presbyterian minister and farmer but had given up the ministry for reasons of health. Both parents were active in the church, hard-working, and somewhat puritanical. Kelly never outgrew his early religious upbringing and remained an active churchman. He was the focus of a good bit of attention as an only child, but his parents had ambitions for him and sent him away to school when he was 13, and he lived away from home for most of the time after that. It can be supposed that his parents, though devoted to him, were wise enough in their religious perspective not to spoil young George, and he unquestionably profited intellectually and personally from his early independence. Out of these early experiences Kelly probably developed the view that life is not so much a matter of objective happenings as it is of what one makes of those happenings. It is difficult to describe Kelly's adult personality without lapsing into the jargon of some other theorist, but at least in this writer's view, in those early days Kelly learned to construe experiences in such terms as strong versus weak; moral versus immoral; clever versus dull; and calm and reliable versus excitable and undependable. Kelly's adult behavior was so unfailingly characterized by the left side of each pair of these terms that, by the application of his own theory, one can only suppose that to him to be otherwise was to be like the right side of the pairs.

It is also probably important that Kelly was born and grew up in Kansas, the heartland of the United States, in the wide open spaces and in an area in which to survive one had to be practical. Not for rural Kansas were debates about angels on heads of pins. Life there revolved around the question "Does it work?" Yet for all that the question is straightforward and practical, it is penetrating. It is, in fact, at the heart of *American* philosophy, pragmatism, which originated with Charles Peirce, William James, and John Dewey. Out of his midwestern rural beginnings Kelly came to construe experience in terms of the practical rather than the useless. He had little regard for the latter, however fancy or elegant.

After three years at Friends University in Wichita, a Quaker school, Kelly moved to Park College where, in 1926, he received a B. A. degree in physics and mathematics. At that point, uncertain about his future, Kelly considered briefly a career in aeronautical engineering, an experience that left him with a lifelong habit of carrying a small slide rule in his shirt pocket. At this point, for reasons which remain obscure, Kelly developed more of an interest in social problems and attended the University of Kansas, where he received an M.A. in 1928, with a major in educational sociology. Kelly's interests shifted in the direction of education, and after several brief teaching positions, including one at a junior college where he met his wife to be and helped coach dramatics, he was awarded an exchange scholarship in 1929 which enabled him to spend a year at the University of Edinburgh. At Edinburgh, Kelly studied under Sir Godfrey Thomson, an eminent statistician and educator, with whose mathematizing of behavior Kelly never agreed but from whom he contracted his interest in psychology.

In 1930 Kelly returned from Scotland with some urbanity grafted onto his Kansas background, although he later claimed never to have gotten all the Kansas mud off his shoes. He entered the State University of Iowa as a graduate student and in 1931 was awarded a Ph. D. with a dissertation on the common factors in speech and reading disabilities. He had also begun some work on physiological psychology while at Iowa. Kelly stated that Carl Seashore and Lee Travis were his intellectual mentors while he was in residence at Iowa, but there is very little indication in any of his later work how they influenced him. One noteworthy thing about Kelly's educational history is that he studied at five different schools, and after his first three years as an undergraduate, he never spent longer than two years in any school. One suspects that Kelly must have been highly flexible and adaptive, and that any influences on his intellectual progress were in terms of breadth rather than depth. He never studied long enough under one man to become "his student."

The beginnings of the depression of the late 1920's and 1930's found Kelly in 1931 back in western Kansas, at Fort Hays Kansas State College. There, under a variety of pressures, including no doubt his own desire to do something useful and humanitarian, Kelly began to develop an interest in psychological services, and he soon established a program of traveling psychological clinics which served the entire state. These clinics were the forerunner of today's psychological consultants who do their work through other people, such as teachers. In his attempts to solve important practical problems Kelly came to see that it was not necessary, or even desirable, to make any distinction between scientific and applied psychology; they were one and the same.

Kelly was also an innovator, an inventor, even a tinkerer. (Kelly's home, automobile, and office provided many examples of his own little inventions to make life more efficient, practical, or even just interesting.) He began to apply his inventive nature to the understanding and solution of human problems and to experiment (again, tinker might be a better word) with new approaches to diagnosis and treatment, as well as new ways of looking at problems. During the 1930s, while at Fort Hays, Kelly produced a remarkable lot of students, several of whom went on to positions of eminence in psychology, although none ever became a "Kellian" because his theory and innovative practices at that time were inchoate. His influence on students arose out of his enthusiasm and dynamic personality.

When World War II began, Kelly entered the Navy along with so many other dustbowl midwesterners. He entered as an aviation psychologist, surely not because of his brief and abortive experience with aeronautical engineering. During his Navy experience Kelly worked closely with other psychologists and with members of other professions in developing an appropriate role in the service for psychology, and particularly for clinical psychology. Consequently, when the war ended, he was reasonably well known to psychologists returning to their academic positions. He accepted a position at the University of Maryland, and a year later, in 1946, he became professor of psychology and Director of Clinical Psychology at the Ohio State University. With the assistance of Julian B. Rotter, himself a social learning theorist of growing stature, Kelly built the clinical psychology program at Ohio State to a point of virtual preeminence in the nation. Recently a survey showed that there are more graduates of Ohio State directing clinical training programs than graduates of any other university.

While at Ohio State, Kelly brought his theory to maturity, slowly at first, then with growing intensity. He held regular meetings with students at which he read drafts of his manuscripts, discussed ideas, argued, and thought through his position. He also encouraged and fostered thesis and dissertation work that became empirical support for his ideas, and his debt to his students was as apparent to him as to anyone. His efforts culminated in 1955 with the publication of his two-volume work, *The Psychology of Personal Constructs*. The publication in the previous year of J. B. Rotter's *Social Learning and Clinical Psychology* (Rotter, 1954) represented a remarkable circumstance in a program involving only four instructors and was indicative of the general intellectual ferment with which Kelly was surrounded.

Almost equally remarkable is the fact that Kelly's two-volume work is very nearly the corpus of his writings. His publications prior to 1955 were limited to a few very practical pieces published in rather obscure places, and after 1955 he published very little. After his death in March, 1967, B. A. Maher, one of his most distinguished students, edited a collection of some of Kelly's more important papers, most of them never previously published. (Maher, 1969) In 1965 Kelly had left Ohio State to take the Riklis Chair of Behavioral Science at Brandeis University. By that time he had traveled extensively and was well known in many foreign countries, particularly Great Britain. Kelly looked forward with great anticipation to a new role at Brandeis. Unfortunately, his career ended quite prematurely with his death in 1967, and we can only speculate as to what he might have produced in the ten years or so longer that should have been his lot.

One last point to be made about Kelly's experiences and their impact on his thinking has to do with the fact that nearly all of Kelly's career was spent in work with relatively young and intact people. He had very little experience with the more severe forms of psychopathology, and most of his direct clinical experience was with people associated in one way or another with universities. To the extent that Kelly's theory may be regarded as cognitive, or rational, or intellective, it is perhaps understandable in terms of the events with which he was trying to deal.

Current Status

In the late 1950s and early 1960s some really

exciting developments growing out of Kelly's theorizing were expected. Jerome Bruner (1956) referred to Kelly's work as the greatest single contribution to the theory of personality functioning of the decade ending in 1955, and Kelly had produced a group of active and dedicated students. Yet, nothing much has happened in the decade since 1965, and the major developments have to do with the utility of the Role Constructs Repertory Test (Bannister & Mair, 1968)[2] rather than with the theory itself. The literature about Kelly's theory in any given year is sparse, and, in the opinion of this writer, not inspiring. It is not clear why. Few of Kelly's students are any longer associated with his theory, and, in fact, his most consistent disciple is now Donald Bannister (Bannister, 1970; Bannister & Fransella, 1971), an Englishman. No doubt many individuals have been influenced indirectly by Kelly, and some of his ideas (e.g., constructive alternativism) find wide acceptance today, indeed are often widely accepted without any special acknowledgment to Kelly. Still, there are no institutes bearing his name, there are no departments or training programs identified with his theory, and one would be hard put to specify any particular impact that Kelly has had on contemporary thinking about personality.

On the other hand, as new textbooks in personality appear, Kelly continues to be included as a major theorist, so that his ideas are apparently surviving, to be presented to successive generations of students in psychology. However, it seems inevitable that the theory will fade and gradually fall into disuse if it is not taken on by at least a small group of dedicated and highly competent persons who can discern and test the many implications it has for personality and for the practice of clinical psychology. In fact, Kelly's theory is one of the most comprehensive and broad theories to be introduced since psychoanalysis, more clearly rooted in clinical experience than most others, so that it is fraught with implications. What the theory seems to lack at present are disciples who will spread the word.

---

[2] The author is indebted in no small measure for his current understanding of Kelly to the fine exegesis of Bannister and Mair. Their work will be cited only on specific points, but their influence is pervasive.

Similar Theories

Where does Kelly's theory belong in the family of personality conceptions? In most textbooks Kelly is referred to as a cognitive theorist, occasionally as a phenomenological theorist. In Kelly's views and recommendations there are similarities to psychoanalytic theory, to other cognitive theories, to Rogerian and other phenomenological theories, in fact, at one point or another, to almost all personality theories, except for those based on understanding personality by way of an individual's location on standard traits or dimensions. That conception of personality is directly antithetical to Kelly's. In any case, however, it should be recognized that in being similar in a few ways to many theories, personal constructs theory ends up being not very similar to any of them. And that is a view that almost any serious student of Kelly's writings would come to. His theory has a lot of second cousins but no siblings. Some readers may even wonder, as does this writer, whether the theory was of parthenogenetic origin, for its lines of intellectual descent are not at all clear.

Kelly himself did not believe that the question of the relationships of his theory to others was of much importance, and he resisted attempts to categorize personal constructs theory. His view was that the theory could be construed for various purposes in any number of ways, depending on one's aims, another example of the reflexivity of the theory. However, Kelly did provide us with a nonparametric factor analysis of the views of six theoreticians about a clinical case (Kelly, 1969). The theoreticians were Samuel Futterman (Freudian), Bruno Klopfer (Jungian), Heinz Ansbacher (Adlerian), Maurice Green (Sullivanian), Solomon Diamond (nondirective), and Kelly himself. The first factor identified was "emphasis on interpersonal relationships," and standings on this factor show Ansbacher, Green, and Kelly with high emphasis on interpersonal relationships when compared to Klopfer, Futterman, and Diamond, who had relatively low emphasis. A second factor particularly sets Kelly apart from Futterman and Klopfer by the way Kelly distinguishes between aggression and hostility; the latter two theorists use the two terms interchangeably. A third factor particularly distinguishes Diamond and Futterman from Ansbacher and Klopfer, with Kelly in the middle, the factor being the result of a difference of opinion as to whether or not the client being interpreted had authority problems (Diamond and Futterman said yes). Kelly believed that the issues revealed by this analysis had to do with the degree to which therapists-theorists put emphasis on interpersonal relationships and the degree to which they distinguish between aggression, in the sense of initiative, and hostility. Kelly's position on both issues was clear, but he ends up rather more like the "social" psychologists Adler and Sullivan than like the Freudians, Jungians, or nondirectivists.

At a symposium in Brunel College, London, held in 1965 (Warren, 1964), Kelly was asked about his philosophical background, and he replied that he had none and denied knowing anything much about philosophy save for some knowledge of John Dewey and William James. However, he said that he had been called a cognitive theorist by Bruner, an emotional theorist by Allport, an existentialist by Murray, a dialectical materialist in Warsaw, a psychoanalyst by a psychoanalyst, a logical positivist, an idealist, and even a behaviorist. One symposium participant then remarked, we think admiringly, that Professor Kelly appeared to be "a projective test" (Warren, 1964, p. 88).

Assertions

More for the psychology of personal constructs than for nearly any other theory of personality, it is easy to state what the theory asserts about personality. However, it is not always so easy to understand just what these assertions mean in other terms. Kelly set forth his theory in a rather formal way, beginning with a Fundamental Postulate and then proceeding to 11 corollary assumptions. Those 12 statements are the content of his theory. Then, since his theory has to do with the ways in which people make sense out of and anticipate experience, Kelly developed 12[3] formal characteristics of constructs, three ways in which constructs exert control over the ele-

___

[3] Here and in other places we follow the excellent presentation by Bannister and Mair (1968), to whom, in general, a debt is owed for a concise and penetrating explication of Kellian theory.

ments with which they deal, 15 constructs diagnostic of the nature of an individual's construct system, and 8 constructs relating to transition or change in an individual and his construct system. Obviously, there are too many terms and too much material to cover Kelly's theory adequately in the space allocated here. Consequently, the presentation which follows will be directed toward achieving a more general understanding of the psychology of personal constructs rather than a technical cataloging of all terms.

To have a good grasp on Kelly's approach to personality, it is necessary to comprehend Kelly's philosophical postion, the essence of which can be stated in the first assertion.

1. ALL OUR INTERPRETATIONS OF THE
    UNIVERSE ARE SUBJECT TO REVISION.
Kelly assumed from the beginning that there is *no* final truth, that there is *no* interpretation of *any* event not susceptible to some other interpretation of events as good as any other. Some views definitely have more usefulness for some purposes than others, but the position which Kelly called *constructive alternativism* meant that individuals with decidedly different views of things were not necessarily divisible into those who are right and those who are wrong.

A parent may view a disciplinary act as a corrective action taken for the good of the child; the child may view the same act as an unavoidable occurrence in a capricious world; and a social worker may view the discipline as cruel punishment. And all three viewers may be "right," and all three may need to recognize that their individual view is not the only tenable one. In terms of final truth, we achieve only successive approximations, each approximation a bit more satisfactory than previous ones, and it is unlikely in the extreme, if not actually impossible, that we would ever know it if we had somehow arrived at the final truth. While Kelly stated his position in terms of the constructs of individuals coping with their lives and experience, the position of constructive alternativism is quite applicable to scientific constructs and systems. Those constructs and systems, too, are only gradually improved and, no matter how persuasive at any one time, are always subject to revision and replacement.

Development

As has been pointed out by others (e.g., Levy, 1970) Kelly's theory is essentially ahistorical, somewhat akin to the phenomenologists in this respect. Kelly did not concern himself with the origins of personal constructs (Sechrest, 1963) for the reason that, as he saw it, the construing of experience is a natural, ongoing process which begins at birth and continues for as long as we live. There is no possibility of an individual *not* construing experience. The only question of interest is in what terms experience will be construed. Kelly expressed no interest in the ways in which some individuals come to construe in different terms than others. He seems to have taken for granted that this would happen. In his theory, what is important is an individual's contemporary view, his construction of reality at a moment in time when a choice must be made. Consequently, the theory of personal constructs may be seen as a here-and-now theory. Kelly did suggest that understanding of a contemporary view might be facilitated by studying the historical processes by which an individual came to that view, that study of changes in the construct system over time could be enlightening, so he did not eschew the study of personal history altogether.

Kelly did not see the need for positing any special processes of development corresponding to developmental stages in children. He viewed the child and his psychological processes as continuous, with the infant preceding and the adolescent and adult following. Kelly did not discern any discontinuities in psychological development, or at least no discontinuities inherent in growth and maturing. He was not overly interested in the "facts" of people's lives, and that disinterest can probably be stated in the form of the single assertion relative to development which can easily be derived from the psychology of personal constructs (Assertion 2).

2.   NO PERSON NEEDS TO BE A VICTIM OF HIS OWN BIOGRAPHY.

Kelly concluded that it is not objective experience that is important for constructions but rather what we tell ourselves about experience. There is no one necessarily correct way to look at things. Every individual may construe or reconstrue his experience differently to anticipate the future. A "difficult" childhood can be viewed as a "toughening" childhood; a physical "handicap" can be viewed by the individual as an opportunity to develop special sensitivities. Kelly never suggested that we are not victimized by experience, but to the extent that we are, we are somewhat willing participants in that victimization.

Do we really have freedom to interpret experience? Isn't our construct system determined to some degree by the nature of our experience? Kelly distinguishes two different problems relative to determinism and freedom. The first he considers relatively trivial. The universe flows smoothly without being divided up into discrete events, and no event ever occurs more than once. To say that an event was an invariant consequent of past events the only time it ever did or will occur is not very helpful. The more important issue has to do with whether events determine our views of them or whether, since our views can vary in infinite ways, those views, or constructs, produce control we have over events. If a man dies from eating a poison berry, Kelly would say that he dies not because of the objective characteristics of the berry, but because of his view of the berry as delicious-looking, hunger-assuaging, relief-producing, or perhaps because he viewed the berry as an object, the eating of which would impress his companions with his bravery.

To quote from Kelly:

> Ultimately a man sets the measure of his own freedom and his own bondage by the level at which he chooses to establish his convictions. The man who orders his life in terms of many special and inflexible convictions about temporary matters makes himself the victim of circumstances. Each little prior conviction that is not open to review is a hostage he gives to fortune; it determines whether the events of tomorrow will bring happiness or misery. The man whose prior convictions encompass a broad perspective, and are cast in terms of principles rather than rules, has a much better chance of discovering those alternatives which will lead eventually to his emancipation. (1955, pp. 21–22)

Kelly points out that culture is often taken to be an important source to explain similarities and differences between people and suggests that persons are often grouped according to similarities in upbringing and environment, a grouping which, to him, implies a stimulus-response theory. However, Kelly notes that culture is also often taken to mean similarity in what members of a group expect of each other, and that view is more compatible with the psychology of personal constructs. Thus, the impact of culture on the development of construct systems is that it provides expectancies about what other individuals may do and also what others expect of the individual whose construct system is being considered. There is, perhaps, a determinism provided by culture, but it is weak in contrast with the views of many other, more patently deterministic theorists.

Maintenance

Since Kelly's theory is essentially ahistorical and supposes that an individual's behavior develops out of his construction and anticipation of events at any given moment, it follows that most assertions made in the theory concern the maintenance or ongoing processes of personality.

3.   A PERSON'S PROCESSES ARE PSYCHOLOGICALLY CHANNELIZED BY THE WAYS IN WHICH HE ANTICIPATES EVENTS (Fundamental Postulate).

Kelly explained every word of substance in the Fundamental Postulate; he chose those words with care. It is not possible to present all his rationale for the postulate as stated (those desiring the complete rationale would do better to consult Kelly in the original), but we can summarize his views (1955, pp. 46–50.) First, the focus of his theory is the individual person (*person's, he*) rather than any part of the person, any group of persons, any particular process within the person, or any nonperson set of phenomena. In choosing the word *processes* as the focus of the theory Kelly centers on a behaving organism, one not requiring any external source of energy. Kelly does not find the concept of motivation useful and thus dispenses with it. *All* living organisms are behaving, acting, moving, metabolizing, and to indicate that they are in a state of motivation or that they are energized is pointless and redundant.

By the third term, *psychologically*, Kelly designates the realm with which he intends to deal; his is a psychological theory. However, it is not the particular events in one's life that are important, but one's unique way of looking at

them. Kelly admits his theory is limited and that some phenomena explained within physiological or sociological systems may lie outside personal construct theory, but he makes no apology for the limitation. A person's processes do not operate in a chaotic or random manner but rather within a system of flexible, modifiable, but restrictive pathways that constitute a network. These pathways channel the processes of an individual so that they go in one direction rather than another. According to Kelly a person's interpersonal processes work in reasonably consistent but modifiable ways. The various processes in interpersonal relations operate as an integral subsystem of the individual, much in the manner of a network.

The network of pathways or channels is purposive in nature. That is what is meant by *ways*; that there is an end, or aim in the system. That aim is the anticipation of real events. Consequently, personal constructs represent a teleological system to some degree. Kelly's conception of man is that he is engaged in an unending attempt to improve his ability to predict and to anticipate the real world. Herein lie the predictive and motivational features of Kelly's view of man: "Anticipation is both the push and the pull of the psychology of personal constructs" (1955, p. 49). Since, like the scientist, any man is constantly striving for better understanding and prediction, the consequence of anticipations which are fulfilled or disappointed is incorporated into the system, which then is modified in terms of outcomes. In short, constructions are constantly being reestablished by experiences.

The basic building block in Kelly's theory is the *personal construct*, the specific way in which a person anticipates certain events. Constructs are *personal*, specific to individuals, and are *constructed* in the sense that they are not "given" to an individual but are created by the person. The process of construing is active. As used by Kelly, *construct* refers to how things are seen as being alike and yet different from other things. For example, friendly is a way that some people may be seen as being alike, and at the same time being friendly differentiates them from people who are hostile, or mean, or not friendly, or whatever the individual who uses the construct thinks is the difference. The characteristics of constructs, how used, how organized, as well as other aspects, are defined in the corollaries to the Fundamental Postulate.

4.   A PERSON ANTICIPATES EVENTS BY CONSTRUING THEIR REPLICATIONS (Construction Corollary).

This assertion (first corollary) indicates that the interpretations man places on his experiences enable him to predict, and hence to control, those things that will happen to him in the future. The process of construing is active but also abstractive. The person develops constructs of similarity and contrast by abstracting from an ongoing flow of events those features that appear to provide meaning. Another person might abstract different features from these events and consequently arrive at a distinctly different meaning.

While we have verbal labels for many constructs, the process of construing is not synonymous with verbal labeling. Kelly points out that if a person is asked how he proposes to digest his dinner, he will probably not be able to answer the question, because such matters seem outside his control. Yet, digestion is a structured process, and what the person anticipates has a good deal to do with the course that digestion takes. Constructs reside in the individual, not in events. Kelly was fond of pointing to the shoes of a member of an audience and alleging that the shoes were "neurotic" and then noting that everyone in the audience tried to get a look at the shoes as if they really might possess neurotic qualities, instead of looking at him, Kelly, to see what it might be about him that would cause him to think of shoes as neurotic.

Whatever a person construes is a process; it is unending and undifferentiated. A person's universe will begin to make sense to him only when he begins to look for recurrent themes, the *replications*. To use Kelly's example, time does not mark itself off into segments, and it does not double back on itself. Today is not yesterday, nor is tomorrow today; but the construct of *day* "is erected along the incessant stream of time—a day which is, in its own way, like other days and yet clearly distinguishable from the moments and years" (1955, p. 53). Only after events have been interpreted in terms of their beginnings and endings and in terms of their similarities and contrasts does it become possible to try to anticipate them. We do not predict that tomorrow will be a duplicate of today, but rather that there are certain ways, which can be predicted, in which tomorrow will replicate today.

5.   PERSONS DIFFER FROM ONE ANOTHER IN THEIR CONSTRUCTION OF EVENTS (Individuality Corollary).

This second corollary is simply an expression of the universally accepted notion that people differ from one another. But here Kelly is saying that people can be seen as differing from one another not only in the events anticipated but in the approaches taken to anticipate the same events. One person with an invitation to dinner with a Vietnamese family may think of having to eat something strange and unpleasant, while another person may think of it as an opportunity to try something new and exciting. No two people play quite the same role in any event, no matter how similar they are, how closely related they may be, or how much they try. Each experiences himself as the central figure in the event, each experiences the other as an external figure, and inevitably each gets caught up in different aspects of the stream of events.

6.   EACH PERSON CHARACTERISTICALLY EVOLVES, FOR HIS CONVENIENCE IN ANTICIPATING EVENTS, A CONSTRUCTION SYSTEM EMBRACING ORDINAL RELATIONSHIPS BETWEEN CONSTRUCTS (Organization Corollary).

This corollary states that construct systems are organized in such a way that some constructs may subsume others, i.e., be more comprehensive. There are several ways in which constructs relate to one another. For example, the construct *extravert–introvert* may subsume the construct *likes parties–dislikes parties* in such a way that, among other things, being an extravert implies liking parties while being an introvert implies disliking parties. However, the construct *likes parties–dislikes parties* might also be subsumed by the construct *social characteristics–nonsocial characteristics*, so that liking or disliking parties would be viewed as a social characteristic and contrasted with other constructs (e.g., *musical–nonmusical*) not having to do with social behaviors. Moreover, at a still higher level, an individual might distinguish between constructs *having to do with human behavior* and those *applicable to nonhumans only.* Each person will develop a construct organization pattern different from that of every other person, e.g., liking parties might imply extraversion for some people rather than the other way around, *musical–nonmusical* might be thought a social characteristic for some persons, and another person might not make any distinction between constructs applicable to humans and others.

7. A PERSON'S CONSTRUCTION SYSTEM IS COMPOSED OF A FINITE NUMBER OF DICHOTOMOUS CONSTRUCTS (Dichotomy Corollary).

Of fundamental importance in understanding Kelly's theory, a view that sets him apart from classical philosophers, is the Dichotomy Corollary. The idea that any given person's construct system is finite poses no difficulties, for we would not suppose otherwise than that any given person would have a limited array of constructs. However, Kelly proposes that constructs are dichotomous, either-or in nature. There are, in fact, two facets of the dichotomy corollary of interest. First, do people actually think in dichotomies? When we hear a person say "John is intelligent," Kelly maintains that the word *intelligent* implies both a similarity and a contrast. The construer abstracts from the overall perception of the object of his attention, John, the characteristic of intelligence, which he must see as a replication of something seen before and, hence, as a way in which John is similar to some other person (or "event," since, presumably, the characteristic of intelligence might have been seen previously in something other than a person). However, to construe John as intelligent also implies a *contrast*. The contrast to intelligence for one person might be "stupid," while for another the contrast might be "not intelligent," two rather different contrasts in terms of their implications. In Kelly's view, it is impossible to see a similarity without at the same time having in mind a contrast, a way in which *some* other events are seen as different.

But, when John is construed as intelligent, similarly, let us say, to Jim and Mary, and different from Joe and Bill, is it necessarily true that the construer can see no gradations in intelligence, that he sees people as either intelligent or

not intelligent, without gradations? That goes against experience and common sense. According to Kelly, at any given moment, for any given construction, the choice must be dichotomous. However, across a series of choices, constructs may be modified slightly so as to produce a gradation of intelligence or any other characteristic in question. Consider, for example, the following set of individuals with their tentative scores: John, 135; Joe, 125; Mary, 115; Helen, 105; Bill, 95; and Sam, 85. The admissions officer for a college might construe John, Joe, and Mary as similar because they are *intelligent* (IQ 115 plus) and Helen, Bill, and Sam as different because they are *not intelligent.* Now suppose this same admissions officer has in mind a special honors program for unusually promising students. He could now construe John and Joe as "highly intelligent" and others, by contrast, as "not highly intelligent." He has a dichotomy still. Mary is now lumped with the others at the low end of the scale. If that same admissions officer were planning a special program for students at the lower end of the scale, he might see Sam as a "slow learner" in contrast to the others as "average or better." Across a series of choices, the admissions officer would have behaved as if he perceived a gradation of intelligence, but at any one moment, his construct would have been dichotomous.

That is how Kelly proposes to construe our thinking. The reader should keep in mind that whether this is *really* the way we think would not interest Kelly very much. He would say, "Well, suppose we *think* of constructs as dichotomous, rather than as continuous, and let's see where that gets us."

A second facet of Kelly's view of constructs as dichotomous which is of critical importance is that there are events which are irrelevant to any given construct and which, therefore, do not need to be lumped together with the contrast.

8. A CONSTRUCT IS CONVENIENT FOR THE ANTICIPATION OF A FINITE RANGE OF EVENTS ONLY (Range Corollary).

Every construct has its focus and range of convenience, just as do theories. Personal constructs, by their nature, are relevant to everything. Constructs evolve around the resolution of certain issues, the anticipation of certain events, and they may be extended with experience to other more challenging events, but eventually one reaches limits beyond which the construct no longer applies. For example, the construct *intelligent–not intelligent* evolves for most people around the issue of anticipating academic success and success in related areas. It can be extended to a variety of problem-solving efforts. One might think of an intelligent sculptor, of an intelligent fish, perhaps of an unintelligent amoeba, or even, stretching considerably, of an "intelligent" plant that seeks out water with its roots and the light with its leaves so effectively. But pies can scarcely be either intelligent or unintelligent, nor can enzymes, or languages, or lights, or smells, or temperatures, or weather conditions. For all these things the construct is irrelevant. Classical logic lumps together the contrasts with the irrelevant; personal constructs theory does not. Things are black *or* white *or* neither. To understand a personal construct it is necessary to know the contrast as well as the construct. To know that a person construes some situations as "nice" is not very comprehensible until one knows that the contrast to the construct is "immoral," "dangerous," "lonely," "financially unrewarding," or some other notion.

9. A PERSON CHOOSES FOR HIMSELF THAT ALTERNATIVE IN A DICHOTOMOUS CONSTRUCT THROUGH WHICH HE ANTICIPATES THE GREATER POSSIBILITY FOR EXTENSION AND DEFINITION OF HIS SYSTEM (Elaborative Choice Corollary).

This corollary is the only direct link in Kelly's theory between an individual's construct system and his specific behaviors. As will be pointed out, even this link is not very dependable. As suggested elsewhere (Levy, 1970; Sechrest, 1963), transition from cognition to behavior is difficult in personal constructs theory. By this elaborative choice corollary Kelly posits a fundamental and continuing human motivation akin to other general, monolithic motives such as self-actualization, self-consistency, and cognitive congruity. In Kelly's view we strive to anticipate events correctly to improve our capacity to predict and control our future. This is the heart of the theory of personal constructs.

One way we improve our ability to anticipate events is (perhaps alternately) to extend and de-

fine our construct system. To *extend* means to be able to account for a wider variety of events, to be able to anticipate events in new settings or with new persons and to develop new constructs. To *define* our system means to eliminate uncertainties, to sharpen predictions, to make clearer the constructs we employ. Kelly believes that individuals build their lives upon one or the other of the alternatives represented in the dichotomies of each construct. People place relative values upon the ends of their dichotomies. Kelly means that people value a pole of the construct, not the specific elements or events subsumed under that pole. For example, an individual may value intelligence as opposed to stupidity quite independently of the value he places on any intelligent or stupid thing, person, or idea. Kelly then proposes that an individual will choose for himself behavioral alternatives that appear to present the greatest possibility for enhancing his ability to anticipate and control future events.

Let us consider an example related to the writer by a clinician colleague. A salesman seemed to apply the construct *aggressive –failure* to a wide variety of events and possibilities having to do with his role as a salesman, and he "chose" for a period of about two years to comport himself as a fairly stereotypically aggressive salesman. He was never successful as a salesman, and, predictably enough, he became inactive, quit his job, began drinking fairly regularly, and regarded himself as a failure. Strangely, however, he did not seem uncomfortable in the role of a failure, and ultimately it seemed to the clinician he was glad to be a solid failure if he could not be a solid success. The clinician came to believe that being a failure rendered much of his life unambiguous and, in fact, even opened some new opportunities to him, such as a chance to try out the role of ne'er-do-well.

Presumably under most circumstances an individual would rather be intelligent than stupid, would rather be friendly than hostile, would rather be sophisticated than naive. However, there may also be circumstances, even if only temporary, in which an individual who usually thinks of himself as intelligent may, if placed in the company of a number of extraordinary persons, see that he may be better able to predict and control what is going to happen if he temporarily abandons his conception of himself as intelligent and thinks of himself as "stupid." What is important from the standpoint of the psychology of personal constructs is that he chooses one or the other of the two alternatives available to him from the construct he sees relevant to the situation at hand, in terms of his general purpose to make sense and fit into the stream of life.

10.   A PERSON'S CONSTRUCTION SYSTEM
      VARIES AS HE SUCCESSIVELY CONSTRUES
      THE REPLICATION OF EVENTS (Experience
      Corollary).

Systems of constructs are not static. Whenever a person makes a prediction, and what he anticipates does not happen, there is an opportunity to reconstrue. If a new construction is not devised, there is a risk that anticipations will become increasingly in error. The succession of events that a person faces represents a continuing test of the validity of the construct system. At any one time a person's construct system may be thought of as a set of working hypotheses, much like those of a scientist, to be revised in the light of experience, outcomes of predictions, and hence to be progressively revised.

A rather important implication of the Experience Corollary reveals Kelly's view of *learning* as a process. It is another given, and like motivation, learning is assumed to take place continuously, and it is assumed that learning is not a special class of psychological processes. Learning *is* psychological processes. It does not happen to a person on occasion; it is what makes that person in the first place.

11.   THE VARIATION IN A PERSON'S
      CONSTRUCTION SYSTEM IS LIMITED BY
      THE PERMEABILITY OF THE
      CONSTRUCTS WITHIN WHOSE RANGE OF
      CONVENIENCE THE VARIANTS LIE
      (Modulation Corollary).

Any variation in a construct system must itself take place within a system: "Even the changes which a person attempts within himself must be construed by him." (1955, pp. 78–79) It is necessary here to introduce the notion of *permeability* of constructs: a construct is permeable if it can be applied to new events not yet construed within its framework. For example, the construct *miraculous–natural* is permeable if applicable to ongoing events. It would be considered imperme-

able if the construer took the position that there was a time when miracles occurred, but that the age of miracles is over. The Modulation Corollary states that if an individual is to change his construct system, there must be permeable constructs within which to fit, or make sense of, the changes. At the present time, to point to an instance, many people in our society are undergoing a change of construction with respect to homosexuality, which has for a long time been construed largely in terms of such evaluative constructs as *good–bad, moral–immoral, strong–weak,* and *healthy–sick*. Now, however, different constructions are being applied, and, while it is difficult to specify both poles of the constructs, homosexuality is being construed as tolerable, nonthreatening, a matter of lifestyle, and as "normal" for certain people. For such changes in construction to occur, the Modulation Corollary states that there must be permeable constructs capable of making sense out of the change. One such construct might be something like *legitimate concerns of the public–legitimate private concerns*. If matters of morality or immorality are reconstrued from being public concerns to private concerns, then it may also be possible to reconstrue homosexuality as a private and tolerable lifestyle for some people and as not especially threatening to the lifestyles of other persons. Another superordinate construct within which change might be construed is *things people choose to be–things people become*. If evaluative constructs such as *good–bad* and *moral–immoral* make sense only when applied to people's chosen behaviors, and if homosexuality comes to be seen as a state of being rather than as a choice, the change from evaluative to nonevaluative constructions may be possible.

12.   A PERSON MAY SUCCESSIVELY EMPLOY A
      VARIETY OF CONSTRUCTION SUBSYSTEMS
      WHICH ARE INFERENTIALLY
      INCOMPATIBLE WITH EACH OTHER
      (Fragmentation Corollary).

The Fragmentation Corollary simply says that people need not be consistent over time in employing their construction systems, although the inconsistencies should be comprehensible in light of the Modulation Corollary. All changes must take place within a larger system, but they need not be particularly consistent at an obvious level. Shifts may occur because construct systems are loose (e.g., a person's definition of a "friendly" gesture may not be very precise), but shifts may also occur because the *regnant* or currently applicable construct switches, as when a "cute" cuddly child comes to be seen as "bothersome."

13. TO THE EXTENT THAT ONE PERSON EMPLOYS A CONSTRUCTION OF EXPERIENCE WHICH IS SIMILAR TO THAT EMPLOYED BY ANOTHER, HIS PROCESSES ARE PSYCHOLOGICALLY SIMILAR TO THOSE OF THE OTHER PERSON (Commonality Corollary).[4]

The idea expressed in this corollary straightforwardly states that people will be psychologically similar in their processes to the extent that they construe experience in the same way. People need not be similar in actual experiences; they need only be similar in the way they have come to construe those experiences. Without regard to any realities, if two people have come to think of the world largely in terms of good as opposed to wicked events, their processes will tend to run in similar channels. They may not agree on what sorts of things are to be regarded as wicked, but they will be similar in their attempts to force events into that dichotomy and in trying to verify that the events do actually fit.

14. TO THE EXTENT THAT ONE PERSON CONSTRUES THE CONSTRUCTION PROCESSES OF ANOTHER, HE MAY PLAY A ROLE IN A SOCIAL PROCESS INVOLVING THE OTHER PERSON (Sociality Corollary).

As Bannister and Mair (1968) so cogently note, in the Sociality Corollary Kelly produces a truly psychological definition of *role*. He states that a person plays a role with respect to another person when he tries to make sense out of what the other person is doing, when he arrives at an interpretation of what the other person has in mind or is intending. Behavior may be described

and understood as behavior, and there need be no implication of role. For example, an announcer may describe all of the complex behavior of a professional athlete in a very insightful and accurate way, but he is not involved in a role with respect to that athlete until he attempts himself to construe the athlete's own experience of what is going on. When the announcer says something to the effect, "Well, he knows he's got to do it this time or else. He is undoubtedly taking a little extra time in order to get himself up psychologically and physically for this next try," the announcer is in a position to play a role in a social process involving the athlete. Similarly, the announcer can call the contest as he sees it, or he can call it in terms of his understanding of what the fans want to get from his description. Only in the latter case is he playing a role in social processes involving the fans. Note that the announcer need not be *correct* in his inferences about the fans or the athlete for him to be playing a role, and he *may* be playing a role even though seemingly totally objective and dispassionate in his description, for it may be his understanding of the athlete and/or the fans that that is the way they want the game called. What is critical to Kelly's notion of role is that the individual attempts to infer the view or outlook of another person.

The foregoing 12 statements—the fundamental postulate and 11 corollaries (in this book, Assertions 3–14)— constitute the basic structure of Kelly's theory. They do not, of course, exhaust the content of the theory. Several other assertions are needed to have a reasonably complete comprehension of what Kelly intended his theory to be and to do. A major criticism of Kelly's theory, made by this writer (Sechrest, 1963) and more recently by Levy (1970), is that nothing in it links an individual's construct system to his behavior. That is, there does not appear to be any provision in the theory for the prediction of specific behaviors. Levy refers to the missing link as the *operation function* and notes that it is absent in most cognitive-perceptual theories. In most other cognitive-perceptual theories *incongruity* results in initiation of action to reduce the tension produced by the incongruity. However, as Levy notes, incongruity plays no part in Kelly's theory. Kelly did not deal at all with the prediction of behavior in terms of his theory, but

---

[4] As Bannister and Mair (1968) point out, Kelly originally stated that it was the "psychological processes" that were similar, but in a later unpublished paper (Kelly, 1966) he realized that what he wished to say was that the processes would be "psychologically similar."

in a posthumously published work, he set forth his views about behavior as an element in his theory (Kelly, 1969). In that paper Kelly makes the following assertion.

15. BEHAVIOR IS MAN'S WAY OF POSING A QUESTION.

How can behavior pose a question? At this point Kelly reverts to his notion of "every man a scientist" and reminds us that the behavior of scientists as scientists is not seen as the outcome of a sequence of unavoidable events. Rather, the scientist intervenes actively in some process, behaving in such a way to get an answer to a question. Why, then, should it be supposed that the behavior of more ordinary men, or that the behavior of scientists in their more ordinary moments, is somehow or other so very different? Our behaviors, Kelly insists, should be thought of as our own independent variables in the experiment of living. It would be virtually impossible to understand the behavior of a chemist testing a substance without taking into account the purpose of the chemist's behavior, the question he would like to answer. Similarly, Kelly suggests, we lack an adequate understanding of an individual behaving in a hostile manner if we do not understand the question he is posing by that behavior. What question? The following are possible: Are these people strong enough to stand up to me when I am nasty, or can I browbeat them? Do these people love me enough that I can be bad when I need to? Are these people really as nice as they have always seemed or do they, too, have a mean streak?

Like the scientist, the man-as-scientist also has in mind some hypothesis about the outcomes expected from his behavior, and consequently his hypotheses may be confirmed or disconfirmed. However, Kelly points out that confirmation and disconfirmation, like other events, depend in part on the way the original question was asked and the way the outcome is construed. Thus, for example, there may be self-fulfilling prophecies for which disconfirmation is scarcely at issue, at least from an outsider's point of view. Other hypotheses (questions) may be phrased so loosely that the nature of the confirmation would appear inappropriate, although to the individual putting the questions, they might seem reasonable and the answers satisfactory. The important

point about confirmations as Kelly sees it is that they suggest that one has a construct system which permits some events to be more or less well anticipated; there always remains the good possibility that the construct system can and will be improved and will do a better job.

Perhaps Kelly never meant personal constructs theory to provide exact predictions of behavior. In his 1969 paper, much of which was devoted to the specific issue of understanding behavior, Kelly did not express any embarrassment concerning the failure of his theory to relate specifically to behavior. Kelly's view was that behavior is to be explained in terms of an ongoing, progressively moving sequence, rather than in terms of discrete units. Viewing behavior sequentially led Kelly to conclude that while it is perfectly possible to describe and perhaps to explain behavior in terms of "stimuli" leading to "responses," it is also possible, and Kelly thinks potentially even more profitable, to interrupt the sequence at a "response" and then observe what stimulus changes follow. For example, a young man may be invited by friends to a party, go with them to the party, find himself in exciting company, put forth some of his best social efforts, and make new friends. Surely it is possible to think of the invitation and the exciting company as stimuli and the attendance at the party and the putting forth of social efforts as responses to those stimuli. But suppose we begin one step further back and discover that the young man originally went to see his friends to ask what they were doing that evening. Then his behavior led to a particular set of stimuli which provided the occasion for another response which further affected his stimulus situation. The sequence of events that follows from a behavior contributes as much, Kelly believes, to our understanding of the behavior as do the antecedents of the behavior. Thus, perhaps behavior is not so much to be predicted as it is to be a focal point of study in order that one can understand the bets a person is placing in his life and the changes he seeks and produces.

Kelly also developed a system for thinking about the properties or characteristics of constructs. We will here follow the lead of Bannister and Mair (1968) in presenting Kelly's views first with respect to the more or less formal characteristics of constructs and then in terms of the ways in which constructs relate to their elements. However, as a general proposition, we might begin with an assertion that Kelly might have made.

16. CONSTRUCTS MAY BE THOUGHT OF IN TERMS OF CERTAIN FORMAL PROPERTIES WHICH HELP TO UNDERSTAND THE PROCESSES OF CONSTRUING.

The most obvious aspect of constructs is the *labels*, usually verbal, that attach to either side of the dichotomy. However, it should be made clear that Kelly did not believe that labels were always necessary, nor that they especially needed to be verbal. He also did not believe that the fact that two persons had constructs with highly similar labels meant that the constructs were actually similar. A construct may be represented by a *symbol* which stands not only for itself but for the construct by which it is abstracted; for example, one of the writer's students employed a construct associated with feelings of near panic which she could only describe as "the blocked doorway situation." The things or events to which a construct applies or which it abstracts are called *elements*, and the *context* of a construct is the set of elements to which the construct usually applies.

Any construct has two *poles*, one on each side of the dichotomy. Whatever elements are abstracted by the construct are like each other at each pole and unlike the elements at the opposite pole. For example, the construct *good quality–poor quality* may abstract a wide variety of elements such as refrigerators, jewelry, beer, and novels. All the things that are abstracted as good quality become in that way alike and at the same time different from those things lumped together on the poor quality side of the dividing line. The term *likeness end*[5] is used to describe that side of a construct which is the focus of attention at any given time, and *contrast end* refers then to the opposite pole. If one describes several items as alike because they are of good quality, then good quality may be thought of as

the likeness and poor quality as the contrast end of the construct. In another instance, however, those descriptors could be reversed. In any given usage or context in which a construct is employed, one side of the construct will often appear to account for the larger portion of the context. When that is so, that side is called the *emergent pole* of the construct. If a student is contemplating the purchase of a motorcycle and says, "The Japanese makes are of good quality." that would represent the emergent pole of his construct. The *implicit pole* of a construct is that which refers to the contrast side and which itself contrasts with the emergent pole. The implicit pole may be or even need not be stated, and in some instances the person may have no ready way of symbolizing it; but its existence is implicit in the emergent term.

The *range of convenience* of a construct refers to the extent of breadth of things or events for which a user of a construct finds it useful, and the *focus of convenience* refers to those things for which the construct would be optimally useful. For example, the construct *threadbare*—one pole of the construct would probably have as its focus of convenience things made of cloth, but still for many persons the notion of "threadbare ideas" or "threadbare plots" is acceptable, that is, ideas and plots lie within the range of convenience of the construct. However, automobiles, dogs, and hamburgers lie well outside the range of convenience of threadbareness, at least for most people.

Another assertion derivable from Kelly's theory is here labeled Assertion 17.

17. CONSTRUCTS MAY BE CHARACTERIZED BY ASPECTS WHICH ACCOUNT FOR DIFFERENCES AND SIMILARITIES IN THE WAYS THEY FUNCTION.

Not only do people's construct systems differ from one another, but even within the same construct system (i.e., one person's system), constructs function in widely different ways. The way constructs function is to be understood in terms of characteristics of the constructs, recognizing that what we are talking about here is constructs about constructs. These constructs about constructs are no more inherent in the constructs themselves than sincerity is inherent in behavior being construed. There are some

---

[5] The writer himself is a bit uncomfortable with the use of either *end* or *pole* to designate one side of a dichotomy, since either term seems semantically to imply a continuum. However, *end* and *pole* are the terms used by Kelly.

ways of thinking about constructs that Kelly found useful in anticipating the application of constructs.

Constructs differ in terms of their *permeability,* the extent to which a construct can take newly perceived elements into its context. The construct *patriotic* is permeable if the user is willing to consider new elements as potentially patriotic. If the user believes that the age of patriotism is past, then the construct would be impermeable. A *comprehensive* construct is applicable to a wide range of events, while an *incidental* construct is applicable to only a narrow range. For most people the construct *good–bad* would be comprehensive, while a construct such as *neat–messy* would be relatively incidental. *Tight* constructs lead to unvarying predictions, while *loose* constructs result in predictions which vary from time to time and occasion to occasion. If the construct *moral–immoral* were a tight construct for a particular individual, it might result in the invariant prediction that any person construed as immoral would be unlikeable. Used loosely, it might result on some occasions in the prediction that a person construed as immoral would prove to be unlikeable and on others that an immoral person would be likeable. A *core* construct is fundamental to an individual's maintenance of himself as a person, and a *peripheral* construct is one with only limited implications for those processes. Core constructs can be changed only with difficulty and with far-reaching consequences, whereas peripheral constructs are more easily changed, and changes do not ramify throughout an individual's construct system. As was suggested earlier, one construct may include another construct as one of its elements, in which case it is a *superordinate* construct; if one is referring to the construct included as an element, the appropriate term is *subordinate* construct. Core constructs tend to be superordinate, and peripheral constructs tend to be subordinate, but the terms super- and subordinate are definitely relative.

Constructs also differ in terms of the obviousness and accessibility of distinguishing labels or symbols. Some constructs lack consistent verbal labels and are called *preverbal.* Such constructs may have been formed prior to the development of high-level language skills. Many constructs that relate to such feelings as security are prever-

bal or are inconsistently labeled. If one or the other pole of a construct is less available for use, it is termed *submerged.* For many people the term *hippie* represents one end of a construct used to construe people who seem to represent that type; the opposite side of the dichotomy is less consistently labeled and is not ordinarily invoked as a description. Sometimes a revision of a construct system will result in the omission from the context of a construct a particular element once subsumed by the construct. Such an omitted element is said to be *suspended.* An example might be a revision in a person's use of the construct *moral–immoral* in such a way that another person once judged immoral is excluded from the context and is simply no longer subsumed under the construct. It was Kelly's belief that some of the phenomena thought of by psychoanalytically inclined clinicians as "unconscious" could involve suspended elements. In general, Kelly believed that *level of cognitive awareness* differs from construct to construct, with some involving a high level of awareness, i.e., with socially effective symbols, readily accessible construct poles, and not involving suspended elements, while others involve lower levels of cognitive awareness.

Another way constructs differ is in how they relate to, or control, their elements. If an element belongs exclusively to the realm of one construct, the construct is then a *preemptive* construct. There is a strong tendency during wartime, for example, for participants to apply the label "the enemy" in a preemptive way. That is: If he is the enemy, then he is nothing but the enemy. He need not be thought of as human, as a father, as a worker doing his job, or as a lover of good music. He is the enemy, and that is it. Somewhat in contrast to the preemptive construct, the *constellatory* construct determines other constructions of its elements. The commonly encountered "halo effect" in ratings of people is a good example of constellatory construction. If a person is construed as successful, then he is also likely to be construed as intelligent, handsome, friendly, and so on. Stereotypes involve constellatory constructs. To complete the set of contrasts here, the *propositional* construct involves no particular assumptions about the applicability of other constructs. The construct *enemy–friend,* used in a propositional way to construe someone as an enemy, does not have any particular implications for other characteristics such as intelligence and quality as a human being. Preemptiveness, constellatoriness, and propositionality are relative terms. Probably every construct is in some degree preemptive and at the same time also in some degree constellatory and propositional. It is a question of which characteristic is predominant.

There is a final general proposition to be considered, again a proposition not stated by Kelly but used here in order to introduce those ideas that relate Kelly's thinking to the more familiar terms of personality and clinical psychology.

18. MANY OF THE IMPORTANT PROCESSES OF PERSONALITY AND BEHAVIOR ARISE AS A PERSON ATTEMPTS TO CHANGE OR IS THREATENED WITH FORCED CHANGE IN HIS CONSTRUCT SYSTEM.

Kelly supposed, probably out of theoretical necessity, that the most important phenomena of personality arise out of the prospects for change or actual changes in construct systems. After all, a perfectly static system, just chugging along in a satisfactory way, would not produce much material of interest. Kelly related the various possibilities for change in construct systems to some of the major constructs or issues that have concerned personality theorists over the years (e.g., 1955, pp. 486–533). However, Kelly related his own ideas to those of others only in limited ways, and while he came to use some of the same terms as other theorists, he used them in special ways, and no direct translations should be contemplated. The problem is something like that of false cognates between languages; there is some sort of a connection, but it is misleadingly indirect or incomplete. For example, the French word *ancien,* meaning *former,* and the English word *ancient* are obviously related but cannot be taken as cognates. Similarly, while it is probably true that Kelly's notion of anxiety is related to the ideas of anxiety held by other theorists, the constructs are clearly not intersubstitutable. It is important for the student of Kelly to understand familiar terms as Kelly uses them and not as they are commonly used.

In the Fragmentation Corollary Kelly indicates that a person may successively employ construct subsystems incompatible with one another. The incompatibility may be tolerable, but it may also lead the person to try to change his construct system to reduce or eliminate the incompatibility. A typical example would be a person whose religious tenets are at variance with his everyday life. There are two opposite processes by which the incompatibility may be reduced. One is to broaden his perceptual field in order to reorganize it on a more comprehensive level, a process called *dilation.* A person might, for example, attempt to develop superordinate philosophical constructs to reconcile apparent contradictions between his everyday behavior and his professed religious principles. There was a time, as an instance, when American businessmen adopted a Calvinist view that wealth was a sign of God's favor and therefore a wide variety of sharp business practices was rationalized and made "right." On the other hand, a person might also try to reduce incompatibilities by narrowing his perceptual field so as to exclude parts of it, a process referred to as *constriction.* A person might give up religious practices, the reading of moral treatises, and so on as a way of eliminating incompatibilities between them and his everyday life.

At times an individual may be faced with the necessity for change in his construct system. Depending upon the extent and nature of the change, the person might or might not be troubled. Presumably most changes in peripheral constructs will be easily tolerated. Invalidation of the prediction that "All Mexican foods are spicy" should not upset anyone, and even a revision of one's food construct system to distinguish "hot" from "heavily seasoned" foods should not present any special problems. However, the prospect of change in core structures, those governing the very maintenance of a sense of personal identity and integrity, is likely to prove troublesome.

Kelly distinguishes three types of reactions to change in core structures: fear, threat, and guilt. *Fear* is the awareness of imminent incidental change in one's core structures. A rider is likely to experience fear when his horse bolts, bringing about thoughts of being thrown and bodily damage. Still the fundamental identity and integrity of the rider would probably not be jeopardized. Even the risk of death might represent a relatively incidental change if it promised only the end of life and not devastating damage to an individual's reputation. *Threat* is defined by Kelly as awareness of an imminent comprehensive change in one's core structures. Death would be relatively more threatening if it carried with it the likely degradation and insult to dignity of the person. If a person had spent his whole life building up a reputation as an expert in some field and if crucial aspects of his identity were involved in that reputation, then what might appear otherwise to be a fairly incidental and ever peripheral change resulting from being wrong about something could be a source of threat.

Guilt is also related to changes in core structure, specifically to changes in core role structures. Those aspects of the core structure which enable the individual to predict and control essential interactions of himself with other persons and groups constitute his *core role.* The experience of guilt lies in one's apparent dislodgement from one's core role structure. For example, a young man may construe himself in relation to his girl friend as a responsible, dependable, and caring lover, and he will enact this role in the light of his understanding or interpretation of his girl friend's behavior. If an important part of his being, of his identity as a person is involved in this role, then it is a part of his core role structure. Suppose one day he can only construe his recent behavior as irresponsible, undependable, and uncaring. Then he will feel guilt.

Another very similar young man may construe women as exploitable objects for the gratification of men, as placed on earth to nurture men, and the same behavior of irresponsibility, undependability, and uncaringness will produce no guilt at all. Kelly states that guilt need not be thought of as awareness of evil, but that notion is not incompatible with guilt as dislodgement from core role structure. Kelly does not insist that dislodgement from core role structure needs to be voluntary. Some Moslem friends of the author have indicated that they would feel equally bad upon learning that they had accidentally eaten pork as they would if they had eaten it deliberately (an act they could scarcely comprehend, however). As defined by Kelly, guilt may as well involve awareness of inadequacy, weakness, or physical limitations as of evil. A person who fails to save a drowning child for want of knowing how to swim may feel as guilty as a person who fails for cowardice. Guilt would depend upon the degree to which being protective in relation to the child (or children) was a part of the core role structure.

Upon occasion we may become aware that perceived events lie mostly outside the range of convenience of our construct systems, in which case we will experience *anxiety.* "Things that go bump in the night," for example, produce anxiety only when they seem to be unconstruable. Once one figures out that the raccoon has knocked over the garbage can again, anxiety disappears. On the other hand, if the noise is clearly construable as an intruder, the experience is fear, not anxiety. Anxiety is not produced merely by being wrong; anxiety is the result of a wrong prediction with no alternative to take its place. Anxiety may be experienced over trivial matters or over critical ones. A chess player bewildered at the unfamiliar and impenetrable strategy of an opponent may be said to be anxious, although probably not to the same degree, as a physician whose patient begins to go into a state of complete physiological collapse for unknown reasons. One defense against anxiety, says Kelly, is a loosening of the construct system so that it can encompass more events by permitting greater variability in construction of them from time to time or by relaxing the requirements by which they are fit into categories. If a chess player's construction system for different strategies can be loosened somewhat, he may see something familiar in his opponent's style that will reduce his own anxiety. Or if the physician faced with a rapidly deteriorating patient can loosen his system a bit, the patient may be construed as simply an anomalous case not fitting textbook patterns and expectations.

When an individual is faced with an enforced change in his core structure, he will be threatened if the change is relatively comprehensive and will experience fear if the change is likely to be only incidental. Any awareness of events confronting him which lie outside the range of convenience of his construct system will make the person anxious. Presumably if the individual is in the process of actively seeking to change his construct system, he will not feel afraid or threatened, although anxiety may be the stimulus to change. One type of change in the construct system which may make it at least temporarily more effective is a conceptual reorganization based on either broadening or narrowing the perceptual field so as to change perspectives and take account of a wider or narrower range of events. Broadening the perceptual field is called dilation, and narrowing it is called constriction.

Two additional maneuvers a person may perform when his construct system proves inadequate or otherwise unsatisfactory are aggressiveness and hostility. When an individual actively attempts to elaborate his perceptual field, Kelly calls this *aggressiveness*. Aggressiveness involves action and initiative rather than attack. The aggressive person takes matters into his own hands, presses issues rather than just letting them lie. Kelly's view of aggressiveness is closer to the usage implicit in speaking of aggressive salesmen or aggressive tennis players rather than criminal behavior and fighting. Kelly thinks of aggressiveness as the active extending and elaboration of the perceptual field so that one can incorporate more and more events into one's construct system. From Kelly's viewpoint an aggressive salesman actively pushes to extend his ability to anticipate, and hence to control, the events with which he must deal, whether they involve other people or more impersonal processes of the marketplace.

Hostility, according to Kelly's theory, is the continued effort to extort validating evidence in favor of a social prediction which is failing or which has already failed. The myth of Procrustes's bed is the archetype for hostility. Procrustes had a bed which he insisted all of his visitors must fit. If his guests were too short, he stretched them some, and if they were too long, he cut off their legs. Procrustes always validated his prediction that anyone could fit his bed. Similarly, says Kelly, forcing people or events to fit our construct system, rather than the other way around, is hostility. A mother who keeps trying to validate her predictions about her "darling little girl," long after it is amply clear that the girl is neither darling nor little, is showing hostility. Bribery is another nonobvious display of hostility, for it amounts to an attempt to extort a confirmation of a prediction that is not working out. Probably most of the things that we would ordinarily think of as hostility would also be called hostile by Kelly, but the commonality of his view of hostility is an attempt to force someone else or some other things to fit one's private view of the world.

Two other processes of change in Kelly's system have no clear counterparts in other personality theories. The *C–P–C Cycle* (circumspection-preemption-control) has to do with how we make construction choices, since there are a variety of ways in which any set of events may be construed. When faced with the necessity for choice, the usual sequence is to apply a series of constructs propositionally, a process termed *circumspection*. For example, a student with a Friday evening facing him may construe the evening successively or simultaneously as an opportunity to rest and relax, or as an opportunity to fulfill obligations by writing letters. Sooner or later, however, if he is not to lose control of the situation altogether, the student must construe the evening *preemptively,* in terms of one or the other of the available constructs. "O.K. To study or not to study, that's it. That is the real issue and nothing else." Then having decided what the crucial choice is, the student will choose that alternative through which he anticipates greater extension or elaboration of his system. If he chooses not to study, then he will have to go through another C–P–C Cycle in order to arrive at another preemptive construct. But the student may also get stuck at the point of exercising *choice* or *control* and be either paralyzed into inaction or thrown back into another C–P–C Cycle.

Kelly describes another important cycle, the *Creativity Cycle,* which starts with loosened construction and terminates with tightened and validated construction. Faced with the question "All right, so we are going out this evening. What will we do?" the student may say, "Well, let's go down to Jack's for a drink and listen to music the way we always do." But if the response is a request to do something different, the student may have to loosen his construction of appropriate Friday evening social activities and try to apply new constructs, leading to new predictions about what would be pleasing for the occasion. The temporary loosening might bring to mind all sorts of possibilities, so that a prediction of the "Hey, I've got a good idea!" sort can be made and validated. As Kelly sees it, many of our important problem-solving efforts can profitably be considered to occur in that way.

In this section we have stated a series of propositions which are either a part of Kelly's theory or derivable from it. The propositions have been presented in a rather uncritical way; they constitute the structure of Kelly's theory, although we cannot do justice to the richness of it within the limitations imposed here. To comprehend Kelly's theory and to think about it in any useful way, one must learn to think, to some degree, in Kelly's terms and to use his language. Not to do so will be to miss the essence of his thought and theory.

Applications

In this section we will consider some applications of Kelly's theory to "real life" and clinical problems, a task made easy by the fact that Kelly was a *clinical* psychologist, firmly rooted in the problems that people brought to him. Kelly was an intensely practical man; if ideas did not have applications, he was little interested in them.

Assessment

"As a whole, diagnosis may be described as the planning stage of therapy" (1955, p. 203). That statement sums up rather well Kelly's views of the purposes of assessment. To get away from a narrow connotation of "therapy," we say that diagnosis is the planning stage of change. Even the intent to do someone harm is likely to involve planning so that the harmful change can surely be brought about. Consistent with his ideas about the ways in which changes are brought about, Kelly points out that while a clinician may attempt to fix a subject with respect to certain static dimensions, such as intelligence, or to type the person, such as "schizoid," a more useful approach is to consider dynamic processes of change. Now, one becomes interested in the subject's freedom of movement, his potentialities, his resources, and what is to become of him. The clinician working within the framework of personal constructs theory attempts to determine the pathways along which

the subject is free to move and the most feasible course of movement.

Kelly's general orientation to assessment is illustrated quite well by five functions which he indicates are served by adequate psychological tests. Such tests must:

1. Define the client's problem in usable terms.
2. Reveal pathways along which the client is free to move.
3. Furnish clinical hypotheses which may subsequently be checked and put to use.
4. Reveal resources of the client which might otherwise be overlooked by the therapist.
5. Reveal problems of the client that might otherwise be overlooked by the therapist.

No particular tests or types of tests were arbitrarily ruled out by Kelly, since he believed that almost any of them might, in the hands of a skilled clinician, serve one or more of the five functions listed. (Bieri, 1961)

Kelly devised psychological assessment procedures closely related to the requirements of his own theory, but only the *Role Constructs Repertory Test* (Kelly, 1955) has received any particular attention. Kelly's masterful account of the clinical, psychological diagnostic procedure deserves attention and exploration. Kelly discusses the appraisal of experiences, the appraisal of activities, the steps in the diagnostic process, elaborating the complaint, and elaborating the personal system in setting forth his overall approach to assessment. He recommends use of interview and observational skills, examination of documents and other products, and consideration of an individual's milieu, among many other procedures. Illustrative of what Kelly strives for is a set of seven basic questions for the elaboration of any complaint:

1. What is the problem with which help is desired?
2. When was the problem first noticed?
3. Under what conditions did the problem first appear?
4. What corrective measures have been attempted?
5. What changes have come with treatment or the passage of time?
6. Under what conditions is the problem most noticeable?
7. Under what conditions is the problem least noticeable?

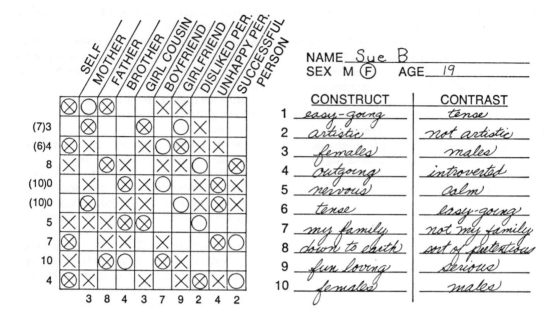

FIGURE 8.1. Role Constructs Repertory Test

INSTRUCTIONS FOR THE ROLE CONSTRUCTS REPERTORY TEST (REP TEST)

Look over and fill in this form. Notice on top we have names of significant persons. If there are any difficulties, you can make changes. Thus if you have no brother you may put name of some one close to you, such as a cousin, etc.

Step 1. Think of some important word that describes two of the three persons circled on line 1. Write that term on Row 1 under *Construct*. Notice that Sue B has written "easy-going".

Step 2. Now write under *Contrast* the opposite of the word. Sue B put in *"tense"* as the contrast to *"easy-going."*

Step 3. Put an X in two of the circles on line 1, for the two who have that construct. Sue B put an X for *self* and *father.* This means she sees herself and her father as *easy-going.*

Step 4. Put additional X's under the names of persons who have that *Construct.* Sue B sees her boyfriend and her girlfriend as also being *easy-going.*

Step 5. Continue in this manner for the rest of the form. Write down an important term under *Construct* and its opposite under *Contrast.* Then make an X in two of the circles and then make an X for all others on the row that fit that construct.

ANALYSIS OF RCRT PROTOCOL FOR SUE B

We suggest that the reader first examine Table 8-1 carefully to try to understand Sue B, who filled out this form. Even this abbreviated form of the REP Test produces more material than can be analyzed in the space available, but this analysis will serve to illustrate approaches that can be made to understand this procedure.

The first construct elicited (*easy-going* vs. *tense*, in this case) often is of special importance and tends to represent a fundamental dichotomy for the subject. Sue B chooses to view people in her life space in terms of how they approach the world. Some in her thinking are "loose," "relaxed," "free flowing," and some are "up tight," "constricted," or "wound up." Since the circles on Row 1 have been put in for *self*, *mother* and *father*, this construct of easy-going vs. tense may be of special significance, perhaps even a core construct.

Note that in Sort 6 (*tense–easy-going*) this construct is repeated, and that Row 5 (*nervous–calm*) is semantically about the same, thus indicating that for Sue this whole area of tension versus calm in people is crucially important. Everyone categorized as easy-going on Sort 1 is calm on Sort 5, and those tense on Sort 1 are nervous on Sort 5. Sort 9 (*fun-loving–serious*) appears to be simply a relabeling of *easy-going–tense*.

We can now conclude that for Sue B there are easy-going, calm, fun-loving people and nervous, tense, serious people. One can be down to earth without being easy-going, and one need not be tense to be artistic.

Most of Sue B's constructs are fairly abstract and "psychological" in nature, but when faced with certain sorts, e.g. self-boyfriend-girlfriend and self-brother-cousin, she comes up only with rather concrete and evaluatively neutral constructs such as *female–male* and *my family–not my family*.

Although Sue B uses eight different sets of verbal labels, we have already seen that three of the eight produce identical sortings when applied to the ten role figures, and female vs. male is repeated with the same results. There are, then, at most seven different constructs. A complete analysis of the test would call for determining the number of "factors" by examining the patterns of checks (Xs) and voids. If two constructs match highly, then they are not considered to be independent. The figures at the left show the number of times that the first construct, Row 1, matches each of the others. As in other correlational techniques, it is possible to have negative values, in which case they are reflected. The numbers in parentheses show the number of matches if the pattern were simply reversed. Note that Sue's

first construct produces a pattern which can account for 69 of the 90 remaining squares, suggesting that Sue's cognitive structure is simpler than might be suggested by the seven sets of construct labels.

Another feature of the REP Test is that it shows similarity. To whom is Sue most similar? Notice that the pattern she has for herself is essentially similar as that for her girlfriend in that only for *my family –not my family* there is a difference, but notice that there are only two matches for successful person. The numbers at the bottom represent the notes that an interpreter might make to find with whom Sue B compares herself.

A clever examiner could elicit a good deal of information about Sue B from this REP Test.

According to Kelly, "The formulation of the questions is designed to get the client (1) to place the problems, if possible, on a time line, (2) to see them as fluid and transient, and then to interpret them as responsive to (a) treatment, (b) the passing of time, and (c) varying conditions" (Kelly, 1966, p. 963).

Kelly also devised a technique for clinical assessment which he called the *Self-Characterization* (Kelly, 1955). While the directions are seemingly simple and the technique quite straightforward, the final directions arrived at by Kelly were the result of many trials and revisions. A verbatim quotation of the directions gives an indication of what is involved. Kelly states that the clinician may say:

> I want you to write a character sketch of Harry Brown (i.e., client's name), just as if he were the principal character in a play. Write it as it might be written by a friend who knew him very *intimately* and very *sympathetically*, perhaps better than anyone ever really could know him. Be sure to write it in the third person. For example, start out by saying, 'Harry Brown is. . . .' (1955, p. 323)

According to Kelly, "The object of this kind of inquiry is to see how the client structures a world in relation to which he must maintain himself in some kind of role." (1955, p. 324)

Analysis of the Self-Characterization is clinical rather than quantitative and is based on several different types of cues to important material, including the sequence of and transition between topics, the organization of the material, terms which are repeated and linked, shifts of emphasis, and different contexts provided for interpretation. The personal constructs clinician is looking, of course, for the dimensions, or constructs, through which the client attempts to make sense of his life and experience. Topical areas covered and themes presented are also important in the analysis.

Neither the Self-Characterization nor the RCRT (REP test) has been standardized or provided with norms to make objective interpretation possible. Aside from research uses which permit rather arbitrary, if quantitative, analyses, both instruments are dependent upon clinical acumen.

Treatment

Applicability is the raison d'etre of Kelly's theory. The major emphasis in Volume 2 of Kelly's work is treatment, and even a fairly cursory reading reveals that Kelly was a flexible, imaginative, "mainstream" therapist. He proposes no tricks, the transcripts that he presents produce no great surprises, and he appears to have thought and worked as a therapist about the same as most other therapists think and work. He attempted to produce changes in patients' cognitions, to get them to explore new forms of behavior and to explore and express their innermost feelings. Yet, in most discussions of Kelly's views about therapy, there has been an almost total concern with *fixed-role therapy*. Kelly devoted a whole chapter to fixed-role therapy in the first, more theoretical volume of his book. Fixed-role therapy represented a considerable departure from standard practice at the time Kelly proposed it, and the prominence he gave it probably led many of his readers to suppose that it constituted Kelly's major therapeutic intervention and, perhaps, his treatment of choice. Yet, fixed-role therapy was never even attempted on more than a handful of cases, was not a major feature of Kelly's teaching about therapy, and was never a focus of any lasting research effort. Because it is so consistent with Kelly's theory, however, it is worthwhile to take a brief look at fixed-role therapy.

Kelly believed that we all are unnecessarily constrained by our view of things, how we construe things. Our health-related behavior, for example, is determined by what we believe about our health rather than by the "objective" facts. People who seek help with their personal problems are likely to be victims of their particular (and not especially useful) ways of looking at things. Their views and resulting choices are what get people into trouble. If people could be led to view things differently and to try new choices or behaviors, their lot in life might improve, along with their views. A shy, timid soul validates his predictions about other people; for example: if he slinks around and keeps out of their way, people leave him alone, and if he asserts himself occasionally, he meets with rebuffs. The problem faced by the therapist is how to get the individual to try new behaviors, to "lay some new bets" on the outcome of which the construct system may be changed, for example, so as to view people in terms other than say *tolerant vs. intimidating*.

Fixed-role therapy was developed as a way of helping therapy clients try out new behaviors. Kelly perceived that people have difficulty in simply "trying out" new behaviors because the therapist tells them to. The suggestion that the client should change himself in fundamental ways is often quite threatening. Kelly wanted a procedure which would permit people to "try on new behaviors for size." He believed trying new behaviors temporarily might facilitate change in the client's construct system. To help the client explore new behaviors and new ways of thinking, the therapist employing fixed-role therapy prepares for the client a role sketch, a prescription for behavior, which the client is to play out in various situations, beginning with role playing. The behaviors are not necessarily behaviors which the therapist thinks the client ought to adopt permanently. Rather, they are behaviors devised to open new possibilities for the client to consider, new ways of looking at things as well as new behaviors. While roles are written with the aim of providing sharp contrasts to a client's usual ways of behaving, the client is afforded the protection of a "make believe" activity which does not require any commitment and hence is thought not to arouse much initial resistance or sense of hopelessness about bringing about lasting change.

In employing fixed-role therapy, extensive use is made of Self-Characterization as a guide to developing the role, with an emphasis placed upon providing interesting and potentially useful contrasts. Therapy sessions are devoted to exploring the implications of the role and actually practicing the playing of the role vis-a-vis the therapist. Later sessions are devoted to discussions of experiences in playing the role and in the changes the role brings about in behavior and outlook.

The emphasis placed on fixed-role therapy by reviewers of Kelly's work is probably understandable, but it is largely misplaced in terms of the more usual ways in which Kelly went about therapy and helped his students learn it. It is clear from the material presented in Volume 2 of *The Psychology of Personal Constructs* that Kelly's therapeutic techniques usually involved heavy reliance on face-to-face interviews, such as might be employed by most other "talk" therapies. Naturally, Kelly's aims in therapy, as well as some of his specific therapeutic tactics, reflected his concerns with the construct systems of his clients and his attempts to understand those systems, to bring his clients to an understanding of them, and to bring about change in them. However, even though it might seem that Kelly's therapy is heavily cognitive—perhaps even intellectualization to some—he was much attuned to the need for *behavior* change, and clients were encouraged strongly and helped in definite ways to try out new behaviors outside the therapy setting. Kelly expressed over and over his conviction that the proof of any theory, including any theory held by a client, is in the accuracy of predictions to be made from it. Consequently, he quite carefully led clients to test the implications of their views of things by altering their behaviors to see whether the anticipated results in fact did occur. He also believed that therapists needed constantly to check their understanding of their clients by making verifiable predictions about them. If a therapist really understood a client, the therapist could predict what the client would talk about in the next therapy session, what happened at home between sessions, and how the client would react to a specific suggestion for new behavior.

Probably the best statement of Kelly's view of the psychotherapy situation is that he thought of it as a laboratory where the client could carry out experiments that might be impossible or hazardous in real life. The client in therapy can test alternative views, can try out different behaviors, in actuality or symbolically, and so on, without fear of dire consequences. The therapist's task is to facilitate such experimentation. Kelly did not, however, think of the therapist as some sort of a passive matrix within which the client's experiments could be carried to conclusion. Rather, he conceived the therapist to be an active facilitator and in some cases even an instigator of the client's experimentation. Kelly described therapy as a carefully planned enterprise and not a spontaneous, "let's see what happens today" activity. It was incumbent on the therapist to know just what was going on at all times, to anticipate what would occur in every session, and to plan the kind of activities that would bring about desired client behavior. In particular, Kelly made heavy use of *enactment* procedures, quite similar to role playing but perhaps more flexible in conception and practice. It was in enacting various problems and possibilities that the client could carry out his within-session experiments and explore new ways of seeing his world.

A good indication of the nature of therapy as Kelly proposed it can be had from suggestions he made concerning ways of encouraging psychotherapeutic experimentation (1955, pp. 1127–1135). The first technique is *permissiveness*. Kelly viewed it as a technique rather than, as for Rogers, a pervasive outlook. He believed that by taking a permissive attitude, the therapist provided the patient with a setting in which experimentation could safely be carried on, without fear of recrimination or embarrassment. The second technique is reaction on the part of the therapist. When the client experiments, something must happen, and that happening is the task of the therapist, whether it be a facial expression, a gesture, a comment, or an invitation to further experimentation. The third technique is the therapist's *creativity* in providing some novel situation in which old, familiar modes of response are not appropriate. While it may at times be advantageous for a client to be in a novel life situation (e.g., a vacation in a new place), the therapist can also provide novelty within the therapy situation itself by such tactics as changing his manner on occasion or changing the rules by which sessions are conducted. A fourth technique which may at times be required is to provide *equipment* which gives the client the "tools" necessary to carry out experimentation. A client may not be able to explore new types of employment or social interactions without proper clothing, and an adolescent may need financial assistance to plan a date. The fifth technique is to get the client to *hypothesize*, preferably in the form of reasonably specific predictions. The client who has stated a fairly specific prediction based on his own behavior will find it difficult to resist carrying out the experiment. *Interpretation* is still another technique for promoting experimentation. In Kellian therapy, this refers to the interpretations made by the client. If the client can be led to interpret the behavior of others, he or she will experience strong pressures to find out more about the views of those people, to fill in gaps of knowledge and understanding. The seventh and eighth techniques involve getting the client to try to portray how another person views himself and how another person *views* the client.

These techniques, along with interpretations, involve role constructs, the client's understanding of another person's construct system in relation to himself, and valuable clues for the client as to what behaviors may be expected from others and what effects his own behavior may have on other people. Still another technique, *biographical hypotheses*, is designed to get the client to elaborate the biographical conditions under which he would behave differently. For example, if the client claims that his behavior is the result of inadequate behavior on the part of parental figures, the client can be asked to describe the sorts of conditions that would have to have existed in order for different behavior to be possible. The therapist can then utilize the hypothesized links between the client's revised biography and the behavior expected to promote experimentation. Finally, Kelly notes that experimentation may be facilitated by the direct approaches of *encouraging* a client directly to experiment, to try something out, and by *manipulation*—putting a client into situations in which there are good social examples of the kind of behavior desired. If a client has difficulty in "letting go," in behaving spontaneously and expressively, exploration with such behavior in some situations is clearly easier than in others.

Mention needs to be made of the "axis" of "tightening" and "loosening" as applied to therapeutic activities. The axis refers to the exactness and variability with which predictions can be made from constructs, (1955, pp. 39–40), and creativity requires an initial loosening of constructs followed by tightening. Given this, it is clear why the loosening and tightening of constructs becomes a major focus of activity for a Kellian therapist. Loosening of thought is characteristic of fantasy, including dreams, and Kelly notes the usefulness of dreams as material for exploration in therapy. However, loosening is also produced by relaxation, by chain association, and by the therapist's uncritical acceptance of the client. When tightening becomes desirable, it is produced by encouraging the client to take a judgmental attitude, by asking the client to "step aside" and take a look at his or her own behavior, to summarize what he or she has been saying and to take a historical approach to his or her thoughts. The therapist encourages tightening by determining whether the client can relate his or her thinking, by asking the client directly to be more explicit, asking for validating evidence, attempting time-binding of constructs, and using other similar techniques.

All of Kelly's therapeutic maneuvers, however similar they may seem to those of some other therapists, have as their aim the altering of a client's construct system in such a way as to make likely more useful and accurate predictions and ultimately more extensive control over the client's fate.

Institutional

Kelly had no questions about the implications of his views for various social institutions. Perhaps the most important implication was that it is necessary for institutions to recognize that the problems they see in their clientele reside in the views of the institutions themselves, rather than being inherent in the clients. When a school regards a portion of its pupils as lazy or as unteachable, that does not change the pupils in any way, and it does not necessarily tell us much about the pupils. What it tells us is something about the school and the way it chooses to see reality. When a school comes to regard its failures as having origins in characteristics of the pupils, that view then determines much of the subsequent response of the school to those failures. As Kelly was fond of noting, the very child labeled "lazy" by a teacher might very well seem extraordinarily active to another observer. The important question is, what kind of a school or teacher views pupils as lazy?

And once pupils are viewed as lazy (vs. industrious), who can doubt that that same laziness will be found again and again? The very label leads to the prediction that if the student is given a new challenge, laziness will be the response, and the prediction works just about every time. What is needed in such a situation is a new way of looking at children, of construing them and their behavior, which will lead to more useful and productive institutional behavior. Note that in Kelly's view, to the extent that a school insists on viewing some of its pupils as lazy and continues to try to produce evidence for the accuracy of its predictions, the school is coming close to what Kelly would call hostility.

It may not be obvious that institutions have construct systems just as individuals do, but it can be useful to think of institutions in such a way. Consider, for example, a prison system. It is likely to be primarily characterized by the superordinate construct of *prisoner–nonprisoner*. The construct ramifies throughout the prison system and affects almost everything that goes on in it. Then, too, the prisoner construct is quite likely to be applied preemptively; that is, an inmate of the prison is a prisoner and nothing but a prisoner. He is, perhaps, scarcely regarded as human, let alone as a husband or lover, a father, a friend, a worker, a fisherman, or a philosophical thinker. The preemptive construct of prisoner is likely, then, also to imply a constellation of other characteristics—such as dangerous, stupid, immoral, prone to escape, potential troublemaker, and animalistic—which leads inexorably to methods of management that all but ensure that the constellation will be validated. Such a construct system (only a part of it has been pointed to here) can be as characteristic of an institution as of an individual and just as surely can determine choices and institutional treatment.

What is needed in institutions are more useful construct systems that could make greater use of propositional constructs (e.g., this man is a prisoner and he may also be a father, a fisherman, and a nice guy—or he may not be) or permeable constructs which can take account of new events (e.g., he is a youthful drug offender and may not have all the characteristics so often found in

other prisoners). Institutions should provide more opportunities for people to change, elaborate, and test their construct systems, occasions on which people can grow. If, for example, some children do not have a chance to change their conception of themselves as "dumb," their behavior is likely to continue in the same old destructive grooves. That does not mean that such children necessarily have to come to think of themselves as "smart" or as standing in some other contrast to dumb. The change might involve tightening up the construct somewhat by delimiting it (e.g., "I'm dumb in math but not in social studies or in fishing"), or it might involve abandoning the *dumb–smart* construct as a major way of differentiating among people, including the self. Schools, prisons, hospitals, mental health clinics, welfare agencies, and probably most other societal institutions all too often construe their clientele—and their own roles—in terms that tend to foster the very behaviors they are in existence to eliminate. These institutions do not often enough provide opportunities for change in construct systems through experimentation and creativity cycles. To the extent that institutions are meant to be therapeutic or to help people change, they need to provide for the same kinds of growth experiences as are provided by psychotherapists.

Self

Both the Self-Characterization and the Role Constructs Repertory Test are so simple in conception and (at least at some levels) in analysis that any reasonably intelligent person could complete them without professional assistance. A careful study of both could well be a fruitful enterprise, perhaps surprising in outcome for many persons. Most of us are too little aware of the nature of our construct systems and of the views and choices that they entail. Consider, for example, the construct *intelligent–stupid* often found on the RCRT protocols of college students. The very fact that people are dealt with in terms of this dimension is of interest when one thinks of the many alternatives that might have been employed. For example, would not *advantaged–disadvantaged* provide equally good predictions in many areas of human functioning, and would not such a construct have quite different implications for the ways in which one might relate to and try to help people? Would the construct *interested in the same things as I—interested in different things* overlap the *intelligent—stupid* construct and be more constructive in many instances? To what extent is the *intelligent—stupid* construct used propositionally as opposed to constellatorily? Is it by any chance used preemptively? If it is a propositional construct, then we may say that an individual is, among many other things, stupid. He may or may not also be friendly, pleasant, unclean, good looking, and cruel. But, in fact, the construct more often than not carries with it a constellation of other traits so that the person construed as stupid is automatically assumed to be unworthy, dirty, cruel, unpleasant, ugly, guilty of poor manners, and a host of other things.

Constellatory constructs often lead to nonconstructive but stubbornly persistent ways of thought and action. When used preemptively, the *intelligent—stupid* construct suggests that an individual need not be regarded as anything *but* stupid (or intelligent). He is stupid, and that is all there is to it! He is not a fine fellow, a good athlete, or someone's sweetheart; he is stupid! It is worth asking ourselves just what kinds of constructs we have and how we ordinarily apply them. Note that the *intelligent—stupid* construct is couched in fairly extreme terms, especially at what we would take to be the unfavorable end. It is probably not without meaning that the construct is rarely, if ever, labeled *genius—stupid* or *brilliant—stupid*, for to do so would be to establish a very discomfiting dichotomy when applied to most of us. And yet, the construct is fairly demanding with respect to the behaviors of most people most of the time, for the alternative to doing something positively intelligent seems to be to do something positively stupid. That is a high standard to expect most people to meet much of the time or to expect anybody to meet all of the time. The range of convenience of the construct is also worth examining, because if it applies only to a very narrow range of behaviors, its implications may be limited; for example, if it applies only to academic behaviors, most of what most people do most of the time will escape the judgment implied. However, if the construct has a very wide range of convenience, it will result in many judgments about many people. The construct might be relatively impermeable with respect to behaviors that are to be accounted for; for example, the construct might be developed in a predominantly academic context and be impermeable to events met later in life outside that context. Thus a former student might be unable to admit such behaviors as throwing a pot, caring for a family, and welding a broken rod to the realm of the *intelligent—stupid* construct. And finally, the construct may be used in either a relatively tight or a loose way, as reflected in the definiteness of the predictions to which it leads. If the construct is a tight one, the person employing it will expect *intelligent* people to be quite consistent in their behavior and to conform fairly closely to expectations. For example, a tight use of the construct might result in the statement, "She is an intelligent woman; therefore, she will not watch stupid daytime soap opera TV programs." A looser construct might lead to such a statement as "She is an intelligent woman; therefore, she will not be overly fond of some of the less intellectual TV programs."

From Kelly's viewpoint, we are constantly evolving our construct systems. However, not all of our construct creation attempts need be accidental or unplanned. Just as the scientist plans deliberate experiments to test his hypotheses, so may we experiment deliberately with our construct systems, trying new ways of looking at things, extending our predictions into previously unexplored areas, and observing carefully the consequences of successive tightening and loosening of our constructs. We may ask ourselves the question "What would happen if . . . ?" and try to get an answer to it. We will ordinarily find it easiest to experiment and try to elaborate our construct systems at times or in areas in which we feel most comfortable and sure of ourselves; we will, correspondingly, find it difficult to experiment elaboratively when we are insecure and will attempt then to achieve greater definition of our systems. For example, the time for a young man to invite a new date is in a situation which he has well under control; the first formal reception he attends, or a dance being given in honor of the mayor's daughter, is a good time to stick with a partner who is predictable and dependable.

The result of our planned experimentation with new constructs should be an elaborated and more useful system, making it possible for us to function effectively in new areas, with new people, and with new problems not previously manageable. Many students, for example, have a great deal of difficulty relating to their college professors, viewing them as aloof rather than friendly, as intellectuals rather than interested in ordinary things, as busy rather than as having spare time, and as uninterested rather than interested in students. However, professors are often lonely, bored, aware of one or two generation gaps, and convinced that nearly all students care nothing for their respective fields. Both students and professors could probably profit from more experimentation with their views of each other. Since this book is addressed to students, however, the point can be made here that suitable elaboration of and change in the construct systems which students apply to their professors and to academic work might very well lead to a more useful and satisfactory system that would promote rather than impede desired interactions and the students' ultimate intellectual and personal development. Similar changes could probably be explored in almost all areas of functioning (e.g., relationships with parents, vocational plans and social interactions). The key to improvement is recognition of the fundamental sense in which the person is a scientist, striving by experimentation to improve his understanding, prediction, and control of the events with which he must deal or chooses to deal.

Validation

Kelly, at least as much as any other theorist, insisted that the proof of any theory lies in the accuracy of the predictions it permits. However, Kelly also recognized that a theory does not make predictions; *people* make predictions, based on a theory, and the accuracy of the predictions depends on the understanding and intelligence of the predictors as well as on the adequacy of the theory. Moreover, the outcome of any prediction will depend on the characteristics of the prediction. Obviously the tighter and more exact a prediction becomes, the greater the probability is that it will be proven wrong. On the other hand, predictions can be made that are so general that they are all but impossible to disprove. There is another problem with a theory as

broad and general as Kelly's—no really direct test of the theory is possible. Only after years of research and application might it become possible to state in a general sort of way whether or not the theory seems tenable and useful. It is early, perhaps, to be evaluating Kelly's theory. It has taken 70 years or so for evidence relevant to the adequacy of psychoanalytic theory to accumulate to any interpretable bulk. Kelly's theory, at a bit over 20 years of existence, is young.

Evidence

It requires no special honesty to admit that the evidence bearing in any direct way on the adequacy of the psychology of personal constructs is thin, disappointingly so. For anyone having any sense of identification with Kelly or with his theory, the history of the past 20 years is disappointing. Kelly's students never produced much work of central and critical relevance to the theory even while they were graduate students, and not one of his students now actively researching and publishing could be identified clearly as a Kellian theorist. A search of *Psychological Abstracts* over the past several years will turn up a handful of relevant articles each year, but most of them have to do in one way or another with the adequacy of the RCRT rather than with the theory itself.

Why this should be so is difficult to say. Perhaps part of the problem is that Kelly was not himself an active research partisan of his own theory. He is not the author of a single piece of research on the theory, and it may be that he did not do a good job of engendering research enthusiasm in his students, at least not enthusiasm for the theory itself. Perhaps also the theory is so novel and so large that it is difficult for single investigators to get a good grasp on it. It may not be evident to a lot of potential researchers just what the important and testable propositions are. And perhaps Kelly was simply not approachable enough as a person to be able to instill in the students close to him a dedication and sense of identification that would keep them working once they had left his direct supervision. Kelly was a formal man, and he could be formidable, too. It is strange, but true, that the one researcher currently working most actively within Kelly's theory is Donald Bannister, an

English psychologist who never studied under Kelly.

The research which has been stimulated by Kelly's theory does not, for the most part, test propositions derived from the theory but provides elaboration of certain points in the theory. There is not space here to do a complete review of the research on psychology of personal constructs, but interested readers may want to consult Bonnarius (1965) for a review of early research and Bannister and Mair (1968) for a slight updating. The material to be presented here is more illustrative of what has been done rather than probative with respect to the theory.

One might begin with the issue whether personal constructs as elicited from individuals are of any particular value in understanding the person, it being possible, often with less effort, to get other comparable information, such as ratings on standard lists of traits or constructs. Kelly's theory proposes that an individual's processes are psychologically channelized by the way *he* anticipates events, not by the way in which events are usually anticipated or ought to be anticipated, or whatever. The issue can be put in concrete terms by asking whether the construct *intelligence* is generally useful, or whether it is more useful for people who spontaneously use it themselves in construing the behavior of other people. In the earliest study bearing on this point, Payne (1956) determined that better predictions about individuals are made from knowledge of those individuals' personal constructs than from rating of those individuals by other persons; that is, knowing the constructs an individual uses in describing others is more useful than knowing the constructs which others apply to him. That finding is of definite interest for the personal constructs theorist, but it is in no way critical. However, other findings generally support the notion that the individual's own personal constructs are of particular value in understanding and predicting reactions.

In a series of studies, Landfield and his associates (Landfield & Nawas, 1964; Nawas & Landfield, 1963; Ourth & Landfield, 1965) have found that it is important for therapists to understand the language systems of clients as reflected in personal constructs and, most interestingly, that clients who improve in therapy tend to become more strongly committed to their own construct

systems rather than coming to adopt the construct systems of their therapists. Messick & Kogan (1966) found that certain aspects of individuals' personalities could be predicted from knowledge of their personal constructs, a finding consistent with data provided by Sechrest (1968) for three different traits. Levy (1954) found that constructs determined to be constellatory by reason of their extensive relationship with other constructs had more information value than did more propositional constructs, and similarly, Williams and Sechrest (1963) found that individuals tended more often to invoke more general constructs and described such constructs as more useful in making interpersonal predictions.

Such findings as the above contribute in general ways to the credibility of Kelly's theory, and they rather clearly suggest that the theory has distinct practical implications in understanding what a person is like, in predicting what a person may do in important interpersonal relationships, and in indicating something about the way in which the most important personal constructs may be determined.

The findings are also of some specific relevance to the Sociality Corollary, which states that an individual can play a role in relationship to another person to the degree that he can construe the construction processes of that other. Apparently to know something of another's construct system is helpful in relating to that person, perhaps more helpful than knowing how that person is viewed by others. One type of role that one may play in relation to the social processes of another person is by *identification* with that person. Jones (1954, 1961) found the RCRT to be of some value in assessing identification, as did Sechrest (1962). Moreover, Jones found that psychiatric patients tend toward either over- or underidentification with others; that is, they see themselves as either too similar or too dissimilar from others, suggesting an inability to play appropriate roles in relation to other people. Shoemaker (1955) found that when people construe others similarly, they predict that they will behave similarly, indicating that the idea that a person's processes are psychologically channelized by the way he anticipates events is tenable. Shoemaker also found evidence consistent with the Sociality Corollary in that his subjects were better able to predict the behavior of people with whom they feel "comfortable" than with whom they feel "uncomfortable," and they are better able to predict the behavior of people to whom they see themselves as being similar.

In many ways a critical issue is what happens when a person makes a prediction that is subsequently invalidated. Unfortunately, perhaps, the theory is not precise on that point; different things could happen. Still, from Kelly's theory it would seem a frequent occurrence that there should be a polar shift in construction. For example, based on my construction of a person as *kind,* I expect that he will affect not to notice when I drop my chicken in my lap; when he does, in fact, note my faux pas and laughs, I might well decide that instead of being *kind,* he is *cruel.* Another possibility, of course, is that I might change constructs, and decide that he is *crude* as opposed to *refined,* however *kind* he might be. In effect, such a switch in constructs suggests that laughing at a faux pas is outside the range of convenience of the *kind–cruel* construct. Another possibility, of course, is that the whole business could seem quite confusing, for example, if the *kind–cruel* construct seemed not to apply and no other construction of the events readily offered itself. In that case, I would experience anxiety stemming from the overall loss of structure, the phenomenal experience being something like "What the hell is going on here?"

Which of the above, or perhaps other, consequences of invalidation of a prediction should obtain is not easy to say. In the earliest study on the topic of invalidation of predictions, Poch (1952) asked students to make sets of predictions based on their personal constructs about acquaintances and then gave them back information designed to make them believe that their predictions about one person were generally correct, while those about the other person were generally incorrect. Poch found that "validated" constructs changed almost not at all during an interim period prior to retesting, but invalidated constructs did tend to change somewhat, although less than had been expected. However, the more important finding was that constructs that were invalidated were less likely than those validated to be invoked for the second set of predictions; that is, the invalidated constructs tended to be dropped. Levy (1954), employing

similar methodology involving invalidated predictions, found that strong invalidation led to more changes in construction than weak invalidation, but he also found that invalidation of *constellatory constructs* (i.e., constructs having many implications for, or connections with, other constructs) produced especially widespread changes in the construct system.

In what is in some ways the most intensive study of construct system yet undertaken, Hinkle (1965) extended the work of Poch and Levy, but he was especially interested in differential effects of changes in superordinate as opposed to subordinate constructs. Essentially Hinkle hypothesized that superordinate constructs would be more resistant to change than would subordinate constructs, but changes in superordinate constructs would have more ramifications when they occurred. In his study, Hinkle limited his attention to what he called "slot change"—the type of change that occurs when an individual is reconstrued as being *cruel* rather than *kind,* for example.

Hinkle first elicited what he assumed to be subordinate constructs from his subjects by having them construe successive triads of people in the ordinary way. He then had his subjects indicate for each construct which pole of the construct was more nearly descriptive of the kind of person the subject would like to be. The technique for eliciting superordinate constructs which followed was to ask subjects *why* they would prefer to be like the pole they indicated. For example, if initially a subject produced the construct *friendly–unfriendly* and indicated a preference for being friendly because the construct *happy–unhappy* was taken to be superordinate to *friendly–unfriendly,* the subject was then asked whether he would prefer to be *happy* or *unhappy* and why. The response then was taken to be suggestive of an event more superordinate construct, as with a person's response that it is better to be happy because that implies a *satisfying life.*

By repeating the procedure described, Hinkle obtained for each subject a set of superordinate constructs. He then presented constructs to subjects two at a time and required them to indicate for which construct a slot change would be more tolerable if they had to change on one construct but could remain the same on the other. Thus he could determine which constructs were most resistant to change, and he found, as expected, that superordinate constructs were most resistant; that is, a person would rather give up being happy than give up having a generally satisfying life and would rather give up being friendly than give up being happy. Finally, by asking subjects to imagine they had changed on one construct and then indicate on which other constructs they supposed they would also have changed, Hinkle determined that superordinate constructs have more implications, in the sense that change on them leads to changes on more other constructs.

At least in a general way the work of Poch, Levy, and Hinkle indicates that some of the general propositions of Kelly's theory lead to testable hypotheses, and the findings are more or less in accord with expectations. However, none of the tests was very stringent, and probably in every case failure to obtain expected results would have been quite inconclusive. Their findings do show quite clearly that methodologically good research can be done on Kelly's theory and that RCRT measurement provides a very useful tool in exploring the theory. On the other hand, the research is obviously "artificial" in important senses, and whether people behave in accordance with expectations from personal constructs theory in everyday life situations remains to be explored by some inventive and determined researcher.

The RCRT itself has been the subject of a fair amount of research, mostly designed to show that it is a reliable and otherwise acceptable measuring instrument. Pedersen (1958) deserves credit for doing the first work on what he called the "consistency" of the RCRT. By administering the measure two times over a period of one week, he found that subjects are fairly consistent in the figures they give for role titles, in the constructs they produce, and in the relationships among their constructs. Kieferle and Sechrest (1961) obtained RCRT protocols from subjects and then showed that efforts to get additional constructs did not produce many that were discriminable from those already produced. Further, giving subjects new construct labels gave results highly similar to those elicited by their own constructs. These findings indicate that the RCRT probably does elicit a good sample of an individual's constructs, maybe in many cases a

fairly complete sample.

Much additional work on the RCRT as a measuring instrument has been done by Bannister and Mair and their students and colleagues and is reported in their book (Bannister & Mair, 1968). They point out that the RCRT is a complex measurement technique, and consequently it is difficult to specify *a* reliability or validity value for it. There are many different aspects which have to be studied separately. For example, the verbal labels attached to constructs might be quite dependable over time and might be indicative of important aspects of an individual's functioning. However, the relationships among those labels, as indicated by the system of checks for their applicability to role figures, might not be especially reliable and might not be a valid index of anything important even if reliable. Bannister and Mair point to a number of important problems still needing investigation and are undoubtedly correct in their assessment of the RCRT as a technique of promise, but one in need of a great deal more research.

Clearly the body of research on personal constructs theory is not large, although we would hasten to point out that we have not surveyed all of it here, by any means. The really important research from a theoretical standpoint has been limited mostly to dissertations and theses; the published research has tended to focus more on the RCRT as a measurement tool. That is unfortunate, for Kelly's theory is not unreasonable. However, it needs to be reiterated that the Fundamental Postulate and the ten corollaries are the *assumptive* structure of Kelly's theory and are, hence, not directly testable. As far as testing the validity of Kelly's theory, all that can be done is to test propositions *derived* from the basic assumptions. It may be a long time before enough evidence accumulates to make it possible to say one way or another whether or not Kelly's theory is generally useful.

Of course, Kelly's ideas are not utterly lacking in precedent. Writers from Epictetus on have noted that what a person *thinks* is real is usually more important than what is real, which is just another way of saying that a person's construction of events will psychologically channelize his processes. The eminent sociologist W. I. Thomas put it rather neatly by saying, "If men define situations as real, they are real in their consequences" (Thomas & Thomas, 1928, p. 512). Such views do not necessarily *prove* anything, but they do suggest a degree of consensual validation for portions of Kelly's theory. Still other parts of the theory are consistent with currently accepted views and research in personality and social psychology. For example, Kelly believed that if his therapy patients could be induced, without any particular pressure, to act in a particular way, their outlook and behavior might very likely be altered in a reasonably congruent manner. That is an expectation very similar to that stated by Festinger in his presentation of dissonance theory (Festinger, 1957) and verified in at least a general way by a 15-year history of research (Wicklund & Brehm, in press). There are, of course, many other points of correspondence between Kelly's theory and both past and contemporary thinking about human thought and behavior; his theory is in various ways supported by both common sense and consensus.

Actually, however, in the opinion of this writer, one of the main reasons for the dearth of research supporting Kelly's theory is the relative disinterest of Kelly himself in such research. It cannot escape the attention of a reviewer of Kelly's work that he rarely in his own writings or speeches, subsequent to publication of his book in 1955, referred to any research of any kind. In the posthumously published volume of Kelly's papers (Maher, 1969), 15 of the 17 papers have no bibliographic citations at all, and the other two have only six apiece, only two of which are research papers. Most of the other citations are to Kelly's own work. Two of the 17 papers set forth Kelly's own view of the proper way to do research, but few trained researchers in psychology would be able to identify a coherent strategy and methodology. A good bit of the substance of each paper is, in fact, an attack on the usual methods of psychological research, but no clear alternative is posed.

It is very likely that Kelly saw the eventual verification of his ideas as lying in clinical practice, in the applications of his theory in clinical settings with real-life cases. Thus he states:

> Translated into the more familiar terms of the psychological laboratory, what I have been saying suggests that the researcher is more likely to mobilize his ingenuities in devising important hypotheses if he goes to where the psychological problems are.

In my own case I interpret this to mean going to where persons are disturbed enough to try to make something new out of their lives as, for example, where children are, for they are continually trying to make something new out of themselves—counting each year as they grow up and making plans for what they will do when they escape the restraints of size, age, vocabulary, and parental control. Or it may mean going to where adults have taken a critical look at themselves as, for example, to the clinic or the psychotherapy room. Wherever man is struggling mightily to make something of himself there is a fertile place for the researcher to be. (Maher, 1969, p. 131)

While one can agree in general with Kelly's prescription for identifying fertile sites for research, the methods that he espouses appear to be more nearly like those of Freud than of contemporary researchers in personality. And like other theorists of a clinical bent, Kelly would have had more pleasure in discovering that his theory had important and constructive implications for bringing about changes in people's lives than any amount of experimental, laboratory evidence could have provided him.

Comparisons

Leon Levy (1970), one of Kelly's students, makes a strong case against thinking in terms of *theories* of personality, on the grounds that what are currently called theories of personality are too loosely structured to qualify as theories and that theories of *personality* are unlikely ever to be achieved, because of the extraordinarily wide range of phenomena encompassed by the term. Levy believes that it is possible to develop theories about different aspects of personality, but an overall, integrative, coherent theory is beyond the realm of probability, if not possibility. What so-called personality theorists since Freud have provided is a set of *conceptions* of personality, "ways of thinking about human behavior that are bases for the development of a variety of methods of scientific research into these phenomena and theories about them" (Levy, 1970, p. 89). Levy also believes that little of either the research or the clinical techniques fostered by the various theories that have been proposed derives in any rigorous way from the propositions of the theories. Rather, the work is more or less consistent with the theories in the same way that a painting of unknown or disputed origin can be said to be "in the style of" some known artist.

In the estimation of this writer, Levy is quite correct, in his assessment of both the theories presented to date and the possibilities for theories in the future. Interestingly, Levy notes that it has been rare for any of the major personality theorists to label their own work as a theory of personality; in most instances it was someone else, often a disciple, who attached the label to the work. Kelly, however, did subtitle his book *A Theory of Personality,* so it is clear what he intended. The same is true of Rogers, who entitled a major presentation of his ideas *A Theory of Therapy, Personality, and Interpersonal Relationships* (1959). Both Kelly and Rogers have been among the few theorists—Rotter (1954) is another—to present their ideas in the form of basic postulates and corollaries (i.e., as formal systems), and for that they are to be commended. In so doing they have made clear much of what it is they assume, and their propositions can readily be examined for logical consistency, heuristic value, points of agreement with other theorists, and so on. However, in neither case do the propositions form a logically interrelated, coherent system. The corollaries do not follow from one another, do not obviously combine to form tight networks, and provide no basis for judging whether the system is complete—that is, whether all the corollaries that are needed within the system are stated.

On the other hand, when one compares Kelly's presentation of his theory with those of other major theorists, it is at least reasonably impressive in the precision with which it is stated, in the care and completeness with which terms are defined or elaborated, and in the internal logic with which each proposition is developed. Kelly was a precise man, perhaps understandably so, in view of his early interests in mathematics and engineering. Moreover, Kelly was not tender-minded about science and the place of his theory in science. He thoroughly intended for his theory to be constructed, and ultimately judged, in terms of the strongest tenets of the philosophy of science. Where some may think he failed, it was not for want of trying. For that reason his theory stands well above others in the explicitness with which it is presented and developed.

Still, one must recognize that if Kelly places well in the science competition, it is in part because some of the other possible competitors never really entered the game. Freud and other theorists of his era were thinking, working, and writing at a time when most of what we now take to be the philosophy of science and scientific methodology had scarcely been imagined, let alone thought through and systematized. Other theorists (e.g., Kurt Lewin, Gordon Allport) never set out to formulate a comprehensive and coherent theory of personality that would meet rigorous tests which might be imposed by critics. Still other theorists have tried rather less to develop a theory of personality than simply to develop a system of description of personality traits which might well be incorporated into any one of several actual theories.

Kelly's theory, perhaps alone among theories developed in the past 50 years, strives for real breadth and scope of the kind that Freud achieved. Even Rogers, for all his pretensions to a theory of "therapy, personality, and interpersonal relationships," did not try for the scope sought by Kelly. To begin with, Kelly, in presenting his theory of personality, really presents also the outlines at least of a theory of human thought and reasoning. It is clear that he did not believe that constructs would be coterminous with the domain of personality. *All* processes are psychologically channelized by the ways in which people anticipate and construe events, including the processes of medical diagnosis, decision making about the purchase of a new automobile, and the development of a theory called the psychology of personal constructs. Kelly's theory was reflexive in a way not even conceived by most theorists; for example, there is nothing in Rogerian theory, in Cattell's theory, or in Rotter's theory that gives a clue as to how the theory itself might have come about. This writer does remember a talk once given by B. F. Skinner in which he attempted to explain the origins of his own theory in terms of that theory; that is, how schedules of reinforcement and so on converged in such a way as to bring about the thoughts and habits that led to the production of his theory.

Beyond its reflexivity, however, Kelly's theory is extraordinary in the range of phenomena with which it aims to deal. Psychotherapy, dreams, moods, psychopathology, creativity, and suicide are indicative of the range of his thought and theorizing. And while not reaching quite the scope of Freud in his *Totem and Taboo* (1952) and *Civilization and Its Discontents* (1930), Kelly even had some thoughts about the cultural and societal phenomena that stemmed from his theory. Such breadth is rare and stands in stark contrast to most other modern theorists and to current trends toward more and more theorizing about narrower and narrower things. Perhaps Kelly pays the price of some degree of precision, but it is often helpful and comforting to be able to see the relationships between separate phenomena with which one is dealing.

Kelly's theory is richest in its clinical origins and implications, perhaps being considerably like Rogers in that respect. His theory is an attempt to deal with whole persons in life settings; it is explicitly opposed to approaches that attempt to represent persons by a set of dimensions which add up to considerably less than the whole person. Kelly might not reject out of hand the value of typical personality tests and the measurement of traits, but they would be regarded as of distinctly peripheral and limited interest, perhaps for what they might show about how a person would choose to present himself when forced to do so in someone else's terms. It is, in fact, difficult to see what the implications are of some approaches to personality. To describe a person in terms of a set of traits tells nothing about whether he ought to change, let alone the ways in which that change might be brought about. Kelly's views of personality come close to those of Allport in terms of the often-made distinction between the *idiographic* and *nomothetic* approach. Kelly's theory is oriented toward the understanding of the individual and his views of things and the choices he might make. That understanding is best achieved by study of the individual in his own terms rather than by comparisons with others on terms of presumed standards, but actually dubious meaning.

Most people who think about personality would probably agree that it is the *self* that is the central issue and the focus of personality. It is an individual's sense of identity, of being himself and no one else, that is the starting point from which the study of personality begins.

Many personality theories deal not at all with the sense of identity, trait theories being especially notable instances but some social learning approaches being especially limited. The individual, his self and his identity, is the focus of Kelly's theory, but his theory has the additional advantage, one not much shared, of providing for the inner view, the view of the world as seen by the person, as well as for the outer view of the person as he is seen by others. While a good portion of Kelly's work is consumed with considerations of the individual's view of the world, Kelly was by no means oblivious to the outer view. Fixed-role therapy, for example, is designed in part with the deliberate aim of changing the impression the client makes on others, and the Sociality Corollary states that one must be able to construe another person's point of view in order to relate in a role way to that person. Unlike most phenomenological theorists (e.g., Rogerian theory), personal constructs theory is not at all limited to comprehension of the individual's own view of the world.

Kelly's theory has been attacked by Bruner (1956) on the grounds that it ignores affect as an aspect of experience and behavior. Bruner alleges, in fact, that the theory is limited by reason of having been formulated largely out of Kelly's experiences with intelligent, articulate, and cognitively facile persons, mainly college students and faculty members. A perusal of the indices of several personality textbooks and sourcebooks on this writer's shelves reveals that neither *affect* nor *emotion* is often indexed as a topic covered in the books. Most writers on personality deal, as does Kelly, with such topics as anger and hostility, anxiety, and guilt, and to a lesser extent with some positive affective states, but little attention is paid in any of them to the phenomenology of affect or its origins. This writer would hazard the guess that most personologists take affect as an aspect of experience pretty much for granted, as not requiring any special consideration. Affect in personality is treated almost as much as a byproduct as ideation is considered to be by Skinnerian psychologists.

Kelly himself is not neglectful of affect and clearly thinks it to be inherent in the choices individuals make and in many nonverbal and preverbal constructs. The emphasis on cognition in personal constructs theory is somewhat illusory, since there is more than ample provision for constructs at low levels of awareness, those lacking in labels, and those with implicit poles, or whatever. Constructs may be symbolized in nonverbal terms or in vague and imprecise ways. However, Kelly admittedly wishes to push the model of man as an active, construing intellect to see how far it may take us, much as the model of "economic man" is pushed by economists, not as a literal image of the way people behave but as a model, a conception, to use Levy's terminology. Can we get along without the explicit formulation of strong affect that Bruner seems to press for? "Try it and see!" might well be Kelly's response.

A final critical point on which Kelly's theory differs from others is that it is ahistorical; the theory makes no provision for the development of construct systems. In that respect Kelly is clearly in the camp of Lewin and much like most phenomenologists, who argue that an individual's behavior at any given moment is determined by his view of things at that moment; how he came to that view is irrelevant. Kelly explicitly states, and makes it a central point in his therapy, that we need not be victims of our own biographies. Our prior experiences may explain how we have gotten ourselves where we are today, but those experiences do not account for where we will be tomorrow. To many psychologists it is something of a disappointment that personal constructs theory does not account for the origins of constructs and for differences between individuals in their construct systems. To Kelly the question was not of much interest, a position he affirmed strongly to this writer, who is among those disappointed at the lack of ontological perspective. To Kelly the preoccupation of psychoanalytic theorists with history and the insistent reversion to historical explanations was unfortunate and unproductive. From Kelly's perspective, every individual's development begins today!

Prospect

As stated earlier in this chapter, Kelly's theory seems to be being kept alive by fairly regular inclusion in textbooks devoted to personality theory. However, it scarcely seems likely that any theory can survive indefinitely without the infusion of new ideas and the thrust provided by new energies from converts. The psychology of personal constructs is not currently being elaborated and tested by empirical research or clinical practice, and there are no new names associated with Kelly's in the promulgation of the theory. It is not unimaginable that the theory will simply die out, to be remembered chiefly by historians of the field as an anomaly in the days of narrow theories based largely on laboratory phenomena of limited scope.

But what if the theory does survive by attracting the interest of a hard-working, brilliant young psychologist; what will it come to be? This writer expects that a way will be found to link an individual's personal constructs more directly to the choices he makes and, ultimately, to his behavior and the impact he has on others. By taking into account the dimensions along which the individual's choices are construed to lie, considerably more accurate predictions should be possible than can be made by other approaches. Additional improvement in understanding, and in the theory itself, can come about through taking into account the constructs an individual applies to aspects of himself and his environment other than persons. For example, knowing what choices an individual sees in a set of situations may add considerably to the knowledge involved in choices about persons. It is not immediately apparent just how constructs may be linked to behavior (if it were, someone would have done it), but one line of investigation of seeming promise is a more careful study of the views that people have of the choices, of the behavioral alternatives that face them at any given time. Most efforts at studying behavior have concentrated, perhaps overly much, on the more or less objective characteristics of behavior, without consideration of its meaning to the actor. Knowing that a person sees his alternatives at a given moment as behaving in either a hostile or a friendly manner is not enough; it is also important to know what behaviors are seen as being hostile and what are regarded as friendly.

Probably the most interesting research stemming from Kelly's theory has been the work on *sociality*, the ability of people to play roles with respect to one another (1955, pp. 32–34). There is, in this writer's view, an excellent chance that more intensive investigation of the relationships between people and the ways those relationships relate to personal construct systems would have a good payoff. Here is an area in which Kelly's ideas might be elaborated into spheres of group relationships and perhaps even international understanding. For example, it appears that Americans tend to apply the construct *freedom–slavery* to a great many governmental actions, while Russians may view the same actions in terms of *order–chaos* (cf. Smith, 1976). Perhaps it should not be surprising that the two countries disagree so strongly on so many issues.

Another promising area of research, and one which would have distinct theoretical implications, is study of the conditions under which people are likely to decide to elaborate rather than to seek further definition of their construct systems. The two responses would seem to be mutually incompatible, and both are likely to be important over the long run. However, in order to comprehend an individual over a briefer time span, it would seem necessary to know whether that individual was at the point of seeking to elaborate his system so as to take into account new phenomena or so as to reorganize a group of constructs by a higher, superordinate construct, or whether he was about to seek further and tighter definition of his system. Theoretically, anxiety, being a loss or lack of structure, would seem to call for tighter definition, while boredom should lead to elaboration, but those are only hypotheses remaining to be tested, along with many others.

Finally, a substantial extension and elaboration of Kelly's ideas about clinical practice would seem to be a virtual certainty if active interest in his theory emerges. The theory was firmly based in ideas about the practice of clinical psychology, and it was directed specifically to clinical applications. Fixed-role therapy is an especially salient and unique contribution to psychotherapy practice, even though it has as yet been little explored. There are many reasons for thinking that fixed-role therapy *ought* to work, at least to some extent, and it deserves experimental testing. However, as we suggested earlier, fixed-role therapy has received disproportionate attention; many of Kelly's other ideas about diagnosis and therapy are likely to have greater importance in

the long run, and many of them are just as novel. A good example is Kelly's discussion of the use that can be made by an accomplished therapist of alternative loosening and tightening of parts of the construct system, to enable a client to explore effectively the alternatives open to him.

Whether any of the above developments will ever come to pass is quite difficult to say at this point. It will require an insightful commitment from a careful thinker and researcher and a devoted clinician to bring much of it to fruition. The combination is rare.

Annotated Bibliography

Primary Sources

Kelly, G. A. *The Psychology of Personal Constructs: A Theory of Personality* (2 vols.). New York: W. W. Norton, 1955.

This is the first and basic presentation of Kelly's theory and its applications. Volume 1 sets forth the basic assumptions and propositions constituting the theory; gives Kelly's views of the clinical setting in which the theory must prove itself; describes the major assessment procedures, the Role Construct Repertory Test and the Self-Characterization; and presents fixed-role therapy as a fundamental clinical derivative of personal constructs theory. The final two chapters of the first volume discuss the basic diagnostic and clinical dimensions employed in the theory. The second volume of the set goes into considerable detail concerning Kelly's views about various clinical problems and ways of dealing with them. Several chapters deal with assessment for psychotherapeutic intervention; others deal with types of problems and psychopathology; and five chapters are devoted to various aspects of psychotherapy. The first three chapters of Volume 1, which present the basic theory, are available as a separate publication from W. W. Norton:

Kelly, G. A. *A Theory of Personality*. New York: W. W. Norton, 1963.

Maher, B. (Ed.). *Clinical Psychology and Personality: The Selected Papers of George Kelly*. New York: John Wiley, 1969.

This book is a posthumously published group of Kelly's papers, most of which were previously unpublished. The book includes a brief biography. One of Kelly's best papers in terms of its contribution to a further understanding of his position is the initial one, "Ontological Acceleration." The book also includes some papers of a rather personal sort which can give the discerning, careful reader some grounds for understanding Kelly as a person and how he came to his views, and some papers indicative of Kelly's views about science and research methodology. Additional papers elaborate on Kelly's views about his theory and clinical practice, and the volume also includes his paper presenting the results of a nonparametric factor analysis of his and several other theorists' views of the same clinical case.

Secondary Sources

Bannister, D. *Perspectives in Personal Construct Theory*. New York: Academic Press, 1970.

This book consists of a series of 12 essays, two being previously unpublished papers by Kelly, and ten being written for this volume by a diverse lot of English, Canadian, and American psychologists and philosophers. The essays are cogent, and several are quite helpful in furthering understanding of George Kelly and his theory.

Bannister, D., & Fransella, F. *Inquiring man: the psychology of personal constructs*. Baltimore: Penguin Books, 1971.

A brief and very readable introduction to Kelly's theory, with consideration of Kelly's views and the implications of the theory for such fields as social psychology, behavior therapy, and schizophrenic thought disorder.

Bannister, D., & Mair, J. M. M. *The Evaluation of Personal Constructs*. New York: Academic Press, 1968.

These authors do an unusually good job of summarizing personal constructs theory and of clarifying and elaborating some of the more obscure points. The remainder of the book is devoted to reviews of research on Kelly's theory and on the RCRT in particular. The book will be especially helpful to those who wish to employ the RCRT for clinical purposes or for research.

Levy, L. *Conceptions of Personality*. New York: Random House, 1970.

This book, by one of Kelly's students, is one of the most thoughtful and insightful books on personality in recent memory. Levy presents the reasons why he believes it incorrect to think in terms of "theories" of personality, preferring "conceptions" as better representing what he thinks are merely different approaches to the problems of personality. Levy places personal constructs theory among the "cognitive-perceptual approaches" to personality, but he shows that there are numerous other connections between Kelly's ideas and those of other persons who have written about personality, including many who are not usually accorded the status of theorist but who are, nonetheless, important.

Rychlak, J. "The Psychology of Personal Constructs: George A. Kelly." In J. Rychlak (Ed.), *Introduction to Personality and Psychotherapy* (pp. 471–499). Boston: Houghton Mifflin, 1973.

Another unusually thoughtful writer about personality who studied under Kelly, Rychlak presents one of the better summaries of Kelly's theory and

manages at the same time to present some insights and clarifications. Unlike many other presentations of Kelly's theory, Rychlak's delves into its implications for clinical matters, including both psychopathology and therapy.

References

Bannister, D. *Perspectives in personal construct theory*. New York: Academic Press, 1970.

Bannister, D., & Fransella, F. *Inquiring man: the theory of personal constructs*. Baltimore: Penguin Books, 1971.

Bannister, D., & Mair, J. *The evaluation of personal constructs*. New York: Academic Press, 1968.

Bieri, J. Complexity-simplicity as a personality variable in cognitive and preferential behavior. In D. W. Fiske and S. Maddi (Eds.), *Functions of varied experience*. Homewood, Ill.: Dorsey Press, 1961.

Bonarius, J. Research in the personal construct theory of George A. Kelly. In B. Maher (Ed.), *Progress in experimental personality research* (Vol. 2). New York: Academic Press, 1965.

Bruner, J. You are your constructs. *Contemporary Psychology*, 1956, *1*, 355–357.

Festinger, L. *A theory of cognitive dissonance*. Evanston, Ill.: Row, Peterson, 1957.

Freud, S. *Civilization and its discontents*. New York: W. W. Norton, 1930.

Freud, S. *Totem and taboo*. New York: W. W. Norton, 1952.

Hinkle, D. *The change of personal constructs from the viewpoint of a theory of implications*. Unpublished doctoral dissertation, Ohio State University, 1965.

Jones, R. *Identification in terms of personal constructs*. Unpublished doctoral dissertation, Ohio State University, 1954.

Jones, R. E. Identification in terms of personal constructs. *Journal of Consulting Psychology*, 1961, *25*, 276.

Kelly, G. A. *The psychology of personal constructs: A theory of personality* (2 vols.). New York: W. W. Norton, 1955.

Kelly, G. A. Ontological acceleration. In B. Maher (Ed.), *Clinical psychology and personality: The selected papers of George Kelly* (pp. 7–45). New York: Wiley, 1969.

Kelly, G. A. *A brief introduction to personal construct theory*. Unpublished manuscript, Brandeis University, 1966.

Kieferle, D., & Sechrest, L. Effects of alterations in personal constructs. *Journal of Psychological Studies*, 1961, *12*, 173–178.

Landfield, A., & Nawas, M. Psychotherapeutic improvement as a function of communication and adoption of therapists' values. *Journal of Counseling Psychology*, 1964, *11*, 336–341.

Levy, L. *A study of relative information value in personal construct theory*. Unpublished doctoral dissertation, Ohio State University, 1954.

Levy, L. *Conceptions of personality: Theories and research.* New York: Random House, 1970.

Maher, B. (Ed.). *Clinical psychology and personality: The selected papers of George Kelly.* New York: Wiley, 1969.

Messick, S. M., & Kogan, N. Personality consistencies in judgment: Dimensions of role constructs. *Multivariate Behavioral Research*, 1966, *1*, 165–175.

Nawas, M., & Landfield, A. Improvement in psychotherapy and adoption of therapist's meaning system. *Psychological Reports*, 1963, *13*, 97–98.

Ourth, L., & Landfield, A. Interpersonal meaningfulness and nature of termination in psychotherapy. *Journal of Counseling Psychology*, 1965, *12*, 336–371.

Payne, D. E. *Role constructs versus part constructs and interpersonal understanding.* Unpublished doctoral dissertation, Ohio State University, 1956.

Pedersen, F. *A consistency study of the RCRT.* Unpublished MA thesis, Ohio State University, 1958.

Poch, S. *Study of changes in personal constructs as related to interpersonal prediction and its outcomes.* Unpublished doctoral dissertation, Ohio State University, 1952.

Rogers, C. A theory of therapy, personality, and interpersonal relationships, as developed in the client-centered framework. In S. Koch (Ed.), *Psychology: A study of a science* (Vol. 3, pp. 184–256). New York: McGraw-Hill, 1959.

Rotter, J. *Social learning and clinical psychology.* New York: Prentice-Hall, 1954.

Sechrest, L. Stimulus equivalents of the psychotherapist. *Journal of Individual Psychology*, 1962, *18*, 172–176.

Sechrest, L. The psychology of personal constructs: George Kelly. In J. Wepman & R. Heine (Eds.), *Concepts of personality* (pp. 206–233). Chicago: Aldine Press, 1963.

Sechrest, L. Personal constructs and personal characteristics. *Journal of Individual Psychology*, 1968, *24*, 162–166.

Shoemaker, D. *Personal constructs and interpersonal predictions.* Unpublished doctoral dissertation, Ohio State University, 1955.

Smith, H. *The Russians.* New York: Quadrangle Books, 1975.

Thomas, W. I., & Thomas, D. S. *The child in America.* New York: Alfred Knopf, 1928.

Warren, N. (Ed.). *The theory and methodology of George Kelly.* Report of proceedings of a symposium on construct theory and repertory grid methodology held at Brunel College, London, 1964.

Wicklund, R., & Brehm, J. *Explorations in cognitive dissonance* (2nd ed.). Hillsdale, N.J.: Erlebaum & Associates, in press.

Williams, T. G., & Sechrest, L. The ascribed usability of personal constructs as a function of their generality. *Journal of Psychological Studies*, 1963, *14*, 75–81.

Existential psychology views the person as a biological, social, and psychological being whose primary task is the search for and establishment of meaning. This distinctively human endeavor goes on within a spatial/temporal context, confronted with limitations such as past experiences, environmental conditions, and the exercise of freedom by others. According to existential psychology, the power of man's consciousness and freedom, and the associated activities of decision making, value postulating, and goal setting, allow the creative and responsible manipulation of these limitations.

The specifically psychological adaptation of this existential view of human nature, originally found in the philosophies of Sören Kierkegaard, Martin Heidegger, Jean-Paul Sartre, William James, Karl Jaspers, and Paul Tillich, begins most notably with the work of the Swiss psychiatrist Ludwig Binswanger (1881–1966), who reacted against the mechanistic psychology of Freud. Other important figures who continue this extension of existential philosophical insights to psychological problems are Medard Boss, Viktor Frankl, Rollo May, R. D. Laing, Eugene Gendlin, and Salvatore Maddi.

Existential personality theory describes two basic personalities. The *authentic* person realizes fully in his behaviors the core existential assumptions about human nature. He exercises vigorously the psychological needs or functions of symbolization, imagination, and judgment and allows these to influence his biological and social experiences. He is well integrated and demonstrates originality and change. Having accepted the givens of his past and present, his basic orientation is toward the future and its associated uncertainty. Uncertainty leads him to experience anxiety, but he accepts this anxiety as a necessary concomitant of vigorous living. He is aided in this acceptance by courage.

The *inauthentic* person, in contrast, inhibits the expression of distinctively human psychological needs; he sees himself as a player of predetermined social roles and the embodiment of biological needs. His behavior is fragmentary and stereotyped and often includes exploitation of others, a rigidly materialistic attitude, and feelings of worthlessness and insecurity. He fears the uncertainty of the future; shrinking from it, he defines himself solely in terms of his past or present, in spite of resultant feelings of guilt and regret.

Existential psychologists discuss how one can get from the inauthentic to the authentic mode of being, from both a psychotherapeutic and a developmental perspective. For them, personality change is an issue across the entire life span and results from the interaction of psychological, social, and biological-physical factors.

Existential Personality Theory

Suzanne C. Kobasa and
Salvatore R. Maddi

Introduction

Existential thinking is at the same time popular and misunderstood. The bases for its popularity are clear. In the midst of the spiritual bankruptcy of modern times, it extends hope not only for psychological survival but even for dignity. Without failing in sympathy for human agonies, it contends that a person can take hold of her or his own life and shape it through an active process of decision making. The existential approach encourages the deepening of consciousness and disentanglement from superficial conventions of society leading to growth in individuality. It counters prevailing views of the human as irrational and impotent and provides a rationale for attempting social change rather than passively adjusting to the status quo. Far from being empty theorizing, it offers psychotherapeutic help as well.

It is not surprising that there should be considerable misunderstanding of the existential approach. One reason for this misunderstanding is that several disciplines or professions are independently involved in developing existential thought. Philosophy has made by far the most rigorous intellectual contributions. Perhaps because of this, psychology and psychiatry have overrestricted themselves to practical applications. Also involved in articulating existential views are writers, dramatists, and film makers; literary, drama, and art critics; sociologists and political scientists. Each profession has its own characteristic vocabulary, emphases, aims, methods, and standards of rigor. There have also been differences in viewpoint about existentialism within each of these professions. No single person or close-knit group has yet dominated existential thought to shape it into a unitary movement. This is true even in philosophy, though the major figures in existentialism have come from that discipline. Popular misconceptions of existentialism stem primarily from this heterogeneity. One person may have read only a bit of existential social criticism, another only the works of one philosopher, a third may have only undergone existential psychotherapy. Each person will have a one-sided view of existentialism but will imagine that he has understood all.

Specifically because of the problem of heterogeneity, the main aim of this chapter will be integrative. It is not sufficient to provide only a lucid summary. The many diversified contributions to existential thought require combination and transposition into a set of coherent and systematic statements about personality. In this attempt to present a coherent existential theory of personality, the work of Ludwig Binswanger will be highlighted. Though hardly the founder or even the principal spokesman of this movement, he did concern himself primarily with the implications of existential thought for personality. This is seen in his theoretical writings and in his application of an existential emphasis in psychotherapy. However, it will be necessary to consider other persons as well as Binswanger to do justice to the existential corpus.

In the pages that follow, a distinct and coherent theory of personality will emerge. The image of the ideal person to be developed is one uncontrolled by others yet socially responsible, sensitive to self yet disciplined, cognizant of life's difficulties yet courageous, individualistic yet capable of intimacy. The emphasis is on personality in a continual process of development. Nonideal persons and their development will also be made understandable. The theory discussed will articulate a technique of psychotherapy, and will be precise enough to serve as a springboard to systematic research.

Most existentialists employ a distinctive vocabulary and style of writing. There are sections in Heidegger and Sartre, for example, which are so highly idiosyncratic in choice of terminology that they seem to demand a special dictionary of existential terms. A deliberate attempt is made in this chapter to define these terms straightforwardly, using simple language. However, like the original sources for the existential vocabulary, this chapter requires the reader to pay close attention to the context or theoretical network within which the terms appear. Recognizing this, but also appreciating the reader's possible need for an easy reference guide, some frequently used existential terms are defined here:

Aesthetic. An inauthentic orientation to self and world characterized by: (1) an emphasis upon the pleasure to be derived from the present, and an attempt to deny the necessary integration of the present with past and future; and (2) a giving over of control of and responsibility for actions to accident or fate. This orientation is similar to the more familiar hedonism.

Authenticity. That form of human behavior which existentialists consider ideal, consisting of the individual's responsible exercise of his powers of awareness and decision making.

Being-for-itself (Sartre), *Dasein* (Heidegger). That mode of existence distinctive to the human being which is never static but is always in the process of revealing new things about itself and its world through decision making as a vehicle for creating meaning.

Daseinsanalysis (Binswanger, Boss). That form of psychotherapy committed to an understanding of the person as continuously involved in the creating and attributing of meaning to himself, others, and his environment.

Facticity. The given facts of a person's existence over which he cannot have total control; examples include physical stature, environmental resources, demands made by employers or teachers, and the inevitability of death.

Fundamental project. The primary choice or orientation about life and one's participation in it which underlies and informs all of the person's other decisions.

Idealistic. An inauthentic orientation to self and world which seeks to deny all of the necessary conflict and limitation in human living through allegiance to one immutable principle or goal.

Possibility. All that a person has not yet become but could be, through active use of his powers of awareness and decision making; that human ability to surpass or transcend limitations which mitigates or seeks alternatives to the specific facticity of each person's life.

History

Precursors

The roots of existential personality theory naturally are found in existential philosophy, a movement which entails a reaction against prior emphases on the impersonal world of nature and its objective order, forces, and essences. Instead, existential philosophy takes the human being, with his or her subjective perceptions, thoughts, feelings, decisions, and acts, as its starting point. In this emphasis on understanding existence concretely realized, existential philosophy adopts a subject matter similar to that of psychology.

The first and perhaps most complete existential philosophy was developed by Sören Kierkegaard (1813–1855). His work was a reaction against the kind of philosophy, best exemplified by Hegel, which attempted to construct a grand view of the universe supported by some external absolute in which the human was a pas-

sive participant. In throwing the serenity of this view into doubt, Kierkegaard focused upon the subjective life of the person. Regarding inner experience as the true reality, he provided an articulate portrayal of such human subjective phenomena as decision making, responsibility, guilt, anxiety, and alienation. He conceptualized the person's life as a series of necessary decisions.

When a person contemplates making a decision in the direction that will change him by throwing him into an unknown future, he experiences anxiety. Persisting in the face of anxiety and choosing to change regardless of circumstances is considered by existentialists as the way of growth and development, with individuality as its reward. Turning away from anxiety and holding on to the status quo is the way of stagnation, with a steady accumulation of guilt which finally constitutes despair (Kierkegaard, 1944, 1954).

Kierkegaard (1959, 1968) provided vivid descriptions of what amount to personality types, or modes of experiencing. The aesthetic, ethical, and religious lifestyles were presented as stages in the development toward maturity. Consistent with his whole approach, emphasizing change and subjectivity, Kierkegaard (1954, p. 173) defined personality as "a synthesis of possibility and necessity." However, common though these ideas may seem now, it should be remembered that Kierkegaard was thereby branded a heretic and ostracized by polite society.

Not many years later, William James (1842–1910), Karl Jaspers (1883–1969), and Paul Tillich (1886–1965) advocated a related view of life as struggle. In the subjectivist tradition, James portrayed the world as a chaos that can only be given order by persons through interpretive actions. The strenuousness of this view of life was echoed by Jaspers in his discussion of "limit situations" which presented the person with conflicts unresolvable in familiar and well-exercised ways. Tillich emphasized how life of necessity was in the grips of anxiety over the human's frail ability to control events. All three philosophers conceptualized a generalized attitude or mode of functioning to help persons meet these life challenges. For James, it was the "strenuous mood," for Jaspers, "transcendence," and for Tillich, "courage." The common element in these views is that as life is by its nature chaotic and threatening, the person lives it best if he recognizes the challenge and responds forthrightly.

Martin Heidegger (1889–1976) provided a thorough analysis of human existence which, though conducted on an abstract philosophical level, contains much that can be interpreted psychologically. Heidegger (1962) described essential conditions of human nature, and, through his concept of *Jemeinigkeit*, or *each-to-his-own-ness*, posited characteristics which differentiate among individuals. Heidegger distinguished *Das man* (conventional or herd mentality) from *Dasein* (ability to reach high levels of consciousness and uniqueness through reflecting upon oneself, others, and the natural world).

The mode of experiencing known as *Dasein* is the special glory of the human being, though it brings with it such discomforting states as anxiety and confrontation with death. Such states are regarded as developmentally valuable, because they spur consciousness and activeness in constructing one's life. *Dasein* can also mediate positive states, such as caring. In this case, caring is not a passive comfort but rather an active, involving, and strenuous matter which takes into account the needs and resources of one's self, one's environment, and the other.

Very definitely a 20th-century figure, Jean-Paul Sartre (1905–   ) emphasizes psychological as much as philosophical considerations. Sartre (1956) criticizes Freudian psychology for viewing the person as the object of the therapist's manipulation, as a static collection of objectively defined inner drives, and as ruled by unconscious forces. In Sartre's sharply contrasting existential view, the person's behavior is determined by his subjective goals which define his "fundamental project" or overall purpose in life. Through the exercise of choice guided by this fundamental project, the person creates meaning and consciousness of what he is and is not. In this manner, the person is continually changing and developing. With this emphasis, it is understandable that Sartre was critical of the Freudian reliance on conceptualizing the person as unconscious of the biological and social forces that supposedly rule him.

For Sartre, a belief in the unconscious provides one with a ready excuse for failure to take responsibility to create one's own meaning and directions through exercise of choice. This failure to exercise choice amounts to irresponsibility, inauthenticity, or *bad faith*. Although Sartre is sometimes seen as a pessimistic existentialist, a good deal of his work involves evangelistic attempts to influence people to exercise choice and thereby achieve authenticity and individuality.

The philosophers mentioned have provided the primary sources for contemporary existential psychology. Among other less directly relevant philosophers are:

1. Friedrich Nietzsche (1844–1900), who emphasized subjective meaning but celebrated the irrational more than the others.
2. Martin Buber (1878–1965), who combined an existential with a Jewish Hasidic perspective, emphasizing interpersonal intimacy and commitment.
3. Gabriel Marcel (1889–   ), whose work is characterized by a strongly theistic conception of the universe.
4. Albert Camus (1913–1960), who pessimistically emphasized the absurdity of attempting to discern meaning in a meaningless world.
5. Edmund Husserl (1859–1938), who provided for existentialism the useful methodology of phenomenology.
6. Miguel de Unamuno (1864–1936) and Nikolai Berdyaev (1874–1948), who adapted existential doctrines to their own cultural contexts in Spain and Russia.

Beginnings

The first three quarters of the 20th century have unfolded in ominous fashion. Ever larger and more destructive wars, the rise of technology concomitant with deemphasis on humanistic enterprises, and corruption in social institutions once considered inviolable have shaken beliefs in traditional, familial, and religious values. Thoughtful persons, in ever-increasing numbers, have begun to question social institutions and look within themselves for grounding and understanding. This dilemma of existence has been fertile ground for the popularization of existential philosophy and its development into personality theory and psychotherapeutic practices.

Perhaps the most influential person in the rise of existential psychology was Ludwig Binswanger (1881–1966). He received a medical degree from the University of Zurich, studied with Carl Jung, and had a psychiatric internship under Eugene Bleuler. In 1911, Binswanger succeeded his father as medical director of the Sanatorium Bellevue in Kreuzlingen, Switzerland. There he specialized in the treatment of psychotics and continued in this work even after his retirement in 1956. Throughout his professional life, Binswanger strove to translate the philosophical concepts of existentialism into a theory of personality which would conceptualize individual differences and psychopathology. Basic to his work was the notion that existential concepts could be useful in identifying and curing mental illness. Showing clearly his debt to Heidegger, Binswanger called his technique of psychotherapy *Daseinsanalyse*, or analysis of the human capability of giving meaning to existence.

Just as Kierkegaard reacted against Hegel's assumption of an objective, impersonal order, Binswanger rejected Freud's belief in unchangeable biological (instincts) and social (protection of the common good) forces. Some of Binswanger's earliest existential formulations appear in a small book entitled *Freud: Reminiscences of a Friendship* (1957). This work questions many central contentions in psychoanalysis, rather than constituting the manifesto linking the Freudian theory of human nature with clinical practice, which Binswanger claims was Freud's assignment for him. Binswanger was particularly critical of Freud's biological emphasis, especially the slighting by psychoanalysis of spiritual elements in philosophy and religion. Freud was also attacked by Binswanger for his mechanistic approach, which left little room for recognizing a person's quest for meaning and construction of his own life through responsible decision making. In a clever argument, Binswanger contended that Freud could never have created the theory and practice of psychoanalysis had his view of the person as ruled by the unconscious and driven by biological forces been true.

Binswanger's (1963) most important and best elaborated theoretical contribution is his discussion of the *existential a priori*, or *fundamental meaning structure*. This concept refers to the universal and unlearned human ability to perceive specific meanings in the world of events and to transcend any concrete situation on the basis of that attributed meaning. The existential a priori associated with a unique individual is a kind of recognizable meaning matrix which, when imposed on reality, allows the distinctive style and life direction of the person to emerge. Like Sartre's fundamental project, the individual's existential a priori underlies all of his choices and gives them their particular form.

Medard Boss (1903–), Binswanger's fellow Swiss who was less a disciple than a colleague, was involved in a similar personological enterprise. Also a physician, Boss served as director of the Institute of Daseinsanalytic Therapy and professor in the medical school at the University of Zurich. Like Binswanger, Boss named his approach *Daseinsanalyse*, derived his interpretations from the works of Heidegger and other existentialists, and criticized Freud for imposing invented abstractions (e.g., instincts) and categories (e.g., the Oedipal complex) upon human actions. For Boss, fantasies, emotions, thoughts, and body organs exist not as separate and static phenomena but rather as a complex and dynamic unity. According to Boss, "the essential structure of man is to be defined as none other than his possible modes of being" (Binswanger, 1963, pp. 20–21). His emphasis is on the construction of personality and individual life through the active investing of events with meaning and decision making which guides action.

Following Heidegger and paralleling Binswanger, Boss (1963) outlines attributes common to all persons, or *existentialia*, and emphasizes individual differences in content and effectiveness of various constructions of self and world which he encountered in clinical practice.

Despite the apparent abstractness of their concepts, Binswanger and Boss are at their best when describing and illuminating case histories. Unfortunately, they were less gifted, or perhaps less interested, in the careful development of a theory of personality. Perhaps both were inhibited from theory development by the vehemence of their reaction to Freud's formalism. The intense concern with the practical activity of psychotherapy may also have distracted them from theoretical tasks. In any event, in neither Binswanger's nor Boss's writings is the interrelationship among their concepts really clear. Nor are relationships between the concepts and laboratory or natural observations always apparent. Consequently, it is difficult to discern how the concepts of these existential psychologists could be tested and further developed through empirical research.

Current Status

No group of followers gathered around Binswanger or Boss. Although the work of both men gained some popularity in Europe during the 1930s, it was only in the late 1950s that their existential writings were translated and read in America. Interest in these writings continued through the early 1960s but now appears to be waning. This decline in interest does not signify a decrease in the influence of existential thinking; rather it indicates a transfer of attention to later existential psychologists more concerned with problems of broad socoiopolitical importance and more willing to be systematic in theorizing about personality.

Contemporary existential thinkers have been influenced as much by Binswanger and Boss as by the earlier philosophers. From the philosophers, they learned the importance of considering the ultimate purpose of human life and have adopted the view that the person creates his own meaning through decision-making and action in the pursuit of possibility. From Binswanger and Boss, they accepted the task of theorizing about psychotherapy. Inevitably, this has required them to consider how and why persons fail to realize ultimate existential fulfillment.

Rollo May is noteworthy not only for his psychological discussions of important existential experiences such as anxiety (May, 1953), love (May, 1967), and power (May, 1972), but also for his introduction of other existential works to the American audience (May, 1950; May, Angel, & Ellenberger, 1958). Although May's primary work has been as a training analyst at the William Alanson White Institute in New York City, he has championed the interdisciplinary nature of existentialism. His books tend to be filled with philosophical and theological references as well as clinical experiences. In an early work, May (*The Meaning of Anxiety*, 1950) developed a lucid approach to personality showing the heavy influence of Tillich (who was his teacher), Binswanger, and Heidegger.

Viktor Frankl (1905-   ) has taught in the medical school and directed the Neurological Polyclinic at the University of Vienna. After being influenced early in his career by Freudian thought, Frankl shifted to existentialism in his attempt to come to grips with the shattering experience of being imprisoned in a World War II concentration camp (Frankl, 1963). He observed that those who did not survive these camps had only conventional meaning to sustain them and had not sufficiently practiced in their lives the human capability of creating one's own individual meaning which existential psychology emphasizes. Out of these insights, he developed a technique of treatment called *Logotherapy*, in which the person is encouraged to ferret out what is meaningful for him in a seemingly indifferent and meaningless world.

Meaning, for Frankl (1965), is expressed through three types of values: *experiential values* (those realized through receptive being in the world); *creative values* (those realized through direct action in the world); and *attitudinal values* (those whose actualization is dependent only upon the person's consciousness and is possible even when the expression of experiential and creative values is blocked). This categorization of values provides an interesting way of distinguishing among persons. Unfortunately, Frankl offers little else to systematic and rigorous theorizing about personality.

The British psychiatrist R. D. Laing (1927–   ) began his formulation of existential psychology while at the Tavistock Clinic in London. His first book (Laing, 1960) is an attempt to apply the philosophy of Sartre in the description and treatment of psychosis. In this, Laing has been acclaimed for an appropriate psychological counterpart of Thomas Szasz's (1961) more sociological critique of psychiatric practice. Maintaining what he calls a strict phenomenological approach, Laing claims that schizophrenia can only be understood from the perspective of the person experiencing it. He accuses the families of patients, the psychiatric establishment, and society in general of failing phenomenologically to understand psychosis and of imposing their own categories and biases on the person diagnosed as schizophrenic. For Laing, misunderstandings and mismanagement lead to prolonging the patient's suffering. Although full of radical implications for psychotherapy, Laing's writings lack the psychological emphasis, precision, and clarity for further elaboration of existential theory.

With a background in both philosophy and psychology, Eugene Gendlin (1928–) combines clinical sensitivity with conceptual sophistication. A professor at the University of Chicago, Gendlin (1962) seeks to construct a new vocabulary to overcome the thought/feeling or mind/body distinction which existentialists have found objectionable. Important is the concept of *felt meaning*, or the intuitive sense of understanding, clarity, or directionality which arises when the person has put aside conventionalities and focuses upon his inner experience. He also attempts to provide a terminology within which personality change can be seen as the rule rather than the exception. Gendlin is also heavily influenced by Rogerian thought, which causes him to deviate from the main tradition of existentialism.

Also a professor at the University of Chicago, Salvatore R. Maddi (1933–) has made recent contributions to existential thought which reflect his concerns with the empirical testing of academic psychology, without losing the emphasis on usefulness and relevancy stemming from psychotherapeutic concerns. Maddi's writings (1967, 1970, 1975b) show clear influence of Kierkegaard, Tillich, Frankl and James, as well as his recognition of what existential psychology requires to become a viable theory of personality. Maddi's use of existential concepts in systematic research (e.g., Maddi, Kobasa, & Hoover, 1976); his formulation of existential personality types (e.g., Maddi, 1970); and his conceptualization of development across the life cycle, focusing on existential matters like the growth-facilitating effects of the acceptance of death (Maddi, 1975a), show his concern for practicality and theoretical rigor.

The impact of existentialism as an approach to understanding personality can be assessed in several ways. It appears to have sustained a good reception among lay readers since the late 1950s. There seems no diminution in the works of fiction and art formulated from an existential perspective. Less impressive is the impact of existential thinking on the professions of psychology and psychiatry. The number of psychologists and psychiatrists claiming to be existential is small. There are virtually no full-fledged programs of graduate study in existential psychology in this country (though one can get some

training in this approach at the University of Saskatchewan, the University of Chicago, Duquesne University, or the William Alanson White Foundation). Over the past three years, there have been some empirical studies (to be discussed in the Evaluation section) which have attempted to operationalize the study of existential concepts. There also appears to be a growing personological interest in existentially relevant variables like decision making and planfulness (e.g., Mischel, 1973).

Similar Theories

The work of the existential psychologists constitutes a distinctive approach to personality and psychotherapy. There are, however, certain similarities with other approaches which it would be useful to describe.

Binswanger and Boss were certainly not the only personologists in Europe initially influenced by Freud who later broke away to form their own views. There are similarities between existential psychology and these other views beyond their common rejected Freudian parenthood. Otto Rank's (1929, 1945) emphasis on the inevitable conflict between *fear of life* (separation, isolation) and *fear of death* (union, conventionality) is similar to the existentialist assumption that in life's necessary decisions, contemplating the choice of the future brings anxiety, and the status quo, guilt. In Rank's and the existentialists' positions, emphasis has shifted from biologically based concerns regarding sex and aggression toward a more mental or spiritual preoccupation with social and personal consequences of one's actions. But where Rank advocates minimizing fear of life and fear of death through artful compromise (e.g., being only as individualistic as can be managed without alienating others), existentialists insist that facing anxiety courageously and choosing the future brings greatest growth and maturity.

Carl Jung (1933, 1953), another great defector from Freudian psychoanalysis, also developed an approach considering the important dilemmas in life to be mental or spiritual. He regarded the achievement of *selfhood* to be the high point of humanness. In this, he shares an emphasis upon unconventionality as a mark of maturity with existentialists. But Jung regarded the *collective unconscious* (essences that have never been and can never be completely conscious) as the major wellspring of human vitality and creativity. Self-hood, according to Jung, is actually a blend of conscious and unconscious determinants of action, with the mystery that this entails being fully accepted by the person. There is no way in existentialism to construe unconscious determiners of action as indicators of maturity, and so here agreement with Jung ends. Also in disagreement with existentialism is Jung's advocacy of compromise to ease the inevitable conflict between the ego (or conscious self) and the collective unconscious.

A third great Freudian critic was Alfred Adler, who emphasized striving toward perfection as more basic and important than sexuality. Adler (1927, 1956) shares with existentialism an emphasis upon the person's effective capacities in the face of difficult demands made upon him by his environment. In both views, the human's virtue is that he struggles and does so through exercise of will. Both Adler's and the existentialists' views reject Freud for failing to conceive of the person as capable of determining his future and that of his society through his own decision making and initiative. In the striving for perfection, considerable individuality and consciousness are implied. Of all Freudian dissidents, Adler is closest to the existentialists. But there are differences in emphasis. In delineating personal and social perfection, Adler relies more on preconceived notions of what is good than do the existentialists. Adler regards certain concrete content characteristics of personality (e.g., goals of service and productivity) and society (e.g., the social institution of marriage) to be invariably worthwhile for everyone. Thus, although Adler emphasizes the person's trajectory into the future as important in evaluating his maturity, it is a rather more specified and determined future than existentialists accept. Although existentialists agree that the person has responsibilities to himself (e.g., to exercise decision making capabilities) and to society (e.g., to care intimately for others), they do not regard any particular life arrangements, determined in advance of the person's experience of them, to be the best ones to aim at. Adler's emphasis upon striving for perfection would seem in some degree inauthentic to the existentialist, who would prefer the connotations of searching for meaning.

In the contemporary United States, existentialism is usually classed with other similar views as a humanistic or third-force psychology. This is certainly a valid classification, in that humanistic approaches are opposed both to the Freudian emphasis on irrationality and the ruling tyranny of immutable biological and social forces, as well as to behavioristic emphasis on mindless subjugation to externally imposed reinforcements which rigidly control behavior. Existentialism joins with other third-force psychologies in emphasizing what is constructive, rational, and self-determined about human beings.

However, there is a distinction separating the actualization position (best exemplified by the theories of Carl R. Rogers and Abraham H. Maslow) from the main thrust of existential thought. For Rogers (1961) and Maslow (1954), development toward maturity takes place through actualization of inherent potentialities. The emphasis for them is making actual what is already present as potentiality. These potentialities, according to the theorists, actualize themselves fairly automatically as long as significant others and society refrain from restrictions or punitiveness toward the person. Very little operation of will, in the form of decision making for the future or courageousness in the face of fear of the unknown, is required. Indeed, according to Rogers and Maslow, the self-actualized or fully functioning person will have a generalized sense of well-being rather than an elaborate consciousness of self. *Conditions of worth* (Rogers, 1961), which could be paraphrased as ideals applied to one's own behavior, are regarded as forebodings of neuroticism by actualization theorists.

In contrast, the existential position advocates self-reflection and self-discipline as necessary if maturity is to be reached, because of the inherent difficulties posed by life. The person must create his own meaning, and this almost invariably requires disentangling oneself from the snares of comfortable but deadening conventionalities and official society. If the person can be so easily derailed by a little punishment and disapproval, how will he ever be able to face fear of the unknown courageously, and to change and grow? Indeed, social ostracism is one of the very things that makes the contemplation of choosing the future worrisome. In being courageous and disciplined, vivid consciousness regarding self and environment is an ally, not mere neuroticism, according to existential thinkers.

Assertions

Development

Most existential psychologists make assumptions about human nature (e.g., Binswanger, 1963, on *a priori conditions*; Boss, 1963, on *existentialia*; Maddi, 1976, on *core considerations*). The first nine assertions are a systematic categorization of what existentialists have said about universal, inherent aspects of humanness. Existential psychologists also consider how individuals come to differ from each other. The next seven assertions (10–16) depict developmental courses, emphasizing interactions that produce changes in personality across the life cycle.

1. PERSONALITY IS PRIMARILY
    CONSTRUCTED THROUGH THE PERSON'S
    ATTRIBUTION OF MEANING.

Human beings are distinctive in their ability to be consciously aware of themselves and the world around them. This involves more than simple perception. People tend, through the active use of their cognitive capabilities, to reflect on and to invest perceived events with meanings. Binswanger (1963) defines the human as the *being-in-the-world* who constitutes the possibility of meaning. The same point is made by Boss (1963), who characterizes *Dasein* (the distinctively human form of existence) as having responsibility for disclosing all forms of reality; and by Frankl (1963) and Maddi (1970), who refer to the search for meaning as the fundamental tendency in all persons.

It is this process of attributing meaning to self, others, and the environment that gives substance to another fundamental yet still more elusive characteristic of human nature—freedom. For existentialists, the terms *consciousness* and *freedom* are equivalent. In creating and recognizing meaning, the person is being free. Sartre (1956) highlights both aspects of the human task in his portrayal of the person as *being-for-itself*. For Sartre, the human is constantly in the process of creating himself and his world. The person, a being conscious of what he is and what he is not, has a never-completed character. His nature is

always changing and always disclosing something new about itself, its environment, and other persons. Sartre distinguishes this distinctively human sort of being from *being-in-itself*, which is complete and never changing. *Being-in-itself*, e.g., a rock, never has to face the task of creating meaning and freedom.

Although the human is essentially constituted as being-for-itself, some people attempt to deny this and aspire after the security of being-in-itself. Sartre calls this process man's attempt to become god. Simone de Beauvoir (1952) views the male in contemporary culture as more easily associated with being-for-itself, while the female is linked to being-in-itself. The degree to which particular persons actively engage in a search for meaning varies greatly. This will be demonstrated in the discussion of individual differences—the concern of the Maintenance section below. It should be kept in mind here that all persons have an inherent capacity for attributing meaning, and personality is an expression of this ability.

2. PERSONS ARE CHARACTERIZED BY
    SYMBOLIZATION, IMAGINATION, AND
    JUDGMENT.

This set of psychological functions directs the universal search for meaning. The explicit emphasis on these cognitive capabilities derives from Maddi's (1967, 1970) usage, but they are implied in the work of other existential psychologists. Symbolization involves the need for abstracting from concrete experience a representative category or idea. The more symbolization is exercised, the more categories there are with which events can be identified and classified. Imagination is the combining and recombining of ideas and categories in new ways, leading to conceptualization of change. Judgment involves assessing experiences with the result being values and preferences.

Much of this is implied in Binswanger's (1963) discussion of *Eigenwelt*, that form of being in which the person is primarily oriented to self. Looked at as a part of personality, *Eigenwelt* most directly reflects the personally or inwardly appreciated aspects of cognitive activities which create meaning. It would not be a misinterpretation to consider *Eigenwelt* a phenomenological sense of self, but it is a common misinterpretation to regard it as the only concern of existential psychology. It is crucial, from an existential perspective, that not only is the person conscious, he is conscious *of* something. The next two assertions clarify this "something."

3. PERSONS ARE CHARACTERIZED BY THEIR PARTICIPATION IN SOCIETY.

The search for meaning goes on in what Binswanger (1963) calls the *Mitwelt*, or the realm of interactions with others. This notion is found in Heidegger's (1962) *care*, Sartre's (1956) *being-for-others*, Boss's (1963) *trust*, and Maddi's (1967, 1970) *needs for contact and communication*. These writers grapple with the question of how a person can freely and responsibly establish meaning for himself and his world while necessarily interacting with the many others involved in the same task. The question of how one's meaning attribution can avoid interfering with that of another person is dealt with.

Existentialists discuss several possible ways in which one person might interact with others. For example, Binswanger (1963) and Boss (1963) provide the alternatives of *communion* and *distrust*; Maddi (1967, 1970), the distinction between *intimacy* and *exploitation*; and Sartre (1956) and Heidegger (1962), the alternatives of *individualism* and *conventionality*. As shown in the maintenance section, these forms of social interaction differentiate the lifestyles of distinct individuals. By evaluating these lifestyles, existentialists arrive at an ethic.

4. PERSONS ARE CHARACTERIZED BY THEIR PARTICIPATION IN A PHYSICAL AND BIOLOGICAL ENVIRONMENT.

Just as it is impossible to think of a human being in isolation from others, so is it impossible to think of him without a body or not occupying physical space. Conceptualizations of this fundamental characteristic appear in Binswanger's (1963) notion of *Umwelt* (the world around us), Heidegger's (1962, p. 133) discussion of the "aroundness of the environment and Dasein's spatiality," Sartre's (1956) and Boss's (1963) explication of the body as an essential structure of human existence, Gendlin's (1962) description of *felt meaning*, and Maddi's (1967, 1970) *biological needs*. In an existential scheme, one's biological or physical mode of being is evaluated in terms of how well the particular environment and its resources (examples include one's voice, sense of touch, and geographical location) serve as the vehicle for, as well as the expression of, one's symbolizing, imagining, and judging to other persons.

Assertions 3 and 4 do not imply that when considering an actual person's life, social, biological, and physical environments can be kept separate. Rather, all are regarded as occurring together. For example, intimacy between two persons is established through a combination of factors such as the exercise of judgment, the act of communication, and the expression of sexuality.

5. TIME IS A NECESSARY CONTEXT FOR THE CONSTRUCTION OF PERSONALITY.

At any given moment, every person has a past, present, and future. Life also has a literal beginning and end. The person has the capacity for incorporating into his or her sense of meaning both the notion that time is not a simple succession of isolated moments and the idea that he or she is not infinite (will die).

Of course, a time sense is not always exercised by people. A certain amount of strenuous effort is necessarily involved in the successful integration of past, present, and future. The person totally involved in the pleasure of the moment resists thinking about the past or the future and the constraints placed upon him by the fact that time is limited. The person secure in a love relationship prefers to consider how well it is going now and to remember the good times of the past, rather than confronting the possibility of the end of the relationship which an undefined future holds.

The vigorous expression of symbolization, imagination, and judgment leads to the awareness of having a clear-cut past, present, and future, and to the integration of these three time periods in the development of personal meaning. By active symbolization, persons bring their past into their present; through imagination, from the present they grasp glimpses of the future; and through judgment, they apply remembrance of the past and contemplation of the future to their present situations.

6. HUMAN LIFE IS BEST UNDERSTOOD AS
     A SERIES OF DECISIONS.

The human activity which best epitomizes the interrelation of the psychological, social, and biological-physical environments and of time periods of existence is decision making. Whether the person realizes it or not, he or she is constantly making decisions which influence actions and have implications for the use of available time.

In understanding personality, the existential psychologist seeks not only the many concrete decisions a person makes, but also the underlying or generic decision that ties all of his decisions together. The universal search for meaning is characterized by some sort of generic or unifying decision. Binswanger (1963) calls it the *existential a priori*, and Sartre (1956), in a somewhat more psychologically accessible discussion, gives it the name *fundamental project*. According to Sartre, the fundamental project is the psychologist's veritable irreducible: the person's ultimate choice about his participation and purpose in the world, which underlies all of his behaviors. To identify a person's fundamental project, the psychologist must consider as many of the person's choices, made in as many possible situations, as can be recaptured. As will be discussed in the section on maintenance, the specific form of the fundamental project—the kind of behaviors it encompasses, and the consistency among these—serves as an important indicator of individual differences.

The emphasis upon the person as decision maker shows existential dynamics in its clearest form. The next three propositions explicate the implications of decision making in the course of human life.

7. PERSONALITY IS A SYNTHESIS OF
     FACTICITY AND POSSIBILITY.

Kierkegaard, (1954, p. 173) points out that in the decision-making process, the person takes into account both the hard facts of his existence (examples include his age and sex, job requirements, and the demands made upon him by a loved one), and his ability to surpass these through symbolizing, imagining, and judging. Personality involves both what one is, in a psychological, social, biological, and physical sense, and what one might become (Jaspers, 1963).

Through including facticity in decision making, existentialists indicate that the person does not have unlimited freedom. The human situation necessarily includes factors over which the person does not have total control. The best example is death. For the existentialists, however, death is not simply the termination of physical functioning or the end point of consciousness and social relations. Death symbolically penetrates all of the person's life and is represented in every limitation, disappointment, and failure of one's attempts to realize meaning.

These limitations and disappointments need not lead to resignation and passivity. When they occur in the life of a person vigorously oriented toward constructing his own life, they serve to establish the dialectic between what is unchangeable and what is possible. In this sense, acceptance of inevitabilities sharpens one's perception of and commitment to what can be influenced through personal effort.

8. A PERSON IS ALWAYS FACED WITH THE
     CHOICE OF THE FUTURE, WHICH
     PROVOKES ANXIETY, AND THE CHOICE OF
     THE PAST, WHICH PROVOKES GUILT.

Although the content of decision-making situations may vary widely, they have an invariant form, according to existentialists (Kierkegaard, 1954; May, 1953; Maddi, 1967, 1970). One alternative in the choice necessitates change and therefore precipitates the person into the future. The other alternative permits him to maintain the status quo; in that sense, he does not change but weds himself to the past. To choose the future brings *anxiety*—what Kierkegaard (1954) called "fear and trembling"—because one cannot predict or control what will happen when one is leaping into the unknown. In contrast, choosing the past brings *guilt,* because in deciding not to change, one is left with a sense of missed opportunity. Emotionally speaking, these are the only two options available to the person. He or she will emerge from every decision-making situation with either anxiety or guilt. Lest this sound overly pessimistic, a further clarification of the existential position is in order.

Existentialists consider anxiety and guilt to be *ontological,* rooted in the nature of being human. Thus, anxiety and guilt associated with decision making are not the result of unfortunate learning and development. They must be accepted as a necessary part of living. The guilt one feels at missed opportunity signifies that growth through changing and even risking is what is ideal for humans. But when changing or the contemplation of it brings anxiety, this is because the person does not live in isolation and must contend with such potentially uncontrollable quantities as other persons and the force of circumstance. Thus he cannot be sure what consequences personal change will bring, and so he becomes anxious. But he also cannot be sure that change will be disastrous, whereas curtailing growth to avoid insecurity will surely lead to stagnation and feelings of guilt. The person's ability to create meaning for himself requires a continual increase in experience that can only come about through change. Thus, to choose the past, the status quo, is to court meaninglessness. Choosing the past once or twice will not cause great damage, but characteristically doing so will lead to an accumulation of guilt. There is a difference between realizing that you have missed one or two opportunities for growth and knowing that you have done so often enough to constitute a commitment to mere security, easy comfort, and personal stagnation. A buildup of guilt will amount to self-condemnation. Existentialists have referred to this as *dread* (Kierkegaard, 1944), *self-surrender* (Binswanger, 1963), and *meaninglessness* (Maddi, 1967).

9.   COURAGE FACILITATES CHOOSING ONE'S
      FUTURE.

The ultimate implications of choosing to stand pat in the past are dire enough that everyone should want to choose the future. But that is not easy to do, because anxiety regarding the unknown is a significant obstacle. The buildup of guilt into despair and meaninglessness does not happen right away, requiring many choices of the past, whereas anxiety is vivid and uncomfortable whenever change takes place or is contemplated. Therefore, *courage* is necessary to choose the future (May, 1953; Tillich, 1952).

In existential psychology, courage has two components. First, courage amounts to faith in oneself as capable, through symbolization, imagination, and judgment, of exercising one's possibility and constructing a meaningful life (Maddi, 1970). This faith mitigates ontological anxiety by

helping the person believe that the risk he takes through change is not foolhardy because he does have influence, though admittedly not complete control, over what change will bring. In addition, he believes that even if there should be dire outcomes (e.g., rejection, ridicule) to change, he can try again because failures do not damage his ability to symbolize, imagine, and judge. The second component of courage is a high consciousness that persons construct their lives through decision making and change, and that the buildup of guilt through choosing the past has worse consequences than tolerating anxiety in the process of choosing the future. In other words, the person must know and believe the existential view of life. If he does, he will reject mere security and easy comfort, though they will certainly have attraction for him. The emphasis shifts from concern over momentary discomfort to a fascination with all there is to be achieved and learned through personal growth.

The following assertions in this section (10–16) concern the developmental process. At the outset, it must be understood that existential psychologists do not regard development to be automatic or simply maturational. Ideal development is difficult and must be stimulated and encouraged. But after the rudiments of courage and toleration of anxiety in decision making have been learned, development becomes much more self-determined and independent of the nurturance of others.

In considering development, existential psychologists scrutinize both facticity and possibility. With regard to facticity, the major question concerns the determining power of the biological, psychological, and social givens as the person moves through life. As to possibility, what is of concern is the person's ability to reinterpret and differentiate his given biological, environmental, and social situation, leading to new creative alternatives for action. This emphasis on the dialectic between facticity and possibility shows that existential psychologists regard development as difficult and strenuous. As mentioned previously, this emphasis differentiates existential psychology from self-actualization positions, which tend to assume that ideal development takes place automatically if adverse experiences are not encountered.

For all its emphasis upon development as shaping life, existential psychology is unfortunately vague as to precise propositions. It will therefore be necessary to elaborate what is rudimentary and render explicit what is implicit.

10. DEVELOPMENT IS BEST UNDERSTOOD AS THE INTERACTION OF PSYCHOLOGICAL, SOCIAL AND BIOLOGICAL-PHYSICAL COMPONENTS OF EXISTENCE.

In seeking to understand personality across the life cycle, existential psychologists investigate changes in the above three areas. Binswanger and Boss demonstrate this in case histories, showing how malfunctioning in one sphere of existence is accompanied by disruption in the other two spheres. For example, in the case of Lola Voss, Binswanger (1963) associates the emergence of schizophrenia with (1) her failure to exercise imagination in her persistent use of one narrow and distorting world-design (psychological sphere); (2) the predisposition for acute anxiety provided by a state of physiological weakness following typhoid fever (biological-physical sphere); and (3) the failure of her parents and teachers to provide adequate moral training (social sphere).

Maddi (1970, 1975a) views development as a series of confrontations between psychological, social, and biological needs and the environments which satisfy or frustrate these needs. All these needs are experienced through all portions of the life span. There is a sharp contrast here with Maslow's (1954) developmental scheme, which organizes needs in a hierarchical form in which higher psychological needs depend upon the prior satisfaction of lower needs (e.g., before a person may exercise his need for creativity, he must satisfy basic physiological needs for food and shelter).

In Maddi's scheme, not only do the three different types of needs simultaneously characterize personality, but the satisfaction of one necessarily affects the others. In what Maddi presents as the ideal developmental course, the child is encouraged to exercise his psychological motivation for meaning. This not only leads to the maturation of the child's ability to symbolize, imagine, and judge, it also facilitates the child's growth in his biological and social realms of being. In ideal development, the child tends to perceive his body as allowing him potential accomplishment of certain goals. He realizes that, through careful exercise, he can become a good basketball player in spite of his small frame. The child who undergoes a nonideal form of development, on the other hand, sees his body as a source of good and bad feelings which he allows to take control—he decides to give up on basketball because he is too short. With regard to the effects of psychological needs on social needs in ideal development, the courageous child is more likely to approach intimate, rather than exploitative, relations with others. At dinner time, the child experienced in the exercise of symbolization, imagination, and judgment is more likely to engage in mutually interesting conversation with his parents and siblings, while the child not skilled in psychological functioning will see dinner as a time only to satisfy his hunger and may consider other persons as threats to his getting enough to eat.

11. IDEAL EARLY DEVELOPMENT IS FACILITATED BY STIMULATING AND ENCOURAGING INDIVIDUALITY.

Although existential psychologists agree that early development necessarily involves socialization (i.e., training of children in culturally shared norms and rules), their emphasis is upon how the child can become a unique individual. Binswanger (1963) utilizes Heidegger's (1962) notion of the inauthentic and authentic forms of caring to explain how adults hinder and facilitate individuality in a child. Individuality results from what Heidegger calls *leaping ahead* of the other person. When parents encourage the child by teaching him that he is really capable of doing more on his own than he has yet accomplished, they are exercising authentic care and promoting ideal development. Individuality in the child is thwarted when parents do what Heidegger calls *leaping in,* when they take over for the child what he is capable of doing for himself, thereby depriving him of a sense of competence and potentiality for greater control over himself and his environment. Joining Binswanger in the emphasis upon training for independence, Maddi (1970, 1975a) recommends to parents and educators the use of exercises in symbolization, imagination, and judgment to foster reliance on personal initiative and release from conventional constraints.

A lot is asked of parents and other developmentally relevant adults by existentialists. They must work hard to foster individuality (e.g., it often takes both patience and imagination to get a young child to see that he can really do an unfamiliar task on his own); and they must also be willing to accept a variety of positive and negative consequences associated with the child's exercise of independence (e.g., his experimentation in areas of life unfamiliar and worrisome to them). Parents must value self-reliance and growth, even though this may mean that their control over their children thereby diminishes.

Through exercising symbolization, imagination, and judgment, and by experiencing intrinsic and extrinsic rewards for acting as a distinct and assertive person, the child is on his way to learning to be courageous, to tolerate anxiety, and to choose his future.

12. THE IMPOSITION OF LIMITS STIMULATES POSITIVE DEVELOPMENT.

An important part of learning that one can successfully influence one's environment is the recognition that one can try again if one fails in initial attempts to be effective. In this sense, it is better for parents to teach their children about facticity through the imposition of limits than to leave them with a false sense that everything is easily possible. Binswanger (1963) and Boss (1963) see the imposition of limits and discipline as necessary for this sort of instruction. They criticize "pseudo permissiveness," indicating that it is growth-inhibiting to allow the child to function without restraints. In Binswanger's view, the child's development of an "inner support" system and the abandonment of "external retreats" is dependent upon his early experience of struggling with something and of being self-reliant in the face of adversities. The imposition of limits leads to the child's recognition that his freedom is not absolute and that there are things beyond his control. His increasingly mature exercise of symbolization, imagination, and judgment in the attempt to carry through on his decisions in completing chosen projects helps his maturation as a self-responsible person. Limits actually facilitate individuality.

13. RICHNESS OF EXPERIENCE STIMULATES POSITIVE DEVELOPMENT.

In seeking to understand the developmental course of a patient, Binswanger (1963) and Boss (1963) ask the basic question: How much has he or she experienced in the psychological, social, and biological-physical spheres of existence? Binswanger evaluates the products of the interaction between the individual's fundamental meaning structure and the other persons, things, and events he encounters. Boss makes a crucial part of every diagnosis an assessment of what was missing from the person's early life; for example, a functional and structural psychosomatic disturbance is explained by Boss as due to lack of sexual experiences in adolescence and young adulthood. Dealing with the same concern, Maddi (1975a) draws comparisons among developmental courses in terms of the breadth, variety, and intensity of the experiences. As noted in Assertion 12, growth-facilitating experiences need not always be positive. Maddi (1975b) discusses creativity as the result of a developmental course involving suffering, conflict, and frustration.

14. PERSONALITY DEVELOPMENT IDEALLY BECOMES INCREASINGLY SELF-DETERMINED.

Although the encouragement of individuality, the imposition of limits, and richness of experience are concerns throughout life, Assertions 11 through 13 focus on the early part of life—the time during which personality and orientation toward living is being formed. At that relatively unstructured time in the child's life, it is necessary to have parental stimulation and guidance for optimal development to take place. Simone de Beauvoir (1948) refers to childhood as a period of inauthenticity, when the person's exercise of freedom is blocked by others who have power over him. But once the child has practiced symbolizing, imagining, and judging and has developed self-reliance, sense of purpose, and courage, he becomes able to develop on his own. His decision making will bring him a continual flow of experience for further symbolization, imagination, and judgment. Existential psychologists do not associate chronological age estimates with the onset of this self-determined development, but it presumably does not occur vigorously until adolescence. Certainly, self-determined development continues throughout life. The emphasis in existential psychology is on continual change and growth. The following two assertions elaborate on self-determined development.

Before going on, it should be noted that to progress from early dependence upon parents and other adults for developmental stimulation, the child must receive the experiences referred to in Assertions 11 through 14. Should he not get independence training, richness of experience, respect for individuality, and imposed limits, his emergence into self-determined development will be jeopardized. He will not have learned to exercise symbolization, imagination, and judgment vigorously, nor will he have learned to rely on himself in making decisions, to accept facticity, and to take responsibility courageously for his own life. Instead, he will change little with the passage of years and will emerge into chronological adulthood without the individualized sense of meaning and purpose that is the special gift of human beings.

15. THE EXPERIENCE OF FAILURE STIMULATES SELF-DETERMINED DEVELOPMENT.

During self-determined development, the limits to a person's exercise of individuality increasingly are recognized as being partially self-imposed. The person who has learned during early development to regard himself as worthy and capable of formulating his own goals and pursuing them successfully continues to learn through observing and evaluating his failures. Failures contain information which can be used to reevaluate goals, to reformulate plans, and to try again. Only for the person who did not get a sound developmental start in early interactions with parents should subsequent failure experiences be avoided or disguised, lest clear appreciation of these failures have an adverse effect on the individual. The following assertion details how failure may spur positive development.

16. SELF-DETERMINED DEVELOPMENT PASSES THROUGH THREE TYPES OF ORIENTATION: THE AESTHETIC, THE IDEALISTIC, AND THE AUTHENTIC.

As soon as a person emerges from the bosom of his family into the wider world with a freshly developed sense of freedom and self-reliance, he is likely to become self-indulgent. The excitement of being free of parental limits and of the mysteries beyond the home is great. The person may use his decision-making powers for pleasure, reveling in the moment, exploiting others and the environment, making no lasting commitments. Kierkegaard (1959) refers to this period as *aesthetic orientation*. This orientation is not merely passivity and dependency but rather the first (and therefore perhaps understandably misguided) attempt at independent functioning made by someone whose early developmental experiences have been beneficial. The self-indulgence of aestheticism comes about because these early child-rearing experiences, though necessary and beneficial, have nonetheless been strenuous. The child has had to strive and to assume responsibility, so he becomes hedonistic at the first opportunity.

Although the person derives pleasure through aestheticism for a while, sooner or later failure experiences will occur. All parties end at some point, and their enjoyment value does not outlive them. Relationships entered into without much commitment or discrimination also end quickly and are soon forgotten. What at first seemed like wonderful freedom becomes emptiness.

The inherent failure experiences deriving from an aesthetic orientation spur self-determined development. Though failures are painful, their import is usually perceived accurately by the person whose early development has given him a good start. Such a person begins to realize that the trouble with self-centered aestheticism is that it involves living in the present only, as if the future and the past are unimportant. Making decisions only for the present involves little by way of planfulness for the future, and the end result, paradoxically, is loneliness and emptiness. Such a person also begins to recognize that aestheticism has led to surrendering control over his or her life to others—to whoever has the next party, to the next one to fall in love with, to the next political cause to be carried away by. The aesthetic lifestyle which seemed to promise such independence has only brought new forms of dependency.

Having learned this, the person in the grips of self-determined development proceeds to the next level—the *idealistic orientation*. The emphasis now is on incorporating the future and the past into the present by making decisions as if current commitments and values have always been and will always remain the same. When the person loves, he insists that it is forever. When he engages in pragmatic activities, such as politics, he does so out of undying beliefs. In his zealousness to overcome his previous lack of commitment, he fails to recognize the real difficulty in determining the most meaningful relationship between ideals and practical activities.

Because the person with an idealistic orientation acts as if he has complete control over events which in reality are too complex to be controlled by any individual, inevitably he encounters failure experiences. A love vowed eternally ends all the more painfully because its end was unexpected. Various practical enterprises force the recognition that shifting loyalties, vested interests, and even accidental factors play a large role in determining the outcome of complex social phenomena.

These failure experiences spur self-determined development once again. The person with an idealistic orientation learns that events are only partially under his control, regardless of his efforts and protestations to the contrary. With the deepening and incorporation of this insight, the final and highest developmental orientation is entered upon: *authentic being*. At this level the person recognizes not only the importance of a time dimension, but also that he is not almighty. He accepts the facticity of his limited control and uses it to gain a clearer sense of what is possible. He commits himself to the possible, incorporating facticity by a vivid sense of urgency to accomplish and experience what is important to him.

Maintenance

This section concerns adult lifestyles which, according to existential psychology, have a number of component parts. The detailing of these parts will help clear what it means to live existentially. In presenting lifestyles, it is necessary to restate existential formulations in a way that might be objected to by some relevant writers. In the works of Laing primarily, but also of Binswanger and Boss, can be found an aversion to categorization and classification. This is clearly a reaction against those psychological approaches that have made rigid use of typologies, which to existen-

tialists seem to do violence to the person's free ability to make decisions and to change. But the existentialists mentioned here have taken their reaction too far, ending in the inconsistent position of denying the utility of any classifications while at the same time themselves engaging in classifications congenial to them. For example, Laing's (1960) notions of *engulfment* and *depersonalization* seem to be classificatory diagnostic statements. Classification is a cognitive act which creates meaning and, as such, is a necessary tool for the mentally active human being. In personality theory, classification of adult functioning necessarily involves statements about lifestyles and their component parts.

17.   ADULTS EXPRESS LIFESTYLES OF
      AUTHENTIC OR INAUTHENTIC BEING.
It might fit the emphases of existential psychology more fully to consider a complex continuum stretching from authentic to inauthentic being. But for purposes of vividness and ease of communication, the continuum is here dichotomized into two general lifestyles.

Authentic being is the end result of facilitative early development and the self-determined development which follows. *Inauthentic being* is the result of inhibiting, destructive early development and a relative lack of self-determined development which is traceable to the earlier trouble. Although the inauthentic being is chronologically an adult, his psychological development is retarded. The sharp differences between inauthentic and authentic approaches to living are pinpointed in the assertions that follow.

18.   THE VALUES, PREFERENCES, GOALS, AND
      VIEWPOINTS OF AUTHENTIC BEING ARE
      DISTINCT AND UNUSUAL, WHEREAS
      THOSE OF INAUTHENTIC BEING ARE
      VAGUE AND STEREOTYPED.
Through a lifetime of exercising the cognitive capabilities of symbolization, imagination, and judgment, the authentic being develops values, preferences, goals, and viewpoints. In this sense, she or he will be a distinct person, with many ways of understanding experience, capable of fine distinctions, and with a richness of reflections upon what is taking place. The more one generates values, preferences, goals, and viewpoints, the more they will be original. In this

sense, the authentic person will also be unusual.

By comparison, the inauthentic person does not strain to exercise symbolization, imagination, and judgment, having been neither stimulated nor reinforced for doing so in early development. No one can exist without some values, preferences, goals, and viewpoints, but the inauthentic person has as few of these as is consistent with the conducting of human life. In that sense, he is a vague person. In addition, those opinions and goals he does possess will be adopted from other persons rather than developed through his own strenuous interaction with the world. In that sense, he will also be stereotyped and conventional.

The inauthentic being is a less conscious person than the authentic person. The inauthentic being will not have clear impressions of what is taking place in his life, or why, and will certainly not be aware that he is able to exercise control over life problems through decision making. In contrast, the authentic being believes that through exercising mentality he can influence what happens to him. This will include recognizing clearly when and how he has been manipulated by circumstances and recognizing the steps that need to be taken for greater personal control. Because of this difference in level of consciousness, the authentic being possesses greater freedom than the inauthentic being.

19.   IN BIOLOGICAL EXPERIENCING, THE AUTHENTIC BEING SHOWS SUBTLETY AND TASTE, WHEREAS THE INAUTHENTIC BEING SHOWS UNDIFFERENTIATION AND CRUDENESS.

For the authentic being, the quality of food, drink, and sex is more important than their quantity. He or she appreciates subtle, tasteful, and unusual biological experiencing. Small variations are recognized as important. The inauthentic being, on the other hand, remains relatively undifferentiated and crude, preferring quantity to quality and refinements.

The authentic being combines the expression of psychological, social, and biological functions, and in this manner achieves a conscious sense of self as someone who can understand and influence his biological experiences. In contrast, the inauthentic being does not have an elaborate consciousness and tends to perceive the biologi-

cal side of his nature as isolated from the rest. Consequently, he assumes and acts as if he is ruled by creature needs, as are the lower animals. Physical survival and the swift satisfaction of biological wants are of paramount importance. Thus, he tends to develop materialistic values, investing importance not only in those things that directly satisfy biological needs (e.g., food) but those that are of indirect relevance as well (e.g., money). In comparison, the authentic being, while recognizing the importance of biological expression, regards the coordination of these needs with psychological and social expression as not only possible but more comprehensively satisfying. The emphasis shifts from survival and satiation at any cost to a less materialistic concern, directed at the priceless qualities of experiencing.

20.   IN SOCIAL INTERACTION, THE AUTHENTIC BEING IS ORIENTED TOWARD INTIMACY, WHEREAS THE INAUTHENTIC BEING IS ORIENTED TOWARD SUPERFICIAL AND CONTRACTUAL RELATIONSHIPS.

For the authentic being, the quality of social interaction is more important than the quantity of conversation, mingling, and people watching. He or she is appreciative of the challenge inherent in relating in depth with other humans. In contrast, the inauthentic person remains relatively undifferentiated in, passive toward, and fearful of social interactions, having little to contribute beyond conventionalities. Consequently, the inauthentic person prefers limited contractual relationships, because their purpose is clearly defined and will therefore not be surprising, threatening, or demanding.

In combining the expression of psychological, biological, and social functions, the authentic being understands and influences his social interactions. The inauthentic person, in contrast, does not have an elaborate consciousness and tends to perceive social interactions as externally determined. Consequently, he defines himself as a player of social roles, with little choice but to adjust. He tends to adopt values and habits stressing similarity to other persons and prefers smoothness of interaction more than he does individuality or uniqueness. Social interaction for the authentic person will emphasize a mutual fostering and enjoyment of unusualness and the exploration of individual differences as a basis for intimacy.

21. IN RELATIONSHIP TO SOCIAL INSTITUTIONS, THE AUTHENTIC BEING IS ACTIVE AND INFLUENTIAL WHEREAS THE INAUTHENTIC BEING IS PASSIVE AND ACQUIESCENT.

The authentic person perceives society and its institutions as having been formed by persons and therefore as properly serving persons. His values regarding the social system tend to be egalitarian. He is able to implement his values through active attempts to convince others of his opinions and thereby have an influence in society.

In contrast, the inauthentic being has only rudimentary consciousness concerning the social system and regards it as an unchangeable entity which rules those living within it. He views himself as a passive player of roles assigned to him by others in this all-powerful social system. In his social behaviors he is acquiescent, trying to play his "assigned" social roles well enough to avoid criticism or rejection. He will quickly go along with the majority and will have only conventional social opinions, if any at all.

22. THOUGHTS, FEELINGS, AND ACTIONS OF THE AUTHENTIC BEING WILL BE UNIFIED AND PLANFUL, WHEREAS THOSE OF THE INAUTHENTIC BEING WILL BE FRAGMENTARY AND AIMLESS.

The preceding assertions have shown how in authenticity there is supportive integration in the biological, social, and psychological components of existence. The authentic being also demonstrates unified functioning and planfulness in her or his orientation toward the future. Not only does he have—through his exercise of symbolization, imagination, and judgment—many values, preferences, goals, and viewpoints, but he arranges these in an order of importance. His priorities organize his actions. Since he is constantly engaged in the comparison, rejection, and ordering of the many components in his self-constructed hierarchy of meaningfulness, his priorities are generic rather than discrete and situation specific. There is a true plan for an entire life in his behaviors, rather than a series of small plans easily reached or characterized by internal contradictions.

The lifestyle of the inauthentic person is fragmentary and disorganized. Because he is aided by neither vigorous symbolization, imagination, and judgment nor by an elaborate consciousness, he is unable to decide what are his values, preferences, goals, and viewpoints. Further, he is unable to recognize the givens in his environment or to make decisions which incorporate them into his general life plan. The result often is fixation on one particular goal, with no appreciation of all there is to learn and do by more strenuous involvement in life. This difficulty is called *extravagance* by Binswanger, to signify self-indulgence. For Binswanger (1963, p. 346), it is only by hierarchically organizing values, preferences, goals, and viewpoints that they can be "weighed against each other in life, art, philosophy, and science and . . . transplanted into words and deeds."

23. THE AUTHENTIC BEING SHOWS CONTINUAL CHANGE, WHEREAS THE INAUTHENTIC BEING REMAINS THE SAME.

The authentic person's manifestation of unity and planfulness should not be mistaken for monotonous and unidimensional activity. Integration features future orientation, originality, change, and creativity. In contrast, the inauthentic being is bogged down in repetitive, monotonous activity supporting the status quo. Whatever values, preferences, and goals she or he possesses are concrete and conventional, providing little basis for change. When change occurs it tends to be fragmentary and unintegrated, giving the appearance of an accidental occurrence.

24. THE AUTHENTIC BEING TENDS TO EXPERIENCE ANXIETY, WHEREAS THE INAUTHENTIC BEING EXPERIENCES GUILT.

The authentic person experiences anxiety as the result of a vivid consciousness that he or she must decide and act without knowing what the outcome will be (Tillich, 1952). This anxiety simultaneously recognizes facticity and possibility. The authentic being faces anxiety because to avoid it would be to shrink from choosing the future and thereby relinquish growth, individuality, and the enactment of values, preferences, and goals.

The inauthentic person experiences anxiety less frequently and less intensely. He does not have the vivid awareness of lonely and unexpected death which Heidegger (1962) attributes to authenticity. He insulates himself from worry over outcomes of decisions and change-producing acts by choosing the status quo instead. He lives a superficial and routine life, never dwelling on the limited ability of persons to actually control occurrences. Having given up the possibility of growth, individuality, and fulfillment, the inauthentic person is inevitably beset by the guilt of missed opportunity and cowardice. As he gets older and guilt accumulates, a general condemnation of self sets in. He can no longer believe that at the next decision point he can make up for past missed opportunities. Rather, he begins to realize that his whole life has been wasted.

This is not to say that the authentic person escapes guilt entirely. It is, after all, impossible to act on every facet of one's possibilities. For example, being involved in one particular relationship, no matter how conducive to change and growth it may be, necessarily means that other possible relationships are ignored. Even choices of the future involve giving up some opportunity. With this in mind, Boss (1963) considers "the call of conscience" to be always present. Even the authentic being recognizes that he is "always in debt." He does not deny this guilt but tries to minimize it by choosing the future regularly and thereby maximizing opportunities. In this fashion, guilt is held to manageable quantities, and there is little risk of despair, meaninglessness, and comprehensive condemnation.

25.   THE EXPERIENCE OF FAILURE
      PRECIPITATES PSYCHOPATHOLOGY IN
      THE INAUTHENTIC BEING.

For one whose early development was positive, the experience of failure has a special ability to stimulate self-determined development in the lifelong process of becoming an increasingly authentic being. But if early development has left the person in self-doubt and relatively unable to exercise symbolization, imagination, and judgment vigorously, her or his self-determined development will be stifled. In such a person, the experience of failure will not spur development but rather will have a further debilitating effect. The extent of debilitation produced by failure experiences will depend not only upon their magnitude and frequency but also upon the degree of the person's inauthenticity.

Maddi (1967, 1970) discusses three extreme experiences of failure: the threat of imminent death, social upheaval, and confrontation with one's own superficiality. For the inauthentic person, debilitation occurs with

1. The threat of imminent death, because he has elevated physical survival to such importance that he has essentially (though implicitly) assumed that he will not die.

2. Social upheaval, because his emphasis upon adjustment and social role playing amounts to assuming that society is absolute and unchanging.

3. Confrontation with one's own superficiality (usually forced by another person who is suffering due to it), because the inauthentic being has spent much effort making himself acceptable and is not able to accept criticism for that very effort.

The three failure experiences mentioned have the effect of disconfirming the inauthentic person's values, preferences, and viewpoints concerning himself and the world (Maddi, 1967, 1970). The breakdown of personality which they produce is elaborated in the discussion of psychopathology in the following section.

Applications

The development of existential psychology owes as much to attempts of practicing clinicians to assess and treat human problems as it does to existential philosophy. It is not surprising, therefore, to find a richness of concrete techniques for the application of existential psychotherapy, amidst some disarray concerning the niceties of formal theorizing.

Assessment

One important part of assessment involves determining a person's degree of authenticity or inauthenticity. This can be accomplished by measuring the various characteristics mentioned in the "maintenance" assertions discussed in the preceding section. To complete the task of assessment, however, attention must also be given to measurement of relevant psychopathological states.

Among the existential clinicians studying psychotic states, Binswanger (1963) has been particularly articulate in identifying symptomatology. He provides four constitutive concepts for use in the analysis of schizophrenia. He advocates looking first for *inconsistency* (fragmentation) in the various parts of existence. Because inconsistencies are bothersome, they are often masked by *extravagance,* or the overemphasis upon one idea or ideology as that which explains and orders everything, and thereby neutralizes all that one experiences. But extravagance is fruitless because it leads to rigidly *dichotomous thinking*, in which the person is totally involved in the struggle between realization of his extravagant ideal or its total denial. The schizophrenic must either actualize his idiosyncratic plan or fall into bottomless despair. Being trapped in dichotomous thinking, the person must then engage in *covering*, or the "Sisyphuslike effort to conceal that side of the [dichotomy] that is unbearable" (Binswanger, 1963, p. 258). The enormous effort involved in covering may finally lead to *being worn away*, a comprehensive resignation and retreat from life.

According to Binswanger, the schizophrenic process involves a progression from the experience of personal fragmentation, through adoption of a single rigid perspective on self and world and a denial of all that contradicts it, to a total surrender of selfhood. The case of Lola Voss stands out among the many Binswanger (1963) offers as examples. Through her inability to face inconsistencies like her anger at her parents for trying to break off her engagement and her simultaneous self-initiated rejection of her fiancé, Lola develops an extravagant belief in herself as ultimately alone, except for her relationship with a supernatural oracle which directs her activities. She attempts to stave off overwhelming despair and anxiety by slavishly following all of the decisions made for her by the oracle, even when this involves extreme behavior like cutting up her clothes. Her resignation is complete when she surrenders all of her decision-making powers to the "enemies" which populate her hallucinations and resigns herself to their persecution.

Maddi (1967, 1970) details forms of existential sickness falling in the neurotic range, all of which involve a breakdown of meaningfulness, as a result of psychological, social, and biological stresses. The most extreme form, *vegetativeness*, is characterized at the cognitive level by inability to believe in the meaningfulness of anything one is doing or can imagine doing; at the affective level, by apathy and boredom, punctuated by periods of depression that become less frequent as the disorder is prolonged; and at the action level, by low energy and general aimlessness. *Nihilism* is a less extreme form of existential sickness, because some sense of meaningfulness remains. The cognitive commitment is antimeaning or paradoxically finding meaning in the meaninglessness of everything. At the affective level, one finds anger and disgust; and at the action level, destructive competitiveness. The least extreme form of existential sickness is *adventurousness*, in which everyday life has lost all meaning. To experience meaningfulness, the adventurer must involve himself continually in extreme, dangerous activities. Maddi discusses these forms of illness in terms of not only their personal implications but their implications for the social system as well.

A word is in order concerning the techniques whereby the major variables of authenticity, inauthenticity, and sickness are properly assessed. Existential psychologists agree that there is no real substitute for open-minded, comprehensive, depth interviewing. Binswanger (1963) advises that accurate assessment requires dropping one's preconceptions about the interviewee, in order to hear what he is saying. In addition, all available aspects of the interviewee's life must be examined, juxtaposed, compared, and integrated. Boss (1963) and Laing (1960) agree with this view. Sartre (1956) suggests a similar procedure for identifying a person's *fundamental project*. This method, which investigates the phenomenology of the patient, is employed with the assumption (agreed to by all mentioned above) that the interviewee cannot accurately assess himself. Assessment is in the hands of the interviewer as an external observer.

In a related assessment technique introduced by Gendlin (1969), the existential psychologist observes the subject's explication of his experience. Through rating this process the psychologist reaches conclusions concerning such relevant existential variables as *felt meaning* and decision making.

Failing more extensive information, questionnaire data are accepted by many existential psychologists. Maddi, Kobasa, and Hoover (1976) have developed a questionnaire measure (the *Alienation-Commitment Test*) of the various forms of existential sickness. Also, Crumbaugh and Maholick's *Purpose-in-Life Test* (1964) is intended to provide a quick paper-and-pencil assessment of several components of authentic being. These are discussed further in the Evidence section below.

Treatment

Whether the client's problem be inauthenticity or psychopathology, the general aim of existential psychotherapy is to help the person who seeks help to achieve authenticity. To move toward authentic being, the client must learn to begin to exercise symbolization, imagination, and judgment and thereby to achieve consciousness of his or her life as being partially under his or her control. He must begin to express these cognitive capabilities in his biological and social experiencing, moving thereby toward subtlety, taste, intimacy, love, and constructive social action. He must accept responsibility for the decisions he makes and attempt to tolerate anxiety so that he can choose to change and grow and thereby avoid accumulations of the guilt of missed opportunities. To learn to tolerate anxiety, he must begin to trust himself and to develop a generic set of goals which can lend direction to personal change. But he must also grow in ability to accept givens and inevitabilities, so that he is clear about what practical possibilities should be pursued.

In helping the client progress toward authentic personhood, the psychotherapist provides a facsimile of the presumably missing beneficial early development. But this does not mean that the past should be dwelt upon. The persistence of past conflicts in an unconscious mind is not an issue for existential psychology. Rather, the subject matter of present life should be dealt with in giving the client the bases for what here may be called *preliminary development* (analogous to early development, but occurring in an adult).

Then, as self-determined development begins to occur in the client, the therapist's task is to support it until it has become vigorous enough to maintain itself as an authentic way of life. At that point, therapy is terminated.

More concretely, in this process of preliminary development, the therapist engages in independence training, shows respect for the client's individuality, encourages him to encounter a rich variety of experience, but also sets limits (see Assertions 11 through 13). Then, as these procedures have their intended effects and self-determined development begins, the therapist helps in interpreting the significance of failures encountered by the client, thereby helping him to chart the life course best for him. Special attention is given to recognizing and formulating generic goals as well as appreciating facticity and possibility (see Assertions 6 and 7).

The discussion thus far has been both more concrete and more comprehensive than that found in the writings of many existential psychotherapists. Nonetheless, in the techniques and case studies reported, much is to be found which falls within this conceptual framework. This is true even though the early existential psychotherapists, Binswanger and Boss, employed many techniques reminiscent of Freudian psychoanalysis. Nonetheless, the general emphases of their Daseinsanalysis was clearly existential.

Although Binswanger and Boss explicate few specific techniques, they do say much about how to encourage clients to disclose subjective experience. Also, they offer suggestions on how to stimulate symbolization, imagination, and judgment. One technique involves asking the client, "Why not?" (Boss, 1963). The therapist raises considerations like: "If you are lonely, why not find some friends? If you are dissatisfied with your job, why don't you start preparing yourself for something more fulfilling?" Through questions of this sort, the client is confronted with his failure to search for meaning in various aspects of his existence. This technique is useful for exposing inauthenticity, stimulating self-reliance, and gaining in appreciation of facticity as well as possibility. Boss regards what he does as different from Freudian interpretation in that the latter tends to dismiss inappropriate behaviors by typing them as left over from childhood, thereby misunderstanding their importance in clarifying what the client is doing in the here and now.

Another technique for stimulating authentic modes of behaving is Gendlin's (1969) *focusing*. He observed that clients do not tend to learn to use vigorously their cognitive capabilities for creating meaning simply as a result of just any psychotherapy. The exercises Gendlin employs involve the client in recalling a memory, or a sense impression. This continuous and dialectical sort of reflection necessarily changes the original mental event. In this fashion, experience is clarified and enriched.

A particularly striking technique for helping the client gain in control over his experiences is Frankl's (1965) *paradoxical intention*. A client troubled by a symptom he cannot control is encouraged by the therapist to exaggerate it rather than minimize it. Frankl has used this technique in cases of phobia, obsessive-compulsiveness, delusions, and even suicidal depression. In one case (Frankl, 1965), a young doctor discloses a phobia concerning perspiration from which he had suffered for years. Whenever the doctor feared he would sweat, the fear itself would precipitate the undesired state. Frankl advised him to try to sweat as much as he could whenever he feared that he would sweat. Whenever the doctor was in a situation with the potential of triggering the phobia, he was to say to himself: "I only sweated out a quart before, but now I'm going to pour at least ten quarts!" After initially reacting to the instructions as absurd, the doctor began trying to sweat. In a matter of days, his fear of sweating and his sweating ceased.

By acting paradoxically in intending that which is feared, the client disengages himself from the overwhelming behavior. This involves what Frankl (1965) calls an exercise of humor. The result is perception of oneself as more than the unwanted behaviors. The attempt to exaggerate the symptom outmaneuvers it, and the client once again establishes control over his thoughts and actions. This reestablishment of control builds self-trust and self-reliance.

A common misconception of existential psychotherapy is that its applicability is restricted to the highly intelligent, relatively healthy and socially secure, those who have the leisure to speculate philosophically. Nothing could be further from the truth. Most existential psychother-

apists, notably Binswanger, Boss, Laing, Frankl, and Gendlin, have treated psychotic clients to a greater degree than did Freud and his followers.

Institutional

There is no major systematic program currently operative whose primary aim is the utilization of existential psychology in prison reform, classroom revitalization, hospital care improvement, and such applications. Nonetheless, in many existential writings there is a call for social reforms and a consideration of how authentic being can be fostered through other than psychotherapeutic means. Of special relevance are the discussions of individualism and the debilitating effect of conformity.

The strongest argument for social reform in existentialism involves the writing and life of Sartre (1949). He has not only advocated needed reforms but has actually worked for them, sometimes through such protests as declining the Nobel Prize. In his later work, Laing (1967) has reformulated and celebrated Sartre's social criticism. Laing maintains that the cure of an individual's psychosis is dependent upon a radical alteration of the society in which he finds himself. Although one may not agree with all Laing says, he does speak for all existentialists when he contends that society will have to become more tolerant and supportive of deviant behavior if authentic being is to be possible for greater numbers of persons. He mounts many specific criticisms of modern industrialized societies.

Maddi (1970) agrees, but he highlights the necessity of persons helping themselves. Social reform cannot be done for the members of a society; they must do it themselves. According to Maddi, the form of government most accessible to change instigated by its members is democracy. But just because a government is nominally democratic does not automatically ensure that the institutionalized channels whereby social change can be brought about are functioning properly. When a democracy becomes large and industrialized, the ensuing bureaucratization and technical complexity increase the likelihood that the public will lose touch with, and influence over, elected officials. If deviation from representational government has existed for some time, it may be difficult to effect social change through legitimized channels. In that case, extreme measures, such as nonviolent confrontation politics, may be necessary to reopen channels for effecting reform. In this, Maddi's viewpoint shows similarity to Sartre's. Maddi does not condone all confrontation politics, only those forms manifesting the clarity, responsibility, and commitment of authentic being. He cautions against endorsing confrontation politics engaged in by inauthentic beings and sufferers of existential sickness and provides an analysis of events in the late 1960s to bolster his points. In the peace, Black Power, and women's liberation movements there were authentic persons striving for social reforms, but also conformists, nihilists, and adventurers attempting desperately to find meaning in their lives rather than seeking constructive social change.

Paralleling the emphasis on participatory democracy should be an emphasis on creativity, for both are ways of producing social reform. Participating in the political process of representative governments—attempting to influence others, lobbying, electioneering—can alter institutions and officialdom. In a less political but nonetheless effective way, creativity can provide new ideas and approaches for dealing with human problems. Sartre (1949) regards creative writing as an example of public responsibility—that is, an identification of the ills of current society and suggestions for their remedy. While Maddi (1975b) contends that creativity provides an antidote for meaninglessness in the creative person, the creative product may well do something similar for others to whom it is communicated. Creative endeavor is a natural activity for authentic persons.

It may seem that the value of creativity is obvious. But most persons are inauthentic, and hence social institutions tend to reflect their commitment to the status quo. All too often, only lip service is paid to creativity. The creative person runs a sociopolitical risk, because the thrust of his endeavor is likely to alter the status quo and hence to be threatening to some people and some institutions (Maddi, 1975b). Creative persons have been persecuted and even killed (Christ, Socrates). Society should take special steps to protect those engaged in creative endeavors so that they can aid in the necessary but painful process of social reform.

A society can reward creative endeavor in many concrete ways. Parents and teachers can foster a view of life as strenuous, with change and anxiety regarded as signs of a maturing process, to help the young grow into adults who truly value creative endeavor and admire rather than condemn creativity in others. Employers can allow workers to utilize personal initiative and give them responsibility for what they produce. In this context, the recent emphasis upon mass production and the assembly line may be shortsighted because it fosters inauthenticity (e.g., irresponsibility) and meaninglessness. Seemingly less efficient procedures in which workers have greater freedom and responsibility may in the long run be best, not only for society but for production of quality work. Public officials should be chosen for their creativity, not their popularity or unthreatening demeanor.

Self

The special message of the existential approach is that each person can construct the unique life he chooses, but doing this is strenuous and involves risk. Giving in to pleasures and settling for comfort is suspect; true fulfillment requires development, and this is inherently a disciplined and stressful process. Although freedom and potency are the promise of humanness, this state is never reached by the timid or the idle.

An example of what the existential approach to life signifies is found in heterosexual relationships. The highest form of love occurs between two authentic beings, with emphasis on exploration in depth of intellectual, social and sexual experiences by persons who trust, admire, and desire each other. Because they know they are individuals and can accept the idea that their relationship may end, they can be intimate without losing the ability to go on alone. The implications of authenticity are violated if one of the persons makes all the decisions or is always dependent. To be fulfilling, an intimate heterosexual relationship calls for mutuality on the part of equal partners. Such relationships are best when integrated into the rest of the participants' lives. Being in love should facilitate being competent and imaginative at work, relating intimately with other persons, acting effectively in one's community, and contributing to one's wider culture.

As a young man, Kierkegaard made a decision to break his engagement for marriage to a young woman, Regina (Lowrie, 1938). It could be argued that the extolling of individuality in his work can be traced to a reaction formation due to the desperate loneliness he felt following this decision. From Kierkegaard's own writings (e.g. 1941), however, it becomes apparent that in Regina he had idolized a frivolous woman who would have interfered with his plans for a career of psychological, philosophical, and theological writing. It would have been difficult for Kierkegaard to compose those brilliantly scathing critiques of conventional Danish middle-class society while also keeping his wife happy by taking her to all the right parties in Copenhagen. Because he judged his own unconventionality and interest in social reform to be crucial to his existence, and he could not encourage Regina to develop out of her conventionality, he decided reluctantly to leave her. Kierkegaard might have considered Regina's conventionality as part of his facticity (something he could not change because of love) and stayed with her. But this would have been what Binswanger calls extravagance, assuming that Kierkegaard had carefully determined that his own individualistic trajectory could not be reversed. Kierkegaard suffered for his lost love but grew by choosing the future.

The point highlighted here is that from an existential perspective, one might indeed be better off proclaiming a relationship—whether friendship, partnership, or marriage—broken if it is based on inauthenticity. The fact that a couple has been together over many years is not reason enough for them to continue if it becomes apparent to all involved that insurmountable inauthenticity exists. Care must be taken, of course, to determine whether the purported inauthenticity is indeed insurmountable. This judgment is based primarily on what each person recognizes as his or her unique set of priorities and crucial values, and on whether these two sets of priorities could possibly flourish in juxtaposition. If there is no way they could flourish together, then separation may be best. What happens as a result of separation is well understood by existential psychotherapists. The persons will feel remorseful and lonely but will also experience a lessening of the guilt of missed opportunity.

Their loneliness will not distract them from engaging in activities which express the previously suppressed values and priorities. With the acceleration of this self-determined development, the loneliness will recede, and the relationship severed will be remembered with fondness but little regret.

Another example of the existential approach involves the life of students. The student-teacher relationship is rightly regarded as necessarily inauthentic; the student must be object and the professor subject. By becoming a student, one proclaims one's lack of knowledge, recognition of another as expert, and willingness (often financially sealed) to be taught, changed, manipulated. Of course, to many students, an educational relationship which allows the student to also act as subject would be most beneficial for both parties. Existentialists agree but add that this kind of encounter must be striven for. A school board's decision to "open up" the classroom or give only "pass-fail" grades is not sufficient. It is up to the individual student to demonstrate through creative activity, and through the exercise of imagination, symbolization, and judgment, that he is also capable of teaching his teacher.

Although the student side of the educational relationship is being focused on here, the teacher should also heed the advice of existentialism. Recognizing the basically inauthentic structure of the educational relationship, the teacher must realize the responsibility of the task he has shouldered. He must have something worthwhile to teach and be able to communicate it effectively, so that it does indeed alter the life of his students. The teacher's role may be considered an exercise of what Heidegger (1962) calls *care*, mentioned in the section on development. In the inauthentic form of care, the teacher "leaps in" for the student—he does everything for the student, presenting the information in finished form and providing no opportunity for integration through use of one's own wits. In authentic care, the teacher "leaps ahead" of the student and stimulates him to produce his own integrations and directions. For example, the inauthentic teacher requires an objective summary of the literature, whereas the authentic teacher emphasizes the student's critique of it.

Validation

Evaluation of existential psychology can be done in regard to its effectiveness in psychotherapeutic settings, as well as through systematic research. Also relevant to validation is a comparison of the existential approach with other personality theories, so that relative merits can be determined from logical inferences.

Evidence

It is a misconception that existential psychology involves no generalizations across persons, simply because it relies upon the phenomenological method. Binswanger (1963), as well as others, agrees that to perceive a client accurately it is necessary to drop preconceptions concerning human behavior. But this phenomenological approach, which stresses idiographic concepts, is not held so rigidly as to obviate arriving at generalizations and even universalizations, as long as they are the end result of an inductive process grounded in sensitive observation. Indeed, many concepts mentioned in this chapter came about in just this fashion. Laing's (1960) extreme (and unrepresentative) unwillingness to generalize, which misinterprets what Husserl (1931) meant in formulating phenomenology, would end in an unworkable solipsism. The fact is that it is not really adhered to even by Laing, who does indeed generalize across persons and thereby contributes to the scientific enterprise.

As a psychotherapy, the existential approach involves a body of concepts and techniques that can certainly claim successes. In the case studies reported by Binswanger (1963), Boss (1963), Frankl (1965), and others, there is convincing evidence that clients, whether neurotic or severely psychotic, can be helped by existential treatment. From all accounts, Binswanger (1963) and Boss (1963) struggle for detailed understanding of the client in his own terms and, in the process, aid him to develop new meaning in life. Often, clients they helped had previously been through one or more other forms of psychotherapy (usually psychoanalysis) unsuccessfully. Frankl (1960) gives example after example of how his technique of paradoxical intention led to swift and complete symptom remission, even when the symptoms were in the psychotic range. Although

there is no evidence presently available with which to compare the relative effectiveness of existential and other psychotherapies systematically, the entire literature indicates that the existential approach helps people. In this practical sense, validity can be claimed.

Until recently, there was a paucity of systematic research on personality employing existential concepts. This can perhaps be traced to the relative disinterest of existential psychologists in performing personality research and to the general unfamiliarity of the existential approach to researchers. But some research of an existential nature is now being done, and many tests of existential personality variables are available.

Gendlin and Tomlinson (1967) have introduced the *Experiencing Scale,* a rating procedure applied by the researcher to verbalizations made by the subject. The ratings concern degree of experiencing, running from the lowest, in which the subject seems distinct and remote from his feelings, through the middle range, in which the subject gets his feelings into clear perspective as his own, to the highest, in which feelings have been scrutinized and explored so that they become a trusted and reliable source of self-awareness. Considering only a few of the findings concerning this test, it appears that the higher the level of experiencing, the better the outcome of psychotherapy and the greater the commitment to creative endeavor (Gendlin, Beebe, Cassens, Klein, & Oberlander, 1968).

Crumbaugh (1968) has developed a questionnaire, called the *Purpose-in-Life Test,* aimed at measuring Frankl's concept of existential vacuum (meaninglessness). Subjects showing existential vacuum on the test had world views rated by judges to be negative, lacking in purpose, and devoid of transcendental goals. In addition, the test shows a positive correlation with the Depression Scale of the *Minnesota Multiphasic Personality Inventory,* as well as with a measure of anomie. Although more research clearly needs to be done, the *Purpose-in-Life Test* shows promise of validity.

Another related test, the *Existential Study,* is under development by Thorne & Pishkin (1973). This questionnaire has been developed factor-analytically to yield seven scales, on self-status, self-actualization, existential morale, existential vacuum, humanistic identification, existence and destiny, and suicidal tendency. Though Thorne has included along with these identifiably existential variables other factors from diverse personality theories, some of the results are of interest to existential theory. On existential morale, for example, followers of Ayn Rand's rational philosophy were highest, followed by students and felons, with alcoholics and unwed mothers appearing demoralized, and schizophrenics disintegrated. Much work remains to be done before the validity of this test can be considered established.

More recently, Maddi, Kobasa, and Hoover (1976) have devised a questionnaire, called the *Alienation-Commitment Test,* which assesses the powerlessness, adventurousness, nihilism, and vegetativeness aspects of meaninglessness which appear in Maddi's theorizing. Each of these dimensions can be measured across relationships to work, persons, social institutions, family members, and self. The test is uncorrelated to intelligence and sex and shows a small relationship to socioeconomic level and age. The scales of the test show negative correlations of varying degree with a measure of creative attitudes toward living. Persons scoring high on meaninglessness in interpersonal relationships describe themselves as enjoying time spent alone. For this test, also, additional research is needed before its value can be fully determined.

Although tests of various aspects of meaninglessness are just at the beginning of their development, there are two substantial bodies of personality research bearing on important aspects of authentic and inauthentic being. Despite the fact that neither body of research began with the special intent to validate existential theory, that is exactly what is emerging.

First is the burgeoning literature on whether a person believes that he has control over his own life or that his life is really under the control of someone or something external to him. A person is said to demonstrate *internal locus of control* when he locates the power for determining behavior within the individual. *External locus of control,* on the other hand, is attributed to the person who locates the control over behavior outside of the individual—that is, in fate or in society, understood in an abstract, nonpersonal sense. The findings are relevant insofar as the authentic person perceives himself as having a mental life through which he can understand and influence his experiences and treats life as a series of decisions he must make responsibly. This would clearly involve an *internal locus of control.* In contrast, an *external locus of control* would signal an inauthentic person, who perceives his life as manipulated by the forces of society or fate uninfluenceable by him.

After several refinements, an *Internal vs. External Locus of Control (I–E) Scale* was made available for general use (Rotter, Seeman, & Liverant, 1962). One group of studies correlated this scale with primarily personal behavior (cf. Maddi, 1976). In general, it appears that internally controlled subjects obtain more information about matters in their world that could affect them, and they utilize this information to influence rather than to be influenced. For example, among hospitalized patients, as the degree of internal control increases, so does the amount of information they seek about their medical condition. In contrast, externally controlled subjects tended to remain ignorant of useful information, though no different in intelligence from their internally controlled counterparts. Internally controlled subjects also choose intermediate risks, banking on their skill to produce successful outcomes, whereas externally controlled subjects prefer large or small risks, wishing certainty or banking on chance. An intriguing study (Alegre & Murray, 1974) demonstrated that externally controlled persons are more susceptible to verbal conditioning, which, of course, uses extrinsic reinforcements. Other results (Cherulnik & Citrun, 1974) suggest that this resistance to external manipulation shown by internally controlled persons can be traced to their greater sense of possibility, compared to externally controlled persons.

Another group of studies using the I–E scale focuses upon social rather than personal behavior (cf. Maddi, 1976). In general, findings indicate that internally controlled persons are social activists, whereas externally controlled persons are acquiescent and conforming. For example, internally controlled subjects signed statements expressing the greatest amount of interest in social action concerning civil rights. That these were not empty statements was shown in another study, in which black social activists were shown to be more internally controlled than blacks who do not take part in civil rights activities.

In a series of studies (cf. Maddi, 1976) comparing scores on the I–E scale across ethnic groups, it was generally found that groups whose social position is low in power, either by class or by race, tend to score high in external control. To judge from the already reported attitudinal and action correlates of the belief in external control, it is easy to see why disadvantage due to class or race tends to perpetuate itself. This raises the possibility that social conditions determine whether one is internally or externally controlled. In contrast, the existential position interprets the belief in internal vs. external control to be a causal influence on action. Fortunately, some experiments have been done by Rotter and his associates which favor the existential interpretation (cf. Maddi, 1976). For example, in one study, two groups of subjects performed the same task of predicting a sequence of events. One group was told that success on the task was due to skill in deciphering the ordering of events, whereas the other group was told that success was due to chance, there being no rational ordering. Despite the fact that both groups received the same number and sequence of reinforcements, subjects with skill instructions changed prediction expectancies more frequently and more in the direction of previous experience than did subjects with chance instructions. The differences in action between the two groups seemed understandable on the basis of whether subjects did or not did not believe that they could influence their own destiny. Similar findings have been obtained with other tasks. Apparently, persons who believe they can influence their own lives act accordingly.

Another large body of research bearing upon existential personality theory concerns the tendency to respond or present oneself in a socially desirable light. This tendency is clearly an aspect of the conformism of the inauthentic being. Among the several available measures of socially desirable responding, the *Social Desirability Scale (SDS)* of Crowne and Marlowe (1960) is especially noteworthy. Much correlational research has been done using this questionnaire.

The higher one's social desirability score, the greater is the tendency to give common word associations and fewer, more concrete responses on tests of fantasy. Subjects high in socially desirable responding are especially rejecting of people but tend to underestimate the extent to which their friends really reject them. Their tendency to perform better on simple, repetitive motor tasks may be due to heightened attentiveness produced by a wish to please the experimenter. Consistent with this interpretation is the finding that subjects high in socially desirable responding are less likely to rate a monotonous task as dull. In general, the picture emerges of a personality characterized by intense interest in appearing attentive, consistent, competent, and acceptable, in the context of conforming, and showing superficial interest in, but lack of deep commitment to, others—in other words, an inauthentic being. In addition, there is evidence of a general unwillingness to face these facts and to engage in defensiveness (Crowne & Marlowe, 1960).

Any information concerning the relationship between social desirable responding and degree of psychopathology should be of interest; Maddi (1967, 1970) has contended that an inauthentic being is predisposed to existential sickness. There is some evidence (Katkin, 1964) that the SDS correlates significantly with various scales of psychopathology as measured by the *Minnesota Multiphasic Personality Inventory*. That the highest correlation is with the Schizophrenia Scale is noteworthy, since Maddi (1967, 1970) assumes that many persons diagnosed as schizophrenic are actually suffering from existential sickness.

Before closing this section, it would be well to mention the gradually developing body of experimental studies relevant to, and for the most part inspired by, existential theorizing. For example, Houston and Holmes (cf. Maddi, 1976) subjected students to conditions of threat involving temporal uncertainty. Some of the subjects were induced to avoid thinking about the threat by immersing themselves in distracting activities, whereas the other subjects were left to their own devices. Physiological measurement showed that the subjects engaging in avoidance thinking actually experienced a greater stress reaction to the threat than the other subjects. Through interviews, it was determined that the subjects who did not engage in avoidance activities spent the time thinking about the threat and reappraising it as less serious than originally believed. Insofar as a temporal uncertainty is not very different from ontological anxiety, this study provides support for the existential belief that accepting such anxiety rather than avoiding it is consistent with personal growth. Liem (cf. Maddi, 1976) permitted some students in an undergraduate course to choose the type of recitation section they preferred and granted them considerable choice in the ongoing conduct of the section, but denied such choice to other students in the course. Subjects permitted choice performed better than others on a course examination and gave higher ratings of satisfaction with their sections than did subjects not permitted choice. This is another demonstration of the value, for personal comfort and growth, of control over one's own life.

Comparisons

Maslow (1962) stated that there are three major themes in contemporary American psychology— the psychoanalytic, behavioristic, and humanistic traditions. The existential approach is strongly opposed to psychoanalysis and behaviorism, and though similar to some other humanistic positions is nonetheless importantly different from them.

Freud (e.g., 1922, 1930) viewed the person as controlled by biological pressures from within and social pressures from without. The biologically determined instincts continually press for expression and are by their nature antisocial. To preserve some semblance of order, society must champion the common good through punishing unmitigated instinct expression. Although this psychosocial conflict cannot be abolished, it must be minimized if organized human life is to be possible. This conflict is invariably minimized if the person goes against his instinctual nature and only acts upon those socially acceptable aspects of his instincts. The compromise must always occur this way, because the individual is weaker than society, the child weaker than the parents.

This is a tragic view of life in which complete fulfillment is impossible and complete consciousness dangerous. Awareness of the real aims of the instincts would bring overwhelming guilt and the temptation to severely punishable action. Even the highest form of development, the genital character type, involves defensive sublima-

tion in which one loves a spouse who unconsciously resembles the opposite-sexed parent, and works diligently to keep out of temptation's way. Although modern ego-psychology has taken some strides away from Freud's original position, pessimism about the individual and his world is still characteristic.

Existential psychology is diametrically opposed to the Freudian view. Freud's assumption of unchangeable biological instincts pitted against equally unchangeable social taboos, with the weak ego having to establish a compromise, actually represents inauthentic being, in the existential view. For Freud, guilt expresses the internalization of social taboos and the perception of oneself as unsocialized. In the existential view, guilt shows a debt to oneself in the form of missed opportunity. Furthermore, the Freudian emphasis on adjustment to society and loss of consciousness concerning antisocial tendencies jars with the existential emphasis on the pursuit of individuality and possibility with heightened consciousness as a guide and a source of freedom. Finally, the Freudian belief in the importance of reducing tension and unpleasant emotions at almost any cost appears as complaisancy, in comparison to existentialism's emphasis upon courageous toleration of anxiety as that which facilitates growth.

Skinnerian behaviorism is equally antithetical to the existential view. According to Skinner (1971), the person is a "black box," about which nothing needs to be known. Behavior can be explained solely in terms of the effects of external stimuli impinging upon the organism. These external stimuli are the cues which precede the behavior and the reinforcements that follow it. When a change takes place in the rate of a particular response through the influence of a reinforcement, learning is said to have occurred, and the response is regarded as explained because controlled. In behavior modification therapy, the behaviorist increases the rate of desirable responses and decreases the rate of undesirable responses by employing various schedules of reinforcement. It is assumed by Skinnerians that what constitutes desirable and undesirable behavior patterns is more or less given by conventional values and role designations.

As was true for Freud, the behavioristic belief that social forces in the form of positive and negative reinforcements control responses, without any possibility of choice on the person's part, represents inauthentic being to existential psychologists. This elevation of inauthenticity to an ideal is also apparent in the behavioristic denial that consciousness and active decision making can have a constructive influence on living. Indeed, Skinner (1971) regards emphasis upon values such as freedom and dignity to be wasteful misunderstandings of the human condition. The existential position also cannot countenance the behavioristic emphasis upon conventionality in determining what are desirable and undesirable responses, and the associated discouragement of persons freeing themselves from control by external reinforcement through knowledge and decision making. It is becoming apparent that the success of behavioristic psychotherapy is based upon the client's exercise of self-control (see Maddi, 1976). That some behaviorists have blithely adopted the terminology of self-control should not dull our realization that such decision-making capability is neither stimulus nor response. Rather, it is a human capability (inside the "black box"), demonstrating the need for an existential formulation.

With its emphases, existential psychology clearly falls into the humanistic or third-force tradition. This does not mean, however, that existentialism agrees completely with all other positions classified as humanistic. In particular, there are distinct and important differences between existential psychology and self-actualization theory. According to Rogers (1959), individuals have a fairly automatic tendency to actualize their inherent potentialities. The inherent potentialities constitute a sort of genetic blueprint which is rendered actual in behavior through the action of the actualizing tendency. According to this self-actualizing view, this will happen without undue effort, socialization, guidance, or stimulation, if no inhibiting social forces are present. For example, a person does not have to grow in the ability to love. He can love from the very beginning and will retain this ability if uninfringed upon by destructive social pressures. Such undesirable social pressures take the form of conditional positive regard from significant others. Conditional positive regard occurs when some of the person's behavior is approved of and rewarded, whereas the rest is disapproved of and

punished. This teaches the person conditions of worth which he will apply to his own behavior, and thereby, he will lose the path to self-actualization. Most self-discipline, striving, and planfulness are regarded as maladjustment rather than self-actualization. The actualized person behaves effortlessly and has a generalized sense of well-being.

In contrast, the existential position regards authenticity as a difficult state to attain and one which must be striven for rather than being simply automatically realized. One way to understand authenticity is as an acquired taste, which yields satisfaction only after it has been developed. This requires stimulation and encouragement from significant others, at least early in life. For example, true loving is difficult, demanding, and ever fraught with insecurity, according to existentialists, and therefore it must be the outcome of much struggle and self-disciplined development. In this view, planfulness, courage, and an acceptance of the strenuousness of life are valuable aids, not expressions of maladjustment. The authentic person tolerates anxiety as the price he must pay for the freedom and potency to create his own life, a possibility available to only the human being. Actualization theory provides a view of life that is indeed pale by comparison.

The comparisons drawn have pinpointed the place of existential psychology among the major trends in contemporary personology, recognizing this viewpoint as a variant on humanism which emphasizes decision making, meaning creation, and life strenuousness. Several personality theories not yet mentioned are similar yet different enough to warrant comment. These theories are associated with Gordon W. Allport, Erik H. Erikson, Erich Fromm, George A. Kelly, and O. Hobart Mowrer.

Both Allport and Kelly assert that life is led through an active consciousness expressed in constructing and shaping experience through choice. But Kelly shows little appreciation of the strenuousness of such a commitment, carried on in anxiety about plunging into an unpredictable future through becoming unconventional. Kelly (1955) comes closest to recognizing such matters when he suggests that persons may make *adventurous* as opposed to *conservative* choices. But he neglects to offer any theoretical basis for understanding why anyone would choose adventurously, since, according to him, unexpected events bring anxiety and are avoided at virtually any cost. Oddly enough, although he extols the value of individuality, Kelly offers no formal theorizing with which to pinpoint its advantages and the disadvantages of conventionality. The apparent similarities between this approach and existential psychology are superficial at best.

Allport's approach may be somewhat closer to existential psychology than is Kelly's. After all, Allport (1955) does include among his *dimensions of maturity* such existentially relevant considerations as well-developed habits of rational coping with problems, and a philosophy of life which includes a generic sense of purpose. But it is far from clear just what role these dimensions are considered to play in decision making and the toleration of anxiety in order to minimize guilt. Even more important, Allport is not convincing on how these dimensions develop. He (Allport, 1955) assumes the importance of parental support and love in spurring psychological growth, and of *functional autonomy* in spurring the detachment of behaviors from their early beginnings as responses to externally imposed rewards and punishments. To existential psychologists, however, it seems doubtful that amorphous parental love and support, undirected toward specifically stimulating the child's creation of meaning through cognitive activity, and unmitigated by the imposition of limits whereby facticity can be appreciated, could lead to the aspects of maturity they agree with Allport in emphasizing. In addition, existential psychologists would regard "functional autonomy" as an inarticulate concept for elucidating the shouldering of risk, toleration of emotional upheaval, and belief in one's own capabilities which must be present if the struggle to transcend conventionality is to occur. For these reasons, his approach must be regarded as rudimentary, if attitudinally congenial.

Both Fromm and Erikson emphasize the importance of a subjective sense of meaningfulness about one's life, and this makes their positions of interest to existential psychologists. There is much in Fromm's (1941, 1947) discussion of the *marketing orientation* and *escape from freedom* which parallels emphases in existential psychology on *conformism* and avoidance of *ontological*

anxiety by shrinking from the future. Erikson's (1950) *ego integrity versus despair* is also reminiscent of the existentialist's emphasis upon *authenticity*, in contrast to *inauthenticity*. But it must be remembered that both Fromm and Erikson approach these concerns out of a basically psychoanalytic frame of reference in which importance is given to Freudian notions of psychosexual development, defensiveness, and a dynamic unconscious. For Fromm, the marketing orientation is traceable to a fixation in the period described rather like what Freud talked about as the latency stage. Further, Fromm's preceding three stages are quite reminiscent of the oral, anal, and phallic stages. Thus, when Fromm talks about his ideal, the productive orientation, as a combination of the valuable behaviors of the preceding stages, this needs to be understood in its implications as closer to Freud's genital character type than the words may signify. The same argument applies to Erikson, as his psychosocial stages lean heavily on Freud's insights. Thus, for existential psychologists, discussions of meaningfulness by Fromm and Erikson emphasize too much the vicissitudes of sex and aggression instincts filtered through libidinized parent-child interactions. Inevitably, Fromm and Erikson put less emphasis than do existentialists upon the creation of meaning through vigorous symbolization, imagination, and judgment as the basic fact of human life. A good example of this is Erikson's view that the crisis of meaning is the last developmental stage, engaged in when the person begins to look backward rather than forward. For existentialists, the earlier in life the person begins to construct his own meaning the better, because the commitment to self-determined development implied is crucial to reaching maturity and personal power.

Finally, Mowrer's (1961) recent emphasis upon guilt and meaninglessness as resultants of failure in accepting social responsibility may appear similar to the existentialist's emphasis. But Mowrer is concerned with something fairly close to conventionality, as the social responsibilities involved are consensually defined, and the guilt is toward others. It is for this reason that the concept of sin has explanatory value for him. In contrast, existentialists emphasize the guilt one feels toward oneself when possibility has been jeopardized. For Mowrer, guilt is best expiated by public disclosure of social selfishness and irresponsibility. For existentialism, guilt can only be reduced by dedicating oneself to choosing the future, and thereby changing and growing. The differences between these two seemingly similar positions are actually vast.

Prospect

For several reasons, existential personality theory has a bright future. First, personology appears to be entering into a new and vigorous phase, after a recent crisis (Bowers, 1973), in which the explanatory value of personality constructs was questioned and situational variables were offered as more powerful for scientific explanation. It is now clear that the person versus situation controversy was a pseudo issue (Carlson, 1975), and the evidence favors approaches that employ concepts concerning the interaction between person and situation variables. The emphasis now is shifting to theories of personality that highlight cognitive processes, consciousness, planfulness, decision making, and the like. Existential psychology is such a theory par excellence. In addition, its emphasis upon the dialectic between possibility and facticity is squarely in the interactionist camp. It can be expected that existential psychology will have a leading role in the coming personalistic renaissance, with other less cognitive and interactionist theories of personality, such as psychoanalysis, declining in importance. This prediction is quite in line with the conclusion reached by Maddi (1976), who found existential psychology to be among the fulfillment theories most supported by available personality research.

Also consistent with the new emphasis upon cognitive, interactionist positions is the recent rise of social learning theory. This approach should not be simply equated with behaviorism. It emphasizes learning that occurs without any responses or reinforcements. It is better understood as an emerging theory of personality in which are highlighted cognitive, interactionist, and strategy variables. In outlining this reconceptualization of personality, Mischel (1973) has not only emphasized such concepts as decision making and planfulness but even goes so far as

to mention the similarity between his approach and existentialism. In the years to come, an accord between existential psychology and social learning theory is likely.

Also prompting the centrality of existential psychology are the recent commentaries on the psychological enterprise by prominent methodologists. Lee J. Cronbach (1975), for example, advocates aims for psychology that take into account the distinctiveness of its subject matter. Personality, he says, is no longer to be constricted by rigid models of causality imposed by the investigator. Instead, the subject is to indicate what about him is worth studying. This is certainly similar to the existential emphasis on beginning with the subjective experience of the person studied.

In this promising future, existential psychology could and should deepen ties with other areas in the field. For too long, existentialism has remained the concern of a few clinicians speaking a language too vague and insular for interaction with academic psychologists. Two fields where the value of cross-fertilization is obvious are cognition and aging. Existential psychology could gain from cognition a better understanding of decision making and symbolization, imagination, and judgment; and from aging, a context within which to specify further concepts such as temporality and the possibility/facticity dialectic. Existential psychology could give to both of these fields an emphasis upon organizing principles whereby research could be systematized and an overall picture of human life could be gained.

Annotated Bibliography

Binswanger, L. *Being-in-the-World: Selected Papers of Ludwig Binswanger.* New York: Basic Books, 1963.

This is the first translation of major writings by the existential psychiatrist-psychologist into English. It is a good collection of representative pieces, including Binswanger's critique of Freud, his description of his reliance upon the work of philosophers, his theoretical innovations in the field of psychopathology, and a case history with descriptive report and existential analysis.

The book includes a lengthy introduction by the translator, Jacob Needleman, which sets the philosophical stage for Binswanger's work, drawing comparisons with the writings of Kant, Heidegger, Husserl, and Sartre. Needleman also provides a systematic consideration of the important concepts which best distinguish *Daseinsanalyse* from traditional psychoanalysis.

Although an essential text for students of existential psychology, this book has its drawbacks. One wishes that Needleman had provided a more extensive consideration of the psychological context within which Binswanger's work should be evaluated. For the psychology reader, the philosophical discussion is insufficient. Also, reading Binswanger's writings is often a rather frustrating exercise. His choice of terms is awkward, and his style of writing is convoluted. Unfortunately, this complaint may be addressed to most existentialists, both psychologists and philosophers. There is clearly an existentialist "jargon" which, although emphasizing the uniqueness of the existentialist concepts, serves often to obscure their intended message.

Boss, M. *Psychoanalysis and Daseinsanalysis*. New York: Basic Books, 1963.

Boss begins this book with a case history of the "patient who taught" him the value of Daseinsanalysis and then cites many varied therapy cases throughout the text as illustrations of his theoretical points. Heidegger's psychological applicability is realized in terms of several diagnostic syndromes. Like Binswanger, Boss presents a systematic critique of Freud and extends it into the psychotherapeutic context. The differences between existential and Freudian analysis are discussed in terms of technique as well as theory. Especially distinctive in Boss's treatment of pathology is his consideration of psychosomatic illnesses from an existential perspective.

Gendlin, E. T. Experiential Explication and Truth. *Journal of Existentialism*, 1965–1966, *6*, 131–146.

Gendlin utilizes both his philosophical sophistication and his psychological skill in this article, which serves as a good introduction to the existentialist orientation. He provides effective discussions of issues like possibility and facticity, the integration of thoughts and feelings in experiential awareness, and existentialism's use of phenomenology. The deliberate intent of several of these discussions is the correction of erroneous assumptions about existential psychology. Among other clarifications, Gendlin convincingly argues that authentic freedom can never be solipsism.

Maddi, S. R. The Existential Neurosis. *Journal of Abnormal Psychology*, 1967, *72*, 311–325.

Maddi, S. R. The search for meaning. In M. Page (Ed.), *Nebraska symposium on motivation*. Lincoln, Neb.: University of Nebraska Press, 1970.

In these two articles, Maddi provides an elaboration of the psychological clarity of existential psychology and a systematic discussion of personality and psychopathology. An articulation between the existential orientation and other psychological systems is found here in the form of Maddi's use of concepts, such as needs, motivation, and personality types, in his existential theorizing, and in his reference to relevant personality research.

May, R., Angel, E., and Ellenberger, H. F. (Eds.). *Existence: A New Dimension in Psychiatry and Psychology*. New York: Basic Books, 1958.

This is a useful text for students. May provides a helpful opening section which introduces basic existential notions and sets the existential movement within the history of psychology. Selections from Binswanger's work are included: a discourse on the nature of *Daseinsanalyse*, and two case histories. The text also includes representative articles by phenomenological psychologists.

Although the authors recommend the reading of the philosophical texts from which existential psychologists draw many of their insights, they also recognize the excessiveness of this assignment in terms of time and energy required, and suggest that the reader might focus on the following selections from important philosophers. In M. Heidegger, *Being and Time* (New York: Harper & Row, 1962), one can focus on the discussions of death, care, and anxiety. In J. P. Sartre, *Being and Nothingness* (New York: Philosophical Library, 1956), the psychologist should read carefully Sartre's section on "Existential Psychoanalysis," in which he provides a critique of Freud, a comparison between Freud's and his own work, and an explication of his distinctive method of psychoanalysis. The introduction from S. Kierkegaard, *The Concept of Dread* (Princeton, N. J.: Princeton University Press, 1944) is also suggested. There Kierkegaard discusses how the psychological investigation of a phenomenon is essential for its understanding and also how this investigation differs from that of the philosopher and religious writer.

A second recommendation directs the reader to two books which present especially lucid summaries of the writings of existential philosophers:

Blackham, H. J. *Six Existentialist Thinkers* (2nd ed.). New York: Harper & Row, 1959.

Grimsley, R. *Existentialist Thought*. Cardiff: University of Wales Press, 1955.

References

Adler, A. *The practice and theory of individual psychology* (P. Radin, trans.). New York: Harcourt, Brace, 1927.

Adler, A. *The individual psychology of Alfred Adler*. New York: Basic Books, 1956.

Alegre, C., & Murray, E. Locus of control, behavioral intention, and verbal conditioning. *Journal of Personality*, 1974, *42*, 668–681.

Allport, G. W. *Becoming: Basic considerations for a*

psychology of personality. New Haven: Yale University Press, 1955.

Beauvoir, S. de. *The ethics of ambiguity* (B. Frechtman, trans.). New York: The Citadel Press, 1948.

Beauvoir, S. de. *The second sex* (H. M. Parshley, trans.). New York: Random House, 1952.

Binswanger, L. *Freud: Reminiscences of a friendship* (N. Guterman, trans.). New York: Grune & Stratton, 1957.

Binswanger, L. *Being-in-the-world: Selected papers of Ludwig Binswanger* (J. Needleman, trans.). New York: Basic Books, 1963.

Blackham, H. J. *Six existentialist thinkers* (2nd ed.). New York: Harper & Row, 1959.

Boss, M. *Psychoanalysis and daseinsanalysis* (L. B. Lefebre, trans.). New York: Basic Books, 1963.

Bowers, K. S. Situationism in psychology: An analysis and a critique. *Psychological Review*, 1973, *80*, 307–336.

Carlson, R. Personality. *Annual Review of Psychology*, 1975, *26*, 393–414.

Cherulnik, P. D., & Citrin, M. M. Individual differences in psychological reactance: The interaction between locus of control and mode of elimination of freedom. *Journal of Personality and Social Psychology*, 1974, *29*, 398–404.

Cronbach, L. J. Beyond the two disciplines of scientific psychology. *American Psychologist*, 1975, *30*, 116–127.

Crowne, O. P., & Marlowe, D. A new scale of social desirability independent of psychopathology. *Journal of Consulting Psychology*, 1960, *24*, 349–354.

Crumbaugh, J. C. Cross-validation of Purpose-in-Life Test based on Frankl's concept. *Journal of Individual Psychology*, 1968, *24*, 74–81.

Crumbaugh, J. C., & Maholick, L. T. An experimental study in existentialism: The psychometric approach to Frankl's concept of neogenic neurosis. *Journal of Clinical Psychology*, 1964, *20*, 200-207.

Erikson, E. H. *Childhood and society.* New York: Norton, 1950.

Frankl, V. E. *Man's search of meaning: An introduction to logotherapy* (I. Lasch, trans.). New York: Washington Square Press, 1963.

Frankl, V. E. *The doctor and the soul* (2nd ed.; R. & C. Winston, trans.). New York: Knopf, 1965.

Freud, S. *Beyond the pleasure principle* (J. Strachey, trans.). London: International Psychoanalytic Press, 1922.

Freud, S. *Civilization and its discontents* (J. Strachey, trans.). New York: Norton, 1930.

Fromm, E. *Escape from freedom.* New York: Rinehart, 1941.

Fromm, E. *Man for himself.* New York: Holt, Rinehart & Winston, 1947.

Gendlin, E. T. *Experiencing and the creation of meaning.* New York: Free Press, 1962.

Gendlin, E. T. Experiential explication and truth. *Journal of Existentialism*, 1965–66, *6*, 131–146.

Gendlin, E. T. Focusing. *Psychotherapy: Theory, Research, Practice*, 1969, *6*, 4–15.

Gendlin, E. T., Beebe, J. III, Cassens, J., Klein, M., &

Oberlander, M. Focusing ability in psychotherapy, personality, and creativity. In J. M. Shlien (Ed.), *Research in psychotherapy* (Vol. 3). Washington, D.C.: American Psychological Association, 1968.

Gendlin, E. T., & Tomlinson, T. M. The process conception and its measurement. In C. R. Rogers, E. T. Gendlin, D. J. Kiesler, & C. B. Truax (Eds.), *The psychotherapeutic relationship and its impact: A study of psychotherapy with schizophrenics.* Madison: University of Wisconsin Press, 1967.

Grimsley, R. *Existentialist thought.* Cardiff: University of Wales Press, 1955.

Heidegger, M. *Being and time* (J. Macquarrie & E. S. Robinson, trans.). New York: Harper & Row, 1962.

Husserl, E. *Ideas: General introduction to pure phenomenology* (W. R. Boyce Gibson, trans.). New York: Macmillan, 1931.

Jaspers, K. *General psychopathology* (J. Hoenig & M. W. Hamilton, trans.). Chicago: University of Chicago Press, 1963.

Jung, C. G. *Modern man in search of a soul* (R. F. C. Hull, trans.). New York: Harcourt, Brace & World, 1933.

Jung, C. G. The relations between the ego and the unconscious (R. F. C. Hull, trans.). In H. Read, M. Fordham, & G. Adler (Eds.), *Collected Works.* Princeton, W. J.: Princeton University Press, 1953.

Katkin, E. S. The Marlowe-Crowne social desirability scale: Independent of psychopathology? *Psychological Reports*, 1964, *15*, 703–706.

Kelly, G. A. *The psychology of personal constructs* (Vol. 1). New York: Norton, 1955.

Kierkegaard, S. *Repetition: An essay in experimental psychology* (W. Lowrie, trans.). New York: Harper & Row, 1941.

Kierkegaard, S. *The concept of dread* (W. Lowrie, trans.). Princeton; N.J.: Princeton University Press, 1944.

Kierkegaard, S. *Fear and trembling and the sickness unto death* (W. Lowrie, trans.). Garden City, N.Y.: Doubleday, Anchor Books, 1954.

Kierkegaard, S. *Either/or* (D. Stevenson & L. Swenson, trans.). Garden City, N.Y.: Doubleday, Anchor Books, 1959.

Kierkegaard, S. *Concluding unscientific postscript* (D. Swenson, trans.). Princeton, N.J.: Princeton University Press, 1968.

Laing, R. D. *The divided self: An existential study in sanity and madness.* New York: Tavistock, 1960.

Laing, R. D. *The politics of experience.* New York: Ballantine Books, 1967.

Lowrie, W. *Kierkegaard.* New York: Oxford University Press, 1938.

Maddi, S. R. The existential neurosis. *Journal of Abnormal Psychology*, 1967, *72*, 311–325.

Maddi, S. R. The search for meaning. In M. Page (Ed.), *Nebraska Symposium on Motivation.* Lincoln: University of Nebraska Press, 1970.

Maddi, S. R. The developmental value of the fear of death. *Proceedings of the American Psychological Association Convention, 1975.* Washington, D.C., 1975. (a)

Maddi, S. R. The strenuousness of the creative life. In I. A. Taylor & J. W. Getzels (Eds.), *Perspectives in creativity*. Chicago: Aldine, 1975. (b)

Maddi, S. R. *Personality theories: A comparative analysis* (3rd ed.). Homewood, Ill.: Dorsey Press, 1976.

Maddi, S. R., Kobasa, S. C., & Hoover, M. *The Alienation-Commitment Test: Reliability and validity*. Manuscript in preparation, 1976.

Maslow, A. *Motivation and personality*. New York: Harper, 1954.

Maslow, A. H. Some basic propositions of a growth and self-actualization psychology. In *Perceiving, behaving, becoming: A new focus for education*. Washington, D.C.: Yearbook of the Association for Supervision and Curriculum Development, 1962.

May, R. *The meaning of anxiety*. New York: Ronald Press, 1950.

May, R. *Man's search for himself*. New York: Norton, 1953.

May, R. *Love and will*. New York: Norton, 1967.

May, R. *Power and innocence: A search for the sources of violence*. New York: Norton, 1972.

May, R., Angel, E., & Ellenberger, H. F. (Eds.). *Existence: A new dimension in psychiatry and psychology*. New York: Basic Books, 1958.

Mischel, W. Toward a cognitive social learning reconceptualization of personality. *Psychological Review*, 1973, *80*, 252–283.

Mowrer, O. H. *The crisis in psychiatry and religion*. New York: Van Nostrand, 1961.

Rank, O. *The trauma of birth*. New York: Harcourt, Brace, 1929.

Rank, O. *Will therapy and truth and reality* (J. Taft, trans.). New York: Knopf, 1945.

Rogers, C. R. A theory of therapy, personality, and interpersonal relationships, as developed in the client-centered framework. In S. Koch (Eds.), *Psychology: A study of a science* (Vol. 3). New York: McGraw-Hill, 1959.

Rogers, C. R. *On becoming a person*. Boston: Houghton Mifflin, 1961.

Rotter, J. B., Seeman, M., & Liverant, S. Internal versus external control of reinforcements: A major variable in behavior theory. In N. F. Washburne (Ed.), *Decisions, values, and groups* (Vol. 2, pp. 473–516). London: Pergamon, 1962.

Sartre, J. P. *What is literature?* (B. Frechtman, trans.). New York: Philosophical Library, 1949.

Sartre, J. P. *Being and nothingness* (H. Barnes, trans.). New York: Philosophical Library, 1956.

Skinner, B. F. *Beyond freedom and dignity*. New York: Knopf, 1971.

Szasz, T. W. *The myth of mental illness: Foundations of a theory of personal conduct*. New York: Dell Delta Books, 1961.

Thorne, F. C., & Pishkin, V. The existential study. *Journal of Clinical Psychology*, 1973, *29*, 387–410.

Tillich, P. *The courage to be*. New Haven, Conn.: Yale University Press, 1952.

Unamuno, M. de. *The tragic sense of life* (J. F. C. Flitch, trans.). New York: Dover, 1957.

Social interactionism, a major tradition within American sociology, emerged late in the 19th century and has constantly maintained a strong interest in social-psychological issues. Early proponents include Charles Cooley, John Dewey, and W. I. Thomas, but the person generally considered to have exerted the strongest influence on contemporary interactionists was George H. Mead.

From the beginning, social interactionism opposed biological determinism, cultural determinism, and reductionism, including stimulus-response theories, as explanations for human behavior. Recently, it has also opposed structural determinism.

Interactionists emphasize that humans live in a world mediated by symbols and that interaction—whether through language or gestures—is symbolic. Meaning is not "in" the object but is linked with behavior. Objects and the social contexts in which they arise via interaction are constantly in emergence.

A central concept of social interactionism is *self*. Each person acts self-reflexively much of the time, taking into account not only himself but the imagined selves of others. These selves arise in interaction and are closely linked with role playing and role taking.

Major contemporary concepts in social interactionism include *impression management* (Goffman), *awareness context* (Glaser and Strauss), *appearance* (Stone), *career* (Hughes), and *labeling of deviancy* (Becker). Some interactionists especially emphasize that face-to-face interaction is never merely interpersonal but involves group or organizational representatives. For example, when a nurse and doctor confront each other, they are not only two individuals handling their differences but are representatives of their respective professions.

Interactionism has not been especially concerned with individuals; hence interactionists are primarily researchers and teachers. Researchers in this tradition tend to rely on field observations and interviewing, primarily to obtain qualitative data and to reach nonquantified conclusions. Quotations and case histories are frequently employed. Critics of social interactionism maintain that this kind of research lacks precision and at best is merely exploratory. Interactionists retort that apparently more precise methodology does not necessarily yield more trustworthy findings on issues important to interactionists.

Recently, social interactionism has had a considerable resurgence among younger sociologists, who believe this perspective and its dominant methodology are more in touch with reality than questionnaire or laboratory research. They also believe that interactionism provides a less strictly deterministic view of human action than alternative perspectives in sociology.

Sociological Theories of Personality

Anselm Strauss

GEORGE HERBERT MEAD

Introduction

Personality theory, generally considered to be the special province of psychologists, is also of considerable interest to other workers in the field of human behavior. Sociologists such as Comte, Tarde, and LeBon who wrote about institutional or group behavior frequently did not explicitly discuss how people either developed as humans in society or maintained themselves. Sociologists of the 20th century, however, have developed a number of theories bearing on personality, and some will be discussed in this chapter.

It will be difficult to communicate in this book with readers as well as with other authors, most of whom presumably will be psychologists or psychiatrists, since many of the terms and concepts used by sociologists are unknown or at least unfamiliar to them, especially if they have not kept up with recent trends in the field. Consequently, in this Introduction we have included a number of definitions of basic sociological terms related to the topic of this book—personality theory. (Note that some of these definitions differ somewhat from those given in the Glossary for this book.) Some of these will be further elaborated in the text of this chapter. We believe this basic lexicon will not only permit the reader to go over the rest of the chapter with greater profit but will also give him or her an understanding of major theoretical items of concern to the sociologist's interest in personality theory of the interactionist type.

Basic lexicon

Accounts or *motivational statements.* Verbal explanations of the purposes of behavior, given to oneself or others when the behavior is problematic.
Actor. Person engaged in interaction.
Assessing. Reading various cues about another person in an attempt to "size him up."
Awareness context. The total combination of what each interactant in a situation knows about the identity of the other person, as well as his own identity in the eyes of the other.
Career. Objective movements a person makes through a social structure (labor market, school, etc.) and subjective aspects which pertain to changes in self-conceptions that accompany such movements.
Deviancy. Behavior which is labeled as deviant (homosexuality, delinquency, etc.) but which is de-

fined, rather than "really" having an objective existence, as wrong or immoral.
Face. The positive social value a person effectively claims for himself by his behavior during a particular interaction.
Field observation. Research done "in the field" based on first-hand observing and interviewing of people.
Functionalism. A sociological position prevalent during the 1950s and 1960s; involves an emphasis on the totality of societies and the interrelationship of each part of society.
Impression management. The organization of the presenting person's cues so as to elicit desired responses in assessing the other person.
Looking-glass self. Imagining another's perception of our appearance, manners, aims, character, and behavior.
Reductionism. Accounting for behavior by reference to assumed neural or physiological processes.
Role playing. The enacting of social roles, which involves the individual's conception of the role as well as others' expectations of how it should be enacted.
Role taking. Imaginatively assuming the point of view of another person.
Self-reflexiveness. Acting with reference to oneself as well as toward oneself.
Status passage. The movement into and out of social statuses (political office or marital status, for example).
Structuralism. Accounting for behavior by reference solely to social factors, such as organizations, institutions, culture, or "society."
Symbolic environment. Reality which is mediated for humans by their symbols rather than through direct encounter.

History

Precursors

Social interactionism is a major tradition within American sociology which has a strong social-psychological emphasis and focuses on interaction among individuals regarded as members of groups rather than as independent individuals. Among the intellectual influences which led to the emergence of social interactionism were the following:

1. *The theory of evolution.* Virtually all social scientists in the 19th century were profoundly influenced by Charles Darwin's theory of evolution. Evolutionary theory contributed such

social-interactionism ideas as: (*a*) emergent evolution (with humans acting at a "higher," more complex "level" than other species), (*b*) communication as a central feature of human relations, and (*c*) the possibilities of rational control in directing societal evolution.

2. *Idealistic philosophy.* Pragmatic philosophers like John Dewey and George Mead, who strongly influenced later social interactionists, reacted against idealistic philosophy but took from it various assumptions, such as (*a*) an essential characteristic of man is his self, and (*b*) man is related to his environment via the mediation of self and self-reflexive action. From idealistic philosophers like G. W. F. Hegel, the pragmatists also borrowed the idea of societal change as evolutionary, with individuals implicated as social beings in the evolutionary process.

3. *19th-century sociology and anthropology.* Both of those fields by the end of the century reflected evolutionary notions of stages of societal development. Societies were said to progress from the simplest toward the most developed. The idea of culture was an especially important one in anthropology, and sociological thinking was strongly colored by the same idea.

Beginnings

From approximately 1890 to 1930, sociologists were deeply engaged in combating biological explanations of human behavior. Some evolutionists had argued for the importance of the struggle for survival among the species, including human behavior. Instincts were often believed to be the main motives lying behind action. Sociologists generally seized on the idea of culture as a counterexplanation for such instinctivist beliefs. Sociological social psychologists like Ellsworth Faris and L. L. Bernard used cross-cultural data in attempts to discredit the reality of instincts. Bernard drew up a list of dozens of supposedly "real" instincts, many of which, he showed, could easily be explained as learned behavior.

In 1902 Charles Cooley attacked biologists and psychologists who maintained that childhood development is essentially a biological unfolding. Like William James and James M. Baldwin—both psychologists—Cooley gave great importance to the development of the child's self, even studying his own children's use of self-reflexive words. He argued that society and self are two sides of the same coin: Persons evolve through their participation in society, and society is what it is because of persons—it is not some reified "thing" over and above its members. "A separate individual is an abstraction unknown to experience, and so likewise is society when regarded as something apart from individuals" (Cooley, 1902, p. 36). In general, sociologists of the time believed environment was far more important than any biological mechanism in explaining human behavior. Environment, however, was regarded as primarily social or cultural, and individuals as relatively open to change. It was believed that human nature is not fixed by genetic structure but is "plastic" and has varied potentials. Dewey (1922) especially influenced sociologists to the dynamic interactional view.

Early in sociological thinking, men like Thomas and Cooley were arguing that the environment does not directly determine behavior. The contrary position had been adopted by many sociologists, including William Sumner, who maintained that folkways and mores determine behavior—period! Anthropologists like A. L. Kroeber held essentially the same position but couched it in terms of "culture." Interactionists, however, believed there is an interaction between a person's self and the social or cultural environment, so that while selves are formed and shaped by environmental influences, they do not simply and directly, or completely, determine behavior.

Another form of environmental determinism against which interactionists reacted was stimulus-response psychology. Thus Dewey (1922) argued that all organisms are active; a stimulus does not directly stimulate an organism's action but rather feeds into its ongoing activity. Later Dewey and others would say stimuli could be related meaningfully to human behavior only through intervening thought processes. In short, humans both are acted upon by the environment and act back to reshape it. This implied a subjective as well as an objective side to human action. In the words of Thomas (Thomas & Thomas, 1928), " If men define situations as real, they are real in their consequences" (p. 572). Another problem with which interactionists and other sociologists wrestled was that of *social order.* How are the regularities, the patterns of human action possible? The interactionists put "communication" at the heart of this problem.

Probably the person who most influences today's interactionists is George H. Mead. Born in 1862, he studied philosophy at Harvard and at German universities. His first position was at the University of Michigan, where he met both Cooley and Dewey. When Dewey shortly afterward went to the University of Chicago, he recruited Mead, who remained at Chicago until his death in 1931.

Mead's influence on sociologists is related to the dominance until the mid-1940s of the University of Chicago's Department of Sociology. Strangely enough, Mead did not publish a single book. His most influential volume, *Mind, Self, and Society* (1934) was edited from students' class notes. Mead did, however, publish many articles which reflect clearly the development of his thought.

During his lifetime of teaching, sociologists at Chicago valued the original contributions Mead was making to that branch of their field known as social psychology. Graduate students flocked to his classes and later were instrumental in introducing his writings on social psychology into the standard sociological literature. His concepts became common property among sociologists; his lines were quoted freely in textbooks. He remains an oft-quoted elder statesman in the field.

A direct line of descent from Mead to contemporary interactionists flows through Herbert Blumer, who took over Mead's class in social psychology. At Chicago and later at Berkeley, Blumer influenced such people as Alfred Lindesmith, Tomatsu Shibutani, Gregory Stone, Orrin Klapp, Anselm Strauss, Howard Becker, Ralph Turner, John Lofland, Stanford Lyman, and Thomas Scheff. Some of Mead's ideas crossed the boundaries into psychology, and social psychologists like T. M. Newcomb utilized some of his concepts (including *generalized other* and *role taking*).

Mead (1932, 1934, 1938) called his social psychology "social behaviorism," rejecting the Watsonian (antimentalistic) behaviorism popular in the 1920s but retaining the behaviorists' emphasis on action. Mead characteristically addressed himself to such topics as self, thought, self-control, role playing, role taking, social interaction, group membership, and society. He tackled

social-psychological issues as a means to getting answers to philosophical problems. While his writing is not easy to master, a growing number of readers find his pages richly rewarding. His ideas and concepts provide continuing stimulation and reference points to many, if not most, interactionists.

One of the best summaries of Mead's thought is by Blumer (1969), who notes that Mead's: "process of self-interaction puts the human being over against his world instead of merely in it, requires him to meet and handle his world through a defining process instead of merely responding to it, and forces him to construct his action instead of merely releasing it." Blumer adds that Mead "saw the self as a process . . . not as a structure" (p. 536).

Current Status

During the 1950s interactionism was politically eclipsed by other trends in sociology, but during the 1960s it had a marked resurgence. In part this is due to younger sociologists' distrust of "the establishment," including the traditional sociological reliance on questionnaires and on statistical methods of analysis, which, on the theoretical side, tend toward functionalism and so seem politically conservative. Interactionists regard persons as having some autonomy in their own destinies and the destiny of their society. These assumptions appeal to many antiestablishment sociologists. Interactionists generally use field research methods and extensive interviews. The interactionists' insistence on getting the actor's views seems much closer to reality than alternative sociological approaches, which often impose the researcher's views on the data. Some interactionists have tended to study politically weak people, including "deviants," and to contest "official" views about those who break laws or customs. This approach appeals to those who have grown up in an era when people took pride in going to jail for good causes or who have enjoyed "playing the bureaucracies" for personal or moral reasons.

Interactionists' writings have recently been quite influential in Europe. In England, interactionism represents a "more in touch with reality than survey research" movement, but interactionists' views of deviancy, occupations, work and organization have also affected the English sociologists. In Germany, interactionists' views seem more to have fed into sociological positions deriving from phenomenological philosophy, while interactionist research seems less influential.

Among the important recent books on the topic is Herbert Blumer's *Symbolic Interactionism* (1969). It attacks social structuralism vigorously, arguing that such concepts as status, role, norm, regulation and values do not determine behavior: "they are important only as they enter into [people's] interpretation and definition" (p. 291).

Another eminent interactionist, Everett Hughes, has recently published *The Sociological Eye* (1971), a collection of influential writings. Hughes is known for such concepts as *status dilemmas* and *career*. The former refers to such situations as introducing women into strictly masculine work settings, where interaction previously rested on an implicit man-to-man basis (sex jokes, swearing), and the woman's presence is subtly (sometimes not so subtly) disturbing. The concept of career will be discussed below; Hughes' writings and teaching about careers have had a major impact on many sociologists.

Another influential interactionist is Erving Goffman. His *The Presentation of Self* (1959) is probably the most widely read volume in contemporary sociology. Goffman's forte is the uncovering of implicit rules which profoundly affect interaction. He emphasizes that even explicit rules are carried out not automatically but through assessments, calculations, strategies, tactics, and actions of the participants, who are self-reflecting, self-referring, and self-evaluating actors. One of Goffman's principal concepts is *impression management*—the organization of the presenting person's cues so as to elicit desired responses in assessing other persons. This management may be completely honest or virtually without awareness. Impressions are created by using a range of gestures and ways of communicating and even by spatial arrangements (as in doctors' offices). Impression management may also involve teamwork, as illustrated in con games.

Howard Becker's *Outsiders* (1973) sparked interest in interactional views of deviancy (often termed *labeling theory*): "The deviant is one to whom that label has successfully been applied; deviant behavior is behavior that persons so label" (p. 9). Becker emphasized that police, governmental, and other official views of deviants (such as homosexuals, delinquents, and political demonstrators) are highly suspect. Officials tend to develop ideologies about the people whom they label as deviant—ideologies which include unverifiable theories of causation along with inaccurate ideas about the harmfulness of deviants "to society." Such labeling, and the powerful agency action based on it, according to Becker, actually creates deviant and even unlawful behavior (for instance, addicts desperate for their high-priced drugs will steal to raise the necessary money). People regarded as deviant sometimes are profoundly affected in their identities because they tend to adopt the prevailing negative evaluations of themselves.

Many sociologists initially encounter social interactionism through the textbook *Social Psychology* (Lindesmith, Strauss, & Denzin, 1975), which systematically spells out, "in English" with empirical data, the Meadian perspective. Anselm Strauss's *Mirrors and Masks* (1958), links the concept of *identity* with group membership, symbolic worlds, language, interaction, and passage in and out of statuses.

While social interactionism does not represent a unitary school or a single line of thought, there are two major streams within it. One stems most directly from Mead, primarily through Blumer, and puts its primary emphasis on the social nature of the self, with a strongly negative reaction to social structuralism. Because of their interest in self-concepts, these Meadian interactionists are more likely to be aware of the writings and theories of psychologists. The second stream derives most directly from Hughes, whose teacher, Robert Park, was one of the chief founders of the "Chicago School" of sociologists. Interactionists in this Parkian tradition tend to be very interested in organizations and their impact on their members. This tradition has especially influenced the work of interactionists who study organizations, professions, work, and deviancy— generally through field research or intensive interviews. Many interactionists are heir to both traditions.

Recently some interactionists have founded the Society for the Study of Symbolic Interaction, thus making a bid to become more visible, both intellectually and politically. The substantive and theoretical writings of interactionists are often of interest to social scientists who would never dream of calling themselves interactionists. Thus people interested in work and professions, for example, can scarcely avoid reading interactionist writings on those topics, and in turn they contribute ideas and findings which then influence interactionists.

Similar Theories

The ideas of interactionists influence other social scientists, who have a tendency to borrow these concepts without understanding the contexts in which they were created. Here are two examples. Some years ago, Robert Merton (1950), a leading functionalist theorist, published a paper on *reference-group* theory in which he aligned Mead's ideas about role playing and the generalized other with the reference-group concept. (Stated at its simplest, a reference group is any group with which an individual identifies, or in relation to which he thinks of himself.) Merton evidently misread Mead, pressing into the service of his own intellectual ends what he thought he had read (Turner, 1962). Similarly, Talcott Parsons (1954), when wrestling with how societal "norms" got "internalized" inside society's members, borrowed from Mead's writings on self and role playing and transformed them to fit a functionalist perspective.

In essence, Mead is transformed by Merton & Parsons into a structural determinist rather than remaining an interactionist. This point has been carefully noted by Ralph Turner (1962), who has addressed himself to the profound differences between a structuralist and interactionist concept of role. He criticized the idea that individuals play roles in conformity with guiding rules or norms as too simple and static (the structuralist view), and emphasized the open-ended nature of interaction (the interactionist view). Turner remarked that the idea of role taking:

Shifts emphasis away from the simple process of enacting a prescribed role to devising a performance on the basis of an imputed other-role. The actor is not the occupant of a position for which there is a neat set of rules—a culture or set of norms —but a person who must act in the perspective sup-

plied in part by his relationship to others whose reactions reflect roles that he must identify. Since the role of alter can only be inferred rather than directly known by ego, testing inferences about the role of alter is a continuing element in interaction. Hence the tentative character of the individual's own role definition and performance is never wholly suspended.(p.23; italics in original)

Interactionism is sometimes confused with another approach called *ethnomethodology* which has emerged during the past decade as a vigorous intellectual movement. It appeals to some younger sociologists because it attacks survey-style research and advocates getting the viewpoint of actors. The roots of ethnomethodology go back to phenomenological philosophy, especially to Edmund Husserl. A sociological forerunner was Alfred Schutz (1962, 1964), whose writings are often cited. Ethnomethodology's chief spokesman is probably Harold Garfinkel (1967), who first made many sociologists aware of this sociological movement.

For the ethnomethodologist, it is necessary to discover the methods used by ordinary people as they formulate definitions of a situation. To discover this seems to involve at least three steps. First, the observer suspends the structuralist assumption that rules, norms, roles, and so on govern interaction. Second, he listens and watches people describe and explain their actions. Third, he must regard these lay explanations as appearances produced so that people can project the image that rules have actually been followed. The ethnomethodologist assumes that individuals produce explanations for their behavior which, in fact, fit everyday conceptions of what the behavior was all about. Ethnomethodologists believe that sociologists should be concerned with how "members of society" go about seeing, describing, and explaining order in their world.

The surface similarities between interactionism and ethnomethodology are clear enough. Both emphasize getting the actor's views, are suspicious of questionnaire-type research, and eschew any form of structural determinism. Beyond those similarities, there is considerable debate and confusion about the convergence of the two positions. This is partly because the writings of ethnomethodologists have been difficult for outsiders to decipher and partly because ethnomethodological findings have been slow in reaching publication. In general, ethnomethodologists believe their approach is much more radical, that interactionists simply do not get to the heart of what interaction and social order are all about. They criticize interactionists for taking for granted how one actually gets to grasp "the actor's viewpoint." That process, they maintain, is difficult and requires new methods for managing it. Thus, interactionists like Blumer do not "provide an answer to the question: How is it possible that man creates a world that he does not recognize as his own handiwork? . . . since actors systematically. . . . obscure from view the work they continuously and endlessly do to provide for the appearance of the world as 'out there' " (Shearing, 1973, pp. 12–13).

In turn, interactionists criticize ethnomethodology as just another derivation from idealistic philosophy: "It shares with all phenomenological philosophy a fundamental ambivalence on the question of reality external to the solitary ego. The world, in this case society, is said to exist but not in any meaningful sense independent of individual consciousness" (Mayrl, 1973, p. 27). The critic quoted above thinks that the "methodological stance" of ethnomethodologists "leads quite logically to idealism and solipsism" (p. 27). Rather than doing what they claim to do—"get at the blood and guts of human existence"—they fail because they rest upon a basically individualistic position. In short, interactionists claim that ethnomethodology returns to a view of society as composed of individuals, thus beginning analysis with an aggregate of individuals rather than with a genuine interplay of society and persons. Since this interplay is what interactionism is all about, interactionists tend to think of ethnomethodology and interactionism as basically incompatible.

Another general theoretical position, called *exchange theory*, has struck some interactionists as partly compatible with their own assumptions, and there have been attempts to align the two positions. One critic of exchange theory, however, has complained that "there is relatively little agreement among sociologists either on the definition of exchange theory or on the works which are supposed to be examples of it" (Heath, 1971, p. 91). The most cited books on exchange are George Homans's *Social Behavior* (1961) and Peter Blau's *Exchange and Power in Social Life* (1964).

In attempting to explain exchange theory—behavior based on the concept of exchange—Homans drew on Skinnerian conditioning theory and on elementary economics. He regards both as encompassing the idea of "human behavior as a function of its payoff: in amount and kind it depends on the amount and kind of reward and punishment it fetches." Here are examples of Homans' propositions:

1. The more often a person's activity is rewarded, the more likely he is to perform the activity.
2. The more often in the recent past a person has received a particular reward, the less valuable any further unit of that reward becomes to him.

Examples of Blau's propositions are:

1. The desire for social rewards leads men to enter into exchange relations with one another.
2. Reciprocal social exchanges create trust and social bonds.
3. Unilateral services create power and status differences.
4. If subordinates collectively experience unfair exercise of power, an opposition movement will develop.

Exchange theory has been criticized as being downright speculative. It is said that many of the propositions are untestable and that the approach is too "psychologistic" and not sociological enough to explain social phenomena (Heath, 1971). Most interactionists would agree but doubtless would add two points. First, exchange theory is merely another variety of drive-reductionistic psychology. Second, its grounding in elementary economics "reflects a focus on aggregate analysis, which will not get us very far either in understanding individuals or the complex social processes in which they participate. . . . the basic notion of 'exchange' is amazingly simplistic, as contrasted with the full range of interactions that take place among men" (Lindesmith, Strauss, & Denzin, 1975, p. 15).

There is one other theoretical position—Marxism—which some sociologists have recently been attempting to reconcile with interactionism, and vice versa. Marxism, which stems from the 19-century writings of Karl Marx, has branched out into innumerable subpositions. Some are very doctrinaire, and others seem relatively open to contributions from non-Marxian traditions such as interactionism.

Some Marxists who are antagonistic to interactionism have levied criticisms along several lines. First, they maintain that interactionism is relatively "structureless" or has an "astructural bias." These Marxists adhere to structural determinism: Social structure determines behavior. Marxist critics also believe that interactionism is simply another version of idealistic, mentalistic theory. Interactionists, naturally, do not accept that criticism (Lindesmith, Strauss, & Denzin, 1975). Marxists are also likely to view interactionism as deeply biased by its political liberalism, which they tend to regard as deriving from philosophic idealism. Most, if not all, interactionists believe "reform" is not only necessary but inevitable, given the continuous interplay between person and society (Becker, 1967).

Some sociologists, including the neo-Marxists, attempt to reconcile Marxism and interactionism. Among the convergencies which have been claimed are the following (Ropers, 1973). Both positions are antagonistic to positivism, which spurns "the subjective" and finds crucial roles for human mentality and actors' viewpoints. Both traditions conceive humans as active agents who shape as well as are shaped by their worlds. Thus, both traditions are truly interactional:

> Marx and Mead .... while focusing upon opposite ends of abstraction were in agreement as to the essential unity and prospective harmony between the individual and society. ... Marx the social structuralist and Mead the social psychologist can indeed "shake hands" in sociology. Both believe in man as maker of society and history and share the conviction that free men in life-nourishing groups can build progressively more human and more just social institutions. (Ropers, 1973, p. 44)

Sociologists who attempt a reconciliation between Marxism and interactionism seem, thus, to emphasize the social-structural strengths of Marx and the social-psychological strengths of Mead. Another sociologist puts it this way:

> On the one hand, if the social psychology of G. H. Mead is found compatible with the dominant assumptions of Marxism, and subsequently could lead to a development of Marxist social psychology, then a further reshifting of "Western" sociological assumptions may be precipitated. On the other hand, an incorporation of Mead's thought into a Marxist social psychology would lead to a sharpening and sophistication of the Marxist paradigm. (Mayrl, 1973, pp. 44–45)

As these quotations suggest, neo-Marxists seem to be attempting to incorporate interactionist views into Marxism rather more than interactionists are turning to Marxism. Probably both trends will continue.

Assertions

Development

1.   BIOLOGICAL VARIABLES DO NOT DETERMINE, BUT ONLY INFLUENCE BEHAVIOR.

Social interactionists do not deny that biological variables affect human behavior, but like all sociologists they are critical of relatively extreme forms of biological determinism. They emphasize learned aspects of behavior, especially the roles of culture, societal participation, and social interaction. Many decades ago they rejected the idea of instincts, and they still look askance at such "instinctual" theories as the Freudians'. The psychologists' distinctions between primary (biological) and secondary or derived (social) needs are also criticized as attempts to ground behavior in biological structures, while greatly oversimplifying the complexity of human experience and conduct.

The variety of desires and aspirations connected, for example, with eating and sexual behavior can be traced back to primary needs or drives only by the most dubious of explanatory tactics. In illustrations, paraphrasing a discussion by Lindesmith, Strauss, and Denzin (1975, pp. 263–264), hunger can mean (1) the sheer fact of biological need, (2) the subverbal appreciation of the connection between the eating of certain substances and relief from hunger distress, and (3) the conscious verbal formulation of an interpretation of a felt biological need The first is unlearned, and the third may be divorced from the physiological: someone may express a wish for food when he doesn't really need it or may believe he is full when poor eating habits have left him malnourished; or he may not even feel hunger when his stomach is distended by nonnutritious substances. In other words, physical need for food and verbalized desire for food are distinct and separate phenomena and are sometimes wholly unrelated. So the interactionist asserts that while physiological and genetic processes are important in explaining behavior, they work only in relation to learned responses, derived in large part from societal and group memberships.

2.   BEHAVIOR IS TELEOLOGICALLY ORIENTED. In accordance with their more sociological views of human action, interactionists have developed the concept of *motive*. Rather than using the concept causally to explain actions, they use it to refer to an actor's stated purposes and his anticipated consequences of his act. People as actors give themselves reasons for acting—that is, *motivational statements*—and when questioned by others, assert such statements (which, of course, may be tailored to others' expectations and anticipated reactions). The interactionist wants to know why these specific explanations are given to oneself or others and how they relate to group memberships.

C. W. Mills (1940) wrote that "Motives are of no value apart from delimited societal situations for which they are appropriate vocabularies. They must be situated.... Motives vary in content and character with historical epochs and societal structures" (p. 904). This remark implies that although an individual may think his motives are entirely personal, in fact many are "in a sense furnished him tailor-made by the society or the groups in which he lives" (Lindesmith, Strauss, & Denzin, 1975, p. 288). For example, in some societies it is believed that men must regularly have sexual intercourse or they will become debilitated; in other societies, a sexual desire for one's aunt is considered due to bewitchment by an enemy. The interactionist claims that it is vitally important to understand motivational assertions—by self and others—both to understand interaction and the actors' own thoughts about themselves.

3.   MOTIVATIONS ARE MOSTLY DUE TO SOCIAL LEARNING.
One implication of this position is that a person cannot use motivational statements which he has not learned. One cannot motivate a man to act by using terms outside his comprehension. Conversely, one cannot properly impute motives (or "rationalizations") when they involve motivational terms which someone has not learned—like ascribing today's monetary notions or "success drives" to medieval men. In common discourse, people do this with some frequency. For instance, men who write novels ascribe various "motives" to female characters, but some women readers may not find these motives valid for women. Such commonsense motivational imputation has its academic counterpart: "Psychoanalysts have reinterpreted the private lives of famous persons such as St. Augustine and Leonardo da Vinci in terms of twentieth-century sexual symbols. They ignore ... that these historical characters viewed the conduct of others and themselves in very different terms than do people of our own era" (Lindesmith, Strauss, & Denzin, 1975, p. 289).

Apropos of rationalizing, Scott and Lyman (1968) have used the term *accounts* to refer to statements which actors make when explaining unanticipated or untoward behavior. They note two types of verbal accounts frequently employed: excuses and justifications. These may or may not be honored or accepted by others, so each person must learn a repertoire of proper accounts to suit appropriate audiences. He must also learn the proper style of couching his statements and how to vary them for different situations and different audiences. Scott and Lyman, for instance, note the "intimate style" (ardent husband's response from his unresponsive wife, "Sorry, pooped out.") as compared with more formal styles of interaction.

The interactionists' emphasis, is definitely not on biological processes; it can even be argued that they are underplayed. This may be attributable to the fact that, like virtually all sociologists, interactionists are principally interested in group behavior and relationships and are interested in individuals mostly as members of groups. This general point can be illustrated by Mead's theorizing about two aspects of the self (1934). What he termed "the I" represents the impulsive side of behavior—what the individual is just as likely to surprise himself as anyone else with. In contrast, "the me" refers to the community internalized in the person; it represents the community's social control of the individual's behavior. Mead sees the self not as an object with two sides but as an interaction between "I" and "me." Translated into the topic of this section, the interactionist is likely to regard biological processes as effective only insofar as they interact with social processes. Mead left the nature of this interaction rather unspecified, and so, generally, have contemporary interactionists.

4. HUMANS LIVE IN SYMBOLIC ENVIRONMENTS.

Social interactionists emphasize that humans are languaged beings, and every known society has generated one or more languages. Indeed, coordinated activity by groups of any size requires group members to share a language. Sometimes groups even develop special languages, jargons, or lingo to refer to important activities and objects. On this point, Lindesmith, Strauss, & Denzin (1975, p. 115) quote de Laguna: "Language singles out for specification only those features which are, in a peculiar sense, common to the social group." Outsiders often do not understand that special terminology. Besides words and phrases, special language may include gestures which have "insider" meaning. Language thus expresses particular points of view, objects deemed important, and ways of life.

In a more profound sense people are not (or so interactionists conclude) merely symbol creators and symbol users and symbol responders; they exist as humans because their symbolization mediates reality to them. Only God can know the "real" reality. As Cassirer (1953–1957) has put it, man does not "confront reality immediately.... Instead of dealing with things themselves man is in a sense constantly conversing with himself. He has so enveloped himself in linguistic forms . . . that he cannot see or know anything except by the interposition of this . . . medium" (p. 25). In other words, humans construct their realities, their worlds: They truly live in symbolic environments (Berger & Luckmann, 1966). Thus, one can certainly say that before microbes were discovered, people were affected by them, but microbes were then not part

of human reality; indeed sickness and death were attributed to everything under the sun except microbes.

Technically speaking, the symbolic environments of different groups are peopled with characteristic "social objects" (Mead, 1934; Blumer, 1969)—that is, with characteristic events, personages, memories, and anticipations, along with appropriate responses to objects, such as fear or hate or hope. Interactionists are also sensitive to the fact that such group stances have a genuine impact on the individuals who compose those groups.

5. SELF-REFLEXIVENESS IS CRUCIAL AND IS LEARNED.

The fact that children learn the languages of their elders—taking over at least some portion of their symbolic worlds—means that eventually they make objects of themselves; they become part of their own symbolic environments. This is called self-reflexiveness. Following Mead, Blumer (1969) states that self-reflexiveness is a cardinal feature of human activity; a process, not a thing. In this reflexive process, the person makes "indications to himself . . . noting things and determining their significance for this line of action" (p. 36). Hence, he "ceases to be a responding organism whose behavior is a product of what plays upon him from the outside, the inside, or both." He has to handle the world "through a defining process instead of merely responding to it, and [this] forces him to construct his action instead of merely releasing it" (p. 37).

Where does self-reflexivity come from? In the 19th century, it was generally believed that it unfolded, along with other biological developments of infants (Cooley, 1902). Nobody any longer believes in that version of biological determinism. Interactionists have rephrased the developmental issue as one involving the typically societal task of transforming a "social neutral infant into a symbolically functioning human being" (Lindesmith, Strauss, & Denzin, 1975, p. 300). This occurs through face-to-face interaction. Although childhood is viewed differently the world over (as undesirable, desirable, inevitable, optional, etc.), children everywhere develop self-reflexivity. Interactionists are somewhat critical of various theories about self-development (theories by Freud, Erik Erikson, Sullivan, for instance), but they have not much studied childhood themselves (Lindesmith, Strauss, & Denzin, 1975). What they have done is generate several useful concepts dealing with self and self-reflexivity.

The Looking-Glass Self. What is commonly called self-consciousness illustrates the close linkage between self-awareness and an imagery of how one looks to some audiences, which may or may not actually be present. Cooley (1962) discussed this phenomena as follows:

> As we see ... our face, figure, and dress in the glass, and are interested in them because they are ours, and pleased or otherwise with them according to as they do or do not answer to what we should like them to be; so in imagination we perceive in another's mind some thought of our appearance, manners, aims, deeds, character, friends, and so on, and are variously affected by it.
>
> A self-idea of this sort seems to have three principal elements: the imagination of our appearance to the other person; the imagination of his judgment of that appearance; and some sort of self-feeling such as pride or mortification. The comparison with a looking-glass hardly suggests the second element, the imagined judgment, which is quite essential. (p. 184)

This ability to visualize oneself through the eyes of others is a capacity learned through interaction.

Taking the Role of the Other. Language is clearly necessary to the development of self-awareness: the child's name, pronouns, terms of address, and the like are particularly important. But Mead believed that among the most important adult vocalizations for the child are those directed at himself. He hears his name said repeatedly by others, who indicate its meaning with appropriate gestures and acts. Beginning with simple words, the child eventually can rehearse conversations in which he has been involved and learns to ascribe motivations and evaluations to his behavior just as others ascribe them. In responding thus to himself, he develops an awareness of his own responses and of some of their consequences.

Given this concept of assuming roles assigned by others, it is easy to see why Mead and the interactionists who have followed him have believed that "No hard-and-fast line can be drawn between our own selves and the selves of others, since our own selves exist only insofar as the selves of others exist" (Mead, 1934, p. 164). That a self seems so inseparable from an autonomous biological organism should not prevent us from noting that it is rooted in social interaction. This means that persons are not carbon copies of each other: Surely they are not. In taking on the roles of others, in meeting the actual and imagined responses of others, every person has unique experiences. The importation of what Mead (1934) called the generalized other—the organization of perspectives of the others out there—is not automatic or easy but is an assimilation marked with anguish, care, concern, and appraisal. The perspectives suggested, and even commanded, by others "are not adopted *in toto* or retained entirely on faith. All perspectives are tested and tried out in action. They are appropriated and possessed" (Lindesmith, Strauss, & Denzin, 1975, p. 308).

Maintenance

6. INTERACTION INVOLVES ROLE PLAYING, ROLE TAKING, DEFINING THE SITUATION.

Much human activity is organized in terms of the roles assigned or assumed. Role enactment (like being a governor, an admiral, or a mother) consists usually of a wide variety of acts played out within a socially accepted general pattern. Since the enactment of any role extends over time, it is interrupted by the person's enactment of other roles. Continuity and unity are given to the role by the person's controlling conceptions of it, to which all of its phases are referred. His role enactment requires him to assess frequently where his action is going, what his next moves should be, what the consequences are likely to be —and how his actions will look, to use H. S. Sullivan's phrase, to "significant others."

It is implicit that role playing occurs in episodes, scenes, and situations. These have to be recognized, named, or at least sensed, so that the person can act appropriately. He must, as W. I. Thomas said, "define the situation." Many situations of course are routine and thus quickly or long-since defined. Other situations are problematic and may be difficult to assess. Even routine situations can be misread or disagreed upon by different actors. An illustrative experiment with animals by Harold Garfinkel (1967), an ethnomethodologist, rendered a routine situation so problematic that the experimental guinea pigs went from making incorrect definitions to complete disarray.

Part of understanding any human interactional situation involves role taking—that is, grasping imaginatively the expected responses of others. An important aspect of role taking is that, in a given interaction between two people, each must determine (1) the other's general intent in the situation, (2) the other's response to himself, and (3) his own responses and feelings toward the recipient or observer of his action. Ralph Turner (1962, p. 40) has used the term *identifying* to refer to still another aspect of role taking, viewing the other's perspective on matters from his actual perspective. Each of these aspects represents a different task requiring different skills. Moreover, the calculating or sensing of different signs of intent, self-feeling, and feeling toward others may change or be reassessed during the course of an evolving interaction. It is not necessarily a once-and-for-all assessment. Actually, little is known about these role-taking processes and their complex interrelationships.

7. PRESENTING AND ASSESSING ARE TWIN,
    SIMULTANEOUS PROCESSES.

In interaction, then, each person assesses the other, though not necessarily with full awareness. This assessment involves the reading of various cues: verbal, nonverbal (gesture, posture), or stylistic (hair or clothing styles). The counterpart of assessment is what Goffman terms "impression management" or presentation of self (1959). The person organizes his presenting cues to make himself out to be what he desires to make himself out to be. This management of the other's assessment need not be fully conscious and certainly not deliberately manipulative. Some people, however, are self-conscious about their impression managements, and even relatively nonmanipulative persons can in certain situations manage, with highly deliberate skill, their self-presentations to achieve desired impressions. Some managements involve teamwork; that is, more than the one actor is involved in the drama of getting the desired presentation projected. Of course, teamwork is also necessary when an entire group presents itself, as when a family offers a solid front to the outside world.

Gregory Stone (1962) has closely analyzed the presentation of self relative to clothing. Both men and women select what to wear and how to wear it to create desired impressions. Style is not necessarily simply a matter of pleasing oneself, wearing what one feels like; it may be more a matter of what Stone calls "appearance." The creation of appearance can involve a complex act: "By appearance, a person *announces* his identity, *shows* its value, *expresses* his mood, or *proposes* his attitude" (p. 101). As for assessment of that presentation, "Identifications of another are facilitated by appearance and are often accomplished silently or unverbally." Of course, appearances are also accomplished by presenting other cues: the types of furniture one surrounds oneself with, the kinds of cars one chooses to drive, even—when one is aware of it—the style of one's walking and talking.

The activity of "passing", getting by with a false identity, depends on successfully presenting a false appearance. Some British people of working-class origin attempt to pass as being of higher origin; to do this calls for deliberate clothes, speech, and gesture management. Passing involves the suppression of true cues and the presentation of false ones, as in many of the activities of spies. Certain presented cues may be so socially convincing that an audience is easily deceived; many an American black has passed as white, provided her or his skin is sufficiently light in color. A white journalist, John Griffin, (1962), once passed for some days as black while traveling in the South, after having his skin treated so he would look black. Griffin had to keep his interactions with blacks quite superficial, or they would have become puzzled or suspicious by disconfirming cues: his ignorance of special lingo or of implicit interactional rules, for instance.

Since interactionists like Goffman or Stone are sociologists, they tend to focus not on individual actors but on group assessments, as well as how an individual's impression management is abetted by teamwork or constrained by social contingencies not much under his control. In any case, interactionists believe that processes like presenting and assessing are central to an understanding of interaction and its impact on the implicated actors.

A further example is the phenomenon of pain —which cannot be directly "seen" but which must be inferred by others from behavioral cues and "expressions" of pain made by the person claiming to be in some degree of pain (Strauss, Fagerhaugh, & Glaser, 1974). Thus there is an assessment problem. Is the person faking? Is he pretending more pain than he actually has in order to get sympathy or to escape work? In hospitals, problems of assessment are magnified by the unfolding interaction which occurs between the patients and the staff. Does this stranger who lies in bed really hurt that much, or must his agonized behavior be discounted? Pain tends to be discounted in some degree for patients who generate dislike for themselves; they are defined as complainers or overanxious or even as psychos, and sometimes, a consulting psychiatrist may even be called in to deal with such patients. In all such interactional dramas, the patient has the problem of legitimating his pain. If his pain is unexpected or unusual, and if there are few overt physical signs of it, then he will encounter difficulties in convincing others of his pain, and his reputation as a good patient will be in hazard. When pain is expected, as after an operation, problems of legitimation are negligible. If one wished to write a script for maximizing the problems of assessment and legitimation, it would be this: unexpected pain, an inarticulate but obstreperous and seemingly not very sick patient, and a busy, harassed hospital staff.

These problems are not, of course, encountered only in the hospital; they affect interactions within families and among friends. People with occasional or acute pain may prefer to control their expression of it, to "cover," so as not to disturb ongoing interactions. They attempt to present a normal appearance. Chronic sufferers also learn to do this or to withdraw or stay out of interaction, and often the consequence is considerable social isolation. People whose pains are relatively unpredictable (as with an arthritic who taught tennis but on certain days was completely incapacitated) have special problems of legitimation. They have problems with their self-conceptions as well, since their lives tend to revolve—at least during peak periods of pain—around the management of life when in pain.

8. INTERACTIONAL STRATEGIES ARE EMPLOYED TO OBTAIN DESIRED ENDS.

Both the presentation of oneself as one wishes and the successful assessment of others' presentations involve the employment of interactional strategies. Situations, indeed entire dramas, are arranged with some deliberateness. The case of the con man hooking "the mark" (the victim) is an excellent exemplification of interactional strategies at work.

Interactional strategies also can be extremely subtle, as one which has been analyzed by Glaser and Strauss (1965), who coined the term "awareness context" to refer to strategies under analysis. Awareness context refers to "the total combination of what each interactant in a situation knows about the identity of the other and his own identity in the eyes of the other. The total awareness is the context within which are guided successive interactions . . . over periods of time— long or short (p. 22)." Four principal types of awareness context are quite relevant to the presentation and assessment which goes on in interaction. An *open* awareness context prevails when each is aware of the other's true identity in the eyes of others. A *closed* awareness context prevails when one interactant knows neither the other's identity nor the other's view of his identity. A *suspicion* context prevails when one suspects the true identity of the other, the other's view of his own identity, or both. A *pretense* context prevails when both are fully aware, but pretend not to be.

The concept of awareness context is applicable to many interactive situations They have, however, the potential for deliberate misrepresentation of self as well as honest presentation of self. Mistakes are inherent in both presentation and assessment, even when each actor attempts a straightforward appearance. Moreover, the need for fictional acting, which everyone recognizes but pretends not to know, is inherent in many situations.

McCall and Simmons (1966) take a rather pessimistic view of the honesty of most interactions, although they mitigate their view with a qualifying phrase: "Owing to the very peculiar nature of knowledge about other persons, relationships necessarily turn on somewhat misguided and misleading premises about the other parties. Social order rests partly on error, lies, deception, and secrets, as well as upon accurate knowledge" (pp. 195-196).

The four types of awareness context are not mutually exclusive but tend to move from one to another, depending on the stage of development to which relationships have evolved. Since interactionists are especially interested in evolving relationships rather than in those that are static or one shot, this idea is of special concern. To illustrate the shifting character of awareness contexts, as well as to underscore that much (if not most) interaction takes place within some kind of organizational setting, the following paragraphs indicate what may happen to a person who is dying in a hospital.

1. Hospitalized patients frequently do not recognize their impending death, although the staff does. Thus interaction between staff members and patient occurs within a closed awareness context about the patient's true identity.

2. Hospital personnel, to prevent the patient's comprehension of their evaluation of his state, utilize a number of "situation as normal" interactional tactics. They act in his presence as if he were only ill. They talk to him as if he were going to live, conversing about his future, thus enhancing his belief that he will regain his health. They tell him stories about others, including themselves, who have recovered from similar or worse illnesses. By such indirect signaling they present him with a false future. They may even directly assure him that he will live, lying with a clear purpose. To supplement such tactics, the staff members use additional techniques to guard against disclosure. They make certain that the patient does not overhear any conversation about his condition and engage in careful management of facial and other gestures so as not to give the show away; they control any expression of sadness they experience over the patient's approaching death. Almost inevitably they attempt, not always consciously, to reduce the number of potentially disclosing cues by reducing the time spent with the patient or by restricting their conversations with him.

3. To accomplish this general strategy of keeping the patient unaware of his fate, teamwork is needed, but the dangers of disclosure are great. Unless the patient dies quickly or becomes permanently comatose, he tends to suspect (or may learn) that others identify him as a dying pa-

tient. Patients do overhear occasional conversations about themselves. Personnel unwittingly may flash cues or make conversational errors which arouse his suspicions. Day and night staff may give him contradictory information or divergent clues. The patient eventually may become more knowledgeable about what is going on around him. In short, the original conditions which sustain closed awareness begin to disappear or are counteracted by new conditions that make for suspicion or open awareness.

4. Some interactants may wish to move him along into other types of awareness contexts and so employ tactics which are the opposites of the nondisclosure tactics. A staff member may give the show away by improper management of face, by carefully obliquely phrasing words, by failing to reassure the patient sufficiently about a hospital prognosis, by changing all talk about the future into concentration upon the present, or by increasingly avoiding both conversation and the patient himself. Of course, occasionally someone may just plain tell the patient that he is dying.

5. The closed awareness that "surrounds" the dying patient has many significant consequences for patient and staff. The patient, unaware of the other's view of his situation, cannot act as if he were dying. Thus, he cannot talk to close kin or friends about his fate; he cannot assuage their grief. Nor can he act toward himself as if he were dying by facing his expected death—gracefully, or with panic and hysteria. In turn, the family, friends and hospital personnel are saved from the possibly stressful scenes that accompany open awareness about death but are also blocked from participating in various satisfying rituals of passage to death. Wives cannot openly take farewells of husbands; hospital personnel cannot share the patient's sometimes ennobling acceptance of death. As a consequence of closed awareness, nurses carry the brunt of stressful verbal interaction with the patient, during which talk of death must be avoided.

Interactionists would point out that, like the situation of dying patients, most social interactions are not merely interpersonal affairs; they frequently involve persons as representatives of groups and almost always in some kinds of groups or organizational setting. The awareness context analysis of the dying patient underlines the point that interactional strategies are socially patterned and not merely personal or interpersonal.

9. INTERACTIONAL RITUALS CONTRIBUTE
   TO THE MAINTENANCE OF
   INTERACTIONAL ORDER.

Goffman (1959) has recommended that special attention be paid to the bizarre behavior of the mentally ill and has suggested that psychotic behavior can be compared to common ideas about proper, decent, appropriate behavior. When the mentally ill seem deranged they are breaking common, implicit rules, which then become visible to the observer. Goffman's position is that social regulations subtly govern interaction and make it the embodiment of social order. These regulations are not especially visible to the actors, who in fact take most of them for granted.

Goffman's paper "On Face-Work" (1955) illustrates his views of what he called the "ritual elements in social interaction." He states that everybody lives in a world of social encounters involving face-to-face interaction, during which people tend to act out "lines"—whether deliberately or not. A line is a pattern of verbal and nonverbal acts by which a person expresses his view of the situation and of the participants within it, including himself. The term *face* is "the positive social value a person effectively claims for himself by the line others assume he has taken during a particular contact." Goffman notes that the line "maintained by and for a person ... tends to be of a legitimate institutionalized kind." During certain socially defined situations "an interactant of known or visible attributes can expect to be sustained in a particular face." He is "out of face" when not ready with a line of the kind that the participants in a given defined situation "are expected to take." When a person is out of face, the ordinary regulated interaction is out of balance: "expressive events are being contributed to the encounter which cannot be readily woven into the expressive fabric of the occasions." Thus, the person may become embarrassed, shamed, or confused. If he can control or conceal these reactions, then he has "poise."

All participants in this interaction share the responsibility of maintaining face. Each "takes on the responsibility of standing guard over the flow of expressive events. ... He must ensure that a particular *expressive order* is maintained." Rules of considerateness and self-respect help him to conduct himself so as to maintain not only his own face but that of the others. Maintaining others' poise, however, is only one important type of interactional tactic. For instance, a person may avoid situations in which threats to his face are likely to occur. Or he may act with studied nonobservance to his own or another's mistakes during an encounter. An important group of tactics pertains to correcting the breakdown of face, like giving the offender an opportunity to correct his offense and thus reestablish the expressive order—for instance, by allowing him to apologize.

This kind of analysis of "interactional rituals" (Goffman, 1967) and tactics tends to be effective when the interaction is relatively nondevelopmental. Thus Goffman sees face-work as contributing to getting people through an encounter "without disrupting the relationships of the participants." However, the analysis has the virtue of focusing on the implicit rules of interaction. The informal control that group membership exerts on interactants is neither rigid nor mechanical but subtle. Goffman's perspective has the merit of emphasizing that interactants must work at keeping their relationships stable—providing they wish them to be nondevelopmental— and that the automatic operation or application of rules cannot ensure stability. Furthermore, the rules are determined only through the assessments, calculations, presentations, tactics, and actions of participants who are self-reflecting, self-referring, and self-evaluating actors. Goffman's perspective on interaction is thus of much interest to sociologists, despite its weakness in analyzing the more unstable, open-ended, emergent, and problematic kinds of interaction.

10. MUCH INTERACTION INVOLVES STATUS
    PASSAGE AND CAREERS.

Social structure often is conceived of as a system of interrelated "offices," statuses, roles, or other designations which stand for social positions. People are said to act in accordance with the requirements of those social positions—insofar as they play those roles, fill those offices, occupy those statuses. We have already remarked that the role playing is not automatic but is variable and is guided by generalized conceptions of the role or position. Sociologists and anthropologists have also focused their attention on how people are induced to fill social positions as well as to leave them at appropriate times. "Insofar as every social structure requires manpower, men are recruited ... to move along through social positions or statuses ... there is an implicit or even explicit date when" a person must leave given statuses (Strauss, p. 162, 1958). This movement in and out of statuses has been referred to as "status passage" (Glaser & Strauss, 1971). Many such passages are governed by fairly explicit rules prescribing when and how the passage is made, who goes through it, what the sequences of steps are that must be followed, and the like. However, a large proportion of passages is much less regulated, prescribed, and organized (for example, nowadays, passage into marriage and out again through divorce or separation). Many passages leave the passagees and the agents who help in the passage with a fair degree of leeway concerning details, including those that relate to sequential steps and to timing.

Interaction during a passage varies considerably in accordance with properties of the passage. Sometimes the passage is undesirable to the person or to others involved in his passage. Sometimes the passage is not very important to him, but it may be central in his life or those of his agents (his parents who insist on his going through college). Passages may be reversible or irreversible (such as parenthood). Other conditions of passage include whether they are inevitable (childhood to adulthood), voluntary or involuntary, and whether the person goes through the passage alone or with others (classmates or draftees). Also, it is left to the person to initiate or consummate some passages; others are actually initiated and controlled by agents. All these properties affect how the participants will act toward one another. In turn, their actions will have consequences for self and other evaluations which will then affect some of the next steps of the passage.

Thus, it can be seen that there is a processual or dynamic side of social structures. Even if given statuses do not change much in character, there is a good deal of movement going on into, through, and out of them. It becomes clear that social interaction has two sides to it: the structural side and the self-other side. To think of interaction without interacting selves is to engage in a species of determinism called social or structural determinism. However, to think of interaction without social-structural considerations is to engage in a species of psychological determinism. How to put these two sides together is a central problem for interactionists.

Linked with status passages are what E. C. Hughes (1971) has called "careers." This concept refers to objective movements which an individual makes through a social structure—that is, through various status passages. Objective careers produce a counterpart, termed the *subjective career*. This refers to the changes in self-conception, sometimes very subtle but sometimes quite manifest, which accompany positional relocations. That is, alterations in the objective career lead to changes in self-conception and self-evaluation. Careers are important not only for getting the business of organizations or entire societies done but also because "they set the stage for the larger redefinitions of self" (Lindesmith, Strauss, & Denzin, 1975, p. 464).

Every individual has multiple careers, in the sense that she or he has several careers going simultaneously; for instance, an occupational career, carried on within an organization or several organizations sequentially; a marital career; and possibly also an associational career which goes from committee positions into official positions. An important feature of careers is that they involve an intersection with the lives and careers of other persons. Some of these others become significant others, influencing one's careers for better or worse. Thus David Wesby (1960), in his study of symphony musicians, quotes one violinist as saying, "I could have gone to (name of a somewhat prestigious orchestra) last year. ... The salary is better there, but I couldn't stomach the conductor" (p. 224).

To have a career is to be involved in commitments to others; hence, trust and its imputation are central to the course of a career. Assessments are not made simply of situations but of the career intentions and strategies of others. Misreadings and misrepresentations can have consequences both for people's careers and for their self-conceptions.

An especially important interactional feature of careers is that as a person moves through any specific career, his "career others" will change.

Thus, as he moves through a preparatory educational phase and on into the business world and up the organizational ladder, he meets different sets of interacting others. At any career phase, some of these are likely to be significant others both for his pursuit or living out a career and for the subjective side of that career.

Another important consideration is that the multiple careers, whether sequential or simultaneous, may be harmonious or in conflict. As Simmel (1953) noted some years ago, people do develop strategies which keep intrusive or competing career demands in some kind of balance. For instance, an art collector needs to keep his avocational career from eating into his occupational career. Some collectors, in fact, eventually become owners of art galleries, thus getting their avocational and vocational careers congruent— or perhaps combined. When these kinds of strategies fail to work, people are in trouble. Of course, the contingencies are often such that people are strategically vulnerable. Again, the interactionist is led to look at the structural conditions making for congruence or conflict of careers: is it easy, for instance, in the United States, to be a good father and to pursue a strenuous business career?

11. DEVIANT ACTIVITY IS LARGELY
     COLLECTIVE ACTIVITY.

The interactionist perspective has also been applied to the question of so-called deviant behavior (homosexuality, delinquency, crime, prostitution, and other forms of "vice," drug addiction, and mental illness). Sociologists generally look askance at psychological or psychiatric explanations of deviancy, perhaps because they are not primarily interested in individual etiology. They commonly raise questions about how certain acts, persons, and groups come to be defined as immoral, sick, dangerous, or otherwise deviant. They wish to know the methods by which those acts, persons, or groups are controlled by other persons or groups who believe that control is necessary. They are interested in the strategies by which deviants fight the law or by which they attempt to avoid the label of deviance. The control apparatus itself (police, courts, mental hospitals) and the range of consequences and possible functions of deviance present other significant sociological problems.

In general, interactionists are skeptical of explanations that posit, in Becker's (1973) words, "mysterious forces" which drive individuals to deviancy. They have also been critical of highly abstract sociological theorizing about deviancy which puts the onus on the deviant and ignores the powerful people and agencies that define the deviant acts *as* deviant and control the apparatus which punishes the transgressor. Interactionists are skeptical, too, of the assumption that there is a special, homogeneous kind of behavior which can be called deviancy, rather than a number of different acts which get defined as "not normal." As Becker says: "The interactionist approach shows ... that a major element in every aspect of the drama of deviance is the imposition of definitions—of situations, acts, and people— by those powerful enough or sufficiently legitimated to be able to do so" (1973, p. 207). He goes on to say that full understanding requires a thorough study of those definitional processes. (Political acts during the sixties which put civil rights or antiwar demonstrators in jail, and 19th-century definitions of Mormon polygamy are good examples of what Becker had in mind.)

The interactionist, then, regards deviant behavior as something that can be understood only by looking at all the interacting actors, some of whom—like the department of the federal government which has vested interest in "the drug problem"—are agencies or organization. Interactionists are concerned with the consequences of defining certain behavior as deviant—consequences for the definers as well as for the defined, although the "deviants" themselves have been more studied than the definers, and of the latter more groups, like prison guards, policemen and mental hospital attendants, have been studied than "their superiors' superiors" (Becker, 1973, p. 205).

In any case, interactionists have been instrumental in pointing out how people who commit deviant acts—or people whose very physical appearance causes them to be defined as queer or strange—may end by regarding themselves as deviant, as well as suffering from feelings of stigma, shame, guilt, alienation, and the like. Deviancy does not cause those reactions: the reactions result from interactional processes such as those discussed earlier. That is to say that the labeling of certain behavior as "deviant" by socially influential people makes it deviant not only in their minds and in the minds of others influenced by them; it also has important effects on the original actors, who thereupon suffer certain consequences attendant on having the label. Users of marijuana are a prime example: official agencies and people of strong social importance who make their statements about "pot smokers" affect not only the law and the apparatus of government but also the self-concepts of the smokers of this relatively harmless weed.

Applications

Like other sociologists, interactionists are mainly engaged in research, teaching at universities and colleges, and developing sociological theory. Some act as consultants to agencies and organizations on topics like delinquency or patients' attitudes toward health. Social interactionism's "applications," thus, are mainly confined to research, consultation, and teaching.

Assessment

While most American sociologists during the past two decades have become deeply committed to quantified research, including data gathering through questionnaires and data analysis via statistical techniques, interactionists have been equally committed to developing a methodology which relies heavily on field observation, intensive interviews, and analysis, primarily of qualitative data. Following the tenet that to understand human action one must first of all get the actor's viewpoint, the interactionist says, or assumes, something like this:

> The researcher MUST get close to the people whom he studies; he understands that their actions are best comprehended when observed on the spot—in the natural, ongoing environment where they live and work. If man creates at least some of the conditions for his own actions, then it can be presumed that he acts in his own world, at the very place that he is. The researcher himself must be at the location, not only to watch but also to listen to the symbolic sounds that characterize this world. A dialogue with persons in their natural situation will reveal the nuances of meaning from which their perspectives and definitions are continually forged. (Schatzman & Strauss, 1973, pp. 5–6)

In other words, interactionist assumptions about the nature of man and human behavior lead to a deliberate choice of *field research* as the preferred method, supplemented, when observation is not possible or is insufficient, with intensive interviews. Since interactionists also focus upon process, on the courses and trajectories of interaction, they prefer to observe sequential interaction. The interactionist "seeks to understand the activities of interacting individuals, and even when the individual is the focus of attention, his behavior is conceived a consequence of past interactional episodes. Process and emergence are stressed" (Lindesmith, Strauss, & Denzin, 1975, pp. 4–5). Allied to the wish to "catch" sequential interaction is a focus on observing and explaining complex interactions among a multiplicity of interrelated actors. Field observation is a superb tool for getting at the networks of relationships which constitute a group or an organization, as well as how groups and organizations function and change.

The precise character of fieldwork varies, depending on the persons, groups, and organizations studied and the aims of the researcher. A common typology of researcher tactics is in terms of the activities of those who are being studied. The field researcher can be seen by the actors but avoids obtruding himself in their actions as much as possible. In the field situation he may actively control interaction along lines designed to provide particular information, as in a formal interview; he can allow himself to be known as a researcher yet participate fully in ongoing activities. He may also, though this is done much less frequently, be a full participant without disclosing his research identity.

Research tactics vary accordingly, but in general most research studies call for at least the following: Actors must be studied at various times of the day, on different days of the week, and even during different seasons. In other words, "time" must be sampled. So must sites, since different kinds of events may occur at different places—as well as at the same places at different times. This means critical decisions must be made about when and where the fieldworker should observe or "be." A fieldworker also must learn what the actors themselves consider to be typical events and make certain that he samples all of them, as well as seizing upon whatever unusual events occur—emergencies or crises. He must attempt to watch and listen to persons who seem relevant to the events he is studying; this means anything from formal interviews, through overhearing conversations in public and watching their behavior, to gaining permission to follow them around during the course of their activities.

Different investigations have different aims, but field researchers try to get data bearing on an organization's or group's "round of life," on its division of labor, major conflicts, attitudes toward key members and toward the impinging of other groups and organizations. Information also is sought on the personal histories and "careers" of group members and their dominant lifestyles.

A rather general feature of field research is its "temporally developing character. The fieldworker usually does not enter the field with specific hypotheses and predetermined research design" (Strauss, Schatzman, Bucher, Ehrlich, & Sabshin, 1964, p. 20). In this regard, field research is rather different from the dominant model of sociological research in this country. Field researchers, whether sociologists or anthropologists (who also rely heavily on this methodology), are trained to make rather quick discriminations among the "things" they see, to begin thinking about what they are seeing, to try to make sense of it. This means that a researcher goes into the field equipped with a background of sociological or anthropological knowledge, but his knowledge may be only general, not specific to the phenomena he is observing. In the words of one set of researchers:

The initial phase of fieldwork is a period of general observation: specific problems and foci have not yet been determined. The fieldworker is guided mainly by sensitivities to data derived both from his professional background and from his general notions about the nature of his research problem. As he surveys the field initially, he is continually "testing"—either implicitly or explicitly—the relevance of a large number of evolving hypotheses, hunches, and guesses. ...The second phase...is marked by greater attention to particular aspects of the field and by an emerging set of propositions. ...A final phase consists of systematic efforts to pinpoint various hypotheses. ...Those hypotheses that survive the informal tests of daily observation are then sub-

jected to more deliberate, controlled inquiry. (Strauss et al., 1964, p. 20)

The phases described above are somewhat artificial, since the investigator may be working within two stages during a single period of time, depending on the particular phenomena on which he is focused. The main point is that the researcher, especially when studying an area he or she knows little about, tends to begin in an exploratory, general frame of mind and then to become increasingly specific in activities and foci.

During the research, copious notes are generally taken. Some are done right on the spot, with the full awareness of the observed or the interviewed, but more frequently the researcher goes home and pounds his typewriter or talks into his tape recorder. This leads to the problem of how to analyze the obtained data. Researchers manage their analyses differently. Most generally, since hypotheses are continually emerging and being checked, analysis begins early and continues until the last word is written. (Analytic methods are complicated, and we shall not consider them here. One widely read account is in Glaser and Strauss, *The Discovery of Grounded Theory*, 1967.)

The reporting of research also varies by the kind of study and the expected audience. In general, a typical presentation includes a certain amount of "raw data"—that is, quotations from the interviews and from the field notes. These quotations function to give credibility to the researcher's analysis and to allow readers to appreciate and "catch" the actors' viewpoints as well as the full flavor of important events, interactions, and social relationships. Lengthy case histories may even be included. In a monograph titled *Identity and Community in the Gay World* (Warren, 1974), for example, even sexually normal readers might learn something from the actors' viewpoint, since the actors are often quoted in this book.

One problem in observational studies which field researchers have debated among themselves, in print as well as in private, is the ethics of fieldwork. Two major problems have emerged. The first is: Should a researcher "pass" unknown to the observed; that is, should he do undisclosed research? The answer to that question depends very much on personal ethics, but there seems to be emerging a tendency to avoid such "concealed" research. This decision is consonant with the increasing trend toward consumer rights (including the right to "consent") and relevant to researchers' feelings about not exposing minority people or other relatively helpless groups to the gaze of officialdom. The second ethical issue pertains to what kinds of information to publish and what kinds to withhold because of the possibility of harming the people studied. This important issue seems to have been handled fairly sensibly by most investigators; some researchers now report first to the implicated people. Such feedback has become a fairly standard feature of field research.

Treatment

Sociologists as such do not treat individuals in one-to-one situations or in small groups, but nevertheless the information they elicit relative to the formation and the maintenance of the personality can be of considerable value to those who do function as psychotherapists. The contribution to treatment made by sociologists of all persuasions is of a general nature; mostly it is through their writings and lectures that helping people gain new perspectives about themselves as well as their clients. This includes data on family life, society, and general interactional relationships. Thus sociologists help change individuals' views in the broader sense, through changing laws and through changing official and unofficial attitudes toward various kinds of behavior.

From the point of view of the individual therapist, regardless of which school he belongs to (such as the Freudians or the Adlerians), the insights afforded by the writings of sociologists can be considerable. As a matter of fact, many founders of psychotherapy in the modern sense (and here again we think of Freud and Adler) attempted sociological explanations of personality. The work of Harry Stack Sullivan, Karen Horney, J. L. Moreno, and especially Erich Fromm, while written mostly from the psychological-psychiatric point of view, very often have elements of sociological thinking and include observations about how society and social groups affect the individual.

The complete therapist presumably would be a physician and would understand how the brain operates; he would be a psychologist and understand how learning occurs and how the mind operates; and he would be a sociologist and understand how the individual is a member of a variety of social groups in interaction, and how, despite the individual's belief that he is an independent individual, he is in reality a member of a variety of groups with distinctive values and styles of life. Adler, for example, in discussing the effects of the family constellation on a child —seeing the oldest as essentially different from the youngest in terms of his ordinal position in the family—was thinking sociologically, but perhaps not enough in cross-national terms. The constitutionalists, who think that the human physique is related to personality, need also consider the stereotypes about how appearances affect people's concepts about constitution. Thus, a fat boy in the United States at this time may be considered unattractive, and this will affect his self-concept one way, while a fat boy in Turkey will be considered attractive, and this will affect his self-concept differently.

In other words, the complete therapist, were he to have a sociological orientation, would have a deep understanding of the patient as a member of a variety of interacting groups. To merely see a person in terms of her or his phenomenological position and not to see that person as affected by society is to be more than half blind. To accept the individual as completely free is as wrong as to see him completely determined. The issues of responsibility, free will, and responsiveness can only be understood by seeing the person simultaneously as actor (as an individual with free initiative) and as actee (as an individual affected by other members of the groups he belongs to). In place of either the indeterminism implied by Carl Rogers or the determinism implied by B. F. Skinner, the typical interactional sociologist would take an intermediate position, saying in effect that both are right—which would also mean that both are wrong.

Finally, sociologists do provide therapy for institutions. They are called on to examine institutions such as churches, business organizations, social clubs, universities, prisons, and mental and somatic hospitals to help relieve these institutions of problems which are essentially sociological in nature. Such treatment usually involves a sociological analysis of the organization, and remedies are suggested to achieve desired goals —even though the goals of controllers of the institutions may be questioned as inconsistent or as undesirable. That is, the sociological "treater" may act as a problem solver and give advice as to how the institution may achieve certain goals, such as, perhaps, greater profit, but the sociologist is likely also to suggest goals in line with his value orientation, such as attempting to get an institution to achieve greater social amelioration.

Institutional

Interactional research findings are sometimes of considerable practical use. The wider public, or at least the publics of particular occupations or industries, can find enlightenment in interactional writings. Thus, interactionist views of deviancy have been found of considerable relevance by those who wish to fight conventional "establishment" views. Sometimes interactionists have fed their writings into particular social movements. A good example is a book published by Stanton and Schwartz (1954) which became part of the movement to reform mental hospitals. Another instance is the research of Glaser and Strauss (1965) on the care of dying patients, published just about the time when the interest of health professionals was beginning to develop into what was to become a considerable "death and dying" movement.

The authors of such interactional studies frequently find themselves called upon to address interested audiences, to participate at workshops, and to consult with relevant organizations and agencies. They may call upon their own findings or those of other researchers or draw mainly upon their general knowledge in attempting to affect either attitudinal or organizational reform. Like other social scientists, they may also attempt to affect legislation, especially by working with reform groups and agencies involved with legislative processes. They also write policy papers and books with titles like "Medical Ghettos" (Strauss, 1970) and *The Addict and the Law* (Lindesmith, 1965), in a direct attempt to influence public policy rather than simply reaching their professional colleagues.

Self

The writings of interactionists can be useful to students. Stylistically, they tend to be down to earth, not particularly heavy on jargon, and quite vivid. The student can get a good sense of the perspectives of people quite unlike himself, who participate in worlds different from his own, and thus can widen his understanding of people and groups. Unquestionably, many a student has had her or his personal horizons broadened by books like *The Professional Thief* (Sutherland, 1937), *Addiction and Opiates* (Lindesmith, 1968), *The Racing Game* (Scott, 1968), *Doomsday Cult* (Lofland, 1966), *Identity and Community in the Gay World* (Warren, 1974), *Passage through Crisis* (Davis, 1963), or *Symbolic Leaders* (Klapp, 1965).

Such books often include enlightening personal observations and colorful case histories which can further understanding. Thus, one can read about a mother, hearing her child's illness diagnosed, who says: "When I heard them say polio, it was like someone was pulling my heart out" (Davis, 1963, p. 32). Or a patient on kidney dialysis who says: "In the beginning it's as if that machine is a human being with a brain and it's *running* you. Then you realize it is only a machine and the brain is *yours*. Then you are suddenly faced with the fact that you're nearly at death's door and you have to depend on that machine to stay alive—that's upsetting" (Strauss et al., 1974, p. 31). Or a homosexual speaking frankly to a researcher, "Lots of men who are straight and do the scene sometimes for fun, they'd do anything for you, but not kiss you on the mouth. That's what they do with their wife" (Warren, 1974, p. 160).

Aside from substantive content, the general interactionist perspective on interaction itself—with its various associated concepts, like career and interactional ritual—unquestionably has affected the views of many readers, especially students. Reading about such matters as recruitment into careers, turning points in careers, sponsorship in careers, downwardly and upwardly mobile careers, leads one to apply such ideas to one's own life. Reading about stigma or deviancy ascription in interaction gives insight into one's own and other's situations.

Because the interactionist perspective so strongly challenges various forms of determinism (including psychological, cultural, and social forms), reading about it provides intellectual weapons against their proponents. More important, it helps students find intellectual justification for believing in their own creative and positive efforts, while recognizing that there are such relevant things as social constraints and disapproving others.

Like everyone else, as the interactionists would say, the reader belongs to groups which constrain his actions; but this does not mean his actions are strictly determined by those memberships. Or as two interactionists (Schatzman & Strauss, 1973, pp. 4–5) have put the issue:

1. Personal perspectives are social in origin and emanate from definitions of countless social situations and processes in which man finds himself, and with which he can identify.
2. Man presents himself with perspectives and definitions that become [some of the] conditions for his own actions; therefore, the "forces" which impel him to act are substantively of his own making.

These authors go on to characterize the situation of the field researcher in ways that definitely apply to the student reading interactionist materials: "The researcher himself must be at the location, not only to watch but to listen to the symbolic sounds that characterize this world. A dialogue with persons in their natural situation will reveal the nuances of meaning from which their perspectives and definitions are continually forged."

Validation

Evidence

Interactionism is a general perspective or approach to human behavior. Of course, as the Assertions section suggests, interactionists have developed a number of major hypotheses about individual and group behavior, along with the concepts associated with these kinds of hypotheses.

Examination of interactionist articles or monographs will show that authors usually follow no specific format in their presentation of hypotheses, findings, and conclusions. Unlike many psychology articles in which a relatively standardized format is found, these sociologists utilize many styles of presentation. Because data tend to be qualitative, the presentation is only

infrequently quantitative (statistical or mathematical). The writing may be "loose" or "tight" but is basically discursive, with hypotheses and evidence and elaborations and illustrations woven together in some personally or conventionally patterned form.

In the concluding section of published articles the researcher almost always presents his main findings or hypotheses in summary statements. An example is Davis (1963, p. 163): "The fundamental issue of identity confronting the families of the handicapped children was how to view, interpret and respond to the many negative meanings imputed to a visible physical handicap in our society." Or, Becker (1973, p. 78): "In short, a person will feel free to use marihuana to the degree that he comes to regard conventional conceptions of it as the uninformed views of outsiders and replaces those conceptions with the 'inside' view he has acquired through his experience with the drug in the company of other users" (Becker, 1973, p. 78). Occasionally, in the final section, specific hypotheses will be listed, along with a summary development of them for quick reader reference. Strauss et al., (1964, p. 362) say: "Our data suggest two hypotheses to account for the patterning of ideology by oppression. . . . *First, ideological commitments are built into professional training*" (italics in original). The explication follows: "While the future professional is engaged in acquiring the specific skills of his trade and the professional identity that will guide his activity, he also acquires convictions about what is important or basic to treatment and what is proper treatment. He learns treatment ideology as an integral part of his professional training."

The text of books and articles on social interactionism tends to be replete with quotations from respondents or people observed and may include lengthy case materials dealing with persons and events. Sometimes these materials are used for simple illustration, to afford the reader a better "understanding" of how things look to the actors. Sometimes they are used as evidence, to "show" that things are as the researcher says they are. It is as if the researcher is saying to his readers: "Here, see for yourselves." When a point is particularly difficult to prove because it runs against commonsense views, the researcher may be inclined to quote many respondents, at great length. In addition, most researchers attempt to link their findings and hypotheses with those of their predecessors and thus give credibility to the presentation.

The issue of credibility in this kind of work is especially thorny. While one can often be skeptical about the claims of experimental or survey researchers, the very style—discursive and "qualitative"—typically employed by interactionists often raises the issue of credibility. Glaser and Strauss (1967), in a chapter titled "The Credibility of Grounded Theory," have written some pertinent paragraphs on this important issue, which many have found persuasive. Here are some excerpts [1]:

> The change of emphasis in sociology toward verification of theory, which has been linked with the growth of rigorous quantitative research, has had the unfortunate consequence of discrediting the generation of theory through flexible qualitative and quantitative research. The qualitative research is generally labelled "unsystematic," "impressionistic," or "exploratory," and the flexible quantitative research "sloppy" or "unsophisticated." These critics, in their zeal for careful verification and for a degree of accuracy they never achieve, have forgotten both the generation of theory and the need for carefully appraising the different degrees of plausibility necessary for sociology's diverse tasks. . . .
>
> This criticism stems from sociologists' taking as their guide to credibility the canons of rigorous quantitative verification on such issues as sampling, coding, reliability, validity, indicators, frequency distributions, conceptual formulation, hypothesis construction, and presentation of evidence. But in this book we have raised doubts about the applicability of these canons of rigor as proper criteria for judging the credibility of theory based on flexible research. We have suggested that criteria of judgment be based instead on the detailed elements of the actual strategies used for collecting, coding, analyzing, and presenting data when generating theory, and on the way in which people read the theory. . . .
>
> A field worker knows that he knows, not only because he has been in the field and because he has

carefully discovered and generated hypotheses, but also because "in his bones" he feels the worth of his final analysis. He has been living with partial analysis for many months, testing them each step of the way until he has built his theory. What is more, if he has participated in the social life of his subject, then he has been living by his analysis, testing them not only by observation and interview, but also by daily living.

> By the close of his investigation, the researcher's conviction about his own theory will be hard to shake, as most field workers would attest. This conviction does not mean that his analysis is the only plausible one that could be based on his data, but only that he has high confidence in its credibility. What he has confidence in is not a scattered series of analyses, but a systematic ordering of them into an integrated theory. He has, in fact, discovered, through principally inductive effort, a substantive theory about delimited arrays of data, which he is ready to publish.
>
> If a research team is involved, then of course their shared knowledge constitutes the final substantive theory offered to colleagues. Each member not only knows his own data and analyses intimately, but has shared his colleagues' observations and experiences during numerous discussions, "talking out," and memo-writing sessions. The inevitable debates among team members have also contributed to the development of a shared conceptual analysis.
>
> The "real life" character of field work knowledge deserves special emphasis, because many critics think of this and other qualitatively oriented methods as being merely preliminary to "real" (scientific) knowing. But a firsthand immersion in a sphere of life and action—a social world—different from one's own yields important dividends. . . .
>
> When the researcher decides to write for publication, he faces the problem of conveying to colleagues and laymen the credibility of his discovered theory so that they can make some sensible judgment about it . . . .
>
> . . . The researcher ought to provide sufficiently clear statements of theory and description so that readers can carefully assess the credibility of the theoretical framework he offers. A cardinal rule for the researcher is that whenever he himself feels most dubious about an important interpretation—or foresees that readers may well be dubious—then he should specify quite explicitly upon what kinds of data his interpretation rests. The parallel rule for readers is that they should demand explicitness about important interpretations, but if the researcher has not supplied the information then they should assess his interpretations from whatever indirect evidence may be available. These same rules apply to

[1] Reprinted by permission from Barney G. Glaser and Anselm L. Strauss, *The Discovery of Grounded Theory.* Chicago: Aldine Publishing Company; copyright© 1967 by Barney G. Glaser and Anselm L. Strauss.

the reading of qualitative materials from libraries and organizational archives, as well as to the writing of those materials. (pp. 225–233).

Comparisons

Interactionism developed not only in response to issues raised in the course of sociological research but in partial response to other "systems." It is worth noting briefly how interactionists feel about some other views about human personality.

Mead's "social behaviorism" was developed partly in opposition to Watsonian and other early forms of conditioning. Though they have in common an emphasis on the great role of the environment, versus biological factors, the interactionists have always believed that conditioning theory is both too simple to account for the complexity of human behavior and that behaviorism (at least in its early forms) tended wrongly to regard humans as rather passive in the face of impinging stimuli. In addition, while interactionists have approved of a comparative psychology (with humans as the most complexly organized species), they have disapproved of theories which are based largely on study of the white rat. Finally, in common with other sociologists, the interactionists prefer to rely on data gotten from people *in situ* rather than in laboratories or in experimentally designed situations.

Another general approach sociologists view with skepticism is Freudianism, in one version or another. The critiques include the following. Freud developed a theory which was "instinctual"—and that is not tenable. His causal models were 19th-century in style, involving a kind of psychological hydraulic system. His developmental theory was basically biological. Insofar as Freudian schemes are applied to group behavior, they tend toward extrapolation of an essentially individualistically based theory, rather than studying group behavior in its own terms. Besides, this kind of theorizing is so difficult to validate or negate! In all these regards, interactionists' criticisms are no different than those of their sociological colleagues.

One would think the social interactionists might be closest in work and perspective to those psychologists who have specialized in social psychology. Despite occasional "convergences," the historical gap between social interactionism and social psychology is evident in that, for many years, "social psychology" has been taught separately and differently in psychology and sociology departments. Interactionists have been traditionally interested in social psychology because they have believed mass or organizational phenomena could not be understood without a proper grasp of their social-psychological underpinnings. (In fact, this position was stated by Thomas in the 1890s and, of course, is quite explicit in Mead's position.) To interactionists, as the authors of a well-known interactionist textbook state, "A maximally useful social psychology has meant one directed toward a number of subjects that are central to the larger discipline. Socialization is one such problem.... Another ... is the nature of interaction ... how groups, institutions, or social structures manage to function ... how they change but manage to persist; and how they may disintegrate and disappear" (Lindesmith, Strauss, & Denzin, 1975, p. 17).

Prospect

This is the most difficult section to write: One wants to claim the world but fears the worst! This author does not dare guess the future but believes his tradition is, at least, on the right trail.

Interactionism successfully avoids certain positions likely to deflect and prejudice inquiry into human behavior. One of these is reductionism, which reduces the complexity of the most complex of creatures, man, to some sort of biological explanation. Every generation attempts a new kind of reductionist explanation, but none succeeds. Likewise, interactionism avoids excessively deterministic explanations which locate explanations for human behavior somewhere "out there" — whether in culture, in the larger society, or in parts of society (like social classes). Interactionists draw on the resources of social science without being overly deterministic. They allow both for human choice and for partial explanations of that choice.

The method utilized by interactionists is also probably on the right track. Rather than attempting to get cues from studying the behavior of rats or other animals, they look directly at the behavior of humans. It is not that comparative psychology is not useful, interactionists would say, but it should not be the chief focus for inquiry into human behavior. Likewise, laboratory experimentation may be useful, but the chief methods for getting information about humans ought to rely on their behavior and their communications. Hence field observation and interviewing of diverse types are the preferred methods.

And finally, interactionism is probably on the right track because of the kinds of concepts that have been coined on the basis of its position and its methods. One can feel both the depth and the breadth of inquiry into human behavior—and the relevance of that inquiry—in concepts such as career, looking-glass self, role playing, role taking, and awareness context. Hopefully, these concepts will lead to related useful ideas and to increasingly relevant inquiry.

On the other hand, this author, in common with most people who put their faith in alternative positions, must admit that the trail to genuinely deep knowledge of humans is a very long one indeed. We are only at its beginning.

Annotated Bibliography

Becker, Howard S., *Outsiders* (Rev. ed.). New York: Free Press, 1973.

A highly influential presentation of the related notions of careers and selves, in relation to the social interactionist views of deviancy and deviant behavior. In the revised edition Becker reviews some of the debate over "labeling theory" which the original edition provoked.

Blumer, Herbert. *Symbolic Interactionism.* Englewood Cliffs, N.J.: Prentice-Hall, 1969.

This collection of papers offers a comprehensive review of Blumer's positions on theory and method from an interactionist perspective. Blumer has been among the most influential spokesmen in defining the implications of interactionism, in interpreting George H. Mead's writings, and in attacking various forms of determinism.

Goffman, Erving. *The Presentation of Self in Everyday Life.* Garden City, N.Y.: Doubleday, 1959.

Goffman's first and probably most influential and widely quoted book. His concepts include the presentation of self, impression management, backstage, front-stage, and teamwork. Many other stimulating suggestions for analyzing interaction, especially implicit rules, are given in this book.

Hughes, Everett C. *The Sociological Eye.* New York: Free Press, 1971.

One of the most exciting books in the interactionist tradition. Contains essays on a number of different substantive areas (race, urban relations, work, profession), almost all oriented toward the development of theory and its grounding in data. Hughes has a very sharp "sociological eye" and relies heavily on field observation.

Lindesmith, A. R., Strauss, A., and Denzin, N. *Social Psychology* (4th ed.). Hinsdale, Ill.: Dryden Press, 1975.

A basic textbook for social interactionists, this includes such chapter titles as: "Symbolic Environments and Cognitive Structures," "Social Structure, Groups and Language," "Language Differentiation and the Learning Process," "The Naming Process and the Internal Environment," "The Origins and Development of the Self," "Interaction and the Self," "Deviance, Conventionality, and Power."

McCall, George, and Simmons, John (Eds.). *Issues in Participant Observation.* Reading, Mass.: Addison-Wesley, 1969.

An excellent reader consisting of papers and excerpts from monographs pertaining to field observation. The editors contribute appropriate introductions as well as a discussion of basic issues in the use and development of this methodology.

Mead, George Herbert. *Mind, Self and Society.* Chicago: University of Chicago Press, 1934.

This is the volume by Mead most widely read by social scientists. Consists of Mead's class lectures, published posthumously and includes discussions of his best known concepts, including the generalized other, roletaking, roleplaying, the self, the I and the me, mind, society.

Strauss, Anselm. *Mirrors and Masks.* San Francisco: Sociology Press, 1971. (Originally published, Glencoe, Ill.: Free Press, 1958.)

An essay which explores the relationship of social interaction, identity, and social structure. It includes discussion of such topics as language and identity, self-appraisals, motivation, transformations of identity, group membership, change, and continuity of identity.

References

Becker, H. Whose side are we on? *Social problems,* 1967, *14,* 239–247.

Becker, H. *Outsiders* (Rev. ed.). New York: Free Press, 1973.

Berger, P., & Luckmann, T. *The social construction of reality.* Garden City, N.Y.: Doubleday, 1966.

Blau, P. *Exchange and power in social life.* New York: Wiley, 1964.

Blumer, H. The methodological position of symbolic interactionism. In H. Blumer, *Symbolic interactionism.* Englewood Cliffs, N.J.: Prentice-Hall, 1969.

Cassirer, E. *An essay on man.* New Haven, Conn.: Yale University Press, 1953–1957.

Cooley, C. *Human nature and the social order.* New York: Scribners, 1902.

Davis, F. *Passage through crisis.* Indianapolis: Bobbs-Merrill, 1963.

Dewey, J. *Human nature and conduct.* New York: Modern Library, Holt, 1922.

Garfinkel, H. *Studies in ethnomethodology.* Englewood Cliffs, N.J.: Prentice-Hall, 1967.

Glaser, B., & Strauss, A. *Awareness of dying.* Chicago: Aldine, 1965.

Glaser, B., & Strauss, A. *The discovery of grounded theory.* Chicago: Aldine, 1967.

Glaser, B., & Strauss, A. *Status passage.* Chicago: Aldine, 1971.

Goffman, E. On face-work. *Psychiatry,* 1955, *18,* 213–231.

Goffman, E. *The presentation of self in everyday life.* Garden City, N.Y.: Doubleday, 1959.

Goffman, E. *Interaction ritual.* Chicago: Aldine, 1967.

Griffin, J. *Black like me.* New York: Signet Books, 1962.

Heath, A. Review article: Exchange theory. *British Journal of Political Science,* 1971, *1,* 90–119.

Homans, G. *Social behavior.* New York: Harcourt Brace, 1961.

Hughes, E. *The sociological eye.* Chicago: Aldine, 1971.

Klapp, O. *Symbolic leaders.* Chicago: Aldine, 1965.

Lindesmith, A. *The addict and the law.* Bloomington: Indiana University Press, 1965.

Lindesmith, A. *Addiction and opiates.* Chicago: Aldine, 1968.

Lindesmith, A., Strauss, A., & Denzin, N. *Social psychology* (4th ed.). Hinsdale, Ill.: Dryden, 1975.

Lofland, J. *Doomsday cult.* Englewood Cliffs, N.J.: Prentice-Hall, 1966.

Mayrl, W. Ethnomethodology: sociology without society. *Catalyst,* 1973, *7,* 15–29.

McCall, G., & Simmons, J. *Identities and interaction.* New York: Free Press, 1966.

Mead, G. H. *The philosophy of the present.* LaSalle, Ill.: Open Court, 1932.

Mead, G. H. *Mind, self and society.* Chicago: University of Chicago Press, 1934.

Mead, G. H. *The philosophy of the act.* Chicago: University of Chicago Press, 1938.

Merton, R., & Kitt, A. Contributions to the theory of reference group behavior. In R. Merton & P. Lazarsfeld (Eds.), *Studies in the scope and method of "the American soldier."* New York: Free Press, 1950.

Mills, C. W. Situated actions and vocabularies of motives. *American Sociological Review,* 1940, *5,* 904–13.

Parsons, T. Psychology and sociology. In J. Gillin, (Ed.), *For a science and social man* (pp. 67–101). New York: Macmillan, 1954.

Reynolds, J., & Reynolds, L. Interactionism, complicity and the astructural bias. *Catalyst,* 1973, *7,* 76–85.

Ropers, R. Mead, Marx and social psychology. *Catalyst,* 1973, *7,* 42–61.

Schatzman, L., & Strauss, A. *Field research.* Englewood Cliffs, N.J.: Prentice-Hall, 1973.

Schutz, A. *Collected papers* (2 vols). The Hague: Martinus Nijhoff, 1962–1964.

Scott, M. *The racing game.* Chicago: Aldine, 1968.

Scott, M. & Lyman, S. Accounts. *American Sociological Review,* 1968, *33,* 46–62.

Shearing, C. Towards a phenomenological sociology. *Catalyst,* 1973, *7,* 9–14.

Simmel, G. *Conflict and the web of group affiliations.* New York: Free Press, 1953.

Stanton, A., & Schwartz, M. *The mental hospital.* New York: Basic Books, 1954.

Stone, G. Appearance and the self. In A. Rose (Ed.), *Human behavior and social processes.* Boston: Houghton Mifflin, 1962.

Strauss, A. *Mirrors and masks.* San Francisco: Sociology Press, 1969. (Originally published, Free Press of Glencoe, 1958.)

Strauss, A. Medical ghettos. In A. Strauss (Ed.), *Where medicine fails.* Chicago: Aldine, 1970.

Strauss, A., Fagerhaugh, S., & Glaser, B. Pain: An organizational-work-interactional perspective. *Nursing Outlook.* 1974, *9,* 560–66.

Strauss, A., Schatzman, L., Bucher, R., Ehrlich, D., & Sabshin, M. *Psychiatric ideologies and institutions.* New York: Free Press, 1964.

Sutherland, E. *The professional thief.* Chicago: University of Chicago Press, 1937.

Thomas, W. I., & Thomas, D. *The child in America.* New York: Knopf, 1928.

Turner, R. Role-taking: Process versus conformity. In A. Rose (ed.), *Human behavior and social processes.* Boston: Houghton Mifflin, 1962.

Warren, C. *Identity and community in the gay world.* New York: Wiley, 1974

Wesby, D. The career experience of the symphony musician. *Social Forces,* 1960, *38,* 223–30.

The term "constitutional psychology" refers to all possible relationships between body and behavior. In this chapter, however, it applies only to the field of personality.

Constitutional theories of personality take three approaches. The *structural* approach assesses character through physical appearance. Its best known advocate today is William Sheldon, who postulates that body build virtually determines personality. This theory maintains that somatotypes, or body structures, are practically unchangeable throughout life and that temperamental or personality types are associated with body types. The structural approach sees maladjustment as stemming either from poor heredity or from failure to accept the personality required by one's bodily form. It advocates social programs to improve heredity and to aid individuals in adjusting to their biological predispositions.

The *experiential* approach, first developed by Paul Schilder and championed today primarily by Seymour Fisher, grew out of other theories, particularly psychoanalysis, but it has acquired its own unique features. It relates body processes to psychological development and emotional organization. Experiential theory is consistent with traditional therapeutic techniques which rely on verbal uncovering and interpretation, but innovative methods, based on exercise and improvement in body awareness, are currently being developed.

The *holistic* approach, proposed initially by Kurt Goldstein, maintains that body and mind are inseparable. Holistic theory describes the person as a complex, self-regulatory system capable of healthy development to maturity if provided with an environment containing an adequate variety of minimally threatening opportunities. The holistic approach advocates freedom for individuals to express themselves in their own preferred ways. It sees disturbances of behavior not as symptoms of illness but as efforts on the part of the organism to restore its natural and rightful integrity.

In general, the structural approach asserts that the body is primary, while personality is derivative and relatively secondary. The experiential approach asserts the primacy of psychological processes and points out that the body becomes psychologically important as it acquires meaning within the personality; this meaning comes from experience, not heredity. The *holistic approach* argues that neither body nor mind is primary but that basic principles (like self-actualization) apply to both and can operate only when the organism is whole, intact, and unconfined. Despite apparent differences, the three approaches complement one another and provide a comprehensive picture of relationships between body and personality.

Constitutional Theories of Personality

Franklin C. Shontz

WILLIAM H. SHELDON

Introduction

Any theory which proposes to take into account the whole of human personality must include consideration of the body and its functions. The human body enters into psychological life in a variety of ways. It is a register of sensory events, an instrument for action, and a source of needs, drives, and motives. It is also a value-loaded stimulus to the self and others, and it is the medium through which self-expression takes place. For most people, the body is the envelope of selfhood; it encompasses events that have always been regarded by society, law, religion (and to some extent, even by science) as taking place within a private and inviolable world of intimate, personal experience (Shontz, 1975).

The significance of the body is obvious in permanent states of physical illness or severe disability. The mutual interplay of mind and body is even more evident in commonly experienced, temporary conditions such as those brought on by pain, fatigue, anxiety, or sexual excitement.

"A sound mind in a sound body" (derived from the Latin saying: *mens sana in corpore sano*) implies several assumptions about the relationship between body and mind. One assumption is that an unsound mind must have its cause in a disordered state of the body. Similarly, obvious physical disability leads many to suspect the possibility of mental disorder. The doctrine that mental stress or conflicts can produce physical illnesses is also currently accepted. Some somatic conditions, such as peptic ulcers or migraine headaches, have come to be called *psychosomatic*, a term which implies that these physical conditions may be taken as evidence of mental distress.

Within the range of normal variation of physiques, stereotypes about the relationship between body structure and personality are pervasive. Dark-complexioned people are reputed to be passionate, emotional, and impulsive. Redheads are said to have fiery tempers. Fat people are expected to be jolly. Long, bony physiques are associated with intellectual abilities or interests and with a tendency to withdraw from social contacts. The ubiquity of stereotypes relating body build to behavior reveals the deep belief in a causal relation between the body and the mind.

Standards for judging personal appearance change, of course. Spectacles, especially those with thick lenses, indicating weak eyes, were once the sign of the intellectual or the absentminded professor, but they are now an accepted accessory for everyday costumes. Among teenagers, braces on the teeth, once a stigma, are commonplace today. Following World War II, many Japanese changed their ancient ways and adopted Western dress and American standards of physical beauty.

Despite its obvious central importance in psychological life, the body has been virtually ignored by most personality theorists. This is especially true in the United States, where theorists tend to regard study of the body as properly done only by biologists or physiologists and to stress nurture over nature so heavily that they relegate body functions to a position of secondary importance to learned behaviors.

Three Theoretical Approaches

The best known theoretical approach to constitutional psychology, the structural, regards the physical body and its functions as the basic, genetically determined framework upon which all subsequent personality development must build. The experiential approach stresses the subjective rather than the objective influence of the body. This approach is best represented by theories about the body image, a hypothetical picture of the body which forms the core of personality as a whole. The holistic approach regards neither body structure nor mental experience as primary but sees them as so inextricably interwoven as to be inseparable. Holistic theories describe a viewpoint extremely useful in clinical practice; they point the way for needed future developments in personality theory.

In the following sections of this chapter we recognize that there is no single constitutional theory and therefore describe the experiential and holistic as well as the structural approaches. Taken together, they provide a comprehensive view of current theories about body-behavior relations.

History

Precursors

The idea that the body determines personality is as old as human thought. Most ancient Greeks believed the heart to be the seat of intelligence, while breath was associated with life itself (Smith & Ross, 1910). The Japanese traditionally have localized the vital centers in the belly. One form of yoga identifies the spinal column as a three-channeled pathway, through which deep-seated spiritual forces can be induced to find their way to ultimate emergence through the top of the head.

Body functions are commonly regarded as mysterious in nonliterate societies. Young adolescent boys endure circumcision or other tests of manhood as a way of being initiated into adult masculine society. Menstruation in girls is assumed to have profound psychological effects. Involving as it does a process that looks like bleeding from a genital wound, it easily becomes associated symbolically with castration or, more obviously, with the mystery of birth.

Humoral Theory. Hippocrates, the famous physician of ancient Greece, was the first to offer a systematic attempt to relate body structure and function to personality. His scheme (called the *humoral theory*) was developed by the Roman physician and encyclopedist Galen into a comprehensive constitutional explanation of body-behavior relations.

This theory associated personality differences with four body humors, or fluids or spirits which affect mood and action as well as physical condition. Accepting the conventional doctrine that the universe is composed of four elements—earth, air, fire, and water—Hippocrates and Galen related each element to a corresponding body fluid and an associated personality type. To the opposed elements, air and earth, they related the body fluids yellow bile and black bile and the personality types choleric and melancholic, respectively. A *choleric* person is like the air: flighty, unstable, quickly aroused but easily calmed down, prone to impatience or irascibility. In contrast, a *melancholic* person is anxious, worried, thoughtful, and depressed. To the opposed elements, fire and water, they assigned the body humors blood and phlegm and the personality types sanguine and phlegmatic. A *sanguine* person is optimistic, sociable, good natured, easily bored, and perhaps shallow in the sense of being unable to take things sufficiently seriously. A *phlegmatic* person is persistent, stable, serious, and unchanging; though not lazy, such a person is hard to arouse emotionally.

One might suppose that no modern psychologist would take such primitive theoretical ideas seriously. Yet, in *Fact and Fiction in Psychology,* (Eysenck, 1965, p. 54) there is a diagram of two straight lines at right angles. The horizontal line is labeled *introverted–extraverted;* the vertical line *stable–unstable.* The quadrant identified by the terms extraverted and unstable is labeled *choleric.* The quadrant identified as introverted and unstable is labeled *melancholic.* Stable extraversion is identified as *sanguine* and stable introversion as *phlegmatic.* Eysenck was writing about psychological traits, not body fluids, and he indicated that his diagram of personality represents conclusions drawn from the results of extensive modern research.

Physiognomy. Humoral theory relied upon postulating internal processes. A simpler theory would result if parallels could be found betweeen outward appearance and personality. The attempt to do this is called the study of *physiognomy,* and the effort to develop a systematic physiognomic science was initiated by John Lavater in the late 18th century. Lavater's (1789) theory relied on such signs of character as the noble nose, the weak mouth, and the cunning eye. Obviously, it was not very scientific.

In the late 19th century, Césare Lombroso (1911) added to the basic physiognomic hypothesis the idea that character is reflected in appearance. Lombroso associated anatomical abnormalities (or *stigmata*) with evolutionary degeneration. He asserted that such throwbacks were related to criminality; thus he promulgated the still persistent idea of a "criminal type" which can be recognized not only by behavior but by appearance and which is genetically inferior to more law-abiding types.

Phrenology. More explicit but no less speculative were the ideas of Franz J. Gall and Johann G. Spurzheim (Gall & Spurzheim, 1809; Spurzheim 1833). Gall, an expert on anatomy and the nervous system, proposed that specific mental faculties are represented by overdevelopment of specific brain centers. These overdeveloped centers could be identified by examining the external contours of the skull, where they were said to appear as bumps. Thus, skull shape could be used to diagnose character, personality, and abilities. Spurzheim extended and popularized this doctrine, which attracted a great deal of attention in the middle of the 19th century and which is not without its followers even today.

Evidence and Theory in Science. The ideas described so far are not scientific because they do not rely upon unbiased and systematically collected empirical data for their confirmation. They therefore represent precursors of scientific theories rather than true theories.

The structural, experiential, and holistic approaches described in subsequent sections of this chapter have been developed by scientists. Their data may in some instances be crude, and some of their ideas are admittedly speculative. But all share a reliance upon careful observation as their source of inspiration, and all respect objective data as the final judgment of the validity of any theory.

Beginnings

Structural Approach. As a scientific method of study, the structural approach began when quantitative measurement was first applied to test hypotheses about physique and behavior. While the use of numbers does not guarantee that findings will be valid, it does reflect an underlying change in attitude and marks the first recognition of the importance of systematic methods of observation and inference.

Anthropometric studies, using quantitative and objective measurements of physique, were begun in Padua, Italy, by Achille de Giovanni. His pupil Giacinto Viola differentiated three body types: the *microsplanchnic* (a type that Hippocrates had called the *phthisic habitus*), with small trunk and relatively long limbs; the *macrosplanchnic* (Hippocrates's *apoplectic habitus*), with large trunk and comparatively short limbs; and the more common and better proportioned *normosplanchnic*. The work of this early Italian school may be illustrated by an investigation conducted in the United States by Sante Naccarati (1921), a student of Viola's. Reasoning that microsplanchnics are developmentally advanced, being more like adults and less like infants in body build, Naccarati hypothesized that microsplanchnic body build is associated with higher intelligence than macrosplanchnic body build. He obtained correlation coefficients of about +.23, indicating a slight tendency (about 5% common variance) for body measures and in-

telligence test performances to be positively related. In 1927 William Sheldon repeated Naccarati's study and found correlations of only about +.13. Sheldon also attempted to correlate body measures with personality traits but had equally disappointing results (Sheldon, Stevens, & Tucker, 1940/1970, pp. 16–20).

In Germany, Ernst Kretschmer (1921) associated psychiatric diagnoses with body build. He observed that patients diagnosed as manic-depressive, who have extremes or rapid shifts of elated and depressed moods, tended to be *pyknics* (Kretschmer's term for the macrosplanchnic type), while schizophrenic patients, whose problems mainly involve disordered thought processes, tended to be *asthenics* (microsplanchnics). Unfortunately, Kretschmer's data were confused and confusing (Paterson, 1930). As Sheldon put it: "With Kretschmer, insight and an observant eye came first, tools of quantification were to be applied later" (Sheldon, Stevens, & Tucker, 1940/1970, p. 24).

Experiential Approach. One source of scientific interest in body experience was the study of unusual behavior which follows damage to the brain or the loss of body parts. Damage to the right hemisphere of the brain produces weakness or paralysis of the left side of the body (left hemiparesis or left hemiplegia). Sometimes associated with this condition is the behavioral disturbance known as *anosognosia*, in which the patient acts as though he or she has forgotten or wished to deny having difficulties with the left side of the body. When questioned about his left arm or leg, the patient claims that nothing is wrong, even though the evidence of his incapacity is in plain view. Sudden denervation or amputation of body parts commonly produces phantom experiences. A phantom limb exists when the person seems to receive sensations from or believes that he can control an extremity that is no longer connected to the sensorimotor centers of the brain. Classic examples of the phantom limb are provided by the patient who tries to catch a ball with an amputated hand or attempts to stand on an absent leg.

Another source of interest in the experiential approach is disturbances of personality, particularly as explained by Freud and his followers. The central component of personality, as Freud described it, is the ego, and Freud himself said that the "ego is first and foremost a body ego" (1927, p. 31), meaning that personality grows primarily from body experience. Fenichel (1945) and others applied this idea within the bounds of orthodox psychoanalytic theory.

More directly relevant to present purposes was the work of Paul Schilder (1935), a psychoanalytic neuropsychiatrist, who expanded psychoanalytic theory by describing in detail the concept of the body image. To Schilder, the body image is not merely a mental picture of the bodily self; it is the core and essence of the whole personality. Furthermore, the body image is not confined to the physical body but is capable of expanding and contracting, or even of merging with the body images of other persons in moments of personal intimacy. Later investigators, like Seymour Fisher, were stimulated by Schilder's thinking to develop ideas described more completely in a subsequent section of this chapter.

Holistic Approach. Philosophically, holism may be traced to Benedict (Baruch) Spinoza (1632–1677), but it was espoused more explicitly in modern times by Jan Smuts (1926), a South African statesman and philosopher. The fundamental doctrine of holism is that mind and body are one and inseparable. The human organism, a complex totality, cannot be analyzed without destroying it; it must be studied whole to be properly understood.

Late in the 19th and early in the 20th centuries, Adolf Meyer (1957), an American psychiatrist, rejected mind-body dualism in the treatment of psychiatric patients and promulgated what has come to be known as the *psychobiological* approach. Other theorists adopted similar views. Notable among psychologists was Wilhelm Stern (1938), who developed an approach that came to be called *personalistic*. Additionally, but from a different observational base, Kurt Goldstein (1939, 1940, 1942) proposed his own *organismic* theory.

Some physicians concentrated on studying the effects of psychological events on bodily states, particularly when the events involve emotional conflicts and when the outcomes are physical diseases. Interest in this subject was first stimulated by H. F. Dunbar's book *Emotions and Bodily Changes,* which appeared in 1935, and by the founding of the *Journal of Psychosomatic Medicine* in 1939. Psychosomatic medicine has been consistently advanced by the efforts of theorists like Franz Alexander (1950), who have applied psychoanalytic theory to the understanding of physical disease (see also Alexander, French, & Pollack, 1968).

Interest in psychosomatics was followed by the definition of its complement, *somatopsychology,* by Barker, Wright, and Gonick in 1946 (see also Meyerson, 1971; Shontz, 1975; and Wright, 1960). This field of study was identified primarily out of concern for the psychological aspects of physical disability, a subject long ignored in psychology and psychosomatic medicine.

Current Status
Generally speaking, the structural approach to constitutional theory has had little encouragement from American psychologists. Experimental psychology in the United States concentrates on the effects of environmental manipulations and emphasizes the plasticity and controllability of behavior. Clinical psychologists and counselors also fail to find constitutional psychology appealing. The "reality" to which they help clients adjust rarely takes into account the clients' unique constitutional endowments. Even the idea of somatically determined sex differences in behavior is currently under attack by the women's liberation movement, which has an obvious interest in altering theories that ascribe personality differences to sex identity.

By and large, American psychologists prefer to be hopeful and optimistic; they like to believe that all behavioral possibilities are open to everyone equally, if only environmental conditions are right for their emergence. American psychologists therefore generally reject assertions that body structures affect behavioral potentialities. Occasionally research on constitutional theory appears in the scientific literature, but no strong movement publicizes or applies constitutional psychology, particularly of the structural type developed by William Sheldon.

Suggestions that culturally valued characteristics, such as intelligence, may be linked to genetic factors arouse indignant responses from social scientists as well as the general population. Jews remember all too well what happened in Nazi Germany when a distorted constitutional psychology was carried to such an absurd extreme that it resulted in the systematic extermination of 6 million persons. No wonder American psychology is reluctant to accept structural constitutional theories of personality. Nevertheless, theories relating body structure and function to personality have always been appealing. They existed among the ancient Greeks, and they exist today. Sheldon observed that the early data of constitutional psychology were never fully convincing but were always suggestive enough to indicate that something important remained to be discovered (Sheldon, Stevens, & Tucker, 1940/1970, pp. 17–20).

The experiential and holistic approaches have been given a more favorable reception. The concept of the body image is popular, especially in the psychiatric literature and in psychosomatics and somatopsychology. Research interest in the body as a stimulus object remains high, particularly in social psychology and in studies of emotional expression and communication through gestures and movement (Birdwhistell, 1970; Spiegel & Machotka, 1974).

Though not clearly articulated or strongly buttressed by laboratory research, holistic theories have had an evident influence on popular clinical practices. Some therapists argue that mental disorders result from disturbances in the flow of energy within the body, while health, happiness, pleasure, and a better world for all come from proper body functioning (Lowen, 1958, 1965, 1972; Reich, 1944). These therapists propose exercises they alleged would restore proper somatic functioning and promote psychological maturity (Feldenkrais, 1949, 1972; Lowen, 1970; 1972; Rolf, 1972). Often such approaches to mental health are even more holistic than conservative scientists would agree is desirable, since the rationale behind the health-through-exercise movement commonly includes not only physical and mental well-being but spiritual development as well.

Constitutional psychologies have one distinctive characteristic. They are virtually all naturalistic. They prefer to develop principles applicable to the solution of real-life problems rather than to concentrate on laboratory experiments. This preference has the disadvantage of basing naturalistic theories on principles that are often imprecise. But it gives to constitutional approaches an air of relevance and immediacy missing in many other specialties of psychology.

Lindzey (1967) pointed out that there are several reasons to expect physique and behavior to be correlated. First, there is the obvious fact that some life events do affect both body and behavior; for example, prolonged stress not only increases anxiety but is also likely to reduce or increase appetite and thus to affect body weight. Second, physique places limits on what it is physically possible or impossible for an individual to do. Third, society pressures people into roles that suit their physiques (a person with an unusual physique may be solicited to work as a "freak" in a carnival) and expects certain behaviors or personality traits to be shown by persons with particular body builds. Fourth, biological factors sometimes determine *both* behavior and physique; obvious examples are cases involving inherited disabilities, like Huntington's Disease or severe mental retardation.

Similar Theories

The similarity of other theories to those described in this chapter may be judged by two criteria: the amount of stress other theories place on body functioning per se, and the extent to which they relate body structure or experience to personality as a whole.

Considering only the emphasis placed on body functions, theories based on laboratory research in biology or physiological psychology (for example, theories of genetics or of sensory or neural functioning) lie at one extreme. They deal mainly with body structures and only to a small extent with behavior. For the most part, also, they concentrate on relatively specific behaviors such as reflex actions or eating, drinking, and maze learning. They do not typically deal with human personality as a whole or with the influence of physique upon overall psychological adjustment. Consequently, although they are important in their own right, they do not receive detailed consideration in this chapter.

To the extent that operant conditioning only describes manifest behavior and does not theorize about physical or mental processes, it lies at the other extreme; it is almost totally unconcerned with physique as a determinant of behavior. Also irrelevant is phenomenology, the study of subjective experience in its most natural and complex forms. For example, George A. Kelly's (1955) theory of personal constructs deals exclusively with cognitive variables (thought processes). As valuable a theory as it is, it is not constitutional in any sense of the term.

Some theories that are called holistic by their originators are given little attention in this chapter because their emphasis has tended to drift away from concern for body structures and processes and toward primary interest in cognitive or phenomenological events. The most obvious example of this drift occurred in the theorizing of Abraham Maslow (1970), who identified his theory as holistic early in his writings but later developed a nearly exclusive concern for cognitive processes. Maslow first argued that human needs exist in a hierarchy; they display a uniform sequence of emergence in development, some being more primary and fundamental than others. At the base of this hierarchy lie the easily recognized physiological, survival-oriented needs like hunger, thirst, and elimination. Next are needs for safety and security. Then come sexual and love needs, followed by needs for esteem from self and others and, ultimately, the need for self-actualization: to develop to one's fullest potential.

Maslow's theory stressed the universality of this hierarchy and the "instinctoid" character of the needs themselves. As his thinking progressed, however, Maslow made it clear that self-actualization is not just another need but involves a kind of transformation or reorganization of the whole personality, a totally new way of thinking. A body need, like the need to escape from pain, is not the same in a self-actualized as in a non-self-actualized person; the difference is one of meaning. Normally, physical pain is avoided, but a self-actualized saint may seek it out as a way to prove his faith or increase his ecstasy. For most of us, pain means danger; for the saint it can mean fulfillment. Thus Maslow's theory turned more toward the study of meaning than toward the study of body states.

Andreas Angyll (1941; 1965), another avowed holist, made significant contributions to personality theory. However, he was more concerned with breaking down the distinction between organism and environment than with the distinction between mind and body. Like the existentialists (such as Barral, 1965; May, Angel, & Ellenberger, 1958; Plügge, 1970), Maslow and Angyll found themselves becoming concerned mainly with solving the distinctive problems of specifically human existence. Many such problems arise because human activities have become relatively independent of body needs and requirements. Hence, theoretical concerns that began with and included body processes soon expanded into involvement with far more inclusive and abstract matters.

Closer to the mark is the work of Hans Selye (1956, 1974) on physiological responses to stress. Selye introduced the concept of the *general adaptation syndrome*: the idea that stress responses occur in stages. The first stage, *alarm*, involves the whole organism. It constitutes a generalized activation and total mobilization of available defensive resources. During the second stage, *resistance*, responses become more localized, more efficiently specialized, and more effectively contained. Finally, in prolonged stress, the third stage, *exhaustion*, occurs when organismic resources are strained beyond their capacity to endure. Exhaustion terminates in the collapse of defenses and the death of the organism.

Selye noted that physiological reactions to foreign substances are of two types, specific and nonspecific. The latter are similar, regardless of the nature of the stress-inducing substance. Part of the process of self-defense involves the hormonal activation of inflammatory reactions which attack the target (threatened) area. An example of an inflammatory response is the redness and swelling that develop around an insect bite or a splinter under the skin. During the initial stages of response, these reactions may be intense and painful in themselves, but as resistance develops, anti-inflammatory responses are initiated to hold them in check. Anti-inflammatory responses are essential because inflammatory responses are harmful to the organism itself if carried on too long or too extensively.

Selye realized that an organism can damage itself by its own uncontrolled inflammatory defense against harm from outside. Should this happen in response to external substances that are not objectively dangerous, the result is a disease of adaptation, such as an allergy. Because allergies, as well as other conditions explained by the theory of stress, had been thought of by one group of theorists as being psychosomatic, Selye's theory was originally of some interest in the study of personality. It became even more interesting when scientists realized that the source of inflammatory stress responses could be psychological as well as physical. However, Selye is not a psychological theorist, and the implications of his thinking have not been developed into a full-fledged explanatory system in the field of personality. Research workers who study the psychological aspects of stress are still far from unanimous about the laws governing the processes they investigate (Appley & Trumbull, 1967).

Most personality theorists acknowledge the importance of body processes, but only Henry Murray's (1938) theory pays explicit attention to them. However, Murray's theory is better described as comprehensive than as holistic. His lists of primary *(viscerogenic)* and secondary *(psychogenic)* needs are more like exercises in taxonomy than a set of theoretical postulates or propositions. Murray stressed that personality has a biological foundation, and his theory attempts to do justice to the full complexity of the human individual. But it presents few broadly applicable principles, and those it does provide cannot be called constitutional, as that term is used here.

Finally, every comprehensive discussion of personality theory must say at least a few words about psychoanalysis. Psychoanalysis recognizes the importance of body processes in psychological life, but it has traditionally been more concerned with mental experiences, especially those of a symbolic nature, than with body structures as such. As has been mentioned, psychosomatic medicine developed in partial compensation for this relative lack of direct concern with physique-behavior relations. Concurrently, body image theory (about which more is said later) came on the scene to fulfill the same purpose.

Traditional psychoanalytic theory has strongly influenced the experiential approach to constitutional psychology. Its newer versions are consistent with the holistic approach, as will be shown by Bakan's concepts of centralization and decentralization. However, the rapprochement of psychoanalysis and structural theory seems to be out of the question, because, from a constitutional point of view, it is a waste of time to promulgate a form of therapy which proposes to change personality but has no effect on constitutionally given traits (Sheldon & Stevens, 1942/1970, pp. 428–429).

Assertions

Development: Structural Approach (Sheldon)

1. THE SOMATOTYPE PROVIDES A UNIVERSAL FRAME OF REFERENCE FOR HOW HUMAN BEINGS GROW AND DEVELOP, INDEPENDENT OF CULTURE.

This assertion points to the *somatotype* as the key construct in William Sheldon's theory. The meaning of the term must therefore be made clear. Though it has implications for the ultimate shape of the body, somatotype is not a static form or fixed structure. It is a theoretical term describing the course of bodily development through which an individual will pass, provided nutrition is adequate and grossly disturbing pathology does not occur. Thus, the somatotype is dynamic rather than static; a process, not a thing.

The underlying structure which assures constancy of the somatotype is the *morphogenotype*. However, the morphogenotype is not observable directly, and it is not the sole determinant of physical appearance. Nutrition and experience play their parts in modifying body structure, though nothing can alter the morphogenotype fundamentally. A person's actual physical appearance displays the *phenotype*, which expresses the influences of both heredity and environment. From careful observation and measurement of phenotypes, inferences are drawn about somatotypes and, hence, about the even more basic, but also more completely hidden, morphogenotypes.

2. THREE POLAR EXTREMES CALLED ENDOMORPHY, MESOMORPHY AND ECTOMORPHY, IDENTIFY THE ESSENTIAL COMPONENTS OF THE SOMATOTYPE.

Endomorphy develops from predominance of the internal (endodermal) embryonic layer, which matures into internal, visceral organs. Extreme endomorphs are round-bodied and blubbery in appearance. In his *Atlas of Men* (Sheldon, Dupertuis, & McDermott, 1954), Sheldon called such persons manatees, dugongs, whales, and ancient hippopotamuses.

Mesomorphy develops from the middle (mesodermal) embryonic layer. An extreme mesomorph shows overdevelopment of muscle, bone, and connective tissue; the physique is rectangular and athletic. Our society values mesomorphy as the ideal male physique. Sheldon identified mesomorphs with aggressive birds of prey, like owls and eagles.

Ectomorphy represents predominance of the external (ectodermal) embryonic layer. Extreme ectomorphs show the greatest development of skin surface and nervous system relative to overall body size. The pure ectomorph is linear and fragile, exposing a relatively large proportion of the body surface to the weather. Sheldon identified such persons with insects like walking sticks and wasps.

In early research, Naccarati had used height divided by weight as a rough index of body type. Sheldon found that a good approximation to somatotype is obtained by height divided by the cube root of weight. When height is taken in inches and weight in pounds, endomorphs tend to score between 11.2 and 11.8; mesomorphs, about 12.5; and ectomorphs, about 14.0 or higher.

Sheldon's classificatory scheme is similar to those that preceded it historically. The endomorph is similar to the macrosplanchnic, pyknic, and apoplectic types described by others. The ectomorph is similar to the microsplanchnic, asthenic, and phthisic types. The mesomorph is like the athletic type described by Kretschmer. An important difference between Sheldon's approach and those of earlier workers is that they tended to see each individual as belonging exclusively to one or another body type. This is not true in Sheldon's theory, as is explained in the next assertion.

3.   SOMATOTYPES ARE NOT EITHER-OR PHENOMENA BUT ARE PRESENT TO A GREATER OR LESSER DEGREE IN ALL INDIVIDUALS.

The best way to represent relations among the somatotypes is by an equilateral triangle, with sides curved slightly outward and with the extreme of one type at each apex (Figure 11-1). Each somatic component corresponds to a line from one extreme, at an apex, to the other extreme, at the midpoint of the opposite side of the triangle. Moderate levels of all components are represented by points near the center of the triangle, where all lines cross.

By convention, the somatotype of a given person is specified by a combination of three numbers, one for each component. The first number represents the degree of endomorphy, the second the degree of mesomorphy, and the third the degree of ectomorphy. Each number may range from 1 to 7, in half-point intervals. The use of half-point values makes it possible to identify 13 points on each component scale. Seven represents the extreme, at the apex of the triangle; 4 is at the center of the triangle; and 1 is at the intersection of the line from the apex at the opposite side. Theoretically, a person may be represented by a point anywhere within the triangular space described by the three numbers. A 117 (read one-one-seven, not one hundred seventeen) is an extreme ectomorph and is located at one apex of the triangle. The commonest male somatotypes lie between 344 and 353. Women tend to be more endomorphic; their average appears to fall somewhere around 433.

Sheldon used a triangular diagram because it conveys more accurately the range of possible somatotypes than does the conventional system of Cartesian, rectangular coordinates. If *X*, *Y*, and *Z* axes were mutually perpendicular, intersecting at the value of 1 on each component, it would be possible to locate a point in space corresponding to a 777 somatotype, even though such a somatotype never appears in a real person and is barely even conceivable theoretically. No such point can be plotted on the triangular coordinates. Other unobservable somatotypes (like the 111) are also automatically excluded by this type of representation. Generally speaking, the sum of the numbers in a description of a somatotype is not less than 9 nor more than 12.

In somatotyping, a set of *second-order* components of physique is also taken into account. These are:

1. *Dysplasia.* The extent of disharmony among somatotypes in different regions of the body.
2. *Gynandromorphy.* The prominence of characteristics of the other sex in the physique.
3. *Hirsutism.* Abundance of body hair.
4. *Texture.* An aesthetic quality, based on such considerations as physical harmony, symmetry, and beauty; it does not refer exclusively or even primarily to the quality of the skin.

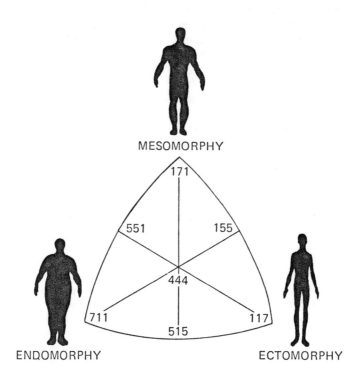

MESOMORPHY

171

551   155

444

711   117

515

ENDOMORPHY   ECTOMORPHY

Figure 11.1: The Somatotypes

Although the second-order components are descriptively useful, their relevance to personality is not as clearly spelled out as is the relevance of the primary components—endomorphy, mesomorphy, and ectomorphy.

4.   EACH SOMATOTYPE PREDISPOSES
      TOWARD THE DEVELOPMENT OF A
      PARTICULAR TYPE OF TEMPERAMENT OR
      PERSONALITY.

Persons whose bodies are high in endomorphy are expected to possess a *viscerotonic* temperament. Viscerotonia is a positive, relaxed, amiable, tolerant, and extraverted orientation with a stable level of emotional flow. Also prominent in viscerotonia is love of polite ceremony, of food, and of physical comfort.

Persons whose bodies are high in mesomorphy should possess a *somatotonic* termperament. Somatotonia is characterized by boldness, love of risk and chance, and Spartan tolerance of pain and discomfort. The somatotonic person is said to be assertive, aggressive, dominant, combative, callous, and action-oriented. In many respects, somatotonia represents the Western cultural ideal of masculinity, or *machismo*.

Persons whose bodies are high in ectomorphy are described as being *cerebrotonic* in temperament. Such persons are tense, restrained, apprehensive, secretive, idea-oriented, and introverted. Though highly sensitive to pain, cerebrotonic persons resist the actions of drugs, even anesthetics. Yet, when cerebrotonics do react, they tend to do so to excess. Therefore, the cerebrotonic is unpredictable as well as extreme, tending to be either underresponsive due to excessive inhibition or overresponsive when nervous discharge predominates.

5. COMBINATIONS IN VARIOUS DEGREES OF THE DIFFERENT TEMPERAMENTAL TYPES ARE COMPONENTS OF A WHOLE PERSON.

An individual may be both viscerotonic and somatotonic, especially if his body build combines endomorphy and mesomorphy. Examples might be a professional wrestler or, perhaps, the television detective Cannon, who superficially displays viscerotonia but who acts in a most somatotonic way when dealing with villains. Sheldon regarded as particularly dangerous for the future of the human race the combination of ectomorphic ideation, which tends to be unrealistic, hyperactive, and theological, with somatotonic ruthlessness and drive for power, which can provide the means for carrying out insane dreams based on cerebrotonic doctrines of world domination or destruction.

Fatalism. Structural approaches to constitutional psychology are often taken to task for being fatalistic (Sheldon & Stevens, 1942, p. 435); they seem not to allow for the possibility of change. Sheldon argued to the contrary: In the long run, constitutional psychology holds out optimistic possibilities. Knowledge of which constitutional components are associated with susceptibility to mental or physical illness and suffering could stimulate social policies to control heredity and produce only healthy, happy, and productive people. With respect to aiding individuals, Sheldon argued that the goal of the constitutional approach is "to develop every individual according to the best potentialities of his own nature" (Sheldon & Stevens, 1942, p. 438). This, he says, is not fatalism but naturalism.

Development: Experiential Approach (Schilder, Fisher, and others)

6. BODY SENSATIONS PROVIDE THE PRIMARY BASIS FOR INITIAL DIFFERENTIATION OF SELF FROM ENVIRONMENT.

Most theorists assume (and assume they must, for there seems to be no way to prove it conclusively) that the human infant does not distinguish initially between self and environment. The distinction is learned through the psychological integration of sensory experience, which changes radically at birth. Sensations from within the body associated with arousal of physiological needs, like hunger, increase noticeably because of the discontinuous schedule of availability of the mother's attentions. Other sensations from within which were not prominent during intrauterine life also become more intense. Among these are sensations generated by the pull of gravity and the anxiety that seems to arise spontaneously as a result of any sudden loss of physical support. Later, internal sensations associated with eliminative needs, and still later with genital sexual needs, become prominent.

Sensations from the surface of the body include active and passive touch; the reactions of sensory receptors such as the tongue, nose, eyes, and ears; and receptors sensitive to heat and cold. These become increasingly important as contact with the environment expands. Because the surface of the body contains all internal sensations, like an envelope, and because it responds immediately to external events, the body surface becomes the locus of separation of self from environment. The child gradually learns to distinguish the inner "me" from the outer world, and when this happens, personality may be said to have begun to form.

7. INITIAL DIFFERENTIATION BETWEEN SELF AND ENVIRONMENT PROVIDES THE BASIS FOR FORMING BODY IMAGE, WHICH BECOMES THE PRIMARY BASIS FOR DEVELOPING BODY EGO, AND THIS, IN TURN, PROVIDES THE BASIS FOR THE FORMATION OF EGO—THE CENTRAL EXECUTIVE OF THE ENTIRE PERSONALITY.

Because the concept of the ego appears in psychoanalytic theory (described elsewhere in this book), this assertion need not be dealt with in detail here. It is sufficient to note that Freud and the early psychoanalysts assumed that body processes, especially those related to sexuality, contributed heavily to personality development; detailed descriptions of how the ego forms out of early experience with the body, however, were provided only by later theorists. Freud was mainly concerned with psychological problems, but it was the observation of disorders of body experience resulting from actual somatic damage that stimulated theorists like Paul Schilder to attempt to unify neurology and psychoanalytic theory by elaborating the concept of the body image.

8.   THE BODY IMAGE IS A MENTAL
       REPRESENTATION OF THE BODY.

The body image is distinguishable from the *body ego*, for the latter has powers of decision and action which the former does not; the ego acts upon the body image or in accordance with the body image. The important point is that the body comes to be represented mentally to the ego. Consequently, when the ego acts it does so not in accordance with the actual physical properties of the body but in response to the image of the body.

As long as image and actuality are in accord, no problems arise; when they differ, actions become unsuitable, ineffective, or unrealistic. Obviously, this proposition is especially important in states like schizophrenia, anosognosia, or phantom limb, where image and actual body fail to coincide. Even in normal experience, however, lack of agreement between image and body may be more common than might be supposed. Fisher and Cleveland (1958) concluded that the body image is not a picture of the real body or its properties and that their theory had almost "taken the 'body' out of 'body image' " by recognizing the overwhelming importance of psychological rather than physical factors in its formation.

9.   THE DEVELOPMENT OF THE BODY
       IMAGE PROCEEDS THROUGH STAGES,
       EACH OF WHICH HAS A LASTING EFFECT
       UPON THE ORGANIZATION OF THE BODY
       IMAGE AS A WHOLE.

T. S. Szasz (1957) identified three stages of body image development, though he indicated that his list is by no means exhaustive. The first stage produces a primary differentiation between ego (self) and nonego (nonself); this occurs very early in life and is prior even to recognition of the body as an object. In the second stage, separate objects (persons or bodies) are differentiated within both the ego and nonego spheres. In this

stage, physical pain comes to be related to the infant's own body, while the mental counterpart of pain, anxiety, is related to the actions of the bodies of others as these threaten the personal ego. This stage occurs between the ages of four and nine months. The third stage (during which most psychosexual phases presumably take place) eventuates in the adult ego, in which the body and its associated feeling states become symbolically significant in the total personality.

There is no need to elaborate on Freudian theory or its derivatives, but it is important to note that the various erogenous zones associated with the phases of psychosexual development are usually regarded as having special significance. Thus, mouth, anus, and genital areas constitute nodal points in the body image and are thought to be especially strongly charged with symbolic meanings and emotional energy. Psychoanalytic theory also recognizes the notion of *displacement*, a defense mechanism by which psychosexual energy is channeled from one body region to another. The concept of displacement explains why regions of the body that are not obviously sexual may be reacted to as if they were, or why regions that are obviously sexual may lose their libidinous charge. For example, genital sexual energy may be displaced to the limbs and extremities, thus accounting for the symbolic equivalence between anxiety over the loss of an arm and the fear of castration. Similarly, the gathering-in quality of visual experience may lead to the displacement of oral energy to the eyes. Vomiting has especially troublesome psychosexual implications, combining as it does both anal and oral implications.

Development: Holistic Approach (Goldstein)

10.   THE NORMAL HUMAN ORGANISM IS
       EQUIPPED TO DEVELOP TO MAXIMUM
       SELF-ACTUALIZATION, PROVIDED
       ENVIRONMENTAL FORCES DO NOT
       INTERFERE.

If there is a single key assertion to all holistic theories, including those of Angyll, Maslow, and Carl Rogers, this is it. What distinguished Kurt Goldstein from others is that he drew his evidence primarily from study of the effects of damage to the body (more specifically to the brain) on adjustment and behavior. Goldstein observed that, despite difficulties in ability to think, speak, perceive, or move about effectively, persons with damage to the brain continue to exhibit strong tendencies to defend their integrity as internally consistent organisms. Actions that others described as symptoms of deficit or loss were explained by Goldstein as attempts to cope effectively with a problem and to retain wholeness in the face of the threat of disintegration.

For example, a common manifestation of brain damage is *perseveration*, the tendency to repeat the same action over and over again. Viewed negatively, as a symptom or as evidence of incapacity, perseveration represents a patient's inability to inhibit action. Viewed positively, as an act of coping (or, at least, as an attempt to cope) perseveration represents the person's tendency to maintain integrity in an uncertain and threatening world by continuing a performance that has been experienced as successful.

Although all behavior is undertaken to enhance or preserve self-actualization, not all behavior is equally effective in doing so. For example, a person may refuse needed medical care because he denies that he is ill, even though evidence of his condition is conclusive. Denial of illness may be thought of as "organic repression", i.e., as a form of psychological maladjustment, a symptom of disorder. Or it may be viewed in the way Goldstein recommended: as an attempt to retain or restore personal integrity, to ward off the catastrophic collapse that threatens to follow recognition of the true situation.

Some such observation is behind Angyll's (1965) more broadly applicable holistic principle of universal ambiguity, which asserts that a neurosis is not like a foreign object in an otherwise healthy personality structure. It is, rather, a property of the personality as a whole, which may be either healthy or neurotic, depending upon how it is viewed. Thus, in a sense all persons are neurotic but, by the same principle, all persons are also healthy. We all have times during which we feel disorganized and unable to cope with our lives, yet there are also times when we feel invigorated and competent. A problem becomes severe enough to require therapeutic intervention only when flexibility is lost and the neurotic aspect of the overall pattern becomes so dominant as to be overwhelming.

11. IN GENERAL, SELF-ACTUALIZATION IS MANIFESTED BY MAXIMUM DIFFERENTIATION AND BY THE HIGHEST POSSIBLE LEVEL OF COMPLEXITY OF AN INTEGRATED ORGANIZATION OF SYSTEMS AND SUBSYSTEMS.

This assertion applies to both bodily and mental aspects of the person. The human organism begins as a relatively undifferentiated union of sperm and egg. This union does not produce first a fully developed leg, to which is later added another leg, then a trunk, and so on. Rather, the organism starts as a whole and grows by differentiating parts and subparts within its overall system.

The model for the building of an organism is not the assembly line of a factory but the unfolding of a plant. For example, the embryo first differentiates into three layers. One of these layers further differentiates into visceral organs; another differentiates into bone, muscle, and connective tissue; the third differentiates into skin and nervous system. The healthy adult human body is a miracle of complexly interconnected structures and functions, each of which is related to all the others throughout the entire course of its development.

The same is true of the person viewed psychologically. The earliest years of development begin a process of differentiation (recall, for example, the primary differentiations of self from nonself and of body from environment) which continues to increase organismic complexity to its maximum potential.

This assertion clearly reflects the influence on Goldstein of the Gestalt psychologists (Kurt Koffka, Wolfgang Köhler, and Max Wertheimer), and evidence of their influence is plain in other holistic theories as well.

12. EVIDENCE OF PSYCHOLOGICAL MATURITY IS THE ABILITY TO ADOPT AN ABSTRACT ATTITUDE.

In Goldstein's theory, an abstract attitude does not mean the person's ability to think like a philosopher; the abstract attitude is not an intellectual capacity but a quality of the behavior of the person as a whole. It means, among other things, taking several points of view into account when making a decision, shifting easily from one task or orientation to another when necessary, appreciating common properties among situations that superficially appear to be different, inferring relationships among things or events that are apparently dissimilar, and planning ahead effectively and realistically. To adopt such an attitude clearly requires, first, that a differentiated field of facts be available and, second, that these be organized by the person so that they can be integrated and reintegrated to serve the needs of the organism as a whole. Failure of the abstract attitude is the most prominent evidence of disruption of the process of self-actualization.

Maintenance: Structural Approach

13. TO THE EXTENT THAT PERSONALITY IS DETERMINED BY PHYSIQUE ALONE, IT IS SELF-MAINTAINING.

Just as the structural theorist maintains that no one can make an ectomorph out of an endomorph (all you would have for your work is a skinny endomorph), so it must also be true that temperamental types are not interchangeable. Sheldon recognized that temperament exhibits greater flexibility than does somatotype. However, there are limits to this flexibility. When pressures become too great for the person to produce behavior that runs counter to the pull of the somatotype, trouble invariably follows. For society, the problem of education or rehabilitation is not to force all misbehavers into a common mold or to change their basic temperaments. Rather, it is to alter situations so that people can express their biologically given temperaments in acceptable and unconflictual ways, thus making misbehavior unnecessary.

A good example of how Sheldon's theory emphasizes the self-maintaining character of the biological determinants of personality is afforded by his comment on a particular case—No. 80 in *Varieties of Delinquent Youth: Constitutional Psychiatry of Delinquency* (Sheldon, Hartl, & McDermott, 1949a/1970, pp. 335–357). The youth had been in serious trouble and had been institutionalized for his misbehaviors. Sheldon noted that a psychoanalyst had previously attempted to explain this case in terms of parent-child relationships, emotional snags, and disturbances of sexuality. Of this, Sheldon said:

All that sort of thing is interesting, and sometimes useful, but in a case like this it is symptomatic of a

profound social sickness. At best, it is cowardly evasion of reality. There is a biological reality in human life which in the end cannot be escaped. Sooner or later, this reality must return to human consciousness, perhaps in the chaos and uproar of a vital revolution (p. 357).

Sheldon recognized the value of self-knowledge in cases where biological predispositions do not create a hopeless situation. He described a nondelinquent, 17-year-old, extreme endomorph who was strongly gynandromorphic—Case No. 100 in *Varieties of Delinquent Youth: Social Psychiatry of Delinquency* (Sheldon, Hartl, & McDermott, 1949b/1970, pp. 416–418). The boy's parents brought heavy pressure upon him to become a boxer, a baseball, football, or soccer player, or a track athlete. The boy felt humiliated because he could not succeed in these. However, he and his parents took a good look at his somatotype photographs, compared them with a few photographs of athletes—and remarkably, within a few minutes, everyone could see the problem and the solution. The parents followed Sheldon's advice to remove the pressure for athletic success, and the boy's career took a sudden, dramatic turn for the better. Freed of the frustrations associated with attempts to become an athlete, he completed high school, performed military service satisfactorily, and prepared to go on to college.

In short, to a structural theorist, maintenance of the personality, at least in its underlying form, is automatic. Personality is as unchanging as somatotype; stability cannot be avoided. The real problem does not even concern individuals; it is much broader in scope, as is shown in the next assertion.

14. THE TASK FOR THE MODERN WORLD IS TO CREATE SOCIAL INSTITUTIONS TO ENSURE REPRODUCTION ONLY BY THOSE CONSTITUTIONALLY ENDOWED WITH THE BEST QUALITIES OF HUMAN TEMPERAMENT.

Sheldon called for a program of *biological humanics* that would promote both science and human welfare by promulgating a moral philosophy based on somatic and temperamental moderation, allowing for full expression of all potentialities. The healthy 444 "is probably about as close as human flesh gets to God" (Sheldon, Hartl, & McDermott, 1949a/1970, p. 93). Sheldon would remove economic incentives to greed by prohibiting hereditary transmission of wealth, thus depriving people of a major reason for money accumulation. His program would face up to the problem of war by establishing an effective, central world government. It would abolish the monogamous family and delegate reproduction (as opposed to individual sexuality) and child rearing to specialists. As early as the 1940s Sheldon recognized the dangers of overpopulation, but he wished to do more than limit numbers; he felt it necessary to control quality as well. His program also would find a way to rescue religion from the quagmire of fruitless theologizing and turn its attention to realistic plans for improving the human species. He saw religion's purpose as providing the moral basis for progress based on science (Sheldon, Hartl, & McDermott, 1949b/1970, pp. 879–881).

Sheldon has not been overly optimistic about the future of the human race. He described modern society as delinquent in its failure to provide conditions (both physical and social) under which individuals can develop fully to the limits of their potential without infringing on the rights of others. In modern society, the successful are the delinquents who steal apples and get over the fence quickly enough to escape. Those who are officially labeled delinquent are no different; they are merely slower runners. To change this situation Sheldon says, requires a change in the whole of society. The needed change can be accomplished through a merger of medicine and religion. The task of psychology is to catalyze the rapprochement between the two.

Maintenance: Experiential Approach

15. THE BODY IMAGE BOUNDARY SUPPORTS AND MAINTAINS THE SELF-CONCEPT IN THE FACE OF THREAT OR STRESS.

A firm body image boundary sharply delineates the self from the environment. Consequently, in modern Western society—which values, even demands, a strong sense of selfhood—a firm boundary facilitates good adjustment by maintaining self-integrity under conditions that would otherwise threaten effective functioning. According to Seymour Fisher, (1970) this seems to be especially true when threats are severe. Be-

cause a well-bounded person is not easily aroused to anxiety, extra strain is required before the coping responses of such a person are activated.

A firm boundary provides almost innumerable benefits. Besides making the person resistant to mild stress, it promotes interest in achievement, desire for independence, greater self-confidence, greater sensitivity to and interest in others, and generalized receptivity to the environment. All in all, a firm boundary is a strong foundation for the personality as a whole.

16. BODY ATTENTION PATTERNS LINK BODY EXPERIENCE TO LIFE SITUATIONS BY ATTACHING LEARNED MEANINGS, THUS GUIDING RESPONSES IN ACCORDANCE WITH PAST LEARNING.

Because the body is the first object with which the person becomes familiar, it remains basic to all later contact with the environment. Body experience provides a background against which all other sensations and all later perceptions are related (Fisher, 1970, p. 595). In fact, internal sensation is more fundamental than external sensation, because without the former, the latter is impossible.

The field or background of internal sensations (body image) is not homogeneous but is articulated and patterned with symbolic meanings. Each meaning is located in a more or less specific body region, so that stimulation of that region arouses its assigned symbolic significance and associated reaction patterns. An obvious example, involving minimal indirect symbolism, is gentle stimulation of the genitals. The aroused sensations surely have obvious sexual meanings, and in most persons they also lead one to approach the stimulating person. Suppose, however, that a child were taught that genital arousal is bad and were punished for it. Genital stimulation would still have the meaning of sexuality (assuming that sublimation or displacement did not occur), but it would acquire the additional meaning of guilt or shame. In that case, the feelings and the behavior they arouse would be in conflict, and if the conflict were too severe the result might be avoidance of sexuality or development of impotence.

A preceding assertion stated that body image growth proceeds through stages. Fisher's version of body image theory also proposes that, as each individual works out attitudes toward essential issues in life during such stages, these attitudes become coded in terms of differential awareness of specific body parts or regions. The pattern of differential awareness becomes self-sustaining and thus remains a permanent structure within the personality. These parts or regions become nodes or "landmarks" in the overall organization of the body image.

Psychoanalytic theory provides an explicit listing of the psychosexual stages through which development proceeds, and body image theorists tend to accept this listing as appropriate. Fisher has collected data that seem to him to be, in some ways, consistent with Freudian theory.

The importance of body attention patterns, however, does not depend upon the validity of psychoanalytic theory. An anger-arousing stimulus could activate sensations in the arms or hands because the person associates hostility with striking out with the fists. Whether psychosexually based or not, the association could lay the foundation for the later arousal of anger or of a tendency to attack (though perhaps in a sublimated way) whenever the hands and arms are stimulated. The same process would also cause all anger, from whatever source, to express itself in increased muscular tension in the arms and hands.

With respect to the maintenance of personality, the critical point is that the body provides continuity for experience and action. Its patterns of sensory responsiveness and its propensities to activate behavioral responses constitute something roughly analogous to the program inserted into a computer. Having automatized behaviors that produced effective coping in the past, the individual may proceed relatively efficiently through the daily affairs of life, in a consistent and generally adequate way.

Just how far automatization of behavior stimulated by body sensation can go is illustrated in a modern psychoanalytic theory of pain (Szasz, 1957). In this view, pain is essentially a psychological signal by which the ego registers the presence of danger to its own integrity. Although physical pain is a signal from the body, the "body" is not the physical organism. In this theory the term *body* means only whatever is recognized as body by the ego. Furthermore, the

important threat in the experience of pain is not damage to the physical body but damage to the psychological *ego*. If the ego's program fails or ceases to regard a particular body part as essential, pain will not be experienced should that body part be damaged or lost.

Szasz's point of view is based on clinical experience rather than systematic research. Indeed, Szasz is inclined to reject systematic laboratory research on pain, because laboratory research cannot take into account complex unconscious determinants of behavior. Fisher's approach relies more heavily on research; however, the two theories are not incompatible. The main difference between them is that Szasz's theory relies upon the concept of the ego to provide an extra theoretical entity which holds the personality together. The term *ego* does not even appear in the indexes of Fisher's major books. Also, it is doubtful that Fisher's psychologizing of body experience, as extreme as it is, extends quite as far as Szasz's. From the broader perspective of constitutional theory in general, these differences are minor.

Maintenance: Holistic Approach

17.   THE KEY TO EFFECTIVE BEHAVIOR IS ADEQUATE FUNCTIONING OF PART-WHOLE RELATIONS.

In Kurt Goldstein's theory, the model of all part-whole relationships is that between *figure* and *ground*. In the development of Gestalt psychology, demonstrations showed that every perception has at least two components: a *figure*, the object toward which attention is directed; and a *ground*, the setting or background with which the figure is contrasted. As you read a single word on this page, the word assumes figural properties: it stands out clearly and distinctly, provided your visual system is functioning well. The page and the other words on it constitute the ground of perception; they are less distinct and recognizable. If you shift attention to the page as a whole, it becomes figure and the desk upon which the book rests becomes ground. Note that figure-ground relations may change even though the physical stimulus array remains constant.

The distinction between figure and ground seems obvious and perhaps trivial. However, it contains the fundamental principle that perception of an object cannot occur in isolation; it is always and inevitably relational, and the ground against which an object is perceived, though usually ignored, is as important as the object itself.

So it is also with behavior as holistic theory sees it. No act is carried out in isolation. Each is influenced by (and in turn influences) the state of the whole organism at the time of its execution. Professional performers, such as actors and athletes, know this. They realize that they must often spend extra time and effort to work themselves up to a high pitch of general physical and mental excitement and must maintain that overall condition if they are to do their best in public. Every action, every thought is invariably a figure against the ground of the state of the organism as a whole. Hence, no action or thought can be explained or understood except in terms of this relationship. As long as figure-ground relations are adequate, behavior proceeds smoothly and effectively. When figure-ground relations break down, behavioral integrity collapses.

18. A MAJOR SOURCE OF BREAKDOWN IN ORGANISMIC INTEGRITY IS DUE TO ISOLATION OR DISRUPTION OF RELATIONSHIPS BETWEEN PARTS AND WHOLES.

Figure-ground relations imply tension between part (figure) and whole (ground). In the normal case, the organism tends to return to a state of equilibrium following stimulation. The process is called *equalization*. The tendency to return to an equilibrated state provides the constancy and order essential to overall integration. Should equalization fail to occur, reorganization fails, and the result is disorder, a state virtually equivalent to maladjustment.

A primary condition which interferes with equalization is *isolation*, or separation of a part process from the whole to which it rightfully belongs. For example, primitive reflexes ordinarily inhibited in the intact, healthy organism may reappear when there is interference or blockage of the pathways to the brain. Reappearance of these reflexes permits the neurologist to diagnose damage to other parts of the nervous system. Impulses that we do not wish to acknowledge may take on an obsessive character; they bother us constantly, yet they seem not to be part of us. They are experienced as coming from outside the self (they are isolated or ego-alien). We may feel compelled to perform acts that we know are irrational and unnecessary but are unable to control.

Any severe environmental, psychological, or physiological disturbance can threaten to bring about disorganization. Experience of threat is called anxiety, and although a certain amount of anxiety is present and necessary in all organisms at all stages of growth, too much is associated with collapse. The ultimate end of a breakdown in figure-ground relations and equilibration is a totally disordered state, which Goldstein (1939) called the catastrophic reaction. Prevention of the catastrophic reaction depends upon how adequately behavior is organized to maintain integrity.

The abnormal organism is particularly vulnerable to anxiety because the abnormal organism is, by definition, ill equipped to deal effectively even with a normal environment. Catastrophic reactions are especially dangerous to the sick person, who must engage in extreme forms of reaction to protect himself against catastrophe and preserve as much integrity as possible. There are many things such a person can do. One is to withdraw from the immediate situation, even to the point of losing consciousness. Another is to avoid dangerous situations, either physically or psychologically, by denying that they are real or threatening. Still another is to find something, no matter how trivial, one can do successfully and to keep on doing it unceasingly (perseveration). A similar reaction is shown in the tendency to become excessively, even fanatically, orderly and intolerant of deviation from prescribed, and therefore comfortingly predictable, plans or rules.

The need for certainty is especially crucial to persons threatened with catastrophic reaction. This need is well illustrated by Goldstein's observation that, in physical disability, partial loss of function is often far more distressing than total loss. One who is totally blind or deaf may regret his loss or be angry about his condition, but he knows what he has to contend with because the condition is stable. The person who is partially blind or deaf is in an ambiguous (hence, partially disordered) state. Not knowing whether to regard himself as sighted or blind, as healthy or disabled, as normal or abnormal, the individual faces problems of adjustment that are far more distressing than those associated with the certain knowledge of even very serious loss.

Goldstein called the process of adapting to threats of disorganization *coming to terms*, and he recognized that the process of coming to terms usually involves adjusting the organism to the environment rather than the reverse. Everyone, normal or abnormal, experiences anxiety, hence everyone must come to terms with the environment. The difference between normality and abnormality is essentially this: the abnormal person comes to terms in ways that block self-actualization, while the healthy person comes to terms in ways that promote it or at least do not prevent it. Maladjustment stems from the isolation of parts from the whole and usually results in increasing the isolation; healthy reactions also require temporary isolation of parts from the whole but usually eventuate in increased differentiation and integrity.

From an entirely different standpoint, Bakan (1968) spelled out a strikingly similar conception of organismic functioning. Bakan was not stimulated by Goldstein but was inspired by the results of research in psychosomatics, by Selye's conception of disease as a response to stress, and by Freud's concepts of personality defense and the wish for death. Yet Bakan's views are remarkably similar to Goldstein's.

Bakan's theory identifies two contrasting aspects or tendencies of organismic functioning. One is telic centralization; the other is telic decentralization. (The word *telic* means purposive.) Biologically and psychologically, *telic centralization* requires subordination of subsystems (parts) to an overriding determinant of form or function (the integrated operation of the whole). For example, centralization in an industrial firm assures that by submitting to a central authority, all departments, from design to sales, work together toward the common end of increasing profits.

Telic decentralization is the opposite tendency for parts or subsystems to develop independently of the whole and to pursue their own destinies. Decentralization is also essential to effective functioning, for subsystems cannot perform adequately unless they have a degree of autonomy. The brain is part of the body as a whole and is subservient to the needs of the total organism. Yet, the brain requires a physical setting in which it can develop as a unique and, to some extent, self-sufficient organ. It cannot be so subservient that its actions are totally governed by changes in other organs or systems, such as the stomach or the circulatory network.

The key to effective functioning is integration or reconciliation of the opposing tendencies toward centralization and decentralization. When a decentralized process (an isolated part-process) begins to act too autonomously for the good of the organism as a whole, it gets beyond the control of the centralizing agencies and threatens breakdown or disorganization of the total system (catastrophic condition). Breakdown is virtually equivalent to sickness, and symptoms may be recognized as actions undertaken by the organism as a whole to restore integrated functioning.

This description is holistic because it recognizes that threat to integrity may arise from psychological or somatic sources or both, and the response may be either mental or physical in character. It goes even further; it draws parallels that seem to apply not only to individual human beings but to social organizations and, perhaps, to ecological systems as well.

19. MAINTENANCE OF ORGANISMIC INTEGRITY AND SELF-ACTUALIZATION DEPENDS UPON THE AVAILABILITY OF CONDITIONS UNDER WHICH THE ORGANISM CAN MAXIMIZE PREFERRED WAYS OF BEHAVING.

In general, holistic theories assume that each person has a kind of "natural wisdom" which will bring about the best possible adjustment if the environment does not interfere too strongly with the process. Therefore, what the individual prefers, when minimally coerced, is what may be assumed to be best for it.

An obvious example of interference with a preferred mode of performance occurs when one tries to teach a naturally left-handed person to become right-handed. It can be done, but the left-handed person feels uncomfortable while learning, never becomes as efficient as possible, and is more likely to become ambidextrous than fully right-handed. That is, he never completely overcomes his left-handedness because it is too much a part of his total organization.

Goldstein realized that freedom has its limits. Social living requires that people exercise some restraint over their impulses. No one should be allowed to actualize himself at the expense of another person. Yet, conformity is not the answer either. In social organization, as in all aspects of human behavior, part processes cannot operate in isolation or in such a way as to damage the whole. Furthermore, it may be safely assumed that the more natural the conditions under which development takes place, the more self-actualized people will be. In the final analysis, that society is best which provides for maximum self-actualization of the greatest number of individuals (Goldstein, 1940). Despite the differences between Sheldon's and Goldstein's theories, both would agree to this.

Applications

Assessment

The structural and holistic views have perhaps made their greatest contributions to psychology by devising techniques of assessment. The appeal of the structural approach has always stemmed from the hope that it can provide a quick, easy way of diagnosing character from personal appearance. History and accumulated evidence show that this hope is vain. Nonetheless, the attempt to relate body build and personality brought about the development of valuable methods for the comprehensive study of individuals.

William Sheldon and Kurt Goldstein were superb methodologists and astute observers; both developed techniques which should serve as guides and models for anyone who studies individuals. A glance at the outline Sheldon, Hartl and McDermott (1949a, 1949b) used in presenting case studies of institutionalized delinquent adolescent males shows the thoroughness with which Sheldon prepared his material. Each study begins with a photograph of the unclothed subject, posed in three standardized standing positions against a plain background; all photographs were taken under uniform conditions for lighting, distance, exposure, type of film, and development. The photograph is followed by a verbal description of the somatotype, including both primary and secondary components. Next

come a paragraph on temperament and separate paragraphs describing the behavior that got the person into trouble with society; his origins and family; his history of intellectual (i.e., academic and vocational) accomplishment; his medical background; a record of his behavior in the institution; quantitative indexes of delinquency, psychiatric classification, and IQ; and, finally, a paragraph of comment which allows the investigator to summarize, draw conclusions and, as Sheldon put it, to preach about the evils of the world and how to eliminate them.

Even more thorough, if possible, were the methods of Kurt Goldstein, who could write a whole book about a single case. Goldstein stressed that close study of individuals is the only way to gain valid information about human behavior. Though by no means an advocate of classical psychological testing methods, Goldstein and Scheerer (1941), developed a set of materials for evaluating patients' abilities to adopt the abstract attitude. These materials are usually presented to subjects in such a way as to permit a wide variety of responses. For example, one set of materials, consisting of a plate, a lock, matches, nails, a pipe, and so on, is used to test the subject's capacities for abstract thinking. The subject might be given one article and asked to select others that belong with it. Or, the examiner might group the items in some way and ask the subject to explain why they are so grouped (knife, fork, spoon, and plate are all used for eating; key, nail, knife are all made of metal, etc.). The examiner might simply ask the subject to group the items in any way he wishes. Follow-up questions and instructions reveal the subject's bases for his or her groupings and determine whether the subject has the flexibility to revise his or her classifications according to different sets of principles.

Tests like this do not yield simple numbers or scores; there are no uniform criteria for deciding whether a given response is right or wrong. In fact, such tests are not designed to yield a score but rather to provide a set of standard materials which a well-trained examiner may use to observe and evaluate behavior in a variety of situations.

Variety is also the key to assessment in recent experiential studies of the influence of the body on personality. Fisher and Cleveland (1958) began by scoring responses to inkblots to obtain indexes of body-boundary definiteness (see the Validation section). In later work by Fisher measures of heart rate, galvanic skin response, and several questionnaires about body experience were added, as well as tests of response to distortions of perception induced by special optical lenses.

In experiential research, the approach to assessment is more classically psychometric, more laboratory oriented, and more analytical than it is in structural or holistic investigation. Experiential studies have tended to study subjects as groups rather than as individuals. This type of research produces volumes of quantitative data, but it deals only with averages and may thus leave open the question of the applicability of the findings to individuals.

Differences in approaches to assessment probably stem from differences in theoreticians' backgrounds. Both Sheldon and Goldstein were medically trained. Schilder, the originator of serious investigation of the body image, was also medically trained and, like Sheldon and Goldstein, relied heavily on case study material. However, Fisher's work shows the influence of his education in research psychology.

Structural and holistic assessments tend to be naturalistic and to allow greater flexibility for the examiner. Laboratory and psychometric methods are more artificial, but they are also more objective and more precise. Because there is no uniform, standard way to assess personality, it is not surprising to find that each investigator uses the techniques with which he is most familiar.

Treatment

The theorists discussed at greatest length in this chapter were not primarily oriented toward treatment. Only the experiential approach seems to justify treating personality by any method that resembles the traditional one-to-one, verbal approach to psychotherapy. Certainly, a psychoanalyst who feels that his patient's problems arise from a disturbance of the body image will focus on discovering the source of the disturbance so that the body image may be revised along more realistic lines. However, the psychoanalyst, like many other therapists, would regard the body image disturbance not as primary but as the product of some more basic difficulty (perhaps an unresolved Oedipal situation). Treatment would therefore be directed at the basic disturbance rather than toward body experience as such.

If the theory of body signals is correct, it follows that conventional psychotherapy is not the most efficient way to proceed. Body image theory suggests that controlled manipulation of the body itself should affect body experience and thereby should alter psychological states in beneficial ways. The basic idea is not entirely new: William James said that we do not run because we are afraid but are afraid because we run. Perhaps, then, we would no longer be afraid if we could only stop running and relax. Furthermore, if the body is the mirror of personality, perhaps a person who knows most about his body, who feels most comfortable with it, and who is most sensitive to its conditions will be most happy psychologically as well.

Since ancient times, physical sports and athletics have been thought of as vehicles for self-development and as devices of benefit to mentally distressed people. Recent developments suggest that interest in sports and physical activity is growing, not always to promote competition or to channel aggression but to develop the self-concept and to promote psychological well-being (Harris, 1973; Kane, 1972).

Courses of exercise to develop the self-image have been outlined by Feldenkrais (1972). Lowen (1972) has integrated exercise into his recommended treatment for depression, a state that is coming to be recognized as the dominant malady of the 20th century. A form of deep massage known as Rolfing, based on the ideas of Ida Rolf (1972), is a method of repositioning the body structure. The concept is that the body tends to assume various typical postures, such as slouching, as a consequence of various attitudes toward life. The body gives the world a message relative to the person's attitude toward himself and others. As the person becomes aware of his own posture this affects, circularly, his self-concept. The massage-type Rolfing treatment is intended to break down tight muscle patterns so that the individual's body becomes free and relaxed. Not only does the body give the outside world a new message about the individual, but the person's attitudes toward himself change as the result of the proprioceptive messages his body gives him.

It has been mentioned that Sheldon rejected psychoanalysis as a serious form of psychotherapy. Indeed, he has not advocated any form of individual therapy but seems to share with Goldstein the conviction that the organism is competent to care for itself, provided only that environmental conditions do not interfere with the process and that the organism is not constitutionally incompetent, as might be the case in severe retardation, for example.

Sheldon turned his attention to society rather than to the individual and to long-term rather than short-term goals. This tendency is paralleled in the study of the psychological aspects of physical disability which began seriously just after World War II. Psychologists and psychiatrists were brought into the rehabilitation movement by medical personnel who determined that rehabilitation often failed because patients lacked motivation to get well. They believed that psychology could resolve patients' mental problems and stimulate clients to desire and to work for greater success. Naturally, the model psychologists applied was the one they knew best: talking with the patient about the patient's problems of adjustment to reality.

After 30 years of less than impressive success, authorities in the field of rehabilitation psychology began to realize that they had been seeking in the wrong place for solutions to their problems. Some patients in rehabilitation or in medical settings do have low motivation for independence. But it is less true than was once supposed that these problems are caused by neurotic disturbances in the mental lives of the patients themselves. Rather, passivity and dependency are rational responses to the dehumanizing, regressive, and often humiliating treatment settings to which such patients are typically exposed. The wonder is not that some patients are unmotivated in these environments but that all are not in that state.

In short, rehabilitation psychology is gradually accepting a view that would have been perfectly obvious to Goldstein and, probably, to Sheldon as well. People treated like children are likely to act like children. People treated like adults are likely to act like adults. The "cure" to problems of adjustment to physical illness and disability, therefore, lies less in changing the internal dynamics of the patient than in altering the societies in which such people are required to live (Shontz, 1975).

Institutional

Constitutional psychology could have important and far-reaching implications for modifying institutional practices. This is true even if one does not go so far as to accept Sheldon's ideas for reorganizing the entire world.

Schools and other organizations for children would do well to recognize more explicitly the special importance of body structure in development. If a physical education teacher gives high grades only to mesomorphs, who easily accomplish what is required, and ignores or downgrades the heroic struggles of endomorphs, who must work much harder to accomplish less, the teacher is not recognizing the importance of physique.

Throughout the school age, but especially from puberty on through the teen years and young adulthood, physical attractiveness is central to social and personal adjustment. The unattractive child may require special help and attention to achieve the self-esteem everyone needs; the too-attractive child may need guidance so that physique will assume a proper role in his or her life. Overattractiveness can be a burden to a child who does not desire to be the center of attention but finds himself thrust into this position despite his wishes.

Information about somatotypes probably cannot be used to predict a child's future precisely. However, in extreme cases, knowledge of the types of activities facilitated or blocked by different body structures can be most useful, as was shown in the case described above of the parents who were trying to create an athlete out of their endomorphic and gynandromorphic son (Sheldon, Hartl, & McDermott, 1949b/1970, pp. 416–418.).

In institutions like the military services, it would make sense to measure, record, and take body type into account when assigning people to duties. Assigning a person who is constitutionally frail to a position requiring heavy labor or exposure to extreme temperatures or severe weather makes little sense. Application of the principles of constitutional psychology would require some loosening of the culturally popular belief that "anyone can do anything if only he tries hard enough." The change would be desirable, because that belief causes more trouble than it is worth in any case.

There is another way in which constitutional psychology, especially in its experiential form, might be used to improve social institutions, and that is through systematically applied programs of physical sport and recreation. The initial reaction to such a suggestion may be negative because it conjures up scenes of masses of people in lines, all dressed alike, and going through routines of calisthenics in unison to the tune of *Deutschland über Alles, The East Is Red,* or *God Bless America.* The proposal becomes more meaningful when one considers the almost infinite variety of psychological meanings and body experiences that can be created through the media of sports, games, and physical activities. Some sports involve one-to-one personal relations and are highly competitive and physically dangerous (boxing, wrestling). Some require intense concentration all the time, but others leave the mind relatively free (jogging, long-distance running). Some require submission to a single leader (football); others demand individual decisions as well as teamwork (basketball). Some are social; some are solitary. In some, one competes against another person; in others, one competes mainly against oneself or against some natural obstacle, such as a mountain or river. Some take more strength than skill; some more skill than strength. The number of possible variations is endless.

Many patients in institutions are unmotivated because they have nothing to do, therefore programs of individualized recreation and physical activity could change the situation dramatically. Granted that this possibility has been recognized for centuries, what has always been lacking and what is still lacking to a large extent is a comprehensive, yet specific, theory to relate particular activities with particular needs and to show how to evaluate outcomes. Constitutional psychology has the potential to provide such a theory.

Self

The preceding section has shown that the three constitutional approaches do not wholly agree in their recommendations for altering or improving social institutions. Sheldon's utopia sounds like something George Orwell or Aldous Huxley might have thought up, while Goldstein's ideas call for maximum self-determination. Despite these differences, however, the three approaches to constitutional psychology are rather consistent in their general recommendations for personal application. All endorse self-knowledge as the key to the enrichment of individual life.

Few people have such extreme body builds that they feel compelled to develop a fitting kind of personality. Fortunately, the average body build is in the neighborhood of the 444, a set of values which provides maximum flexibility of potential. Nevertheless, nearly everyone has experienced private fantasies in which the body appears as extraordinarily handsome, strong, or virile. In mature adults, such fantasies are usually harmless, because adults have learned their real limits; experience has taught them not to require the impossible of themselves. But everyone can probably also remember the misery of those times when heroic fantasies were dashed. The sooner one learns one's potentialities and limitations, the more effective one becomes in using the body to best advantage. Coming to terms with the body seems to be most difficult during periods of transition: at birth, puberty, during sickness, and at the approach of old age and death.

For many, the critical changes yet to be faced are those associated with aging. This is no small matter, and it poses problems poorly handled in American society, which is almost wholly youth oriented. We do not advocate preoccupation with aging and death, but young adulthood is none too soon to begin thinking about and planning for later years: not only economic preparations for retirement, but concern for such matters as sexuality, health, diet, exercise, religion, and the unpleasant possibilities of physical disability as well as the certainty of death. Unfortunately, no extensive formal educational opportunities are as yet provided for this purpose, but interest is growing rapidly, and the day may come when society places as great importance on preparing citizens for aging as it now does on preparing them for young adulthood. One of the best popular sources that can serve as a starting place for thinking about the myths and realities of this subject is Simone deBeauvoir's *The Coming of Age* (1972).

Of more immediate concern to most readers is the fact that anyone can avoid a great deal of grief by examining closely and critically his or her own standards of physical presentability. How much anxiety is justified that perspiration will show on clothing or that one may occasionally reveal one's organicity by way of odors? How necessary is it to be expensively or elegantly dressed, and how much hard-earned money spent on deodorants, mouth washes, foot powders, depilatory creams, colognes, special soaps, shampoos, rinses, sexy toothpastes, hair colorings, and other cosmetics is justified? Because modern life forces close personal contacts, it is well to be considerate of the impression we make. Efforts to be physically inoffensive are surely justified. But it is not psychologically healthy to so completely reject biological reality that we heed every advertisement or commercial which sells body-care products as if they guaranteed escape from nature and assured success in a world of artificial people.

Within recent years, interest has developed in techniques to increase body awareness and control over body functions. One approach employs yogic practices—a systematically organized course of exercises designed to make the practitioner more sensitive to the body and more responsive to its urgings. Many such programs were originally designed to help achieve spirituality by overcoming the needs and demands of the body. However, it is not necessary to seek *nirvana* to derive psychological benefit from a program which promotes relaxation and increases personal sensitivity. Many yogic exercises develop freedom from the body by attaining mastery over it. In this regard, the recent development of techniques of biofeedback appear to have considerable potential, particularly in making more efficient the teaching of relaxation and control over autonomic functions (Brown, 1974; Green, Green, & Walters, 1970).

On an interpersonal level, some psychotherapists have established encounter groups, which use body contacts to reduce defensiveness and raise levels of self-awareness. Problems with body experience are likely to manifest themselves in disturbances in sexuality. Some therapists specialize in treating this type of difficulty,

no longer a taboo subject and one which can be handled quite matter-of-factly. Homosexuality, once identified as a symptom of deep and serious underlying personality disturbance, is now coming to be accepted as a matter of personal preference rather than of internal, emotional compulsion. These developments have made it increasingly easier for people seeking help with behavioral or emotional problems related to body experience to find help and for people who are merely atypical to assert their right to social acceptance. Naturally, caution must be used before entering into a program of yoga, biofeedback, sensitivity training, encounter groups, or sex therapy. In these newly emerging fields, charlatans are likely to be abundant and difficult to detect. Examination of the qualifications of persons offering such programs is essential and will, of course, be welcomed by any ethical professional.

People who merely wish to increase their self-awareness may benefit from courses of exercises described in books by therapists like Alexander Lowen (1958, 1965, 1970, 1972) and Moshe Feldenkrais (1949, 1972). Some of their recommendations will give the reader an idea of what is involved. Lowen (1972) pointed out that most people are not well "grounded"; they struggle too hard against gravity and are insufficiently aware of the lower regions of their bodies. One simple exercise that helps overcome this involves standing barefoot with knees slightly bent, arms hanging loosely at the sides, mouth slightly open, and belly, buttocks and pelvis completely relaxed. While in this position, the person is instructed to attend to sensations in the legs and feet and to try to keep the weight balanced between the heels and the balls of the feet. If tremors occur in the body or legs, they are not to be fought or resisted but are to be allowed to develop, so long as the subject does not feel uncomfortable.

Feldenkrais (1972) suggests a set of exercises in imagining, designed to increase awareness of parts of the body of which the person is not normally aware. In one, the subject, in a prone position on the floor, and with the head resting on crossed hands, imagines that a finger is pressing on the heel of the right foot and being drawn, under considerable pressure, up the calf to the knee. Then he imagines a heavy iron ball rolling along the same path, to the buttocks and back several times. As the exercise progresses, he imagines the ball rolling up to the shoulders, along the arms, and up and down the spine.

These exercises are not designed to develop physical strength or stamina but to increase self-awareness. Unlike many courses of exercise they require full participation of the mind. One is not asked to expend physical energy at a high rate in automatic, repetitive fashion but to combine modest expenditures of both physical and psychological effort in a project involving the whole organism. The effect of the exercises is intended to be pleasurable and stimulating, not painful and fatiguing.

Undoubtedly, full awareness of body experience requires contact with discomfort as well as with pleasurable sensations. But almost all authorities seem to assume that uncomfortable experiences are common and familiar enough in everyday life. Few people in the modern world need to learn how to be tense; nearly everyone can benefit from learning how to relax.

Validation

Evidence

Structural Approach. Sheldon's primary task was to observe physique in such a well-controlled and thoroughly standardized way that he could identify the primary components of variations in somatotypes. His overall strategy was to examine photographs of large numbers of persons and to extract from his observations a set of conclusions about the nature of these components and a set of procedures which could be applied to produce standard assessments of body build. Examination of these photographs showed to his satisfaction that only three extreme types stood out as distinctive. These he identified as the basic components of physique.

Complete somatotyping involved gross visual inspection of a standard, three-view photograph. This yielded a preliminary estimate of the somatotype, which was checked against tabled values for the overall index: height divided by cube root of weight. Next, region-by-region determinations were made. Finally, region estimates were averaged to produce the final three somatotype values. A kind of primitive computer cranked out somatotype values for five body regions

when values for a total of 18 indexes were fed into the machine.

Somatotyping developed quite early into an objective, reliable procedure. By the time of the publication of the *Atlas of Men* (Sheldon, Dupertuis, & McDermott, 1954), data had been collected on 46,000 subjects; no one can argue that the size of the sample Sheldon used was small.

Assessments of temperament were made on rating scales which were devised by Sheldon and used to evaluate individuals he interviewed and observed. The three well-known clusters of traits (viscertonic, somatotonic, cerebrotonic) emerged and were incorporated into a 60-item rating scale. For the benefit of future investigators, Sheldon recommended that ratings of temperament with this scale be based on at least a year of observation of each subject, and 20 or more interviews. This suggests how thorough Sheldon was when making observations for his own research.

As might be expected, when Sheldon compared somatotype with temperament ratings in a group of 200 persons, he found the relationship to be strong (Sheldon & Stevens, 1942/1970, p. 400). They ranged from 0.79 to 0.83, values that are far higher than those obtained in most psychological studies. His research has been criticized because Sheldon performed ratings of temperament and somatotypes himself. Sheldon replied that it would certainly be unreasonable to expect a rater to get to know a subject well without ever seeing him.

At any rate, this study alone is hardly responsible for the high level of interest Sheldon's theory aroused. Much more impressive are the 200 case studies presented in detail in *Varieties of Delinquent Youth* and the comprehensive series of photographs and psychological sketches included in the *Atlas of Men*. Here Sheldon showed his skill as a naturalistic observer of human beings. His writings convey such assurance, such exceptional sensitivity and stylistic color, that he creates the impression of being a supreme authority on his subject. When the apparently universal appeal of the physiognomic hypothesis is combined with his superb expository skill, the result is nearly irresistible.

Other investigators followed up on Sheldon's work and managed to confirm his findings, although the correlations they obtained between body type and personality were not as high as those reported by Sheldon (Child, 1950; Cortés & Gatti, 1965, 1966; Fiske, 1944; Walker, 1962). Sheldon himself has been less prolific, having produced only one major publication since 1954 (Sheldon, Lewis, & Tenney, 1969).

Sheldon's interest in delinquency was reflected in a classic study by Glueck and Glueck (1956), who found an extraordinarily high incidence of mesomorphy in a group of delinquent boys. This finding has been confirmed by at least two other independent investigations (Epps & Parnell, 1942; Gibbens, 1963).

Experiential Approach. Early evidence for the idea of the body image was largely clinical in origin. Mention has already been made of the disorders of body experience associated with anxiety, schizophrenia, brain damage, and denervation of body parts. Case studies provided early investigators like Schilder (1935) with ample illustrative material, and case studies are still prominent in many theoretical articles on the subject. Recent years have seen a tendency to rely more heavily upon systematically collected research data and to employ some techniques of laboratory research in the study of body experience. For example, much of Fisher and Cleveland's early work (1958) was devoted to developing a measure of body image boundary properties based on subjects' responses to the Rorschach inkblot plates. Inkblots are presumed to be meaningless stimuli; consequently, all meaning perceived in them is regarded as coming from the perceiver. That is, the subject *projects* meanings which have their origins in personal experience.

Fisher and Cleveland reasoned that subjects would project their own body images into their perceptions of inkblots. A firm body image boundary is therefore represented in responses that stress the surface properties of the object. Examples are: man in armor; snail in a shell. The total of such responses constitutes the *barrier* score. Other responses represent the breakdown of barriers (e.g., bullet going through flesh); the total of these constitutes the *penetration* score. In general, the barrier score is believed to reflect more permanent psychological states; it is therefore more important to a theory about personality structure than is the penetration score, which is more sensitive to transient conditions. Re-

search has shown that barrier and penetration scores correlate modestly with measures of many other personal characteristics, from anxiety proneness to type and location of physical illnesses.

Other tests of body image have been developed, and some have achieved considerable popularity. Best known is the draw-a-person test (Machover, 1949), designed on the premise that people project their personalities into their drawings of human figures. Obviously, the body image was assumed to play an important role in this process. A related development required subjects also to draw pictures of a house and a tree, each of which was expected to represent the self, though in less direct and therefore more symbolic form (Buck, 1948).

The draw-a-person technique has become most popular among clinical psychologists and psychiatrists, many of whom find it useful for diagnostic purposes in individual cases. It has also been the subject of considerable research, which has failed to be definitive because two problems have arisen. The first is that results are seldom clear and consistent: indeed, they are often contradictory. Second, and perhaps more important, no single investigator has taken responsibility for developing a systematic, long-term program of research with the draw-a-person test and defending it against the critics. If a theory lacks clear and indisputable data, it needs a strong advocate willing to devote an entire career to the cause. In psychology, theoretical progress tends to be made not on the basis of a sequence of classic experiments, each of which proves some fundamental point for all time, but through the appeal of forceful, committed, authoritative individuals who present ideas that strike responsive chords in others.

Fisher and Cleveland's research has been criticized on two grounds. First, the validity of responses to inkblots as measures of the body image has been questioned; in fact, the validity of the theoretical concept of the body image itself has been doubted (Wylie, 1974). Second, although the results of most of the research performed on body image are statistically significant, their magnitude is not very great. Data often show small average differences between groups or low correlations between measures, but such findings are too weak to justify statements about psychological processes taking place in individuals (Shontz, 1971).

Fisher replies to these criticisms by noting that the body of research evidence, all pointing in a consistent direction, is too large to be cast aside summarily. Inconsistent findings are few and can all be explained away. Also, it is unreasonable to expect powerful experimental outcomes in a field of research where the number of irrelevant variables determining behavior is so great and the possibilities for controlling them are so low. Virtually no experiments anywhere in the field of personality have ever been able to account for more than 20% to 25% of variation in their data; body image research is no exception, and it should not be condemned on that basis (Fisher, 1971).

Holistic Approach. Some of the most important points Goldstein made had to do with the methodological processes of scientific investigation; he was highly critical of conventional modes of collecting scientific data. His criticisms strongly influenced the first chapters of Maslow's primary work, *Motivation and Personality* (1970).

Goldstein objected to the study of organs or behaviors in isolation from the total, living person. For example, in a classic experiment of the 17th century, William Harvey, often called the father of modern experimental biology, demonstrated that the blood circulates in a closed system. This finding generated the modern idea that blood circulation takes place in a closed circulatory network, in which the heart acts as a pump. A holist would claim that this conception is woefully incomplete. Everyone can recognize immediately that it is modeled on the assumption that the body is a machine, and it leaves no room for descriptions of the relationships between blood circulation and the rest of the organism. For instance, it does not recognize that, within limits which are greatly expanding now that biofeedback techniques are available (Green, Green, & Walters, 1970; Brown, 1974), the operation of the circulatory network can be controlled psychologically; given proper training, some persons can even control the expansion and contraction of surface blood vessels. It leaves no room for considering the interaction of blood and air in the lungs, or of blood and nutrients in the viscera. It can only explain these by proposing

new mechanical analogies and by assembling its conception of the whole body piece by piece. Not surprisingly, the result is a view of the person as being nothing more than a gigantic, complex machine.

This mechanistic conception of the person might be all right were it not for the fact that intact persons display characteristics which are not apparent in machines, certainly not in isolated parts separated out for dissection and analysis. Examples of characteristics shown only by intact organisms are preference, intentionality, abstraction, and (above all) self-actualization.

Had Goldstein been entirely negative in his criticism, his views would have gained little ground. However, he developed and used his own methods to obtain evidence to support his theory. Essentially, these methods involved close and systematic study of single individuals. It is sometimes said that Goldstein advocated the use of case studies (Hall & Lindzey, 1970, pp. 311–314), but that is true only in a limited way. To Goldstein, there really was no such thing as a "case" of brain damage or schizophrenia. There were only people, some of whom had special problems induced by damage to the central nervous system or disorganized from functional sources. Goldstein therefore studied persons, not diseases, and he studied each person systematically and completely, often for years.

While most scientists in psychology try to discover the particular by studying the universe, or as large a sample of it as possible, Goldstein sought to discover the universal by studying the particular. Unlike the scientist who measures only single attributes of personality (e.g., body image boundary) and who relies on large samples of subjects to cancel out errors and yield overall estimates of correlations, Goldstein studied every attribute of a single individual, seeking by intensive investigation to gain complete and error-free understanding of one subject at a time. Furthermore, he argued, certain phenomena of human existence can be studied only in this way. Goldstein's theoretical views have been widely influential. Regrettably, the implications of his methodological arguments have never been fully exploited.

Comparisons

Because constitutional psychology does not

present a single monolithic theory to which all advocates adhere, it cannot easily be compared to other, more unified, self-contained systems. The breadth and inclusiveness of constitutional psychology is its major asset.

Unlike orthodox psychoanalytic theory, constitutional psychology does not sidestep the issue of the mind-body relationship but faces it squarely. Not that any simple answers have been forthcoming; but, as has been shown, the experiential approach does attempt to fill an important gap in psychoanalysis. It does not merely assume that body structures and processes influence personality, it attempts to describe how such influences operate. Even Freud did not undertake that task, though he was medically trained and eminently qualified to do so.

A purely structural approach sees little need for psychoanalytic concepts. For, if personality is an expression of body structure, little is to be gained by penetrating to the depths of the psyche in search of hidden problems or unconscious conflicts. Sheldon would certainly have argued that time is better spent devising programs of social control to improve personality by improving heredity.

On the question of psychoanalysis, holism would agree, for neither Goldstein nor those holists who came before or after him had any use for the idea of the unconscious. Goldstein recognized the reality and importance of subjective experience; in fact, his own thinking became progressively more phenomenological as time went by. (As we have seen, that was a common fate for holistic theorists.) Goldstein also recognized that some contents of thought are more prominent, more in focus (figure) than others (ground), and that a person might attempt to isolate certain ideas so that they could never come clearly into the center of attention. Of course, isolation is a source of disorganization and disturbance of behavior, but it in no way implies the operation of unconscious forces, as the psychoanalysts describe them.

For the holist, perhaps the least useful (and possibly actually harmful) psychological theories are those that derive from the study of conditioned responses. Nothing exemplifies the type of science a holist opposes more clearly than do theories based on the conditioned response. Conditioning procedures violate nearly all the re-quirements that must be fulfilled if the organism is to function effectively. Most crucial is the fact that conditioning requires the experimenter to exert such complete control over environmental conditions that the organism is not free to behave according to its own preferences; it is confined and virtually coerced to do not what is best for its own self-actualization but whatever the experimenter requires it to do. Small wonder that conditioning theorists do not recognize self-actualization as a legitimate motive; they never observe organisms under conditions that permit it to be displayed.

Also deleterious is the specificity of conditioned-response-type learning. A child may learn multiplication tables by rote, but memorization alone does not teach the child the relation between multiplication and addition or why 6 times 2 equals 4 times 3. Similarly, a child may be conditioned to say *please* and *thank you* and still be anything but polite, for true politeness resides in the abstract capacity to appreciate the situations of other people, not in the automatic recitation of verbal formulas.

The holist completely rejects the behaviorist dogma that observable acts alone comprise the subject matter of psychological science. To the holist a specific act has meaning only as it relates to the total organization of the person in his life situation. In this respect, holism and the structural approach tend to be similar; both are avowedly naturalistic in their orientation. The experiential approach also directs itself to understanding people in real-life situations, but, as has been shown, its methods are more likely to borrow from the laboratory than are the methods of structuralism or holism.

The essence of naturalism is its unwillingness to simplify or manipulate the processes it studies and its appreciation of the complexity of events which occur outside the confines of the laboratory. Mention has been made of the tendency on the part of holistic theorists to drift away from the biological determinants of behavior and toward the study of subjective experience and the phenomenology of human existence. One might guess that the drift occurs as a way of escaping the complexity of the mind-body problem by leaving the body behind. More probably, however, it occurs because these theorists realized that the real complexities of human life do not

stem from common problems of satisfying biological needs; these are well taken care of in
modern Western society. Rather, life is complex
because today's human beings are more troubled
by the problem of the meaning (if any) of human
existence than ever before. This problem affects
the highest level of human existence; it truly involves self-actualization in its most abstract
form.

Prospect

Constitutional psychology has never been a dominant force in American theoretical thought, nor
is it likely to become so in the near future. This
author recently obtained a computer-assisted
search of the scientific literature in psychology
for 1968–1975 which uncovered only four published studies that related somatotypes and personality profiles. None provided strong support
for the structural approach. While people will
probably always be fascinated by the idea that
personality, temperament, or character can be
read from the appearance of the body, the continued lack of success in demonstrating, under
controlled conditions, that correlations of any
magnitude can be consistently found causes
most investigators to regard this field of study as
unpromising for future work.

Even if American psychologists can be induced
to take constitutional factors in personality seriously, they would be more likely to regard the
as challenges than as obstacles or as fixed co
tions or limits. If Sheldon says that endom
cannot become track stars, some other
will be stimulated by that remark to fi
to train endomorphs to break track
the very least, this expert may we
every endomorph has the right to
run as fast as possible, even if he
age the four-minute mile.

The experiential approac
firm place for itself in mo
choanalytic theory. Howe
pied at the expense of
tity. Eventually, cur
will probably not be
points of view bo
hancement of t
short, the futu

a new body image theory of personality, though
theorists will continue to use the term bo
image in their writings.

By contrast, the influence of holism will
ably become broader and more pervasive.
the term itself may well disappear a
Perhaps holistic theories will be re
newly developing general systems th
tically no theorist today would d
influences mind or that mind af
holistic position has become so
vincing to anyone who wor
clinical situations that de
validity is out of the que
problem of holism is t
philosophical conclusi
rather than truly sci
havior. Though th
holism have beer
veloping expe
remains unres

There ma
something
rists tha
human
tract
ulti
ti

op into a major, unified theory on its own, the problems it raises will persist in the treatment or rehabilitation of people in trouble. As long as people suffer psychosomatic disorders and physical disabilities, questions must be raised about the relationships between mind and body. Unless and until other answers come forward, some form of constitutional psychology will be needed to deal with them.

Annotated Bibliography

Structural Approach

Sheldon, W., Dupertuis, C. W., and McDermott, E. *Atlas of Men: A Guide for Somatotyping the Adult Male at All Ages.* Originally published, Harper & Row, 1954.

Sheldon's basic writings, which originally appeared between 1940 and 1954 were republished in 1970 by Hafner Publishing Co., Darien, Conn., as a matched set of five volumes. Naturally, anyone who wishes to learn about the structural approach in detail should read them all, but the best introduction and overall view of Sheldon's later ideas and of his inimitable style is the *Atlas of Men.* It begins with a survey of the philosophy and theory of the structural approach and then provides photographs and psychological descriptions of men who were selected because they display the widest possible variations in physique. This book presents Sheldon at his best.

Sheldon, W., Hartl, E. M., & McDermott, E. *Varieties of Delinquent Youth.* Vol. 1, *Constitutional Psychiatry of Delinquency;* Vol. 2, *Social Psychiatry of Delinquency.* Originally published, Harper & Row, 1949.

The two volumes called collectively *Varieties of Delinquent Youth* consist of case studies of young men, most of whom have been in some kind of trouble with society and have therefore been institutionalized. Both volumes display Sheldon's naturalistic methods and interest in whole persons.

Sheldon, W., Stevens, S. S., & Tucker, W. B. *The Varieties of Human Physique: An Introduction to Constitutional Psychology.* Originally published, Harper & Row, 1940.

The Varieties of Human Physique provides historical background and describes how Sheldon developed techniques for somatotyping.

Sheldon, W., & Stevens, S. S. *The Varieties of Temperament: A Psychology of Constitutional Differences.* Originally published, Harper & Row, 1942.

The Varieties of Temperament describes the three personality types and the results of Sheldon's attempts to relate each to its corresponding somatotype.

Experiential Approach

Fisher, S., and Cleveland, S. E. *Body Image and Personality* (2nd ed.). New York: Dover Publications, 1968.

Fisher, S. *Body Experience in Fantasy and Behavior.* New York: Appleton-Century-Crofts, 1970.

Originally published in 1958, *Body Image and Personality* describes research conducted by Fisher and Cleveland which used measures of body image boundary *barrier* and *penetration* derived from subjects' interpretations of inkblots. It also provides a useful historical survey of body image theory and outlines the early version of experiential theory developed by the authors from their findings. By and large, the research is correlational: It relates scores on measures of body image to a variety of other indexes, from evaluations of subjects' behavior in groups to body sites of cancer and measures of physiological reactivity.

The second book, by Fisher alone, describes more recent, elaborate and extensive research which used a broader array of body experience indexes and measures of other personality and behavioral characteristics. In addition, it presents relatively newer developments in Fisher's formal theoretical thought.

Holistic Approach

Goldstein, K. *The Organism: A Holistic Approach to Biology Derived from Pathological Data in Man.* New York: American Book, 1939.

Goldstein, K. *Human Nature in the Light of Psychopathology.* Cambridge, Mass.: Harvard University Press, 1940.

These are the two basic books describing Goldstein's holistic approach. *The Organism* is an English version of his original work, which was published in German in 1934. *Human Nature in the Light of Psychopathology* was drawn from lectures Goldstein presented at Harvard University.

Both books show clearly the two essential aspects of Goldstein's work: his critical attacks on analytic, atomistic, mechanistic, reflex-centered methods and theories of biological science, and his positive assertion and defense of holism as a more inclusive and therefore more satisfactory view of human nature. The influence of early Gestalt psychology on Goldstein's thinking, as well as the reasons for Goldstein's later profound influence on other more phenomenologically and existentially oriented holistic theorists such as Maslow and Angyal, is apparent in both volumes.

References

Alexander, F. *Psychosomatic medicine.* New York: Norton, 1950.

Alexander, F., French, T. M., & Pollack, G. H. (Eds.). *Psychosomatic specificity*. Chicago: University of Chicago Press, 1968.

Angyll, A. *Foundations for a science of personality*. New York: Commonwealth Fund, 1941.

Angyll, A. *Neurosis and treatment: A holistic theory*. New York: Wiley, 1965.

Appley, M. H., & Trumbull, R. (Eds.). *Psychological stress: Issues in research*. New York: Appleton-Century-Crofts, 1967.

Bakan, D. *Disease, pain, and sacrifice: Toward a psychology of suffering*. Chicago: University of Chicago Press, 1968.

Barker, R. G., Wright, B. A., & Gonick, M. R. *Adjustment to physical handicap and illness: A survey of the social psychology of physique and disability*. (Rev. ed.). New York: Social Science Research Council, 1953 (Originally published, 1946.)

Barral, M. R. *Merleau-Ponty: The role of the body-subject in interpersonal relations*. Pittsburgh: Duquesne University Press, 1965.

Birdwhistell, R. L. *Kinesics and context: Essays on body motion communication*. Philadelphia: University of Pennsylvania Press, 1970.

Brown, B. B. *New mind, new body; biofeedback: New directions for the mind*. New York: Harper & Row, 1974.

Buck, J. N. The H-T-P technique: A qualitative and quantitative scoring manual. *Journal of Clinical Psychology*, 1948, *4*, 317–396.

Chein, I. *The science of behavior and the image of man*. New York: Basic Books, 1972.

Child, I. The relation of somatotype to self-ratings on Sheldon's temperamental traits. *Journal of Personality*, 1950, *18*, 440–453.

Cortés, J. B., & Gatti, F. M. Physique and self description of temperament. *Journal of Consulting Psychology*, 1965, *29*, 432–439.

Cortés, J. B., & Gatti, F. M. Physique and motivation. *Journal of Consulting Psychology*, 1966, *30*, 408–414.

De Beauvoir, S. *The coming of age*. New York: G. P. Putnam's Sons, 1972.

Dunbar, H. F. *Emotions and bodily changes*. New York: Columbia University Press, 1935.

Epps, P., & Parnell, R. W. Physique and temperament of women delinquents compared with women undergraduates. *British Journal of Medical Psychology*, 1942, *25*, 249–255.

Eysenck, H. J. *Fact and fiction in psychology*. Harmondsworth, England: Penguin Books, 1965.

Feldenkrais, M. *Body and mature behavior*. New York: International Universities Press, 1949.

Feldenkrais, M. *Awareness through movement: Health exercises for personal growth*. New York: Harper & Row, 1972.

Fenichel, O. *The psychoanalytic theory of neurosis*. New York: W. W. Norton, 1945.

Fisher, S. *Body experience in fantasy and behavior*. New York: Appleton-Century-Crofts, 1970.

Fisher, S. Complexity reflected. *Contemporary Psychology*, 1971, *16*, 744–745.

Fisher, S., & Cleveland, S. E. *Body image and personality* (2nd ed.). New York: Dover Publications, 1968. (Originally published, Van Nostrand, 1958.)

Fiske, D. W. A study of relationships to somatotype. *Journal of Applied Psychology*, 1944, *28*, 504–519.

Freud, S. *The ego and the id.* (J. Riviere, trans.) London: Hogarth Press, 1927.

Gall, F. J., & Spurzheim, J. G. *Récherches sur le système nerveux*. Paris: Schoell, 1809.

Gibbens, T. C. N. *Psychiatric studies of borstal lads*. London: Oxford, 1963.

Glueck, S., & Glueck, E. *Physique and delinquency*. New York: Harper, 1956.

Goldstein, K. *The organism: A holistic approach to biology derived from pathological data in man*. New York: American Book, 1939.

Goldstein, K. *Human nature in the light of psychopathology*. Cambridge, Mass.: Harvard University Press, 1940.

Goldstein, K. *After-effects of brain injuries in war*. New York: Grune & Stratton, 1942.

Goldstein, K., & Scheerer, M. Abstract and concrete behavior: An experimental study with special tests. *Psychological Monographs*, 1941, *53* (2), 1–151.

Green, E. E., Green, A. M., & Walters, E. D. Voluntary control of internal states: Psychological and physiological. *Journal of Transpersonal Psychology*, 1970, *9*, 1–26.

Hall, C. S., & Lindzey, G. *Theories of personality* (2nd ed.). New York: Wiley, 1970.

Harris, D. V. *Involvement in sport: A somatopsychic rationale for physical activity*. Philadelphia: Lea & Febiger, 1973.

Kane, J. E. (Ed.). *Psychological aspects of physical education and sport*. London: Routledge & Kegan Paul, 1972

Kelly, G. A. *The psychology of personal constructs* (2 vols.). New York: W. W. Norton, 1955.

Kretschmer, E. *Physique and character*. (W. J. H. Spratt, trans.). New York: Harcourt, 1925. (Originally published, 1921.)

Lavater, J. C. *Essays on physiognomy* (H. Hunter, trans.), London: John Murray, 1789.

Lindzey, G. Behavior and morphological variation. In J. N. Spuhler (Ed.), *Genetic diversity and human behavior* (pp. 227–240), Chicago: Aldine, 1967.

Lombroso, C. *Crime, its causes and remedies*. (H. P. Horton, trans.). Boston: Little, Brown, 1911.

Lowen, A. *Physical dynamics of character structure*. New York: Grune & Stratton, 1958.

Lowen, A. *Love and orgasm*. New York: Macmillan, 1965.

Lowen, A. *Pleasure: A creative approach to life*. New York: Coward, McCann, 1970.

Lowen, A. *Depression and the body: The biological basis of faith and reality*. New York: Coward, McCann, 1972.

Machover, K. *Personality projection in the drawing of the human figure: A method of personality investigation*. Springfield, Ill.: Charles C Thomas, 1949.

Maslow, A. H. *Motivation and personality* (2nd ed.). New York: Harper & Row, 1970.

May, R., Angel, E., & Ellenberger, H. F. (Eds.). *Existence: A new dimension in psychiatry and psychology*. New York: Basic Books, 1958.

Meyer, A. *Psychobiology: A science of man*. Springfield, Ill.: Charles C Thomas, 1957.

Meyerson, L. Somatopsychology of physical disability. In W. M. Cruickshank (Ed.), *Psychology of exceptional children and youth* (3rd ed.; pp. 1–74). Englewood Cliffs, N. J.: Prentice-Hall, 1971.

Murray, H. A. (Ed.). *Explorations in personality*. New York: Oxford University Press, 1938.

Naccarati, S. The morphologic aspect of intelligence. In R. S. Woodworth (Ed.), *Archives of Psychology*, 1921, *6* (45), 1–44.

Paterson, D. G. *Physique and intellect*. New York: Appleton-Century, 1930.

Plügge, T. The ambiguity of having and being a body. *Human Inquiries: Review of Existential Psychology and Psychiatry*, 1970, *10*, 132–139.

Reich, W. *The function of the orgasm*. New York: Orgone Institute Press, 1944.

Rolf, Ida. *Structural integration*. New York: Viking Press, 1972.

Schilder, P. *The image and appearance of the human body*. New York: International Universities Press, 1950. (Originally published, 1935.)

Selye, H. *The stress of life*. New York: McGraw-Hill, 1956.

Selye, H. *Stress without distress*. Philadelphia: J. B. Lippincott, 1974.

Sheldon, W., Dupertuis, C. W., & McDermott, E. *Atlas of men: A guide for somatotyping the adult male at all ages*. Darien, Conn.: Hafner, 1970. (Originally published, Harper & Row, 1954.)

Sheldon, W., Hartl, E. M., & McDermott, E. *Varieties of delinquent youth* (Vol. 1, Constitutional psychiatry of delinquency). Darien, Conn.: Hafner, 1970. (Originally published, Harper & Row, 1949). (a)

Sheldon, W., Hartl, E. M., & McDermott, E. *Varieties of delinquent youth* (Vol. 2, Social psychiatry of delinquency). Darien, Conn.: Hafner, 1970. (Originally published, Harper & Row, 1949.) (b)

Sheldon, W. H., Lewis, N. D. C., & Tenney, A. M. Psychotic patterns and physical constitution: A thirty-year follow-up of thirty-eight hundred psychiatric patients in New York State. In D. V. Siva Sankar (Ed.), *Schizophrenia: Current concepts and research* (pp. 838–912). New York: PJD Publications, 1969.

Sheldon, W., & Stevens, S. S. *The varieties of temperament: A psychology of constitutional differences*. Darien, Conn.: Hafner, 1970. (Originally published, Harper & Row, 1942.)

Sheldon, W., Stevens, S. S., & Tucker, W. B. *The varieties of human physique: An introduction to constitutional psychology*. Darien, Conn.: Hafner, 1970. (Originally published, Harper & Row, 1940.)

Shontz, F. C. Body image: Data galore. *Contemporary Psychology*, 1971, *16*, 362–364.

Shontz, F. C. *Psychological aspects of physical illness and disability*. New York: Macmillan, 1975.

Smith, J. A., & Ross, W. D. (Eds.). *The works of Aristotle* (Vol. 4, *Historia animalium*, D. W. Thompson, trans.). London: Henry Frowde, 1910.

Smuts, J. *Holism and evolution*. New York: Macmillan, 1926.

Spiegel, J. P., & Machotka, P. *Messages of the body*. New York: Free Press, 1974.

Spurzheim, J. G. *Phrenology in connexion with the study of physiognomy*. Boston: March, Copen & Lyon, 1833.

Stern, W. *General psychology from the personalistic standpoint* (H. D. Spoerl, trans.). New York: Macmillan, 1938.

Szasz, T. S. *Pain and pleasure: A study of bodily feelings*. New York: Basic Books, 1957.

Walker, R. N. Body build and behavior in young children: I. Body build and nursery school teachers' ratings. *Monographs of the Society for Research on Child Development*, 1962, *27* (3, No. 84).

Wright, B. A. *Physical disability—A psychological approach*. New York: Harper & Row, 1960.

Wylie, R. C. *The self-concept* (Rev. ed.; Vol. 1). Lincoln: University of Nebraska Press, 1974.

Soviet personality theory has its fundamental bases in the philosophical concepts of dialectical materialism of Karl Marx, Friedrich Engels, and Vladimir Ilich Lenin and in the neurophysiological findings of Ivan P. Pavlov. Its practical applications as well as its experimental research approaches have been largely guided by the work of A. S. Makarenko, an educator who in the 1920s had remarkable success in restructuring personalities and rehabilitating delinquent youth. As a result, the guiding principles of Soviet personality theory today are Makarenko's dicta:

1. Personality can most effectively be developed and maintained in, by, and for the collective.
2. The collective is *the* developer of personality.
3. Study the child while teaching him and teach the child while studying him.

The major research tool in Soviet Personality procedures is the "transforming experiment," which changes the phenomenon while studying it. Other specifically Soviet areas of research include human typology based on Pavlov's conditioned-reflex theories and the study of the theory of "set" of the Georgian school of psychology headed by D. N. Uznadze, which Soviet personality theorists see as the key to understanding unconscious psychic processes. Meticulous laboratory studies are also carried out on the development of speech, thought, perception, attention, and so on.

One thing readers of this book will inevitably note is the Soviet theorists' harsh criticisms of Western personality theory. They proclaim the superiority of their "unified" approach over the "babble of voices" (*raznoboi*) of the numerous Western personality theories, which they see as evidence of a "crisis" in Western psychology. However, in recent years this criticism has been moderating, and Soviet psychologists are becoming increasingly open to the rich store of data and concepts available from Western personality theories.

CHAPTER 12

Soviet Personality Theory

Isidore Ziferstein

ANTON S. MAKARENKO

Introduction

Soviet personality theory employs a set of concepts and a terminology which appear strange to the uninitiated reader. However, the effort involved in familiarizing oneself with this terra incognita can prove to be stimulating and thought-provoking.

The Western reader of Soviet writings on personality theory is puzzled, and often put off, by the insistence of Soviet psychologists on proclaiming the correctness of the philosophical foundations of their Marxist theory, by the injection of political partisanship (*partiinost'*) into their formulations, and by the sometimes harsh polemics against "incorrect" philosophical foundations and what they consider the reactionary political applications of most, if not all, Western personality theories.

Soviet psychologists justify their emphasis on a correct philosophical, dialectical materialist orientation, and their struggle against "bourgeois idealist" or "vulgar materialist" personality theories, by maintaining that there cannot be valid practice without a proper philosophical base. Soviet personality theorists also maintain that the work of all scientists, including personality theorists, is based on a matrix of philosophical concepts, explicit or implicit, and that this matrix determines the direction that scientific research takes. For the Soviet personality theorist, one such basic philosophical question is the relationship of mind and matter.

The American psychologist Gardner Murphy (cited in Simon, 1957, p. 3) takes an analogous position:

> Perhaps the most prevalent attitude of contemporary psychologists is to regard the problem [of the relationship of mind and matter] as outside the scope of psychology as at present defined. This attitude, however, very naturally means in practice a refusal to admit that any such problem exists. This again turns out upon closer examination to mean among many psychologists that the answer to the problem is quite simple, and that philosophy has made itself much trouble over many unproductive and unreal problems. When we turn to ask what this simple and obvious answer is, we find persisting, without great alteration, a variety of answers prevalent in the nineteenth century, indeed, a number of them prevalent in the ancient world.

Similarly, Raymond A. Bauer (1952) writes,

> The theories of psychologists and prevailing political and social ideas act upon each other. The findings of psychological research carry political and social implications and influence social and political ideas, just as social and political ideas influence the areas of interest of the psychologist and often condition his basic assumptions. . . . There can be no doubt, however, that the psychologist's theories of personality and the assumptions about human nature prevalent in society are related. (p. 3)

And he adds (p. 10), "The psychologist—usually unconsciously—adopts the assumptions of his culture as 'natural' or 'self-evident' truths."

Soviet personality theorists insist on "making the unconscious conscious" (to paraphrase Freud). They maintain that the philosophical underpinnings must be made explicit. Otherwise, errors and biases creep in which vitiate theory and eventually lead to bad practice. Thus S. L. Rubinshtein writes, "One of the most important conditions for the successful development of psychology is a profound and penetrating analysis of theoretical questions" (Rubinshtein, 1957, p. 264).

Soviet personality theorists also insist that the basic philosophical problems of psychology must be solved before experimental work can get underway. "Experimental investigation is blind unless its course is illumined by theory. If theory is despised it always takes a cruel revenge; the abandonment of theory usually means the dominance of bad theory" (Rubinshtein, cited in Payne, 1968, p. 167).

That they are philosophical materialists is often stated explicitly in the writings of Soviet personality theorists. They make certain to distinguish their materialist philosophic position from "vulgar" or "mechanistic" materialism, and they often discuss in detail the meaning of their philosophy, which includes dialectical and historical materialism. (See Assertion 1 below.)

History

Precursors

Historiographers of Soviet personality theory generally cite M. V. Lomonosov (1711–1765) as the earliest precursor of materialist personality theory. He interpreted sensations in a material-istic-mechanistic way, as a combination of physiological particles ordered according to mechanical laws. In his studies of personality, Lomonosov manifested "a profoundly progressive approach, in which he clearly recognized the enormous significance of speech and of verbal communication among people in the development and vicissitudes of human personality" (Boryagin, 1957, p. 163.)

The tradition of materialism in the study of human personality was continued by three professors at Moscow University. One of these was Ye. O. Mukhin (1766–1850), a basic feature of whose scientific *Weltanschauung* was his conviction that the material world is real and knowable:

> Nature does not hide anything. She expresses everything significant by signals. We discover and determine these signals through the appropriate use of our developed sense organs. Of course, there are many things in nature which we cannot grasp because of the grossness of our perceptions: for example, gravity, the forces of centripetal and centrifugal force, magnetism, etc. But no one doubts that these natural forces indeed exist, because we all clearly see their effects. (Shumilin, 1957, p. 288)

A second member of this troika was I. Ye. Dyad'kovskii (1784–1841), who, along with Mukhin, formulated the concept of *nervism* (the central nervous system is *the* regulator and coordinator of all the other bodily systems). This concept later became a central theme of the work of Ivan P. Pavlov. Dyad'kovskii wrote:

> We know that the higher (i.e., central) nervous system has connections with all the other systems, and directly merges into the material of these systems, which are subordinated to it, such as the muscular, circulatory, reproductive, absorptive, and cellular. Hence we see that any change in the subordinate system can easily produce a change in the higher system. (1830/1954, p. 194)

A third precursor of Soviet materialist thinking in psychology was A. M. Filomafitskii (1807–1849), who enunciated a principle which later became a fundamental tenet of Soviet materialist personality theory: the unbreakable connection of thought to speech. He wrote, "Animals cannot form words, not because they lack the necessary organs, but because they have nothing to say" (Filomafitskii, 1836, p. 90).

Related to these outstanding physicians-physiologists-psychologists were a number of Russian clinicians who were interested in the psychological treatment of somatic illnesses and are credited by Soviet historiographers as the founders of scientific psychotherapy. Thus, Lebedinskii (1971) writes:

> The most distinguished representatives of Russian medicine and physiology did extraordinarily much for the development of psychotherapeutic ideas. The tendency to take full account of the psychic aspect of any illness was characteristic of the foremost figures of Russian medicine. The scientific understanding of the role of the psyche in the causation, progression, and treatment of diseases was actively developed for almost two centuries. In Russia, as nowhere else, the most prominent figures in general medicine directly developed psychotherapy and advocated its use. In 1794, Skiadan, who was profoundly influenced by Lomonosov, refuted the pronouncements of many authorities of his day, and pointed to the cerebral cortex as "the abode of the soul." Skiadan noted that passions of the spirit may produce both a harmful and a beneficent effect on the organism, and he cited case histories of patients with various somatic illnesses who were cured by psychic influences. (p. 75)

An important precursor whose work had a strong influence on subsequent personality theory was I. M. Sechenov (1829–1905), known as "the father of Russian physiology." In his classical work *Reflexes of the Brain*, Sechenov (1863, p. 106) stated the proposition that "all acts of conscious and unconscious life are reflexes by origin." However, he was not really a reductionist who attempted to explain all psychic phenomena as due solely to reflex activity. In subsequent writings he distinguished between two classes of reflex: one in which "conscious feeling" plays no part (as in decerebrate frogs and unconscious humans), and another class in which:

> ... conscious feeling is an indispensable factor, determining now the beginning, now the course, now the end of every act. Take, for instance, the evacuation of the bladder and of the rectum determined by the urge to urinate and defecate.... It is owing to the will that the actions of man are not machine-like, especially in the higher stages of psychical development. (Sechenov, 1904/1973, pp. 344–345)

Another significant current in Russian philosophical and psychological thinking was contributed by a group of major 19th-century philosopher-writer-activists. Pavlov (1904) writes in his autobiography that he and his comrades were influenced by these thinkers to adopt an interest in the natural sciences.

One member of this group, V. G. Belinskii (1811–1848), stressed the special importance of social influences in the development of personality. A. I. Herzen (1812–1870) espoused materialist monism but maintained that the psychic processes, although derived from material physiological processes, were qualitatively distinct and were not reducible to physiology. Herzen viewed personality basically as the resultant of physiological and historical necessity and repudiated freedom of the will. N. G. Chernishevskii (1828–1889), a consistent monistic materialist, contended that human sensations impart to the personality a knowledge of the real material world, which has objective existence. N. A. Dobroliubov (1836–1861) viewed psychic processes as reflections from material objects existing in the external world and regarded them as being produced by the activity of the cerebral hemispheres. He considered sociohistorical factors, rather than biological factors, to be primary in personality development. Character traits were acquired, he taught, as a result of sociocultural and historical influences, rather than by inherent, genetic or biological factors.

Another basic element in the development of Soviet personality theory consisted of the writings of the "Classics of Marxism," Karl Marx, Friedrich Engels, and V. I. Lenin, whose concepts are called dialectical and historical materialism. Soviet personality theorists would agree with the following formulation by V. N. Myasishchev (1958), a leading exponent of Soviet materialist personality theory:

Without a scientific, materialist psychology, it is impossible to solve the problem of psychogenesis and psychotherapy. Modern Soviet psychology is developing on the foundation of the general theory of dialectical and historical materialism and on the foundation of the teachings of I. P. Pavlov. It takes as its point of departure the sociohistorical and natural historical understanding of man.... Man is not only an object, but a subject, whose consciousness reflects reality and at the same time transforms it. (pp. 7–8)

Beginnings

Present-day Soviet personality theory is the result of contributions by six outstanding scientists: Makarenko, Pavlov, Rubinshtein, Vygotskii, Myasishchev, and Uznadze.

Anton Semyonovich Makarenko (1888–1939) has had the greatest impact on Russian personality theory and practice. His major work, *The Road to Life—an Epic of Education*, published in 1933–35, as well as his others are cited in practically all Soviet writings on personality development and in books on education and pedagogical manuals.

In 1920, at 32, Makarenko had the challenging assignment of rehabilitating children made homeless by the 1917 revolution and the civil war. In the course of his successful work in rehabilitating young delinquents, he developed a set of theories about personality development and character building which became keystones for Soviet personality research and educational practices. Makarenko stated the essence of his principle as follows: "To make the greatest possible demands of each person, and to show the greatest possible respect for each person." He enunciated his system of the upbringing of the collective and of the individual personality as "the pedagogy of parallel influence."

In 1888, Ivan Petrovich Pavlov (1849–1936) began a study of the physiology of digestion in healthy, intact animals. He elucidated the neuromechanisms regulating digestive activity and the dependence of digestive activity on the nature of the ingested substances. In 1904, he received the Nobel Prize for this work.

In his experiments with the salivary response to foods, Pavlov observed a phenomenon which at first he considered a nuisance—the dog salivated not only in response to the introduction of food into its mouth, but also to a variety of neutral stimuli which coincided temporally with feeding. A systematic study of this learning process led to Pavlov's formulation of unconditioned and conditioned reflexes. Eventually, Pavlov formulated a conditioned-reflex theory, according to which all psychic activity of animals and man is due to the activity of the cerebral hemispheres and of the nearest underlying subcortical structures. The basic unit of this psychic activity is the neural reflex arc, involving three parts: (1) the receptors (or, as Soviet psychophysiologists call them, "the analyzers") and afferent nerves, (2) the central nervous system, and (3) the efferent nerves and effectors, such as the voluntary musculature.

In his experimental work with dogs, Pavlov arrived at the following hypotheses about human personality: Unconditioned, biologically fixed reflexes are mediated by subcortical structures and by the spinal cord. These structures can therefore be regarded as the seat of the instincts. The infant, having available a limited number of such inborn, "instinctual" responses in reaction to a few specific stimuli, has a limited capacity to adapt to its environment and is therefore dependent on others. As it grows and develops, the infant begins to elaborate an increasing number of conditioned reflexes which involve the cerebral cortex, resulting in a progressive enhancement of its ability to adapt to environmental changes.

A new element is decisive for personality development: the elaboration of the "second signal system"—human speech. Pavlov (1941) described two distinct systems of stimuli, or "signals" as effective in elaborating conditioned reflexes. The first is the direct sensing of objects in the environment, and the second is constituted of speech.

Pavlov attributed maladaptive behavior to a breakdown in the responsiveness of the reflex activity to changes in external reality. By manipulating the environment he was able to produce experimental neuroses in dogs. He later applied these laboratory findings to the study of human patients.

Another basic contribution by Pavlov to personality theory is his study of individual differences in dogs, which ultimately led to conjectures about individual differences in humans. He discovered that experimental animals differed in terms of the ease with which conditioned reflexes were established, the rapidity with which they could be extinguished, and also the ease with which experimental neuroses could be induced by subjecting the dogs to traumatic experiences. He then classified "types of higher nervous activity." By "type," Pavlov meant a definite complex of fundamental properties of higher nervous activity, resulting from a blend of congenital and acquired characteristics. Experimental work in which puppies from the same litter were subjected to different environments and different methods of rearing convinced Pavlov that in this blend of the congenital and acquired, the latter characteristics were decisive.

Sergei Leonidevitch Rubinshtein (1889–1960) contributed more than any other psychologist to the efforts toward a philosophical integration of dialectical materialism and Pavlovian psychophysiology. In 1935 he had published his first effort at a rounded, integrated formulation of the new Soviet psychology and personality theory, *Fundamentals of General Psychology*. This effort was refined with the publication of his most important work, *Foundations of General Psychology* (1940), in which he enunciated the basic principles of the application of dialectical materialism to the theory of personality. (These will be described in Assertion 1.)

Lev Semyonovich Vygotskii (1896–1934) had an extremely fruitful career as an original thinker and experimenter in personality theory, and his work has been continued by two distinguished pupils, A. R. Luria (1902–   ) and A. A. Leontiev (1903–   ). Vygotskii is credited with originating the sociohistorical origin theory of higher mental functions in man and being the first to demonstrate the Marxist thesis of the sociohistorical nature of human consciousness.

Vladimir Nikolayevich Myasishchev (1893–1973) made major contributions to the study of personality and to medical psychology. He was the founder of the "Leningrad School" of pathogenetic psychotherapy, which treats neuroses by elucidating those psychological causes of the illness of which the patient is unaware.

One major contribution of Myasishchev was his detailed study of the role of interpersonal relations in personality development. Myasishchev was aware of the work of H. S. Sullivan on interpersonal relations, but he criticized Sullivan for being too much under the influence of the "biologizing" concepts of psychoanalysis. A second major contribution to personality theory was Myasishchev's study of the role of the patient's personality in the development of mental illness and his emphasis on restructuring the patient's personality in the course of psychotherapy.

Dmitrii Nikolayevich Uznadze (1886–1950)

who contributed highly original work on the *theory of set* (1949) found many followers in Georgia, and this has become almost the exclusive preoccupation and domain of Georgian psychologists. For many years little was known abroad (or even in the Soviet Union) about the work of Uznadze and the Georgian school, because their researches were exclusively published in the Georgian language.

Current Status

Present-day Soviet personality theory continues to draw heavily on "the heritage of Makarenko," the philosophical works of the "classics" of Marxism, and the conditioned-reflex theory of Pavlov. In practice, the emphasis is mainly on pedagogy. The majority of Soviet personality theorists have been associated with pedagogical institutes and the Academy of Pedagogical Sciences of the U.S.S.R. and of the Russian Soviet Federated Socialist Republic.

However, beginning in the late 1950s (apparently in connection with the "thaw" which followed the denunciation of the cult of Stalin), there has been a progressive expansion of personality studies into areas other than pedagogy and a broadening of the theoretical and experimental base. Concomitantly, there is an increasing willingness to acknowledge that the teachings of Makarenko, Marx, and Pavlov, while seminal, are not in themselves sufficient to cover so complex a phenomenon as human personality.

More and more voices are heard expressing dissatisfaction with the present state of Soviet personality theory:

> Although the term "personality" is frequently used, it is not adequately defined and is often used as a synonym for consciousness, or self-awareness, or "set," or for the psyche as a whole. (Bozhovich, 1968, p. 131)
>
> [This symposium] has demonstrated that in this problem [of personality theory] there are vaguenesses and slipshod definitions of personality; there remain discrepancies and contradictions. (Banshchikov, Rokhlin, & Shorokhova, 1971, p. 33)

The expanding interest in a many-sided study of personality has been demonstrated in recent years in the publication of a number of books and monographs devoted exclusively to problems of personality. (Myasishchev, 1960; Kovalev & Myasishchev, 1957; Kovalev, 1965; Kon, 1967; Tugarinov, 1965; Bozhovich, 1968.)

Indicative of the active interest in personality research was a three-day All-Union Symposium on Problems of Personality which was held in Moscow in March 1970. Under the auspices of the Institute of Philosophy of the Academy of Sciences of the U.S.S.R. and the All-Union Society of Neuropathologists and Psychiatrists, 600 participants from all parts of the Soviet Union met to discuss three aspects of personality research: (1) personality as an interdisciplinary research problem, (2) philosophical and psychological aspects, (3) medicobiological aspects.

As a basis for discussion at this symposium, a two-volume work containing the latest researches on personality was published (Banshchikov, Rokhlin, & Shorokhova, 1969 and 1970.) The proceedings of the symposium were published in 1971 (Banshchikov et al., 1971.) These three volumes give the most complete overview of the current status of personality theory in the Soviet Union. A survey of the views of the more than 70 discussants whose presentations were published leads to the conclusion that they would probably agree with Gardner Murphy's summing-up of the present status of personality theory, East *and* West: "Since the data-taking can never be complete, and since the perspectives constantly change with the advent of new methods, current personality theories cannot be regarded as anywhere near complete or exhaustive" (Murphy & Kovach, 1972, p. 429).

Similar Theories

Although Soviet historiographers emphasize philosophical materialism in Russian personality theory, dating back to Lomonosov in the early 18th century, there was also, at the time of the 1917 revolution, an influential current of philosophical idealism. The most influential idealist personality theorist was G. I. Chelpanov (1862–1939), who regarded the spirit as independent of matter. Chelpanov and fellow idealists developed experimental techniques for studying "spiritual" properties of personality. They maintained that the world was perceived by the soul, aided by the brain (Chelpanov, 1915). This school of thought included the distinguished personality theorist N. N. Lange (1858–1921), founder of one of the first psychology laboratories in Russia (Lange, 1893).

After the 1917 revolution, the majority of the younger personality theorists set themselves the task of developing a new Soviet psychology of personality. Since Marxism contends that all aspects of a society, including its science, are based upon economic relationships and that science serves the interests of the ruling class, these personality theorists had to free themselves of bourgeois influences to found a science of personality which would reflect the interests of the new "ruling class," the working people. Thus science was to serve the new society and the "new Soviet man": "From the beginning of the Soviet regime, it was recognized that the remaking of human personality was an integral part of the social, political, and economic revolution that Bolshevism represented" (Bauer, 1952, p. 80). The unlimited plasticity of the human personality, even at a mature and advanced age, was assumed, and there was heavy emphasis on those areas of personality theory applicable to child rearing and education, vocational guidance, motivation of workers, improvements in industrial productivity, and the mental health of the "toiling masses."

Soviet personality theorists also had to concern themselves with the special psychological problems of revolutionary transition and with depicting the new Soviet man "so that the superiority of the socialist order can be made evident to all" (Wortis, 1950, p. 24). This was clearly a tall order, and in their enthusiasm, Soviet personality theorists welcomed all theories which gave promise of fulfilling these tasks.

From 1917 to 1929, numerous schools of personality theories, with wide-ranging experimentation and a search for new approaches to personality theory, emerged. Although suspicious of bourgeois psychology, Soviet personality theorists were open to all new "progressive" trends that were critical of the "European bourgeois psychology." Thus behaviorism was hailed as materialist, and John B. Watson (1927) was invited to write an article for the *Great Soviet Encyclopedia* (2nd ed., 1949). Gestalt psychology also was welcomed because its concept of holism was considered compatible with the philosophy of dialectical materialism. In the early 1920s, in fact, Soviet psychologists considered psychoanalysis "progressive"—a methodological application of historical materialism—and young personality theorists of the day wrote laudatory articles about it (Reisner, 1924, 1925; Bykhovskii, 1923; Petrovskii, 1967, p. 87).

Acrimonious Soviet polemics were carried on against the still influential idealist psychologists and Wundtians. When G. I. Chelpanov was deposed from his position as head of the Institute of Psychology and replaced by N. N. Kornilov (1879–1957), the event marked the demise of idealism in Soviet personality theory. The personality theories that survived in the 1920s were marked by an extreme mechanistic interpretation of Marxism, such as the *reactology*, elaborated by Kornilov, which became the dominant personality theory of the early 1920s. In 1926, Kornilov wrote a *Textbook of Psychology from the Standpoint of Dialectical Materialism*, in which he tried to synthesize the various concepts which then prevailed in personality theory throughout the world and to put them under the aegis of a Marxist materialist philosophy. His (1921) studies of the relationship between intensity of reactions and reaction time opened the way for the later Pavlovian investigations of the signaling functions of sensations.

Two other trends in the development and application of Soviet personality theory were psychotechnics and pedology. They flourished during the twenties and early thirties but were later rejected as being too mechanistic. Both resulted in theoretical and practical contributions to the later development of Soviet personality theory, however.

Psychotechnics is analogous to Western industrial psychology and was emphasized because work was looked upon as a central element in life. S. L. Rubinshtein (1940), for example, said: "For us man is defined primarily not by his relationship to his possessions, but by his relationship to his work." *Pedology*, the science of childhood, attempted to synthesize, through a study of "age syndromes," the anatomical, physiological, and psychological characteristics of the child. On the basis of his experimental work with school children, P. P. Blonskii (1935) concluded that thought comes about directly as a result of the child's activities: "Thought is not an a priori activity, and cannot emerge from an empty intellect." Many of Blonskii's theoretical formulations and practical applications were later repudiated, but his work on the theory of behavior became the foundation for the cultural-historical concepts of personality later elaborated by Vygotskii.

In the middle 1930s, psychotechnics and pedology were severely criticized by the Communist Party as being "pseudo-scientific and anti-Marxist." The pedologists were accused by the Central Committee of carrying out what "amounted to pseudoscientific experiments, and numberless investigations on pupils and their parents in the form of senseless and harmful questionnaires, tests, etc., long since condemned by the Party" (Resolution of the Central Committee, 1936 (1950). The Central Committee also condemned the so-called "two-factor theory," which holds that human personality is determined by heredity and environment, stating that this "law" was a heritage of bourgeois pedology. Instead, it enunciated a "three-factor theory" which stated that personality development is determined by inheritance, environment, and *vospitaniye*, a Russian word for which there is no exact English equivalent but which subsumes upbringing in the family, education and upbringing in the school, and training at work.

Later there was added the element of *samovospitaniye*, i.e., self-upbringing. In the struggle against the concept of the "all-powerful influence of the environment," it was maintained, the environment is changed by the child, who enters into active relationships with it and thereby alters its influence (Leontiev, cited in Bauer, 1952, p. 149). This concept became known as autogenetic movement (*samodvizheniye*). According to the concept of *samovospitaniye*, "a man takes part in the shaping of his own character, and he himself bears a responsibility for that character" (Rubinshtein, 1940, p. 475). In the process of development, new internal conditions for self-development are gradually created (Kostiuk, cited in Bauer, 1952, p. 149). Self-training comes about as the individual develops ideals and a definite image of the lifestyle he will adopt. For this reason, ideology and "communist morality" are intrinsic parts of education in the Soviet Union. The individual is taught to aid in molding himself to a "correct" lifestyle through self-encouragement and constantly practicing those traits of character he is trying to develop in himself (Selivanov, cited in Bauer, 1952, p. 149).

Soviet personality theorists contend that not only can the child be shaped from birth but that the human being remains plastic as an adult and can continue to shape his character even at a mature age, provided he is equipped with an adequate ideological picture of himself and the world. According to Rubinshtein:

> The early years of childhood play an essential role in the development of character. However, the Freudian notion that character is fixed in early childhood is erroneous. This error arises from the failure to understand the role of consciousness in character development. Man takes an active part in reshaping his own character to the extent that it is related to a Weltanschauung.... (1940/1946, p. 475)

A school of thought which played a significant role in the development of personality theory in the 1920s was *reflexology*, initiated by V. M. Bekhterev (1857–1927). Bekhterev attempted to study objectively the effect of physical, biological, and social factors on psychic functioning by recording external reactions of the individual, such as facial expressions, gestures, and speech, and relating them to the provoking stimuli. He maintained that all psychic phenomena, conscious and unconscious, must be made manifest sooner or later by external behavior, and therefore it should be possible to investigate them by purely objective observations of behavior.

In many of his writings (1907, 1917, 1921), Bekhterev expressed an extreme reductionist, mechanistic view, positing that mental and physiological phenomena represent a single neural process and that consciousness and conscious activity are manifestations of neural energy or neural electricity, the same energy as is manifested in heavenly bodies and animate and inanimate organisms. He postulated that psychic processes resulted from tension which accumulated when the current of neural electricity encountered obstacles and was "detained."

Bekhterev investigated the reflex responses of voluntary musculature in humans. He noted that reflexes are elicited not only by adequate stimuli (for example, electric shock for retraction of the finger) but also by "associated stimuli." Bekhterev suggested that the complex behavior of human beings consisted of the compounding of these associated motor reflexes, and that thought processes depended on the inner activities of the musculature of speech, essentially a complex associated reflex: "Thought is an inhibited reflex. . . ."

During the 1920s, Bekhterev's reflexology was more influential in Russia than was the similar work of Pavlov. After his death in 1927, however, the influence of his work declined. The Second All-Union Conference of Marxist-Leninist Research Institutes concluded that reflexology was "a revisionist trend which deviated from the true Marxist-Leninist position" (Editorial, 1929).

Assertions

Soviet personality theorists attach great importance to explicit statements of the philosophical basis on which personality theory is founded. Therefore, in this chapter we begin with the relationship of mind and matter before proceeding to specific personality theory assertions.

Philosophical

1. PSYCHIC PROCESSES ARE A FUNCTION OF THE BRAIN, THE HIGHEST FORM OF ORGANIC MATTER.

This crucial statement of the philosophical-materialist point of view means that mental phenomena derive from, and are subordinate to material processes. Matter is primary to, and exists independently of, any perceiving mind. The external material world is real and would continue to exist even if there were no mind to perceive it.

This philosophical-materialist concept opposes philosophical idealism, which holds that mental processes are primary and that human beings can be sure only of their own perceptions. In this concept, sensations, perceptions, thought, consciousness, and other mental processes derive from, and are dependent on, material reality in two ways: (1) they are a product of matter in motion, i.e., of the various physical processes which take place in the central nervous system, and (2) their contents are a reflection of the external material reality.

To understand mental processes, according to the philosophical-materialist view, the psychologist must study cerebral processes and must take into account the objective reality these mental processes reflect: both the material environment and the social environment—the history and traditions of a given society, its economic organization, class structure, and ideology. However, psychic processes and consciousness are *not* merely an epiphenomenon. The psyche actively interacts with external reality, in the process of which it is modified but also actively changes the environment. In addition, human consciousness can voluntarily produce changes in itself, thus promoting progressive development of its own personality (the principles of *samodvizheniye* and *samovospitaniye*—autogenetic movement and self-upbringing—discussed above).

This leads to the principle of the unity and interaction of consciousness and activity. Consciousness is formed in practical activity (most significantly, to the Soviets, in social labor). Since consciousness is revealed in the course of activity, it can therefore best be studied in that course. Furthermore, changes in the form and content of practical activity produce changes in the organization and development of mental processes. This leads to emphasis on upbringing and education as decisive influences on personality development and on collective living and work as decisive in the maintenance of desirable personality development in adults.

Development

2. FROM THE MOMENT OF BIRTH, THE CHILD IS A SOCIAL BEING.

Because of the infant's helplessness, all its relationships to the environment have to be mediated by an adult. Every need of the infant is a need for another human being—that is, a social need. The adult becomes, for the infant, the psychological center of every situation and consequently the child develops a need for communication as the most important factor in his psychic development.

3. THE INFANT'S MOST IMPORTANT PRIMAL NEED IS FOR NEW STIMULI.

N. M. Shchelovanov (1960) states that this need appears during the first month of life. The absence of stimuli, even if the infant is healthy, well-fed, and well-attended, will provoke crying which can only be stilled by presenting new stimuli. He explains that anatomical and functional development of the brain requires stimuli to provoke it into activity, for, as is true for all organs, it only develops properly through functioning.

4.   PSYCHIC DEVELOPMENT IS A GENUINE PROCESS OF AUTOGENOUS MOVEMENT.

The need for stimulation emerges as the inner core of the process of psychic development, rather than being due to outside stimulating forces, as would be the case if other primal needs were to be considered the leading ones. This concept of the social nature of development, and those needs that stimulate the infant's psychic development (the need for stimuli and for communication and activity), depicts the psychological aspect of the infant differently from those theories that give primacy to the infant's biological needs and drives. If the primary need of the infant is stimulation, then the infant represents a being completely turned toward the outside world and constantly in need of its stimulation to bring him joy or satisfaction. Knowledge of the outside world is thus necessary for life in the infant and more required than the satisfaction of any other need.

In this view the needs for knowledge and for communication are also primary in all other stages of psychic development. In every stage these needs acquire a different content, a different structure, and a different embodiment in the behavior and activity of the individual. And at every age level, there is a specific functional complex of needs and strivings, which are genetically related to the primal needs of the child. This complex finds expression in forms of behavior and activity which are specific for individuals of that particular age.

5.   THE SECOND SIGNAL SYSTEM HAS A BASIC SIGNIFICANCE IN PERSONALITY DEVELOPMENT.

In animals, connection among stimuli occurs on the level of the first signal system, and for that reason it can lead, at most, to the formation of reflexes of only the second or third order. However, because man possesses the second signal system—speech—he is able to establish long series of associations. As a result of these he can be active in areas only remotely related to stimuli which have a direct, vital significance for the organism. This explains why unconditioned reflexes (i.e., the primitive, primal drives) rarely determine the behavior of man. Rather, it is determined by signals far removed from primal drives, because conditioned reflexes are produced in response to signals which are remote but still sufficiently significant to be effective. For animals, temporary associations are based on biologically significant stimuli; in man, influences of a social nature become "personally significant."

The presence of the second signal system brings a new principle into the higher nervous activity of man and determines the new character of man's interrelationships with the environment. It leads to another important function: because it permits generalization and systematization of experience, man can behave not only actively but also consciously, on the basis of his understanding of the social significance of his actions. This qualitatively distinguishes the conditional, temporary connections or associations of man from animal behavior. Speech enables man not only to adapt to the conditions of life but also to change them.

These concepts of the second signal system bring into personality theory consideration of the real needs, motivations, interests, and strivings of man as a determining factor in his psychic life. They elucidate the conscious activity of man, its sources, and its significance.

6.   THE ADULT IS THE MAJOR FACTOR IN THE CHILD'S EARLY PERSONALITY DEVELOPMENT.

During early childhood, the support and approval of the adult is seen as essential for the child's "equilibrium" with his environment and for his emotional well-being. This powerful social need induces the child to behave in ways for which he does not feel a direct need but which are likely to gain desired adult-parental approval. Consequently, "sanctions" by adults are both important regulators of the child's behavior and stimuli for his moral development.

Cognitive activity progressively increases during early childhood. Walking extends the child's spatial and motor range; by mastering speech, his learning is no longer restricted to his own direct, personal experiences. The ever-increasing and complex cognitive activity which accompanies growth, even in the absence of systematic teaching or obligation to work, leads to a specific activity, roleplaying or creative play. This activity satisfies the basic requirements for the psychic development of the child: the needs for communication and for practical activity. Play gives the child an opportunity, in the "pretend" situation, to engage in those activities that, while attractive, are not yet accessible to him in reality. Thus play leads to learning and eventual mastery of more advanced forms of behavior. Play also gives the child the opportunity to maintain direct contact with adults, entering, on a level of pretending, into their world and considering their relationships, and interests. Since play embodies the age-appropriate development of needs, it is seen as the principal activity through which the preschool child masters the adult culture.

The direct connection of play with the satisfaction of the child's needs makes possible its use in education and upbringing. By converting the demands of adults and parents into the goal of the child's play, the need to fulfill these demands is evoked in the child. In this way, play can be employed as a specific technique for translating adult demands into the child's own need—a precondition for the child's fulfilling adult demands and making them his own.

7. THE PEER COLLECTIVE BECOMES INCREASINGLY CRUCIAL IN PERSONALITY DEVELOPMENT.

Starting school at age seven marks a turning point in the social development of the child. He has new rights and obligations and for the first time begins to engage in socially significant activity. Soviet researchers find that toward the end of the preschool period, the child develops an insistent desire to go to school. The major needs of the child, cognition and social communication, take the form of a wish to fulfill important, socially significant activities which have value not only for the child but also for the adults around him. This results in a rapid formation of various personality traits essential for the successful fulfillment of school obligations.

In school, the teacher is an influential authority, while the child's association with his peers assumes ever-greater significance. Toward the end of the early school period, at about age 11, the child's need for approval of his peers becomes stronger than his need for adult approval. This new, overriding role of the peer collective creates significant changes in the child's social situation and prepares him for transition to adolescence.

In adolescence the demands and opinions of the peer collective become the most important factor in psychic development. Typically, the adolescent wishes to win acknowledgment and to gain and maintain a position of authority among his comrades. This creates a vividly expressed need to respond to peer demands as well as possible. In this situation, if the adult upbringer succeeds in becoming the senior member of the collective, the moral norms he presents will be adopted by the collective, thus ensuring that the development of the children's personality will accord with the norms of the adults. If, however, adult demands are imposed from without, by external pressure, the members of the collective will tend to resist them, and on this foundation there can develop wrong norms of behavior which have a negative effect on the formation of personality.

Association with peers and comparison of self with others result in the most important aspect of the psychic development of adolescence: the development of self-awareness. The adolescent manifests a great interest in his own personality and in demonstrating and evaluating his potentials. As a result, he develops a relatively stable self-appraisal and level of aspirations, and these give rise to a new need—the need to reach the level of the demands of those around him as well as of his own demands and self-appraisal. If the adolescent is unable to fulfill these aspirations, he experiences acute suffering, and his demands of himself become a new factor in his social personality development. Thus, a correct balance between the adolescent's aspirations, his self-assessment, and his potentials is decisive for his emotional well-being and his further development.

Another factor during adolescence is the gap between the adolescent's objective situation and inner position, between his psychic development and real-life opportunities. This gives rise to a striving to break out of the limitations of school and to be included in the life and activity of adults. Psychologists generally designate this trait as a striving for adulthood, for independence, and for self-affirmation. When these strivings are frustrated, suffering typical for this age group and conflicts within self or with others result. Research by T. Ye. Konnikova (cited in Bozhovich, 1968, p. 434) indicated that when there are opportunities for the adolescent to participate in the adult collective and to engage in socially valuable work, this not only eliminates sufferings and conflicts but produces an upsurge of vital activity, evokes positive life experiences, and stimulates creativity.

Assertions 6 and 7 are considered crucial by Soviet personality theorists because of their insistence on the preeminence of the social environment in determining the course of personality development and their repudiation of those personality theories (particularly psychoanalysis) that attribute primacy to instinctual, unconscious, irrational forces within the individual.

8. SEXUAL MATURATION IS ANOTHER IMPORTANT FACTOR IN PERSONALITY DEVELOPMENT IN ADOLESCENCE.

Soviet personality theorist I. S. Kon (1967) states that in the process of sexual maturation, the adolescent begins to experience erotic needs. But this need and the need for emotional closeness with another person are not yet unified; eroticism is directed toward a member of the opposite sex and closeness to a peer of the same sex, because of common experiences.

The fantasies of the adolescent about love, Kon continues, are also contradictory. On the one hand, the adolescent fantasies a sublime, "pure" love in which there is nothing base or petty. On the other hand, conceptions of the physical side of love, which are largely drawn from vulgar anecdotes and are "reinforced" by masturbation experiences, seem appealing but also somewhat dirty. This dichotomy is further reinforced by lectures on moral themes by unqualified persons which are limited to the statement that sexual attraction is in contrast to romantic love: a variation on the theme of divine love versus carnal sin. The essence (and basic difficulty) of sexual maturation involves the psychological and practical overcoming of this false dichotomy.

The psychophysiological and the moral reality —the down-to-earth quality of individual love, with its intensity, vividness, and drama—is to be discovered not by moralizing phrases but by a rigorously scientific analysis of the physical aspect of love. Kon states that while there are unclear areas and theoretical difficulties in knowledge of sexual maturation, one thing is undeniable: the degree of gratification experienced in the process of sexual activity is in direct relationship to the depth of feelings. While social maturity presupposes sexual maturity, mature sexuality presupposes social-psychological maturity, which the individual achieves as the cumulative result of prolonged development and interaction with others. According to Kon (1967, p. 157, ff.):

There is no full correspondence between these two aspects. The development of the human personality is contradictory. Not in vain does Erikson call his schema a utopia, emphasizing the difficulty of its realization. It is not only that the stages of sexual and social development may not coincide in time, but not infrequently a person who has been crippled by incorrect upbringing will prove incapable of deep and all-enveloping love; and this aspect of his life will perforce be limited to less perfected forms. However, this may not prevent him from being a useful member of society, nor from achieving outstanding successes in his chosen field. Likewise, the talent for loving may, in certain cases, be the only and exclusive gift possessed by an individual, subordinating to itself all his other qualities. We know nothing about the breadth of the socio-political horizons of Juliet, but this fourteen-year-old girl symbolizes for us all of the beauty of romantic love. People differ, and one must not try to include all under one category, and then blame them for a disharmony, of which they themselves, without knowing it, are victims. However, it is essential to strive for harmoniousness, and this striving the older generation hands on to the younger one. (p. 157 ff.)

The above assertion is as far as Soviet personality theorists are willing to go, at present, in acknowledging the role of sexuality and sexual conflicts in personality development.

9. PERSONALITY TRAITS OF SOVIET ADOLESCENTS DIFFER FROM NON-SOVIET PSYCHOLOGICAL DESCRIPTIONS OF THE ADOLESCENT.

Soviet researchers maintain that the character traits traditionally attributed to the adolescent by Western observers—for example, that continuous sense of isolation attributed to the discovery by the adolescent of his own self and his experiencing of himself as a unique individual—are absent in Soviet youth. Instead, these young people report episodic but not continuous feelings of loneliness. The distinction between this kind of loneliness and the traditional descriptions of adolescent isolation is illustrated in the following statement by a Soviet adolescent girl:

> Nikolenka [the hero of L. N. Tolstoy's classic story, "Childhood, Adolescence, and Youth"] was lonely because he considered himself better than others, and could not include himself into any group of comrades. According to his viewpoint, some were beneath him, others he shunned because he felt inferior. I don't understand this. I sometimes feel lonely, when I quarrel with someone, or when I'm convinced that something is being hidden from me, which means that they don't like me. Everybody knows something, and I do not. It is so vexing! And sometimes you feel lonely because it seems that everybody has forgotten you. Then you feel sad and you want to cry. (Bozhovich, 1968, p. 357)

For Soviet personality theorists, such a statement illustrates the thesis that the experience of loneliness in Soviet adolescents is fundamentally different; these feelings are episodic and concretely based, rather than chronic, and are not the result of dissatisfaction with reality and a wish to retreat from it but instead stem from occasions in which the need for communication with the peer collective is not concretely gratified. Episodic loneliness occurs in adolescence because that is when one most intensely experiences the need to be (and to feel that one is) a member of a collective. At this age constant participation in the life of the collective, actual communication with comrades, and common, practical activity are needed. The adolescent may experience an acute feeling of loneliness in circumstances when, for reasons often connected with excessive sensitivity, he feels temporarily excluded from the collective.

10.　FORMATION OF A SCIENTIFIC AND MORAL WORLD VIEW IS CRUCIAL IN POSTADOLESCENCE.

The tasks the postadolescent sets for himself are joined into a unified system and embodied in a moral model. These tasks are stimuli for his be-

havior and also fulfill the function of organizing his other needs and aspirations. The resultant world view represents a significant qualitative change in the psychic development of the postadolescent.

Thus in postadolescence the motivational sphere becomes the decisive factor in personality development. In the course of the individual's development, needs increase in number, are enriched, and become sources for the development of new needs. As in all other psychic processes, primal needs change to mediated needs, which then acquire a conscious voluntary character. For the postadolescent, the moral world view organizes all motivations and resulting behavior.

The moral world view begins to be established long before postadolescence, however. It is determined in part by the development in the adolescent of ideal models whom the adolescent wishes to emulate. However, only in the postadolescent phase does the moral world view begin to represent a stable system of ideals and principles which becomes a continuously acting moral stimulus mediating her or his entire behavior.

11.　SOCIALLY DESIRABLE PERSONALITY DEVELOPMENT IS ACCOMPLISHED IN THE COLLECTIVE, BY THE COLLECTIVE, AND FOR THE COLLECTIVE.

Following the teaching of A. S. Makarenko and his thesis that the collective is the connecting link between the individual personality and society, Soviet personality theorists have conducted many researches investigating the influence of the collective on personality. They have given particular attention to those characteristics of the collective that have a desirable influence on personality development, the most important of which ensure for each person a definite place in the collective and an opportunity to demonstrate independence and self-reliance.

Many researchers have investigated the development of individual personality traits under the conditions of life and activity in the collective. The development of persistence was investigated by N. I. Sudakov (1950); of self-confidence, by F. I. Ivashchenko (1952); of setting high standards for the self, by A. A. Bodalev (1957). The researches of L. I. Bozhovich and her co-workers were concerned with how best to use the collective as a positive character builder. Special attention was directed to the impact of the collective on the structure of the personality, goal orientation, self-awareness, self-evaluation, and level of aspiration.

12. CONSCIOUSNESS IS FORMED DURING PRACTICAL ACTIVITY AND REVEALED IN THE COURSE OF ACTIVITY.

Changes in practical activities can influence changes in the organization and development of mental processes: This is the principle of the unity of consciousness and behavior enunciated by Rubinshtein (1934). Soviet personality studies are aimed at organizing the life of the child so that his personality will develop in accordance with the aims of upbringing (vospitaniye). This task dictates a corresponding methodological principle: The laws of the formation of personality should be studied in the course of the pedagogical process, in the actual conditions of upbringing. For this reason, the major methods used are not nomothetic, or quantitative analysis of the material, but longitudinal observation of the pedagogical process and generalization and analysis of idiographic experience, based on many-sided studies of individual children.

Another characteristic trait of Soviet research is that it is not limited to a passive observation of the developing child. Researchers strive actively to form desired character traits and qualities, applying pedagogical principles to achieve certain desired goals based on specific psychological hypotheses. In accordance with this action-research conceptualization, one of the basic methods is the "transforming" experiment, which involves studying the personality of the child during the process of goal-directed upbringing. Research carried out in this way meets an important requirement of Soviet science—to guide those very processes whose laws of development are being investigated.

Kovalev (1949), in early research, describes how a classroom teacher who encounters undesirable behavior (shyness, impulsivity, rudeness), can achieve the reeducation of the child by employing appropriate pedagogical measures. The case histories cited demonstrate how negative character traits are produced by life situations and conditions of upbringing of the child, and also how a correctly structured pedagogical approach brings about positive results.

Maintenance

13. PERSONALITY MEANS A CERTAIN LEVEL OF PSYCHIC DEVELOPMENT.

In the process of achieving self-knowledge, the individual begins to perceive himself or herself as distinct from others. This level of psychic development is characterized by distinct outlooks and attitudes and particular moral demands and values, as a result of which he becomes relatively stable and independent of influences alien to his own convictions. Having achieved this level of development, he has the ability to purposefully affect the surrounding reality, to change it to suit his purposes, and also to change himself.

The Soviet viewpoint holds that the person, as a completed personality, is capable of regulating his own behavior and actions and, to a certain extent, his own psychic development. When he has achieved that level of development where he can be called a personality, all psychic processes and functions, all qualities and properties have attained a specific structure. At the center of this structure are stable, dominant motivations which determine his hierarchical arrangement of needs. Such a level of development is achieved only in the adult personality.

14. THE PSYCHE IS SOCIAL IN NATURE.

On a certain level of development, the human being becomes a personality. Thus in Soviet psychology, personality is seen not as some kind of spiritual essence but as the product of sociohistorical development. (This is a basic contribution to Soviet personality theory by L. S. Vygotskii.) The major determining condition for the maintenance of the personality is the place one occupies in the system of social relations and the activity one carries out within that system.

15. MAN REPRESENTS A PRODUCT OF HISTORICAL DEVELOPMENT.

Only within the framework of a sociohistorical conception of personality is it possible to account for the distinctive features of personality in different historical epochs. Analyzing the development of the psyche in correlation with a particular epoch and its connection with the class struggle and the entire dynamic of the historical process makes it clear not only that human personality depends upon the class to which an individual belongs but also that the psyches of the representatives of classes change as society changes.

Study of the development of personality (its interests, needs, tastes, aspirations, and views) during the past century indicates how the representatives of different classes (workers, bourgeoisie) have undergone enormous personality changes during that period. At the beginning of this century in Russia, the working man was still half peasant; later he became a proletarian, with an as-yet-dim social consciousness, and finally he became a revolutionary fighter. In the policy of the Communist Party, the working man in Soviet society is the conscious builder of a socialist society. In the same way, the bourgeois of the French Revolution was substantially different, psychologically, from the capitalist-imperialist of the 20th century.

In personality studied as a whole gestalt, in the course of history and as it is included in the entire system of social relationships, changes in all interpersonal relationships can be noted. Although the abstractly studied functions seem unchangeable, the entire structure—the whole dynamic, the whole content of the personality— does change as a result of historicocultural change. In short, personality is a function of the society.

16. MOTIVATION ASSURES MAINTENANCE OF
     AN INTEGRATED RELATIONSHIP TO
     REALITY.

Motivation ensures the integrated character of the individual's relation to reality. All a person's reactions, the entire structure of his or her affective life, are determined by motivational properties of the personality which develop in the course of social experience. Vygotskii (1936) states, "Only pathology, only a personality disorder, can bring about a primitive reaction, which represents direct affective discharges which are not mediated by the complex structure of the personality" (p. 30).

This concept of personality characterizes the approach of Soviet psychologists and psychopathologists to investigations of the formation and disintegration of personality. In these investigations, an important element is the study of the dependence of individual psychic processes on the needs and motivations which stimulate the individual to bring these processes

about. The first to carry out such investigations were A. N. Leontiev (1948), A. V. Zaporozhetz (1948), and their collaborators (Zaporozhetz & El'konin, 1964). Later they were carried out on a very large scale, and there emerged a significant number of facts demonstrating how individual psychic processes (for example, memory, or organization of behavior) are changed significantly by the motivations that stimulate them.

The concept of a personalistic approach also penetrated investigation of the disintegration of psychic activity. B. V. Zeigarnik (1965) writes, "In destroying the psychic activity of man, disease often changes precisely the personal component of man. For this reason, in analyzing psychopathological phenomena, we must take into consideration the disturbances in the personality of the patient, the changes in his orientation, his needs, his interests" (p. 9). Zeigarnik contrasts this point of view with another approach in which the psychopathological symptom is looked upon as a disturbance of individual psychic functions and this in turn is explained by the disturbance of physiological processes:

> And yet, the patient frequently has a memory-loss for certain material, precisely because of his changed attitude toward this material, and toward his activity with this material. . . . The pathological changes were in the motivational sphere, in the sphere of their attitude toward the activity to be carried out, and in their attitude toward others. These patients were profoundly indifferent to all that went on around them, to the consequences of their own activity, and this absence of a relationship produced their "forgetfulness." (1965, p. 10)

17. DISTINCTIONS MUST BE MADE BETWEEN
     MEANING AND SIGNIFICANCE.

This assertion derives directly from research findings about the role of motivation in maintaining an integrated relationship to reality. Motivation is determined by the significance to the individual of a given event or activity. Significance, then, is distinct from meaning.

Meaning denotes something *objective* in a phenomenon which can be observed in the system of its objective connections, relationships, and interaction. Significance, in contrast, denotes a *subjective* experience of the psyche. This concept derives directly from the Soviet formulation that the psyche is an adaptive instrument which is derivative from the material in two ways: its *processes* are a manifestation of the reflex activity of a material entity—the central nervous system—and its *content* is a reflection of material reality.

According to Pavlov, a conditioned reflex is forn..ed only if it is reinforced by directly useful or directly harmful stimuli—that is, stimuli which are significant to the organism. Therefore, the mistake of associationism consists in its lack of understanding of the active principle in the formation of associative bonds. For the formation of a conditioned reflex, (i.e., of an associative connection), it is not sufficient that stimuli merely coincide in time. It is essential that one of them has significance; only then will other stimuli connected to it also acquire significance.

18. PSYCHIC ACTIVITIES ARE NOT
     LOCALIZED BUT ARE PRODUCTS OF
     FUNCTIONAL CORTICAL SYSTEMS.

Functional interacting systems of the cortex develop as a consequence of the organism's interactions with the environment. Damage to a localized area of the cortex need not produce permanent loss of a psychic function, because it is possible, by appropriate training, to organize a new functional cortical system which will successfully carry out the "lost" psychic activity.

Research by Luria (1969) demonstrated that a given psychological activity may be performed by one of several functional cortical systems, so that, if one system is damaged, another can be trained to take over its function. Man's adaptive functions (speech, computation, abstraction) are mediated by functional cortical systems which are acquired rather than innate. The most important determinant of the functional cortical systems in man is the organization of the social environment.

19. WORK IN, AND FOR, THE COLLECTIVE IS
     ESSENTIAL FOR MAINTENANCE OF A
     HEALTHY PERSONALITY.

Soviet personality theorists maintain that love of work is essential for the emotional health of the "new Soviet man." It is understandable, they say, that under capitalism, where the worker is exploited, work cannot generally give the worker joy or pleasure. However, even in a society divided into antagonistic classes, there are individuals who find work a joyful need rather than merely an unhappy necessity, who see in work the meaning of their lives. Mainly, these people are involved in intellectual work and in the so-called "free professions"—artists, writers, musicians. People like Lomonosov, Darwin, and Tolstoy worked not for material gain but primarily under the pressure of filling a creative need. Tolstoy stated that he wrote because of an irresistible need to create and because of his awareness of the social significance of his work.

The emancipation of physical and intellectual work brought about by the October Revolution radically changed attitudes toward work, according to the Soviets, who maintain that the opportunity to work in accordance with one's abilities under conditions of comradely cooperation and mutual help gave birth to enthusiasm for work in the masses and the flowering of their creative abilities. They acknowledge that they have not yet achieved the ideal communist society, where the principle "from each according to his abilities, to each according to his needs" will become a reality and where work will be a primary life need. They quote Lenin (1963): "Communist work will be voluntary, without any consideration for reward; work as a habit for the common good, and as a conscious attitude (which becomes a habit), which recognizes the necessity to work for the common good; work as a basic need of the healthy organism" (p. 199).

The psychological readiness to work in the Communist way has a complex structure which includes (1) consciousness of the social and personal meaningfulness of work; (2) the wish to work not only as a social duty, but also because of the love of work; and (3) the ability to work *po-kommunisticheski*, which means the ability to work in the collective, collectively, and in the interests of the whole collective. To satisfy these requirements, the mature, developed personality must possess the following qualities: (1) discipline, or the ability, consciously and responsibly, to relate to one's tasks; (2) collectivism, or the ability to give aid to one's comrades in the interests of achieving the goals and tasks of the collective; and (3) a creative attitude toward work, or not being content with what one has achieved but constantly striving to raise the productivity of labor by mastering greater skills.

20. THE NEEDS OF MAN ARE OF TWO KINDS: IMMEDIATE AND MEDIATED.

Human needs differ not only in content and dynamic properties (force, stability, mobility) but also in structure. Some needs have a direct, immediate character, and others are mediated by a long-range goal. The structure of needs also determines how they stimulate action. For direct, immediate needs, the stimulus moves directly from the need to action and is related to the immediate desire to carry it out. This kind of stimulus is best represented by physiological needs. When there is a mediated structure of needs, the stimulus emanates from a consciously established purpose which may be in conflict with immediate desires. Mediated stimuli occur in cases where a powerful need cannot be directly satisfied but requires intermediate activities the individual may not have a direct ability to carry out immediately.

The presence of indirect needs (that is, of stimuli which originate from a consciously established purpose) characterizes that phase of development of the motivational sphere of the individual which makes it possible for him to consciously direct and regulate his own needs and strivings.

21. SOVIET PSYCHOLOGY REJECTS THE STUDY OF PERSONALITY BY TESTS AND QUESTIONNAIRES.

The mechanistic approach to man, the subjective nature of the interpretation of the results, the attempt to "study," by means of primitive and standardized techniques, an extremely complex object, quantifying personality traits and manifestations—all these factors, which are organically inherent in tests and questionnaires, have forced Soviet psychologists to reject once and for all this antiscientific method. (Krutetski, 1962)

Soviet psychologists have established a number of principles for the scientific study of personality:

1. Character should be studied in an analytic-synthetic manner, with due regard for its wholeness.
2. Character can be studied only on the basis of objective data, i.e., one should proceed from concrete reality, from man's behavior, and the motivations thus revealed.
3. Character can be studied only by taking into account the determining influences of external and internal conditions (conditions of life and upbringing, condition of the organism and its vital activity).
4. Character traits should be examined in their development and changes.
5. Individual personality can be studied only in the collective, through the collective, and against the background of the collective in which the personality is formed and developed.
6. Character should be studied on a plane involving plans for its development.

In addition, personality must be considered not only as an object of study but also as an object of upbringing; the study must have the practical purpose of controlling the processes of personality formation.

The basic method for studying character in Soviet psychology involves observation, under natural conditions, of the individual. The natural experiment usually assumes the form of an instructional or transforming experiment which combines a psychological study of the child with the bringing about of desired results. Laboratory experiments, biographical methods, talks, and an analysis of the products of activity are other research means. Usually several methods are combined, so that they supplement, correct, and control each other.

Summary

The above assertions have led Soviet personality theorists to optimistic conclusions about the individual's relationship to his or her physical and social environment and to self, and about the future:

1. The individual can know the true nature of his material and social environment, and the true nature of his own physical and psychic functioning.

2. This knowledge gives him the power to change his material and social environment and himself for the better.

3. There is a continuous reciprocal ("dialectical") interaction between the person and his environment. By improving his environment, he makes possible his own self-improvement, and by improving himself, he furthers the improvement of his environment.

4. The plasticity of the individual's brain and his personality makes changes for the better possible at all ages.

5. The individual's "higher" social, ethical, and moral needs are more compelling than his "lower" animal needs.

6. In the process of upbringing, these "higher" needs can be used to inculcate socially desirable character traits in children.

7. This process of "correct" upbringing will be continued by the individual himself, by autogenetic movement (*samodvizheniye*) and self-upbringing (*samovospitaniye*). Thus, the individual who has been given a proper start by collective upbringing will continue to bring himself up, improve himself, and improve his society, thus creating a self-perpetuating upward spiral.

8. A collective society provides optimum conditions for the improvement of mankind, by providing for collective upbringing of children and for a collective milieu throughout life.

Applications

Assessment

Personality assessment is carried out in the Soviet Union in a number of ways. In the 1920s and early 1930s a proliferation of specially devised tests was widely applied in assessing the aptitudes of children to determine whether they should be assigned to regular schools, special schools for the emotionally or intellectually handicapped, or schools for the gifted. Tests were also widely used in industry to determine the aptitudes of workers for specific occupations. In the middle thirties, many of these tests fell into disrepute, and the Resolution of 1936 against pedology effectively curtailed their use.

Zeigarnik (1962, 1965) and her associates continued to employ various testing techniques in the diagnosis and treatment of patients with organic brain lesions, and defectology became an important area of research and practical application. Defectologists like Luria (1961, 1962, 1969) published extensively on the application of personality theory to the diagnostic study and education of children with organic brain defects and the rehabilitation of patients with organic brain lesions.

In recent years there has been renewed interest in the use of tests in clinical diagnosis, including tests developed in the Soviet Union as well as adaptations of tests like the Rorschach, Thematic Apperception Test, and Minnesota Multiphasic Personality Inventory (Myasishchev, Bespal'ko, & Gilyasheva, 1969). Soviet clinicians have also made extensive use of conditioned-reflex techniques to determine the type of higher nervous activity of patients, in accordance with the meticulous experimental work on human typology by Pavlov, Teplov, and Nebylitsyn.

However, in keeping with their adherence to the principle of the unity of theory and practice, most Soviet personality theorists hold that the most valid techniques of personality assessment involve the use of the "natural experiment." They prefer this method to laboratory techniques, tests, or questionnaires, concluding that personalities can best be assessed by studying behavior and responses in the natural setting of the collective. There is an enormous literature about the transforming experiment (*preobrazuyushchii eksperiment*), in which individual personalities are assessed in the process of experimental efforts to change personality and behavior in a specified, desired direction. Similarly, Soviet personality theorists hold that assessment for purposes of vocational guidance is best accomplished by longitudinal observation of the child and young person in his natural setting, rather than by vocational aptitude testing. However, there has been a renewal of interest in recent years in the use of tests and questionnaires in assessing vocational aptitudes and motivation (Lomov, 1966).

Treatment

Psychiatric treatment in the Soviet Union leans heavily on Soviet personality theory. For example, Myasishchev, a leading Soviet psychotherapist, cites Makarenko's work as a paradigm for his conclusion that:

> ... the principle of treatment by the method of psychotherapy consists in the reconstruction of the personality through the process of social intercourse and working and living in common. The creative work of A. S. Makarenko exemplifies the feasibility and the realization of this approach. Psychotherapy

represents a border zone which combines the treatment, rehabilitation and upbringing of man. . . . The psychiatrist is the teacher of life to the patient. (1973, pp. 15–16)

Soviet psychiatric treatment rests on the same three theoretical pillars as Soviet personality theory:

1. The philosophical orientation of dialectical materialism.
2. The Pavlovian doctrine that mental disorders are caused by disturbances of the reflex activity of the central nervous system.
3. Myasishchev's interpersonal relations approach to the study of personality and the elucidation of intra-psychic conflicts.

In accordance with the principle of studying the personality while influencing (or shaping) it, and influencing it while studying it, Soviet psychiatrists and psychotherapists take an active role in treatment. They may intervene directly in the patient's life situation by manipulating his environment, occupation, or residence. They actively strive to maintain a positive therapeutic climate by giving the patient emotional support, warmth, and help. They try to reeducate the patient and guide him toward the development of such "socio-moral qualities as moral fibre, social consciousness, collectivism, and the ability to be guided by the collective and with its help to see and correct his mistakes"(Myasishchev, 1961, p. 44).

Since work is considered a central element in personality development, work therapy is a major tool in treatment. Most psychiatric hospitals and clinics maintain well-equipped workshops where patients produce, for pay, articles to be sold to retail outlets. Soviet psychiatrists hold that work therapy is an important socializing factor; that it helps the patient retain contact with reality and prevents emotional isolation and retreat from the real world; that engaging in socially useful work and getting paid for it helps restore and enhance the patient's self-esteem; and that the protected conditions of the therapeutic workshop prepare the patient for a return to life outside the hospital.

Because of the close interrelationship between psychology and neurophysiology, and between psychotherapy, psychiatry, and medicine, Soviet psychotherapists invariably combine psycho-

therapy with physiotherapy and medication. The psychiatrist carries out not only a psychiatric evaluation but also a thorough physical and neurological examination in a search for neurological and somatic causes of a mental illness—such as infection, trauma, malnutrition, or toxic manifestations in the central nervous system. The psychiatrist also becomes, in effect, the personal physician of the hospitalized patient, treating whatever somatic illness he may present or develop.

In keeping with the optimistic tone of Soviet personality theory, with its emphasis on the unlimited potential for change and rehabilitation, the psychiatrist demonstrates a great deal of therapeutic optimism and vigor in his approach and in the liberal use of various medications and physiotherapeutic modalities. Because of their Pavlovian orientation to the mental patient as someone suffering from a weakening of the cortical nerve cells, Soviet psychiatrists prescribe various tonicizing and roborant ("generally strengthening") medications, therapeutic physical exercises, hydrotheraphy, and acupuncture.

Basing themselves on Pavlov's formulation that mental illness is a manifestation of "protective inhibition," whereby the weakened cortical cells protect themselves "from the danger of being destroyed as a result of excessive stimulation" (cited in Andreev, 1960, p. 3), Soviet psychiatrists for many years made wide use of various techniques for inducing prolonged sleep, in order to reinforce the already existing protective inhibition and give the weakened cortical cells rest and an opportunity to recover. In recent years, with the introduction of modern psychotropic drugs, the use of prolonged sleep has diminished.

Since the collective is considered to be a central factor in the security system of the individual, in the satisfaction of his material and emotional needs, and in the furthering of his growth and development, the Soviet psychiatrist calls upon the various collectives in the society to help in therapeutic work. A psychiatric history of the patient is obtained not only from the patient and his family but also from members of his trade union collective, who are called on to maintain contact with the patient during hospitalization. The collectives of fellow patients and of the staff are consciously employed as an encouraging and supportive, but also pressuring, corrective and reality-testing medium.

In accordance with the Pavlovian concept that speech (the second signal system) is a powerful stimulus in the formation of conditioned reflexes and of the "dynamic stereotype" of the personality, Soviet psychotherapists avoid giving patients interpretations which involve their negative feelings. The rationale is that such negative interpretations reinforce the already existing unhealthy "dynamic stereotype" of the patient and thus have an antitherapeutic effect. Instead, they give the patient countervailing suggestions to help extinguish the unhealthy stereotype (Ziferstein, 1965, 1966). In line with their emphasis on the crucial role of the collective, Soviet psychotherapists make extensive use of group ("collective") psychotherapy. The combination of collective psychotherapy and collective work therapy has become one of the hallmarks of Soviet psychotherapy (Ziferstein, 1972).

An important application of personality theory to the treatment and rehabilitation of patients with organic brain disease, and of the mentally retarded and the handicapped, is based on the research of A. R. Luria (see Assertion 18). These studies demonstrated that if a given function (e.g., reading) is lost because of damage to a localized area of the brain, a different cortical functional system can be trained to take over the "lost" function. Therapists have found that handicapped patients can be trained to develop alternate cortical systems which enable them to function much more effectively. In the case of mental retardation, the assumption is that certain functional cortical systems are not operative because of genetic or congenital damage, and appropriate training of new functional systems can enable the mentally retarded person to function more effectively in his environment.

Institutional

From the days immediately after the revolution, from the time of Makarenko, the major emphasis in the application of personality theory has been on rearing and educating the new Soviet man. Therefore, the large bulk of research and application has been in crèches (day nurseries), nursery schools, kindergartens, children's homes, and schools. Brackbill (1962) reports that "at present, a higher proportion of developmental

behavioral research cannot be found in any other country."

The concerted, practical applications of personality theory to the task of rearing a physically, mentally, and morally healthy Soviet citizen begin almost from birth. In the crèches connected with factories, to which working mothers bring their infants at two months, one can observe nurses massaging, exercising, and verbally stimulating their charges. Every day the same nurse massages and exercises "her" child and talks to him. During a lengthy exercise period there is a great deal of nonverbal social stimulation and physical contact between nurse and child.

Several infants are usually placed in one playpen, to encourage early socialization. There they are exposed to new, stimulating, colorful toys, and when the *orienting reflex* is brought into play as one infant focuses on a toy, the object is moved to refocus his attention on his neighbors.

At the toddler stage, socialization and cooperation are encouraged by providing large blocks and toys which cannot be handled by only one child. Throughout the period of infancy a variety of techniques is employed to improve the children's visual, tactile, and other sensory discriminatory powers and to develop coordination, agility, and motor and verbal skills. Toddlers are also taught to attend as much as possible to their own needs: to feed themselves, to pick up their toys at the end of playtime, to socialize with their table companions at meals, to prepare themselves for a nap.

Stress is laid early on social ownership: "Mine is ours, ours is mine." Children are taught to engage in criticism and self-criticism for the good of the collective, and to build a self-upbringing and self-disciplining collective.

Manuals for teachers describe in minute detail the daily class routine and the techniques to be employed by the teacher at each grade level, to achieve "the objectives of upbringing; namely: communist morality, a responsible attitude toward learning, cultured *(kul'turnoye)* behavior, aesthetic culture, and physical culture" (Boldyrev, 1960). For example, instructions for first-grade students are detailed in one official manual as follows:

> *In school.* All pupils are to arrive on time, wipe their feet before entering, greet the teacher and staff

members by name, give a general greeting to class-mates and greet seatmate by name....

At home. On awaking, greet parents and thank them after breakfast...take care of your own things; sew on buttons, iron clothes, shine shoes, keep desk in order....

In public places. Behave calmly. Obey all requests of adults...Dissuade friends from behaving bad-ly....Learn about the work the adults in your fam-ily do for the common good.

Other manuals describe techniques to be em-ployed by teachers and school administrators to develop "socialist competition"; for example, the rows in one classroom may compete with one an-other in areas such as orderliness, neatness, scholarship, and cooperation. Similar competi-tion is developed among classrooms and even-tually among a number of schools.

Another prevalent application of personality theories which stress the role of the collective is in trade-union organizations, housing commit-tees, and so on, where the guiding principles are applied not by professionals but by the members of the collectives themselves. One example is the "comradely court" *(tovarishcheskii sud),* which tries individuals for infractions of a collective's rules. It has no judicial powers but effectively uses the pressures of the collective to halt unde-sirable behavior. In recent years there has been a renewal of interest in the application of person-ality theory to problems of industrial psychology and to specific issues involving motivation, im-provement of attitudes toward work, and devel-opment of work habits and skills.

Self

A Western reader might ask what value there is to him personally in learning about the personal-ity theories and practices of a culture so differ-ent from his own. At first glance it may seem that the social conditions and ideology of the Soviet people, and their concepts and attitudes, are so different that they cannot possibly have any applicability to his life.

A major benefit of any cross-cultural study is that it may cause the reader to confront his own ethnocentrism, as well as that of the other cul-ture. It can make explicit attitudes and values about others that have been accepted as a matter

of course. Reexamination of these attitudes can result in a deeper, more objective self-exploration and self-understanding, not only as an individual but as a member of a particular culture. Uri Bronfenbrenner, after visiting Soviet schools and reading some of Makarenko's writings, concluded:

...the results of this inquiry indicate that the rather different Soviet approach to the upbringing of the young is not without significance for our own problems.... perhaps we have reached the point of diminishing returns in allowing excessive autonomy and in failing to utilize the constructive potential of the peer group in developing social responsibility and consideration for others.... What is called for [is] ...greater involvement of children in responsi-bility on behalf of their own family, community, and society at large. (1970, pp. 164–166)

And in an introduction to Makarenko's book *The Collective Family: A Handbook for Russian Parents* (1937/1967), Bronfenbrenner writes:

The question therefore arises whether we cannot profit by taking to heart Makarenko's injunction re-garding the constructive influence of imposing com-munal responsibility within both family and peer groups.... [These responsibilities] should involve the full range of human beings who make up the so-ciety, including those who most need and deserve the service of others—old people, young children, the handicapped, and the underprivileged. ...We too must teach morality through the imposition on chil-dren of concrete responsibilities and expectations consistent with the welfare of all and the dignity of each. (pp. xvii–xix)

This perhaps presents an overidealized picture of Soviet child-rearing and educational methods, and an equally overidealized prescription for us. Bronfenbrenner himself issues a caveat about not subscribing to Soviet insistence on the pri-macy of the collective over the individual or adopting their practice of shifting major respon-sibility for upbringing from the family to public institutions. Furthermore, one cannot simply transplant practices that may work for one society and expect them to work in an entirely different society, with different traditions and different values. However, this in no way invalidates the fructifying effects of cross-cul-tural exchanges of data and theoretical concepts.

Validation

Evidence

Soviet personality theorists validate their theories in several ways. One is by citing the soundness of the philosophical and sociohistorical concepts on which they base their hypotheses and which dictate the direction of their research and its methodology. They cite the writings of the "classics" of Marxism and the continuing elaboration of the concepts of dialectical and historical materialism by contemporary Marxist scholars and by psychologists like Vygotskii and Rubinshtein.

A second type of validation is the large body of meticulous experimental work on conditioned reflexes initiated by Pavlov and continued by psychophysiologists like Ivanov-Smolenskii, Bykov, Teplov, Nebylitsyn, and many others. This work, involving animal and human subjects, continues to be done in many psychophysiological laboratories. Soviet psychologists maintain that these carefully controlled laboratory studies demonstrate the correctness of the materialist approach to the study of personality and of human typology, and that they prove that psychic activity is a function of the "higher nervous activity," of processes in the cerebral hemispheres and in the neighboring subcortex.

They further cite the careful experimental studies in typology, initiated by Pavlov and continued by Teplov and Nebylitsyn, in which human subjects were studied for such properties of the nervous system as strength or weakness, mobility and speed of the appearance and cessation of the neural process, and the equilibrium of excitation and inhibition. They maintain that these studies lay the foundations for a truly scientific typology of human personality.

A third source of validation cited by Soviet personality theorists is the careful study of developmental psychology, under laboratory conditions, by specially devised experimental designs such as Vygotskii's "technique of dual stimulation," and in real-life settings. For example, the conclusion that the newborn has a primal "social" need for new stimuli and communication has been buttressed by observations of infants in the first month of life by Peiper (1962), Figurin and Denisova (1949), Shchelovanov (1960), Lechtreman-Abramovich (1949), Rosengart-

Pupko (1948), and many others. Vygotskii's innovative studies of the development of thought and language (1934)—which were continued by his students Luria and Leontiev (El'konin, 1969) and by experimental studies like those of Smirnov and Zinchenko on the psychology of memory, Zaporozhetz on sensory training, and Kasatkin on the development of conditioned reflexes in early childhood (Cole & Maltzman, 1969)—are cited as evidence for Vygotskii's dictum that the child is a social being from the moment of birth.

Another type of validation of Soviet personality theory is the contention that Soviet techniques of collective upbringing, combined with the influence of living in a collective society, produce healthier and "better" citizens. Some Soviet writings cite Western psychiatric sources on the high incidence of neurosis and juvenile delinquency in the West and maintain that the incidence is much lower in the Soviet Union. Myasishchev (1974) and other personality theorists state that the new Soviet man demonstrates such desirable qualities as: concern for the common welfare, pride in the achievements of the collective rather than in self-aggrandizement, cooperativeness, a new attitude of respect for work, and heroism on a mass scale.

Other evidence cited as validating Soviet personality theory is Makarenko's achievement in dramatically restructuring the personalities of several thousand delinquent youths through the influence of the peer collective. These successes led to the development of the type of experimentation and validation which is most prevalent among Soviet personality theorists and which they consider to be the most productive—the transforming experiment.

A typical experiment described by N. F. Prokina (1961) proposed to validate the hypothesis that the child develops specific personality traits by incorporating aspects of his social activity. The experiment was carried out in a class of 30 first-graders at a boarding school in Moscow, chosen because it was particularly disorganized and the teacher had had difficulty in getting the children to abide by the school rules. One bit of behavior was selected for investigation, in the course of which the behavior was to be improved: having the children leave the classroom in an orderly fashion. This was chosen because it had practical importance: Much time was lost out of each school day due to the disorganized activities of the children. (This is one of the major characteristics of Soviet personality theory; the psychologist's work must not only have purely theoretical significance but must, even in the course of the investigation, make a direct, practical contribution.)

The experiment consisted of several stages. In the first, the desirability of leaving the room in an orderly fashion was presented to the children. The investigator outlined in detail what was required: standing up promptly when the bell rang, moving into the aisles and forming straight rows, and so on. Immediately after this explanation the children were able to respond to the bell in the desired manner, although they had not previously done so.

In Stage 2, which involved motivating the children to use this ability consistently, audiovisual techniques were employed. The class was divided into six groups, and for each a chart was drawn on which a staircase was represented. The number of steps on the staircase equaled the number of line-ups required each day. When a group lined up in the desired manner, the leader of the group had the honor of pinning a red flag to the step representing that line-up. This introduced the incentive of "socialist competition"— that is, competition on a group basis rather than by individuals vying for recognition. This motivation had the immediate effect of more orderly line-ups, but it did not produce lasting results.

Stage 3 involved efforts to make the results more durable by adding more motivation, in this case by introducing the element of play. Each team was designated as aviators, sailors, and so on and then motivated to carry out the task in an orderly fashion, "the way pilots (e.g.) do." This additional motive helped to improve performance but did not achieve the desired durability. An additional element was introduced in the form of a three-minute hourglass to time the children as they lined up. Each step in the process of lining up was timed, and the teams were awarded points for being the first to complete each step, such as standing up, moving into the aisle, or walking out the door.

As a result of this combination of techniques, the average time for dismissal of the class was reduced from ten minutes to one and a half minutes. Lasting results were achieved in that the improved performance was maintained for the remaining three months of the school year.

Prokina concludes that this was a successful experiment because it accomplished a desirable practical result, and it advanced the theoretical understanding that three basic conditions are needed to produce lasting improvements in behavior:

1. Strong motivation must be established in the form of "socialist competition" combined with pleasurable play activity, to evoke a strong desire to engage in the approved behavior and to continue it.
2. To facilitate learning of this behavior, it had to be analyzed into easily learned and timed components.
3. The child had to be taught how to carry out each of the behavioral elements in the time interval allotted.

This approach is invariably encountered in books and articles on Soviet personality theory and in conversations with Soviet personality theorists and pedagogues. In essence, Soviet personality theorists prefer this kind of practical, qualitative, holistic action-research approach to the quantitative statistical studies which characterize many schools of Western personality theory.

Soviet personality theorists declare that this research approach is superior to Western procedures. Thus, in a recent paper, Myasishchev (1974) states:

> In personology, the investigation of the social ontogenesis of personality is especially essential. It seems to me that the socio-historical elucidation of the ontogenesis of personality will most likely be achieved by Soviet psychology.... The socialist system is the system of Soviet humanism. Only on the foundation of this system is a genuinely scientific psychological understanding of personality possible.
> ... The historical-materialist concept is the only scientific concept of personality and its relationships.... The relationships of man are studied as processes of genesis, formation, development and disintegration, in the course of his life, in the course of his social being. These relationships are the most dynamic products of his life and of his life experience. Therefore, the study of man in his relationships satisfies to the highest degree, the require-

ments of the genetic, dynamic, historical concept of personality. (pp. 5–25, passim)

Comparisons

Soviet psychologists severely criticize prevailing Western personality theories. For example, Myasishchev (1974) states:

Capitalist society stifles personality, and its science and philosophy cannot but distort the concepts of this most important problem of the history of social development and psychology. . . . In the polar tendencies on the one side of negation of the personality and of the mass depersonalization of the toilers in capitalist society, and on the other side, the cult of the individualistic "I", of the "unique superman," of the cult of the personality of the property owner, of the bourgeois, are shown most clearly the class tendencies and contradictions of the structure of capitalist society which is built upon the principle "everything for the few, nothing for the masses." (p. 21)

In these attacks on Western personality theory, the prime target most often is Freudian psychoanalysis. Myasishchev (1974) states:

Taking as our point of departure the definition of consciousness as the highest stage of the development of the personality, we perforce come to the conclusion that the psychology of the personality and of its relationships is essentially the psychology of consciousness. Therefore, the psychology of personality and its relationships is the exact opposite of the current reactionary bourgeois psychology of the unconscious, the typical expression of which is the psychology of Freud. (p. 8)

Until recently, the attacks on Freudian psychoanalytic personality theory were extremely harsh. One example is this statement by Ye. V. Shorokhova (1963): "The social function of Freudian depth psychology consists of an attempt to poison the minds of the intelligentsia and of the common people." Another example is Lebedinskii and Myasishchev (1966):

In the final phase of the development of his concepts, Freud arrived at the affirmation that the most powerful drive is that of the death instinct. Of significance here is not so much this assumption itself, which totally lacks any experiential validation, but its mystic pessimistic essence, which harmonizes with the decadent world view of the epoch of capitalism in decline. (p. 354)

And Svyadoshch (1959) says: "Freud and his students founded a pseudo-scientific school based upon neo-Kantian philosophical conceptions, which biologize the human personality" (p. 25).

In more recent Soviet writings on personality theory criticisms of Freudian psychoanalysis have been moderated, and they even speak positively about some aspects of psychoanalytic personality theory. A consensus of present-day Soviet criticism of psychoanalysis may be stated as follows: Psychoanalysis created an illusion that it had finally discovered an objective method for uncovering the deep, hidden roots of human experience. Since there was a need for a scientific conception of personality and for an adequate research methodology, the psychoanalysts unjustifiably broadened the conclusions at which they had arrived. And so, while the data obtained by the psychoanalytic method were true, the interpretation of these facts was invalid.

Soviet personality theorists generally applaud the efforts of Alfred Adler and Carl Jung to move away from Freud's biologizing interpretation of human personality and to find a place in theory for the social factors in the development of the personality by limiting the role of the sexual drive and identifying other, nonsexual forces as motivating human behavior. During the Stalin era, official Soviet personality theory was critical of Adler, labeling his writings as "idealist" (*Great Soviet Encyclopedia*, 1949), but more recent Soviet evaluations of Adler are much more positive (e.g., Lyalikov, 1970). The Soviets now point out that there is a close parallelism between Adler's conclusion that personality is social in its formation and the Soviet formulations that the psyche is social in nature and that the major determining conditions for the maintenance of the personality are the place occupied in the system of social relations and the activity carried out within that system. (See Assertion 14.) They agree with Adler that the motive forces in man's behavior are social in nature and that there is in man a genuine need to find his place in life, in society.

Jung attempted to reform classical Freudianism by putting forth independent concepts related to the motive forces of man's behavior and the formation of his personality. He correctly noted the enormous power of man's moral strivings, but he posited them as yet one more drive (along with the sex drive) which determines the psychic development of man. Jung convinced himself, from his clinical experience, of the importance of moral attitudes of which the person himself is often unaware and which often act not only independently of conscious intentions but even in opposition to them. He should have tried, then, to understand their real nature— that is, the psychological mechanisms of the functioning and development of these attitudes —but he evaded this. In accordance with his philosophical world view, and because he did not have the materials necessary for a truly scientific analysis, he preferred to see them not as norms and rules of social morality which had been so deeply ingrained as to give the appearance of being instinctual, but rather as an innate category of divine origin *(bozhestvennoye proiskhozhdeniye)*.

Soviet personality theorists are also critical of the personality theories put forth by the neo-Freudians, such as Erich Fromm, Karen Horney, H. S. Sullivan, although they acknowledge that these theories generally have a clearly defined social direction. Some Soviet psychologists see the attempts of contemporary neo-Freudians to introduce a social interpretation of human conflicts into psychoanalysis as a genuine response to the rapidly developing social sciences and particularly to social psychology. But others, including Soviet social psychologists like Ye. V. Shorokhova and N. S. Mansurov, look upon this change as merely a bow in the direction of what is in vogue and consider the propositions of the neo-Freudians about the social conditioning of the human psyche as mere lip service which adds nothing to the understanding of the social nature of human personality.

The neo-Freudians maintained that the most acute and most difficult conflicts to be overcome are people's conflicts with themselves, with their own aspirations and with their over- or undervaluing of their personality. In Horney's (1939) words, it is specifically in the clash between self-idealization and self-realization that the sources of those inner conflicts that cannot be eliminated lie. While Horney's proposition concerned the role of the relationship between the "idealized self" and the "real self" for the formation of personality, Sullivan investigated

the influence of various early "personifications" (emotion-laden images of the self and others) on the formation of character. For Fromm, the determining factor in personality development is the striving to "escape from freedom," since, in his view, freedom imposes personal responsibility and renders the individual helpless in a world of struggle and competition.

Soviet psychologists agree with Hall and Lindzey (1957) that the neo-Freudians' acknowledgment of the significance of the social environment, their refutation of the all-encompassing role of the libido, and their striving to find new motive forces for behavior and personality development helped to create an intellectual climate conducive to the development of contemporary social-psychological investigations. Further, this new direction is one in which the unconscious, while significant, no longer occupies the leading role. Horney, in particular, emphasizes the significance of those goals the person sets for himself and by which he is consciously guided. In addition, the neo-Freudians do not consider man to be inherently aggressive and inclined toward destructiveness but see defects in the existing life conditions and flawed human relationships as the source of such impulses. On that basis, Fromm, Horney, and Sullivan are quite severe critics of their own society and even propose measures for changing it, although from the point of view of Soviet psychologists these proposals are usually naive and ineffectual.

In spite of these steps in the right direction, the neo-Freudians have not succeeded in creating a new, original conception of personality; they did not employ their new-found facts to overcome Freudianism. Instead, Freudianism proved to have such a strong influence on them that they subordinated their data to theories which in essence were close to Freud's. According to Soviet personality theorists, Hall and Lindzey are quite right when they say that the neo-Freudians, Adler, and Jung all stand on the shoulders of Freud.

The neo-Freudians did not succeed in "socializing" Freudianism, because Freudianism in essence cannot be socialized. Such a system cannot be reformed or reworked; it must either be developed further or repudiated. And if it is to be repudiated, exactly the opposite of the neo-Freudians efforts must be made. One must not repudiate particular conclusions of Freud's while preserving the overall conception; on the contrary, one must preserve the concrete findings and data he uncovered but incorporate them in a basically different theoretical conception. Central to such a theoretical conception, according to Soviet theorists, must be the dialectical materialist understanding of the psychic development of man and of his relationship to his social environment.

Soviet personality theorists generally view the personality theories of Carl Rogers and Kurt Lewin favorably because they pay greater attention to the effects of the social environment on the development of personality, and they study the personality from a holistic viewpoint. The Soviets credit Lewin with refuting the mechanistic concepts of associationism and demonstrating that the process of association takes place only when it is a necessary link in a series of activities directed toward the satisfaction of a person's needs. However, they criticize Lewin's general psychological conception of the personality as being far-fetched, artificial, and unproductive. They also feel that the "behaviorization" of Lewin after he emigrated to America caused him to lose a crucial direction, namely, the investigation of the internal psychological structure of the personality and of the role of the social environment in its formation. In Lewin's later work, both the personality and the environment were attenuated and replaced by the hypothetical reality embodied in his concept of the locomotion of the subject in his "life space", a concept which represents a mixing of the subject and the object, of the personality and the environment, in some kind of artificial conglomerate of quite abstract forces.

Soviet personality theorists also take favorable note of the work of Rudolph Dreikurs because of his practical interest in pedagogical work with children and his emphasis on the significance of the activity of the child himself in the process of child rearing. They applaud his view that the individual is not merely a reactive mechanism but an active participant in the resolution of the conflicts around and within him or her. However, they are critical of Dreikurs' concept that a basic motivation in the behavior of children, and a fundamental element of their experience, is the feeling of inferiority which inevitably arises in

the child because he lives "in a world of giants" and therefore feels weak and helpless. According to Dreikurs, this incites the child to compete with others in a struggle for a definite position in the group, and the Soviets note that the development of a dog-eat-dog society is therefore inevitable. While they agree that the child "as a social being, invariably strives to find his place in the peer collective, that he wants his merits acknowledged and he wants the approval of those around him" (Bozhovich, 1968, p. 106), they counterpropose that "correct" child rearing in a cooperatively oriented society enables the child to find his proper place among his peers by cooperation rather than competition.

Despite this criticism, Soviet personality theorists are appreciative of the contribution made by Adlerians such as Dreikurs in their studies of the affective life of the child and its connection with the influences of the environment. They believe these studies "have contributed incomparably more toward the solution of problems of child rearing than the numerous experimental investigations carried out in the spirit of traditional empirical psychology" (Bozhovich, 1968, p. 107).

Soviet personality theorists are extremely critical of existential personality theory. They state that contemporary existentialism, as a philosophical basis for psychology and psychiatry, represents a trend of militant idealism which counterposes the doctrine of existence and essence to the Marxist-Leninist doctrine of being and consciousness. They argue that existentialism is an extremist reactionary-idealist doctrine which considers that awareness of essence is primarily introspective self-knowledge. "This doctrine is in the sharpest contradiction to dialectical and historical materialism and does not contribute anything new to the question of the relationship between the external (i.e., appearance) and the genuine essence of phenomena" (Myasishchev, 1960/1963, pp. 410–411).

In conclusion, Soviet personality theorists maintain that "incorrect" Western theories have had a negative influence on the practice of childrearing. For example, American pedagogues claim that rearing children in institutions inevitably results in defective personality formation, because the child is deprived of satisfaction of its instinctual need for the mother. Soviet workers, on the contrary, find that children reared in well-run institutions are frequently more advanced, socially and intellectually, than peers brought up in their own families. They conclude, therefore, that the negative results observed by Western workers are due to inadequate institutional setups and *not* to frustration of the child's instinctual needs.

Prospect

Soviet psychology has undergone a number of vicissitudes, beginning with the acrimonious struggles for supremacy among the several schools of psychology in the twenties, continuing with the synthesizing contributions of Vygotskii and Rubinshtein in the thirties and forties, through the repressive era of Stalinism and to the relative "thaw" of the post-Stalin era. Throughout this period the development of Soviet personality theory has been hampered by two factors described by T. R. Payne (1968, pp. 168–169):

1. The construction of psychology on the basis of Marxism-Leninism has meant not merely adherence to its principles but even to the very words used by the Classics, when referring to psychological subjects.
2. The attempt to "Pavlovize" psychology, beginning in 1950, as a result of which Pavlov was raised "to the status of a 'Classic' whose ideas were quoted but never questioned.

Payne points out that these factors "acted as a brake on the normal development of psychological theory, . . . forced Soviet psychology into a theoretical strait-jacket, and produced a vast crop of purely exegetical problems."

Fortunately, there is increasing evidence that Soviet personality theorists are beginning to free themselves of rigid adherence to dogma. For example, F. V. Bassin, a leading Soviet personality theorist, is openly critical of Soviet "dogmatism in the social and natural sciences, [the] uncritical attitude toward scientific authorities, and the resort to meaningless quotations as a substitute for independent research." He observes that "Instead of solving scientific problems in an atmosphere of free discussion among competent specialists, the declaration of theoretical postulates became more or less the rule" (Cited in Wortis, 1962).

Bassin criticizes the overemphasis on Pavlov's teaching and the neglect of other approaches, such as cybernetics, information theory, and factor analysis:

> The theory of the higher nervous activity should not be considered as the only possible method for the study of the functions of the higher regions of the nervous system. Other approaches to the problem must also be used. . . . Both method and theory should be developed not only through a variety of disciplines, but also on the basis of diversified positions and from the point of view of diverse trends. (Cited in Wortis, 1962)

As part of this "thaw," there has been an increased interest in unconscious mental processes (Bassin, 1963, 1968, 1969) and in the affective aspects of personality. It is likely that the immediate future will see further development and refinement of the set theory of the Uznadze school, because it is seen by Soviet psychologists as a fruitful approach to the exploration of unconscious mental processes. In addition, it is likely that the studies of typology initiated by Pavlov and continued by Teplov and Nebylitsyn will be carried forward as part of the further development of personality theory based on precise laboratory observations and experimentation.

Both of these specifically Soviet approaches to personality theory will probably be enriched by a willingness to incorporate the wealth of experimental, clinical, and testable data being made available by the numerous Western personality theory approaches. There is evidence that this is already happening, but this does not mean that Soviet personality theorists will abandon their fundamental materialist philosophical position that there is only one material reality. They will continue to adhere to the ideas that man's consciousness, including his scientific findings and theories, are a reflection of the single material reality; that these scientific theories can and must progressively become more accurate reflections of this reality; and that only a dialectical materialist philosophy, explicitly stated and employed, can assure such a "correct" scientific understanding of reality.

However, Soviet personality theorists can be expected to recognize that the material reality they are investigating is extremely complex and cannot be understood by a simplistic, one-dimensional approach. As they give up their fear that the purity of their dialectical materialist orientation will be "contaminated" or "subverted" by utilizing the vast store of data and formulations Western personality theory has to offer, they will acknowledge that it is in keeping with the tenets of dialectical materialist philosophy to employ in the study of a very complex reality a multiplicity of approaches and tools, including those available in the West.

Annotated Bibliography

Bozhovich, L. I. *Personality and Its Formation in Childhood.* Moscow: Izdatel'stvo Prosveshcheniye, 1968.

Although this book has not yet been translated into English, it is included here because it is the most well-rounded and most readable presentation of current trends in Soviet personality theory. In the preface, the author writes, "This book contains a resumé of the many years of research on the problems of personality development which were carried on in the Laboratory of Upbringing of the Academy of Pedagogical Sciences of the U.S.S.R. These researches reveal the conditions and the moving forces of personality development in children. The book also includes a critical analysis of various viewpoints on personality and its investigation in Western and Soviet psychological literature."

Cole, M. & Maltzman, I. (Eds.). *A Handbook of Contemporary Soviet Psychology.* New York/London: Basic Books, 1969.

Although this book covers the entire field of Soviet psychology, not limiting itself to personality theory, it contains contributions by leading Soviet psychologists which provide an excellent cross-section and convey the flavor of contemporary Soviet psychological thinking. The editors' introduction analyzes this thinking and discusses Soviet developmental psychology.

Makarenko, A. S. *The Road to Life: An Epic of Education* (I. & T. Litvinov, trans.; 3 vols.). Moscow: Foreign Languages Publishing House, 1951. (Originally published, 1933.)

Presents a detailed account and theoretical analysis of Makarenko's work in rehabilitating delinquent youth at the Gorky Colony in the early 1920s.

Myasishchev, V. N. *Personality and Neuroses* (J. Wortis, Ed. and trans.). Washington D.C.: U.S. Department of Commerce, 1963.

To date this is the only Soviet book dealing specifically with the question of personality which has been translated into English. In this collection of articles published in various journals and books during the period 1935–60 are papers on the importance of personality in psychology and psychiatry,

the problem of psychological type in the light of Pavlov's teaching, and the pathogenesis of the neuroses.

Pavlov, I. P. *Lectures on Conditioned Reflexes.* Vol. 2, *Conditioned Reflexes and Psychiatry* (W. H. Gantt, Ed. and trans.). New York: International Publishers, 1941.

A selection of Pavlov's works, during the period 1930–36, when Pavlov's interest turned to applying his conditioned-reflex theory to the study of neuroses and psychoses in humans. The individual chapters are republished from various journals and include a description of experimental neuroses in animals, with an introduction by the translator and editor, who worked for many years in Pavlov's laboratory.

Payne, T. R. *S. L. Rubinshtein and the Philosophical Foundation of Soviet Psychology.* Dordrecht, Holland: D. Reidel Publishing Co., 1968.

A penetrating analysis of Rubinstein's attempt to reconcile the various schools of psychology in the Soviet Union which competed with one another during the 1920s and 1930s, and to produce a synthesis of dialectical materialist and Pavlovian doctrine. Payne's obvious admiration for Rubinstein's genius does not prevent him from objectively and critically noting gaps in Rubinstein's theoretical reasoning and unresolved philosophical problems facing Soviet psychology.

Uznadze, D. N. *The Psychology of Set.* (B. Haigh, trans.). New York: Consultants Bureau, 1966. (Originally published in the Georgian language in 1949.)

This book consists of two monographs which describe in detail the author's highly original experimental work, beginning in 1923. In the second monograph, considerable attention is devoted to the application of laboratory findings to personality theory and psychopathology.

Vygotskii, L. S. *Thought and Language* (E. Hanfmann & G. Vakar, Eds. and trans.). Cambridge, Mass.: M.I.T. Press, 1962.

Written by Vygotskii during his last illness, this book was published posthumously and represents an effort to sum up his life work. He describes his experimental work on the development of thought and its relationship to "internalized speech" and takes issue with many of Piaget's formulations in this area of child development.

References

*Andreev, B. V. Sleep therapy in the neuroses (B. Haigh, trans.). New York: Consultants Bureau, 1960.

*Bibliographic references preceded by an asterisk are available in English.

Banshchikov, V. M., Rokhlin, L. L., & Shorokhova, Ye. V. *Problems of personality* (Vols. 1 and 2). Moscow, 1969 and 1970.

Banshchikov, V. M., Rokhlin, L. L., & Shorokhova, Ye. V. *Personality.* Moscow, 1971.

Bassin, F. V. Consciousness and "the unconscious." In P. N. Fedoseyev (Ed.), *Philosophical problems of the physiology of higher nervous activity and psychology* (pp. 425–474). Moscow: Izdatel'stvo Akademii Nauk SSSR, 1963.

Bassin, F. V. *The problem of the unconscious.* Moscow: Izdatel'stvo Meditzina, 1968.

*Bassin, F. V. Consciousness and the unconscious. In M. Cole & I. Maltzman (Eds.), *A handbook of contemporary Soviet psychology* (pp. 399–420). New York/London: Basic Books, 1969.

*Bauer, R. A. *The new man in Soviet psychology.* Cambridge, Mass.: Harvard University Press, 1952.

Bekhterev, V. M. *Objective psychology.* St. Petersburg, 1907.

*Bekhterev, V. M. *General principles of human reflexology.* New York: Arno Press, 1973. (Originally published, 1917.)

Bekhterev, V. M. *Collective reflexology.* Petrograd, 1921.

Blonskii, P. P. Memory and thinking. In *Selected psychological works.* Moscow: Izdatel'stvo Prosveshcheniye, 1964. (Originally published, 1935).

Bodalev, A. A. On the development of self-exactingness in school-children. In *Papers of a conference on psychology.* Moscow: Izdatel'stvo APN RSFSR, 1957.

Boldyrev, N. I. *The program of upbringing in the school.* Moscow; Izdatel'stvo APN RSFSR, 1960.

Boryagin, G. I. The psychological views of M. V. Lomonosov. In M. V. Sokolov (Ed.), *Essays on the history of Russian psychology* (pp. 102–164). Moscow: Moscow University Press, 1957.

Bozhovich, L. I. *Personality and its formation in childhood.* Moscow: Izdatel'stvo Prosveshcheniye, 1968.

*Brackbill, Y. Research and clinical work with children. In R. A. Bauer (Ed.), *Some views on Soviet psychology* (pp. 99–164). Washington D.C.: American Psychological Association, 1962.

*Bronfenbrenner, U. *Two worlds of childhood: U.S. and U.S.S.R.* New York: Russell Sage Foundation, 1970.

Bykhovskii, B. On the methodological foundations of Freud's theory. *Pod Znamenem Marksizma,* 11/12: 158–177, 1923.

Chelpanov, G. I. *Introduction to experimental psychology.* Moscow: Kushnerev, 1915.

*Cole, M., & Maltzman, I. (Eds.). *A handbook of contemporary Soviet psychology.* New York/London: Basic Books, 1969.

Dreikurs, R. & Soltz, V. *Children: the challenge.* New York: Durell, Sloan & Pearce, 1964.

Dyad'kovskii, I. Ye. *Symptomatology.* Moscow: 1954. (Originally published, 1830.)

Editorial: A new phase: On the results of the Second All-Union Conference of Marxist-Leninist Research Institutes. *Pod Znamenem Marksizma,* 1929, *5,* 1–5.

*El'konin, D. B. Some results of the study of the psychological development of preschool-age children. In M. Cole & I. Maltzman, (Eds.), *A handbook of contemporary Soviet psychology* (pp. 163–208). New York/London: Basic Books, 1969.

Figurin, N. L., & Denisova, M. P. *Developmental stages of children from birth to one year.* Moscow: Medgiz, 1949.

Filomafitskii, A. M. *Physiology* (Vol. 1). Moscow, 1836. *Great Soviet encyclopedia* (2nd ed.). Moscow: Aktsionernoye Obshchestvo "Sovietskaya entsiklopediya," 1949.

*Hall, C. S., & Lindzey, G. *Theories of personality* (2nd ed.). New York: Wiley, 1970. (Originally published, 1957.)

*Horney, K. *New ways in psychoanalysis.* New York: W. W. Norton & Co., 1939.

Ivashchenko, F. I. *Development of self-confidence in poorly progressing school-children.* Author's abstract of Kandidat dissertation. Moscow, 1952.

Kon, I. S. *Sociology of personality.* Moscow: Izdatel'stvo Politicheskoi Literaturi, 1967. (German translation, Berlin: Akademie Verlag, 1971).

Kornilov, K. N. *A theory of human reactions from the psychological point of view (reactology).* Moscow: Gosudarstvennoye Izd., 1921.

Kornilov, K. N. *Textbook of psychology from the standpoint of dialectical materialism.* Moscow: Gosudarstvennoye Izd.,1926.

Kovalev, A. G. *The role of the classroom teacher in the study of the child's personality.* Simferopol', Crimea: Krimizdat, 1949.

Kovalev, A. G. *Psychology of personality* (2nd ed.). Moscow: Izdatel'stvo Prosveshcheniye, 1965.

Kovalev, A. G., & Myasishchev, V. M. *Psychological features of man.* Vol. 1, *Character.* Leningrad: Izdatel'stvo Leningradskovo Universiteta, 1957.

* Krutetskii, V. A. Problem of character in Soviet psychology. In B. G. Ananiev (Ed.), *Psychological science in the U.S.S.R.* (Vol. 2, pp. 63–102). Washington, D.C.: U.S. Government Printing Office, 1962.

Lange, N. N. *Psychological investigations: The law of perception; The theory of voluntary attention.* Odessa, 1893.

Lebedinskii, M. S. *Essays on psychotherapy* (2nd ed.). Moscow: Meditzina Publishing House, 1971.

Lebedinskii, M. S., & Myasishchev, V. N. *Introduction to medical psychology.* Leningrad: Izdatel'stvo meditsina, 1966.

Lechtreman-Abramovich, R. Ya. *Stages of development of play and activity with objects in early childhood.* Moscow: Medgiz, 1949.

Lenin, V. I. *On Communist morality* (2nd ed.). Moscow: Gospolitizdat, 1963.

Leontiev, A. N. Psychic development of the preschool child. In *Problems of the psychology of the preschool child.* Moscow/Leningrad: Izdatel'stvo APN RSFSR, 1948.

Lomov, B. F. *Man and technology. Studies in engi-*

neering psychology (2nd ed.). Moscow: Izd. Sovietskoye Radio, 1966.

*Luria, A. R. An objective approach to the study of the abnormal child. *American Journal of Orthopsychiatry*, 1961, *1*, 1–16.

*Luria, A. R. Study of brain affections and the restoration of damaged functions. In B. G. Ananiev (Ed.), *Psychological science in the U. S. S. R.* (Vol. 2, pp. 611–656). Washington, D.C.: U. S. Government Printing Office, 1962.

*Luria, A. R. The neuropsychological study of brain lesions and restoration of damaged brain functions. In M. Cole & I. Maltzman (Eds.), *A handbook of contemporary Soviet psychology* (pp. 277–301). New York/London: Basic Books, 1969.

Lyalikov, D. N. Alfred Adler. In the *Great Soviet encyclopedia* (3rd ed.). Moscow: Aktsionernoye Obshchestvo "Sovietskaya entsiklopediya," 1970.

*Makarenko, A. S. *The road to life—an epic of education* (I. & T. Litvinov, trans.; 3 vols.). Moscow: Foreign Languages Publishing House, 1951. (Originally published, 1933–1935.)

*Makarenko, A. S. *The collective family: A handbook for Russian parents* (R. Daglish, trans.). Garden City, N.Y.: Doubleday, 1967. (Originally published, 1937.)

*Murphy, G., & Kovach, J. K. *Historical introduction to modern psychology* (3rd ed.). New York: Harcourt Brace Jovanovich, 1972.

Myasishchev, V. N. Some problems of the theory of psychotherapy. In M. S. Lebedinskii (Ed.), *Problems of psychotherapy*. Moscow: Medgiz, 1958.

*Myasishchev, V. N. *Personality and Neuroses* (J. Wortis, Ed. and trans.). Washington, D.C.: U. S. Department of Commerce, Joint Publications Research Service, 1963. (Originally published, 1960.)

Myasishchev, V. N. The nature of neuroses and the basic problems of combating them. In O. Janota & E. Wolf (Eds.), *Neuroses* (I Congressus psychiatricus bohemoslovenicus cum participatione internationali, 1959, pp. 41–45). Prague: Statni Zdravotnicke nakladatelstvi, 1961.

Myasishchev, V. N. Psychotherapy as a system of techniques for influencing the psyche of man for the purpose of restoring health. In B. D. Karvasarskii (Ed.), *Psychotherapy in nervous and mental illness* (pp. 7–20). Leningrad: Bekhterev Psychoneurological Research Institute, 1973.

Myasishchev, V. N. The problem of personality in psychology and medicine. In M. M. Kabanov and I. M. Tonkonogii (Eds.), *Current problems of medical psychology* (pp. 5–25). Leningrad: V. M. Bekhterev Psychoneurological Research Institute, 1974.

Myasishchev, V. N., Bespal'ko, I. G., & Gilyasheva, I. N. Methods of personality assessment abroad. In V. N. Myasishchev & B. D. Karvasarskii, (Eds.), *Assessment of personality in the clinic and in extreme conditions* (pp. 69–96). Leningrad: Bekhterev Psychoneurological Research Institute, 1969.

*Pavlov, I. P. *Autobiography*. In *Selected Works* (pp. 41–44). Moscow: Foreign Languages Publishing House, 1955. (Originally published, 1904.)

*Pavlov, I. P. *Lectures on conditioned reflexes, Vol. 2: Conditioned reflexes and psychiatry* (W. H. Gantt, Ed. and trans.). New York: International Publishers, 1941.

*Payne, T. R. *S. L. Rubinshtein and the philosophical foundations of Soviet psychology*. Dordrecht, Holland: D. Reidel Publishing Co., 1968.

Peiper, A. *Specificities of the activity of the child's brain*. Leningrad: Medgiz, 1962.

Petrovskii, A. V. *History of Soviet psychology: The development of foundations of the psychological science*. Moscow: Izd. Prosveshcheniye, 1967.

Prokina, N. F. Conditions of formation of organized behavior while implementing the regime of a boarding school. In *Problems of the psychology of personality of school children*. Moscow: Izdatel'stvo A. P. N., R. S. F. S. R., 1961.

Reisner, M. Freud and his school on religion. *Pechat' i Revolyutsiya*, 1924, *1*, 40–60 and 1924, *1*, 81–106.

Reisner, M. *Problems of social psychology*. Moscow: Burevestnik, 1925.

*Resolution of the Central Committee of the Communist Party on pedological distortions in the commissariats of education, July 4, 1936. In J. Wortis, *Soviet Psychiatry* (pp. 242–245). Baltimore: Williams & Wilkins, 1950.

Rosengart-Pupko, G. L. *Speech and development of perception in early childhood*. Moscow: Izdatel'stvo A.M.N. S.S.S.R., 1948.

Rubinshtein, S. L. Problems of psychology in the works of Karl Marx. *Psikhofiziologiya truda i psikhotekhnika*, 1934, *1*, 3–20.

Rubinshtein, S. L. *Fundamentals of general psychology*. Berlin: Volk & Wissen, 1959. (Originally published, 1935.)

Rubinshtein, S. L. *Foundations of general psychology* (2nd ed.). Moscow: Uchpedgiz, 1946. (Originally published, 1940.)

*Rubinshtein, S. L. Questions of psychological theory. In B. Simon (Ed.), *Psychology in the Soviet Union* (pp. 264–278). London: Routledge & Kegan Paul, 1957.

*Sechenov, I. M. *Reflexes of the brain*. Cambridge, Mass.: M.I.T. Press, 1965. (Originally published, 1863.)

*Sechenov, I. M. *Biographical sketch and essays*. New York: Arno Press, 1973. (Originally published, 1904.)

Shchelovanov, I. M. *Crèches and children's homes: Problems of upbringing* (4th ed.). Moscow: Medgiz, 1960.

Shorokhova, Ye. V. *Contemporary psychology in the capitalist countries*. Moscow: Izdatel'stvo Akademii Nauk S.S.S.R., 1963.

Shumilin, Ye. A. Russian precursors of I. M. Sechenov. In M. V. Sokolov (Ed.), *Essays on the history of Russian psychology* (pp. 272–367). Moscow: Moscow University Press, 1957.

*Simon, B. (Ed.). *Psychology in the Soviet Union*. London: Routledge & Kegan Paul, 1957.

Sudakov, N. I. *Psychological characteristics of persistence displayed by senior students*. Author's abstract of Kandidat dissertation. Moscow, 1950.

Svyadoshch, A. M. *The neuroses and their treatment.* Moscow: Medgiz, 1959.

Tugarinov, V. P. *Personality and society.* Moscow: Izdatel'stvo Mysl', 1965.

*Uznadze, D. N. *The psychology of set* (B. Haigh, trans.). New York: Consultants Bureau, 1966. (Originally published in the Georgian language in 1949.)

*Vygotskii, L. S. *Thought and language* (E. Hanfmann & G. Vakar, Eds. and trans.). Cambridge, Mass.: M.I.T. Press, 1962. (Originally published, 1934.)

Vygotskii, L. S. *Diagnosis and pedological clinical considerations of emotional problems of childhood.* Moscow: Izd. Eksperimental'noi Defectologii In-ta im. M. S. Epshteina, 1936.

Watson, J. B. Behaviorism. In O. Ya. Schmidt et al. (Eds.), *Great Soviet Encyclopedia* (Vol. 6, pp. 434–443). Moscow: Aktsionernoye Obshchestvo "Sovietskaya Entsiklopediya," 1927.

*Wortis, J. *Soviet Psychiatry.* Baltimore: Williams & Wilkins, 1950.

*Wortis, J. A "thaw" in Soviet psychiatry? In *American Journal of Psychiatry,* 1962, *119,* 586.

Zaporozhetz, A. V. Development of logical thought in the preschool child. In *Problems of the psychology of the preschool child.* Moscow/Leningrad: Izdatel'stvo APN RSFSR, 1948.

Zaporozhetz, A. V., & El'konin, D. B. (Eds.), *Psychology of preschool children: The development of cognitive processes.* Moscow: Izdatel'stvo Prosveshcheniye, 1964.

Zeigarnik, B. V. The tasks of psychopathology. In *Problems of experimental pathopsychology.* Moscow: Gos. Nauch. Issled. In-t. Psikhiatrii, 1965.

*Zeigarnik, B. V., & Rubinshtein, S. Ya. Experimental-psychological laboratories in psychiatric clinics in the Soviet Union. In B. G. Ananiev (Ed.), *Psychological science in the U.S.S.R.* (Vol. 2, pp. 657–690). Washington, D.C.: U.S. Government Printing Office, 1962.

*Ziferstein, I. Direct observations of psychotherapy in the U.S.S.R. In *Sixth International Congress of Psychotherapy, London, 1964: Selected lectures* (pp. 150–160). Basel/New York: S. Karger, 1965.

*Ziferstein, I. The Soviet psychiatrist: His relationship to his patients and to his society. *American Journal of Psychiatry,* 1966, *123,* 440–446.

*Ziferstein, I. Group psychotherapy in the Soviet Union. *American Journal of Psychiatry,* 1972, *129,* 595–599.

CHAPTER 13

Asian Personality Theory

Paul B. Pedersen

Asian personality theory includes aspects of Asian religion, philosophy, and social theory which explain human behavior and provide systems that support or justify Asian styles or modes of behavior as more acceptable than others. As contrasted with Western psychology, Asian psychology borrows readily from religions, such as Hinduism, Buddhism, Confucianism, Taoism, and Zen. While each region of Asia developed its own original variation, the spread of religious, philosophical, and psychological theory moved from India to China and from China to Japan in the last 2,000 years. Asian psychology has succeeded in adapting outside influences in an eclectic mode combining both Asian and Western ideas. Western psychology, however, has largely ignored Asian theories of human behavior as being unsubstantiated by scientific validity, although some aspects have recently attracted popular interest.

The assumptions underlying Asian psychological thought relate to the basic philosophical assumptions of human existence and the concept of self. There is much less emphasis on individualism and more on corporate identity in the various Asian psychologies, but there is also more emphasis on a positive interpretation of their interdependencies and dependence upon one another. The family plays a significant role in shaping personality in Asian cultures; clearly defined roles provide models of institutionalized social behavior in adult relationships.

YIN and YANG

Attempts to measure Asian personality have depended on using Western psychometric methods and assumptions in attempts to bend Asian data according to Western constructs. Extensive testing of Asian populations has produced few conclusive results. Indigenous modes of psychotherapy are being rediscovered in Asian systems of mental health care. *Measured* validity, however, is unavailable for most Asian theories of psychology.

There are significant differences in the assumptions of Asian and Western psychologies. Western theories, such as psychoanalysis, rational-emotive therapy, reality therapy, Gestalt therapy, Rogerian theory, and existential psychology, stress the individual, achievement motivation, rationally defined evidence, the scientific method, and direct self-disclosure. Asian theories, in contrast, emphasize corporate welfare, experiential evidence, intuitive logic, religiophilosophical methods, and subtle indirection in personal relationships. Extreme care should be used in comparing Asian and Western theories of psychology.

Increased interest in Asia is likely to influence Western psychological theory, incorporating concepts of Asian psychology in the interpretation of human behavior. And as Asian psychological theories become more popular in Asia, they are providing a basis for regional identities.

Introduction

It is impossible to give an adequate one-chapter representation of Asian thought relative to what Westerners call "personality" or to summarize Asian ideas about how the organism becomes and remains human. Nevertheless, the world's Asian majority has its own explanation of human behavior, and all psychologists should have some acquaintance with Asian theories of personality. This chapter thus gives non-Asians a brief introduction to Asian alternatives in psychological thought about personality.

Research on Oriental cultures has generally been of two different types: explanations of Asian phenomena using Western theoretical constructs, or "uniquely" Asian phenomena viewed in comparison to Western norms. In this chapter we will identify ways in which *individualistic* Western assumptions underlying the construct *personality* differ from Eastern assumptions. For example, in Asian cultures the basic structure of personality is *relational,* focused on the space *between* individuals, rather than *individualistic,* as is the implicit assumption in Western thought about personality.

Human fulfillment psychologies in Asia predate Western culture. Though the psychologies of Asia are largely philosophical, political, or religious, their function contains insights appropriate to psychological phenomena. The emphasis in Oriental systems is mainly on the structure of family, clan, class, and state through which individuals relate to one another.

The task of making Asian psychology indigenous has been particularly difficult for Western-trained Asian psychologists who are writing about their own cultures and attempt to adapt, amend, or explain the categories and rationale of non-Western cultures in terms of Western theories of psychology. In this regard, psychology is perhaps the most culturebound of the traditional disciplines (Surya, 1969; Pedersen, 1976).

This does not mean that the interface of culture and personality has been neglected by social scientists. Kroeber and Kluckhohn (1952) listed 150 different definitions of culture, while Allport (1937) provided 50 definitions of personality, suggesting that there are at least 7,500 ways of considering the relationship of culture and personality. Price-Williams (1968) divided all personality theories into two groups: the individualistic, wherein the individual shapes culture; and the culturological, whereby the culture shapes individuals.

In reviewing the field of culture and personality, Singer (1961) identified three major problem areas: the relation of culture to (1) human nature, (2) the typical personality, and (3) individual personalities. While the study of culture and personality has typically been located in departments of anthropology rather than psychology, recent publications on cross-cultural psychology have broadened the cultural scope of psychology.

The separation of Asian and Western, Oriental and Occidental cultures sometimes obscures more than it illuminates. Nakamura (1964) discounts various attempts to identify cultural traits that contrast East and West. He claims the common features of one hemisphere are either partly or imperfectly understood in the other hemisphere or were conspicuous in a particular country at a particular time and then generalized to include the whole hemisphere. Thus, he says, "we must acknowledge the fact that there exists no single Eastern feature but rather that there exist diverse ways of thinking in East Asia characteristic of certain peoples but not of the whole of East Asia" (p. 19). The whole idea of national character is in some disrepute among social scientists, as are research findings suggesting innate racial differences in personality. There is, however, empirical evidence of differences in suicide rate, character, mental illness, alcoholism, calorie intake, and other phenomena in different cultures (Lynn, 1971). There is indeed a unique, special emphasis, evolved for whatever reason, in particular cultures, such as India's emphasis on the spiritual, China's emphasis on the social, and Western emphasis on the rational aspects of human behavior. At the same time, we must realize that Asia includes a wide range of distinctive cultures, and this precludes accurate generalizations about the thinking of Orientals.

This chapter can at best only hope to stimulate Western students toward greater interest in Asian ways of thinking. Examples of Asian thought are arbitrarily chosen and are in no way comprehensive enough to cover the many great traditions of India, China, and Japan, not to mention the abundance of less well-known systems in other parts of Asia.

History

It is difficult to untangle the concept of personality from the complicated histories of Asian cultures, religions, and philosophies without oversimplifying each unique tradition or artificially imposing non-Asian categories of thought. India, Japan, and China each perceive "history" quite differently within their own traditions—from emphasizing what happened in the past in Indian mythologies, to the detailed, factual chronologies of China. After surveying the separate traditions, the cultural systems of India, China, and Japan will be contrasted with one another and with Western notions of psychology, emphasizing similarities and differences.

Precursors

Psychological explanation is not a Western invention. Ancient India had developed a variety of personality theories, originally based on the *gunas* or attributes of the mind, dating back to Vedic literature of about 800–500 B. C. Each succeeding religiophilosophical system in India modified views of personality in its own way, generally emphasizing practical aspects of organizing, classifying, and understanding persons in relation to the family, society, and abstract values.

These Indian systems were developed into specific ways of thinking through the classical Hindu literature of the Rg-Veda, the Upanishads, Yoga, and the Bhagavad-Gita. The revolutionary teachings of Gotama Buddha, born in 563 B. C., spread throughout Asia to China and Japan, carrying, modifying, and adapting original ideas of the Aryans who invaded India between 1000 and 2000 B. C.

From Aryan philosophy there is the notion of mind, soul, or spirit rooted in the changeless reality of an inner self or *atman*, considered to be the core of reality both for individuals and for a Cosmic Unity. Murphy and Murphy (1968) observe: "From this philosophy of the *atman* develops a conception of purity, changeless nobility, freedom from deception, freedom from passion, deceit, and delusion which reappears in almost all the forms of Indian philosophy" (p. 6). The emphasis in Oriental thought, however, is not on the *atman* as an individual entity or basic unit but rather on the principle of an Absolute which approximates the Western notion of God.

Beginnings

India. The development of psychological concepts in India went through the period of magic, in which people tried to control nature by recourse to mysticism, the period of gods, as in Hinduism, in which people tried to understand nature; and the period of man, as in Buddhism, in which inner harmony and psychic consciousness became the key to freedom (Govinda, 1961). Awareness of suffering is a constant theme of Indian psychology whereby the wise person escapes enslavement to selfishness by realizing the true nature of the universe.

Four basic concepts are needed to understand Indian psychology:

1. *Dharma.* Codes and rules which define goodness, maturity, and appropriateness of behavior.
2. *Karma.* The propulsion from previous incarnations, present deeds, and future destiny (which has been wrongly characterized as "fatalism").
3. *Maya.* The *illusion* of real knowledge and causes (which Westerners might describe as "reality").
4. *Atman.* The person, not as an individual and separate "self" but as part of an ultimate Cosmic Unity or Absolute.

These concepts were taught in the legends of the *Ramayana* and the *Mahabharata* and in the religious literature of the Upanishads and Bhagavad-Gita and are concerned with the struggle between good and evil.

The Upanishads ask the question "Who am I?" in a variety of contexts. The person is variously described as the one who sees, who speaks, who discriminates; the ear of the ear, mind of the mind, agency for memory and volition, austerity, and self-control. The Upanishads emphasize the *connection* between an individual and the Cosmic Absolute rather than taking any aspect separately.

Yoga likewise discriminated between self and the time-defined context in which self exists. The person was considered to exist outside the sphere represented by pure self. Undifferentiated consciousness separated self as "knower" from the object "known" which contaminated pure self. The separation of individual self—serene and changeless—from thought process is evident in disciplined self-training through the system of *Raja-yoga* (royal yoga) and the physiological discipline of *Hatha-yoga* (yoga of force), concerned with cultivating extraordinary bodily control (Murphy & Murphy, 1968).

The Bhagavad Gita presented three classifications of goal orientation and modes of existence (*gunas*) for persons: the *Tamas, Rajas,* and *Sattwa* systems. The *Tamas* and *Rajas* emphasized self-diminuation, while the *Sattwa* emphasized self-enhancement and self-realization. "Individuals abiding in *Tamas* prefer to lead an easygoing life. They are generally sluggish and lethargic and totally indifferent to any constructive action which calls for a rigorous discipline in life" (Beg, 1970, p. 13). The state of *Rajas* more clearly defined goals of power and the accumulation of wealth, perceiving others as objects for exploitation. Both *Tamas* and *Rajas* emphasize a closed system, depriving human relationships of harmony, happiness, and dignity. *Sattwa* stressed the goal of cosmic awareness, ecstacy, bliss, altruism, unitive consciousness, and spiritual enlightenment, emphasizing the value of knowledge, altruism, and nonattachment. The *Sattwa* emancipated human mind and body from bondage of passions, pride, anxiety, and the wasteful action of biological needs. There was an emphasis on human and transcendental values, ethical behavior, and "self-actualization" beyond the physical or psychological realities of life in a "transpersonal" psychology of personality.

Buddhism emphasized the four noble truths and the eightfold path. The four noble truths were: (1) all life is subject to suffering, (2) desire to live is the cause of repeated existences, (3) only the annihilation of desire gives release from suffering, and (4) the way of escape is through the eightfold path. The eightfold path was: right belief, right thought, right speech, right action, right livelihood, right effort, right mindfulness, and right concentration to escape from desire. These ideas spread throughout Asia to influence the understanding of personality in a variety of settings (Sangsingkeo, 1969).

China. When Buddhism was imported to China around the 1st century B.C., it was modified to emphasize the social responsibility of Buddha's ethical teaching. The Chinese have been fairly characterized as valuing commonsense and utilitarian ways of thinking. Even their philosophical teachings were based on practical subjects and included everyday examples of morality, politics, and a lifestyle that would result in successful living:

> Many of the teachings of Taoism dwell on the art of self-protection, on the method of attaining success, or on the right way of governing. Confucianism, which occupied the highest position in Chinese thought, is also largely a system of ethics for the governing class and a set of precepts for governing the people. (Nakamura, 1964, p. 234)

The indigenous Chinese view of personality developed from the teachings of Confucius (551–479 B.C.), emphasizing aspects of "characterological theory" (Hiniker, 1969). The basic aspects of this view emphasize the notions of face, filial piety, and proper conduct. The notion of face brings out an individual's felt moral worth, assessed according to his loyalty to his group rather than according to universal principles, with social deviance controlled more by public shaming than private guilt. Filial piety describes a compliant and submissive posture toward authority in a personalistic rather than legalistic understanding of human behavior. Proper conduct (*Li*) defined the duty of persons and the necessity of observing proper forms of conduct for each social situation. These truths were described in four books: *Confucian Analects,* the *Book of Mencius,* the *Great Learning,* and the *Doctrine of the Mean.* The task of Chinese philosophy is to describe the "way" (*Tao*) to perfection of the personality along practical lines, synthesizing Confucian this-worldliness and Taoist other-worldliness to achieve sageness within and kingliness without. Chinese philosophy can be described according to five basic social relationships between (1) sovereign and subject, (2) father and son, (3) elder and younger brother, (4) husband and wife, and (5) friend with friend. Each contrasting layer of Chinese philosophy, from early Confucianism to contemporary Maoism, has emphasized variants of these basic themes.

Japan. The Japanese way of thought was strongly influenced by both India and China, particularly in the period before the Meiji Restoration in 1868. Evidence of these influences is apparent both in the language and philosophies of the Japanese culture. Chinese writings and thought were introduced in the sixth century, with particular emphasis on Confucianism and Buddhism. The Japanese selectively adapted these viewpoints to develop their own unique way of thinking, emphasizing what Nakamura (1964) calls the limited social nexus of the Japanese people themselves.

Current status

Most studies of culture and personality have been written by anthropologists, who generally have taken a relativist position in classifying and categorizing psychological phenomena, identifying deviations as culturally unique, allowing multiple notions of acceptable behaviors to coexist with one another, and examining each culture as a separate configuration (Singer, 1961; Hsu, 1961, 1972; Child, 1968; Caudill & Lin, 1969; LeVine, 1974). Psychologists, on the other hand, have tended to link social characteristics and psychological phenomena with a minimum of attention to intercultural maps of differentiated cultural values. The number of psychologists writing on cultural difference has increased remarkably recently (Triandis, Malpass, & Davidson, 1973; Brislin, Bochner, & Lonner, 1975; Price-Williams, 1969; Pedersen, Lonner & Draguns, 1976).

Currently, there is a growing interest in the ideas and practices of the Orient. For understanding Oriental thought, Nakamura (1964) and Murphy and Murphy (1968) are probably the best books to start with. Nakamura provides a comprehensive description of Asian thought from an Asian point of view, while Murphy and Murphy give a good introduction to Asian psychology from a Western viewpoint, with extensive references to classical Asian literature. The series of books on mental health in Asia and the Pacific (Caudill & Lin, 1969; W. Lebra, 1972, 1974) gives the most comprehensive survey of authorities on Asian psychology. *The Journal of Cross Cultural Psychology* and the Japanese publication *Psychologia* are the two best sources for current articles.

Popular literature on transcendental meditation (TM) has developed psychological insights from Asian religions. The popularity of TM in the United States starting in the 1960s suggest that these insights are particularly attractive today to the Occidental world. While there is the quality of a fad in the rapid popularity of TM, nevertheless it conveys some basic viewpoints of Asian psychology which are rooted in centuries of tradition. Yoga likewise appears to be increasing in popularity in the West as a system of meditation and as a discipline of exercise. The practice of Zen meditation has also gained importance. Increased attention to Asian religions in the West seems to be introducing a new era wherein Asian religion, philosophy, and culture will provide alternative ethical, philosophical, scientific, and psychological viewpoints in Western cultures.

Zen Buddhism can be divided into *Bompu, Gedo, Soojo, Daijo,* and *Saijojo,* each offering a meditative technique aimed at a different level of consciousness. They are united in the Zen belief that if a person is "emancipated from the dualistic bondage of subjectivity and objectivity, of mind and body . . . he can be . . . awakened to his . . . true self" (Mills & Campbell, 1974, p. 192). This condition is intended to lead to a condition of enlightenment or *Satori,* a state in which the person is completely tuned to the reality outside and inside of himself, in which he is fully aware of reality and fully grasps it.

Yoga has been divided into the subsystems of *Mantra, Laya, Bhakti, Raja* and *Hatha* yoga. Each system aims toward meditative techniques with eyes closed and employs a repeated sound (*mantra*) to help the person meditating achieve *Samadhi,* or knowledge of the absolute, by becoming oblivious of external or internal sensory stimuli.

Yoga consists of meditation practices and physical techniques performed in a quiet environment, with the participant typically seated in the "lotus" position and concentrating on the repetition of a special mantra. Transcendental meditation grew out of Yoga as taught by the contemporary Maharishi Mahesh Yogi, which in turn grew out of the Vedic tradition in India. The technique requires no physical or mental control and can be accomplished in brief (15–20-minute) sessions daily. Zen resembles Yoga in its objectives, although the two modes are significantly different. The emphasis of this technique is on five areas of body control: (l) muscle tension; (2) blood flow and blood pressure; (3) heart rate (EKG); (4) body temperature; and (5) brain waves (EEG) (Stewart, 1974).

These systems apparently demonstrated their effectiveness not only according to the subjective criteria of their religiophilosophical traditions but also through the hard data provided by scientific experimentation.

Biofeedback techniques, currently employed with sophisticated electronic equipment, also have developed from Asian techniques of psychology. They have been used to treat muscle tension problems, to control heart rate and blood pressure, and to solve sexual problems as well as a variety of other difficulties, such as control of epilepsy. In addition, they are cited as aiding creativity, psychic integration, and improved learning and problem-solving abilities, according to Jacobson's (1974) and Brown's (1974) review of the literature. Kanellakos (1973) cites a number of supportive studies in a bibliography on TM.

The literature on "transpersonal psychologies" (Tart, 1975) is exploring a range of philosophical assumptions behind Western and non-Western psychologies previously considered to be outside the mainstream of modern psychology, in an attempt to enlarge the scope of psychology beyond its culturally narrow focus.

Similar Theories

This section views the East-West differences in personality theory in broader contexts. The "Occident" is supposed to be materialistic, analytic, and objective, while the "Orient" is supposed to be spiritual, introverted, and synthetic. Nakamura (1964), who objects to this simplification, nevertheless recognizes that East and West do have certain differences, as well as internal similarities. Data-supported stereotypes provide some justification for the notion of less emphasis by Asians on the normal Western criteria for logical rules to define reality. But Asian thought is by no means irrational. It contains in linguistic organization, for example, a logical consistency as rigorous as any Western culture. Modal stereotypes of Asian thought ignore the complex variations that are at least as important for Asian as they are for Western ways of thinking. Neither all Asians nor all Westerners think alike.

A major difference between the East and the West is supposed to be attitudes towards religion. However, we note an interesting paradox. The supposedly more pragmatic West developed the concepts of heaven and hell and a whole pantheon of gods and near gods, saints and angels, while the supposedly more spiritualistic East has not. The Chinese, for example, have no concept of god in the Western sense.

Westerners are supposed to be more rational than Easterners, but if rationality means practicability, the Chinese may be the most rational and practical of all people in terms of the strictly nonrational religious beliefs of the West. Asians are supposed to be more passive and Westerners more dynamic; if true in the past, this is certainly untrue now. The Indian philosopher Rabindranoth Tagore, who visited China in 1924, preached the superiority of Eastern spirituality over Western materialism. He was attacked by his audience as a living symbol of the futile passivity of Eastern religions that had reduced India to colonial and China to semicolonial status (Nakamura, 1964, p. 243). The predilection for tolerance and mutual concession in Asian thought is often mistaken for passivity, however. Asians are mistakenly supposed to be escapist and indifferent toward social or political action and to place more emphasis on contemplating nature or man in meditation, while Westerners are supposedly more interested in conquering nature. In view of contemporary China and Japan's rapid political, industrial, and social development, this stereotype is hardly to be taken seriously any longer.

Asian systems are mystical and practical at the same time. Each major Oriental religious system incorporates a psychological aspect of defining ethical practices by speculating on how the mind works and how it can be freed of delusion and self-imposed misery. Asians have been described as more pessimistic in contrast to the Westerner's gusty and lusty belief in the possibility that life is good and not bad or painful. Asian psychologies have attempted to find a sense of goodness in the timeless and limitless universe and in the self freed of personal striving. "The goal is freedom from individual frustration and suffering, a process possible only when the battle of self against non-self is given up and cosmic order reigns within as it does without" (Murphy & Murphy, 1968, p. 228).

Contrasts between Asian and Western psychology oversimplify both systems and may betray the unwary reader. We could easily neglect the wide range of alternative points of view within each system and the extent to which the basic assumptions are so totally different that apparent similarities are almost wholly a function of random chance. Western methods of defining psychology seek evidence to verify external experience in objective, linear categories. Asian alternatives suggest that we look inward, applying our discipline and training to better understand subjective reality in a more philosophical or even religious mode: "The Oriental psychologist carries his laboratory within him" (Murphy & Murphy, 1968, p. 230).

Assertions

Some unique Asian points of view about personality development and maintenance will emerge as we examine assertions which differ significantly from Western points of view. Many of these assertions will challenge the basic assumptions of personality theory as we know it, substituting concepts we have normally relegated to the areas of philosophy or religion. The Asian psychologies do not fit easily into Western categories, sometimes providing answers to questions not being asked by Western psychologists. The first three assertions describe basic assumptions which define reality and the goals of personality development in Indian and Chinese society. The next three describe assumptions in parent-child relationships, and the final seven deal with maintenance strategies.

Development

In examining the development of personality, it is appropriate first to establish the nature of individuality itself. The very construct of *personality* assumes a particular view of the individual as a basic unit in the structure of psychology. Some examples from Indian, Chinese, and Japanese thought clearly contrast with that understanding by Western psychologists.

1. A NEWBORN INFANT, AS A RESULT OF ITS PREVIOUS LIVES, HAS CERTAIN PERSONALITY AND CHARACTER TRAITS WHICH, AFTER HIS PRESENT LIFE, ARE TRANSMITTED TO ITS NEXT EXISTENCE.

This reincarnation assertion about the trans-

migration of souls raises obvious difficulties for the definition of personality. If you were someone else and are to become someone else again, then it would seem unreasonable, according to any ordinary logic, for you to remain yourself. To understand this basic Hindu assertion it is necessary to recognize the way Indian thought has developed the concept of the individual. We think of an individual starting his personality at birth and ending it at death. The Hindu concept is that the personality extends before the birth and after the death of a particular individual, a process of identity which extends over many generations. The Sanskrit equivalent of "individual" is *vyakti*. However, the concept was defined as a transitional state. To the extent that the individual is a self, it has independent reality. The ultimate end of spiritual freedom guides that individual's behavior in a particular way. To the extent that the self is embodied in the particular body as a product of nature, with a capacity to produce offspring, there is an indissoluble bond between the embodied individual and all other individuals. An individual caught in an otherwise hopeless web of misery can always hope for a better world after rebirth which gives him a degree of hope for the future. Contrariwise, there is the possibility that an individual will be reincarnated into a more painful existence. There is also the frustrating possibility that in spite of noble aspirations, one's unavoidable *karma* will shape one's destiny through a long series of rebirths before the basic "badness" within can be purged away. Thus, the individual is important because he or she has the metaphysical status of "permanent substance coeternal with God" (Nakamura, 1964, p. 46). This concept should not be unfamiliar to the Westerner who believes the individual soul is created by God and is co-eternal with God.

The profoundly Asian implications of that doctrine are the rejection of the reality "mine," or one's own possessions up to and including one's own body. All these possessions are regarded as changeable, passed on to others after death and therefore impermanent or temporary. What, then, is left to transmigrate from one existence to the next? "Life is like fire: its very nature is to burn its fuel. When one body dies it is as if one piece of fuel were burned: the vital process passes on and recommences in another, and, so long as there is desire of life, the provision of fuel fails not" (Murphy & Murphy, 1968, p. 22).

2. SELF, AS THE SUBSTANCE OF
INDIVIDUALITY AND THE REALITY OF
BELONGING TO AN ABSOLUTE COSMIC
SELF, ARE INTIMATELY RELATED.

The self or *atman* is regarded as identical with the Absolute or ultimate Ego throughout Indian philosophy. While there is disagreement among the various Indian religions about the essence of the *atman* as a metaphysical principle, there is no disagreement regarding the *atman's* significance as the moral agent for individual action. The ultimate goal of the process of emancipation is the recovery or discovery of one's true self. "Hell" is continued bondage to others; "heaven" is mastery of one's self. Thus the true *Atman* is the ultimate or pure wisdom without internality or externality, indestructible and imperishable. The self therefore participates in this condition of unity with all things, with the changing manifestations of the phenomenal world being illusory and temporary.

In the contemporary emphasis of humanistic psychology on rediscovering the nature of "real self," some religiophilosophical teachings of Indian thought have demonstrated their attractiveness. The emphasis is less on individual or particular surface qualities of the self and more on the relational meaning of personality to all other realities. This provides an unchanging stability at the core of personality which is genuinely eternal, participating in ultimate reality and demonstrating the unity of all things. Consequently, the more an object is individualized, the less it participates in the essence of reality. This basic monist view was developed in the Rg-Veda and developed to the Upanishads as a major theme throughout most of Indian thought.

The Indian view of self takes an ontological rather than an epistemological view of truth, leaning in the direction of monistic idealism and contending that all reality is ultimately One and ultimately spiritual. The emphasis is on the underlying features or "essence" of the individual, rather than on surface qualities of the self. The individual or particular self is dependent on the universal which supports and defines reality, emphasizing the *relational* meaning of a person or

thing rather than its fundamental uniqueness. By fixing limits between self and not-self, the person limits and defines a place in the universe that gives him an identity. There is thus a balance due to the harmonious tension between self-affirmation and self-negation.

> In terms of modern psychology: the tendency of self-affirmation is extravertive, directed toward the external world; the tendency of self-negation is introvertive, i.e., directed toward the inner world, within which the ego-illusion is dissolved (because an ego can only be experienced in contrast to an external world). The extravertive and introvertive movements are as necessary in the life of humanity as inhalation and exhalation in the life of an individual. (Govinda, 1961, p. 29)

3. ASIAN THEORIES OF PERSONALITY
GENERALLY DEEMPHASIZE
INDIVIDUALISM AND EMPHASIZE THE
IMPORTANCE OF SOCIAL RELATIONSHIPS.

Western views of personality see it as a separate entity, distinct from society and culture (Hsu, 1971, p. 23). Society is seen as composed of individuals who express and create that society. The extreme Eastern view concentrates on relational cultural differences without specific reference to individuals. Traditional Western definitions of personality move from a central core of the unconscious, through preconscious and unexpressed conscious, to the expressible conscious behavior. Hsu (1971), representing Asian thought, goes beyond these "layers" of personality into the relationships of social and cultural being. He substitutes the term *psychosocial homeostasis* as the basic unit to be studied, instead of personality. These relationships are central in the Chinese concept of *jen*, which translates as "person" but emphasizes the person's transactions with fellow human beings. Western concepts of personality emphasize what happens within an individual's psyche, while external behavior is seen as the overt effects or expressions of these forces. *Jen* emphasizes interpersonal transactions and evaluates the central core of individuality according to how well it serves to enhance interpersonal adjustment.

This humanistic trend caused the Chinese to deemphasize discrimination between the individual and human organization to which the individual belongs. *Jen* defined the core of morality and humanity itself. A person was considered a person only when he observed the right behavior, so that birds, animals, barbarians, and extremely immoral individuals were excluded from *jen,* or the definition of human. Hsu (1971) contends that the concept of *jen* is superior to the Western concept of personality, illustrating a more "Galilean" view than the "Ptolemiac" view of personality theory. The locus of cultural change or resistance is not in the individual personality but in the circle of humanity, ideas, and things that define goodness in interpersonal relationships. This notion is close to a field theory concept of personality in the Western world, most specifically like Kurt Lewin's gestalt concept of personality as the summation of vectors of force.

While Indian psychology describes the world as impermanent and mortal, with very little difference between persons and other living beings, Chinese thought attaches considerable importance to individual human beings as the highest form of existence. As a result, Chinese psychology emphasizes practical ethics, while Indian psychology makes individuals subject to discipline of a spiritually religious character. Chinese psychology is "situation centered" and socially controlled, with less "inward" introspection. In this connection Hsu (1963) provides an elaborate chart comparing Chinese, Hindu, and U.S. orientations on situational emphases.

4. THE HINDU IDEAL OF MATURITY EMPHASIZES CONTINUOUS DEPENDENCY RELATIONS.

In the Hindu extended family the child and, to a lesser degree, the adolescent occupies special status, rarely being required to wait for anything or tolerate prolonged frustration. The child is praised and compared favorably to other children. This permissive style of child rearing results in adults with a low tolerance for frustration and a consuming need for reassurance.

> If no one has the time or patience to say that he is a good lad, then he himself has to proclaim it. Friends, events, and the like exist and are valued only to the extent that they supply these narcissistic needs. Deep, durable friendships become difficult and threatening especially outside the family in-group. (Surya, 1969, p. 388)

A therapist working with such a person would seek to reconcile independency strivings or to submerge the individual's complex interdependence. The concept of "mine–not mine" applied to material objects, time, thoughts, and emotions is branded as selfishness inside the extended family. A Western therapist working with a Western person would probably move in a nearly opposite direction.

In the enlarged Indian extended family, social relations are diffused among parents, aunts, uncles, grandparents, and siblings. Each stage of the person's development marks a new network of dependency relations, with never a final emergence into "adulthood" and the independent responsibility or freedom implied in that concept in the Western sense. Each dependency relation is marked by a more or less rigid inherent status which perhaps is most apparent in the caste system. Caste places strict limitations upon the liberty of the individual and constrains him to unalterable conformity with what is called *jati-dharma,* the rule of the caste (Anant & Shanker, 1966). As a result, different personality patterns emerge for each of the different caste groups.

The *Kshatriyas* tend to be dominant, the *Brahmins* to be devoted to religious duties, the *Vaishyas* to be parsimonious, and the *Sudras* to be authoritarian. Rapid social change has diffused these caste distinctions, but the intricate network of dependency relations is continued in modern India.

The goals of maturity in India are satisfying and continuous dependency. Independency longings are considered to lead to neurosis, contrary to Western concepts of mental health and adjustment. The notion of *dependency* is viewed positively in the Indian notions of *bandha, sambandha,* or *bandhavya* (bond, bondship, kinship) and does not have the negative connotations of *immaturity.*

5. INTERDEPENDENCE IN PARENT-CHILD RELATIONSHIPS IS THE CHINESE IDEAL FOR PERSONALITY DEVELOPMENT.

Differences between Chinese and American cultural child-rearing practices are reviewed by Chiu (1972). Chinese elders employ more severe discipline than American parents; Chinese parents emphasize mutual dependence in the family rather than self-reliance and independence; Chinese children see the world in terms of relationships rather than with an individualistic self-orientation; Chinese are more strongly tradition oriented and more situation centered, as well as more sensitive to environmental factors—all of which results in a more passive than active attitude towards life. Consequently, Chinese children develop a cognitive style attuned to interdependence of relationships, while American children prefer to differentiate, analyze, and classify a stimulus complex in a more independent manner (Chiu, 1972). A key aspect to understanding these cultural differences lies in the parental role.

Chinese babies are normally breast fed whenever they cry, even in public, and are carried on their mother's back and sleep in their parents' bed. Breast feeding is prolonged, and the mother is typically extremely protective of the baby's bodily health, giving it herbs or medicines even when the baby is not sick. Continuous and immediate gratification is the ideal form of child rearing. Toilet training is very permissive. "It is the mother who 'trains' herself and sensitizes herself to the baby's rhythm. She does not train the infant to control himself. The Chinese mother assumes that she is responsible for her baby's function" (Tseng & Hsu, 1971, p. 7).

The Chinese child is taught to handle hostility without expressing anger. Aggressive behavior is severely punished. Sharing and collaterality is encouraged, thereby developing a "shame-oriented" conscience in the child. There is little sibling rivalry for parental favoritism, since both children would be punished for aggressive, competitive behavior toward one another. The handling of the child changes abruptly by about school age (six years old), at which time the teacher is expected to assume control over the child's discipline. The contrast between indulgence for young children and subsequent harshness to instill discipline in maturing youngsters indicates a way of handling aggressive impulses through the basic social rhythm of *ho-p'ing* (harmony) and *hun-luan* (the confusion of vented aggression). The earlier permissiveness instills a strong sense of self-esteem and feelings of self-worth in children, just as subsequent discipline teaches commitment to family above self. "Thus the subsequent harsh disciplines of youth represent the parents' effort to arrest the develop-

ment of that self-esteem which is the legacy of an indulged infancy. The child matures with a 'selfish' longing to recapture the oral pleasures and the sense of power known early in life" (Solomon, 1971, p. 80).

The system of filial piety resembles a mutual exchange. Parents devote themselves to children, who in turn are expected to support the parents in old age. Relationships among family members provided a model for moral virtue in all areas of society, with the ideals of family government becoming the basis of national statesmanship, sanctioned not merely by the family's emotional needs or political necessity but also by intellectual rationales with inherently religious meaning. Western parents send their maturing child into the world to gratify hostile or pleasure-seeking impulses outside the family. "The Confucian solution, however, rejects 'abandonment' as a solution to generational conflict in favor of the greater ends of parental security and the integrity of the family group. The son is to realize his social identity in a lifelong prolongation of his original state of dependency" (Solomon, 1971, p. 36). In this interdependent relationship, the child depends on parents and, later, the aged adult depends on his children, in a full cycle of reciprocity.

Currently, in the People's Republic of China, the breakdown of authority relations and equalization of the power of men over women or parents over children is expressed in new kinship terminology. The husband and wife now refer to each other as *ai jen*, or "loved one," suggesting equality. The wife now normally retains her maiden name, and children may assume either the mother's or the father's name. While traditional concepts of filialism are still evident, particularly in overseas and Nationalist Chinese society, through respect and obedience of children to parents, the arbitrary authority of parents over children has diminished. The child is encouraged to become relatively independent at an early stage, and this lack of parental supervision is reinforced by the mainland regime's manuals on child rearing (Vogel, 1969).

6. JAPANESE PERSONALITY IS MOLDED BY GUILT SANCTIONS THROUGH PARENTAL SELF-SACRIFICE.

The principal controversy in the field of Japanese culture and personality has revolved around different interpretations of child-rearing practices on the formation of adult personalities. Recent explanations have shifted from emphasizing formal customs, such as use of the cradle or toilet training, to less formalized but more complicated factors. The current emphasis favors affective relations between parents and child, measured by the length of time a child sleeps with its parents, who bathes a child, and other means of gratifying or expressing affective impulses (Norbeck & DeVos, 1961).

In Japan, mothers view their babies as extensions of themselves, with the psychological boundaries between mother and child more blurred than in Western cultures. Compared with Western models, there is less emphasis placed on verbal communication and more on physical contact, with the expectation that the mother will be totally devoted to the child. For the first five years the Japanese child experiences unconditional love for what he or she is, rather than what he or she does. As the child approaches school age and must represent the family to the outside world, there is a shift to emphasizing the child's obligation. The duty to repay implies a duty to achieve in a cooperative framework, on behalf of the family and within the family, contrasted with a competitive stance toward outsiders. The Japanese mother contributes to this sense of obligation: "by exhibiting an uncomplaining striving and endurance on behalf of her family, and by taking upon herself responsibility for their failures, she demonstrates that there is really something which deserves repaying" (DeVos, 1973, p. 156).

These obligations continue through the adult Japanese person's life until retirement. When old age is reached, the individual is again free. As Benedict (1946) points out, this developmental curve allows most freedom at infancy and old age and most control during the middle range of years, and so it is the *opposite* of the developmental responsibility curve of Western society. The Japanese concept of *ie* or "family system" implies closely guarded family relationships as a model of total involvement and commitment to a group, with other social commitments approaching this final commitment. While modernization has eroded the *ie* tradition, it continues to serve as an ideal in Japanese society (Nakane, 1972).

At the present time there are coexisting traditional and modern family styles in Asia, as a consequence of rapid social change. Traditional values are less rigidly adhered to in nontraditional families, and self-direction displaces passive compliance to parental commands; differential role expectations are allowed for men and women; and role differences of age-graded siblings place less responsibility on the eldest son. At the same time, the traditional values are maintained to some extent as ideals and thereby continue to influence the development of personality.

Maintenance

The categories of development and maintenance assume a dichotomy that to some extent forces Asian psychologies along some artificial continua, and a uniformity that disguises the tremendous variation among Asian cultures is implied. Several of the assertions in this section consequently reflect the development of personality as well as its maintenance. The first three deal with maintenance of interpersonal relationships in Japan, the next two with authority relationships and consciousness in India, and the final two assertions emphasize the importance of balance in applied psychology for Chinese personality maintenance.

7. JAPANESE SOCIAL BEHAVIOR PATTERNS ARE MAINTAINED THROUGH MODELING THE UNIQUE RELATIONSHIP BETWEEN PARENTS AND CHILDREN.

In Japan, *amae* means to expect and to depend upon another's benevolence. The term is generally used to describe a child's relationship toward parents, particularly the mother, but it can also describe a special relationship between two adults, such as husband and wife or master and subordinate. There is no such concept in English, which reflects a difference in psychological viewpoint between the two cultures.

The unique aspect of Japanese dependency is the fluidity of relationships without fixed roles of inferiority and superiority. There is rather a mutuality in the bond of *ameru*, implying the tendency and necessity to presume upon another person. This dependency need is both accessible and acceptable to the consciousness of a Japanese adult, and in fact social sanctions encourage it. The positive value of dependency sharply contrasts with Western views which characterize dependency negatively (Doi, 1969, p. 339). This positive attitude toward dependency is greatly influenced by an emphasis on immediate personal relations as a basic principle of Japanese culture.

Doi (1969) reviews the importance of *amae* relationships for understanding Japanese culture. With the decline of loyalty to the emperor, and deemphasis on repaying one's "*on*," or spiritual debts to emperor, parents, and ancestors which had regulated the psychology of *amae,* the delicate balance of powers maintaining Japanese personality are being disrupted. The result is present-day moral chaos, according to Doi (1974).

8. PERSONALITY MAINTENANCE IN JAPAN DEPENDS ON ROLE PLAYING SOCIALLY APPROVED INTERACTIONAL PATTERNS.
Relationships in Japanese culture stress groups rather than persons. While the basic social unit in the West is the individual, and groups of individuals compose the state, the Japanese society is more accurately understood as an aggregation of family units. Considerable importance is attached to esteem for the hierarchical order, with each person well defined in his role. Special attention is given to the family, clan, and nation as instrumental in defining loyalty through mutual exchange of obligation.

In abstract terms, human relations are divided into "vertical" categories, such as the parent-child and superior-inferior relationship, or "horizontal" ones, such as that between siblings or collegial associates. While the horizontal relationship has contributed to the formation of concepts of caste, as in India, or of class, as in America, the vertical relationship in Japan has taken the form of *oyabun-kobun,* as for example patron and protege, landlord and tenant farmer, or master and disciple in the Japanese bureaucracy. Hierarchy in the group is usually determined by a seniority system, and this frustrates modern Japanese management systems, which emphasize individual competency. The sense of Japanese honor is closely tied to high esteem for a hierarchical order. Nakamura (1964) claims this hierarchy motivates the moral faculty of Japanese self-reflection and identity: "It posits

before man the ideal of the infinite good that he should strive for, it induces him to reflect, by contrast, upon the sorry fact that he himself is too weak and helpless to refrain from doing evil; and thus it awakens within him the consciousness of man's sinfulness" (p. 513). Nakane (1972) contrasts the notion of *attribute*, or any specific quality of an individual, with the notion of *frame*, or groups of individuals who share the same situation by living in the same neighborhood, working in the same company, or belonging to the same organization. The practical significance of a Japanese individual's identifying himself according to his frame reference rather than his individualized attributes is readily seen.

Role behavior, therefore, becomes the means of self-realization for even the modern Japanese. The individual is dedicated to and inseparable from his role, probably dating back to basic Confucian values embodied in the *samurai* elite of the 19th century. Carefully prescribed role relationships, beginning with the family, have significantly contributed to the stability of Japanese society in spite of rapid social change, at the cost of deemphasizing a sense of personal self. Achievement is not considered an individual phenomenon but rather the result of cooperation, both collaterally and hierarchically, in the combined and the collective efforts of individuals. De Vos (1973) notes that "Internalized sanctions make it difficult to conceive of letting down one's family or one's social groups and occupational superiors. In turn, those in authority positions must take paternal care of those for whom they have responsibility" (p. 185).

The importance of human relations is further evidenced in elaborate rules of propriety. The exchange of greetings, for example, is elaborate rather than simple. There is an abundance of honorific words and phrases in the Japanese language. "It is said that if all such honorific words were taken out of Lady Murasaki's *Tale of Genji,* the book would be reduced to one half its length" (Nakamura, 1964, p. 407). At the same time, there is an acknowledgment and acceptance of natural desires or sentiments as they are. It is in the social realm that conduct is carefully regulated; within one's inner self one can think whatever one pleases. The strong collectivity orientation in Japanese culture stresses stability and security but can result in stagnation; while the American adjustment, through self-orientation and individual freedom, can result in anomie.

9. INTERNAL CONTRADICTIONS IN JAPANESE CULTURE RESULT IN PARADOXICAL PERSONALITIES FROM THE NON-JAPANESE POINT OF VIEW.

Nakakuki (1973) discusses the psychodynamic mechanisms in Japanese culture which are reconciled in a balance of contrasting tendencies. In the title of her book on Japan, Benedict (1946) juxtaposed the symbolism of a "chrysanthemum" for the soft, tranquil delicacy of aesthetic character in tension with the militaristic, authoritative attitude of a "sword." There is a similar dynamic balance throughout Japanese culture which reconciles self-expression against conformity throughout the society. These contrasts are related to a basic tension between narcissism and masochism (Nakakuki, 1973).

The narcissistic element is indicated by achievement orientation, competitiveness, and ambitiousness in a self-centered, omnipotent, and grandiose manner. The Japanese self-consciously strive for higher goals to realize their ego-ideal and are further motivated in this direction by a family-related, shame-oriented drive to be successful. The masochistic lifestyle is demonstrated in attitudes toward work, illness, and death whereby the person is duty bound to repay obligations. The ideals of self-denial are prominent in Japanese culture. The traditional Japanese family provides models in a narcissistic father through his omnipotence in the household and a masochistic mother whose task it is to maintain harmony in the family. The narcissistic pattern is related to shame and the masochistic pattern to guilt, as these two tendencies coexist in Japanese culture. The individual reconciles this tension by living in accord with prescribed roles within family and society. The source of conflict most likely to occur is between individual ambition and role responsibility.

Mental health therefore depends on keeping these two opposing tendencies in balance, so that the individual can move freely from masochistic hard work in the daytime to narcissistic relaxation at home, without either tendency taking control of him. It is necessary for the individual to transcend these categories by balancing them

without weakening either tendency. The notion of balance is familiar in other Asian cultures as well, as, for example, the harmonious tension between *Yin* and *Yang*, the female and male principles of Chinese philosophy. This emphasis on harmonious balance of forces once more underlines the basic theme of this chapter—human behavior in Asian countries requires an understanding of *relational* units instead of the individualistic assumptions of Western personality theory.

10. RIGID AUTHORITY RELATIONSHIPS DO NOT NECESSARILY INHIBIT ACHIEVEMENT-ORIENTED INDIVIDUALITY.

While motivation patterns are greatly affected by family structure and ecology in any culture, the studies of families in non-Western countries have not confirmed predictive findings from Western research on the family (Chaubey, 1972). This may relate to the different role and function of the family in different societies. The Indian extended family usually includes husband, wife, children, husband's brothers, their wives, children, sisters, parents, and so on, living corporately. This system has been cited as an obstacle to economic development because it inhibits the growth of personalities motivated toward development (Sinha, 1968): "It is argued that the joint family reduces incentives for hard work, promotes idleness and irresponsibility among the members. It is associated with 'dependence proneness' rather than 'achievement' orientation."

However, there is evidence that extended families may lead to enhancement of family agricultural success (Chaubey, 1972), and large families also may contribute to the entrepreneurial spirit in a village. A spirit of cooperation is required to achieve harmony in the shared living accommodations of a joint family. This cooperation is assumed to be voluntary, since members of a joint family are always able to separate with honor. There is no clear evidence that the joint family is more favorable than the nuclear family in promoting achievement-oriented personality types. But the support provided in this joint family system and caste-based social organization maintains uniquely Indian personality traits of respect for authority and conformity. Sundberg, Rohila, and Tyler (1970) discovered that while Indian adolescents were higher than Americans on deference and conformity, Americans were not significantly more individualistic or autonomous.

Cultural orientation toward "authority" relations is different in India than in the West. In analyzing Indian school textbooks for orientations toward authority, Kakar (1971) discovered the "traditional-moral" source of authority to be the most popular. *Dharma* is the Hindu counterpart of traditional-moral, which prescribes duties through modes of conduct at different stages of the human life cycle. This traditional-moral base is supported by the "person" of the superior, as illustrated in the *Mahabharta* and other classical Hindu legends. The image of the superior in Kakar's findings was modeled after the paternal image of control or the maternal image of support, but rarely in the fraternal mode. The sanctions to maintain obedience included the arousal of guilt and the promise of emotional rewards. The "nurturant" mode appeared more effective than "assertive" styles of enforcement, resulting in an "actively submissive" mode of dependency in the core personality of Indian youth. Authority is often associated with the inhibition of freedom in Western psychology, while in India and elsewhere in Asia it can itself be a liberating element. Progress and achievement are possible under either system, depending on how these concepts are defined.

11. EXPERIENCE RATHER THAN LOGIC CAN
     SERVE AS THE BASIS FOR INTERPRETING
     PSYCHOLOGICAL PHENOMENA.

There are 121 classes of consciousness in Buddhism classified into an intricate structure containing wholesome, unwholesome, and neutral factors of consciousness (Govinda, 1961, p. 155). While Western psychology seeks to integrate personality functions, the Indian ideal is toward dissociation and even detachment of higher from lower functions. The ego has a "witness function" in Indian thought—watching the body suffer, but essentially as a nonparticipant. This structure requires explicit acceptance of a higher consciousness beyond human control, with a capacity to influence behavior, as well as the individual's capacity to be in communication with power.

The more subjective method can be compared to a man looking out over the landscape from a high mountain watchtower, searching for the route he must travel to get where he wants to go. He does not study the total landscape; only those aspects pertinent to his route, which is almost certainly not going to be a straight line. Thus while "reality" in the higher sense might be unobtainable within the confines of logical thought and reason, the alternative criteria, through experience, seek to go beyond the boundaries of logically abstract cognition. Even abstract ideas are expressed in concrete terms, endowed with substantiality in most schools of Indian philosophy. The idea of "being" is more important than the more abstract notion of "becoming." The universal tendency is more important than the individualistic attitude. By looking at psychological phenomena in terms of experience rather than logic, Buddhist psychology deals with criteria of reality that do not always differentiate between actual and ideal, or fact and fantasy.

Existence is compared to a river which has its source in birth and its mouth in death, winding through a continuous process of existence in which consciousness unites persons with one another and brings together the different moments or phases within one's life. All components are constantly changing in relationship to one another, giving the illusion of constancy, of "ego-identity," or of an unchangeable personality: "The relation between subject and object is that of two moving systems: if their movement is exactly of the same kind, it creates the impression of non-movement; if their movement is of different kinds, that system which is the object of perception appears to move, while the system of the perceiving subject seems to be stationary" (Govinda, 1961, p. 130).

The aim of spiritual training is to achieve higher stages of consciousness through experience and exploring inner potentials through meditation. Once the person understands the relativity of the objectively perceived world and the facility of consciousness to expand beyond this ordinary level of experience, he has moved toward the goal of liberation. Ultimately the goal is to participate in higher and higher levels of consciousness, approaching the final state of *Nirvana*.

12. LIFE IS A DIALECTICAL, PARADOXICAL PROCESS RECONCILING OPPOSING FORCES.

While authority provides security against conflict and material deprivation through reliance on a united, dominant, and personalized political leadership, there are limits to the manipulative or harsh qualities of that authority. The five moral or natural relationships of the Chinese (*wu-lun*) describe a pattern of deference and obligation between ruler and subject, father and son, husband and wife, brothers and friends. Solomon (1971) differentiates between this expectation and the notion of an individual's social role, because unlike a role, which is defined in terms of the action of the *individual,* the Chinese emphasis is on the *relationship* between individuals. The Confucian tradition defined an individual's social identity not so much by what he had achieved as by those to whom he was related through ties of kinship or personal loyalty.

There is a dependence on hierarchical authority rather than self-assertion, reflecting the authoritarianism of China's social tradition, wherein order is maintained through a structured, hierarchical series of relationships. The need for social harmony and peace is balanced with the need to express hostility and aggression. The child develops a fear of expressing hostility toward those in authority through his early experiences with harsh parental authority. He learns to "put into his stomach" the pain of parental discipline and to "eat bitterness" rather than to act out dangerous emotions when provoked by an older member of the family. At the same time, the child learns that hostile feelings can be appropriately released against those subordinate in status or power. In status-equal relationships, the intense expectations of friendship to embody the gratification of dependency needs, especially in times of difficulty, are so strong that even friendship takes on the flavor of a hierarchical obligation (Solomon, 1971, p. 133).

The irony is that the strength of authority or dependent submission to it which is designed to create harmony actually generates tensions by inspiring the holding in of resentments and hatred of oppressive authority. At some point the critical flash point will be reached, and the system will explode into unrestrained conflict, overthrowing the superior authority and allowing an-

other power to reorganize the confusion in a new hierarchical ordering of social relationships. Thus in China early-life experiences and political orthodoxy are combined in tension to give cyclic and balanced coherence to otherwise contradictory forces.

13. CHANGES IN POLITICAL SYSTEMS AFFECT THE INTERPRETATION OF PERSONALITY STRUCTURES.

The Chinese revolution grew out of a potential for unrestrained violence in the Chinese people. It stressed political education as a way of redirecting consciousness of the aggressive response to purposeful political action. The revolution combined emotional manipulation and political education as complementary dimensions of mass mobilization. By 1949 China's revolution on the mainland was providing an idealized, nonhierarchical brotherhood of friendship as a solution to problems of anger. However, the possibility of peer conflict, even in this idealized system, gives renewed meaning to the need for strong political authority, and the sense of ambivalence and tension remains unalleviated (Solomon, 1971, p. 122).

The Confucian order stressed emotional restraint and "eating bitterness" as the appropriate response of subordinates, but the revolution rejected this dependency orientation.

> Where Confucianism alluded to the virtues of tranquility and interpersonal harmony, Mao [Tse-Tung] has made activism the key to the behavior of the ideal Party cadre. Where fear and avoidance of conflict characterized the "cultivated" response to social tension in the traditional society, Mao has stressed the importance of criticism and controlled struggle in resolving those issues which block China's social advance. (Solomon, 1971, p. 513)

We have reviewed various assertions relative to the formation and maintenance of individual lifestyles or personality patterns in the three Asian cultures. These assertions give evidence that the Western view of man as an independent person beginning with his life at birth and ending at death, as having freedom of will, being entirely responsible for his life, and moving upwards in the social scheme, is not the only possible way of seeing life and truth. Such views produce Western man. The Eastern person is surrounded by different traditions, different views of mind as right and wrong, different notions of proper relations, and is treated differently by his parents and relatives in childhood. Consequently, the Asian personality can be expected to develop a world view guided by relationship strategies rather than individualistic strivings, family and group identity rather than selfish ambitions, and submission to authority rather than rebelliousness.

Applications

All Asian psychologies do not subscribe to the assumption that psychological theory is justified by its usefulness. However, usefulness need not be seen only in terms of material accomplishment. Some examples of how these Oriental psychologies are applied will show that Asian psychologies are useful and valuable by other than pragmatic criteria.

Assessment

The extensive literature on applying Western tests of personality measurement to Asian populations is readily available in standard journals of psychology. Excellent reviews of the cross-cultural psychometric literature generally are available in Brislin, Lonner, & Thorndike, (1973), Spiro (1972), Spain (1972), and Triandis et al. (1973), who include personality measures in their broad review of cross-cultural psychological research. Brislin et al. (1973) discuss controversial issues in measuring personality factors from different cultures, such as the trend toward criterion-oriented (empirical) or construct-oriented (theoretical) measures. They cite numerous examples of both measurement styles and their strengths and weaknesses.

One of the problems of criterion-developed tests is that the criterion itself may be culture-bound. As an example, Kikuchi and Gordon (1970) point out that leadership in Korea is primarily defined in terms of one's relationships with one's *superiors* rather than with *subordinates*. There are other examples of how extraneous variables can affect test response. Klineberg gives an example from Chinese culture. Some years ago a group of Chinese psychologists ap-

plied a number of the standard inventories developed in the West to Chinese students and concluded that Chinese students were neurotic. From this evidence they appealed for more mental hygiene facilities in the universities. Klineberg (1949) reports this as follows:

> What had happened, of course, was that the specific items in the inventory were interpreted quite differently by the Chinese. One question went like this. "Do you allow others to push ahead of you in line?" Of course all the Chinese said "yes," which apparently is marked on the neurotic side. Well, there are no such lines in China: they all gather around together. So everybody turned out to be neurotic. (p. 103)

Perhaps the most promising application of Western psychological assessment technique to non-Western populations is Osgood, May, & Miron's (1975) measurement of affective meaning through extensive cross-cultural research which used a semantic differential to measure cultural universals of "affective cross-cultural meaning." A second example of the use of Western tests in Asia is the cross-cultural use of the Minnesota Multiphasic Inventory (MMPI) reviewed by Butcher and Pancheri (1976), who cite numerous examples of these tests being used appropriately as well as inappropriately. They state that profiles from normal populations in Japan and Pakistan (the only two Asian populations in their sample) were elevated one to two standard deviations above the normal mean profile, particularly for males and particularly on the scales measuring depression and schizophrenia. However, when appropriate new norm levels were determined for these Asian populations, the MMPI was highly predictive for clinical diagnosis.

There is a continuing controversy over whether Asian cultures are "guilt" or "shame" oriented. While the Chinese are more likely to direct their symptomatology outward, to act out against others and to perceive the outside world in unreal ways, the Japanese are more likely to turn against themselves and to see the major source of their problems as within themselves. T. Lebra (1972) cites research in central Japan which indicates that guilt arises from a breakdown in social reciprocity, while shame occurs when a person finds himself in a situation incongruous with his status. There is no agreement whether Japanese culture should be regarded as a shame or a guilt culture. DeVos (1973) argues that the strong achievement drive noted among the Japanese is linked with a deep undercurrent of guilt, as well as a shame-oriented concern with community standards. Guilt is derived from a system of loyalties which cements the structure of traditional society, especially in complicated family relations. "The keystone toward understanding Japanese guilt is held to be the nature of interpersonal relationships within the Japanese family, particularly the relations of children with the mother. The Japanese mother, without conscious intent, has perfected techniques of inducing guilt in her children by such means as quiet suffering" (Norbeck & DeVos, 1961, p. 26). Culturebound aspects of Western personality theories are particularly evident in the attempts to assess non-Western personalities by Western criteria.

Treatment

In a study of "culturebound reactive syndromes" Yap (1969) describes a great variety of mental disorders unique to various cultures in Asia but largely undetected elsewhere. Just as the norms for personality are assessed differently for each culture, the nature of abnormality is likewise distinctive, requiring an adjustment of style for the therapist as well as the psychometrist. Pedersen (1976) surveys the literature on counseling "across" different cultures, while other chapters in the same book (Pedersen et al., 1976) identify how counseling practice differs from one culture to another. Draguns (1976) discusses four questions related to the counseling process in different cultures:

1. Are psychological phenomena generally shared across cultures, or are they specifically unique to each separate cultural group?
2. Does effective counseling depend more on the relationship with a therapist or on sophisticated skills and techniques?
3. Should the counseling relationship be bilateral or hierarchical?
4. Should counseling attempt to change the individual to fit the environment or the environment to fit the individual?

Western treatment generally emphasizes teaching persons how to act appropriately in problem situations, while the emphasis in Asian therapy systems concentrates on how the client can become a better *person* who will then incidentally know how to act appropriately. There seems to be more of a partial, symptomatic emphasis in Western approaches, contrasted to a more total approach in Asia. Murphy and Murphy (1968) point out:

> In cosmic terms, order, truth and justice depend on right relationships of all the parts to one another and to the whole. Right conduct is not only the chord by which the individual responds to a cosmic symphony: it creates the symphony. Man and woman act in accord with truth; and truth alters the world. Psychology is a sort of rhythm of soul to world; and a rhythm which changes the world. (p. 39)

There are many forms of indigenous treatment for mental health throughout Asia, particularly in rural areas where the functions of mental health are closely related to spiritual well-being (Kiev, 1964). Literature on indigenous psychotherapy is readily available in journals such as *Transcultural Psychiatric Research Review*. As Torrey (1972) points out, indigenous healers in both Western and non-Western cultures use similar approaches in providing a "name" for the affliction, in depending on personal therapeutic qualities, in using credentials to gain a patient's confidence, and in applying well-defined techniques to change a patient's behavior. While the approach to treatment is similar, there are also differences. Several examples of indigenous therapy in Japan will illustrate different approaches to treatment.

In Japan *Morita* psychotherapy is employed to treat the patient who worries obsessively about his mental ability or physical health. Iwai and Reynolds (1970) describe the treatment, which takes place in a removed hospital setting.

> Hospitalization customarily lasts four to five weeks and consists of four stages of treatment. The first is absolute bed rest (four to seven days). During this period the patient is not allowed to smoke, read, write, talk, work, or engage in any activity other than biological functions. He is instructed to sleep, suffer, and worry with complete acceptance of any experience that might occur. During the remaining three stages, the patient is permitted to take on increasingly difficult and tiring jobs; at the same time he is asked to keep a diary upon which his therapist comments. During these periods the patient receives ad-

vice from his doctor, learning that because man's meaning in life results from work, he must evaluate himself in terms of his work, not in terms of emotions or symptoms of illness. To work well and behave normally despite symptoms is the proper course to recovery and a satisfactory life. (p. 156)

The technique of *Morita* therapy is theoretically based on Zen Buddhism philosophy and emphasizes *arugamama* or "the accepting of phenomenological reality" as it is, rather than the more Western notion of rationalistic idealism, wherein objective reality must be brought in line with the patient's needs and desires.

In another form of therapy called *Naikan*, patients are assigned to small individual rooms away from external stimuli and do not communicate with anyone but a *sensei*, or teacher, for about one week during treatment (Sato, 1968). Except for sleeping, meals, and bodily functions, they sit from about 5:00 A.M. until about 9:00 P.M., and devote themselves exclusively to self-observation. The *sensei* visits their rooms every hour or two and gives them instruction or advice. This concentrated self-observation is called *Shuchu Naikan*, but after the patients return home they are encouraged to practice *Bunsan Naikan*, or distributed self-observation, for some hours every day. The instructions by a *sensei* are for the patient to examine one by one the past experiences with people who have molded her or his personality—mother, father, brother, and sister, grandparents, friends, teachers, or co-workers, with primary emphasis on the mother. The *sensei's* hourly visits encourage a patient to redirect his attention on self-examination through his relationship to these significant persons rather than on the persons themselves.

The key to reevaluation of personality is through better understanding of the patient's relationships to these significant persons. The patient will normally at first concentrate on grievances, resentments, and hatreds toward these significant others, but in a later phase he acknowledges his deep indebtedness to parents and significant others and becomes more sympathetic to others' viewpoint toward him. A Japanese therapist, Nishimaru (1965), shows how this orientation is uniquely Japanese.

A truly Japanese psychotherapy would have patients strive to accept life as it immediately is—good, bad, and ugly and beautiful are false and tormenting dichotomies and there is no personality to get sick at all. In such terms the goal and problem of psychotherapy for the Japanese is how to live in the midst of this sad transitoriness of all things—one does not struggle against this, but becomes one with it. There is no need to look backward as in Western psychotherapy to seek for past causes which no one can prove to have really taken place. (p. 24)

Both of these techniques are indebted to Zen Buddhism for their origin and emphasize a nonduality point of view which tends to confuse our conceptual abstractions of the world with the real world itself. Zen opposes the notion of subject-object distinction. In the West we become aware of ourselves as subject and the rest of existence as object; Zen teaches that this dualism is not real, that both self and nonself are unified in the totality of existence so that the self is not an entity separate from experiencing but part of that experiencing itself (Sato, 1968). Instead, Zen recommends the condition of "Nothought" where the mind functions on its own, free of distractions and the illusions around us. Berger (1962) discusses this notion in the practice of therapy, where the

... counselor allows his total organism to act on its own, to experience and respond and to act without any attempt to achieve any special effect, without standing outside the relation and viewing either the client or self or the relationship objectively for the purpose of analyzing, manipulating or evaluating what is being done. (p. 18)

The developments of therapy in Asian psychologies apply to problems of mental health in our own Western culture as well.

Institutional

Rather than describing the social institutions—such as schools, military, or voluntary organizations—for each Asian society, this section will focus on basic assumptions which define institutional and social relationships in Asia as a whole. There is a wide range of styles by which the different Asian cultures relate to social institutions of their societies. Hsu (1963) characterizes the Hindu approach to the world as supernatural centered, or unilaterally dependent, while the Chinese emphasize individual centeredness, or self-reliance, and situation centeredness, or mutual dependence. As an extension of the family, the most important secondary interpersonal relationship in China is the clan, while for the Hindu the most important secondary group is the caste.

The Chinese situation-centered world is characterized by permanent ties which unite family and clan and allow the individual to experience and exchange mutual dependence with others in that group:

> The individual enmeshed in such a human network is likely to react to his world in a complacent and compartmentalized way; complacent because he has a secure and inalienable place in his human group, and compartmentalized because he is conditioned to perceive the external world in terms of what is within his group and what is outside it. (Hsu, 1963, p. 1)

Each individual clearly knows his role and place in society and is taught the skills of how to improve his position, with few incentives to change or attack that system. The individual is much more likely to accept his role, whatever it is, without complaint.

The Indian supernatural-centered world places less emphasis on family and kin and more on absolute ideals as a guideline. Each individual knows his place in society, and there is little chance of changing his status relative to the society. Individual behavior is of less importance, since temporal existence is, after all, transitory and illusory, and differences are reconciled in a future reincarnation. The Chinese and Hindu cultures differ: the Chinese allow for more reciprocity, while the Hindu tend to be more one-sided in their interpersonal relationships. Dependence in Chinese society is limited to well-defined channels and limits, while in India there is an all-embracing and more widely diffuse dependence. Hsu (1963) points out that: "the situation-centered outlook did in fact lead the Chinese to consolidate themselves within their clans, the supernatural-centered orientation prevented the Hindus from any significant development of their clans" (p. 60). The centripetal or cohesive tendencies of a Chinese family contrast with the centrifugal or divisive tendencies of the Hindu family and are further reflected in the contrast between cohesive Chinese clans on the one hand and amorphous caste groups on the other.

There is a tendency toward conformity in Chinese culture in the direction of a group norm. Meade and Barnard (1973) suggest that Chinese are more sensitive to group stress and thus, in conflict situations, tend to change their opinions, seeking harmony or balance, more frequently than would Americans. It is important to live in harmony and peace with one's surroundings, combining the powers of nature and the power of ideas or the role of the individual and the human organization as two aspects of the same universe. Consequently, they do not regard nature as opposed to humanity, emphasizing harmony with nature, an attitude which may have held China back in the development of natural sciences (Nakamura, 1964).

The basis of institutional relationships in Japan relates to a profound sense of duty or obligation described as *on* (Suzuki, 1962). While there is no corresponding English term, it approaches the notions of gratitude, favor, or obligation. In its Christian religious connotation it would translate as *grace*. It relates the individual to all existence in a "friendly" interaction. Suzuki, as quoted by Sato (1960), thus explains the concept:

> We are living on earth with the support of the universe, and it is our awareness of this support and our appreciation for it shown to the universe (and its elements) which may be called the *shujo-no-on*. If ever those of non-Buddhist countries thought about the debt which we owe to the universe for our existence, it would not be difficult to arrive at this feeling of gratitude and appreciation. (p. 243)

This sense of obligation is applied to family, work, and other social relations to define the boundaries of closed groups of reference. Less value is placed by the Japanese on individualistic self-realization and more on bringing pride to one's family. This is most evident in the use of honorific forms in the language.

This incredibly complicated social system emphasizes the code of behaviors which define interpersonal relationships. The well-adjusted person appropriately applies the honorific system in relationships. Inappropriate use of honorific terms, perhaps more than any other clue, reveals the person's level of maladjustment to a situation. However, the Japanese businessman, for example, behaves much differently with his colleagues and co-workers in the company office than he would with the same individuals late at night in a teahouse. Thus formal relationships are a function of the social situation and are not frozen. To the Western observer, it is a wonder to see a dignified executive operating with considerable formality during the day in relation to subordinates who know their place and are evidently subservient and these same individuals playing nursery-level games in a teahouse in the evening, evidently with complete familiarity. In Japan, this is how traditional relationships function for the same individuals in two different settings.

Wagatsuma (1973) discusses "instrumental" and "expressive" interpersonal dimensions, relative to the Japanese. Instrumental role behavior is motivated toward achieving a goal or meeting a standard of judgment, while expressive behavior operates in terms of immediate feeling. It is important to understand both aspects as implemented in the Japanese conception of appropriate "role" in the various institutions of society. It is very difficult for the Japanese to think of "self" as separate from a carefully defined and appropriate role.

The Japanese, Chinese, and Indian cultures differ considerably in their organized, institutional, interpersonal relationships. We may wonder why Japan so easily adapts the technological revolution with an achievement motivation which resembles, but is significantly different from, the Protestant ethic of capitalism. We may be puzzled at mainland China's seemingly deliberate and needless abortion of progress in a Cultural Revolution, wherein the institutional machinery valued so highly in Western society is deliberately brought to a halt. We may be offended by a society which allows starvation to exist alongside opulence, as in India. Only when we understand assumptions and goals of each society—both those similar to and different from our own—can we hope to accept each culture on its own terms.

Self

Some of the so-called "mysticism" in Asian psychology as experienced by Westerners is due to our lack of understanding of their values, goals,

and aspirations. The same kind of misunderstanding applies to Asians who characterize Western culture as merely "materialistic." The specific differences between Asian and Western psychologies should be evident, and the simplistic and dehumanizing stereotypes of "strangeness" in Asian psychology can be rejected. The big difference betweeen the psychologies of the East and the West, as Pande (1968) points out, is that for Asian psychologies the ultimate goal is consciousness or awareness, while for the West the ultimate goal is achievement. Western theories of cognition emphasize the resolution of emotional conflict, while Asian psychologies seek to transcend conflicts and restore a sense of relatedness between individuals and their environment. Asian psychology offers a new set of assumptions and, alternately, a new lifestyle.

These differences in lifestyle have practical implications for our own high pressure society as well. Matsumoto (1970) develops a hypothesis to explain the low rate of heart disease in Japan. He credits this to the Japanese being able to express a variety of feelings more freely than Americans. "Thus the Japanese man is free to relax with his co-workers and indeed is provided plenty of opportunity for recreation and informal relationships with them." (p. 9). There is a stronger sense of "personal community" in Japan than in countries like the United States, with its higher rates of heart disease.

Tseng and Hsu (1971) comment on the lower frequency of depression among Chinese patients. The Chinese are provided satisfaction and security in the early years of life: The strong tie between members of the extended family provides a feeling of belongingness, overt mourning is encouraged, and the Chinese are simply not used to expressing depressive affect verbally. On the other hand, they are especially likely to have somatic symptoms such as headaches, stomach aches, or other pains.

There is a new emphasis in the Occidental world relative to subjective as well as objective psychological phenomena and humanistic as well as experimental, process as well as content, and non-Western as well as Western cultural points of view. In some areas of the social sciences and certainly the humanities, the West is beginning to perceive itself as "underdeveloped" in contrast to Asian cultures. In the search for new solutions to our problems Asia offers new assumptions and conceptual frameworks which have improved the quality of life for participants. Gilbert (1973) discusses some of the potential contributions of Asian psychology in increasing our awareness of the world around us, both through incorporating Asian content into the field of psychology and through better understanding the techniques applied in that context.

Asian psychology has typically been disregarded in Western texts on human behavior, in spite of the popularity of Asian ideas in even the Western consumer culture. The logic of isolating psychology to a narrow cultural enclave is more readily questioned by the student than by the teacher of psychology. As we come to understand the rich resources of alternative Asian psychologies we might well expect to find aspects of our own science of psychology overshadowed, even when those alternatives are tested by our own cultural criteria of truth.

Asian theories will help break down the cultural encapsulation by Western cultural values that has largely defined modern psychology. The constructs of *healthy* and *normal* are assumed to have a universal meaning, when in fact each culture defines them differently. By studying psychological theories radically different from our own we learn not only about cultural differences but about our own cultural bias as well.

Why should the individual play such an important role in the Western psychology of human behavior? Perhaps as we prepare for the future, a psychology of human interdependence will be more appropriate to our needs. We have valued freedom a great deal in our ideological thought, but it has been an externalized freedom from control by one another and not inner freedom, as defined in the religiopsychological thought of Asian philosophies. We have emphasized scientific and empirical evidence as the source of validation. If we can't measure it, it doesn't exist. These assumptions can function as blinders, limiting our sight to a narrow tunnel of existence. Asian psychology spends less time on the process of rushing around to accomplish things and more time teasing out the original assumptions which motivated us in the first place and pointed us in one direction rather than another. Most of all,

Asian psychology will put us in touch with the majority of the world's population outside the splendid isolation of Euro-American experiences.

Validation

It would be difficult to ignore systems of Asian psychology that have been actively serving most of the world's population for several thousand years. The endurance of ideas central to the psychological point of view in India, China, and Japan must be considered as evidence of their vitality. Many aspects of Asian psychology, as they gain popularity in the West and among Western-trained Asian psychologists, have demonstrated their validity outside their Asian environment also, even when subjected to the judgment of non-Asian criteria.

Evidence

There is a profound difference in the assumptions relative to personality theory made in India, China, and Japan, compared to those of the West. Asian psychology emphasizes the inner person's awareness as the ultimate goal, while Western theories of personality concentrate on the reality of the outside world. Asians seek to transcend conflict, while Western psychology tries to resolve emotional conflict. The individual Asian personality is absorbed into other primary relationships as the basic units of human behavior, rather than seeing others as hostile counterparts to one's self.

Evidence supporting self-induced altered states of consciousness as resulting in better mental or physical health and increased ability to deal with tension or stress has encouraged a growing interest in Zen, Yoga, transcendental meditation and biofeedback systems which have grown out of essentially Asian psychologies (Benson, Beary, & Carol, 1974). These techniques have emphasized greater dependence on inner resources rather than external controls of behavior, resulting in the self-actualization of trained participants. Though they have been popular in Asia for centuries, they are being discovered by modern Western medicine as effective in their results (Brown, 1974).

One of the most popular adapted techniques

has been transcendental meditation, or TM. The measured response to this technique is described by Benson, Beary, and Carol (1974):

> During the practice of one well-investigated technique called Transcendental Meditation, the major elements of the relaxation response occur: decreases in oxygen consumption, carbon dioxide elimination, heart rate, respiratory rate, minute ventilation, and arterial blood lactate. . . . . The electroencephalogram demonstrates an increase in the intensity of slow alpha waves and occasional theta wave activity. (p. 38)

Benson, Beary, and Carol provide a comparative table describing the effect of TM, autogenic training, hypnosis, Zen, Yoga, and other relaxation techniques.

The very need to evaluate and demonstrate a personality theory's usefulness can assume a bias foreign to Asian psychology. Western psychologists as a rule both dislike and distrust a pessimistic view which questions the value of life.

> They [Europeans] can accord some sympathy to a dying man who sees in due perspective the unimportance of his past life or to a poet who under the starry heavens can make felt the smallness of man and his earth, but such thoughts are considered permissible only as retrospects, not as principles of life: you may say that your labor has amounted to nothing, but not that labor is vain. (Murphy & Murphy, 1968, p. 28)

Our belief in progress is so strong that asceticism and the contemplative life are immediately suspicious or even offensive. As a result, when Western psychologists study Asian psychology, they tend to look for evidence of its usefulness in either a Western or an Asian context, measured objectively by external criteria (Wittkower & Termansen, 1969). They ask: "Does the Oriental way of life with its emphasis on social and emotional withdrawal, on meditation and contemplation, increase or reduce a tendency to develop mental disease?" or "To what extent is mental morbidity affected by prevailing Eastern value orientations—such as the traditional family structure, role and status of women—compared with prevailing Western value orientations?" To evaluate these points of view, they look at criterion factors affecting rates of mental disorder and the measured effects of rapid social change

on behavior, social organization, and mental health.

Even from this achievement point of view, Asian psychology has gained importance in the West and promises to continue doing so. In part, this new popularity relates to a reorganization of our own values in Western societies and in part to the recognition of the need for alternatives. The increased international exchange of professional psychologists and international students has contributed to greater awareness, as has the increase of publications through cross-cultural writing and research. Increased political dependence by Western countries on Japan and China is likely to result in more attention to their social and cultural organization, as well as a better understanding of Asian behavior styles.

Sato (1968) documents a list of benefits from the Japanese point of view as validating Zen training. They include promoting vitality; helping to cure chronic disease; adjusting nervous functions and helping to cure neurosis; changing temperaments; heightening self-control of the will; promoting work efficiency and preventing accidents; heightening intellectual functions; integrating the individual's personality into a "flexible and serene mind"; achievement of *Satori*, or realization of the interdependence between self and the universe; a deepened sense of compassion; and peace of mind. The emphasis in validating Zen within its own framework is on freedom from worries of life and death, in a variety of forms.

The ultimate task of validation is locating criteria sensitive to both the Asian and the Western criteria of importance. As the various systems exchange ideas with one another, such superordinate criteria may emerge. In the meantime it will be necessary to understand each system from its own assumptions and point of view to evaluate its importance adequately.

Comparisons

The notion of *personality* as described in Western theories is a direct product of preliterate concepts of Mediterranean, Greek, Hebrew, and finally Judeo-Christian ideas, shaped and structured through the Roman and Holy Roman Empires and finally delivered to the world in the plastic package of "better-things-through-better living" consumerism. The assumptions which define this concept of personality are that the individual is not only free but somehow aloof from the rest of the universe. When this structure of reality is viewed in context—e.g., in perspective with the beliefs of non-Western societies—we can see that there are alternative ways to look at human behavior which emphasize not the individual but rather the lively space between individuals in relationship with one another. While we may meaningfully look at the outside world through direct observation, there are other cultural traditions that emphasize self-examination and subjective truth, beyond accepting apparent reality around us as the criterion of truth.

We may now ask the central question as to which tradition is more valuable, if indeed it is possible to compare them. Murphy and Murphy (1968) suggest that both viewpoints are valuable.

So, after three centuries of observation of the outer world in a form which we know as science, we are coming around to a psychology which uses knowledge of the external world—physics and physiology—as a primary clue to the methods most suitable for the study of the world within. . . . The basic human nature which is tapped, displayed, or distorted, or whatever you believe happens during such conditions, is apparently much the same in the East and in the West, but the East has made these special states so far from immediate, everyday, palpable reality, something to be sought; the West hands them to the aspirant or the casual inquirer as a gift from biological chemistry. (p. 231)

We can describe the intention of mobilizing, changing, or modifying individual behavior through therapy as ultimately similar to the basic goals of Asian psychology in arranging for a better understanding of human relations. Pande (1968) describes the "mystique" of Western psychotherapy, when viewed from an Asian perspective of how we seek to accomplish these ends. The emphasis on insight as a goal of psychotherapy, for example, is a way of uncovering the dynamics of behavior. The special dependency relationship with a counselor or therapist is legitimized by the medical model of seeking "treatment" to become "healthy." Much of the structure in this relationship is self-perpetuating, with both patient and therapist reassuring one another that their roles are profound. The functions of therapy or counseling are accom-

plished through other significant relationships in non-Western cultures which have not resorted to the invention of psychotherapy. The spontaneous dependence on other relationships in modes of Asian psychology fill much the same function as the professional dependence on a therapist. The function is similar, although the source of help is different.

Pande (1968) further discusses how the categories of personality are different in the East and West. Western culture emphasizes rationality, an intellectual understanding of reality, the separation of work and play, and the perceiving intelligence as separate from the other parts of a person. This categorization is most clearly seen in our separation of stages in human development.

Comparatively speaking, in the psychological and physical growth of the child into adulthood in the Eastern setting less of an issue is made of growth; a relatively smaller premium is placed on becoming an adult. Consequently, the continuum is smoother, and, instead of an either-or here is the caterpillar and here is the butterfly dichotomy, a looser, both-and-neither child in man and man in child view exists. (p. 429)

As a consequence, childish values in the Western world are discouraged in a attempt to lure adolescents into the adult world, with all the implicit values and responsibilities this commitment entails. Much of therapy, consequently, relates to working through unresolved conflicts in personality from childhood experience, rather than accepting the real presence of the child in the adult personality.

In many other ways, Western psychology assumes a separation and even opposition of the individual and environment, building a system that assumes the ego to be the actively independent observer and controller of the environment. Watts (1961) describes the Indian alternative of intuitively assuming the unity of all life as central, substituting self-transcendence for self-assertion, and the Chinese assumption of nature's balanced harmony for the individual who follows Confucian rules of social responsibility. The task for Asian psychology is not to separate ego from environment but to relate these two elements meaningfully and harmoniously to one another. The emphasis is not on the autonomy of the ego, of distinctiveness of the individual, but rather, as in the Japanese culture, on individual ego and society becoming one interdependent unit.

Asian psychology provides an alternative series of assumptions for understanding, evaluating, and shaping human behavior. Pande (1968) mentions other contrasts such as the Western

> ... emphasis on work rather than relationships and love; self-direction and independence in life rather than interdependence and acceptance of guidance from others; a directional and linear attitude toward time rather than an ahistorical view of time; encapsulated individual consciousness rather than social if not cosmic consciousness; and a problem-solving, cerebral approach to life's conflicts rather than one emphasizing absorption and integration of experience. (p. 432)

Sometimes an apparent similarity between Western and Asian behavior leads Western psychology to assume similar motivation in the two cultures. Wagatsuma (1973) asserts that need achievement in Japanese society is as strong a work ethic as that guiding Northern European Protestants. While this may be true, DeVos (1973) cites the Japanese example of industrial productivity as an argument against McClelland's theory of motivation as depending on individualistic assumptions: "Principally, I attack the theoretical approach of David McClelland and his associates for the way it generalizes a relationship between need achievement and individualism that is recurrently apparent in West European culture" (p. 167). DeVos characterizes the economic and psychological understanding of Western countries as too dependent on individualistically motivated behavior.

To explain Zen to English-speaking readers, Sato (1968) attempts to identify parallels from Western systems of psychology. He compares some of the stages of Zen meditation with heightened awareness through psychedelic drugs and suggests that under controlled conditions drugs could contribute to a better understanding of Zen. He draws parallels with Rogerian emphasis on "an accepting and permissive attitude," suggesting that Rogerian theory could enhance its effectiveness through a better understanding of Zen.

Rogers discussed about that self which one truly is. Away from facades, Away from oughts, Away from meeting expectations, Away from pleasing others, Toward self-direction, Toward being process, Toward being complexity, Toward openness to experience, Toward acceptance of others, Toward trust of self, are the directions toward his true self. (Sato, 1968, p. 18)

Carl Rogers (Meador & Rogers, 1973) himself acknowledges his debt to Asian psychological thought. Sato compares the "true self" of Rogerian theory with the bottomless bottom of the "True Self" in Zen. He believes that in some other respects Zen provides much more direction than Rogerian theory would allow. Zen is described as more encompassing and broader, less restricted than Rogerianism.

A comparison of Zen and psychoanalysis is in Fromm, Suzuki and DeMartino (1960). Erich Fromm (1959) describes Zen as a blending of Indian rationality and abstraction with Chinese concreteness and realism, which makes it uniquely Eastern, in contrast with the equally unique Western notion of psychoanalysis. While Zen is a more or less religious technique or way to achieve enlightenment and spiritual salvation, psychoanalysis is an emphatically nonreligious therapy for mental illness. Therefore, while the aim of "transforming the unconscious into consciousness" may approximate the Zen notion of enlightenment, the method of achieving that goal is entirely different. There is perhaps less flexibility in psychoanalytic theory than we find in Zen's ability to accommodate diverse approaches to the same goal. Many of the basic concepts of psychoanalysis, such as have been discussed in the Assertions section of this chapter, are closely tied to European cultural values.

Jungian analytical theory has borrowed some of its imagery and symbols directly from Asian cultures and would therefore seem to be most adapted to Asian cultures. The differences between Asian and Western interpretations of the unconscious, the self, sexuality, and paradoxical tensions such as Yin and Yang are sufficiently profound, however, that Carl Jung's interpretations often change or distort the Asian understanding of the same phenomena. Jung appears to apply Asian concepts to the non-Asian world, standing on the outside of Asia looking in. The

Asian theorist, standing on the inside looking out, is not constrained by having to fit his experiences into non-Asian categories or explanations.

Rational-emotive therapy sees "irrational beliefs" as the source of emotional disturbance. But whose rules for rationality are being applied? Even though the process of deduction may be eminently rational, it can begin from different basic assumptions about reality which lead two rational individuals in completely different and emotionally disturbing directions. In emphasizing the rational process of thinking, Albert Ellis neglects the diverse underlying cultural assumptions as well as the norms for cultures, deemphasizing rationality as the ultimate measure of reality. Rather, he requires us to accept *his* definition of rationality, reasonableness, and reality. Nonrational or irrational tendencies are viewed as destructive and evaluated as ineffective, so that "all serious emotional problems with which humans are beset directly stem from their magical, superstitious, empirically unvalidatable thinking" (Ellis, 1973, p. 172). Rational-emotive therapy may not only be depending on Western assumptions; it appears to evangelize these assumptions to the less fortunate majority of the world's population.

Behavior therapy appears insensitive to the sociocultural context of behavior, attempting to isolate the individual from family, society, and significant relationships which Asian culture imposes and which deemphasize the individual self. Thus, while behavior therapy can successfully identify unadaptive behavior and learning processes, there is a mechanistically scientific assumption about factors motivating the individual (Goldstein, 1973, p. 245). The Asian is likely to be less concerned about factoring out behaviors in adaptive and maladaptive categories. From the Asian point of view, behavior therapy may well be asking the wrong questions.

Gestalt therapy is more all-inclusive in its emphasis, adapting to a wide range of personality styles and cultures to disclose the individual to himself and others. There is a directness and sometimes embarrassing openness implied in Gestalt which can easily become offensive and insensitive to the less direct stabilities of Asian relationships. Gestalt successfully captures the paradoxical and complex polarization of Asian motivation but then "demands the active expres-sion of what one is and not a description of what one is" (Kempler, 1973, p. 260). Gestalt's emphasis on explicit awareness appears almost clumsy in its objectified analysis of human behavior. The gestalt-oriented therapist working with Asians could easily violate the limits of self-disclosure and become more terrifying than the original problem for clients.

Reality therapy emphasizes personal responsibility for one's own behavior and is insensitive to family and social relationships which are more constraining in Asia than in Western culture. William Glasser "feels that blaming their failure upon their homes, their communities, their culture, their background, their race or their poverty is a dead end..." (Glasser & Zunin, 1973, p. 291). Such a view disregards the influence of *karma* in Indian society, the situation-centeredness of Chinese culture, and the *amae* model of relationships discussed earlier. There is success-oriented optimistic emphasis on mankind's basic goodness and individual responsibility which must seem naive to many Asians. To this extent, reality therapy does indeed impose value judgments on non-Western clients.

Other experiential or existential theories of personality place more emphasis on the present, disregarding many traditions of critical importance to Asian culture. There is an emphasis on concrete experiencing that denies the mystic complexity of Asian psychology, as it includes both the past and future through philosophy and religion. The emphasis on experience is authentic to Asian thought, making this view perhaps the most adaptable to Asian culture. At the same time, there is an analysis and explanation of human behavior in Asia which, while different from Western theories, nonetheless goes beyond experience. The existential or experiential explanation is not likely to satisfy the troubled Asian who would prefer to go beyond this immediate awareness to some external reality.

The Japanese are known for adopting ideas from India and China, as well as the West, to synthesize their own culture as an extension of tolerance and conciliation with their environment. Other aspects, such as the familistic custom, are deeply entrenched against change. Foreign ideas have been adopted in the context of a Japanese emphasis on an almost supernatural ethnocentrism. The traditional Shinto worship of Japan places less emphasis on the moral distinction between good and evil and more on submission or nonsubmission to the authority of a corporate whole or the Emperor. The Japanese militaristic ultranationalism of World War II emerged from this basic idea. Unlike the Indians and Chinese, the Japanese depended on a more concrete, tangible, and less abstract source of final authority. There is a "contempt for rational thinking and the worship of uncontrolled intuitionism and activism" (Nakamura, 1964, p. 400). The Japanese emphasis on loyalty and responsibility is limited to their own family, community, and ultimately country, but it tends to neglect the context of humanity as a whole and presents a serious weakness of traditional thought in dealing with the social confusion of contemporary international relations (Nakamura, 1964, p. 521).

Murphy and Murphy (1968) characterize European psychology as less pessimistic than Asian psychology, offering a belief in the possibility of realizing some modicum of happiness in this life. Asian psychologies have been more skeptical of this goal.

> Whether we take the disparagement of the body and of the world as we find it in the Upanishads, or the retreat into an inner discipline as expressed in the Bhagavad-Gita and in yoga, or the belief that a middle course, involving Buddha's noble eightfold way, must lead one into a loss of individuality, a state of *nirvana*, we seem to find very little faith that life is really good. (p. 226)

Since the actions of an individual are supervised and regulated by the ideas of *karma* and *Samsara*, there is a tendency toward submissiveness to whatever inequities exist in the present system and an escape to some future transmigration under better conditions. In this respect, Indian thought resembles Western romanticism's vague and undefined attraction to a distant Truth.

The subjective emphasis on infinite being offers both advantages and disadvantages. The disadvantages lead to tolerance for injustice and inequity, so that one may accept the ideas that one's efforts need not be commensurate with rewards. You may work more but eat less than your neighbor, but that is all right. This notion of acceptance of reality in a passive manner explains what is generally considered Oriental fa-

talism. It also demonstrates the nonimportance of suffering. As Surya (1969) points out, "if you work ten times harder than the next, it is no special virtue" (pp. 387–388). Some personal social benefits derive from viewing human relations as a fusion of self with others into a corporate identity. Nakamura (1964) quotes Albert Schweitzer in acknowledging the importance of acceptance, calmness or equanimity of mind. "The Indian people comprehend the essential weak point in the faith of modern Christianity. We Europeans believe that Christianity is only dynamic in its religious activity. There are too few occasions when we reflect on our deeper selves. We Europeans are usually devoid of equanimity of mind" (p. 79). In a context of activism the ideas of inner peace have become increasingly attractive to Western peoples.

Prospect

This chapter has introduced alternatives to Western psychology from Asian cultures and directed the reader to resources which adequately analyze them. In a sense, the whole chapter has been critical of the cultural bias in traditional Western psychology, attacking the culturally limited assumptions on which a construct such as *personality* is based. The examples cited have been more or less arbitrarily chosen, omitting other vitally important aspects of Asian culture and oversimplifying the wide diversity of thought within each of the major cultural traditions of Asia. The goal is to make readers aware of Western psychological theory as one—but not the *only*—way of understanding how personality contributes to human behavior.

In the cross-cultural understanding of personality, qualitative and not merely quantitative patterns differentiate one group from another. Although we all may share the same personality dimensions, we do not share them in the same context, which frustrates the accuracy of communication of culturally universal psychological statements. We are becoming more aware of the specific ways an individual's behavior is linked to the environment. Traditional societies tend to be more restrictive in patterning personalities toward sameness, while more open societies encourage individuation.

Because of this the discipline of psychology

will eventually become enlarged to accommodate a variety of viewpoints and assumptions. We will invent new constructs to interpret human behavior. With the invention of new terminology, or perhaps rediscovery of parallel systems in non-Western cultures, psychology as a discipline will better interpret the varieties of human behavior in many cultures. Several changes are likely to occur.

1. Modernization and "Westernization" will contribute to cross-cultural similarity through the demands of industrialization, technological expansion, and military expediency. This does not mean that the traditional cultures will disappear. The phenomenon De Vos (1973) calls *psychological lag* continues despite changes. For example, the traditional notion of arranged marriages in Japan runs counter to popular opinion, but most marriages in Japan, even today, are arranged by the families. There is an underlying system of basic traditional and indigenous assumptions which in principle do not change but do in fact define change by their own stability. These basic cultural principles become disguised by the apparent similarity of modernization but will continue to influence behavior through their cultural entrenchment.

2. The need to establish an Asian identity for the Japanese, the Chinese, and Indian will result in the maintenance or perhaps even the deliberate reinvention of cultural traditions to separate and distinguish Asians from non-Asians. These cultural differences will be more similar within nationality groups or linguistically defined dialect groups. Modernization is unlikely to destroy cultural uniqueness, beyond fairly superficial and superordinate goals of expedient necessity. If psychology is to be accurately applied to understanding behavior in a variety of cultures, we will need to develop expertise *both* in the cultural universals shared by all people *and* the unique circumstances of Asians on their own terms.

3. Western cultures will increasingly borrow ideas from Asian models of behavior that might apply to our own culture as well. We will learn about ourselves not just by comparison with other cultures in Asia but from within the assumptions of an Asian psychology. The popularity of Asian psychologies of meditation provides an immediate example of how Asian psychological insights might provide a more "advanced" and sophisticated alternative to our own traditional systems of mental health. The "development" assumption has otherwise too easily measured progress in underdeveloped countries by their approximation to the Western ideals of modernization. As non-Western countries increase in their political and economic influence, our increased dependence on them will no doubt extend to modeling aspects of their social organization in the future, as many of these countries have modeled themselves after ours in the past.

We need most of all to see history in a perspective of thousands rather than hundreds or tens of years. In that perspective our notions of psychology are relatively recent. Arnold Toynbee may have been right in predicting the rise of the East and the decline of Western civilization. Our survival and theirs will depend largely on our flexibility and evolutionary adaptability to the changing world around us. By increasing our awareness of the alternative cultures available to us, we might increase the likelihood of our survival in a future culture which is not known.

Annotated Bibliography

The resources cited in this chapter include materials in anthropology, philosophy, and religion as well as psychology, although each reference contributes to a uniquely "psychological" point of view on human behavior. While there is an abundance of material on separate and specific psychological aspects of Asian cultures, there are few books which provide an overall structure for comparing Asian psychological traditions with one another or with the West. The best books surveying Asian thought are Nakamura (1964), Caudill and Lin (1969), Hsu (1972), and Murphy and Murphy (1968). The best books for getting at each separate Asian tradition are De Vos (1973) for Japan, Solomon (1971) for China, and Govinda (1961) for India.

Nakamura, Hajime. *Ways of Thinking of Eastern Peoples: India, China, Tibet, Japan.* (Philip P. Wiener, Ed.). Honolulu: University Press of Hawaii, 1964.

Professor Nakamura's book developed from conferences at the East-West Center in 1962–63 and was updated and revised by Philip Wiener. The book's theme is that there is no "Asia" in the singular sense, but that there is a wide range of traditions which touch all extremes; just as there is in Western thought. The genius of Nakamura is to look at each culture's language as the key to a better understanding of their thought and psychology. The language provides a rich source of hard data for specific nuances of differences between cultures. While each cultural tradition is discussed comparatively with Western thought, each is approached from within its own assumptions and no attempt is made to enforce or impose evaluative criteria of Western traditions. The book is written from primary materials in Asian languages not otherwise readily available and is perhaps the best single resource on Asian psychology.

Caudill, William, and Lin, Tsung-Yi (Eds.). *Mental Health Research in Asia and the Pacific*. Honolulu: East-West Center Press, 1969.

The 30 articles in this book were written by leaders in the area of Asian psychology. The chapters review the issues in identifying mental illness cross-culturally and cultural effects on human behavior. The chapters are largely self-contained, but there is some effort by authors to cross-reference with one another; Doi and Surya, for example, compare one another's comments on "dependence" as it is different and similar in Japan and India. The specialized focus of each chapter samples the diversity of Asian psychology. This book is part of a three-book series; the other two volumes were edited by William Lebra (1972, 1974). The more recent volumes continue the tradition of sampling a wide range of specialized topics in Asian psychology.

Hsu, Francis L. K. (Ed.). *Psychological Anthropology*. Cambridge, Mass.: Schenkman, 1972.

Francis Hsu is the anthropologist who is perhaps best known for his books in the area of Asian psychology. His publications are helpful for understanding the structure and systems of Asian psychology. This particular 14-chapter book is an updated revision of a popular 1961 edition. The chapter authors represent leading authorities from Western countries who have widely published articles interpreting psychological phenomena in Asia. The book surveys non-Asian cultures as well as cultures of Asia and the Pacific, reviewing psychological methods, techniques, processes, and assessment procedures in cross-cultural psychology. Asian psychology is seen, along with Western psychology, in the larger world perspective.

Murphy, Gardner, and Murphy, Lois (Eds.). *Asian Psychology*. New York: Basic Books, 1968.

This book is part of a series exploring the possibility of some sort of "universal psychology" around the world's cultures. Whether or not such a phenomenon exists depends largely on how terms are defined. At times the book may oversimplify the complexity of Asian cultures, but generally it pro-vides an interesting introduction to Asian psychology in a comparative framework. The authors enlisted help from well-known Asian authorities from the major areas in India, China, and Japan for the three sections of the book. Original translations of Asian traditional literature are widely quoted to illustrate psychological insights and to at least introduce the major psychological ideas in each culture.

De Vos, George A. (Ed.). *Socialization for Achievement*. Berkeley: University of California Press, 1973.

With the help of Hiroshi Wagatsuma, William Caudill, and Keiichi Mizushima, De Vos has assembled essays that explore all aspects of Japanese cultural psychology. The book elaborates aspects of personality theory specific to human psychosexual and cognitive maturation, looking at the psychological structure of Japanese culture. While it admits to a psychoanalytic bias, and the influence of sociologists such as Max Weber and anthropologists such as Emil Durkheim, there is open criticism of these viewpoints as well. The authors provide valuable and unique insights into Japanese culture, although within the framework of fairly traditional personality theory.

Solomon, Richard. *Mao's Revolution and the Chinese Political Culture*. Berkeley: University of California Press, 1971.

Chinese psychology covers a wide range of systems and contrasting viewpoints from the traditionalism of Confucius to the revolutionary writings of Maoism. Solomon draws out the unity underlying this wide contrast with lengthy reference to both the more accessible traditional writings and a perceptive interpretation of the politically oblique psychological thought in the People's Republic of China. Psychology is applied to political and social processes in a way that illuminates the logic of modern Chinese thought. While many other books deal with the religiophilosophy and psychology of China no other single volume gives as perceptive a discussion of the relationship of traditional and modern China to one another.

Govinda, Lama Anagarika. *The Psychological Attitude of Early Buddhist Philosophy*. London: Rider, 1961.

Indian psychology is perhaps the most philosophically obscure of all Asian psychologies, though it contains the roots of ideas developed later throughout Asia. The book carefully sorts out the particularly psychological aspects of Indian thought to demonstrate the complex sophistication of a psychological system thousands of years old, predating many "modern" discoveries of contemporary psychology. The close connection between religion and psychology is particularly apparent and may be disconcerting to the traditional psychologist because it answers questions not being asked in modern Western psychology. The book provides a rich background for understanding popular psychologies of meditation and subjectivity from within the Asian psychological system.

None of the books annotated here presumes a profound acquaintance with Asian philosophy or religion. Any of these references will provide an easily read introduction to non-Western alternatives in psychology.

References

Allport, G. *Personality: A psychological interpretation.* New York: Holt, Rinehart & Winston, 1937.

Anant, S. S., & Shanker, P. Intercaste difference in personality pattern. *Psychologia,* 1966, *9,* 225–231.

Beg, A. The theory of personality in the Bhagavad Gita: A study in transpersonal psychology. *Psychologia,* 1970, *15,* 12–17.

Benedict, R. *The chrysanthemum and the sword.* Boston: Houghton Mifflin, 1946.

Benson, H., Beary, J., and Carol, M. The relaxation response. *Psychiatry,* 1974, *37,* 37–46.

Berger, E. Zen Buddhism, general psychology and counseling psychology. *Journal of Counseling Psychology,* 1962, *9,* 122–127.

Brislin, R., Bochner, S., & Lonner, W. (Eds.). *Cross-cultural perspectives on learning.* New York: Wiley, Halstad, 1975.

Brislin, R., Lonner, W., & Thorndike, R. *Cross-cultural research methods.* New York: Wiley, 1973.

Brown, B. B. *New mind, new body: Biofeedback: New directions for the mind.* New York: Harper & Row, 1974.

Butcher, J., & Pancheri, P. *A handbook of cross-national MMPI research.* Minneapolis: University of Minnesota Press, 1976.

Caudill, W. and Lin, T. Y., (Eds.). *Mental health research in Asia and the Pacific.* Honolulu: East-West Center Press, 1969.

Chaubey, N. Indian family structure and risk-taking behavior. *Indian Journal of Psychology,* 1972, *47,* 213–221.

Child, I. L. Personality in culture. In E. F. Borgatta & W. W. Lambert (Eds.), *Handbook of personality theory and research.* Chicago: Rand McNally, 1968.

Chiu, L. H. A cross-cultural comparison of cognitive styles in Chinese and American children. *International Journal of Psychology,* 1972, *7,* 235–242.

De Vos, G. (Ed.). *Socialization for achievement: Essays on the cultural psychology of the Japanese.* Berkeley: University of California Press, 1973.

Doi, L. Japanese psychology, dependency need and mental health. In W. Caudill and Y. Lin (Eds.), *Mental health research in Asia and the Pacific.* Honolulu: East-West Center Press, 1969.

Doi, L. Amae: A key concept for understanding Japanese personality structure. In R. LeVine (Ed.), *Culture and Personality.* Chicago: Aldine, 1974.

Draguns, J. Counseling across cultures: common themes and distinct approaches. In P. Pedersen,

W. Lonner, & J. Draguns (Eds.), *Counseling across cultures.* Honolulu: University Press of Hawaii, 1976.

Ellis, A. Rational-emotive therapy. In R. Corsini (Ed.), *Current psychotherapies* (pp. 167–206). Itasca, Ill.: F. E. Peacock, 1973.

Fromm, E. Psychoanalysis and Zen Buddhism. *Psychologia,* 1959, *2,* 79–99.

Fromm, E., Suzuki, D. T., & De Martino, R. *Zen Buddhism and psychoanalysis.* New York: Harper & Bros., 1960.

Gilbert, A. Essay on the history of Asian psychology. *Proceedings, 81st Annual Convention,* American Psychological Associations (Vol. 8, Part 2). Washington, D.C., 1973.

Glasser, W. & Zunin, L. Reality therapy. In R. Corsini (Ed.), *Current psychotherapies* (pp. 287–315). Itasca, Ill.: F. E. Peacock, 1973.

Goldstein, A. Behavior therapy. In R. Corsini (Ed.), *Current psychotherapies* (pp. 207–250). Itasca, Ill.: F. E. Peacock, 1973.

Govinda, L. A. *The psychological attitude of early Buddhist philosophy.* London: Rider, 1961.

Hiniker, P. Chinese reactions to forced compliance: Dissonance reduction or national character. *Journal of Social Psychology,* 1969, *77,* 157–176.

Hsu, F. L. K. (Ed.). *Psychological anthropology.* Homewood, Ill.: Dorsey Press, 1961.

Hsu, F. L. K. *Clan caste, and club.* Princeton: Van Nostrand, 1963.

Hsu, F. L. K. Psychosocial homeostasis and Jen: Conceptual tools for advancing psychological anthropology. *American Anthropologist,* 1971, *73,* 23–44.

Hsu, F. L. K. (Ed.) *Psychological anthropology.* Cambridge, Mass.: Schenkman, 1972.

Iwai, H., & Reynolds, D. Morita psychotherapy: The views from the West. *American Journal of Psychiatry,* 1970, *126,* 1031–1036.

Jacobsen, L. Feedback on biofeedback. *Human Behavior,* 1974, *3* (7), 47–51.

Kakar, S. The theme of authority in social relations in India. *The Journal of Social Psychology,* 1971, *84,* 93–101.

Kanellakos, D. The psychobiology of Transcendental Meditation. Annotated bibliography by P. C. Ferguson, MIU International Center for Scientific Research (rev. 1973).

Kempler, W. Gestalt therapy. In R. Corsini (Ed.), *Current psychotherapies* (pp. 251–286). Itasca, Ill.: F. E. Peacock, 1973.

Kiev, A. *Magic, faith and healing.* New York: Free Press, 1964.

Kikuchi, A., & Gordon, L. Japanese and American personal values: Some cross-cultural findings. *International Journal of Psychology,* 1970, *5,* 183–187.

Klineberg, O. General discussion on methods. In S. S. Sargent & M. W. Smith (Eds.), *Culture and personality.* New York: Viking Fund, 1949.

Kroeber, A. L., & Kluckhohn, C. Culture: A critical review of concepts and definitions. *Papers of the Peabody Museum of American Archeology and Ethnology,* 1952, *47,* 181.

Lebra, T. Intergenerational continuity and discontinuity in moral values among Japanese: A preliminary report. In W. Lebra (Ed.), *Transcultural research in mental health* (pp. 247–275). Honolulu: University Press of Hawaii, 1972.

Lebra, W. (Ed.). *Transcultural research in mental health.* Honolulu: University Press of Hawaii, 1972.

Lebra, W. (Ed.). *Youth, socialization and mental health.* Honolulu: University Press of Hawaii, 1974.

LeVine, R. (Ed.). *Culture and personality.* Chicago: Aldine, 1974.

Lynn, R. (Ed.). *Personality and national character.* Oxford: Pergamon Press, 1971.

Matsumoto, Y. Social stress and coronary heart disease in Japan: A hypothesis. *Millbank Memorial Fund Quarterly,* 1970, *48* (1), 9–36.

Meade, R., & Barnard, W. Conformity and anticonformity among Americans and Chinese. *Journal of Social Psychology,* 1973, *89,* 15–24.

Meador, B., & Rogers, C. Client-centered therapy. In R. Corsini (Ed.), *Current psychotherapies* (pp. 119–165). Itasca, Ill.: F. E. Peacock, 1973.

Mills, G., & Campbell, M. A critique of Gellhorn and Kiely's mystical states of consciousness. *Journal of Nervous and Mental Disease,* 1974, *159,* 191–195.

Murphy, G., and Murphy, L. *Asian psychology.* New York: Basic Books, 1968.

Nakakuki, M. *Japanese culture and mental health: Psychodynamic investigation.* Paper presented at the 9th International Congress of Anthropological and Ethnological Sciences, Chicago, September 1973.

Nakamura, H. *Ways of thinking of Eastern peoples: India-China-Tibet-Japan* (Philip P. Wiener, Ed.). Honolulu: University Press of Hawaii, 1964.

Nakane, C. *Human relations in Japan.* Tokyo: Ministry of Foreign Affairs, 1972.

Nishimaru, S. Mental climate and Eastern psychotherapy. Transcultural Psychiatric Research Review, 1965, *2,* 24.

Norbeck, E., & De Vos, G. Japan. In F. L. K. Hsu (Ed.), *Psychological anthropology.* Homewood, Ill.: Dorsey Press, 1961.

Osgood, C., May, W. H., & Miron, M. S. *Cross-cultural universals of affective meaning.* Urbana: University of Illinois Press, 1975.

Pande, S. The mystique of "Western" psychotherapy: An Eastern interpretation. *Journal of Nervous and Mental Disease,* 1968, *146,* 425–432.

Pedersen, P. The field of intercultural counseling. In P. Pedersen, W. Lonner, & J. Draguns (Eds.), *Counseling across cultures.* Honolulu: University Press of Hawaii, 1976.

Pedersen, P., Lonner, W., & Draguns, J. (Eds.). *Counseling across cultures.* Honolulu: University Press of Hawaii, 1976.

Price-Williams, D. The philosophy of science and the study of personality. In E. Norbeck, D. Price-Williams, and W. McCord (Eds.), *The study of personality: An interdisciplinary appraisal.* New York: Holt, Rinehart, & Winston, 1968.

Price-Williams, D. R. (Ed.). *Cross-cultural studies.* Baltimore: Penguin Books, 1969.

Ramadevi, S., & Rao, S. Personality investigations in India. *Psychologia,* 1967, *1,* 86–91.

Sangsingkeo, P. Buddhism and some effects on the rearing of children in Thailand. In W. Caudill & T. Y. Lin (Eds.), *Mental health research in Asia and the Pacific.* Honolulu: East-West Center Press, 1969.

Sato, K. The concept of "on" in Ruth Benedict and D. T. Suzuki. *Psychologia,* 1960, *2,* 243–245.

Sato, K. Zen from a personalogical viewpoint. *Psychologia,* 1968, *11,* 3–24.

Singer, M. A survey of culture and personality theory and research. In B. Kaplan (Ed.), *Studying personality cross-culturally.* Evanston: Row Peterson, 1961.

Sinha, J. B. P. The construct of dependence proneness. *Journal of Social Psychology,* 1968, *76,* 129–131.

Solomon, R. *Mao's revolution and the Chinese political culture.* Berkeley: University of California Press, 1971.

Spain, D. A supplementary bibliography on projective testing. In. F. L. K. Hsu (Ed.), *Psychological anthropology* (pp. 609–623). Cambridge, Mass.: Schenkman, 1972.

Spiro, M. An overview and a suggested reorientation. In F. L. K. Hsu (Ed.), *Psychological anthropology* (pp. 573–609). Cambridge, Mass.: Schenkman, 1972.

Stewart, R. Self-realization as the basis of psychotherapy: A look at two eastern-based practices, Transcendental Meditation and Alpha Brain Wave Biofeedback. *Social Behavior and Personality,* 1974, *2,* 191–200.

Sundberg, N., Rohila, P., & Tyler, L. Values of Indian and American adolescents. *Journal of Personality and Social Psychology,* 1970, *16,* 374–397.

Surya, N. C. Ego structure in the Hindu joint family: Some considerations. In W. Caudill & T. Y. Lin (Eds.), *Mental health research in Asia and the Pacific.* Honolulu: East-West Center Press, 1969.

Suzuki, D. T. *The Essentials of Zen Buddhism* (selected from the edited writings of B. Phillips). New York: Dutton, 1962.

Tart, C. *Transpersonal psychologies.* New York: Harper & Row, 1975.

Torrey, E. *The mind game.* New York: Emmerson Hall, Bantam Books, 1972.

Triandis, H. C., Malpass, R., & Davidson, A. Psychology and culture. *Annual Review of Psychology,* 1973, *24,* 355–378.

Tseng, W. S., & Hsu, J. Chinese culture, personality formation and mental illness. *International Journal of Social Psychiatry,* 1971, *16,* 5–14.

Vogel, E. F. A preliminary view of family and mental health in urban Communist China. In W. Caudill & T. Y. Lin (Eds.), *Mental health research in Asia and the Pacific.* Honolulu: East-West Center Press, 1969, 393–405.

Wagatsuma, H. Status and role behavior in changing

Japan: Psychocultural continuities. In G. De Vos (Ed.). *Socialization for achievement: Essays on the cultural psychology of the Japanese.* Berkeley: University of California Press, 1973.

Watts, A. *Psychotherapy East and West.* New York: Pantheon Books, 1961.

Wittkower, E. C., & Termansen, P. E. Cultural psychiatric research in Asia. In W. Caudill & T. Y. Lin (Eds.), *Mental health research in Asia and the Pacific* (pp. 433–477). Honolulu: East-West Center Press, 1969.

Yap, P. M. The culture-bound reactive syndromes. In W. Caudill and T. Y. Lin (Eds.), *Mental health research in Asia and the Pacific.* Honolulu: East-West Center Press, 1969.

In planning this book, I hoped that the authors of the preceding chapters would include information about other personality theories, in addition to the 12 that were featured. This was the reason for the two sections in each chapter entitled "Similar Theories" and "Comparisons." After the various chapters were in, it was evident that many important theorists had hardly been mentioned at all, and therefore I decided to add another dozen theories. These summaries appear in this chapter; for reasons of time and convenience I wrote them myself, but experts were asked to read and approve each one. In some cases, as you can tell from the credits in the preface, the originator of the theory gave his approval.

CHAPTER 14

A Medley of Current Personality Theories

Raymond J. Corsini

Selection of Theories for This Chapter

For this chapter I selected only those theories which I felt were important, which I knew fairly well, and which did not overlap. As a consequence, the selection is idiosyncratic. Investigating the coverage other textbooks gave to the theories selected, I discovered that Erik Erikson, Hans J. Eysenck, Karen Horney, Abraham Maslow, and Henry Murray were frequently mentioned, and there was usually some coverage of Albert Bandura, Albert Ellis, and J. L. Moreno. But I found practically no coverage of the theories of Eric Berne, William Glasser, Harold Greenwald, or Frederick Perls.

Some of the dozen theories in this chapter are well established and stabilized, but others are up and coming, in their "childhood" or "adolescence" in the process of growth and development. You will find in this chapter a medley of current theories in active use by therapists. Some short comments about the theories and the theorists may be of interest.

I used to listen to Karen Horney lecture while I was a graduate student at the New School for Social Research. She is the only woman theorist in this book and, indeed, the only woman personality theorist of any note. Trained as an orthodox Freudian psychoanalyst, she developed her own psychosocial theory after coming to this country. Most people who label themselves "psychoanalytically oriented" are really followers of Karen Horney, as well as of Erich Fromm and Harry Stack Sullivan.

I knew J. L. Moreno quite well. He was a highly original and spontaneous individual whose ideas have been labeled "sociometric theory." I believe his major contribution was the development of therapeutic roleplaying and psychodrama. I had many encounters with Moreno on the psychodrama stage and I authored two books on roleplaying, one of which I dedicated to him. Moreno's writing and thinking are so diffused that it is difficult to follow his thought; various summaries differ from one another considerably. Since I knew him fairly well, I believe I have been able to capture the essence of his thinking.

Abraham Maslow, who developed the theory of self-actualization, was a research psychologist with a mission in life. He was essentially a social

reformer, dedicated to improving the condition of mankind. Unlike most psychiatrists and clinical psychologists, he dealt with superior individuals and worked from a health rather than a sickness model. Maslow is important as a founder of humanistic psychology. He was no impartial researcher, but rather a man with a vision of the good life.

Frederick (Fritz) Perls, like Moreno, was an original and also was extremely difficult to understand. Essentially a lonely person and difficult to get close to, he was nevertheless a warm and helpful individual, and in my judgment he was superb as a therapist. Perls' Gestalt therapy has practically no structure and operates mostly on the basis of feeling. It is a theory that accords well to the rootless temperament of the times and is congenial to the dispossessed living in a mixed-up world.

Eric Berne, who is rarely mentioned in personality theory texts, probably is the most influential current personality theorist in this group, with the possible exception of Albert Ellis. Through his popular texts on transactional analysis, he has made the terms *games* and *OK* well known and has led to the training of a considerable number of personality specialists from fields outside psychology and psychiatry.

Henry A. Murray represents a unique but nevertheless eclectic theory of personality with his need-press theory. Essentially biologically oriented (as might be expected in one trained as a surgeon), he is probably best understood in his taxonomic attempts to organize personality into its constituent parts.

Erik Erikson, like Karen Horney, was trained as a Freudian psychoanalyst, and like her he diverged from the Viennese master and generated his own developmental theory. He sees himself still as a psychoanalyst, but most textbook authors (as I do) see him as having developed his own original theory. Increasingly, it is being used in work with adolescents and the aged.

Albert Ellis is the relentless expositor of rational-emotive therapy. Unlike most theorists who start with one idea and then expand on it, going on and on, he has done exactly the opposite. Trained as a psychoanalyst, he soon turned away and began to develop his own theory. As time has gone on, his R-E-T theory has been condensed to its absolute limit, and all of humanity has been contracted within it. Ellis is one of the most influential of all personality theorists through his popular books.

William Glasser represents a somewhat different type of person and a different type of theorist from the others discussed so far. He seems to have been more or less a homegrown product, thinking out his own theory, which is probably the simplest in this book. That it is the essence of common sense is indicated by its name: reality theory. Essentially, he is best described as a hard-headed pragmatist.

Albert Bandura's social learning theory is based on the notion that personality is mostly learned through observation. A learning theorist and behaviorist, Bandura utilizes a complex model which includes the individual processing the information received. This theory has considerable laboratory-type confirmation and is in the process of conceptual and research expansion.

Hans J. Eysenck is one of the world's most productive, imaginative, and controversial psychologists. He has done research in heredity, criminology, mental disease, political attitudes, and education, and has produced dozens of books and hundreds of articles. He is a strong critic of psychoanalysis and psychotherapy generally and is most strongly attached to the concept of objective evidence. For this reason he has been inclined recently to a behavioristic treatment of specific conditions which makes objective evidence obtainable. Attention will be given in this chapter mainly to his work on personality typologies.

Harold Greenwald, the last personality theoretician included, is probably the least well known of all the individuals discussed in this book. Paradoxically, however, he may represent more working therapists with his direct decision theory than any of the other theorists. Essentially, he is a third-generation theorist-therapist with an eclectic orientation. He has assembled, as do most people who work with others, a variety of articulated ideas that make sense to him, most of them taken from other theorists, to generate a consistent system of thought. The evidence is that relatively few people in the field of psychology or psychiatry, broadly defined, take any individual's model hook, line, and sinker; rather, they make modifications and alterations

to suit their concepts and experience, as Greenwald has done.

A final statement: In no way should any of these theories be considered inferior to those discussed in the separate chapters. Every theorist calls the shots as he sees them and attempts to explain all of life. Whether it be as complex a theory as Freud's or Carl Jung's or as simple as Ellis' or Glasser's, each theoretician tries to tell the whole story and the total truth. No one can judge the value of theory objectively. There is no way of knowing whether Freud's views are more close to the truth than, say, Greenwald's. As Alfred Adler said: *Omnia ex opinione suspensa sunt* (It is all a matter of opinion).

In closing this section, I want to acknowledge another dozen theorists whom I would have liked to include and who are worth searching out. They are Andreas Angyll, Trigant Burrow, Karl Bühler, Raymond A. Cattell, Erich Fromm, Rollo May, O. Hobart Mowrer, Wilhelm Reich, Julian Rotter, Harry Stack Sullivan, Adrian Van Kaam, and Joseph Wolpe.

Psychosocial Theory

When the big three of Freud, Adler, and Jung went their separate ways, each began to recruit associates and followers. However, the lion's share of the recruits to the new science and methodology of psychic treatment—which was called psychoanalysis (with a small *p* to indicate any kind of mental treatment) and Psychoanalysis (with a large *P* to indicate Freud's special theory)—went over to Freud. One of Freud's pupils was Karl Abraham, who taught psychoanalysis at the Berlin Psychoanalytic Institute, and one of Abraham's trainees was Karen Horney (1885–1952). She was associated with this institute from 1918 to 1932, a total of 14 years.

In 1932 she came to the United States, where for two years she was associated with the Chicago Psychoanalytic Institute, later moving to New York. She reported that in the United States the types of problems her neurotic patients presented were not what she had been trained to deal with: Causes, symptoms, and outlooks were different. Her training had placed great emphasis on sex-related causes, the standard psychoanalytic thinking of the time, but in the United States (remember this was during the Great Depression), problems were mostly about jobs, housing, careers, education, and relationships with people rather than with sexual hangups.

She found herself in the situation of many other people who had been trained in psychoanalysis: Reality did not accord to theory. The first American psychoanalyst, Trigant Burrow, finding this to be the case, had also deviated from psychoanalysis and started his own system, which he called Phyloanalysis.

Of the big three leaders, Adler became an ego-psychologist, stressing consciousness, self-control, common sense, and the impact of social and cultural factors. Jung became introverted, as it were, stressing the unconscious, internal conflicts, and inner reality. Freud concerned himself with the conflict between instincts and society. Karen Horney, Harry Stack Sullivan and Erich Fromm went in the sociocultural direction, following Adler's lines, and can be called Freudian disciples who became neo-Adlerians.

Horney was a seminal thinker, a good observer, and her intellectual progress can be observed by reading her five books: *The Neurotic Personality of Our Time* (1937), in which she stresses cultural factors in neuroses; *New Ways in Psychoanalysis* (1939), in which she further contrasts sexual versus social causes of maladjustment; *Self-Analysis* (1942), an attempt to present her modified theories with a self-treatment methodology; *Our Inner Conflicts* (1945), her most important book, in which she presents her trichotomy of social movements; and *Neurosis and Human Growth* (1950), in which she summarizes and generalizes her theory.

Assertions

1. MAN HAS A DESIRE TO DEVELOP TO PERFECTION.

This teleological statement, reminiscent of Adler, is one of the cornerstones of Horney's theory. A person, she asserts, is driven to attain perfection, wants honor and glory, and drives forward in terms of dimly perceived goals of attainment. Potentially, he has the capacity to deal with life and adjusts to situations as they arise.

2. PEOPLE DEVELOP STRATEGIES TO COPE WITH LIFE.

In view of a person's goal, and in terms of the roadblocks in life, people develop general ways of operating, habituated responses, or typical strategies. In some cases the procedures are not healthy (neurotic), a result, in part, of finding incorrect ways of getting along early in life. For example, a child who learned to operate on the basis of getting pity from others later could become a hypochondriac. Using inadequate strategies which worked early in life after one has grown up is what a neurosis amounts to.

3. PEOPLE TEND TO FORM A GENERALIZED MOVEMENT SOCIALLY.

This is one of Horney's unique contributions. People tend to move toward others (love), away from others (distance), or against others (aggression). The more clearly the person is in one of these three corners, the more maladjusted he or she is. To be able to move freely between these three positions is a mark of normality. If one has, say, a strong need for affection from others, then one may move toward others through pleasing people, giving in to others, sacrificing one's self for others and letting one's self be dominated. If one wants freedom, then one may move away from people, refuse to accept responsibility, and become a loner. If one desires to be important, to be first, then one may take an aggressive stance toward life, be an exploiter, and have a me-first attitude. The neurotic is not well balanced and tends to move to one of these three primary social positions.

4. PERFECTION IS THWARTED BY SOCIETY.

The child has a kind of dream or vision of what he might become, and lives this dream in his head. His idealized conception of himself is shown by his fantasies. But the inner daydream life is brutally affected by reality; things do not work out the way the person wants them to. Now the individual, thwarted by society, has the task of adjustment.

5. THERE ARE TWO REALITIES, INNER AND OUTER.

Normality is a function of keeping the inner ideal reality and the outer realistic reality in focus. The person must be aware of himself to keep on an even keel. There are a variety of images the person has: what he thinks himself to be, what he is, what others see him as. Adjustment calls for knowing and dealing with all these views. If one emphasizes the ideal rather than the real self, then one is alienated from reality.

Applications

Horney did not set out to establish a personality theory. A clinician and a teacher, her aim was to help people understand themselves, and her book *Self-Analysis* is an indication of this. We can best view Horney's applications as a correction of Freudian psychoanalysis and, as is the case with Sullivan and Fromm, as a presentation of alternate views attached to old ideas. Horney's views appear to have been incorporated by people who call themselves neo-Freudians or psychoanalytically oriented therapists and who assemble a melange of ideas from Freud as well as from other psychoanalytic deviationists, such as Fromm and Sullivan.

Evaluation

Horney is generally held in high regard by those who label themselves "psychoanalytically oriented," and she appeals primarily to those who generally like the ideas of psychoanalysis but who do not accept the theoretical underpinnings of Freud. Horney carefully traces the psychological development of children in a sympathetic and understanding way and combines common sense, careful observation, and a feeling for the development of individuals. Consequently, in evaluating her theory, one must deal with impressions of the logic and reasonableness of her position, as well as the acceptance of her views by many psychoanalytically oriented clinicians. The trichotomy of social movements leading to three orientations of life (toward—away—against) seems to have been her major theoretical contribution; this too makes intuitive good sense and is quite useful clinically. She has many ideas close to those of others. For example, Ellis's concern that people load themselves with all kinds of "shoulds" in a search for supremacy is closely related to Horney's idea of the neurotic demands people make of themselves.

Summary

Horney presented a complex but compact view of life. While she was essentially treatment oriented and dealt with neurotics rather than normals, her position was optimistic, forward moving, and humanistic. She stressed social fac-

tors in personality formation and the effects people have on each other, but at the same time she was aware that the person's inner life is a reality. The concept of strategies as resulting from the interaction of a person's internalized goals, and the idea that the reality of life leads in some cases to inadequate and incorrect solutions —which have the general movements of toward, against, and away from people—will probably remain as solid and enduring contributions. Other important features are the human being's self-corrective potentiality and the notion that essentially all therapy is self-therapy.

We see Horney's major contribution as affirmation of the dignity of the person; a sympathetic view of the striving person, burdened with goals for perfection, facing a harsh world, and trying to find happiness, honor, and glory, while struggling for sanity regardless of disparate and discordant inner and outer realities.

Sociometric Theory

J. L. Moreno (1892–1974), like Perls and Wilhelm Reich, was a European-born psychiatrist who, because of his unusual personality and unusual ideas, never was fully accepted in the mainstream of personality theory or psychiatry. Each of the three developed idiosyncratic theories and therapies.

Moreno had diverse interests. He was a poet who was attracted to the theatre and saw himself at one time as a religious innovator who wanted to start his own church. He had many unusual ideas about life and society and was constantly concerned with meetings, publications, conferences, and organizations devoted to the betterment of the world. One of his earliest notions, developed in Europe before he came to the United States in 1925, was that people in post–World War I relocation camps should be permitted to form their own natural groups rather than being allocated places. In 1932, he advanced the same idea relative to prisoners, suggesting that if they were allowed to find their own mates to associate with, this would be "group therapy."

Moreno was a man of action who traveled the world, constantly lecturing and demonstrating. His lectures were sometimes impossible to understand, especially with themes that had religious or mystical implications. His demonstrations of psychodrama were generally most fascinating, but they often resulted in criticisms due to his tendency to expose people's weaknesses and foibles and then move on to his next assignment.

Assertions

Moreno, who wrote voluminously and who published most of his own writings (1934, 1946, 1951), made an exceedingly large number of assertions. Because he was thoroughly unsystematic, however, it is difficult to understand what was important or enduring for him, and, due to his difficulties in communication, it is often difficult to know just what he is saying. Nevertheless, some themes do occur frequently enough to be worth stating as his major assertions.

1. LIFE IS A STRUGGLE BETWEEN
   CREATIVITY AND THE CONSERVE.

Moreno viewed life as process. The essence of goodness and normality is represented by movement, while the essence of badness is staticity. The individual, in his adjustment to life, can either operate in terms of the past, the conserve, or in terms of the present, which calls for spontaneity and creativity. The individual who solves new problems by old methods is frozen into past behaviors. A truly living person operates spontaneously, finding good new solutions to new problems. Thus the individual must avoid operating on the basis of habits, or getting into ruts, instead remaining alert, creative, and spontaneous and finding his way through life dynamically.

2. LIFE CONSISTS OF COMPLEXES THAT
   HAVE TO BE MET IN THE MOMENT.

Moreno was an exponent of the here-and-now school of thought: He felt one should do all things at the same time, not first do this and then do that and then do other things. Reality is not thinking and feeling and acting but thinking-feeling-acting. So a person is always in the arena of life, meeting all kinds of problems in all kinds of dimensions simultaneously. One runs, looks, thinks, has emotions and plans—all at the same time. One cannot really analyze behavior piece by piece or bit by bit: the reality is the whole, integrated, moving unit. In this sense, Moreno is a holistic theorist.

3. INDIVIDUALS HAVE NO REALITY IN AND
   OF THEMSELVES.

Moreno was group oriented and did not see individuals as such but rather as actors in relationship to others. The reality is the relationship between people. A person really does not have any kind of constant self, since he operates differently in different situations. However, most individuals develop an accretion of other individuals with whom they have related in a relatively stable manner. Each person is a nucleus of those around him, and the total group is called a social atom.

4. *Tele* IS THE BASIC RELATIONSHIP UNIT.

Moreno developed the concept of *tele*, a term which means about the same as *magnetism* and represents either a positive or negative force between individuals. People who meet and like each other immediately have a lot of positive tele. While Moreno never explicitly said so, the impression is that normality is a function of a great deal of tele—that is, positive feelings to and from others. Moreno gave the impression that tele is a physiological entity, but it could be developed.

5. LIFE IS ROLE PLAYING.

Moreno viewed how people relate to one another as the result of each individual's perceptions of the roles in which others have placed him. Consequently, people behave generally as they think others expect them to. This, as he saw it, was the original sin. The individual should be himself, and while perhaps caring for others and not hurting them, he or she should not yield to the "cultural conserve," which he saw as the repressive aspect of society.

The successful person (to return to an earlier concept) is one who is able to play the role in life according to the needs of the situation but also in terms of one's own needs. This calls for creativity and spontaneity.

Applications

In trying to understand Moreno, who was quite contradictory as well as complex, we must acknowledge that his vision was affected by an inability to communicate clearly. For example, he called his personality theory a "sociometric" theory—he had developed a method of measuring interactions between individuals known as "sociometry." Now, the meaning of "sociometry" is quite clear, but how a personality theory can be called sociometric is not clear at all.

To put this in another way: Moreno did develop a number of applications within psychology of considerable value, but the relation of these techniques and procedures to the theory he presented is at best tenuous.

Sociometric Testing. Sociometry is an ingenious and useful method of measuring the degree of relationships between people in a particular universe. The procedure is essentially simple: each person is asked to select one or more people within that particular universe in terms of some function, say "working together" or "going on a trip together." The results can be charted on a so-called sociogram which will indicate who wants to be with whom. Thus we can locate the most popular person in any group; we can locate isolates, mutual pairs, and cliques. In two groups, say orchestras A and B, both of the same size, we can determine the total degree of tele within each one. If, for example, when each person is asked to name his three best friends, if 10 percent of the people in orchestra A select people within that orchestra and 50 percent in orchestra B select people within that orchestra as their best friends, it is evident that there is more tele in B than in A. This may mean that orchestra B has greater mutuality, higher morale, and perhaps will play better. The values for this sociometric procedure in summer camps, kindergartens, and industrial and military organization should be evident.

Roleplaying. However, Moreno is best known for (and his greatest impact has been in terms of) a method of a psychotherapy he developed which has the generic name of *role playing* and the specific name of *psychodrama* when used for the direct treatment of a patient. Roleplaying essentially is a method of make-believe. One can roleplay with an absent person, as in the "empty chair" technique (which incidentally Fritz Perls used, calling it the "hot seat") or with one other person, as with a therapist in his office, or one's own role on a stage in front of many

people. If one is roleplaying himself for therapeutic purposes, this is known as psychodrama. If one roleplays to illustrate something, such as a social problem or how to sell a product, then this is generally known as sociodrama. In psychodrama, the person doing the acting is the patient; in sociodrama, the observers are those whom the action is designed to instruct.

Roleplaying, a powerful technique, calls for spontaneity and creativity, not only for the client but also for all others involved—the psychodramatist and the various therapeutic assistants who play various roles in the patient's social atom. Its major purpose is to help a person break away from the cultural conserve and spontaneously find new and creative ways of dealing with problems. Moreno felt psychodrama to be the most natural of the therapies, since it called for the individual, as in real life, to think and act and feel on his feet rather than lying down on a couch and free-associating.

Evaluation

It is difficult at this point to assess Moreno's contributions. It would appear that a great many of his thoughts are not original, but his language was. As such, these concepts were already in the common domain and will remain so, probably with other names. Tele, for example, is not used by anyone, but terms such as *empathy* or *chemistry* to express degree of relationships in terms of feelings between people have more or less the same meaning. Eventually, we suspect, the techniques of sociometry and role playing will be incorporated into psychology generally.

Summary

Moreno is an example of an individual who gets a private vision of how the world really is and how it should be and decides to express his views to all. He had a truly gigantic view of what he could accomplish. One of his aims was the explanation of human nature, his concept of personality. While his views were provocative, practically no one has taken them on or is moving forward with them. This is also the situation with George Kelly, for example, another highly original thinker.

The contributions of Moreno to psychology are not so much his theories as they are his techniques, which could be called "theories in concrete"—the technique of sociometry and of roleplaying, one for diagnosis and the other for treatment. The notions of tele, cultural conserve, spontaneity, creativity, and social atom will probably merge into general personality theory, and indeed they already have to some extent.

Self-Actualization

Abraham Maslow (1908–1970), like Gordon Allport and Albert Bandura, was a researcher, not a clinician. He developed his personality theory from studying superior self-actualized people. A liberal and humanitarian with utopian ideas, Maslow represents an optimistic point of view, concerned with betterment of life. With Charlotte Bühler, Carl Rogers, and Rollo May, he helped establish the American Association of Humanistic Psychology, which had four tenets:

1. The primary study of psychology should be the experiencing person.
2. Choice, creativity, and self-realization, rather than mechanistic reductionism, are the concern of the humanistic psychologist.
3. Only personally and socially meaningful problems should be studied—significance, not objectivity, is the watchword.
4. The major concern of psychology should be the dignity and enhancement of people.

Some of the terms Maslow stressed give an idea of his interests: "full humanness," the utmost expansion of a person; "peak experience," a high feeling of ecstacy, and "eupsyschia," a world of fully realized people. He was concerned with the fully functioning person, an individual who realizes his full potentials. His theme was that only those individuals who are fully realized internally—free, healthy, and fearless—could be fully functioning in society. He came to this point of view rather suddenly, in terms of his admiration for two of his teachers: Ruth Benedict and Max Wertheimer, saying of them: " . . . they were most remarkable beings. My training in psychology equipped me not at all for understanding them. It was as if they were not quite people but more than people. . . . I realized in one wonderful moment that their two patterns could be generalized. I was talking about a kind of person, not about two noncomparable individuals" (1972, p. 41).

Maslow's contributions to personality theory fall into two parts: (1) his concept of a hierarchy of needs, which stipulates that people must first fulfill certain lower needs to be able to aspire to higher needs (1970), and (2) his description of self-actualizing people (1950). Maslow was not an experimentalist in the usual sense. He was more an observer and a philosopher. There is no doubt that he imposed his own values on his observations and that his conclusions were not forced on him by his data. In short, he found what he was looking for.

Assertions

1. NEEDS ARE ARRANGED ON A HIERARCHY OF POTENCY.

The human being has a basic need, and this is to actualize himself. We can see this as the tip of a pyramid (Figure 14-1), where perfection is achieved. But there are lower levels, and the tip can only be reached if these levels have been realized.

In order of priority, first the individual has a need for physiological maintenance. To give a gruesome example, if a person is at a dinner as the guest of honor and if some food lodges in his throat so his air supply is choked off, his need for esteem gives way to his need to breathe; he forgets everything else and is solely concerned with getting the food out of his throat. In general, after physiological needs are attended, next come safety needs, such as a desire to be financially secure; and then belonging and love needs, such as a mate and family. When these are met, esteem needs emerge, and the achievement of glory and fame become of concern. Finally comes the need to be free to create.

This contribution of Maslow probably has generality but must not be seen as absolute. How would one explain self-sacrifice, which may call for an individual to suffer, go on hunger strikes, go to war, or even commit suicide for some ideal? Also, some self-actualizing people seem to be relatively free of affiliation or love needs; artists such as Pablo Picasso seem to deny the generality of Maslow's hierarchy of needs.

2. THE SELF-ACTUALIZED PERSON HAS 17 ATTRIBUTES.

Maslow established a private definition of self-actualization and then searched for individuals

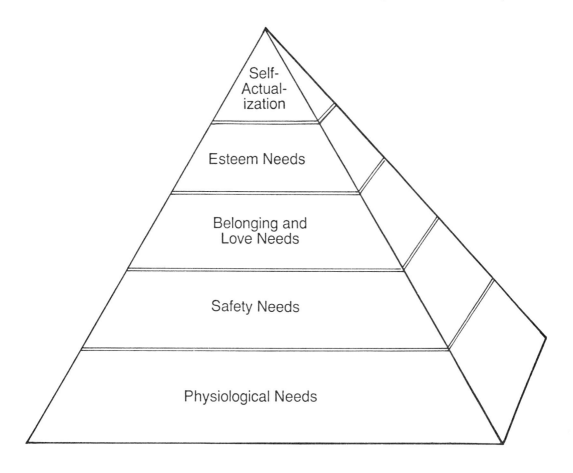

Figure 14-1: Pyramidal Conceptualization of Maslow's
Hierarchy of Needs

who fitted his definition and attempted to discover what they had in common. It was a kind of self-reflexive research, based on interviews, biographies, accounts, and so on. While the final result "makes sense," the technique must not be confused with standard research. Rather, it is a kind of attempt to locate general parameters of highly competent and successful individuals. Maslow (1950, pp. 156–174) found that self-actualizing people:

1. Perceive reality accurately.
2. Accept reality readily.
3. Are natural.
4. Focus on problems.
5. Have a need for privacy.
6. Are self-sufficient and not dependent.
7. Appreciate and enjoy life.
8. Have peak experiences, attain transcendence.
9. Have *Gemeinschaftsgefühl*—brotherly love, social interest.
10. Make strong friends.
11. Have a democratic, egalitarian attitude.
12. Have values, know the difference between right and wrong.
13. Have a broad philosophical sense of humor.
14. Are inventive and creative, see things in new ways.
15. Resist the pressures of society or conformity.

16. Are well integrated, total and entire.
17. Transcend dichotomies, bring together opposites.

Applications

Since Maslow did not establish any system of psychotherapy or of education, applications of his theory by others amount to an acceptance of the validity of his ideas relative to their use in practical situations. To give an illustration, a person dealing with another and concerned about the other's nonachievement (such as a teacher dealing with a child) might examine whether his "lower" needs, such as for belonging and love, are being met. Or a therapist concerned with a client's progress may use the 17-item list of signs of self-actualization to check how things are going. From a research point of view, either of these conceptualizations can have value.

Evaluation

It must be remembered that these major contributions of Maslow's are essentially armchair theorizing, based on observations and wishes. This does not mean that they are not "true," but their truth is not the replicable type based on objective measures. They are true to their own credo, as stated earlier in terms of the four tenets of humanistic psychology. It is evident that Maslow was a "do-gooder" of the highest type, and he may essentially have been a religious reformer rather than an objective scientist, at least in these respects.

Those who are interested in growth centers and in personal development and greater awareness, moving from a situation of general comfort and average effort and medium success, will find Maslow's ideas useful for self-implementation and dealing with others. Social reformers, educational theorists, and the like find his ideas can provide a superior goal.

Maslow's ideas, as in the case of Allport, who resembles him in many ways, have already been absorbed in general psychology and in personality theory.

Summary

Maslow's theories about motivation, the good life, the nature of humans, and the direction in which people should move are all part of his optimistic and altruistic viewpoint. Essentially, they state that individuals should feel good about themselves and should move upward, as they are destined by their essential nature. This "growth" concept, found in the work of almost every theorist, is a kind of metapsychology which approaches the status of philosophy.

Personology (Needs-Press Theory)

Henry A. Murray (1893–   ) has an unusual background. By age 32, when he met Carl Jung (and thereby had his life changed), he had earned an M.D. from Columbia University, had had two years of surgery training, and been awarded a Ph.D. in physiological chemistry from Cambridge. He went into psychiatry and for 35 years was an instructor in psychology at Harvard University, until his retirement in 1962. During the World War II years he was in charge of evaluating people for counterespionage work in the Office of Strategic Services.

In 1938 his book *Explorations in Personality* appeared, and in 1948, *Assessment of Men*. He is perhaps best known for his co-development, with Christiana Morgan, of the projective instrument the *Thematic Apperception Test*, (1943), called the TAT (pronounced T-A-T).

At Harvard, Murray worked closely with Gordon W. Allport. Murray's need-press theory (also known as personology) is similar to Allport's *personalism* in that both are primarily concerned with understanding individuals. Murray's theory resembles the eclectic stimulus-organism-response (S-O-R) theory of behavior; it also resembles William McDougall's instinct theory and has a family resemblance to Abraham Maslow's theory of self-actualization. On the other hand, Murray's need-press theory, while essentially simple in general structure, is complicated in its details.

Murray's theory can be seen as a theory of motivation: The inner person and the outer world interact to lead to differential behavior. This means we must consider what is in the brain of the individual in terms of what gets there from inside (needs) and what gets there from outside (press), which combine, fuse, interact, and lead to differentiated action.

Behavioral units (*actones*) are thus a function of the individual and the environment, but they are expressed via *vectors*, or particular modes of behavior or patterns of habits. These units are also affected by the individual's uniqueness, his values. The total picture of the individual's functioning is known as his *thema*.

Needs are constructs, or inferred conditions, but they are considered to be real. Murray developed a list of 12 primary (physiological) and 28 secondary (psychological) needs. Four of each are listed below, with some explanatory comments. Note that the letter *n* precedes the name of each of these needs.

Primary Needs	Comments
n water	Deficiency need for liquids.
n sex	Inner tension need, due to secretions.
n urination	Inner tension need, due to expulsion pressure.
n harm avoidance	Negative need, due to threat from environment.
Secondary Needs	
n abasement	Need to passively submit to others.
n affiliation	Need to behave cooperatively with others.
n dominance	Need to be in control.
n play	Need to have fun.

The concept of *press* (this word is spelled the same for singular and plural) relates to the reality of the outside world (*alpha press*) and the outside world as subjectively interpreted by the individual (*beta press*). An example of this is that to marry a person requires a marriage license (alpha press), but one who wants to marry a particular person may believe that person will not want him (beta press).

The various needs may interact and summate or fuse, and the same can occur with the various press elements leading to units of behavior, the actones.

Assertions

1. OPTIONAL BEHAVIOR (ACTONES) IS A FUNCTION OF NEEDS.

In Murray's thinking, every internal element (need) has a kind of power or valence which will affect the total final act. Consequently, in understanding personality, the behavior of the individual must be understood in terms of the needs of the individual, which are often quite complex.

2. OPTIONAL BEHAVIOR (ACTONES) IS A FUNCTION OF PRESS.

The other half of the picture is the pressure of reality, not only pure reality (alpha press) but interpreted reality (beta press).

3. NEEDS AND PRESS ARE DIRECTED BY UNITY-THEMAS.

As the individual develops, he forms certain patterns of behavior and establishes certain values which form a kind of supercontrol of the individual, leading him to behave in ways not necessarily explained by the needs and press. Thus, X can have exactly the same need-press pattern as Y and yet operate quite differently, because he established in his earlier life a particular *unity-thema* which will direct the particular actone.

4. NEEDS IN CONFLICT PRODUCE TENSION.

Were humans calculating machines, or as John Stuart Mill asserted, capable of hedonic calculus, human behavior would be simple to predict, since it is a function of the various forces, plus and minus, consisting of needs, press, vectors, values, and themas. Such is not the case. Needs can conflict with one another, and the individual may not be able to deal with these internal conflicts. Thus, a person may have *n affiliation* and *n dominance* at the same time to such a degree that he may not be able to function effectively. When a person has this problem, he can be said to be in psychological difficulty, in that he is conflicted.

5. THE PRIMARY MOTIVE IS TENSION REDUCTION.

Murray views the organism as fluctuating between periods of contentment (homeostasis) and activity (Funkstionsluft). The individual at times wants to be at rest and at other times wants to be in action. The pressure of needs and of press motivate the individual to seek tension reduction.

Applications

Murray's theory is mostly employed in reference to two tests: The Thematic Apperception Test and Edwards' Personal Preference Schedule (1953). While the TAT can be interpreted in many ways, including subjectively, without any kind of scoring system, it is frequently employed with some sort of check-off system in attempts to locate the various needs and press in the individual's conceptions which lead to various themas. The TAT is an especially popular instrument, not only in Murray's original form but in countless variations.

Evaluation

Curiously, in terms of the specificity of the theory and the popularity of the TAT, one might expect considerable research had been done to validate Murray's hypotheses. While there have been studies on specific needs, especially the work of D. C. McClelland (1961) on *n achievement*, there has been relatively little research of any substance on Murray's theory.

Evidence for the validity of Murray's personology comes from two major sources: the continued use of the TAT, and Murray's relative popularity with personality theorists. After the theories to be discussed in this book had been selected, a count was taken of the number of times each of the theorists covered in this chapter was mentioned by seven textbook authors. The most popular theorist was Abraham Maslow, who was mentioned by all seven authors on a total of 125 pages. Murray was a close second, being referred to by six authors on 121 pages, and Erikson was third, with 97 pages.

Summary

It is an intellectual and aesthetic treat to read the works of H. A. Murray. His point of view is extremely persuasive, and one can get the impression that he is right. Yet, his theory does not have any great degree of specific research, and it is not employed, as far as this writer knows, by any clinicians in counseling or psychotherapy. Part of this may be because the theory is static, since it is mostly taxonomic and consequently is perhaps a theory of motivation rather than a theory of personality.

Murray is still, at the time of this writing, working on his theory and undoubtedly more will be pouring from his facile pen. It is hoped the theory will gain the further dimensionality it now lacks.

Transactional Analysis

Transactional analysis (TA) is essentially a procedure for evaluating interactions between people systematically which is especially suitable for group therapeutic endeavors. Developed initially by a psychiatrist, Eric Berne (1961, 1964) and popularized by Thomas Harris (1969), also a psychiatrist, TA has become increasingly popular for a variety of reasons. One of these is a new vocabulary which apparently simplifies the conceptualization of human relationships, such as the concept of the person playing the role of Parent, Adult, or Child in relationship to another person's Parent, Adult, or Child.

The notion that a person may have several selves or different levels of functioning—say mature in one respect and immature in another; honest in dealing with customers, dishonest with relatives; bold with friends and shy with strangers—is an old one, and this phenomenon of apparent inconsistency has been well understood. In medieval religious thought, for example, people were thought to be influenced by a guardian angel and a guardian demon, and the person was said to listen at one time to messages from God and at another to messages from the Devil.

The partition of the self into parts, however, is best represented by the psychoanalytic notion of ego, id, and superego. Berne imitated Freud in this respect, and indeed his system may be said to be equivalent: Parent = superego, Child = id, and Adult = ego. Berne had been associated with psychoanalysis for 15 years, and it is highly likely that he was influenced in this respect by Freud's original conception. However, according to Rozsnafszky (1974), Berne was influenced more by Alfred Adler than by Freud. Adlerian psychology and transactional analysis are similar in these respects (and differing from psychoanalysis): The individual is considered responsible, and the aim of therapy is to control the ego; the major problem in Adler is identified as feelings of inferiority and in TA as feeling "not OK." Adlerians talk about a person having a lifestyle and a life goal, while transactional analysts discuss scripts and payoffs, which appear to be equivalent terms. Individual psychology is essentially a social psychology, in contrast to Freud's instinctual psychology, and Berne's transactional psychology is also a social psychology. Finally, treatment methods are quite similar in Adler's Individual Psychology and Berne's TA. The therapist plays the role of teacher rather than doctor. The patient is seen as a cooperating colleague wanting to learn about himself and how he functions. The influence of the past is reduced. Diagnoses are avoided. TA (and Glasser's reality therapy and Ellis's rational-emotive therapy) is directive, rational, and didactic.

Transactional analysis, as is true for a number of other of the schools of thought considered in this chapter, is an "aggressive" system, fighting for its place in the sun. This is shown by the establishment of a national society, The International Transactional Analysis Association, with its own *Transactional Analysis Journal*. The membership of this group already exceeds that of some older societies, such as those for Adlerians and Jungians.

Assertions

1. PHYSIOLOGICAL NEEDS BECOME CONVERTED TO SOCIAL HUNGERS.

The infant needs physical attention to survive. For example, a child must be physically manipulated to live; this handling helps him to digest his food, to burp gasses, to defecate, and so on. Later this physiological life need changes to social symbolism; while the adult may no longer need physical handling, he needs it symbolically and so develops hungers. Stroke hunger, as shown by friendly greetings, smiles, and gestures, develops from prior physiological need.

2. A COMMON HUMAN PROBLEM IS THE STRUCTURING OF TIME.

People have to do something with their time, and keeping apart the time spent for physiological needs, such as eating and drinking, they must spend their time in a meaningful manner. Consequently, the individual attempts to maximize his time and activities to achieve the greatest return. This concept is quite similar to hedonistic calculus, which holds that a person so operates to get the greatest pleasure out of life.

3. INDIVIDUALS ESTABLISH LIFE PLANS AT AN EARLY AGE.

The concept of *script* is equivalent to the Adlerian notion of a lifestyle or Freud's repetition compulsion and serves to explain the dynamics

of emerging personality patterns and goals. It is a *modus operandi*, something that represents the individual's individuality, his unique way of operating, a basic life position. This script is usually developed as a result of parental guidance, directions, and injunctions, as interpreted by the child and the self-confirming nature of his behavior.

4. AS PART OF LIFE SCRIPTS, PEOPLE ENGAGE IN RACKETS.

The term *racket* refers to an individual's attempt to achieve certain results emotionally. To attain these results, called *stamps* (in the same sense as a housewife collecting trading stamps), the individual tends to play certain stereotyped roles called *games*. Games are transactions between people, usually at two levels, leading to some sort of payoff, which may be pleasant or unpleasant.

To illustrate, a person may be apologetic and deferential and even self-abasing. Those who deal with him find his abjective self-deprecating manner uncomfortable and unwittingly "feed it" (kick him). This whole procedure is his game, playing inferior is his con, the strokes he gets are his payoff, and the payoff is his racket.

5. PEOPLE OPERATE RITUALISTICALLY IN MANY TRANSACTIONS.

To avoid real interactions and confrontations, people structure their time socially by engaging different exchanges. These are preestablished ways of dealing with others and prescribing correct rituals. Two people meeting for the first time may smile at one another, shake hands for a predetermined length of time, and then engage in conversation intended to keep them at a distance.

6. THE PERSON TENDS TO TAKE AN OK OR A NOT-OK POSITION RELATIVE TO SELF AND OTHERS.

The four possibilities (Harris, 1969) are:
1. I'm OK, you're OK.
2. I'm OK, you're not OK.
3. I'm not OK, you're OK.
4. I'm not OK, you're not OK.

These four attitudes tend to be part of the life script and to maintain themselves tenaciously, since they represent fundamental beliefs re self and others. Thus, if we think we are basically OK and others are OK, we tend to be courageous and friendly, and the type of games we play are quite different from those of people who see themselves as not OK and others as not OK.

7. THERE ARE THREE EGO STATES: CHILD, ADULT, AND PARENT.

An individual is seen as having potentials in all three of these ego states, but in any particular situation with another person he may be found usually in one of those states. Thus, John may be a Child in relationship to his wife, dealing with her symbolically as though she were his mother; and with his friends he may be a Parent taking a supervisory and caring role. But, the other person may or may not go along with him. Thus, if he treats his wife as though he were her child, and if she were to reply similarly, acting as though he were a child, a reciprocal relationship would exist, and the relationship could go on. But let us say that at the office, he deals with others as adults but that he is treated as a child; then we have a crossed relationship, and this would be mutually unsatisfactory.

Applications

Transactional analysis was started as a form of group psychotherapy, although some practitioners employ its insights in individual therapy. In terms of the concept of structural analysis, the therapy is between two Adults, and the participants are viewed as partners, equally valuable, and at the same level.

Usually, the first step in the treatment process is a clear statement of the problem and the goals of the patient; then comes a structural analysis to attempt to see the person as he views himself and others; the patient's transactions with others are analyzed; their games are uncovered; and individual scripts are identified and discussed. In a manner of speaking, the therapist puts a mirror in front of his patient or perhaps draws him a diagram so he can see himself clearly in terms of this particular system of conceptualization.

Techniques used in addition to the interview or the circular discussion group include psychodrama, fantasy exercises, and a whole variety of methods developed by imaginative group leaders. For example, a person may put a sign on his sweatshirt to indicate the message he gives the world, such as: I Love Everybody, and then on his back is the message he really has, such as: Go To Hell! There is no orthodox way of operating, and practitioners are free to use whatever procedures they feel best will achieve their goals.

As in the case of Ellis's and Glasser's theories, the main object is to give patients a rapidly objective view of themselves relative to the presenting theory, to unconfuse these individuals who are wandering about in trouble, not knowing where they are or what they want or where they want to go. The therapist sees himself as a teacher and operates, again as in the case of Moreno, Ellis, Glasser, and Greenwald, on a here-and-now basis.

Evaluation

The value of this system is evident to practitioners who usually begin with a contract with the patient who wants to achieve certain goals and who, at the end of the relationship, is asked whether he did, in fact, receive what he was looking for. Thus far, there have been no really meaningful research studies of the nomothetic type—only case histories.

Summary

In summarizing, Eric Berne's transactional analysis is a rather simplified version of some aspects of Alfred Adler's Individual Psychology, with elements of Freud's psychoanalysis and parts of encounter methodology (Schutz, 1973). Relatively simple to understand, it provides the client with a clear-cut picture of where he is in relation to his feelings about himself and others and how he relates to others structurally and dynamically. In use, the client is given a diagram of his behavior and an analysis is made of the games he plays. The general intention is to develop the individual as an OK person who deals with others, typically at an adult level and owning feelings and behavior, through helping the patient see the errors he makes in interacting with others.

While still mostly a method of psychotherapy, the literature of TA is growing, and while at the present time most of the substantive writing of a theoretical nature is Berne's (1961–1964), some other popular publications, such as Harris's *I'm OK, You're OK* (1969) and Steiner's *Games Alcoholics Play* (1971), are engaging the attention of professionals and the public in this dynamically growing theory and procedure.

Developmental Theory

Erik H. Erikson (1902–   ) is an unusual person. Without any academic degrees, he has taught at Harvard, the University of California and Stanford University. He is one of the best-selling authors on psychoanalysis and is best known for (1) his developmental theory of personality, (2) his book *Childhood and Society* (1963), and (3) his brilliant biographical studies of Gandhi (1969) and of Martin Luther (1958).

To understand Erikson's contribution requires some historical orientation. Trained as a psychoanalyst, he has always maintained a loyal allegiance to the theory of Freud but has operated mainly within one aspect of psychoanalysis: the development of ego. This makes Erikson an ego-psychologist, as with so many others who were trained originally in psychoanalysis. Many personality theorists have offered a sequential concept of the individual as maturing from stage to stage in a kind of psychological metamorphosis. Freud himself suggested that individuals move from an oral to an anal to a genital stage, and we have seen this notion in Maslow's self-actualization theory. But the most explicit and comprehensive view of development of self is offered by Erikson, who was most concerned with the development of personal identity.

Assertions

1. THE EGO IS SHAPED BY SOCIETY.

The Freudian notion of the development of ego was that it is between the forces of the id and the superego. Erikson more or less disregards these two forces and sees the ego as an autonomous function within the society in which the individual finds himself. This provides a simpler conceptualization of how personality functions: the self against society. Instead of considering personality as primarily affected by instincts or by parents, Erikson focuses on all of society, which includes parents, siblings, and other individuals. In addition, instead of stopping at early child-

hood and believing that the personality is essentially shaped by age four or five, Erikson's view is that personality is constantly emerging and developing in relation to society.

2. THE INDIVIDUAL IS IN A CONSTANT PROCESS OF CHALLENGE AND GROWTH.

Instead of viewing the individual as the plaything of social forces, Erikson presents the concept of the emerging individual, challenged by the crises of life, from which he can emerge victorious and strengthened. This means that he views the person as in charge, the captain of his fate rather than a crew member who has to do another's biddings. Erikson has an optimistic-creative view of personality.

3. THE INDIVIDUAL IS PREPROGRAMMED TO GO THROUGH VARIOUS DEVELOPMENTAL STAGES.

Erikson is best known for his eight stages of development, which is part of his epigenetic principle. Before studying these, it is important to understand the concept of *epigenesis,* which means that the individual, under normal conditions, will develop inevitably from stage to stage. The fully matured and realized individual will have gone through these stages successfully, passing through the various crises inherent in each stage in a proper manner. To move from one of these stages to another means that the individual has to struggle, since there always is some sort of conflict in the transition from stage to stage.

Figure 14–2, which illustrates Erikson's eight stages of ego development, should be studied carefully, with the following comments:

I. *Trust vs. distrust.* During the first year of life the baby has a crisis problem of learning whether to trust or mistrust life. Naturally, his solution depends a great deal on his parents, especially the mother. If mothering is inadequate, he may develop basic mistrust that may never leave him. Not only should a child develop a trust in the outside world, he should also develop trust in his own ability to meet some of life's demands himself. The consequences of success or failure are either *hope* or *fear.*

II. *Autonomy vs. shame and doubt.* At ages one to three, the child has a problem with self-control and ability to move around and to be

Figure 14-2: The Eight Stages of Ego Development According to Erikson

		Ages	Stages $\rightarrow$	Consequences
I.		Early infancy (birth-1)	Trust vs. Mistrust	Hope Fear
II.		Infancy (1-3)	Autonomy vs. Shame and doubt	Self-control Self-doubt
III.		Early childhood (4-5)	Initiative vs. Guilt	Responsibility Unworthiness
IV.		Middle childhood (6-11)	Industry vs. Inferiority	Competency Incompetency
V.		Puberty and adolescence (12-20)	Identity vs. Confusion	Loyalty Uncertainty
VI.		Early adulthood (20-24)	Intimacy vs. Isolation	Mutuality Promiscuity
VII.		Middle adulthood (25-65)	Generativity vs. Stagnation	Caring Selfishness
VIII.		Late adulthood (65 plus)	Integrity vs. Despair	Acceptance Meaninglessness

self-sufficient. As the exploration drive shows itself, the child has to learn to move away from the protection of the parent. He or she learns to be more independent and to make decisions. He is no longer a baby and develops confidence as he expresses his ability to decide. He develops *self-control* or *self-doubt*.

III. *Initiative vs. guilt.* In this third stage, ages four to five, the "play age," the child increases the degree of initiative and self-responsibility. He gives up his mother and develops a sense of right and wrong. He moves on to creative play, and life begins to have purpose. He develops a sense of *responsibility* or *unworthiness*.

IV. *Industry vs. inferiority.* This is the school-age period, running from about 6 to 11, the age at which the child must begin to prepare himself for an occupation. He has broken away from his home, at least for part of the day, and has to compete with his peers without the protection or domination of his parents. He now

learns to "work" and gains recognition by his achievement, not just for being himself. During this period the child becomes vulnerable to feelings of incompetency, since no longer does he get credit or praise for inconsequential things. Success leads to *competency*, failure to *incompetency*.

V. *Identity vs. confusion.* It is for this period, from ages about 12 to 20, that Erikson has made the greatest contribution. The youth begins to separate from his family and at the end of the period should be an adult, having established his own values, associates, and way of life. Changes in the body, development of sexuality, and demands of peers lead to the crucial problems of deciding his identity. Successfully meeting this crisis leads to the development of *loyalty*, the ability to remain faithfully in love; failure leads to *uncertainty*.

VI. *Intimacy vs. isolation.* This is the period of adulthood, moving past adolescence. The individual now has the ability not only for love but for commitment and can achieve mutuality with one other person at a genital level of relationship. The inadequate or immature reaction is to remain apart from others, unable to sustain a deep or abiding relationship. The consequence of success in this stage is *mutuality;* failure leads to *promiscuity*.

VII. *Generativity vs. stagnation.* An interesting period of later life is middle adulthood, characterized by generativity or stagnation. Generativity relates to feelings for others, concern with the younger generation. Usually it refers to proper parenting, bringing up children. Stagnation refers to inability to care for others, selfish self-concern. Such people, with excessive self-love, have no ability to give to others and are stale. Success here leads to *caring*, but failure leads to *selfishness*.

VIII. *Integrity vs. despair.* To achieve ego integrity, the various prior stages must have been successfully handled. At this stage the individual has wisdom, self-acceptance, a feeling of the rightness and fitness of life, and the ability to face death with dignity and fortitude. The end result is either *acceptance* or *meaninglessness*.

Applications

Erikson's theory has found applications at all levels of development. Perhaps because he is one of the few who have taken up adolescence and later maturity, it has been specially favored by those working in these areas. It is based on psychosocial rather than psychosexual concepts and is therefore useful to eclectic counselors. Erikson's (1968) concern for the "identity crises" of adolescence have seemed particularly appropriate in recent years as the problems of teen-agers have increased. In recent years, too, this issue of identity seems to have become a concern for adults. The women's liberation movement, for example, has taken up the issue of whoness and whatness, as adults are rethinking their aims and ambitions, goals and values. Erikson's concepts relative to these eight stages of life relate to these problems, and we find Erikson quoted in popular periodical literature in terms of his general thoughts on adult stages of development.

Evaluation

In attempting to evaluate Erikson's work, the first issue is whether it really is an extension of psychoanalysis. Despite Erikson's assertions, it seems that he is his own person, a seminal thinker, who has not really accepted much of Freud's basic concepts. A good example has to do with determinism. Erikson makes an interesting contradictory point: while these stages are more or less determined biologically, nevertheless they are not inevitably decided either by biology or by the environment. True, both have a factor in the emergence of the stages, but the solution of the crises belongs essentially to the individual. Erikson's position is a variety of soft determinism. Also, Erikson does not depend much on the unconscious. As an ego-theorist, he concerns himself with the rational aspects of individuals.

There has not been much research on Erikson's theories. Bronson (1959) demonstrated that Erikson's concept of ego identity has meaning with reference to college students. Waterman, Beubel and Waterman (1970) provided further evidence that successful identity crisis solutions are related to normal personality.

Summary

Erikson started, as did so many others in psychotherapy and personality theory, as a Freudian psychoanalyst but then went on to develop his own theory. In Erikson's case, unlike such other theorists as Burrow or Sullivan, he does not call his views his own creation but states, in effect, that they are a natural outgrowth (not a contradiction) of psychoanalysis. Erikson's thesis is the effect of society on the maturing individual, how the person goes from role crisis to role crisis trying to find successively the answer to the questions: "Who am I? What should I be doing?"

Overall, the greatest impact of Erikson's thoughts seem to be on those counselors who deal with the problems of adolescence and early maturity.

Gestalt Therapy Theory

Of the various systems in this book, possibly the most difficult to explain is the Gestalt Personality System, and the reasons are several. First, the name itself, hastily chosen, has nothing whatever to do with the Gestalt psychology developed by Max Wertheimer, which dealt with perception and learning, and this creates immediate confusion. Second, the founder of the modern Gestalt personality theory, Frederick (Fritz) Perls (1893–1970), was so idiosyncratic and wrote such disjointed works that they do not appear to hang together. Even the titles indicate this: *Gestalt Therapy Verbatim* (1969b), *In and Out of the Garbage Pail* (1969c), and *Ego, Hunger and Aggression* (1969a). His best known book (probably mostly written by one of his collaborators) is *Gestalt Therapy* (Perls, Hefferline, & Goodman, 1958). Third, there are a number of individuals who claim to be Gestalt therapists who do not necessarily seem to agree and who do not seem to regard it as important that they do agree. Their motto can be said to be the essence of philosophical anarchy: "Do your own thing." Indeed, Gestalt therapy appears to appeal to anarchistic individuals who resent order and discipline and are in interminable search for the uniqueness within themselves.

Gestalt theory emphasizes awareness, just as Adlerian theory emphasizes togetherness, existentialism emphasizes authenticity, and psychodrama emphasizes spontaneity. Gestalt theory, which is concerned with confrontations between contesting, contending, or discordant functions, makes the strange assumption that if contending forces were brought together, both elements would disappear. In illustration we quote from Walter Kempler (1973), whose account of Gestalt we shall follow: "Theoretically, at least, a completely successful course of treatment could result in the total physical disappearance of both patient and therapist" (p. 255). The discordant elements within an individual or between individuals are brought to confrontation to achieve harmony. The Gestalt approach is of the here-and-now variety, deals with behavior, and calls for considerable participation by the therapist who guides his client to fuller awareness.

Perls himself was unique, *sui generis,* and no one could really work as he did. He was the guru, highly active and very authoritarian in his work, although quite the opposite personally. He was not an organizer, was not methodical, and did not try to establish any school in any sense, always emphasizing the individuality of everyone. Following his death, a kind of consistent disorganization persisted in the Gestalt world. There were a number of Gestalt institutes, and true to their general philosophy, each did his own thing. Consequently, there was little in common between them or even between individuals within the various institutes.

Assertions

1. MAN IS PROCESS.
The concept of the Greek philosopher Heraclitus that man is in the process of constant change is assumed here. Man is but energy within a sea of energy. "To recognize man as a process is a beginning. To see him as a composite of processes in an endless universe of processes is to define him" (Kempler, 1973, p. 255).

2. PERSONALITY HAS THREE PHASES: SOCIAL, PSYCHOPHYSICAL, AND SPIRITUAL.
These are sequential steps of development, each existent from birth as potential. The first, smaller one is the social phase, which relates to awareness of others; the second, containing the social within it, is the psychophysical phase, in which the individual becomes aware of himself; and the third, containing the psychophysical (with the social within it), is the spiritual, in which there is awareness of extrasensory matters. Most people stop at the second step and are intuitively aware

of this third aspect of reality but do not know how to experience it. Religious institutions and drugs have the power of generating belief in this third aspect but are not strong enough to put one in that phase. The process of moving from stage to stage is difficult to explain, but by becoming more fully what one is, one becomes ready to move on to the next higher level of integration.

3. PERSONALITY CONSISTS OF BEING, SELF, AND SELF-IMAGE.
The individual at first is being without awareness. During his early existence the child bumps into identifiable objects and learns adaptation. By interaction with reality, what Kempler calls "Mother Earth," the individual discovers his self to some extent, but, more importantly, he does this through "acknowledgment," which means being given attention for being just what he is, a valueless appreciation of the child. What is potentially harmful is "approbation," which is a means of setting standards for the child that are not his own, but another's. The child, to gain approval, splits off from what he is to what others want him to be. He develops a social face, a self-image, in order to survive. He has to appear to be what others want him to be rather than just being himself.

Applications
Gestalt theory has been utilized mainly in psychotherapy. The therapist in the Kempler version sees his task as confrontations leading to the resolution of discordant elements in some process. The therapist himself should be in a good place, not discordant, not in trouble, in harmony with himself. He applies himself to the patient who is in conflict, with elements of his life not going the way he wants them to. His therapeutic objective is to extinguish all troubling symptoms, so that the patient will be at peace with himself. This is done by getting the patient to confront his discordant elements. In the therapeutic process the therapist recognizes what really causes this symptom (that is, what is discordant about the patient) and then gets the polar opposites lined up so that they can be brought into apposition and thus reduced. As Kempler states it, "Persuading the patient to face himself or whoever he identifies as his oppressor . . . requires all the personal and profes-

sional skill the therapist can muster" (Kempler, 1973, p. 268).

The therapeutic process involves asking questions at a practical level so to get closer to the problem, narrowing down the field of inquiry, as it were, and then, on reaching an impasse, using fantasy to attempt resolution. The therapist tries to lead the patient so that self-help will occur. A question such as, "Well, imagine that you were to ask some fellow for a date, what you think might happen then?" leads the patient to fantasy a reply. The therapist not only listens for the answer but watches the patient carefully to get an awareness of the degree of discomfort. He relentlessly attempts to get to central polarization, looking for process discordance.

The therapist does not play the doctor role but tries to be himself authentically. Should he feel bored by the patient, he might simply yawn and tell him "I am bored by you," or he may even pick up a book and start to read it. Quoting from Kempler again, "Telling a patient what you think of him in a fit of pique is as important as recognizing a polarized conflict . . . admitting your fear of telling him off even more important" (Kempler, 1973, p. 271).

Evaluation

As is true with most of the personality theories in this section, validation of Gestalt theory comes from individual clinical cases. That is, the therapist who applies this method and gets success realizes that he and his method succeeded in achieving desired results, and since how he operates is a function of his central beliefs, this necessarily confirms in him that his basic concepts are correct. Therefore, the Gestalt therapist—as is true for the psychodramatist, the transactional analyst, or any other therapist with a special theory—finds confirmation of the validity of his theory from clinical experience.

Summary

We want to emphasize that Gestalt theory does not have the central unity or clearness of definition that say rational-emotive or Adlerian theory have. In this section we have utilized the views of one person (Kempler), who identifies himself as a Gestalt therapist and whose ideas are not necessarily those of others who identify themselves as Gestaltists. We can attempt to classify Gestalt

therapy as a variety of existential thinking which emphasizes the uniqueness of persons struggling for identity and awareness. The student of personality theory will be interested to watch its development which at the present time has a quite uncertain future.

Rational-Emotive Theory

Albert Ellis (1913–   ), a psychologist, is the founder of Rational-Emotive Therapy. Originally trained as a psychoanalyst, he became dissatisfied operating within this theory because he discovered that after successful analysis, when a client came to understand his problem, he was likely to still have the problem, and insight alone was not enough. He threw over the whole complex psychoanalytic system in favor of an extremely simple basic concept. Behavior is due, he said, not to events but to interpretation of events. This statement is formally made as follows: Consequences (that is, behavior) are not a function of Activators (that is, stimuli) but rather of Beliefs (that is, interpretations). The reader may see the similarity of this A–B–C formulation to the concept of S–O–R, that Reactions are a function of the Organism's interpretation of Stimuli.

Ellis is fond of quoting Epictetus's statement, "Men are not disturbed by things, but by the view they take of them," and Shakespeare's Hamlet, "There is nothing either good or bad, but thinking makes it so." In short, according to Ellis, it is not reality—the environment or heredity—that must be considered the explanation of personality in action. What counts is the cognitive process: how one interprets reality.

Thus, in reacting to any stimulus situation, the understanding of the individual lies in his intellectual, interpretative apparatus: the messages the person gives himself. This is why insight is not enough. As regards modifying behavior through psychotherapy, Ellis concluded that lack of change results when people actively reindoctrinate themselves with self-denigrating statements, such as "I should be better than I am," and consequently reinfect themselves through their beliefs. He sees humans as self-reflecting—talking to themselves, evaluating themselves, giving themselves propaganda, and then responding appropriately in a circular manner. The problem of behavior change, as Ellis sees it, is to break this cycle which has the result that people keep themselves disturbed.

As a consequence of this belief, Ellis developed his rational-emotive system and has been most active in expounding his message. The author of more than 35 books and monographs, Ellis actively organizes and expands his school of thought. *Reason and Emotion in Psychotherapy* (1962) and *Humanistic Psychotherapy: the Rational-Emotive Approach* (1973) are probably the most comprehensive accounts of his system. He maintains a training center in New York City and is a frequent lecturer around the United States.

His system is probably most similar to Alfred Adler's Individual Psychology (Rozsnafszky, 1974). He is a member of the American Society of Adlerian Psychology, but his theory does differ in some respects from that of Alfred Adler.

Assertions

From Ellis's writings, various theoretical statements can be extracted.

1.   HUMANS HAVE THE POTENTIAL TO BE
        RATIONAL OR IRRATIONAL.

This basic notion differs considerably from the underlying concept found in many other systems —including Individual Psychology, person-centered theory, and Goldstein's holistic theory — that people are essentially growth- and health-oriented and if permitted to grow on their own, will inevitably aim for perfection, health, and so on. Ellis's position parallels Freud's concept of opposing forces of life and death instincts, but there is a difference in that Ellis posits that the individual is equally likely to go in one direction or another. In his terminology, people are equally vulnerable to straight or to crooked thinking.

2.   PEOPLE LARGELY CREATE THEIR
        EMOTIONAL DIFFICULTIES, BUT WITH
        SIGNIFICANT HELP FROM THEIR
        ENVIRONMENT.

Ellis's position here is that the individual must take responsibility for his thoughts, feelings, and acts, but at the same time his situation relative to his mental status is affected by others. The implication is that as the individual grows up he must begin to take responsibility relative to the acceptance/nonacceptance of the messages given to him by others and that he should become more and more his own person as he develops from childhood to maturity. Yes, one is affected by one's family (for instance) in terms of values, but one cannot keep on blaming them for one's incorrect ideas.

3.   THE TOTAL INDIVIDUAL
        FUNCTIONS HOLISTICALLY IN THE AREAS
        OF COGNITION, AFFECTION, AND ACTION.

As we shall see in the next assertion, while Ellis views the person as functioning as a whole, and theoretically and philosophically he is a monist, nevertheless he values cognition as being the most important function relative to personality maintenance and change. This means, according to him, that in a true system of psychotherapy the total person must be changed in behavior, thoughts, and feelings; while one-sided systems may work, they are relatively ineffective, and it is the total being that is changed primarily by dealing with his rational congitive aspect.

4.   BECAUSE HUMANS ARE SINGULARLY
        COGNITIVE CREATURES, THEY HAVE THE
        CAPACITY TO UNDERSTAND THEIR
        IRRATIONAL THINKING.

Ellis makes the assumption that human behavior operates in the sequence (1) thoughts, (2) actions, and (3) feelings. This means that, logically, the best way to break up the chain of behavior patterns is to begin with thoughts. That is, people can think about their thinking. This is the fastest, cheapest and most effective way of changing people: asking them to evaluate their own thinking.

5.   WHEN PEOPLE CHANGE DYSFUNCTIONAL
        THINKING, BEHAVIOR, AND EMOTING,
        THEY FREQUENTLY RETURN, AT LEAST
        TEMPORARILY, TO THEIR FORMER
        PATTERNS.

This concept out of learning theory—namely, that old habits persist—can be analogized with the property of a rubber band which enables it, after being stretched and released, to return to its prior shape. The implication is that personality change calls not only for insight but for constant vigilance against relapses.

6. PEOPLE GET HABITUATED TO SELF-
DEFEATING PATTERNS.

Ellis's position differs from the so-called growth psychologists, who see humans as constantly moving towards perfection, since he sees people as adjusting to their insanities and neuroses and even struggling to maintain them. This theoretical point explains resistance to change as found commonly in therapy. The client or patient may know his thinking has errors, and yet he will persistently hold on to ideas he knows are irrational.

7. TO ACHIEVE OPTIMAL LIVING, PEOPLE
SHOULD NOT EVALUATE THEMSELVES
BUT ONLY CHANGE THEIR BEHAVIOR.

Watching one's self and judging one's self and others tends to be self-defeating. One should only try to do the right things (those actions that achieve what one really wants) and should be unconcerned with self-regard, others' judgments, or outside evaluations. In this sense, Ellis wants people to be inner directed, or authentic, rather than other directed, or inauthentic.

Applications

While Ellis is primarily an individual therapist who operates on a one-to-one basis, he also utilizes group therapy. With evaluation and treatment techniques he is eclectic, employing the interview, objective and projective tests, tape recordings, role playing, questionnaires, assignments, written autobiographies, readings, and so on.

Evaluation

In a summary account of his system (Ellis, 1973), 53 investigations of rational-emotive concepts are reported, and more than 100 other studies are said to be in progress. Consequently, in addition to many case studies which give idiographic evidence of the validity of rational-emotive theory, there are many nomothetic sources of supportive evidence.

More than most other theorists about human behavior, Ellis comes closer to commonsense versions of how people think and act and feel. This has generally been the case with most second- and third-generation theorists who generally followed Freud. Ellis, who had been trained in Freud's theory came to take a relatively simple, cognitive, ego-oriented position, with a here-and-

now viewpoint. People are in trouble; they are not succeeding in life; they are unhappy. This is due to poor actions based on poor thinking. Once we find out the errors in thinking and change them, we can get people to act properly.

Ellis's theory can be criticized not so much in terms of what may be wrong with it but rather for its apparent narrowness. As yet it may not be considered a fullblown theory of human nature but rather a more limited approach to treatment.

Ellis takes an aggressive attitude toward other systems (Ellis, 1957, 1973), saying in effect that the proof of the value of any theory is how it works. He argues that all systems probably work, but efficiency is the key word. Since his system, in his view, is the most efficient of any, therefore it is the most valid. He backs such statements with the opinions of his many colleagues and a number of comparative studies.

Summary

Ellis's rational-emotive system comes from a long tradition: Socrates's maieutic method of questioning, and the ordinary man-in-the-street's attempt to talk common sense are in the same family. In this sense, Ellis is only doing, in a more systematic way, what people have been doing for ages: changing other people's behavior through changing their thinking by questioning, giving parallels, agreeing, disagreeing, and so on. His basic concept that behavior is a function of thought and that feelings are a result of behavior is also an old one, as is the concept that the total person—thinking, feeling, and acting—must be dealt with simultaneously.

In view of this, Ellis's genius seems to be in taking old concepts and organizing them into a complete system. The A–B–C theory does not cover the total person's growth and development, but it offers a time-tested and experimentally proven method of helping individuals achieve a better adjustment to life through a here-and-now procedure.

Reality Theory

Reality theory was developed by William Glasser, (1925–   ) a psychiatrist. As the name indicates, it is a here-and-now theory related to behavior. The major concept in practice is that the therapist and the patient agree on relatively small segments of desired behavior, establish contracts covering specified elements, discuss procedures fully, and then proceed to fulfill the contracts. Doing this successfully tends to give the individual a success orientation and permits her or him to tackle other, more difficult problems with a greater probability of success. The aim is acceptance of personal responsibility for one's behavior, which is seen as the major criterion of mental health.

Probably no other theory discussed in this book is as simple or as old in its foundations as Reality Therapy, which can be readily explained by well known clichés such as: Walk before you run; The longest trip begins with the first step; A stitch in time saves nine; and Make up your mind. It is the essence of common sense, the kind of advice a parent would give a child.

Paul DuBois, a Swiss physician who may be called the father of modern psychotherapy, took a commonsense attitude toward mental problems. He believed that it is possible for therapists to talk sense to the insane, and he operated essentially in this manner. Certainly, hundreds of thousands of eclectic counselors—in schools, industry, the military institutions—who operate on commonsense principles employ these techniques of person-to-person advice. In this regard, most of the other theories discussed in this chapter have a close relationship, in part, to reality therapy, the difference being that in the latter the therapist doggedly refuses to look at the big picture or to be concerned with conceptualizations and generalizations. From the first, she or he is concerned only with the successful completion of specific miniprojects.

According to Roznafszky (1974), of the original big three (Freud, Jung, Adler) Reality Therapy is closest to Adler's Individual Psychology, in its pragmatic common sense, relatively simple theory, and procedures. However, according to Glasser and Zunin (1973) Glasser began formulating his ideas with very little knowledge of the prior work of others.

The first instance of the use of this theory was in 1962 with psychotic patients in a Veterans Administration hospital in Los Angeles. Glasser, together with G. L. Harrington, discovered that the discharge rate in a particular building had been two patients a year. They found what they believed to be a kind of unspoken contract be-

tween staff and patients for the latter to remain "peacefully psychotic." When Glasser's system was employed, the discharge rate of this unit of 210 patients went up from the original 2 a year to 45 the first year, 85 the second, and 90 the third. Soon after Glasser published his first book, *Mental Health or Mental Illness?* (1961). After he moved on to the Ventura School for Girls, a correctional institution, he first employed the term *reality therapy*. Glasser's book with this title was published in 1965.

Later the Institute for Reality Therapy was established, offering courses in the theory and practice of Glasser's ideas. Glasser became interested in elementary education and had published a book (*Schools without Failure*, 1969); eventually, a unique master's degree program in education was offered through LaVerne College.

Assertions

1. THE INDIVIDUAL MUST FIRST TAKE RESPONSIBILITY FOR HIMSELF.

Reality Therapy is essentially ahistorical. While there may be reasons and explanations and excuses for where the patient is now, going backward to try to find out what happened to make the person what he is is generally regarded as a waste of time. The important first step is for the patient or client to take an attitude that he is in charge of his life, that what he does is his responsibility, and that he must look forward, not backward. This means also he must not depend too much on the therapist.

2. THE UNSUCCESSFUL INDIVIDUAL MUST BE DIRECTED TO FEASIBLE GOALS.

If there is one generalization important for the patient it is that he think of himself as a successful person. Past failures tend to make the individual generalize himself as unsuccessful. Part of this may be due to the patient trying to do more than one can. So, the patient should be directed to relatively small and readily achievable goals in life which in turn will give him a feeling of success and of responsibility.

Glasser believes that this failure identity tends to occur at the time children enter school, and his concept of a school without failure illustrates this notion.

3. PEOPLE WITH A FAILURE ORIENTATION
ARE LONELY.

Glasser sees individuals having either a success or a failure orientation, which incidentally is quite similar to Berne's OK–not OK. Those who have this personal failure orientation tend to avoid others, are unwilling to accept responsibility, and find it difficult to love themselves or others. Separation from others tends to occur, and the individual begins to live his fantasy life and tends to move toward frank mental illness.

4. THE PERSON'S MOST BASIC
PSYCHOLOGICAL NEED IS SOCIAL
IDENTITY.

As a normal person grows up he should begin to see himself as a separate individual, having clear-cut values, knowing his worth, feeling secure, being able to relate to others as an independent person. The adult has an internal value system, an authenticity. This concept is similar to a notion expressed in existential theory.

The following points refer to the theory of the Reality Therapy.

5. FOCUS ON PRESENT BEHAVIOR RATHER
THAN FEELINGS.

Note that in the above sentence the three elements of cognition, behavior, and emotion are stated or implied; the word *focus* indicates cognition. The order also is important: first the conceptualization, and then the behavior, and leave the feelings alone. The logical progression is not, "When I feel better I do better", but rather "When I do better I feel better." In Reality Therapy, some acknowledgment may be made about feelings, but the main thrust is on better behavior. Here there is a distinct difference between Glasser's theory and Rogers' person-centered theory.

6. SUCCESS ORIENTATION COMES FROM
SUCCESSFUL PLANNING.

Again there is the notion of the primacy of the intellect. Closely related to this notion is a parallel idea from behavior modification—the shaping of behavior is best done in small steps. However, instead of disregarding the individual's phenomenology, as occurs in classical behavior therapy, the patient in Reality Therapy is asked to go over in his mind, to role play cognitively, what he will do and then, step by step, to be prepared to follow some preestablished routine.

Thus, a man may plan (1) to ask at least five girls to go to the movies with him this weekend, (2) to then take out his date (if he gets one) to a bar, (3) to kiss her goodnight, and (4) to call her the next day to thank her for a pleasant evening.

7. THE CRUCIAL ELEMENT IN ATTAINING A
SUCCESS ORIENTATION IS A NO-EXCUSE
COMMITMENT.

The heart of the system is simply making up one's mind. Visualize a woman who wants to jump from a high board and is afraid to do so. Either alone or with the help of an instructor she plans (1) to climb up the ladder to the board, (2) to walk to the end of the board, (3) to hold her nose with her right hand, (4) to step off the board, and (5) to remain stiff and straight. However, she does not begin to climb up toward the diving board until she has made an absolute commitment to do exactly everything she has planned.

8. NO EXCUSES FOR NONPERFORMANCE
ARE ACCEPTED.

The therapist working with a client is not interested in hearing why a person did not do what he promised to do. His sole concern is replanning the program suggested for the success orientation, perhaps modifying it. Excuses are seen as retarding progress.

Applications

In the foregoing discussion, how the system is applied is indicated. The therapist takes a personal, friendly, helpful attitude. The overall generalization he may state to his patient is as follows:

Find out what you want to do; and if I agree with you that what you want to do is mentally healthy, then I will plan with you a program so that you can attain success in a small but important aspect of your life, and together we will determine how you can succeed, and I will work with you until we both have some kind of contract. You then will have an assignment which you are to fulfill.

Thus the therapist's attitude toward his client is friendly but limited. Their main goal is to set goals, establish plans, come to a strict determination of procedures, and then, if there is success, to move toward other goals and plans. If there should be failure, the two will go back to reexamine how to achieve success and make new plans. The therapist is concerned with operations and with details: When will you do this? How will you do this? So he asks when, where, how, what, trying to be detailed and exact, planning a campaign. The therapist may take a strong position, refuse to baby the client or to accept excuses, use shocking language, confront the client, and watch carefully that he does not get manipulated by the patient into accepting nonsense.

Evaluation

While evidences of success on a nomothetic basis can be determined (for example, the statistics given earlier for discharges from a mental unit), Glasser's position is that evaluation is on a case-by-case basis and is essentially evaluated by the client's subjective estimate of his success. Some statistical evidence of the success of Glasser's educational program has been obtained (English, 1970; Hawes, 1971).

Summary

Reality Therapy, while it is a distinct theory and philosophy and is relatively simple in conceptualization, has a considerable degree of overlap with other systems. It is a practical theory with little concern for how a person came to be what he is now and major concern for what to do to help the person achieve precisely formulated goals and change his self-concept from a failure to a success orientation. In terms of its elements the system is essentially cognitive, in that the person is to see himself realistically, to determine what he wants to achieve, to make detailed plans to achieve desirable and feasible goals, and then to make up his mind to proceed according to established plans. If the plans work out successfully, the patient and therapist then plan again, always moving forward and upward toward successful accomplishment.

This theory of learning is applicable not only to psychotherapy but to life success in general, whether it be learning to swim, learning to get a new job, or learning to have a successful mar-

riage, and it represents essentially a commonsense approach with very little fancy language. It is about as far away from Jung's analytical psychology or Freud's psychoanalysis as any system can go.

Social Learning Theory

Albert Bandura (1925–   ) a psychologist and past president of the American Psychological Association, has been and still is busy in the development of a social learning theory of personality (Bandura & Walters, 1963). To understand his system, a bit of review may be helpful. In the Introduction, three views of personality were cited: (1) *phenomenological*—one's self, (2) *social stimulus value*—the views of a person by others; and (3) *veridical*—true but unknowable. We also discussed two ways that personality theories are "proven": by citing cases, the *idiographic* approach, and by group experiments, the *nomothetic* approach.

Methodologically, Bandura assumes a wider stance than almost any other personality theorist, in that he makes phenomenological statements indicating what goes on in a person's head, depends strongly on observations, cites individual cases in evidence, conducts group studies, and comes to conclusions based on both idiographic and nomothetic evidence. Essentially, he operates as an inductive scientist, setting up verifiable hypotheses that emerge from his general theory and then obtaining evidence from individuals and from groups to support the theory.

Bandura's theory of social learning has three major elements:

1. People learn their personality through the vicarious process of observation—that is, through imitation.
2. To achieve this they make use of symbols.
3. People are self-regulators in a complex interaction with the environment.

The following incident illustrates Bandura's social learning theory:

Jim, age five, found a dead rat, picked it up by the tail, and brought it over to Rita, also age five, waving it in front of her, and evidently hoping to frighten her. Rita showed interest in the rat and wanted to touch it, much to Jim's apparent disappointment.

He then took the rat to Dorothy, age seven, who reacted with apparent disgust and fear and ran away from Jim and toward Rita, screaming. When Jim pursued Dorothy, Rita also ran away from Jim and the rat and began to scream. Later, when Jim showed up with his rat, Rita ran and showed fear even though Dorothy was not around any more.

This incident summarized Bandura's theory: People model their social behavior (evident personality) according to their interpretations of the behavior of people they deem worthy of imitating. This is called vicarious or *observational learning*.

Assertions

1. ONE'S PERSONALITY IS LEARNED THROUGH OBSERVATIONS.

Bandura does not say that this is the only way personality is developed, but rather that it is a major method. Inherited predispositions and reward and punishment do have a part in personality formation, but a most important way they do so is by simply imitating the behavior of significant others. Anyone who has watched children role play, spontaneously imitating adults in the game of "playing house," realizes that they are good observers and can closely imitate others.

What does this mean about phenomenology, or one's inner aspects of thinking and feeling? According to Bandura, emotional reactions can be transmitted vicariously by observing the affective reactions of others. In studies of vicarious affective learning (Bandura, 1965), changes in autonomic reactivity are the dependent measures. Changes in cognitive functioning can be promoted by abstract modeling, or having people observe others performing various responses which embody a certain rule or principle. Through repeated exposures, the observers learn the rules from the modeled exemplars. Thus, people learn judgmental orientations, linguistic styles, conceptual schemes, information-processing strategies, and standards of conduct. In brief, according to Bandura, modeling influences can be highly effective in altering affective and cognitive functioning, as well as overt behavior. In our example, Rita learned overt behavior from the older girl, Dorothy, but later she felt fear within herself.

2. SOCIAL LEARNING IS A FUNCTION OF MODEL STRENGTH.

From whom one learns and how much one learns depends on the prestige or the "strength" of the individual who is the model. Thus Rita, age five, might not have imitated the reaction of a two-year-old, but she did imitate Dorothy, who was older than she.

3. BEHAVIOR PATTERNS ARE LEARNED IN CONTEXT.

Children do not simply learn indiscriminate patterns; rather, they interpret the appropriateness of the situation. The person who is learning is a complex individual who functions on many levels and in terms of the situation. Thus, in one context, when a child is with adults, it is proper to cry, but it is not proper when with children of his own age. An adult, male or female, reacts one way with men and another way with women.

4. BEHAVIOR CAN BE MODIFIED VIA SYMBOLS.

Social learning theory places special emphasis on the symbolic environment in personality development. Most of our actions are based on our images of reality, which are largely derived from symbolic media. The growth of symbolic technology, especially television, has increased the importance of social observational learning.

Applications

Bandura's social learning theory confirms well-known ideas: Parents want to move to a "good" neighborhood, with "good" schools, so their children will be exposed to "good" influences. Because research proves what we have always known does not mean it is useless, however. After all, everyone once knew that the world was flat!

Bandura's theory can be called a variety of behaviorism: modify the environment and you modify the personality. However, it is more complex than simple behaviorism; he insists that the individual processes information and makes use of it in terms of expectations.

A number of research studies have been reported by Bandura (1976) which show the effectiveness of changing behavior through the processes of (1) having the individual observe model behavior, (2) having the person enact the desired behavior, and (3) permitting favorable consequences to result from the new behavior. Thus, a person who is afraid of snakes is (1) shown that another person can handle them without negative consequences and (2) is then asked to touch the snake while it is held firmly by the model; (3) eventually the fearful person can handle the snake without any harm. This process is quite well known to those who train people to undertake feared activities, such as swimming or flying. It has been discussed in various ways by others, including Mary Cover Jones (1924), who got a child to discard his fear of a rabbit; Joseph Wolpe (1969), who employs symbolic procedures to modify emotional reactions to special situations; and J. L. Moreno (1946), who uses psychodrama to achieve personality changes through symbolic behavior.

Evaluation

Bandura, either alone or with collaborators, has conducted a considerable number of impressive research studies relating to the validity of his social learning theory. Some of these are summarized below:

1. *Children imitate those they regard as having power.* In a study by Bandura, Ross, and Ross (1963), children were exposed to several adults' behavior. They tended to imitate those who exhibited signs of having power or control rather than those adults who were seen as "weak." This finding relates to the general belief that children generally imitate the stronger or more powerful parent.

2. *Children can learn to delay gratification.* A research study by Bandura and Mischel (1965) dealt with children who were given a choice of a small reward immediately or a better reward later on. The issue was the ability of children to resist immediate gratification in favor of greater but later rewards. The top 25 percent and the bottom 25 percent of children, in terms of this "delay" ability, were then exposed to observations of adults who acted exactly the opposite of how they had behaved. When the children were retested, the low-delay children were able to delay more and the high-delay children tended to want immediate gratification.

3. *Children can generalize in terms of conse-*

quences observed. Bandura (1965) showed a film to children in which an adult showed aggressive behavior to a Bobo doll, knocking it down, hitting, and kicking it. Some of the children then saw one consequence for such behavior as the adult was punished, while others saw the adult being rewarded. Still other children observed no consequences for the aggressive behavior. As expected, those who saw the aggressive behavior rewarded themselves demonstrated greater aggressiveness, those who saw it punished acted later with relatively little aggression, and those who saw no consequences administered were intermediate in aggression.

4. *Learning behavior does not necessarily lead to actual behavior.* In this same study (Bandura, 1965) the question arose whether the children who had not shown aggressive behavior had really "learned" from watching the film. The issue was settled by giving the children incentives to be aggressive. As a result, all children were able to demonstrate aggression: that is, they knew what to do, even though some did not show this aggression in their usual behavior.

Summary

Bandura's commonsense theory that we learn from observing others has important implications for child training as well as for institutional dealing with adults, as in prisons, mental hospitals, or the military. It does not necessarily conflict with other theories that emphasize biological determinants of personality or with theories that depend on rewards and punishment. That is to say, Bandura's theory could "live with," for example, Sheldon's or Skinner's theory and not be contradictory to them. Indeed, if they were contradictory, in view of the strong experimental evidence adduced by Bandura and associates, the other theories would have to give way.

This theory also depends on reciprocal determinism: the child affects the environment just as the environment affects the child during early personality development. Also, for adults, they interact and thus affect others in their environment, just as others affect them. That is to say, internal personal factors (cognition and affection), the individual's own behavior, are the nature of the environment (including other people, books, television, laws, social standards): All are in a complex interaction.

Behavior is influenced by environmental events, but these events are partly of the making of the individuals affected. In other words, everything comes into the mix. For example, people's expectations influence how they behave, and then the outcome of their behavior affects their later expectations. From the social learning perspective, psychological functioning is a continuous, reciprocal interaction between personal behavior and environmental determinants, each affecting the other.

What does this do to the concept of the veridical personality? If personality is a function of the environment, then people can be changed simply by modifying the environment. Then there is no true innate personality, merely individuals who adjust to their society, going along with its models of behavior. Through social modeling, individuals learn certain patterns of behavior, and also patterns of thinking and feeling, so that they are modified in particular directions without having much control over how they think or act or feel. That this is true is quite evident from anthropological findings: individuals in various societies do tend to behave and think and feel in standardized ways, and certainly this degree of conformity to norms is due to vicarious learning.

It may be worth editorializing at this moment to say that undoubtedly Bandura's observations are correct, in terms not only of his experimental evidence but of commonsense conclusions about the importance of the social environment to changing personalities. However, just as his views are correct, so too are other views! This is what makes this subject of personality so fascinating. One is constantly convinced of opposing views. The simple answer is that they are all correct—and that none of them are complete.

People do learn from others; they do learn from experience; they are affected by the total environment. Nevertheless, all social learning is not uniform: Children in the very same environment do differ from one another. Even the so-called Siamese children, with absolutely identical heredities and practically identical environments, do differ from one another in personality. In terms of statistical theory, the variance of personality is not completely determined by the environment. This point of view is shared by Ban-

dura, who states that some of the variance of personality is determined by the environment as experienced by the individual.

Typology Theory

Perhaps the oldest and certainly the most common way of dealing with personality is to type people. It is common to hear individuals described by a single summary word such as *kind, nice, sweet, weird,* and so on. The typology established over two thousand years ago by Hippocrates is an example. All people were put into one of four categories in terms of the proportion of bodily fluids (humors) in their bodies (see Chapter 1).

Current typologies generally are elaborations of this primitive concept that there is some sort of relationship between the biological basis of the individual and his personality type. We have seen several illustrations of typologies. Jung typed people as introverts and extraverts, the former people who tend to live within themselves and the latter those who tend to be oriented to the outside world. Another example of a typology is Karen Horney's, which typed individuals as being oriented *toward* people, *against* people, and *away* from people. Sheldon typed people in terms of their body shapes.

In recent years a number of statistically oriented psychologists have attempted to make sense out of the complexity of personality by establishing various kinds of taxonomical systems, schemes for classifying and organizing personality in terms of types of people or traits of people. Hans J. Eysenck (1948, 1952) has been most active in typologies, while Raymond B. Cattell (1957) has done much work on locating basic traits. We will summarize some of Eysenck's work in this section; while Eysenck has been extremely productive in general psychology as well as personality theory, in this section we will discuss mostly his work on typology.

Assertions

1. A SCIENCE OF PERSONALITY MUST BE
    NOMOTHETIC.

This first assertion mows down practically all the theories in this book. Eysenck would say that people who deal with people must consider them one by one and consider each person's individuality, operating idiographically. But while this clinical procedure is necessary in terms of the uniqueness of each individual, it is not the method of science. A scientific attitude would be to determine, on the basis of large groups, generalizations about human nature.

2.   A PRIMARY NEED FOR PERSONALITY THEORY IS A DEPENDABLE TAXONOMY.

When personologists or clinicians or the man in the street characterize people, they use words. Allport and Odbert (1936), in doing a dictionary summary of trait names, found no fewer than 17,000 terms. When several adjectives are used to describe a person, the possibilities of typing people into millions of possible combinations are raised. There is just too much material to deal with. What is needed is the same type of typology that exists in biology: Life is divided into plants and animals, and then animals are divided into classes: insects, birds, mammals, fishes, and so on. But to devise such a taxonomic personality scheme based on rational scientific methodology is a challenge. If this could be achieved, people would know what is meant when a particular type is mentioned.

There are many problems involved in this kind of thinking. For example, while it is evident that some members of the animal kingdom are birds and some are reptiles, and such classification seems easy, nevertheless even in biology there are difficulties. How can one classify viruses? Birds lay eggs; the platypus lays eggs but is a mammal. Further, humans do not differ radically from one another. Even with sexuality, the most apparently clean-cut difference, there are problems of classification. While most children at birth are clearly boys or girls, some are difficult to classify if they are born with undifferentiated sexual organs, the so-called pseudo-hermaphrodites. Thus human differences are not clear-cut for the most part, but are to be seen on a scale. There really are not tall or short people, but mostly average people with relatively few extremes.

Nevertheless, some sort of rational categorization is needed as a first step in classification, to generate a scientific typology.

3.   THE BEST WAY TO ACHIEVE A SCIENTIFIC TYPOLOGY IS OBJECTIVELY.

Suspicious of the intrusion of opinions and values, those who have been concerned with statistical personality theory, which attempts to define personality through research methods, have in a sense thrown into the pot everything that seems important relative to human differences and stood back to see whether patterns of personality will develop as a result of statistical research. In this method there are four steps: (1) a large population of individuals is obtained; (2) from each person various kinds of measures or variables are determined, each translated into some form of numbers; (3) usually, intercorrelations are obtained between all the classes of data, and (4) the data are analyzed by factor analysis to yield more-or-less objective information. In short, the human element of judgment is reduced as much as possible.

Applications

In terms of the general theory of such research, there can be a final solution to understanding personality types through the use of statistical procedures, since the human element can be reduced by the usual hypothetical-deductive procedures, and a universal rational taxonomy can be established. This utopian concept, at least for the present, does not appear to be reality. There are at least three reasons for this disappointment.

First, the various statistically oriented researchers do not agree among themselves what form such a taxonomy should take. Eysenck would prefer a typology of people, while Cattell (1957) prefers a taxonomy of traits. Second, different statisticians have obtained different taxonomies, even though they have used more-or-less the same methodologies. Third, different statisticians give different names to more-or-less the same findings.

French (1953) reviewed 70 research studies on personality and found that no fewer than 450 factor names had been suggested. Studying these terms, he noted that some of the names could be combined, since they were essentially synonyms. Thus, if one experimenter found that people could be classified on a bright-dull continuum and another asserted they could be classified on an intelligent-nonintelligent continuum, French felt that these experimenters were saying the same thing but using different words. After he made his summary of summaries, he still had 50 different factors! In examining the various conclusions of the typologists and traitologists studied, he found very little agreement.

For those who hope that mathematically oriented personologists will show a greater convergence than clinically oriented psychologists have done, the evidence is that at present this is not so. In addition, the individual multivariate personologists are equally insistent that they are correct in their formulations, as is the case with the clinicians.

One useful end product of these statistically derived taxonomies are personality tests. Edwards, who developed his Personal Preference Schedule in terms of Murray's need-press theory, is an example of a test constructor who employed a clinical theory as a model. Eysenck, with his Maudsley Personality Inventory (1952) and Cattell with his Personality Factors Test (Cattell & Eber, 1964) have developed personality questionnaires based on rational statistical principles, even though the two tests evidently measure different modalities.

What is Eysenck's personality typology? It seems a disappointment. After all the research he has done, he has come up with a simple, double-dichotomous classification: people are either normal or neurotic, and people are either extraverted or introverted. These two dimensions, he found, are orthogonal, that is are independent of each other, with a correlation approaching zero. One might think that Eysenck has affirmed Jung's introversion-extroversion categorization of people oriented internally and people oriented externally, but such is not the case. Eysenck's extraversion is not the same as Jung's extroversion (notice the spelling difference). Based on research, Eysenck (1952) found that a certain number of objective, nonequivocal variables went together to form a specific dichotomous typology which he labeled introversion-extraversion. For example, the introverts in his grouping had certain characteristics which contrasted to the extraverts. They were: (1) easier to condition, (2) liked repetitive tasks more, (3) held on to learning for a longer time, (4) remembered drawings for a longer time, (5) were

more difficult to inhibit, (6) smoked less than did the extraverts, and so forth.

What name should be given to people who exhibited these objective tendencies? Eysenck labeled such people *introverts,* which he had a perfect right to do. In doing so, however, he illustrated one of the most important problems of personality theory: the tyranny of words, the difficulty of unequivocal communication.

Later research indicates a possible third dimension of psychotocism—nonpsychotocism.

Evaluation

It is difficult to determine how a taxonomy can be validated. The most evident way would be confirmation through independent studies, but as we have already pointed out, this has not happened. Consequently, there has been no conclusive evidence of reliability of any taxonomy based on confirming studies. This means that anyone is free to choose his own system of taxonomy.

Summary

What appears to be needed is communication between the multivariate personologists in defining their terms, in standardizing their procedures, and in replicating their experiments. But statistical personologists are humans and have human failings, and like the clinical personologists, each believes that he is on the right track and others should accept his findings as correct. Therefore there is just as much discord and confusion among the mathematicians as among the clinicians.

Nevertheless, the work of Raymond B. Cattell, Hans J. Eysenck, J. P. Guilford, F. C. Thorne, and L. L. Thurstone, who have worked generally in the statistical tradition established by Charles Spearman in the early 1900s, holds more promise for eventual convergence than do clinical systems. The absolute hope for a real science of personality will be achieved with the merging of idiographic clinical theorizing and nomothetic experimental research.

Direct Decision Theory

Any system of psychotherapy has inherent in it a theory of personality, since it must have some systematic view of people: how they get to be what they are, how they maintain themselves, and how they can change or be changed. Counselors and psychotherapists who do not belong to any particular school of personality theory in effect make up their own eclectic theory.

An example of an eclectic theory is Direct Decision Therapy (1975), as formulated by Harold Greenwald (1910–   ). Not only is this theory interesting by itself, but it has special value for this book in that it is an example of the most common type of theory of all: the eclectic theories of most working counselors and psychotherapists, who when they do not claim loyalty to any particular school of thought, tend to put together bits and pieces of other theories with some elements of their own, to come up finally with some uniquely formulated conception of human nature.

It is worth making this point: many individuals in the professional helping fields started off with some particular theory as a result of their training, but as time goes on they may keep their old language but think a bit differently. The result is that when professional people of different orientations meet they usually can accommodate their thoughts with one another and find one another's ideas rather sensible, even though they may have some difficulty with words and concepts.

Greenwald was originally trained as a Freudian psychoanalyst by Theodore Reik. When he began to practice, he found that his indoctrination and his experiences did not exactly jibe, and he began to make various additions and modifications. Finally he had established an entirely new way of thinking which held together, had its own rationale, but was far from his original psychoanalytic orientation. However, instead of labeling himself a psychoanalytically oriented therapist, he took the plunge and named his developing system Direct Decision Therapy.

His general view about personality goes somewhat as follows: a person operates in terms of his perceptions of the payoffs of anticipated actions. However, his judgments are imperfect, for a variety of reasons. One is that his experience has given him certain habitual patterns, and he is likely to operate according to a well-established *modus operandi*, even if not quite appropriate. Second, he may have a narrow vision and see

very few alternatives for action when there are actually many. Third, he may simply be afraid to try something new. Life is a process of voluntary behaviors. We have to make decisions constantly: whether to get up, what to wear, what to eat, when to go to work or to school, what to read, and so forth. In some cases, decisions are crucial: whether to continue to get an education, and if so what courses to take; whom to date and whom to marry; whether or not to accept a job, and so forth and so on.

Every person has an idealized concept of himself and his goals and strives to achieve the greatest amount of success. However, some people constantly make poor decisions: They say the wrong things at the wrong times; they make hasty judgments of poor quality; they select the wrong types of friends; and, as the current saying goes, they are "losers" in the game of life.

Now, how does it come that a person becomes a loser rather than a winner? Why is it that some people always make the same kinds of mistakes and do not seem to learn from experience? How is it that some people, despite all advice, bullheadedly continue to follow incorrect paths?

The questions that Greenwald asks have a somewhat different flavor from the questions other theorists and therapists ask, because he zeros in on the moment of decision as the focus of personality. This is where the past ends and the future begins. While Greenwald is teleologically oriented, he also gives due attention to the past: it is in the past that one has learned certain patterns and pathways which continue.

The total picture of human behavior goes somewhat as follows: in the past the individual made a basic mistake at a turning point in life, and he "went off the track" and found an inferior solution. Diagrammatically, this is shown in Adler's diagram shown in Figure 3-2 in Chapter 3. This inadequate solution—be it telling a lie, avoiding a problem, walking away from a conflict, or getting excited—"worked" in that the person thereby avoided a painful confrontation, but he thereby paid the "price" of having learned an inaccurate and useless habit. In the future, faced with a similar problem, the individual is again likely to lie, avoid conflict, or get excited, since he has not learned a more useful or superior method. Given time, the person undertakes a sort of generalization of errors and gets enmeshed in his mistakes, and his life becomes increasingly twisted and distorted.

This would be the basic formulation that a person trained in Greenwald's theory would have about her or his client: He has a pattern of self-defeating behavior, due to incorrect patterns supported by mental gymnastics to uphold the validity of his patterns. The therapist sees his task as getting to understand the poor decisions his client makes, learning how this process started, educating his client so that he can see for himself the mistakes he makes, and then getting him to change his behavior to a more satisfactory pattern.

At this point you may see the essential similarity of Greenwald's theory with other here-and-now, practical, problem-oriented theories and schools of psychotherapy, especially those of Ellis and Glasser.

Assertions

1. BEHAVIOR DEPENDS ON ESTIMATES OF VARIABLE SUCCESS.

The individual is seen by Greenwald as weighing the advantages and disadvantages of various decisions and constantly trying to win in the game of life. This statement has several implications: the person is teleologically oriented, since he is planning constantly for the future. The individual operates in a cognitive rather than an emotional manner and makes "bets" about the relative advantages of various behaviors.

2. BEHAVIOR IS A FUNCTION OF EXPERIENCE.

While the individual may see the advantages of certain forms of behavior (for example, he may realize the value of keeping quiet in a social situation), he is nevertheless highly likely to go against his own better thinking and operate in a manner he is used to, since this is a safer even though more inadequate way of operating.

3. POOR BEHAVIOR HAS ITS ORIGINS IN A FAILED CRISIS SITUATION.

Greenwald sees the individual as having somewhere in his past been in a crisis situation which may have caused him to panic and to fail to meet a problem in a satisfactory manner. This crucial error generates a kind of compulsion to repeat the error—and having gone in the wrong direction, he tends to maintain it.

4. POOR DECISIONS CALL FOR PAYING A PRICE.

As a result of poor decisions, the individual moves constantly farther and farther from the goal of mental health and success, becomes more persistent in his neurotic behavior, and goes off center more and more. The analogy is similar to a person who is heading north and starts to walk to the northeast; each step actually takes him farther away from his goal.

Applications

Greenwald's Direct Decision Therapy has been applied to counseling and psychotherapy. It has been used by his students and trainees and is well-known in the Scandinavian countries where Greenwald taught and lectured.

The "set" of the counselor or therapist has been stated: The client is viewed as having made errors in judgment in the past, and these errors have become concretized and established. The general plan of treatment involves (1) forming a good relationship with the client so that trust is established, (2) carefully examining the client's behavior for evidence of common and constant mistakes, (3) locating, if possible, early examples of poor thinking and poor behavior, and then (4) putting a kind of mirror in front of the client and making him see himself as he is: a kind of self-confrontation. A counselor might say, "Can you see that in social situations, you wrongly assume that you must take the lead at all costs, and that if you are not in charge you believe you have been defeated?"

The counselor or therapist using Direct Decision Therapy may be directive or nondirective, may use tests and projective techniques, and may employ any system of behavior modification, including interviews, humor, examples, role playing, or assignments. The essence is to get the individual to see his generalized errors, to attempt to get a feeling of continuity from his first remembered example of this kind of error, to get him to see new alternatives, and then to get him to start to act in a more mature and successful manner.

For example, a client may ask: "What shall I do with my wife? Should I kill her or myself or divorce her or live with that monster?" The counselor may lead the counselee to understand that these four choices are not the only possible ones. After suggesting new possibilities, the probable consequences are examined.

Evaluation

Greenwald believes that his therapy is amazingly rapid. He goes immediately for the heart of the problem of neurosis, which he sees as constantly making poor judgments and poor decisions, and is not concerned with background information unless it relates to the problem. The analogy would be a physician and a patient with a splinter. The doctor who goes immediately for the splinter and removes it can be compared with Greenwald. The doctor who chooses to do a full physical and mental status examination, believing that the splinter is only the symptom of a bigger problem, may be the archetypal analyst.

The value of the theory of direct decision, as far as this book is concerned, is that essentially it is an eclectic system, and relatively little is original except that the arrangement is new. Greenwald may be seen as a third-generation theorist, who found that practically everything had already been explored, and his task was to pick and choose and assemble what had been already found. This eclectic selection of elements to make a new theory is representative of what many other counselors and therapists actually do, and this relatively clear and simple system has the advantage of appearing to meet the dictates of common sense.

Summary

Harold Greenwald's Direct Decision Therapy is a simple and logical view of man, rather narrow and inchoate as a theory but in general accordance with almost every theory discussed so far. This theory is essentially cognitive: The person thinks incorrectly and so acts incorrectly and so feels badly. Treatment also is cognitive: The person is led to see his errors and to commit himself to new, superior behavior.

This eclectic system may be a forerunner of the theories of the future: a putting together of elements from other theories, in which each theory has its own logical and reliable articulations with its various elements. Consequently, and paradoxically, although Direct Decision

Theory is the least well known of any in this book, it is probably more representative of what working counselors and therapists actually do than any of the theories that are more-or-less generated by idiosyncratic concepts. In a sense, as a type, it may represent the personality theory of the future.

References

Allport, G. W., & Odbert, H. S. Trait-names: A psycholetical study. *Psychological Monographs*, 1936, 47 (No. 211).

Bandura, A. Influence of models' reinforcement contingencies with the acquisition of imitative responses. *Journal of Personality and Social Psychology*, 1965, 1, 589–595.

Bandura, A. Effecting change through participant modeling. In J. D. Krumholtz & C. E. Thoresen (Eds.), *Counseling methods.* New York: Holt, Rinehart & Winston, 1976.

Bandura, A., & Mischel, W. Modification of self-imposed delay of reward through exposure to live and symbolic models. *Journal of Personality and Social Psychology*, 1965, 2, 698–705.

Bandura, A., Ross, D., & Ross, S. A. Imitation of film-mediated aggressive models. *Journal of Abnormal and Social Psychology*, 1963, 66, 3–11.

Bandura, A., & Walters, R. H. Social learning and personality development. New York: Holt, Rinehart & Winston, 1963.

Berne, E. Transactional analysis in psychotherapy. New York: Grove Press, 1961.

Berne, E. Games people play. New York: Grove Press, 1964.

Bronson, G. Identity diffusion in late adolescence. *Journal of Abnormal and Social Psychology*, 1959, 59, 414–417.

Cattell, R. B. *Personality and motivation structure and measurement.* Yonkers, N. Y.: New World Book, 1957.

Cattell, R. B., & Eber, H. W. *Handbook for the sixteen personality factor questionnaire.* Homewood, Ill.: Dorsey Press, 1964.

Corsini, R. J., *Roleplaying in psychotherapy.* Chicago: Aldine, 1966.

Corsini, R. J., Shaw, M. E., & Blake, R. R. *Roleplaying in business and industry.* Glencoe, Ill. 1971.

Edwards, A. L. *Personal preference schedule.* New York: Psychological Corporation, 1953.

Ellis, A. *How to live with a neurotic.* New York: Crown, 1957.

Ellis, A. *Reason and emotion in psychotherapy.* New York: Lyle Stuart, 1962.

Ellis, A. *Humanistic psychotherapy.* New York: Julian Press, 1973.

Ellis, A. Rational-emotive therapy. In R. J. Corsini (Ed.), *Current psychotherapies.* Itasca, Ill.: F. E. Peacock, 1973.

English, J. *The effect of reality therapy on elementary school children.* Paper presented at the meeting of the California Association of School Psychologists and Psychometrists, Los Angeles, March 1970.

Erikson, E. *Young man Luther.* New York: Norton, 1958.

Erikson, E. *Childhood and society.* New York: Norton, 1963.

Erikson, E. *Identity: Youth and crisis.* New York: Norton, 1968.

Erikson, E. *Gandhi's truth.* New York: Norton, 1969.

Eysenck, H. J. *Scientific study of personality.* New York: Macmillan, 1952.

Eysenck, H. J. *The biological basis of personality.* Springfield, Ill.: C. C. Thomas, 1967.

French, J. W. *The description of personality measurements in terms of rotated factors.* Princeton, N. J.: Educational Testing Service, 1953.

Glasser, W. *Mental health or mental illness?* New York: Harper & Row, 1961.

Glasser, W. *Reality therapy.* New York: Harper and Row, 1965.

Glasser, W. *Schools without failure.* New York: Harper & Row, 1969.

Glasser, W., & Zunin, L. M. Reality therapy. In R. J. Corsini (Ed.), *Current psychotherapies.* Itasca, Ill.: F. E. Peacock, 1973.

Greenwald, H. *Direct decision therapy.* New York: Knapp, 1975.

Harris, T. *I'm OK, You're OK.* New York: Harper & Row, 1969.

Hawes, R. M. Reality therapy in the classroom. (Doctoral dissertation, University of the Pacific, 1971)

Horney, K. *The neurotic personality of our time.* New York: Norton, 1937.

Horney, K. *New ways in psychoanalysis.* New York: Norton, 1939.

Horney, K. *Self-Analysis.* New York: Norton, 1942.

Horney, K. *Our inner conflicts.* New York: Norton, 1945.

Horney, K. *Neurosis and human growth.* New York: Norton, 1950.

Jones, M. C. The elimination of children's fears. *Journal of Experimental Psychology,* 1924, 7, 382–390.

Kempler, W. Gestalt therapy. In R. J. Corsini (Ed.), *Current psychotherapies.* Itasca, Ill.: F. E. Peacock, 1973.

Maslow, A. *Self-actualizing people: A study of psychological health.* New York: Grune & Stratton, 1950.

Maslow, A. H. *Motivation and personality* (2nd ed.). New York: Harper & Row, 1970.

Maslow, A. H. Self-actualizing and beyond. In A. H. Maslow, *The further reaches of human nature.* New York: Viking Press, 1972.

McClelland, D. C. *The achieving society.* Princeton, N. J.: Van Nostrand, 1961.

Moreno, J. L. *Who shall survive?* New York: Beacon House, 1934.

Moreno, J. L. *Psychodrama* (Vol. 1). New York: Beacon House, 1946.

Moreno, J. L. *Sociometry.* New York: Beacon House, 1951.

Murray, H. A. *Explorations in personality.* New York: Oxford University Press, 1938.

Murray, H. A. *Thematic Apperception Test Manual.* Cambridge, Mass.: Harvard University Press, 1943.

Murray, H. A. *Assessment of men.* New York: Holt, Rinehart & Winston, 1948.

Perls, F. *Ego, hunger and aggression.* New York: Random House, 1969. (a)

Perls, F. *Gestalt therapy verbatim.* Lafayette, Calif.: Real People Press, 1969. (b)

Perls, F. *In and out of the garbage pail.* Lafayette, Calif.: Real People Press, 1969. (c)

Perls, F., Hefferline, R. F., & Goodman, P. *Gestalt therapy.* New York: Julian Press, 1958.

Roznafszky, J. The impact of Alfred Adler on three "free-will therapies" of the 1960's. *Journal of Individual Psychology,* 1974, *30,* 65–80.

Schutz, W. C. *Joy.* New York: Grove Press, 1967.

Steiner, C. *Games alcoholics play.* New York: Grove, 1971.

Waterman, C., Beubel, M., & Waterman, A. Relationship between resolution of the identity crisis and outcomes of previous psychosocial crises. *Proceedings of the Annual Convention of the American Psychological Association* (Vol. 5). Washington, D. C.: 1970.

Wolpe, J. *The practice of behavior therapy.* New York: Pergamon Press, 1969.

Glossary

Abreaction. Responding emotionally to the memory of a past experience or repressed event.

Accounts. Verbal statements intended to be explanatory relative to problematic behavior.

Actone. Unit of behavior.

Affection. Relating to feelings or emotions. Psychology is sometimes divided into three parts: cognition, (knowing). conation (willing) and affection (feeling).

Anima. The inherited potential carried by the male to experience the image of woman.

Apersonal. Not relating to a specific individual, such as a phenomenon which affects all people or events over which the individual has no control.

Approach-avoidance conflict. A conflict situation in which the organism simultaneously wants to go in opposite directions. A baby who wants a desired candy offered by a feared stranger is an example of an approach-avoidance conflict.

Archetypal image. An activated, transpersonal nucleus of any emotionally charged complex that is symbolically filled out by collective conscious cultural experience and shared symbolic representations.

Archetype. An innate capacity of the mind to apperceive core emotional human experiences in nearly universal ways accumulated during the experiences of ancestors.

Archetype "as such". Content of the collective unconscious which is the psychological counterpart of instinct; inherited formal property of the human brain to experience typical figures, situations, or behavior patterns.

Autism. Living and thinking in a self-centered manner, in terms of one's internal aspects, unrelated to reality. Usually used as a synonym for childhood schizophrenia.

Autochthonous. Coming from within; self-generated. See *autogenous*.

Autogenous. Originating from within, self-induced. See *autochthonous*.

Awareness context. Knowledge of self and of others relative to role behavior in any situation.

Behavior modification. A system of changing behavior based on rewards and punishments.

Behaviorism. The study of raw or pure behavior without concern for mental contents or introspection. An objective and rigidly controlled system of dealing with organisms to check hypotheses and measure behavior under a variety of conditions.

Biofeedback. The process of informing an individual of the status of some variation of an ordinarily unknown internal event, such as heart rate or brain waves, ordinarily done so that the person can control these events.

Black box. Name given by behaviorally-oriented psychologists to those processes internal to the individual organism (psychological, neurological, and physiological), which they consider unobservable and, therefore, outside the subject matter of psychology.

Career. Relative to an individual, the pattern of movements and thoughts in proceeding through social situations, roughly equivalent to lifestyle and strategies.

Catharsis. Literally, "cleaning out"; the process of emotionally experiencing past events that have been repressed.

Cathexis. An investment of psychic energy in mental representation that may vary in interest or value.

Causality. The relationship between an act and its consequence; the necessary results of the actions of one entity on another.

Cognition. Intellectual functions such as remembering, thinking, planning, recognizing, reasoning. See *affection* and *conation*.

Collective. All psychic contents that belong not to one individual but to the whole group, such as to a society or a race; also the group that is most meaningful to an individual, especially one's gang, the bunch, friends. In Soviet usage, this term implies an enduring community of persons united by common goals.

Collective unconscious. The transpersonal aspect of the psyche, what Jung called the "objective psyche," where archetypes exist but are not necessarily activated by personal life experiences.

Compensation. The tendency of an organ or an individual to make up for a lack by increasing its function or its efforts.

Complex. An emotionally charged group of associated ideas and memories unconsciously organized around an activated archetypal image; always exists in unconscious dynamic relationship to other complexes having bipolar positve and negative emotional significance.

Conation. The "willing" or "wanting" aspect which "pushes" the person onward. See *affective, cognition*.

Conserve. Term employed by Moreno to refer to habits or deposited wisdom from the past; the sum of past learning.

Constellatory construct. Statement relative to a person with the implication of other associated aspects. See *preemptive construct, propositional construct*.

Construct. Generally, a hypothetical entity (such as Intelligence)treated as though actually in existence.

Contrasexual. Images, feelings, memories, and behavior patterns associated with the opposite sex; *anima* and *animus* are contrasexual *archetypal images*.

Crèche (French). A child-care nursery.

Cryptomnesia. The unconscious production of something read, heard, or seen at any earlier period of time and then forgotten.

CS. Conditioned stimulus.

Daseinsanalysis. In German *Daseinsanalyse*. Literally "analysis of existence", a school of psychotherapeutic theory and practice viewing the individual as constantly growing and enfolding, responsible and interactive.

Defectology. The study of human defects, especially relative to aberrations in children.

Defense mechanism. A procedure employed by the ego to protect itself against changes. *Repression* and *idealization* are examples. See *safeguarding tendency*.

Deintegration. A maturational process, beginning with birth, when a primary self or state of original wholeness and integration is disrupted in the service of growth.

Depressive anxiety. An anxiety derived from the fear of one's own wishes and capacity to destroy, harm, or damage an ambivalently loved object; originates in the depressive position.

Depressive position. Achieved when the infant recognizes his mother as a whole object; an early developmental achievement that peaks around the seventh month of life, resulting in the ego's capacity to tolerate ambivalent feelings of love and hate simultaneously toward the same object.

Depth psychology. Any psychological school of thought which assumes that people operate in terms of unconscious forces.

Determinism. The idea that any event is completely explained or controlled by prior events. This implies perfect prediction of behavior if all antecedent elements were known.

Dialectical materialism. A kind of reasoned argument based on the concept of the priority of the reality of matter, and the philosophy of Hegel that theses is followed by antithesis and the result is synthesis. See *dialectic process*.

Dialectic process. A method of discovering truth through contrasting arguments, known as the thesis (statement) and antithesis (contrasting or opposing statement), leading to the emergence of a new proposition based on the integration of the two opposing positions.

Drive. A physiological demnd due to tissue being out of balance; reaction to deprivation, such as the hunger drive.

Drive reductionism. The concept that human behavior is ultimately best exlained by reduction of tensions associated with needs that arouse the drive.

Dualism. The notion that life is composed of two substances, usually body and mind or body and soul. See *monism pluralism*.

Dyad. A pair, two.

Dynamic psychology. Usually seen as the equivalent of *depth psychology*, relating to the supposed effects on behavior of unconscious drives.

Ego. In Freudian psychoanalysis, one part of the total psyche, the part that is conscious and in touch with reality. In Jung's formulation, ego is seen as the totality of the psyche. One's sense of self-identity. See *superego, id*.

Encounter. A meeting; In psychotherapy usually used to mean a stressful interaction leading to emotional display plus insight; a controntation. Encounter groups tend to be noisy and emotional and usually call for physical touching.

Endogenous. Originating within the body. See *exogenous*.

Epigenesis. The notion that for an individual there are preplanned stages of development.

Epiphenomenon. An event that accompanies another event but has no causal or dependent relationship with it.

Epistemology. The study of knowledge or understanding.

Eros. The life instinct. See *Thanatos*.

Ethnomethodology. A sociological procedure for understanding people's ordinary behavior through interviewing and observing people's attempts to make sense out of their cultures.

Eugenics. The improvement of mankind through selective breeding. See *euthenics*.

Eupsychia. A society of fully realized people.

Euthenics. The improvement of mankind through improving the environment. See *eugenics*.

Exchange theory. The concept that people's social interaction is a kind of transaction, with various payoffs related to operant conditioning and economic interactionism.

Existentialism. A philosophical movement which is primarily involved with the analysis of existence, specifically the existence of individual human beings. Its central problems include freedom, exercise of the will, choice, and responsibility.

Exogenous. Originating outside of the body. See *endogenous*.

Extravert. A person whose libido tends to turn naturally outward toward the interaction of external objects. See *introvert*.

Face. A kind of positive social value that a person assumes during which he expresses "lines" appropriate to the situation. When out of face, a person does not behave according to social expectations.

Facticity. The givens of life. Elements that cannot be affected by the individual: one's sex, body type, parents, history, etc.

Family constellation. The arrangement by age and sex of the siblings in a family, from oldest to youngest. The underlying concept is that the oldest male tends to play one role, the oldest female another, and so on.

Field theory. Any system of thought that concerns itself with vectors or forces of influence between the elements in the field. Lewin's Gestalt-oriented personality theory is an example of a field theory.

Finalism. The notion that human behavior can best be explained in terms of the future, with the individual seeking to achieve goals. See *teleology*.

Free association. A method of psychic investigation and psychotherapy devised by Freud in which a patient talks, without any self-censorship, about whatever comes to mind.

Functional autonomy. A behavior which formerly operated in terms of some purpose but now operates on its own, having become its own purpose.

Functionalism. A school of psychological thought, in contrast to structuralism, which emphasizes the importance of activities rather than static elements. American psychology is essentially functionalistic.

Geisteswissenschaften (German). Psychology as a social science. See *Naturwissenschaften*.

Gemeinschaftsgefühl (German): Literally, a feeling for community, usually translated as "social interest."

General adaptation syndrome (GAS). A series of reactions to stress calling for alarm, resistance, and then collapse.

Generativity. Interest shown in others, especially those in another generation. Roughly equivalent to *social interest*, altruism, or *Gemeinschaftsgefühl*.

Generalized other. The conception that an individual has of others, "the average man."

Genotype. The general characteristics, from inheritance, of any class of individuals. See *phenotype*.

Gestalt theory. The position that perceptions are organized by the perceiver into organized wholes which are more than the sum of their parts.

Gestalt Therapy. Form of psychotherapy with associated theory as developed by Perls; has little to do with Gestalt theory as developed by Wertheimer.

Hedonistic calculus. Behavior explained as dependent on the calculation of anticipated pain/pleasure involved in the consequence of anticipated acts.

Heuristic. Procedure that leads to discovery; a mode of investigation.

Holism (also wholism). Gestalt concept that a living organism is best understood as a unified entity rather than as a summation of parts.

Homeostasis. The tendency of a body to maintain itself in balance; for example, the human body tends to have a constant level of water, salt, and other elements. Also used in terms of psychological balance; the tendency to be in a state of quiet, peaceful rest.

Humoral theory. A theory proposed by Hippocrates that personality is a function of certain body fluids (humors).

Hypothetical-deductive method. A means of attempting to determine the truth of theories by establishing testable hypotheses from theories and then finding evidence for or against the hypotheses.

Id. The part of the psyche that contains instincts; the Unconscious; the seat of pleasure demands. See *ego, superego*.

Idealism. A philosophical position that the ultimate reality is in the mind. See *realism*.

Idealization. A defense mechanism in which the unwanted aspects of an object (person) are denied and the individual's own standards are projected onto the object.

Idiographic. Having to do with the lawfulness of individual cases. See *nomothetic*.

Imago. Internal object, frequently an image of a subjective functional complex rather than the external object itself; not identical with the outer object. Created by a combination of an introjected outer object, archetypal fantasies, and instinctual needs.

Impression management. Behavior on the part of an individual designed to generate a particular response or reaction from another.

Indeterminism. The notion that behavior cannot be perfectly predicted or explained, even if all prior events were known.

Individuation. The process of becoming differentiated as an individual.

Interactionism. Concept of reciprocal relations between mind and body, each of which influences the other.

Introjection. One of several mental mechanisms. Essentially, it means taking in, absorbing aspects of the outside world, and incorporating them into one's own psyche.

Introspection. Self-analysis; examination of one's internal status; dealing with the conscious mind.

Introvert. A person whose libido tends to turn predominantly inward toward the world of inner objects and subjective reality. See *extrovert*.

Labeling theory. Giving names, usually critical, to social behavior of an undesirable sort, thereby often making that behavior deviant by definition.

Libido. Sexual energy.

Limbic system. Part of the brain in which emotional aspects are supposed to be located.

Longitudinal method. Study of people by following them up over a considerable period of time, such as testing them from infancy through adulthood with intelligence tests.

Looking-glass self. Imagining how another person sees one's self; seeing one's self through the eyes of another.

Mandala. A Sanskrit work used by Jung to describe an image representing the self-archetype, a psychic process of centering, and a symbol of a center of the total personality. Also, a formal structure or container in which psychic organization takes place around a center.

Manic defenses. Developed, as the depressive position is achieved, as a protective reaction of the ego against experiencing feelings of guilt and loss that go with depressive anxiety.

Masculine protest. According to Adler, a desire to be more powerful or to dominate, to be like a "real man." Can occur in women as well as in men.

Materialism. The view that matter is the only reality. See *idealism, realism*.

Metaphysics. A branch of philosophy which attempts to explain the nature of being and reality.

Metapsychology. Literally "beyond psychology"; any theory that attempts to encompass all the facts of psychology by philosophical generalizations about the nature of reality, the ultimate causes of events,

ultimate truth, and so on. Freud used this term to indicate that psychoanalysis went beyond conscious experience to explain behavior.

Modeling. Process of changing someone to someone else's desires. Used mostly in modifying behavior to meet outside specifications.

Molar behavior. Unit of behavior, generally thought of as a completed act.

Molecular behavior. Behavior in terms of units of function within the behavior; seen as the totality of contributing elements to the behavior, physiologically and psychologically.

Monism. The position that life is based on one substance.

Naturwissenschaften (German). Psychology as an objective biological science. See *Geisteswissenschaften*.

Nomothetic. Relating to general laws, or based on group norms. See *idiographic*.

Numinous. Awe-inspiring, overwhelming feeling, thought, sensation, or intuition, related to some thing archetypically experienced as having intense symbolic significance beyond simple, everyday personal concern.

Object. In psychology, this word has a variety of meanings. In personality theory it may refer to another person.

Object relations theory. The complicated interaction of internal objects and archetypal images in psychic reality; emphasizes the original mother—infant relationship in the first two years of life.

Oedipus complex. Psychoanalytic notion that male children have a desire for sexual relations with their mothers. This desire is repressed and so is in the Unconscious. In females the analogy is called the Electra complex.

Ontology. The science of being. A branch of metaphysics relating to the kinds and relations of being.

Operant conditioning. Type of learning whereby the organism's responses are modified by the consequences of the behavior. Essentially, the organism repeats rewarded behavior and discontinues unrewarded or punished behavior.

Organismic. Pertaining to the organism usually emphasizing an holistic response.

Paradoxical intention. The psychological process in which one chooses to perform behavior which one sees as pathological, as well as out of one's control. By willing to perform it, one regains control, and the undesired behaviors, e.g., perspiring in anticipation of meeting new persons, cease.

Paraphrenia. General term meaning abnormal, insane, psychotic thinking.

Parapraxes. The so-called "Freudian slips," errors

one makes in life which are dynamically caused by unconscious wishes, such as forgetting names, slips of the tongue or of the pen.

Part object. Omnipotent and needy experience of the breast or penis and their symbolic equivalents. At about seven months the infant who views the mother as a series of previously separated feelings now perceives her as a whole object, that is, a person.

Passage. A sequence of steps invovled in social movements, a kind of expected protocol of operations regulating how one changes situations.

Pedagogy. Science of teaching.

Persona. A false self or social mask that represents a facet of the personality turned toward the external world; pathological when the ego rigidly identifies with mask and is unrelated to the reality of the true self and inner world with its unconscious needs and fantasies.

Personal unconscious. Repressed fears, wishes, memories, and emotions of an individual nature; preconscious perceptions of subliminal personal nature that can be recalled.

Pedology. The study of children.

Phenotype. The actual appearance of a person, having particular characteristics. See *genotype.*

Phobia. Strong fear of an unreasonable or irrational type.

Phrenology. A spurious conception that personality is based on the shape of the skull which in turn has its shape affected by the brain.

Phylogenetic. Hereditary elements in a group of people, such as what is common for the whole human race.

Physiognomy. The study of the personality as a function of the appearance of the body, especially the face.

Pluralism. The notion that reality consists of more than two ultimate substances. See *monism, dualism.*

Pragmatism. A basically American philosophical movement which finds the meaning of conceptions in their practical implications, the function of thought in the guiding of action, and the test of truthfulness in the practical consequences of belief.

Preemptive construct. Statement relative to a person which has the implication that the statement tells all about the individual, all that need be known. See *constellatory construct, propositional construct.*

Press. A term employed by Murray to refer to external forces in life. Alpha press indicates objective forces, while Beta press indicates subjectively seen external forces. The word *press* is singular and plural.

Primary self. The basic psychosomatic unit existing in the infant at birth; an integration disrupted and reestablished again and again at crucial developmental points along the life cycle; precursor of the ego and the archetypes that are derived from deintegration.

Primordial image. Jung's earlier term for archetypal image.

Preconscious. Area of the mind where memories exist which can be brought readily to awareness; in between the unconscious and the conscious.

Prodromic. Tending to predict, an early sign or warning.

Projection. Attributing certain aspects of self to others without awareness.

Projective identification. A state describing fusion characteristic of the earliest mother-infant relationship; referred to by Jung as a state of "participation mystique" or "primary identity" which can be negatively regressive or lead to growth.

Propositional construct. Statement relative to one aspect of an individual among other aspects of the person. See *constellatory construct, preemptive construct.*

Proprium. Term suggested by Allport as essentially meaning the same as self or ego; one's individuality.

Psychic reality. The experience of one's inner world, including the dynamic relationships between complexes, unconscious fantasies, and archetypal images.

Psychosomatic. Relating to a physical disorder which originates in or is influenced by the emotional state of the person.

Q-sort. Usually a group of cards (perhaps with words or sentences) that are to be sorted according to some preplanned distribution and then mathematically correlated to determine degrees of correspondence.

Range of convenience. The range of events conveniently subsumed by a construct without stretching or distorting it.

Rationalization. A plausible explanation for some behavior that comes after the decision or the act, but not the real reason.

Realism. A philosophical position that the world exists apart from the mind; that it is objectively a fact. See *idealism, materialism.*

Reality testing: Checking out hypotheses relative to people and events; a validation of reality usually done in psychotherapy.

Reciprocal inhibition. Interference of two items with one another, leading to lack of memory of either.

Reductionism. The view that large events are ultimately explained by elements; the attempt to explain complex units in terms of their constitutent interacting parts.

Reflexology. A system of psychological thought that human behavior can be explained on the basis of reflexes as the fundamental unit, with other processes building on these basics.

Reification. Conceptualizing that something which is abstract is concrete; presupposition of the real existence of concepts.

Reinforcement. Strengthening various behavioral responses through rewards.

Replication. Repeating an experiment to check the accuracy of prior conclusions.

Repression. Unconscious exclusion of events: also includes such events as instinctual drives, and conflicts between such drives and defense mechanisms. A *defense mechanism* or a *safeguarding tendency*. More or less equivalent to the term *blocking*.

Respondent. Relating to behavior that is the effect of, or identified with, a particular stimulus.

Role playing. This word has four meanings: (1) theatrical acting, (2) social role taking, (3) dissembling, and (4) acting a part for educational-therapeutic reasons, such as psychodrama.

Role taking. Imagining another's point of view; a kind of empathy.

Rorschach test. Best-known of the projective personality tests; consists of ten standard inkblots, five black-and-white and five chromatic plates, which people observe and report what they see in them.

Safeguarding tendency. Means used by individuals without awareness or intention to preserve self-esteem, through such processes as distortion, repression, and regression. See *defense mechanisms*.

Schedule. Planned program, used mostly in terms of behavior modification, experiments in which predetermined intervals and rewards and/or punishments are given to various behaviors.

Self The archetype of order, centering, and integration; also the totality of the personality.

Self-reflexivity. Process whereby a person defines his own behavior rather than simply responding to stimuli.

Set. A determining tendency a kind of preparation to behave in particular ways; a habitual kind of response preparation.

Shadow. The unconscious "natural" instinctual dark side of a person, often guilt-laden.

Sign. Expression that stands for a known thing, created from known associations, in contrast to a living symbol pregnant with ambiguous, hidden, unconscious meanings.

Social atom. Term used by Moreno to refer to the people in one's social group. Each person is the nucleus of his social atom.

Social interactionism. Doctrine that people do not interact with others in terms of themselves as individuals but as members of groups.

Soft determinism. Acknowledgement of the influences of both the individual (indeterminism) and the environment (determinism) to generate consequences.

Social stimulus value. How the person is generally seen by others.

Solipsism. A theory which states that the self is the only existent thing; and that the self can know nothing but its own modifications.

Somatotype. Classification of body structure. There are a variety of systems in use, all arbitrary in nature.

Splitting. Dichotomizing, such as the distinction between the good and bad self.

Status dilemma. A social situation which raises a problem because the individuals do not know the proper ways to act, since norms for that situation have not been established.

Status passage. Regulated movements according to prescribed protocol in social relations.

Structuralism. School of thought relative to elements or structure in the mind, such as the quality of cold. In sociology, behavior in reference to social entities. See *functionalism*.

Subception. Perception without awareness.

Superego. Psychoanalytic term referring to the incorporation of social standards within the mind of the individual more-or-less corresponds to the term "conscience." See *ego, id*.

Symbol. Distinguished from a sign; a "living" symbol expresses something relatively unknown to consciousness that is pregnant with meaning which cannot be characterized in any other way; formulates an essential, unconscious factor, not something already conventionally known.

Tabula rasa (Latin). A blank slate, referring to John Locke's concept that children are born with no memories and their minds are like a clean piece of paper.

Tele. Term developed by Moreno to refer to a kind of gravitational force which brings people together (positive tele) or keeps them apart (negative tele); roughly equivalent to empathy.

Teleology. Purposive; the concept that behavior is best understood in terms of the organism's prediction of or orientation to the future; goal orientation.

Thanatos. The death instinct; opposed to *Eros*, the life instinct.

Thema. The unifying "plot" behind behavior in Murray's system; a constant general aim of the individual. Also, the relationship between a press and a need.

Thermodynamic theory. Relationship between energy and heat.

Third-force psychology. Term referring to a group of psychological schools of thought distinguished from depth psychologies, such as pschoanalysis, and behaviorism; generally humanistic in tone, best represented by Maslow.

Token economy. Method of training organisms by teaching them first that tokens can be used to obtain various gratifications and then that tokens can be obtained by a variety of behaviors.

Trait. Any more-or-less permanent aspect or characteristic of an individual; a person's reliably consistent ways of operating.

Transaction. A relationship event depending on the transfer of forces between participating parties.

Transcendental. Going beyond normal understanding and human potentialities.

Transcendent function. Cognitive process which unites two psychological opposites in the mind, giving rise to a new level of symbolic awareness, attitude, and integration. Also, a process by which unconscious contents are made accessible to consciousness.

Transference. Displacement of feelings for one person, such as a parent, toward another, usually one's therapist, without awareness that the feeling is inappropriate.

Transitional object. Anything that serves as a link between infant and mother; the infant's first separate "not me" possession which contains qualities of both mother and child.

Transpersonal. Archetypal, symbolic meaning which cannot be explained in terms of individual or personal life experience alone; collective psychic contents which are typical or nearly universal.

UCR. Unconditioned response.

UCS. Unconditioned stimulus.

Unconscious. That portion of the psyche of which one is unaware which contains desires and drives. See *id*.

US. Unconditioned stimulus.

Vector. Force going in a particular direction. Somewhat similar to the term *cathexis* in psychology when referring to an emotional charge.

Veridical. Truthful; absolutely accurate; corresponding to fact.

Weltanschauung (German). One's total view of the world; one's personal values.

Whole object. Perception of the mother as good and bad in the same person; perception of another person as a whole person occurs with the achievement of the depressive position when the ego is strong enough to tolerate ambivalence and guilt.

Word association test. Projective test developed by Jung in which a person responds to words given one at a time. The response given plus time taken to respond, when interpreted correctly, gives the examiner an idea of the *complex* the examinee may have.

Zeitgeist (German). Spirit of the time. Cultural, social, artistic values of any society at any particular period of time.

Name Index

Abelson, R. P., 9
Abraham, Karl, 24, 25, 401
Adler, Alexandra, 49
Adler, Alfred, 1, 4, 5, 6, 9, 45-78, 85, 87, 89, 97,
    103, 107, 109, 112, 117, 119, 127, 131, 141,
    158, 169, 172, 173, 209, 250, 296, 358, 401,
    402, 410, 411, 412, 418, 420, 428
Adler, Gerhard, 119
Adler, Kurt, 49, 76
Agel, J., 65
Ainsworth, M. D., 106
Alegre, C., 268
Alex, W., 89
Alexander, Franz, 16, 20, 51, 307
Allers, Rudolf, 49
Allport, Floyd, 156
Allport, Gordon, 1, 2, 4, 5, 9, 50, 51, 131, 144,
    153-173, 209, 236, 237, 271, 272, 368, 406,
    408, 426
Anant, S. S., 375
Andreev, B. V., 353
Angel, E., 248, 274, 300
Angyal, A., 131, 309, 314, 315
Angyll, Andreas, 9, 401
Ansbacher, Heinz L., 9, 45, 48, 51, 57, 59, 65, 66,
    68, 69, 70, 71, 76, 208
Ansbacher, R. R., 51
Appley, M. H., 310
Aristophanes, 17
Aristotle, 205
Asch, Solomon F., 56
Aspy, D. N., 130, 146
Assiogoli, Roberto, 9
Atkinson, J. W., 74
Ayllon, Teodoro, 181, 188, 192
Azrin, Nathan, 181, 185, 189

Bachofen, Johann, 85
Back, J. A., 141
Baer, D. M., 192
Bakan, D., 310, 320
Baldwin, James M., 279

Balint, Michael, 113
Bandura, Albert, 9, 148, 187, 400, 401, 406, 422,
    423, 424, 425
Bannister, Donald, 208, 209, 216, 217, 231, 232,
    234, 240
Banshchikov, V., 340
Barker, R. G., 307
Barnard, W., 385
Barral, M. R., 309
Bassin, F. V., 361
Bastian, Adolf, 85
Batt, C. F., 69
Bauer, Raymond A., 226, 341, 342
Baxter, J. C., 74
Beary, J., 387, 388
Beauvoir, Simone de, 251, 256, 325
Bechterev, V. M., 177
Becker, Ernest, 72
Becker, Howard, 277, 281, 284, 293, 298, 301
Beebe, J., III, 267
Beecher, Willard, 69
Beg, A., 370
Bekhterev, V. M., 342, 343
Belinskii, V. G., 338
Benedict, Ruth, 377, 379, 406
Benson, H., 387, 388
Berdyaev, Nikolai, 246
Berger, E., 384
Berger, E. M., 74
Berger, P., 286
Bergson, Henri, 47, 205
Bernard, Claude, 22
Bernard, L. L., 279
Berne, Eric, 9, 77, 118, 400, 410, 411, 412, 421
Bernheim, Hippolyte, 18, 112
Bertocci, Peter A., 156
Bespal'ko, I. G., 352
Bettelheim, Bruno, 36
Beubel, M., 415
Bieri, J., 223
Bijou, Sidney, 181
Biller, H. B., 7

Binet, Alfred, 85
Binswanger, Ludwig, 4, 9, 51, 77, 106, 131, 243, 244, 245, 246, 247, 248, 249, 251, 252, 253, 254, 255, 256, 258, 260, 262, 263, 264, 266, 267, 273
Birdwhistell, R. L., 308
Birnbaum, Ferdinand, 49, 51, 68
Bischof, L. J., 173
Blackham, H. J., 274
Blake, R. R., 9
Blau, Peter, 283
Bleuler, Eugen, 85, 86, 87, 106, 247
Bloombaum, Milton, 9
Blonskii, P. P., 341
Blough, Donald S., 181, 198
Blumer, Herbert, 280, 281, 282, 286, 301
Bochner, S., 371
Bodalev, A. A., 347
Boldyrev, N. I., 354
Bonnarius, J., 232
Boren, J. J., 198
Boring, Edwin, 156
Börne, Ludwig, 17
Bornstein, B., 26
Boryagin, G. I., 227
Boss, Medard, 9, 51, 106, 151, 243, 245, 247, 248, 249, 251, 252, 255, 256, 258, 261, 262, 263, 264, 267, 274
Bottome, Phyllis, 49, 69
Bowers, K. S., 273
Boyer, B., 106
Boyer, L. B., 18, 33
Bozhovich, L. I., 340, 346, 347, 360, 362
Brackbill, Y., 354
Bradway, K., 107
Branden, Nathaniel, 9
Brawer, F., 106
Breen, D., 74
Brehm, J., 235
Brenner, C., 21, 41
Breuer, Josef, 18, 24, 34
Bridgman, Percy, 205
Brink, 70
Brislin, R., 371, 382
Brofenbrenner, Uri, 355
Bronowski, Jacob, 70
Bronson, G., 415
Brown, B. B., 325, 328, 372, 387
Brown, Claude, 69, 189, 190
Brucke, Ernst, 17
Bruner, Jerome, 155, 208, 209, 237, 238
Buber, Martin, 246
Bucher, R., 295
Buck, J. N., 327
Buddha, Gotama, 369

Bugenthal, James, 131
Buhler, Charlotte, 9, 406
Bühler, Karl, 9, 165, 401
Burkhardt, Jakob, 85
Burrow, Trigant, 9, 401, 402, 415
Burt, Cyril, 172
Burt, F. D., 70
Burton, A., 131
Butcher, J., 382
Bykhovskii, B., 341
Bykov, 356

Calkins, Mary W., 153, 154
Call, J. D., 113
Cameron, N., 188
Campbell, M., 371
Campbell, R., 109
Camus, Albert, 51, 70, 246
Cannon, A., 109
Cantril, Hadley, 155, 156
Carlson, R., 273
Carol, M., 387, 388
Cartwright, D., 146
Carus, Carl Gustav, 85
Cassens, J., 267
Cassier, E., 286
Cattell, R. B., 6, 9, 73, 107, 165, 172, 236, 401, 425, 426, 427
Caudill, William, 371, 393, 394
Chadwick, B. A., 196
Chaplin, J. P., 70, 75
Charcot, Jean, 18, 112
Chaubey, N., 379
Chein, I., 330
Chelpanov, G. I., 340, 341
Chernishevskii, N. G., 338
Cherulnik, P. D., 268
Child, I. L., 327
Chiu, L. H., 375, 376
Chomsky, Noam, 113
Citrun, M. M., 268
Clark, Kenneth B., 69
Cleveland, S. E., 314, 321, 327, 331
Coan, R. W., 10, 12, 13
Cohen, M., 37
Cole, M., 356, 362
Combs, A. W., 9, 131
Comte, Auguste, 205, 278
Confucius, 370
Cooley, Charles, 277, 279, 280, 286, 287
Copernicus, 17
Corsini, R. J., 1, 6, 68, 399
Cortes, J. B., 327
Coulson, W. R., 141
Cranit, R., 144

Cronbach, Lee J., 273
Crowne, O. P., 269
Crumbaugh, J. C., 263, 267
Cruzer, Georg Friedrich, 85

D'Abro, A., 37
Danton, G. J., 70
Darwin, Charles, 17, 56, 278, 350
Davidson, A., 371
Davidson, D., 109
Davis, F., 297, 298
Day, R. C., 196
DeMartino, R., 390
Dement, William D., 66
DeMontaigne, Michel Equem, 399
Denisova, M. P., 356
Denzin, N., 281, 283, 284, 285, 286, 287, 292, 294, 300, 301
Descartes, René, 203
Deutsch, Danica, 49
DeVos, George, 377, 378, 383, 390, 393, 394
Dewey, John, 47, 72, 128, 129, 205, 206, 209, 277, 279, 280
Diamond, Solomon, 208, 209
Dicks-Mireaux, M. J., 107
Dilthey, Wilhelm, 154, 155
Dobroliubov, N. A., 338
Doi, L., 378
Dollard, J., 9, 56, 177, 181, 182, 199
Doob, Leonard, 156
Dostoyevsky, Fyodor, 19
Draguns, J., 371, 383
Dreikurs, Rudolf, 49, 66, 67, 68, 71, 121, 360
DuBois, Paul, 420
Dunbar, H. F., 307
Dunn, J., 108
Dupertius, C. W., 310, 326, 331
Dyad'kovskii, I. Ye., 337
Dymond, R. F., 137

Eber, H. W., 427
Eckstein, R., 33
Edinger, E., 99, 101
Edwards, A., 109
Ehrlich, D., 295
El'konin, D. B., 349, 356
Ellenberger, Henri F., 16, 18, 26, 49, 69, 77, 84, 87, 106, 112, 248, 274, 309
Ellis, Albert, 4, 6, 9, 51, 70, 391, 400, 401, 411, 412, 417, 418, 419, 429
Empedocles, 205
Engels, Friedrich, 335, 338
English, J., 422
Epictetus, 234, 417
Epps, P., 327

Erikson, Erik, 6, 9, 20, 22, 26, 89, 99, 157, 271, 272, 286, 400, 413, 414, 415
Eysenck, H. J., 6, 9, 73, 107, 165, 172, 305, 400, 401, 425, 426, 427

Fagerhaugh, S., 289
Fanon, Frantz, 69
Farberow, N. L., 72
Faris, Ellsworth, 279
Farson, Richard, 130, 140
Federn, E., 47
Feldenkrais, Moishe, 9, 308, 322, 325
Felker, D. W., 75
Fenichel, O., 26, 40, 114, 307
Ferenczi, S., 20, 50
Ferguson, E. D., 70
Ferster, Charles B., 180, 181, 190
Festinger, L., 9, 235
Figurin, N. L., 356
Filomafitskii, A. M., 337
Fine, R., 114
Fisch, R., 67
Fisher, Seymour, 9, 303, 307, 313, 314, 317, 318, 321, 322, 327, 328, 331
Fiske, D. W., 327
Flournoy, Theodore, 85
Foa, U. G., 74
Ford, D. H., 50, 51
Fordham, Frieda, 95, 98, 108, 119
Fordham, Michael, 92, 93, 97, 104, 108, 109, 114, 119
Foster, C. M., 141
Frankl, Vistor, 9, 49, 51, 72, 77, 153, 157, 158, 173, 243, 248, 249, 251, 264, 267
Franklin, Benjamin, 70
Fransella, F., 208, 240
French, J. W., 426, 427
French, Thomas M., 20, 77
Freud, Anna, 30, 114
Freud, Sigmund, 1, 4, 6, 9, 15-28, 31-35, 38-40, 45, 48, 50, 53, 56, 66, 71, 72, 73, 75, 76, 77, 83, 85, 86, 87, 88, 90, 93, 94, 101, 103, 104, 106, 107, 112, 113, 114, 115, 116, 117, 127, 157, 164, 167, 168, 172, 184, 199, 205, 236, 237, 247, 249, 250, 264, 270, 272, 286, 296, 300, 306, 313, 320, 358, 359, 360, 401, 402, 403, 410, 411, 412, 418, 419
Frey-Rohn, L., 88, 110
Frobenius, Leo, 85
Fromm, Erich, 9, 20, 51, 71, 77, 88, 89, 112, 117, 155, 271, 272, 400, 401, 402, 403
Fürtmuller, Carl, 49, 53, 69
Futterman, Samuel, 208, 209

Galileo, 141

Gall, Franz J., 305
Garfinkel, Harold, 282, 288
Gatti, F. M., 327
Gendlin, Eugene, 9, 127, 130, 141, 143, 243, 249, 250, 262, 264, 267, 274
George, Alexander I., 70
George, Juliette, 70
Gewitz, J. L., 192
Ghougassian, J., 173
Gibbens, T. C. N., 327
Giegerich, W., 85
Gilbert, A., 387
Gilyasheva, I. N., 352
Giovacchini, Peter L., 15, 18, 27, 32, 33, 34, 37, 41
Giovanni, Achille de, 306
Glaser, Barney G., 277, 289, 292, 295, 299
Glasser, William, 9, 77, 391, 400, 401, 411, 412, 419, 420, 421, 422, 429
Glueck, E., 327
Glueck, S., 327
Goethe, Johann Wolfgang, 85
Goffman, E., 277, 281, 288, 291, 301
Goldfried, M. R., 74
Goldiamond, Israel, 181, 194, 195
Goldstein, A., 391, 418
Goldstein, Kurt, 9, 157, 303, 307, 314, 315, 318, 319, 320, 321, 322, 323, 324, 328, 329, 331
Gonick, M. R., 307
Goodman, P., 415
Gordon, L., 382
Gordon, R., 98, 101, 104, 109
Gould, S., 68
Govinda, L. A., 380, 393, 394
Gray, H., 107, 112
Green, A. M., 325, 328
Green, E. E., 325, 328
Green, Maurice, 208
Greenwald, Harold, 6, 9, 400, 401, 412, 427, 428, 429
Griffin, John, 288
Grimsley, R., 274
Grinker, R. R., 130
Guevara, 74
Guilford, J. P., 6, 9, 73, 107, 427

Haley, J., 74
Hall, C. S., 47, 51, 73, 75, 104, 167, 173, 332, 359
Hallowell, I., 106
Hanfmann, E., 362
Hanna, Thomas, 127
Harlow, H. F., 133
Harrington, G. L., 420
Harris, D. V., 322

Harris, Thomas, 410, 411, 413
Hart, J. T., 137, 143, 149
Hartl, E. M., 316, 317, 321, 323, 331
Hartmann, H., 22, 33
Harvey, O. J., 9
Harvey, William, 328
Hawes, R. M., 422
Heath, A., 283
Hefferline, R. F., 415
Hegel, G. W. F., 205, 245, 247, 279
Heidegger, Martin, 85, 243, 244, 245, 246, 247, 248, 252, 255, 261, 266
Heider, Fritz, 9, 72
Helson, H., 144
Henderson, J., 94, 107, 109
Henry, G., 43
Heraclitus, 205, 416
Hernstein, Richard, 181
Herodotus, 16
Herzen, A. I., 338
Hiniker, P., 370
Hinkle, B., 107
Hinkle, D., 233, 234
Hippocrates, 16, 62, 305, 425
Hitler, Adolf, 110
Hoffman, E. T. A., 85
Hold, E. B., 177
Holdstock, T. L., 125, 126
Holland, J. G., 180
Holmes, 269
Holsopple, James, 106
Holt, R. R., 50, 106
Homan, George, 283
Hoover, M., 249, 263, 268
Horney, Karen, 5, 6, 9, 20, 26, 51, 71, 77, 88, 112, 117, 155, 163, 172, 296, 359, 400, 402, 403, 425
Horton, D. L., 74
Houston, 269
Hsu, F. L. K., 371, 374, 375, 384, 385, 393, 394
Hsu, J., 376, 386
Hubbard, H. Ron, 9
Hughes, E. C., 277, 281, 292, 301
Hull, Clark L., 154, 164, 177, 181, 182
Hunter, W. S., 177
Husserl, Edmund, 85, 127, 246, 267, 282
Huxley, Aldous, 324

Irving, J., 70
Isaacs, W., 195
Ivanov-Smolenskii, 356
Ivashchenko, F. I., 347
Iwai, H., 383

Jackins, Harvey, 9

Jackson, Don, 9
Jackson, M., 96, 109
Jacobi, J., 91, 94
Jacobs, Laurence, 9
Jacobson, L., 372
James, William, 47, 60, 153, 154, 159, 164, 165, 167, 168, 205, 206, 209, 243, 245, 249, 279, 322
Janet, Pierre, 85, 86, 112
Janov, Arthur, 9
Jaques, E., 98
Jaspers, Karl, 127, 243, 245, 253
Jelliffe, Edith Ely, 48
Jones, E., 17, 18
Jones, Mary Cover, 179, 180, 424
Jourard, Sydney, 9
Jung, Carl, 1, 4, 9, 19, 28, 83-118, 119, 159, 166, 172, 247, 249, 250, 358, 359, 390, 401, 402, 408, 425

Kakar, S., 380
Kane, J. E., 322
Kanellakos, D., 372
Kankeleit, O., 48
Kant, Immanuel, 47, 85
Kardiner, Abraham, 77
Kasatkin, 356
Katkin, E. S., 269
Kaufmann, Y., 97
Kelley, D., 72, 106
Kelly, Charles, 9
Kelly, George A., 1, 2, 9, 51, 52, 66, 73, 203-239, 271, 272, 308, 405
Kelman, Harold, 50
Kempf, Edward, 77
Kempler, Walter, 131, 416, 417
Kettner, M., 93
Kieferle, D., 234
Kiell, N., 70
Kierkegaard, Sören, 85, 121, 243, 245, 247, 249, 253, 254, 257, 266
Kiev, A., 383
Kikuchi, A., 382
King, M., 75
Kinkade, K. A., 193
Klages, Ludwig, 47
Klapp, O., 297
Klein, George S., 76
Klein, Melanie, 20, 33, 89, 92, 96, 113, 116, 117, 267
Klineberg, O., 382
Klopfer, Bruno, 48, 50, 106, 208
Kluckhohn, Clyde, 93, 368
Kobasa, Suzanne C., 243, 249, 263, 268
Koch, Robert, 16

Koffka, Kurt, 50, 315
Köhler, Wolfgang, 50, 315
Kon, I. S., 340, 346
Konnikova, T. Ye., 346
Kornilov, N. N., 341
Korsybski, Alfred, 9
Kostiuk, 342
Kovach, J. K., 340
Kovalev, A. G., 340, 348
Kramer, B. M., 172
Krasner, L., 201
Kretschmer, Ernst, 166, 306, 311
Kris, Ernst, 33
Krishnamurti, 127
Kroeber, A. L., 279, 368
Krogan, N., 232
Krutetski, V. A., 351
Künkel, Fritz, 49

Laguna, de, 286
Laing, Ronald D., 131, 243, 248, 258, 262, 264, 267
Lambert, K., 109
Landfield, A., 232
Lange, N. N., 340
Lashley, Karl, 177
Lasswell, Harold D., 70
Lavater, John, 305
Lazarfeld, Sofie, 49
Lazarus, A., 148
Lazarus, Moritz, 47
Lebedinskii, M. S., 337, 358
LeBon, 278
Lebra, W., 371, 382
Lechtreman-Abramovich, R. Ya., 356
Lecky, P., 9, 131
Lefcourt, H. M., 73, 79
Leibnitz, Gottfried, 85
LeMay, M. I., 75
Lemere, F., 195
Lenin, Vladimir I., 335, 338, 350
Leonardo da Vinci, 19
Leontiev, A. A., 339, 342, 349, 356
LeVine, R., 371
Levi-Strauss, 113
Levy, Leon, 205, 210, 214, 216, 232, 233, 234, 235, 236, 238, 240
Lewin, Kurt, 9, 48, 72, 74, 154, 155, 236, 360, 375
Lewis, N. D. C., 327
Liem, 270
Lin, T. Y., 371, 393, 394
Lindesmith, A. R., 281, 283, 284, 285, 286, 287, 292, 294, 297, 300, 301
Lindon, J., 33

Lindsley, O. R., 185
Lindzey, G., 51, 73, 75, 104, 155, 170, 173, 308, 328, 359
Liverant, S., 268
Lofland, J., 297
Lombroso, Césare, 305
Lomonosov, M. V., 336, 337, 340, 350
Lomov, B. F., 352
Long, I. M. K., 50
Lonner, W., 371, 382
Lorenz, Konrad, 113
Low, A. A., 9
Lowe, R., 68
Lowen, Alexander, 9, 308, 322, 325
Lowenstein, Rudolph, 33
Lowrie, Regina, 266
Lowry, R., 50
Luckmann, T., 286
Lundin, Robert W., 177, 178, 181, 200
Luria, A., 339, 350, 352, 354, 356
Lyalikov, D. N., 358
Lyman, S., 285
Lynn, R., 368

Machotka, P., 308
Machover, K., 327
MacKinnon, D., 106
Maddi, S. R., 50, 51, 75, 243, 249, 251, 252, 253, 254, 255, 256, 261, 262, 263, 264, 265, 268, 269, 270, 271, 273, 274
Maduro, Renaldo J., 83, 89, 95, 96, 99, 101, 109
Maeder, Alphonse, 85
Maharishi Mahesh Yogi, 371
Maher, B. A., 207, 235, 239
Maholick, L. T., 263
Mair, J., 208, 209, 216, 217, 232, 234, 240
Mairet, P., 70
Makarenko, Anton S., 335, 338, 340, 347, 352, 354, 355, 356, 362
Malpass, R., 371
Maltz, Albert, 9
Maltzman, I., 356, 362
Manaster, G. J., 75
Mansurov, N. S., 359
Mao T'se Tung, 381
Marat, Jean Paul, 70
Marcel, Gabriel, 246
Marlowe, D., 269
Marmor, Judd, 51, 71, 76
Marrone, R. I. M., 192
Martin, P. L., 196
Martinez, C., 89
Marx, Karl, 47, 283, 284, 335, 338, 340
Maslow, A. H., 6, 9, 51, 71, 72, 89, 131, 141, 153, 155, 157, 158, 164, 172, 250, 270, 309, 314, 328, 400, 406, 407, 408, 410, 413
Masters, J. C., 200
Matson, F. W., 51, 71
Matsumoto, Y., 386
Maugham, Somerset, 70
May, Rollo, 51, 71, 131, 243, 248, 253, 254, 274, 309, 401, 406
May, W. H., 9, 382
Mayrl, W., 283, 284
Mazlish, B., 70
McCall, George, 289, 301
McClelland, David, 390, 410
McCully, R., 106
McDermott, E., 310, 316, 317, 321, 323, 326, 331
McDougall, William, 56, 168, 408
McGuire, W., 87, 103
McLaughlin, J. J., 70
McReynolds, P., 74
Mead, George H., 9, 277, 279, 280, 281, 282, 284, 285, 286, 287, 300, 301
Meade, R., 385
Meador, B. D., 127, 129, 390
Meerloo, J. A. M., 77
Mees, H. L., 195
Meier, C. A., 107
Merton, Robert, 282
Mesmer, Friedrich, 18
Messick, S. M., 232
Metzger, Wolfgang, 50
Meyer, Adolf, 9, 51, 307
Meyerson, L., 307
Miale, Florence, 106
Michael, J., 188
Miley, C. H., 75
Mill, John Stuart, 59, 409
Miller, N. E., 9, 56, 177, 181, 182, 199
Mills, C. W., 285
Mills, G., 371
Mindness, H., 106
Minton, H. L., 72
Miron, M. S., 382
Mischel, W., 249, 273, 424
Mitchell, K. M., 146
Monroe, Marilyn, 70
Montagu, Ashley, 75
Moreno, J. L., 6, 9, 71, 296, 400, 403, 404, 405, 412, 424
Morgan, Christiana, 408
Mosak, B., 49, 70, 79
Mosak, H., 49, 70, 127
Mosher, D. L., 74
Mowrer, O. H., 9, 51, 75, 177, 181, 182, 183, 184, 199, 271, 272, 401
Mukhin, Ye. O., 337
Munroe, R. L., 77

Murasaki, Lady, 378
Murphy, Gardner, 9, 78, 153, 336, 340, 369, 370, 371, 372, 373, 374, 383, 388, 389, 392, 393, 394
Murphy, L., 369, 370, 372, 373, 374, 383, 388, 389, 392, 393, 394
Murray, E., 9, 268
Murray, H. A., 73, 106, 107, 153, 157, 158, 209, 310, 400, 409, 410, 427
Mussolini, Benito, 70
Myasishchev, V. N., 335, 338, 339, 340, 352, 353, 356, 357, 358, 362
Myers, I., 107

Naccarati, Sante, 306, 311
Nagel, E., 37
Nakakuki, M., 379
Nakamura, H., 368, 370, 371, 372, 373, 378, 392, 393
Nakane, C., 377, 378
Napoleon Bonaparte, 3
Nawas, M., 232
Nebylitsyn, 353, 356, 361
Neumann, E., 85, 91, 96, 99
Neumann, Johannes, 49
Neuringer, C., 74
Newcomb, T. M., 280
Newton, K., 109
Nietzsche, Friedrich, 17, 47, 50, 85, 86, 246
Nishimaru, S., 384
Noguchi, Hideyo, 16
Norbeck, E., 377, 383
Nunberg, H., 47

Oberlander, M., 267
O'Connell, W. E., 76
O'Connor, R. D., 187
Odbert, H. S., 426
Oden, T. C., 127
Olds, J., 192
O'Leary, K. D., 200
Orgler, Hertha, 49, 69
Orwell, George, 324
Osgood, C., 9, 382
Osterman, E., 93
Ottenheimer, Hilde, 69
Ourth, L., 232

Pancheri, P., 382
Pande, S., 386, 389, 390
Papanek, Ernst, 69, 76
Papanek, H., 68
Park, Robert, 281
Parnell, R. W., 327
Parrott, M. C., 200

Parsons, Talcott, 282
Pasteur, Louis, 16
Pastore, N., 5
Paterson, D. G., 306
Patterson, C. H., 127, 131
Pavlov, Ivan P., 38, 177, 178, 179, 182, 184, 185, 335, 337, 338, 339, 340, 341, 343, 350, 352, 353, 354, 356, 361, 362
Payne, D. E., 232
Payne, T. R., 361, 362
Pederson, F., 234
Pedersen, Paul B., 367, 368, 371, 383
Peiper, A., 356
Peirce, Charles, 206
Perls, Frederick (Fritz), 6, 9, 71, 77, 118, 400, 403, 405, 415, 416
Perry, J., 90, 94
Perry, Ralph Barton, 57
Perryman, T. B., 75
Petrovskii, A. V., 341
Pettigrew, Thomas, 155
Phillips, E. L., 51
Piaget, Jean, 9, 113, 157
Picasso, Pablo, 406
Piskin, V., 267
Planck, Max, 37
Plato, 154
Plaut, A., 92, 109, 116
Plugge, T., 309
Poch, S., 233, 234
Pollack, G. H., 307
Postman, Leo, 155, 168, 171
Pratt, S., 195, 198
Price-Williams, D., 368
Progoff, I., 110
Prokina, N. F., 356, 357

Rablen, R. A., 137
Rachman, S., 73, 196
Rado, Sandor, 77
Ramos, S., 69
Rand, Ayn, 268
Rank, Otto, 9, 20, 50, 51, 128, 129, 249
Rapaport, D., 22
Raskin, N. J., 139, 146
Raynor, Rosalie, 179, 184, 186
Redfearn, J., 92
Reich, W., 9, 308, 401, 403
Reik, Theodore, 77, 428
Reisner, M., 341
Reynolds, D., 383
Rice, L. N., 130, 150
Rimm, D. C., 200
Risley, T., 195
Robespierre, Maximilien de, 70

Rodin, J., 145
Roebuck, F. N., 130, 146
Rogers, Carl, 1, 4, 6, 9, 51, 75, 89, 118, 125, 126,
    127, 128, 129, 130, 149, 153, 158, 167, 169,
    173, 205, 227, 236, 237, 250, 271, 296, 314,
    360, 406, 421
Rogers, William, 141
Rohila, B., 379
Rokhlin, L. L., 340
Rolf, Ida, 9, 308, 322
Rom, P., 51, 70
Ropers, R., 284
Rorschach, Hermann, 106
Rosenblith, W. A., 144
Rosengart-Pupko, G. L., 356
Ross, D., 424
Ross, S. A., 424
Ross, W. D., 305
Roth, Sydney, 49
Rotter, J. B., 9, 72, 73, 74, 77, 207, 236, 268, 269,
    401
Roznafszky, J., 410, 418, 420
Rubinshtein, Serge L., 336, 338, 339, 341, 342,
    348, 356, 361
Rühle, Otto, 49
Rühle-Gerstel, Alice, 49, 70
Rychlak, J. R., 50, 53, 240
Ryle, A., 74

Sabshin, M., 295
Sahakian, William S., 78, 153, 173, 174
Sangsingkeo, P., 370
Sarbin, Theodore, 9
Sartre, Jean Paul, 51, 77, 173, 243, 244, 245,
    246, 247, 251, 252, 253, 262, 264, 265
Satire, Virginia, 77
Sato, K., 384, 385, 388, 390
Saul, Leon J., 76
Schaefer, H. H., 196
Schaffer, Herbert, 49
Schatzman, L., 294, 295, 298
Scheeling, Friedrich, 85
Scheerer, M., 321
Schilder, Paul, 303, 307, 313, 314, 322, 327
Schiller, Johann, 85
Schnachter, Stanley, 145
Schopenhauer, Arthur, 85
Schutz, Alfred, 282
Schutz, W. C., 9, 412
Schwartz, M., 297
Schweitzer, Albert, 392
Schwitzgebel, R., 195
Scott, M., 285, 297
Searles, H. S., 33
Seashore, Carl, 206

Sechenov, I. M., 337
Sechrest, Lee, 203, 210, 214, 216, 232, 234
Seeman, J., 146, 268
Segal, H., 92, 98, 116
Seif, Leonhard, 49
Selesnick, S., 16
Selivanov, 342
Selye, Hans, 309, 310, 320
Shakespeare, William, 1, 303, 417
Shanker, P., 375
Shchelovanov, N. M., 343, 356
Sheldon, William, 9, 303, 306, 307, 308, 310,
    311, 313, 316, 317, 321, 322, 323, 324, 326,
    327, 330, 331, 424, 425
Shlien, J. M., 146
Shneidman, E. S., 72
Shoemaker, D., 232
Shontz, Franklin, 303, 304, 307, 323, 328
Shorokhova, Ye. V., 340, 358, 359
Shulman, R. H., 66, 70
Shumilin, Ye. A., 337
Sicher, Lydia, 49
Simmel, G., 293
Simmons, John, 289, 301
Simon, R., 336
Singer, M., 368, 371
Sinha, J. B. P., 379
Skiandan, 337
Skinner, B. F., 1, 4, 9, 76, 154, 177-200, 236,
    270, 271, 296, 424
Smirnov, 356
Smith, Brewster, 155
Smith, H., 239
Smith, J. A., 305
Smuts, Jan, 307
Snygg, D., 9, 131
Socrates, 17, 154
Solomon, R., 376, 381, 393, 394
Sonstegard, M., 68
Sorokin, Pitirim, 169
Spain, D., 382
Spearman, Charles, 172, 427
Sperber, Manes, 49
Sperry, R. W., 145
Spiegel, J. P., 308
Spiegelman, J. M., 106
Spiel, Oskar, 49, 68
Spinoza, Benedictus, 17, 205, 307
Spiro, M., 382
Spitz, Rene, 113
Spranger, Eduard, 155, 170
Spurzheim, Johann, 305
Staats, Arthur, 181, 200
Stanton, A., 297
Stein, 91, 115

Steiner, C., 413
Steinthal, Heymann, 47
Stephenson, William, 137
Stern, A., 51
Stern, Wilhelm, 307
Stern, William, 50, 153, 155, 159
Sternbach, R., 145
Stevens, S. S., 306, 308, 310, 313, 326, 331
Stewart, R., 372
Stone, Gregory, 277, 288
Strauss, Anselm, 277, 281, 283, 284, 285, 286, 287, 289, 292, 294, 295, 297, 298, 299, 300, 301
Sudakov, N. I., 347
Sullivan, Harry Stack, 9, 20, 51, 71, 77, 88, 89, 113, 117, 167, 172, 209, 286, 287, 296, 339, 359, 400, 401, 402, 403, 415
Sumner, William, 279
Sundberg, N. D., 51, 379
Suomi, S. I., 133
Surya, N. C., 368, 375, 392
Sutherland, E., 297
Suzuki, Daisetz T., 367, 385, 390
Svyadoshch, A. M., 358
Szasz, Thomas, 51, 248, 314, 318

Taft, Jessie, 128
Taft, R. A., 73
Tagore, Rabindranoth, 372
Taintor, Z., 75
Tarde, 278
Tart, C., 372
Tate, D., 92
Tausch, Reinhard, 130
Taylor, J. A., 75
Teasdale, J., 196
Teichman, M., 74
Tenney, A. M., 327
Teplov, 352, 356, 361
Termansen, P. E., 388
Thibaut, 72
Thomas, D. S., 234, 279
Thomas, J., 195
Thomas, W. I., 167, 234, 277, 279, 287, 300
Thompson, Clara, 51, 77
Thomson, Sir Godfrey, 206
Thorndike, Edward Lee, 179, 182, 184
Thorndike, R., 382
Thorne, F. C., 6, 9, 51, 72, 131, 267, 268, 427
Thurstone, L. L., 9, 427
Tillich, Paul, 243, 245, 249, 254, 260
Tolstoy, Leon, 350
Tomlinson, T. M., 149, 267
Tooley, J. T., 195, 198
Torrey, E., 383

Toynbee, Arnold, 393
Trandis, C. H., 382
Travis, Lee, 206
Triandis, H. C., 371
Trotter, W., 56
Troxler, Ignaz, 85
Truax, C. B., 146
Trumbull, R., 310
Tseng, W. S., 376, 386
Tucker, W. B., 306, 308, 331
Tugarinov, V. P., 340
Turner, Ralph, 282, 288
Tyler, L. E., 51, 379
Tyler, V. O., 189, 190

Ullman, L. P., 201
Unamuno, Miguel de, 246
Urban, H. B., 50, 51
Uznadze, D. N., 335, 338, 339, 361, 362

Vaihinger, Hans, 47, 50
Vakar, G., 362
Van Dusen, W., 51
Van Kaam, Adrian, 9, 401
Vernon, Philip E., 155, 170
Viola, Giacinto, 306
Virchow, Rudolf, 16, 46
Vockell, E. I., 75
Voegtlin, W. L., 195
Vogel, E. F., 376
Von Békésy, G., 144
Von Franz, M. L., 95, 110
Von Hartmann, Eduard, 85
Von Schubert, Gotthilf, 85
Vygotskii, L. S., 338, 339, 342, 348, 349, 356, 361, 362

Waelder, R., 21, 29, 31, 41
Wagatsuma, H., 386, 390
Wagner-Juaregg, Julius, 16
Walker, R. N., 327
Walters, Bernard, 9
Walters, E. D., 325, 328
Walters, R. H., 422
Wapner, 144
Ward, James, 153
Warren, C., 295, 297
Warren, N., 209
Waterman, A., 415
Waterman, C., 415
Watson, John B., 5, 36, 177, 179, 180, 183, 184, 186, 341
Watts, A., 389
Watzlawick, P., 67
Weakland, J., 67

Weissmann, Eric, 49
Werner, Harold, 68, 144
Werner, Heinz, 9
Wertheimer, Max, 50, 315, 406, 415
Wesby, David, 292
Wexberg, Erwin, 49
Wexler, D. A., 130, 139, 145, 147, 150
Wheelwright, Joseph B., 83, 107, 112
White, Robert W., 51, 72, 75, 77
White, William Alanson, 48
Whitehead, C., 112, 116
Whitmont, Edward, 102, 119
Wickes, F. G., 97
Wicklund, R., 235
Wilder, J., 78
Wiley, R. E., 74
Williams, C. D., 186, 198
Williams, M., 91
Williams, T. G., 232
Wilson, G. T., 200
Wilson, Woodrow, 70
Winnicott, D., 33, 41, 104, 116

Wittkower, E. C., 388
Wolf, M. M., 195
Wolpe, Joseph, 9, 194, 401, 427
Wood, J. K., 138
Wortis, J. A., 341, 361
Wright, B. A., 307
Wundt, Wilhelm, 154
Wylie, R. C., 327

Yap, P. M., 383
Youngdale, J. M., 70

Zagona, S. V., 10
Zaporozhetz, A. V., 349, 356
Zeigarnik, B. V., 349, 352
Ziferstein, Isidore, 335, 354
Zillborg, G., 43
Zimring, F. M., 146
Zinchenko, 35
Zinkin, L., 108
Znaniecki, Florian, 167
Zunin, L. M., 391, 420

Subject Index

Ability, 57, 58
Abnormality, 320
About Behaviorism, 180
Abreaction, 18, 34
Absolute, 369
Absolute or ultimate ego, 374
Abstract attitude, 315-316
Academy of Pedagogical Sciences of the U.S.S.R. and of the Russian Soviet Federated Socialist Republic, 340
Accounts (Motivational statements), 278, 285
Achievement motivation, 74
Acquired characteristics, 339
Activators, 417
Active therapy, 20
Activity, 61, 62, 63; energy, 62; unity with consciousness, 343, 348
Actones, 408
Actor, 278
Actualization, 250; self, *see* Self-actualization
Actual neuroses, 27
Adaptive hypothesis, 23
Adlerian movement, 49
Adolescence, 345-347; developmental theory, 414, 415
Adventurousness, 262
Aesthetic type of orientation, 244, 257
Affection, 190
Affective functions, 5, 204
Affective theories of personality, 13
Aggression, 189, 222, 424; Chinese child-rearing practices, 376
Aging, 324-325
Alarm stage of stress response, 307
Alcoholism, 195
Alienation-Commitment Test, 262, 268
Allergy, 309
Allport-Vernon Study of Values Test, 155
All-Union Conference of Marxist Leninist Research Institutes, 343
All-Union Symposium on Problems of Personality, 340

Altruism, 169
Amae, 377, 378, 391
American Academy of Psychoanalysis, 88
American Association of Humanistic Psychology, 406
American Psychological Association, 200
American Society of Adlerian Psychology, 45, 49
Anal phase of psychosexual development, 25; obsessive-compulsive person, 32
Analytical psychology, 9, 83-118
Anima-animus, 95, 112
Animals: behavior research, 178, 179; personality, 160; theories of human behavior, 172
Anosognosia, 306, 314
Anthropology, 118, 279
Anthropometric studies, 306
Anxiety, 18, 221; authentic person, 261; existentialism, 253, 254; experiences contrary to self-concept, 136; neurosis, 27; punishment, 189; signal theory, 28; theory, 27-28; threat experience, 319
Apoplectic habitus (body type), 306, 311
Appearance, 277, 288
Applications of personality theories: analytical psychology, 106-112; Asian theories, 382-387; behaviorism, 193-197; constitutional theories, 321-326; developmental theory, 414-415; direct decision theory, 429-430; existential psychology, 261-266; Gestalt therapy theory, 416-417; individual psychology, 65-71; personal constructs theory, 223-231; personalism, 166-169; person-centered theory, 137-143; personology, 400-410; psychoanalysis, 33-37; psychosocial theory, 403; rational-emotive theory, 419; reality theory, 421-422; self-actualization, 408; social interactionism, 294-298; social learning theory, 423; sociometric theory, 404-405; Soviet personality theories, 353-355; transactional analysis, 412; typology theory, 426-427

Applied behavior analysis, 197
Approval, 190
Aptitude, 57, 58
Archetypes, 89, 90, 93-94, 113; analyst, 91; child, 95; transference, 109
Aryan philosophy, 369
Assessment methods of personality theories: analytical psychology, 106; Asian personality theories, 382-383; behaviorism, 193-197; constitution theories, 321-322; existential psychology, 261-263; individual psychology, 65-66; personal constructs theory, 223-226; personalism, 166-167; person-centered theory, 137-138; psychoanalysis, 33-35; social interaction, 294-296; Soviet psychology, 352
Assertions concerning personality theories: analytical psychology, 89-106; Asian theories, 373-382; behaviorism, 183-193; constitutional theories of personality, 310-321; developmental theory, 413-414; direct decision theory, 429; existential psychology, 251-261; Gestalt therapy theory, 416; individual psychology, 51-65; personal constructs theory, 209-223; personalism, 158-166; person-centered theory, 131-136; personology, 409; psychoanalysis, 7, 20-33; psychosocial theory, 402-403; rational-emotive theory, 418-419; reality theory, 420-421; social interactionism, 284-294; social learning theory, 423-424; sociometric theory, 404-405; Soviet theories, 343-352; transactional analysis, 411-412; typology theory, 425-426
Asian personality theory, 367-393; child-rearing, 375-376; contrast with Western theory, 372-373, 374, 375, 379, 380, 382, 386, 387-392
Assessing, 278, 288, 289; group, 288
Asthenics (microplanchnic body type), 306, 311
Atlas of Men, 310, 326
Atman, 369, 374
Attention, 190
Attitude, 3, 165
Attitudinal values, 248
Attribute, 387
Authenticity, 245, 257-258, 259
Authentic person, 243, 258-259; social interaction, 260
Authority: China, 381; Dharma, 380; India, 380; Japan, 392
Autoerotic instincts, 23, 24
Autogenetic movement, 342, 343; training, 388
Autonomous functions, 101
Autonomy, 19; psychoanalysis, 37, 40
Aversive stimuli, 177, 188; therapy, 195-196

Avoidance behavior, 188
Awareness context, 277, 278, 289, 290

Balance of energy, *see* Homeostasis
Balance theory, 9
Becoming: Basic Considerations for a Psychology of Personality, 157
Behavior, 45, 160, 217-218; Asian vs. Western, 390; brain damage, 306; control, *see* Behavior control; direct decision theory, 429; environmental influence, 425; implicit and explicit, 204; laws of, 178; personology, 408, 409; prediction, *see* Behavior prediction; psychoanalysis, 19; rational-emotive theory, 417-418, 419; relation to body, 303, 305, 308; responsibility for, 420, 421; social learning theory, 423; teleological orientation, 285; *see also* Behaviorism
Behavior control, 177, 178, 183, 184
Behaviorism, 5, 177-200; constitutional theories of personality, 329; existential view, 270; individual psychology, 76; person-centered psychology, 148; personalism, 157; social learning theory, 423; Soviet view of, 341
Behavioral modification, 38-39, 177, 270; psychoanalysis, 36
Behavior of Organisms, The, 180
Behavior predictions, 177, 178, 183, 184, 232; invalid, 233
Behavior theory, 9
Behavior therapy, 180, 194, 391
Being-in-itself, 251
Being-for-itself, 245, 251
Beliefs, 417
Beyond Freedom and Dignity, 180, 193
Bhagavad-Gita, 369, 370, 392
Bhakti-yoga, 371
Biocentrism, 9
Bio-energetics, 9
Biofeedback, 144; systems, 387; techniques, 372; yogic exercises, 325
Biographical hypothesis, 228
Biological determinism, 284, 286
Biological humanics, 316-317
Biosocial theory, 9
Bipolar dynamics, 54-55
Birth order, 65-66, 75
Bisexuality of human beings, 112
Body: altering psychological states, 322; arousing stimuli, 318; build, 324; human personality, 304; patterns of sensory response, 318; relation to behavior, 303, 305, 318; techniques for control, 325
Body awareness, 9

Body ego, 91, 314

Body image, 307, 314; boundary, 317, 327; stages of development, 314, 317-318; tests, 327; theory, 9, 322

Brain research, 144-145; relation to behavior, 306, 314-315

Bribery, 222

Buddhism, 369, 370, 380

Bunsan Naikan, 384

Cannibalistic phase of psychosexual development, 25

Career, 277, 278, 281, 292-293; multiple, 292, 293; objective and subjective, 292

Caring, 139, 246, 266

Caste, 385

Castration anxiety, 25

Catastrophic reaction, 319, 320

Catharsis, 18

Cathexis, 22; loss of, 30-31

Center for the Studies of Persons, 128

Cerebrotonic temperament, 312-313

Character, 2, 160-161; physical appearance, 303

Character analysis, 9

Characterological disorders, 18, 27; psychological regression, 32

Characterological theory, 370

Chestnut Lodge, 36

Chicago Institute for Psychoanalysis, 19

Chicago Psychoanalytic Society, 39

Chicago school of sociologists, 281

Child development, 36, 64-65, 96-98; China, 375-376; ego development, 413-414; existential psychology, 255-257; institutional rearing, 360-361; Japan, 376-378; Jungian psychotherapy, 110; modeling, 187; pedology, 341-342; positive reinforcement, 197; sensation, 313; Soviet psychology, 343-347, 354-355, 360-361

Child guidance clinics, 68

Child symbol, 95

"Chimney sweeping", 34

China, 368, 372, 374, 375; authority, 381; history of personality theory, 370; interpersonal relationship, 384-385, 386; psychology compared to Western, 386-387; revolution, 381

Choleric personality type, 305

Circumspection-preemption-control cycle (C-P-C cycle), 222

Clan, 385

Class, 349

Client-centered personality theory, 125

Client-centered therapy, 39; counseling, 129

Client-Centered Therapy, 129

Clinical psychology, 403; constitutional theory

of personality, 307; personal constructs theory, 223; psychoanalysis, 18, 26

Closed awareness context, 289, 290

Coenesthesis, 163

Cognition, 5, 204; relation to personality development, 418

Cognition dissonance, 9

Cognitive theories of personality, 13

Collective, 347, 348, 353, 355

Collective Family: A Handbook for Russian Parents, 355

Collective psyche, 116

Collective unconscious, 89, 113, 249, 250

Collective upbringing, 356

Coming of Age, 325

Coming to terms, 320

Commonality Corollary, 216

Common sense, 66, 419, 420, 424

Communication, 280; psychic development, 344

Community, 58

Community psychology, 141

Comparison between personality theories, 7-8; analytical psychology, 114-117; Asian, 388-392; behaviorism, 198-199; constitutional theories, 328-330; existentialism, 270-273; individual psychology, 75-77; personal construct, 235-238; personalism, 172; person-centered theory, 147-149; psychoanalysis, 38-39; social interactionism, 300; Soviet, 358-361

Compensation, 100

Complexes, 85, 89, 90, 91

Comradely court, 355

Conation, 5

Concepts, 2; definition, 186

Conceptual systems, 9

Condensation, 32

Conditional regard, 134

Conditioned reflex, 179, 335, 338, 339, 344, 350, 356; constitutional theories of personality, 329

Conditioned stimulus, 178, 179, 195

Conditioning, 184

Conditions of worth, 134, 250

Conflict, 181

Conformity, 38-39, 40

Confucianism, 370; family, 376; rules of social responsibility, 389; social identity of individual, 381

Congenital characteristics, 339

Congruence, 140, 147

Congruity theory, 9

Conscience, 25

Consciousness, 4-5, 52; altered states of, 387-388; existentialism, 251; psychoanalysis,

15, 21; relation to activity, 343; theories of personality, 13; unconscious affecting, 38; unity of, 348

Consequences, 417

Constellatory construct, 219, 220; invalidation, 233

Constitutional theories of personality, 303-331; experiential approach, *see* Experiential approach to constitutional psychology; holistic approach, *see* Holistic theories of personality; structural approach, *see* Structural approach to constitutional psychology

Constriction, 220, 222

Construct, 205, 211, 212, 218; characteristics, 217-220; institutional systems, 229; permeability, 215, 219

Construction Corollary, 212

Constructive alternativism, 209

Construe, 205, 210, 212

Contracts, 195

Conversion, 30

Conversion hysteria, 30

Core construct, 219

Core role, 221

Cosmic Unity, 369

Counseling, 68, 383; direct decision personality theory, 429

Courage, 254

Creative regression, 108

Creative values, 248

Creativity, 52, 104, 265

Creativity cycle, 222

Crime and delinquency, 69

Criminal personality, 75

Cross-cultural psychology, 368

Cross-cultural psychometrics, 382

Cultural borrowing, 393

Culture, 210-211; personality, 368

Culturebound reactive syndromes, 383

Current personality theories, 399

Dasein, 245, 246, 251

Daseinanalysis, 9, 245, 247, 263

Day residue of dreams, 32

Death, 253

Death and rebirth, 94-95

Death instinct (Thanatos), 26, 89, 104

Decathection, 22, 30

Deduction, 5

Defectology, 352

Defense, 28-31, 32; mechanism, 102

Deintegration, 92, 93, 114

Delayed gratification, 424

Delinquency, 316, 317, 327

Denial, 29

Dependency, 377-378; Chinese society, 385; India, 385

Depreciation tendency, 74

Depression, 27, 64; regression in psychosexual development, 32; treatment, 322-323

Depression Scale, 267

Depressive position, 89, 92, 116

Deprivation, 191, 192

Determinism: behavior theory, 148, 178, 183, 193-194; biological, 4; developmental personality theory, 415; environmental, 4, 279; personal constructs theory, 210, 211; reciprocal, 424-425; social interactionism, 300; soft, 4, 415

Deterministic-indeterministic theories of personality, 13

Developmental personality theory, 9, 413-415; evaluation, 415

Developmental process, 254, 255-257; children, 255-257; discipline, 256; experiencing, 256; failure, 257; preliminary, 263; self-determined, 256, 257, 263

Development of personality, 7; analytical psychology, 89-99; Asian theories, 373-377; behaviorism, 183-189; existential psychology, 251-258; individual psychology, 51-55; personal constructs theory, 210-211; personalism, 158-165; person-centered theory, 131-134; psychoanalysis, 20-26; social interactionism, 284-287; Soviet theory, 343-348

Deviancy, 278, 281, 293-294; labeling, 293

Dharma, 369, 380

Dialectical materialism, 338, 361-362

Dichotomy Corollary, 213

Differentiation, 187, 195-196

Dilation, 220, 222

Dimension, 165

Direct decision theory, 9, 401, 427-430; evaluation, 430

Discipline, 256; Chinese child rearing, 378

Discovery of Grounded Theory, 295

Discriminative stimuli, 186, 187, 190

Disorganization of organism, 319, 320

Displacement, 30, 32, 181, 314

Displasia, 311

Disposition, 2

Draw-a-person technique, 327

Dread, 254

Dreams, 32-33, 38; interpretation, 66, 88, 100

Drives, 22, 53, 55; acquired or secondary, 181; innate or primary, 181; primal, 344; regulation and control of, 101

Drugs, 36; behavior, 192, 198; physiological changes, 145-146; psychedelic, 113

Duquesne University, 249

Dynamic organization, 159-160
Dynamic theories of personality, 13
Dynamic unconscious, 15, 18, 22, 37, 100, 112

Early recollections, 65, 75
Eclecticism, 9
Eclectic personality theories, 428, 430
Ectomorphy, 311, 312
Education: aversive stimuli control, 188; Jungian psychotherapy, 109-110; operant conditioning, 196; person-centered theory, 141-142; psychoanalysis, 36
Edwards's Personal Preference Schedule, 409, 427
Effect, law of, 179, 184
Ego, 15, 21, 22, 33, 89, 91; anxiety, 28; Asian and Western views of, 389-390; autocratic instincts, 24; body experience, 306-307, 318; developmental personality theory, 413-414; dialogue with unconscious, 90; formation, 23; functions, 101; innate, 113; proprium, 162, 164; sexuality, 24; transactional analysis, 410-412
Ego development, 413; stages of, 413-414
Ego-enhancement, 163
Ego-extension, 163
Ego identity, 91-92
Ego-psychology, 19, 114
Ego-self polarity, 101
Ego states, 412
Eigenwelt, 251-252
Eightfold path, 370, 392
Elaborative Choice Corollary, 214-215
Elementaristic theories of personality, 13
Elements of the universe, 305
Emotionality, 73
Emotional disturbances: organic causes, 16; psychoanalysis, 20, 21
Emotions and Bodily Changes, 307
Empathy, 139, 146-147, 167, 405
Encounter groups, 76, 325
Endogenistic theories of personality, 13
Endomorphy, 310, 311, 312, 313
Energy, 22, 62; neutralized, 33; psychic, 91, 99; sexual, 22, 33
Enuresis, 182-183
Environment, 161, 178; adjusting organisms to, 320; body, 317; human behavior, 279, 423-424; personality variance, 425; Soviet psychology theories, 342
Environmental determinism, 4, 279
Environmental stimuli, 184
Epigenesis, 413
Equalization, 319
Erogenous zones, 23-24, 314

Escape, 188
Ethical nature of man, 46
Ethnocentrism, 391-392
Ethnomethodology, 282, 283
Ethos, 84; observational studies, 295-296
Eupsyschia, 406
Evolution, theory of, 278-279
Exchange and Power in Social Life, 283
Exchange theory, 283
Executive apparatus of ego, 33
Exercises, 325-326
Exhaustion stage of stress response, 309
Existential a priori, 247, 253
Existentialism, 9
Existential psychology, 50, 243-273; applications, 261-264; Asian personality theory, 391; comparisons, 270-273; developmental process, 254, 255; person-centered theory, 131; prospect, 273; self, 265-266; Soviet psychology, 360; treatment, 263-264; validation, 266-273
Existential Study, 267
Existential vacuum, 267
Exogenistic theories of personality, 13
Exorcism, 16
Experience Corollary, 215
Experiencing, 129-130, 135, 143-146; bodily sensing, 132, 133; development of personality, 256; external integrated with internal, 133; organismic, 144, 145; self-concept, 136
Experiencing Scale, 267
Experiential approach to constitutional psychology, 303, 304, 308, 313-314, 327-328; psychoanalysis, 310, 330
Experiential psychotherapy, 127, 143, 391
Experiential research, 321-322
Experiential values, 248
Experimental neuroses, 178
Experimental psychology, 307
Experimental theory, 9
Experimentation, 4, 178, 183; behaviorism, 197
Expressive movements, 170-171
Expressive order, 291
External locus of control, 268
External objects, 90
Extinction, 185, 186
Extravagance, 260
Extraversion, 73, 105, 106, 427
Extroversion, 425, 427
Eysenck-Rachman typology, 73

Face, 278, 291; Confucianism, 370
Fact and Fiction in Psychology, 305
Facticity, 245, 253, 254, 256, 258
Factors, 165, 172

Factor theory, 9
Failure, 74, 257, 258, 261; orientation, 420-421
Family, 65-66, 68; abolishment, 317; Asian personality theories, 376; China, 385; India, 379-380; Japan, 377, 378; person-centered theory, 142
Family Education Centers, 68
Fantasies, 96, 110
Fatalism, 313, 392
Father: animus image, 95; child's attitude toward, 25; mother's attitude toward, 74
Fear, 181, 220-221; of death, 249; of life, 249
Feeling, 105, 106
Felt meaning, 249
Field observation, 278, 294-296, 301
Field-theoretical psychology, 45
Field theory, 130
Figure, 318-319
Filial piety, 370, 376
Fixation, 32
Fixed role therapy, 226-227, 237, 239
Focusing, 264
Foundations of General Psychology, 339
Four noble truths of Buddhism, 370
Fragmentation Corollary, 215, 220
Frame reference, 378
Free association, 15, 16, 35
Freedom, 194; existentialism, 251, 253; personal constructs theory, 210
Freedom to Learn, 141
Free will, 194
Full humanness, 406
Functional autonomy, 165
Functional cortical system, 350, 354
Functionalism, 153, 278
Function pleasure, 165
Fundamental meaning structure, 247
Fundamental project, 245, 246, 253, 262
Funktionlust, 9
Future orientation, 158

Galen, 305
Games, 411, 412
Games Alcoholics Play, 413
General adaptation syndrome, 309
Generalization, 181, 186
Generalized other, 287
General semantics, 9
Genetics: endowment, 178, 183; factor in human characteristics, 307-308; human behavior, 279; hypothesis, 22-23
Genital phase of psychosexual development, 25; hysteria, 32
Genuineness, 140, 147

Georgian school of psychologists (Soviet Union), 340
Gestalt psychology, 5, 50; figure and ground model, 318; person-centered theory, 130; therapy theory, 415; Soviet view, 341
Gestalt therapy theory, 9, 400, 415-417; evaluation, 417
Glossary, 433-439
Goals, 53, 258, 259
God, 369
Gratification, 23, 424
Gray-Wheelright Questionnaire, 107, 112
Grid theory, 9
Ground, 318-319
Group leadership, 69
Group psychology, 110; social interactionism, 285
Group psychotherapy, 354; transactional analysis, 412
Growth motivation, 164, 172
Growth psychologists, 408, 419
Guilt, 21, 189, 221, 272, 273; Asian culture, 382; authentic or inauthentic person, 268; existential, 253, 254
Guttman Multidimensional Scalogram Analysis Method, 9
Gynandromorphy, 311

Habit, 2, 165, 179, 181
Halo effect, 219
Hatha-yoga, 370, 371
Hedonism, 244
Here-and-now viewpoint, 419
Heredity, 4, 161, 178, 183; improvement, 303; Soviet psychological theories, 342
Hierarchy of needs, 255, 309, 406, 407
Hinduism, 369-370; literature, 369; reincarnation, 373; relation to social institutions, 384-385
Hirsutism, 311
Historical materialism, 338
History of personality theories, 7; analytical psychology, 84-89; Asian personality theory, 369-371; behaviorism, 178-183; constitutional theories, 304-308; existential psychiatry, 245-251; individual psychology, 47-51; personal constructs theory, 205-209; personalism, 154-158; person-centered theory, 126-131; psychoanalysis, 16-18; social interactionism, 218-284; Soviet, 336-340
Holistic theories of personality, 5, 13, 45, 330; constitutional psychology, 303, 304, 307, 308, 314-316, 318-321, 322, 328
Homeostasis, 5, 22, 23, 91, 99
Homosexuality, 40, 325

Honorific system, 385-386
Hospitalization, 36
Hostility, 22
Humanistic psychology, 9, 51, 72, 76, 157, 172, 173; existentialism, 250, 271
Human relations: Japan, 378; propriety, rules of, 378-379; vertical and horizontal, 378
Humoral theory, 305
Hunger, 55
Hypnosis, 17-18, 112-113, 388; psychoanalysis, 34
Hypostatization, 2
Hypothetico-deductive method, 154
Hysteria, 18, 27, 32; repression, 30

Id, 15, 21, 22, 23, 410; anxiety, 28
Idealism, 279, 340, 343, 360
Idealistic orientation, 245, 257-258
Identification, 30, 232
Identifying, 288
Identity crisis, 415
Identity system of ego, 33
Idiographic method of personality investigation, 4, 169-170, 422, 427; morphogenic, 170; personal constructs theory, 237; Soviet studies, 348
Id-psychology, 19
Imagination, 251, 252, 253; authentic and inauthentic persons, 258-259; development, 255-256, 261
Imitation, 423, 424
I'm OK, You're OK, 413
Impression management, 277, 278, 281, 288
Inauthenticity, 243; behaviorism, 271; development, 256, 259; social interaction, 260
Incest, 25, 97
India, 368, 372, 374, 375; authority, 380; family, 379-380; history of personality theory, 369-370; social relationships, 385, 386
Individual, 19; social interactionist, 285-286; sociometric theory, 404
Individual and His Religion, 157, 168
Individualism, 368, 387; Asian personality theory, 381-382; Confucianism, 381-382
Individuality, 153; child development, 255-256; nature of, 373, 374; personal constructs theory, 212
Individuality Corollary, 212
Individual psychology, 9, 45-78; meaning of name, 46; person-centered theory, 127, 131; rational-emotive theory, 418; reality theory, 420; transactional analysis, 410, 411, 412
Individual Psychology of Alfred Adler, 77
Individuation, 98, 99, 108, 111-112
Induction, 5

Industrial psychology, 341
Inferiority complex, 53-55
Inflammatory stress response, 309, 310
Initiation, 94
Innate ego, 113
Instincts, 15, 22, 23-24, 279; anal-sadistic, 25; part, 24; sexual, 22, 23; social interactionism, 284
Instinctual discharge, 23
Institute for Reality Therapy, 420
Institutional applications of psychotherapy: Adlerian psychology, 68-70; analytical psychology, 109-110; Asian theory, 384-386; behaviorism, 168-169; child-rearing, 360-361; constitutional theories, 323-324; individual psychology, 68-71; Jungian psychology, 109-110; personal constructs theory, 228-229; personalism, 168-169; person-centered theory, 140-142; psychoanalysis, 35-36; social interactionism, 296; Soviet theories, 354-355
Integrative system, 33
Integrity of personality, 5
Intellectualization, 31
Intelligence, 2, 161
Interactional rituals, 291
Interactionism: mind-body, 5; social, *see* Social interactionism
Intercranial self-stimulation, 192
Internal locus of control, 268
Internal object psychology, 89
Internal objects, 90
Internal vs. External Locus of Control Scale (I-E), 268, 269
International Association of Analytical Psychology, 88
International Association of Individual Psychology, 49
International Association of Jungian Trainees and Newly Qualified Analysts, 88
International Congress of Individual Psychology, 48
International Journal of Individual Psychology, 49
International Psychoanalytic Association, 87
International Transactional Analysis Association, 411
Interpersonal relations, 339
Interpersonal theory of psychiatry, 9, 167
Interpretation, 228, 416, 447
Intrapsychic processes, 19
Introjection, 31; depression, 32
Introversion, 73, 105, 106, 425, 427
Intuition, 105, 106
Isolation, 30-31, 319, 320; obsessive-compulsive person, 32

Japan, 368, 372; body-personality theories, 305; child-rearing practices, 276-278; guilt and shame, 382-383; history of personality theory, 370-371; human relations, 378-379; institutional relations, 385, 386; psychotherapy, 383-384; role playing, 378-379

Jen, 374-375

Journal of Cross Cultural Psychology, 371

Journal of Humanistic Psychology, 173

Journal of Individual Psychology, 49

Journal of Psychosomatic Medicine, 307

Judgement, 251, 252, 253; authentic and inauthentic persons; development, 255-256, 259, 261

Karma, 269, 373, 391, 392

Kleinian school of analysis, 89; theory, 98

Korea, 282

Labeling of deviancy, 277, 281, 293

Language, 55, 286, 287

Latency phase of psychosexual development, 26

Latent dream stage, 32-33

Laya-yoga, 371

Leaping ahead, 255, 266

Leaping in, 255, 266

Learning, 5; behaviorism, 178, 181, 182; psychology of, 162

Learning theory, 9

Least effort personality theory, 9

Leningrad School of pathogenic psychotherapy, 339

Letters from Jenny, 167

Libido, 22, 103-104; theory, 22

Life instinct (Eros), 26, 104

Lifestyle, 64; assessment, 65-66; authentic and inauthentic persons, 260; comparison of Asian and Western, 386-387; Japanese, 379; script, 410, 411; Soviet psychological theories, 342

Literary criticism, 69

Logotherapy, 9, 72, 248

Loneliness, 347

Longitudinal observation, 348, 352

Looking-glass self, 278, 287

Love-hate (Eros-Phobos), 104

Machismo, 69, 312

Macroplanchnic body type, 306, 311

Magnetism, 405

Mahabharata, 369, 380

Maintenance of personality, 7; analytical psychology, 99-106; Asian theories, 377-382; behaviorism, 190-193; constitutional theories, 316-321; existential psychology,

258-261; individual psychology, 55-65; personal constructs theory, 211-223; personalism, 165-166; person-centered theory, 134-136; psychoanalysis, 26-33; social interactionism, 287-294; Soviet psychological theory, 348-352

Male-female roles, 112

Manifest content dream stage, 32-33

Mantra, 371

Maoism, 370

Marital relationships, 112; person-centered theory, 142

Marxism, 336, 341, 356

Masochism, 379

Masturbation, 26; neuasthenia, 27

Materialism, 336, 337, 343

Maudsley Personality Inventory, 427

Maya, 369

McNaghten rule, 3

Meaning, 243, 248, 349; felt, 249; neuroses, 262; search for, 251, 252, 253

Meaninglessness, 254, 267, 268

Medical psychoanalyst, 39, 40

Melancholia, 64; personality type, 305

Memory traces, 21

Menninger Clinic, 36

Mental disorders, 66; body build, 306; physical disability, 304; role of personality, 339

Mental events, 198, 199

Mental health: Asia, 383; holistic theories, 308; Japanese psychiatry, 379; self-determination, 73-74; usefulness as criterion, 59

Mental retardation, 354

Mesomorphy, 310-311, 312, 313

Metapsychology, 20, 75-76

Metrics, 6

Microplanchnic body types, 306, 311

Middle age, 98

Military services, 323-324

Mind, 5; Adler's view, 46; behaviorist view, 177, 178; composition of, 21; holistic theory, 303; psychoanalytical view of, 15

Mind, Self and Society, 280

Minnesota Multiphastic Personality Inventory, 267, 352; use in Asia, 382

Mirrors and Masks, 281

Modeling, 187, 423, 425

Modernization, 393

Modulation Corollary, 215

Money, 190

Monists, 5

Mood, 2

Moral development theory, 9

Moral world view, 347

Morita psychotherapy, 383, 384

Morphogenotype, 310
Morphological theory, 9
Moses and Monotheism, 115
Mother: anima image, 95; attitude toward father, 74; child's dependence on, 25; complex, 90; influence on development of child, 64; Jung's theories, 116; primitive identity, 92; relationship with child, 97-98
Motivation: behavior, 191-193; functional autonomy, 165; growth, 164; personology, 408; psychophysical systems, 160; social interactionists, 284; Soviet psychology, 349
Motivational statements (Accounts), 278, 285
Motivation and Personality, 328
Multivariate experimental theory, 9
Myers-Briggs Type Indicator, 107
Mysticism, 386

Naikan, 384
Narcissism, 24, 379
Narcissistic neuroses, 27; psychosexual regression, 32
National Accreditation Association for Psychoanalysis, 88
Naturalism, 329-330
Nature of Prejudice, The, 157, 172
Nazi Germany, 307-308
Need achievement, 390
Need-press theory, 9, 408-410
Needs, 22; bodily, 310; gratification, 23; hierarchy, *see* Hierarchy of needs; personality development, 255; personology, 409
Negative reinforcement, 185, 188
Neo-Freudians, 20, 89, 359-360, 403
Neo-Jungian psychology, 89
Neo-Marxists, 284
Neo-Reichian theory, 9
Nervism, 337
Neurasthenia, 27
Neuroses, 27; actual, 27; behaviorist explanation, 179, 182; choice of, 32; direct decision theory, 430; experimental, 178, 331; holistic personality theory, 315; organic causes, 16; psychoses, 136; sexual factors, 24
Neurosogenesis, 32
Neurotic Condition, The, 48
Neurotic paradox, 182
Neutralized energy, 33
Nihilism, 262
Nirvana, 380, 392
Nomothetic approach to personality investigation, 4, 169-170, 422, 429; personal constructs theory, 237; typology theory, 425-426
Nonconformity, 59
Nondirected personality theory, 125

Nondirective counseling, 129
Normality, 3, 320
Normoplanchic body type, 306
Nosology in psychoanalysis, 26
No-thought, 384

Objective psyche, 93
Objective theories of personality, 13
Object relations 98, 101, 113, 114, 116
Observation, 4
Observational learning, 9, 423
Obsessive-compulsive neuroses, 27, 32
Occupation, 55-56
Oedipus complex, 25, 26, 37, 97-98; psychoneuroses, 32
OK position, 411-412
Old age, 99, 108
Oneupmanship, 74
Open awareness context, 289
Open encounter, 9
Operant behavior, 184, 196, 197
Operant conditioning, 9, 197, 200
Operant conditioning chamber, 180
Operant reaction, 189
Operant reinforcement, 177-200
Operational methodology, 45
Operation function, 216
Oral satisfaction, 24
Organic repression, 315
Organismic experiencing, 144, 145
Organismic personality theory, 9, 307
Organismic valuing, 132, 133, 134
Organization Corollary, 212-213
Organization of personality, 159-160
Orthogenic School of the University of Chicago, 36
Overcompensation, 31
Overdeterminization, 32

Pain, 289, 318
Pampering, 64-65
Pan-sexualism, 24
Paradoxical intention, 264, 267
Parallelism, 5
Paranoia, 27
Paraphrenia, 27
Parapraxes, 38
Parent education, 68
Participation mystique, 92
Part-object psychology, 89, 92, 113, 116; relations, 98
Passive-dependent stage of psychosexual development, 24-25
Past-future theories of personality, 13
Pathobiography, 19

Pattern and Growth in Personality, 157
Pavlovian conditioning, 184
Pavlovian doctrine of mental disorders, 353
Payoff, 411
Peak experience, 406
Pedagogy, 340
Pedology, 341, 342
Peer group, 345-346, 347
People's Republic of China, 376
Perceptive processes, 101
Perfection, 402, 419
Peripheral construct, 219
Permissiveness, 227; Chinese child-rearing, 376; pseudo, 256
Perseveration, 315, 319
Persona, 102-111
Personal constructs theory, 9, 203-239; Commonality Corollary, 216; Construction Corollary, 212; Dichotomy Corollary, 213; Elaborative Choice Corollary, 214-215; Experience Corollary, 215; Fragmentation Corollary, 215-216; Fundamental Postulate, 211-212; Individuality Corollary, 212; Modulation Corollary, 215; Organization Corollary, 212-213; origin, 210; Range Corollary, 213-214; Sociality Corollary, 216-217
Personal dispositions, 166
Personal documents, 166-167
Personalism, 9, 50, 153-173, 307, 408
Personality: animals, 160; behaviorist views of, 178, 179; biologically defined, 162; body type, 303; character, 160-161; cross-cultural understanding, 392-393; culture, 368; definitions, 2, 131, 157-158, 159-160; maintenance, *see* Maintenance of personality; measurement, 382; phases in development, 416; phenomenological view, 422; social stimulus value, 422; sociohistorical conception, 348-349; theories, *see* Personality theories; unity of, 159
Personality and Psychotherapy, 181
Personality Factors Test, 427
Personality: A Psychological Interpretation, 156
Personality syndrome, 157
Personality theories, 235, 237, 247; apersonal and personal, 13; Asian vs. Western, 387-392; courses taught, 156; definitions, 2, 84; list of, 9; ratings of, 12-13; scientific methods applied to, 9-10; Soviet, 340
Personality types, 62, 155, 165
Personal Preference Schedule, 409-410, 427
Personal unconscious, 89, 90
Person-centered personality theory, 9, 125-149; comparison with other theories, 147-149; research, 146

Personology, 408-410; evaluation, 410
Phallic phase of psychosexual development, 25; curiosity of child, 26; psychoneuroses, 32
Phallocentrism, 116-117
Phantom limb experience, 306, 314
Phenomenology, 9, 45, 204, 423; view of personality, 422
Phenotype, 310
Philosophy, 126; existentialism, 244, 245; Soviet personality theory, 343
Phlegmatic personality type, 305
Phobias, 27
Phrenology, 305-306
Phthisic habitus (body type), 306, 311
Phyloanalysis, 9, 402
Physical appearance, 303
Physical sports and recreation, 324
Physiognomy, 305
Physiological arousal, 145
Physiological reactions to stress, 309
Physique, 161, 162; behavior correlation, 308; measurement of, 306; second-order components, 311
Play, 345
Population control, 317
Positive regard, 133, 134, 147; unconditional, 133, 134, 139-140
Positive reinforcement, 185; education, 197; freedom, 194
Possibility, 245
Posthypnotic phenomenon, 38
Preconscious, 21
Preemptive construct, 219, 220
Preferences, 258-259
Pregenital sexuality, 24
Prejudice, 69, 157, 171-172
Presentation of self, 288, 289
Presentation of Self, 281
Pretense context, 289
Preverbal construct, 219
Primary narcissism, 24, 113
Primary process thinking, 35
Primary self, 92
Primitive identity, 92
Private sense, 66
Process scale, 137-138
Procruste's bed, 222
Productive Thinking, 50
Programmed learning, 180, 196
Projection, 31
Projective identification, 89, 92
Projective technique, 106; Thematic Apperception Test, 107
Proof, 4

Proper conduct, 370
Propositional construct, 219-220
Propriate striving, 164
Proprium, 162, 163; definition, 165; rational agent, 164
Prospects for personality theories, 8; analytical psychology, 117-118; Asian theories, 392-393; behaviorism, 199-200; constitutional theories, 329; existentialism, 273; individual psychology, 117-118; personal constructs theory, 238-239; personalism, 173; person-centered theory, 149; psychoanalysis, 39-40; social interactionism, 300-301; Soviet theories, 361-362
Psyche, 23, 83; defenses, 28; energy distribution system, 91; fantasy creation, 96; individuality, 91; self-realization, striving for, 102; sociohistorical development, 348; structure of, 87
Psychic energy, 91, 99, 103-104
Psychic equilibrium, *see* Homeostasis
Psychoanalysis, 9, 15-40, 401-402; acceptance, 18; behaviorist view, 183, 199; body processes, 310, 318; constitutional theories of personality, 303, 329, 330; developmental personality theory, 412, 415; evaluating potential patients, 33-34; fundamental rule of, 35; institutional, 35-36; Jung, 87; neo-Freudians, 403; nosology, 26; Soviet view of, 341, 358; person-centered theory, 128, 148-149; philosophy, 37; therapy, 34-35; Zen compared, 390
Psychobiography, 9, 70, 307
Psychocybernetics, 9
Psychodrama, 400, 405
Psychodynamic self, 89
Psychodynamic viewpoint, 22
Psychoeconomic hypothesis, 22, 23
Psychohistory, 19, 70
Psychologia, 371
Psychological testing, 34
Psychological Types, 87
Psychology, 204; defined, 204; existentialism, 249
Psychology of Personal Constructs, 205, 207, 227
Psychology of Radio, 170
Psychology of Rumor, 168
Psychology of use, 64
Psychometrics, 106; cross-cultural, 382; experiential research, 322
Psychoneuroses, 18, 27
Psychopathology, 15, 20, 66-67
Psychopharmacology, 198
Psychophysical phase of personality development, 416

Psychophysical systems, 2, 160; research, 145
Psychoses, 27; misunderstanding of, 248; organic causes, 16; neuroses, 136; psychoanalysis, 18
Psychosexual development, 23; stages, 24-25
Psychosocial homeostasis, 374
Psychosocial personality theory, 401-403; evaluation, 40
Psychosomatic illness, 304; body image, 308; medicine, 5, 307
Psychosynthesis, 9
Psychotechnics, 341, 342
Psychotherapy: Adlerian, 67-68; Asian theories, 383-384, 389; direct decision theory, 429; existential, 261-265; Gestalt theory, 416-417; group, 354; Jungian, 107-109; personal constructs theory, 226-228; personalism, 167-168; person-centered, 138-142, 147-148; psychoanalysis, 15-40; Soviet, 337, 352-354
Puberty, 26
Punishment, 188-189
Purpose-in-life test, 263, 267
Pyknic (body type), 306, 311

Q-sort, 137
Quantitative-qualitative theories of personality, 13

Racial memory, 115
Racket, 411
Rajas, 370
Raja-yoga, 370, 371
Ramayana, 369
Range Corollary, 213-214
Rational-emotive psychotherapy, 9, 71, 391, 400, 417-419; evaluation, 419
Rationality, 372
Rationalization, 29, 30, 285
RCRT, *see* Role Construct Repertory Test
Reaction formation, 31
Reactology, 341
Reality, 402-403
Reality testing, 35, 101
Reality theory, 9, 391, 419-422; evaluation, 422
Reciprocal determinism, 424-425
Reciprocal inhibition, 194
Reductionism, 5; social interactionism, 278, 300
Reevaluation counseling, 9
Reference group theory, 282
Reflexes, motor, 342
Reflexes of the Brain, 337
Reflexology, 342, 343
Regression, 32, 103; creative, 108, 109
Rehabilitation, 323

Reification, 2
Reincarnation, 373, 385
Reinforcement, 177; conditioned, 190; generalized, 190; intermittent, 190; operant, 177-200; positive and negative, 185; primary, 190, 191; principle of, 179, 184; scheduled, 190-191; selective, 177; therapy, 194-195
Relational personality structure, 368, 379, 381, 382
Relaxation, 194
Religion, 69; Asian psychology, 367, 372; behaviorist influence on, 183; moral base for scientific progress, 317; personalism, 156-157, 168, 171; person-centered theory, 126-127, 128
Religious instinct, 104
Repetition compulsion, 411
Repressed unconscious, 89
Repression, 21, 28, 56, 182; defense, 30; latency phase of psychosexual development, 26
Research, 294-296; analysis, 295; ethics, 295-296; quantitative-qualitative, 299; reporting of, 295; tactics, 294-295
Resistance in psychoanalysis, 34
Resistance stage of stress response, 309
Respondent behavior, 177, 184
Respondent conditioning, 184, 195
Respondent reaction, 189
Responsibility, 3-4; individual, 158
Rites de passage, 94
Rituals, 411
Road to Life— an Epic of Education, 338
Role, 216
Role Construct Repertory Test, 66, 208, 223, 224, 225, 226, 229, 234
Role playing, 39, 226, 232, 400; Japan, 378, 379, 386; social interaction, 278, 287, 291-292; sociometric theory, 404, 405, 406
Role taking, 278, 288
Role theory, 9
Rolfing, 322
Rorschach Psychodiagnostic Inkblot Test, 34, 106, 327
Rorschach Thematic Apperception, 352
Rumor, 168-169, 171

Sadistic-anal phase of psychosexual development, 25
Samadhi, 371
Samsara, 392
Sanguine personality type, 305
Satiation, 191, 192
Satisfying consequences, 184
Satori, 371
Sattwa, 370

Scapegoat theories, 110, 171
Scheduled reinforcement, 190-191
Schizophrenia, 27, 248, 262, 314; body type, 306
Schizophrenia Scale, 269
Schools, 68, 323
Science, 37
Science and Human Behavior, 180
Scientology, 9
Script, 410, 411, 412
Secondary dynamic characteristics, 57
Secondary narcissism, 24
Secondary process thinking, 35
Selective reinforcement, 177, 186, 187
Self, 7; Adlerian psychology, 70-71; analytical psychology, 110-112; Asian personality theories, 374, 386-387; behaviorism, 196-197; body image boundary, 317; constitutional theories of personality, 324-326; Eigenwelt, 251-252; existential approach, 265-266; individual psychology, 70-71; Jung's view, 110-112, 114; personal constructs theory, 229-231, 237; personalism, 153, 169; person-centered theory, 142-143; psychoanalysis, 36-37; social interactionism, 297-298; Soviet psychology, 355; Zen Buddhism, 384
Self-actualization, 9, 125, 134, 271, 321; attributes, 407-408; behavior, 315; hierarchy of needs, 309; personality theory, 406-408
Self-analysis, 403
Self as coper, 164
Self as knower, 164
Self-awareness, 345
Self-characterization, 225, 226, 229
Self-concept, 133, 134; conflict with experiencing, 136
Self-consistency, 9
Self-control, 194
Self-deception, 67
Self-determination, 73-74
Self-development, 99, 342
Self-discipline, 250
Self-esteem, 163
Self-estrangement, 135
Self-experience, 133
Self-extension, 163
Self-help, 70-71
Selfhood, 249, 250
Self-identity, 163
Self-image, 163
Self-observation, 384
Self-reflexiveness, 278, 286
Self-regard, 133
Self-representation, 33
Self-surrender, 254
Self-understanding, 110-111

Self-upbringing, 342, 343
Semantics, 5; theory, 9
Sensation, 105, 106, 313
Sensing, 132, 133, 144; signal system, 339, 341
Set, theory of, 340, 361
Sex-role identification, 74; personality differences, 307
Sexual disorders, 195-196
Sexuality, 18; adolescence, 346; anxiety, 28; energy, 22, 33; female, 20; instinct theory, 24; libido, 22; oral phase, 24; pregenital, 24; social problems, 55
Shadow, 90, 101, 110
Shame, 382-383
Shaping, 194-195, 197
Shinto, 391-392
Shock therapy, 36
Shuchu Naikan, 384
Signal system, 339, 341, 344
Significance, 349-350
Sign learning, 182
Situational neuroses, 27
Skinner Box, 180, 270
Skinnerian theory, 172
Social Behavior, 283
Social Behaviorism, 280
Social desirability Scale (SDS), 269
Social determinism, 292
Social hunger, 411
Social identity, 421
Social interaction, 9, 252, 259-260, 277-301
Social interest, 56-64, 75; activity, 62-64; mother's influence in development, 74; relation to mental health, 59; social usefulness, 59
Socialist competition, 355
Sociality, 238-239
Sociality Corollary, 216-217, 232, 237
Socialization, 354-355
Social Learning and Clinical psychology, 207
Social learning theory, 9, 273, 401, 422-425; evaluation, 424
Socially oriented psychology, 45
Social morality, 359
Social movement, 402, 403
Social order, 279-280, 291
Social phase of personality development, 416
Social position, 291-292
Social problems, 55-56
Social psychology, 300; transactional analysis, 410
Social Psychology, 281
Social reform, 264-265
Social responsibility, 141, 272
Social structuralism, 281

Social usefulness-uselessness, 59-64; personality type, 62
Social work, 68-69
Society for Free Analytic Research, 48
Society for Individual Psychology, 48
Society for the study of symbolic interaction, 281
Sociohistorical conception of personality, 348-349
Sociological Eye, The, 281
Sociology, 279
Sociometric testing, 405
Sociometric theory, 9, 400, 403-406; evaluation, 405
Sociopolitical viewpoint, 5
Sociopsychological theory, 9
Socrates, 419
Soft determinism, 4, 415
Solution learning, 182
Somatic approaches to psychotherapy, 36
Somatopsychology, 307, 308
Somatotonia, 312, 313
Somatotype, 303, 310, 311, 312, 323, 326
South End Urban Renewal Project of Boston, 141-142
Soviet personality theory, 335-362
Space, psychology of, 159
Speech: personality development, 339, 344; relation to thought, 337; stimulus to conditioned reflex, 354
Spiritual phase of personality development, 416
Static theories of personality, 13
Status dilemmas, 281
Status passage, 278, 292
Stimulation, 344
Stimulus-organism-response (S-O-R) theory, 408, 417
Stimulus-response (S-R) theory, 178, 279
Stream of consciousness, 154
Stress, 309, 310
Structural approach to constitutional psychology, 303, 304; assessment, 322; character diagnosis, 321; validation, 326-327
Structural determinism, 282, 284, 292
Structural hypothesis in psychoanalysis, 21, 22
Structural integration theory, 9
Structuralism, 278
Student-teacher relationship, 266
Studies on Hysteria, 18
Study of Values, 155, 170
Subjective theories of personality, 13
Sublimal perception, 144
Sublimation, 31
Submerged construct, 219

Submission, 190
Subordinate construct, 219
Success, 74; orientation, 421
Superego, 15, 21, 22; conscience, 25; transactional analysis, 410
Superiority complex, 53-55
Superordinate construct, 219, 233, 234
Suppression, 28; punishment, 189
Suspended construct, 219
Suspicion context, 289
Symbolic environment, 278
Symbolic interactionism, 281
Symbolization, 32, 84, 86, 100-101, 115; authentic and inauthentic persons, 258-259; death and rebirth, 94-95; development of children, 255-256, 261; existentialism, 251, 252, 253; reality mediation, 286
Symbols of Transformation, 87, 103, 116
Symptoms, 38
Synthetic functions, 101-102
Systematic desensitization, 194
Systems theory, 9

Tamas system, 370
Taoism, 370
Taxonomical personality systems, 425, 426, 427
Teaching machine, 180
Tele, 404, 405, 406
Telic centralization and decentralization, 320
Temperament, 2, 62, 161, 162; assessments, 326; body types, 303, 316; somatotypes, 312-313
Tension, 158, 409
Tests, 321-322, 351, 352; body image, 327; personality, 409, 426, 427; Personal Preference schedule, 409-410; psychological, 34; sociometric, 405; Thematic Apperception, 409-410
Textbook of Psychology from the Standpoint of Dialectical Materialism, 341
Texture component of physique, 311
Thema, 409
Thematic Apperception Test, 107, 408, 409-410
Theory, 154, 336
Therapeutic institution, 36
Therapist attitudes, 138-140, 146-147, 227-228
Thinking, 105, 106
Third-force psychology, 157, 169, 172, 173; existentialism, 250, 271
Three-factor theory of personality development, 342
Threat, 221
Time, 4; existentialism, 252; psychology of, 159; structuring of, 411
Time-out, 189, 197

Token reinforcement, 190, 196
Tonic-sensory theory of perception, 144
Topological psychology, 9
Totem and Taboo, 116
Traditional-moral source of authority, 380
Trait, 2, 165, 166, 172, 199
Transactional analysis, 9, 39, 400, 410-413; evaluation, 412; person-centered theory, 130
Transactional Analysis Journal, 411
Transcendental meditation (TM), 371, 372, 387-388
Transcultural Psychiatric Research Review, 383
Transference, 6, 15; analysis of, 90; archetypal, 109; psychoanalysis, 34-35, 39; psychoses, 27
Transference neuroses, 27
Transforming experiment, 335, 352, 356
Translations, 5-6
Transmigration of souls, 373, 392
Transparency theory, 9
Transpersonal psyche, 93
Transpersonal psychology, 9, 372
Treatment, psychotherapeutic; analytical psychology, 107-109; Asian psychology, 383-384; behaviorism, 194-196; constitutional theories, 322; existential psychology, 263-264; individual psychology, 66-68; personal constructs theory, 226-228; personalism, 167-168; person-centered theory, 138-140; psychoanalysis, 34-35; social interactionism, 296-297; sociologists, 296-297; Soviet psychology, 352-354
Trend, 2
Twin Oaks community, 193
Two-dimensional personality theory, 73
Two-factor theory of personality development, 9, 342
Types of Men, 155, 170
Type theory, 112, 166
Typological theory of personality, 155, 425-427; evaluation, 427
Typology; Eysenck-Rachman, 73; Pavlovian, 356, 361

Ultimate ego, 374
Unconditional positive regard, 133, 134, 139-140
Unconditioned reflexes, 339, 344
Unconditioned stimuli, 179, 195
Unconscious, 4-5, 17, 84, 110; consciousness, 38, 52; creative, 96; dynamic, *see* Dynamic unconscious; ego, 90; operations of, 32; psychoanalysis, 15, 21; theories of personality, 13
Understanding Human Nature, 70

Underevaluation, 74
Undoing, 31
Unitas multiplex, 155, 159, 162-163
Unity of composition (Unitas compositionis), 155
Universal ambiguity, 315
University of Chicago, 249; sociology department, 280
University of Saskatchewan, 249
Upanishads, 369, 392
Upbringing, 348; self, 342, 343
Upward displacement, 30
Usefulness, uselessness, *see* Social usefulness-uselessness

Validation of theories: Adlerian psychology, 71-77; analytical psychology, 112-117; Asian theories, 387; behaviorism, 197-199; constitutional theories, 326-330; existentialism, 266-273; individual psychology, 71-77; Jungian psychology, 112-114; personal constructs theory, 231-238; personalism, 169-172; person-centered theory, 143-147; psychoanalysis, 37-38; social interactionism, 298-300; Soviet psychology, 356
Value in element of personality, 104-105
Values, 3; authentic and inauthentic persons, 258, 259; existential, 248
Variable, 165

Varieties of Delinquent Youth: Constitutional Psychiatry of Delinquency, 316, 326
Varieties of Religious Experience, 167, 168
Vegetativeness, 262
Verbal Behavior, 180
Veridical view of personality, 422, 425
Vicarious learning, 423, 424
Vienna Psychoanalytic Society, 48
Viscerotonia, 312, 313

Walden Two, 180, 193
War, 317
Wealth, 317
Westernization, 393
William Alanson White Institute, 248, 249
Will theory, 9
Women: psychology of, 118; repression, 112; rights, 69
Word Association Test, 106
Work, 350; therapy, 353
Workaholism, 111
World view, 84

Yin and Yang, 112, 279, 390
Yoga, 127, 144, 305, 325, 369-370, 371, 387, 388

Zeitgeist, 5
Zen Buddhism, 127, 371, 387, 388, 390; Morita therapy, 384

THE BOOK MANUFACTURE

Current Personality Theories was typeset, printed and bound at R. R. Donnelley & Sons Company, Elgin, Illinois, and Crawfordsville, Indiana. Internal and cover designs were by Herbert Pinzke, Design, Inc. The type is Century Schoolbook with Helvetica Medium display.